BRIT G

ORLANDO

& WALT DISNEP World

2011

Simon & Susan Veness

foulsham
LONDON • NEW YORK • TORONTO • SYDNEY

foulsham

The Oriel, 33 Bath Road, Slough SL1 3UF

Foulsham books can be found in all good bookshops or direct from www.foulsham.com

ISBN: 978-0-572-03627-0

Look out for the latest editions of Foulsham travel books:
Brit Guide to Las Vegas, Karen Marchbank with Richard Evans
Brit Guide to Disneyland Resort Paris, Simon and Susan Veness
Brit Guide to New York, Amanda Statham

Dedication: To our special three-boy research team – Ben, Anthony and Mark – who help make our work fun!

SPECIAL THANKS
Special thanks for this edition go to: Orlando/Orange County Convention and Visitors Bureau, Kissimmee Convention and Visitors Bureau, The Walt Disney Company, Universal Orlando, Busch Entertainment Corporation, St Petersburg/ Clearwater Convention & Visitors Bureau, Seminole County Convention & Visitors Bureau, Mary Deatrick, Nigel Worrall, Allan Oakley and Bill Cowie.
Our sincere thanks also go to all the hard-working people at Foulsham who help to bring our work to life every year.

Printed in Dubai

CONTENTS

FOREWORD

Simon says... Well, knock me off my broomstick! The opening of the *Wizarding World of Harry Potter* at Universal's Islands of Adventure Park in June 2010 was one of the biggest things we've seen in Orlando for a LONG time, and the knock-on effect is likely to be felt well into 2011, with the increased publicity and focus bringing even more Hogwarts-influenced visitors. Those who do flock this way – many of them for the first time – will also find a LOT of other new development either underway or ready to open. Disney's huge redevelopment of the Fantasyland area of the Magic Kingdom Park is startling, while Busch Gardens is likely to wow visitors with another eye-catching roller-coaster, Cheetaka; and we will also be closely monitoring the construction of Legoland Florida, on the site of the old Cypress Gardens in Winter Haven and incorporating some of the better elements of the old Florida attraction. Once again, it serves to underline the fact nothing stands still in this region of central Florida that we call Orlando, and you need to keep your wits about you to keep track of it all. Fortunately, that's what we at the *Brit Guide* specialise in. We keep our finger on the pulse of Disney and Co pretty much 24/7, hence you can be sure that if you are taking us along, you will have the best possible preparation, insight, help and advice for everything that's in store. No one else has the overview of this amazing holiday destination that we do, and no one else can steer you through all the possibilities, lures and delights of what is still the 'holiday of a lifetime' as well as we can. Pay attention, now!

Susan says... Orlando in 2011 is all about scale. At one end of the spectrum is the massive edifice of Hogwarts, the enormous emotional impact when you walk into Hogsmeade for the first time, and the off-the-charts excitement the whole of the *Wizarding World of Harry Potter* has generated in Central Florida (and around the world, for that matter). At the other end of the spectrum are the smaller gems found in more obscure places: Pure Magic in Kissimmee, where they flash-freeze your ice cream from liquid to solid right in front of you; Island Boat Lines Eco Tour in Cocoa Beach, where you may just spot a baby manatee floating alongside its mother; and even that special little smile that special someone gives you as you watch Disney's classic Main Street Electrical Parade make its long-awaited return to the Magic Kingdom.

Between the highly anticipated opening of a whole new land and the surprising little touches that add a bit more sparkle to your holiday, Orlando is more addictive than ever, with so many new things to discover! And if you want to make sure you get the very best out of your holiday without wasting time or money, let us help with our Itinerary Planner Service (see page 49).

And now, on with the planning!

Simon and Susan Veness (visit us at **venesstravelmedia. com** or email **britsguide@yahoo.com**)

Greetings from Susan and Simon

1 Introduction

or Welcome to the Holiday of a Lifetime

On your marks, get set; and Go! for the world's most exciting holiday experience – and we'll take no arguments on that score! The area of central Florida we call Orlando is a vast mix of adventure rides, thrills, fun and fantasy with no equal anywhere else on earth. And we're not talking just about the amazing *Walt Disney World Resort.*

First off, this is a BIG venture in every sense and you must be aware of the extensive and complex nature of this tourist wonderland. Disney is the leading attraction, but there is a strong supporting cast, led by Universal Orlando and SeaWorld. There's something for all tastes and ages – young and old; families, couples and singles – but it exacts a high toll. You'll walk a lot, queue a lot and probably eat a lot. You WILL have a fabulous time, but you'll probably end up exhausted, too. It is a holiday – but it's also something of a military campaign!

The gang's all here

Eight theme parks

In simple terms, there are 8 essential major theme parks, and at least 1 will require 2 days to make you feel it has been well and truly done. Add a day at a water park, a trip to see some of the wildlife or other nature attractions, and the lure of the nearby Kennedy Space Center, and you have 12 days of pure adventure mania. Then mix in the nighttime fun of *Downtown Disney*, Universal's CityWalk and a host of dinner shows, plus world-class shopping, and you have an idea of the awesome scope of the place. Even with 2 weeks, something has to give – just make sure it isn't your patience, wallet, – or sanity.

> **BRIT TIP**
> All website addresses in this book are preceded by **www.** unless they begin with **http://**.

So, how do you get full value from this truly magical holiday? The basic answer is Good Planning – read, reflect and prepare. At the back of this book is a handy outline guide for all you might want to do. Be aware of the time demands of the parks and make sure you build in a quiet day or two by the pool or at one of the smaller attractions. With SO much on offer, it just isn't possible to 'do it all', so try to ensure you get full value from your choices. Also, don't underestimate the vast scale involved. Everything is well spread out and it takes time even to get from park to park. But do stop to admire the imagination and clever detail of what's on offer as they are simply world class.

Orlando

Orlando itself is a small but bright young city, now synonymous with *Walt Disney World* in its south-west corner. When Walt's dream of a vast resort opened in 1971 with the *Magic Kingdom Park* (sadly, he never saw it realised as he died in 1966), it led to a massive tourist expansion that has never stopped. New attractions pop up all the time, which vary from terrific to tacky.

The name 'Orlando' has grown to encompass much of Central Florida. It comprises 7 counties: **Orange County** is home to the city of Orlando, but part of *Walt Disney World* is also in **Osceola County** to the south, with Kissimmee its main town; **Seminole County**, home of Orlando Sanford International Airport, is north-east of Orange County; **Lake County** is to the north and west, with Mount Dora its principal town; **Polk County** lying to the south-west is home to many vacation villas and the new Legoland Florida; and **Brevard** and **Volusia Counties** are on the east (Atlantic) coast, home to the Kennedy Space Center and Daytona Beach. The local population of Greater Orlando (Orange, Seminole, Osceola and Lake counties) numbers 2.1 million and 375,000 are employed in the tourist business. Each year, more than 45 million people visit Orlando on holiday, spending more than $30. Britain accounts for 40% of foreign visitors, and in 2009 that was 845,000 of us. Orlando International Airport has seen traffic boom from 8 million passengers in 1983 to a record 36.4 million in 2007 (2009 was 33.6 million). The area boasts around 115,000 hotel rooms, 26,000 vacation homes, more than 4,000 places to eat and 30 malls. Here's a taste of the main attractions.

Walt Disney World Resort

This is where the 'magic' really starts – and the effect is vividly real. This vast resort actually consists of 4 separate theme parks, 22 speciality hotel resorts, a camping ground, 2 water parks, a sports complex, 4 18-hole golf courses, 4 mini-golf courses and a huge shopping and entertainment district (*Downtown Disney*). It covers 47sq ml/122sq km. The likes of Alton Towers and Thorpe Park would comfortably fit into its car parks! Indeed, Alton Towers, Britain's biggest theme park, is 60 times smaller. At peak periods, there are estimated to be 200,000 visitors throughout the Resort. The Disney organisation does things with the most style, and there are always new projects on the drawing board. It maintains an extremely high level of customer service, where everyone who works for them is officially a Cast Member, not just staff, and they take that ethic to heart.

Magic Kingdom Park: This is the essential Disney, including the fantasy of its wonderful films, the adventures of the Wild West and Africa, the excitement of thrill rides like Space Mountain (an indoor roller-coaster), the 3-D film fun of Mickey's PhilharMagic and splendid daily parades and fireworks.

Epcot: Disney's 2-part park, with the technology-inspired Future World, plus a potted journey around the globe in World Showcase. Though more educational than adventurous, it still has some memorable rides, including Test Track, Mission: SPACE and the superb Soarin', along with excellent dining options.

Disney's Hollywood Studios: Here you can ride the movies in style, meeting Star Wars™, the Muppets and Indiana Jones; drop into the fearsome Tower of Terror or the high-speed Rock 'n' Roller Coaster Starring Aerosmith; and learn the tricks of the trade at the epic Lights, Motors, Action!™ Extreme Stunt Show, try the Toy Story Mania ride and the American Idol Experience.

Disney's Animal Kingdom: This delivers another contrasting and entertaining scenario. With realistic animal habitats, including a 100-acre/40.5ha safari savannah, captivating shows and terrific rides, like the grand Expedition Everest, it offers a pleasant change of pace.

Florida

0   50 mile

N

JACKSONVILLE

Atlantic

Ocean

St Augustine

Ormond Beach
Daytona Beach
New Smyrna Beach

Silver Springs
Ocala

Mount Dora

Homosassa Springs

Sanford

Titusville

Cape Canaveral
Kennedy Space Center

ORLANDO

Walt Disney World

Kissimmee

Cocoa Beach

New Port Richey

Winter Haven
Legoland Florida
(opening Dec 2011)
Lakeland

Melbourne

Clearwater Beach

Lake Wales
Bok Tower Gardens

TAMPA

St Pete Beach

FLORIDA

FLORIDA TURNPIKE

Vero Beach

Gulf of

Bradenton

Mexico

Sarasota

Venice

*Lake
Okeechobee*

Charlotte Harbor

Fort Myers

Captiva

Palm Beach

Delray Beach

Boca Raton

Sanibel

Florida

Naples

Everglades

Fort Lauderdale

Marco Island

MIAMI

Key Largo

How far from Orlando to . . .

	mls - km
Bradenton	130 - 210
Clearwater Beach	110 - 176
Cocoa Beach	40 - 64
Daytona Beach	60 - 97
Fort Lauderdale	205 - 330
Fort Myers	190 - 306
Jacksonville	155 - 250
Kay Largo	294 - 470
Key West	375 - 604
Miami	220 - 354
Naples	230 - 370
Sarasota	140 - 225
Silver Springs	80 - 129
St Augustine	120 - 193
St Pete Beach	105 - 169
Tampa	75 - 120
Venice	160 - 257
Winter Haven	40 - 64

Florida Keys

Key West

© Steve Munns 201

Disney's Typhoon Lagoon Water Park: Bring your cozzie and spend a lazy day splashing down waterslides and learning to surf in the world's biggest man-made lagoon.

Disney's Blizzard Beach Water Park: The big brother of all the water parks, this has a massive spread of rides in a 'snowy' environment.

Downtown Disney: This incorporates a near mile-long spread of themed restaurants, bars, unique shops, a cinema multiplex, the DisneyQuest arcade of interactive games, House of Blues music venue and world-famous Cirque du Soleil® company.

Wedding Pavilion: Walt Disney World even boasts a fairytale venue overlooking Bay Lake for picture-perfect marriage ceremonies.

ESPN Wide World of Sports: This is a huge sporting venue to both play and watch top events.

The other parks
However, if you think Orlando is all about Disney, you'll be amazed by the range of other attractions on offer.

Universal Orlando: The other big resort development, this has 2 theme parks, an entertainment district and 3 speciality hotels. The parks are *Universal Studios*, where you Ride The Movies as you encounter The Simpsons, Jaws, the Shrek 4-D show, the Hollywood Rip Ride Rockit roller-coaster and Revenge of the Mummy ride, plus Woody Woodpecker's KidZone and amazing Terminator 2: 3-D show; and *Islands of Adventure*, featuring the new *Wizarding World of Harry Potter*, with a superb blend of thrill rides, family attractions, shows, eye-catching design and high-tech features such as the Amazing Adventures of Spider-Man and Harry Potter and the Forbidden Journey.

Wet 'n Wild: Although on International Drive, this water park is Universal owned and offers plenty of fun rides and slides.

SeaWorld: This is THE place for creatures of the deep, with killer whales the main attraction, a bright,

refreshing atmosphere, the amazing Blue Horizons and Believe shows and a serious ecological approach, plus thrill rides like the new Manta 'flying' coaster and huge Kraken, plus an area of rides and activities just for kids.

Discovery Cove: Its exclusive neighbour offers the chance to swim with dolphins, among other things.

Aquatica: A fab water park that provides even more fun and animal encounters in a colourful South Seas environment.

> ### BRIT TIP
> Beware travel-agent pressure to buy more tickets than you need. You simply won't get full use out of, say, a 14-day Disney ticket and the Orlando FlexTicket Plus in a 2-week holiday.

Busch Gardens: The sister park to SeaWorld (in nearby Tampa) offers creatures of the land, with a good mix of rides and shows. Highlights are the SheiKra mega-coaster, the Rhino Rally ride, Myombe Reserve, a close-up look at the endangered central African highland gorillas, the Edge of Africa 'safari' experience and Jungala 'village' of rides and animal exhibits. A real family treat, plus a must for coaster fans.

Other key attractions
These include the Kennedy Space Center, the dramatically upgraded home of space exploration, with the Shuttle Launch Experience; the surprisingly fun and humorous Gatorland; Silver Springs, a close look at Florida nature via various boat journeys on the crystal-clear Silver River; and Fantasy of Flight, an aviation museum experience that includes the world's largest private collection of vintage aircraft, plus fighter-plane simulators.

Disney tickets
Most people buy the multi-day passes that allow you to move between the theme parks on the same day and provide most flexibility and value for a 2 or 3-week visit. But don't be fooled into thinking you can walk between

the parks (they can be miles apart). Trying to do more than one a day is also hard work. The choice of tickets is bewildering, so be sure to buy ONLY what you need.

BRIT TIP
Buy your theme park tickets in advance, NOT at the park gates. You will save time AND money, as most outlets offer an advance purchase discount.

Disney's basic ticket system is called *Magic Your Way* and is horribly complicated. Happily, there is a simplified choice, sold in advance, for UK visitors. All multi-day passes offer good savings against 1-day tickets but unused days DO expire unless you buy an upgrade.

Magic Your Way: If you just turn up at the ticket booths, you must choose from the Magic Your Way menu:

• Choose the number of days (1–10).

• Decide if you want *Park Hopping* (letting you visit more than 1 park on the same day for a $54 flat rate).

• Decide if you want the *Water Park Fun & More Option* (1–10 visits to the water parks, *DisneyQuest* and *ESPN Wide World of Sports*™) for $54. Disney also offers 1 free round of golf at its 9-hole Oak Trail course (book in advance on 407 939 4653); club hire NOT included.

• Decide whether you want the *Non-expiration Option* (at $22–213, depending on the number of days of ticket). This option can be added *after* the initial purchase, but what you pay is still based on the original length of the ticket; e.g., if you buy a 7-day ticket and decide after 4 days you won't use the rest of it on this visit, you can add non-expiration for $142 and save the remaining 3 days for the future. You must upgrade within 14 days of first use.

• Per-day ticket savings increase with the more days you buy: 1 day = $82 plus tax; 10 days = $262 plus tax, or $26.20/day.

UK tickets: Pre-buy in the UK and there are only 4 main tickets to

consider (2 exclusively in Britain), and all good value. They are the 5 and 7-day **Premium Ticket**, and the 14 and 21-day **Ultimate Ticket** (see chart on page 12). At the time of writing, only Theme Park Tickets Direct offered the 3, 4, 6 and 10-day Disney tickets in the UK. The 1 and 2-Day tickets can be bought *only* in the US.

BRIT TIP
Need to buy your Disney tickets in Orlando or exchange vouchers for tickets? Use the Guest Services at Downtown Disney to save time and queuing.

Other tickets

When it comes to Universal Orlando, Wet 'n Wild, SeaWorld, Busch Gardens and Aquatica, the choice can be equally complicated as, along with 1-day tickets, there are various multi-day and multi-park options, plus periodic special offers (check with Orlando Ticket Deals, opposite).

• The **Orlando FlexTicket** provides 14 consecutive days to both Universal parks, Wet 'n Wild, SeaWorld and Aquatica; or those 5 plus Busch Gardens with the **FlexTicket Plus**.

• For Universal alone, select from **1, 2, 3, 4** or **7-day Tickets** either for **One Park** per day or park-to-park access to **Both Parks** each day.

• Look out in the UK for Universal's **2** and 3-Park Bonus Ticket that offers 14 days at Universal Studios and Islands of Adventure or those 2 plus Wet 'n Wild.

• SeaWorld and Busch Gardens have **2** and **3-Park Tickets**, combining SeaWorld and Busch Gardens, or SeaWorld and Aquatica, or all 3, for a full 14 days.

• A day at **Discovery Cove** includes a **14-Day Pass** for SeaWorld, Busch Gardens or Aquatica; the **Discovery Cove Ultimate Ticket** includes SeaWorld, Busch AND Aquatica for 14 days for an additional $70.

• For CityWalk, there is also a **Party Pass** ($11.99 plus tax) or a **Party Pass with Movie** ($15 plus tax), as the centre has a 20-screen cinema.

- Many UK ticket brokers now offer a 14-Day **Combo** or **Mega Pass** for Disney & Universal or Disney & SeaWorld parks, plus a **Freedom Ticket**, or similar name, bundling all 8 parks together. This does NOT provide a single ticket but rather a bundle of 2 or 3 tickets.

- Yet another choice is the **Go Orlando Card**, which offers 1, 2, 3, 5 or 7 days of visits in the space of 14 days to more than 50 Florida attractions and activities, including Kennedy Space Center, Gatorland, WonderWorks, airboat rides, mini-golf, dinner shows and more ($74.99–219.99 adults, $54.99–179.99 3–12s). You'd have to work hard to get full value for the 7-day card, but the 3 or 5-day ones are a good catchall for some of the smaller attractions. It also comes with a handy guidebook to the attractions. Look up more on **goorlandocard.com**.

With price hikes each year, try to buy your tickets as soon as you can, being aware that some discounted tickets must be used for the first time in the year of purchase (eg, first use by Dec 31, 2011). Shop around as many outlets have periodic sales and special offers, but stick with a reputable agent and use your credit card for added security. These all come well recommended.

BRIT TIP
Save money on some of the smaller attractions, dinner shows, restaurants, shops and more with the FREE Orlando Magicard from the Orlando Tourism Bureau at **orlandoinfo.com/uk**. Download online, order it directly, or call in to the Official Visitor Center on International Drive.

Attraction Tickets Direct: Britain's top direct-sell Florida ticket broker, with a sharp bookings team, has no credit card fees, free delivery in 7 days and a promise to match any other UK brochure price (plus a full range of dinner shows, excursions, sports, many theme park backstage tours and a keen online **Florida Forum** and info centre to which we also contribute).

It also offers Disney hotels, with the same price-match guarantee tickets (0800 975 0002, **attractiontickets-direct. co.uk**).

Keith Prowse Attraction Tickets: Also offering the full range of theme parks, with a **2-week All You Need Package** that bundles an Orlando FlexTicket with a Disney 7-Day Premium ticket, plus a number of excursions, notably to the Kennedy Space Center, Clearwater, Cocoa Beach, Orlando Shopping, airboat rides and sporting events (0844 209 0381, **keithprowse. com/uk**).

Orlando Ticket Deals: A keenly priced and extremely helpful broker that also issues real tickets (not vouchers), has a 'Next Day' delivery service and offers a significant Price Promise for all its attractions, including all the parks, dinner shows and many excursions (0845 678 1682, **orlando-ticket-deals.co.uk**).

Theme Park Tickets Direct: Another well-priced specialist (part of Theme Park Holidays Ltd, 1800 809 4348, **themeparkticketsdirect.com**).

There are others, but beware of the lure of 'free' tickets in Orlando as these are usually timeshare scams. And NEVER buy resale tickets from a booth in Orlando – they are often unusable. Stick with one of these main brokers, who offer good products, service and local knowledge. And don't forget to plan with our sample Busy Day Guide on page 361. You'll be exhausted if you try to do the parks in one big chunk!

BRIT TIP
For all your theme park tickets, be sure to check out *Brit Guide* partner **Orlando Ticket Deals** first, as it features an exclusive money-saving offer for our readers (see inside back cover).

The climate
The next decision is when to go. Florida's weather varies from bright but cool winter days from November to February, with the odd drizzly spell, to furiously hot and humid summers punctuated by torrential

Choosing a ticket

Ticket type	Park	Allowance
1-Day Ticket	Any Disney park, Universal Orlando parks, SeaWorld or Busch Gardens	Access to 1 park ONLY for 1 day; not available in advance
5-Day Premium Ticket	*Magic Kingdom, Epcot, Disney's Hollywood Studios, Disney's Animal Kingdom*	Access for 5 days, with multiple parks on same day; plus 4 visits to water parks, *ESPN Wide World of Sports™* and *DisneyQuest*; and 1 round of at 9-hole Oak Trail golf course (clubs not included); valid for 14 days after first use; non-expiration option available
7-Day Premium Ticket	*Magic Kingdom Park, Epcot, Disney-MGM Studios, Disney's Animal Kingdom Theme Park*	Access for 7 days, with multiple parks on same day; plus 6 visits to water parks, *ESPN Wide World of Sports™* and *DisneyQuest*; and 1 round of at 9-hole Oak Trail golf course (clubs not included); valid for 14 days after first use; non-expiration option available
14-Day Ultimate Ticket	All Disney parks	Unlimited access to all Disney attractions, including water parks, *DisneyQuest, Wide World of Sports™* and 9-hole Oak Trail golf course (clubs not included) for 14 days after first use; NO non-expiration option; available only in advance in the UK
21-Day Ultimate Ticket	All Disney parks	Unlimited access to all the attractions, including water parks, *DisneyQuest, Wide World of Sports™* and 9-hole Oak Trail golf course (clubs not included) for 14 days after first use; NO non-expiration option; available only in advance in the UK
Annual Pass	*Magic Kingdom, Epcot, Disney's Hollywood Studios, Disney's Animal Kingdom;* plus discounts for shops, dining and tours	Unlimited admission and free parking for 365 days after purchase date. If ordered online, you get a voucher which must be activated at a park; the 365 days start on the first day you activate the pass
Premium Annual Pass	All Disney parks; plus numerous discounts for shops, dining and tours	Unlimited admission and free parking for 365 days after purchase date; plus discounts on sports and recreation
1, 2, 3, 4 or 7-Day 1-Park Ticket	Universal Studios, Islands of Adventure	Access to 1 of the Universal parks each day for 7 days, plus CityWalk on 2-Days or more
1, 2, 3, 4 or 7-Day 2-Park Ticket	Universal Studios, Islands of Adventure	Access to both Universal parks each day for a 7-day period, plus CityWalk on 2-Days or more
2-Park Bonus Ticket	Universal Studios, Islands of Adventure, and CityWalk	14 consecutive days' access to both Universal parks, plus CityWalk clubs
3-Park Bonus Ticket	Universal Studios, Islands of Adventure, Wet 'n Wild and CityWalk	14 consecutive days' access to both Universal parks and Wet 'n Wild water park, plus CityWalk clubs
Orlando FlexTicket	Universal Studios, Islands of Adventure, SeaWorld, Wet 'n Wild, Aquatica	Access to all 5 parks, with multiple parks on same day, for 14 days from first use, plus CityWalk clubs
Orlando FlexTicket Plus	Universal Studios, Islands of Adventure, SeaWorld, Wet 'n Wild, Aquatica, Busch Gardens	Access to all 6 parks, with multiple parks on same day, for 14 days from first use, plus CityWalk clubs
2-Park Ticket	SeaWorld and Busch Gardens	14 consecutive days' access to both parks
2-Park Ticket	SeaWorld and Aquatica	14 consecutive days' access to both parks
3-Park Ticket	SeaWorld, Busch Gardens and Aquatica	14 consecutive days' access to all 3 parks

tropical downpours. The most pleasant option is to go between the two extremes, in spring or autumn – and you also avoid the worst of the crowds. However, as most families are governed by school holidays, Easter and July–August remain the most popular months for British visitors, so we have plenty of advice on how to stay ahead of the high-season crush. If you do need to go in summer, opt for late August as some US schools have resumed by then and the crowds drop off somewhat.

BRIT TIP
The humidity levels – up to 100% – and fierce daily rainstorms in summer take a lot of visitors by surprise, so carry a lightweight, rainproof jacket or buy a cheap plastic poncho locally.

The mood
Orlando is big, brash and fun, but above all it's American and that means everything is well organised, but with some cultural differences such as tipping (see below). It's clean, well maintained and eager to please: Floridians generally are an affable bunch, but they take affability to new heights in the theme parks, where staff are almost painfully keen to make sure you 'have a nice day'.

BRIT TIP
Tipping guide

Bill	Suggested tip
$15	$2.25
$20	$3.00
$25	$3.75
$30	$4.50
$40	$6.00
$50	$7.50

Tipping
Close to every American's heart is the custom of tipping. With the exception of fast-food restaurant servers, just about everyone who serves in hotels, bars, restaurants, buses, taxis, airports and other public amenities will expect a tip. In bars, restaurants and taxis, the usual rate is 15% of the bill, while porters expect $1/bag and chambermaids $1/day per adult. It's

important to know and remember that all service industry workers are taxed on the basis of receiving 15% in tips, whether they're given it or not.

ESTA, immigration and new $10 'entry fee'
Anyone flying to the USA on the Visa Waiver Programme MUST register online via the Electronic System for Travel Authorization (ESTA) no later than 3 days before departure. For all flights to the USA, this has now replaced the old green Visa Waiver form (I-94W). However, it also now requires (as at the end of 2010) a $10 fee per person (plus admin and credit card fees, that will take the final cost to around $15/person).The ESTA form simply requires the input of your basic immigration info – passport, address in the USA, flight details, email address and a few security questions – and is then valid for any visits in the next 2 years (i.e. you do NOT need to pay the $10 fee again in that period). ESTA is a pre-authorisation process prior to arriving at US immigration and should generate an almost immediate response of 'Authorization Approved' or 'Pending'. However, if the response 'Travel Not Authorized' is generated, it indicates that the applicant is unable to travel under the visa waiver programme and must apply for a Visa in advance. Apply for ESTA at **https://esta.cbp.dhs.gov**. Remember to have your holiday address details available both for the ESTA and, later, for your flight check-in. Ask your tour operator if you don't have a specific address (e.g. for a villa allocated on arrival) as it will have a formula for this. NB: Remember to record your Application Number during the online process so you can amend it for future visits inside 2 years. You can also print it out for reference.

BRIT TIP
Beware unofficial websites that offer to fill in the ESTA form for you – for a fee. Stick with the official US government website and just pay the $10/person entry fee (or 'Travel Promotion Act fee' as they call it).

INTRODUCTION

Main Attractions & Routes

↟ Sanford International Airport

Sanford Airport via Interstate 4 has no tolls,
but can be far busier, especially during rush-hou...

Sanford Airport via 417 has
a few tolls, but is much quieter

Daytona

Mount Dora

ALTAMONTE SPRINGS

⬜⬜⬜ Toll road (from 25c to $4.50)

Lake Apopka

94

92

4

436

429

90

441

WINTER PARK

88

87

OCOEE

417

WINTER GARDEN

50

WEST COLONIAL DRIVE

50

DOWNTOWN ORLANDO

← Silver Springs

EAST - WEST EXPRESSWAY

84

83

82

408

Orange County History Center

KIRKMAN RD

FLORIDA TURNPIKE

79

80

WINDERMERE

78

SEMORAN BOULEVARD

429

77

441

Universal Studios 🏰
CityWalk ■
Islands of Adventure 🏰

75

74B

Cocoa Beach

Kennedy Space Center —

■ Wet'n Wild

74A SAND LAKE RD

528

BEACHLINE

■ Ripley's Believe
It or Not

north exit

TURKEY LAKE RD

INTERNATIONAL
DRIVE

✈ **Orlando International Airport**

Magic Kingdom

535

435

72

🏰

71

■ Aquatica

ORANGE BLOSSOM TRAIL

SeaWorld 🏰

4

Discovery Cove **423**

south exit

BOGGY CREEK ROAD

PALM PARKWAY

Lake Buena Vista

Downtown
Disney

CENTRAL FLORIDA GREENEWA...

EPCOT DRIVE

Epcot

BUENA VISTA DRIVE

68

JOHN YOUNG PARKWAY

Disney's Hollywood Studios

■ Typhoon Lagoon

67

Animal Kingdom

■ Blizzard Beach

65

417

Gatorland ■

MainGate
West

64

OSCEOLA PARKWAY

FLORIDA TURNPIKE

WORLD DRIVE

63

■ Old Town

_Toll road

OLD LAKE WILSON RD

62

Celebration

KISSIMMEE

East Lake Tohopekaliga

60

WESTERN BELTWAY

192

IRLO BRONSON MEMORIAL HIGHWAY

Champions
Gate

58

Kissimmee Airport ✈

17

BOGGY CREEK ROAD

↙ Busch Gardens, Fantasy of Flight, Bok Tower Gardens

ST CLOUD

Tampa, Clearwater, Gulf Coast

Lake Tohopekaliga

© Steve Munns 2010

0   5 miles

Miami

N ↗

Although the ESTA process now has the official $10 fee, it DOES speed up the Immigration process and also does away with much of the old form-filling. You still need to complete the white Customs form en route (which should be given to you on the plane or at check-in; it is also available on arrival but it's better to have completed it in advance).

An ESTA form MUST be completed for every member of your group or family travelling under the visa waiver programme. Those who have a US visa because they are not eligible to travel under the visa waiver programme (i.e. because of a criminal record – see page 15) still need to fill in a white I-94 form en route (fill in the front only) but they do NOT pay the $10 entry fee. However, anyone with a US visa for work purposes and who is travelling to America for a holiday, WILL need to fill in an ESTA and pay the fee. Only one Customs form needs to be filled out per family group, with some of the same basic info but also the value of any goods that will stay in the USA (put $0 unless you are arriving with gifts for friends). Hand the document(s) with your passports to the Immigration official who checks you through and takes a fingerprint scan and photo. The Customs form will be handed back to you to present to another official when you exit the Baggage Hall.

Visa requirements

Holiday visitors to America do not need a visa providing they hold a valid machine-readable passport (MRP) showing they are a British citizen. Any passport issued from 26 October 2005 must include a digital photograph (not glued or laminated). All passports issued from 26 October 2006 must include the new biometric data. Each family member must have their own passport that does not expire for 90 days from the time of entry. Provided your passport conforms to the above, all you do is fill in a green Visa Waiver form and hand it in with your passport to the US Immigration official after landing. However, British subjects, those without an MRP or those who fail to meet the photo/biometric data criteria DO need a visa ($131), and should apply at least 2 months in advance to the US Embassy.

Some travellers may NOT be eligible to enter under the Visa Waiver Programme and will have to apply for a special restricted visa or they may be refused entry. This applies to those who have been arrested in the past (even if it did not result in a conviction), have a criminal record (the Rehabilitation of Offenders Act does not apply to US visa law), have a serious communicable illness (and the US includes AIDS sufferers in this category), or have previously been refused admission into, been deported from, or have overstayed in the US on the Visa Waiver Programme. Minor traffic offences that did not result in arrest and/or conviction do not count.

In England, Scotland and Wales, write to the Visa Office, US Embassy, 24 Grosvenor Square, London W1A 1AE (020 7499 9000). In Northern Ireland, write to US Consulate General, Danesfort House, 223 Stranmillis Road, Belfast BT9 5GR (028 9038 6100). You can call 09042 450 100 (£1.20 per minute; 8am–8pm Mon–Fri, 9am–4pm Sat) for more detailed advice, or visit **usembassy.org.uk**.

BRIT TIP

If you need to fill in the white I-94 immigration form for Visa holders, do so carefully in block capitals. Mistakes are often sent to the back of the queue. Please be courteous to Immigration officials – they do a difficult job in demanding circumstances, and jokes about terrorism are NOT appreciated.

BRIT TIP

US immigration now requires ALL visitors aged 14–79 to give fingerprint and photo ID on arrival. It slows things down, but the process is simple – first, left index finger then right index finger on the glass panel, then stand still for the camera. Some US gateways require a full 10-finger scan.

Travel information

Luggage is now liable to random searches in the US and you are advised NOT to lock your suitcases or bags at check-in for the flight home as TSA officials have the authority to break into them. Using zip-lock seals that can easily be snipped open is permissible and some airlines provide them free, while you can also buy TSA-approved reusable locks at some travel shops. Leave any gifts unwrapped in case screening requires them to be opened; don't put film in checked bags as screening equipment can damage it; and put scissors and other sharp items in checked bags, never in your hand luggage.

 BRIT TIP

Cabin baggage restrictions often change, so check with your airline in advance for up-to-date info.

Central Florida festivals

This region stages some excellent annual events and festivities. Here are some worth looking out for in 2011.

Blue Spring Manatee Festival: 22–23 Jan. Beautiful Blue Spring State Park is home to the wonderful manatee, and special celebrations are staged around its seasonal migrations, with craft shows, park tours and interpretive programmes. This park in Orange City is worth seeing at any time of year (off exit 118 of I-4; **themanateefestival.com**).

36th Annual Arts Festival: 5–6 Feb. The charming town of Mount Dora, north-west of Orlando, hosts 16 major festivals each year, of which this is one of the best, a nationally ranked fiesta with worldwide artists (take Florida Turnpike, the Western Beltway 429 and Highway 441 to Mount Dora; **mountdora.com**).

Florida State Fair: 3–14 Feb. This 107-year-old fair just outside Tampa (right on I-4) draws big crowds to its fairground rides, arts, crafts, livestock and live entertainment, with a variety of contests and competitions (**floridastatefair.com**).

Mount Dora Music Festival: 17–20 Feb. Outstanding offering of jazz, classical and big band sounds in the pretty outdoor setting of the Lakeside Inn (**mountdoramusicfest.com**).

Silver Spurs Rodeo: 18–20 Feb, 4–5 Jun. A twice-yearly celebration of an original American sport at Osceola Heritage Park in Kissimmee, it features top-quality events, plus associated crafts and activities (just off the eastern end of Highway 192; **silverspursrodeo.com**).

Florida Strawberry Festival: 3–13 Mar. One of the most unusual and fun events, a country fair in Plant City based on the local produce but with concerts, shows, exhibitions and parades (off exit 19 of I-4; **flstrawberryfestival.com**).

Daytona Beach Bike Week: 4-13 Mar. A lively celebration of all things 2-wheeled and mechanical, with races at Daytona Speedway, concerts, parades and street festivals (**officialbikeweek.com**).

Sidewalk Arts Festival: 18–20 Mar. Winter Park hosts one of America's most prestigious arts festivals, with arts, food, music and children's events (exit 87 of I-4; **wpsaf.org**).

Spring Collectibles & Arts Show: 26–27 Mar. A unique fiesta of art, antiques and more in the second of Mount Dora's major festivals. Almost a 2-day street party (**mountdora.com**).

Fun 'n Sun: 29 Mar–3 Apr. Annual aviation spectacular in Lakeland, with exhibits, vintage planes, aerobatics and more; one of America's biggest (off exit 27 of I-4; **sun-n-fun.org**).

Spring Fiesta In the Park: 2–3 Apr. Arts, crafts, food, music and family fun highlight this event around Lake Eola that typically draws 100,000 per weekend (**fiestaintheparkorlando.org**).

Sail Boat Regatta: 2–3 Apr. Florida's oldest yachting regatta is an eye-catching event with weekend fun for the whole family (**mountdorayachtclub.com**).

Independence Day: 4 July. A huge US national holiday, but watch out for big special events at Lake Eola

Simon and Susan say...

As our quick annual message, we like to highlight a few trends that we think are worth noting.

Orlando remains a world-class destination in general terms, but we're concerned at the growing tendency of the parks to try to squeeze a few extra dollars out of their customers. This is evident in a meteoric rise in car parking fees in recent years - just $8 in 2006, but up to $14 in 2010. It's a fee that's hard to avoid (though it makes sense NOT to visit Universal AND Disney or SeaWorld on the same day, as you do at least pay only once per day for all Disney parks), but some costs can be avoided with pre-planning, like taking a bottle of water with you and refilling it as you go.

The most invidious thing we have noticed creeping in is charges for sun-loungers and umbrellas in 'premium' spots at the water parks. When you consider Disney has never charged for these before, to suddenly start putting a $40 fee on 2 loungers, a table and umbrella (OK, they do throw in 2 towels, but big hairy deal, hey!) in the best spots around Typhoon Lagoon and Blizzard Beach seems horribly unfair. You should still find a decent spot if you arrive early enough, but late-comers now risk not finding anywhere to place themselves.

Likewise, the price for pushchair hire is another example of sheer avarice, in our eyes, and it definitely pays to bring your own (or even buy one here). Price increases at some of the most sought-after restaurants in peak periods (like Cinderella's Royal Table and Chef Mickey's) is another awful trick to play on your customers, especially if they have no ability to visit outside those times. Much better, therefore, to have your main meals outside those parks where it can be MUCH cheaper to feed the family (or take your own picnic to the water parks).

Meal portions continue to be too large in many places, hence splitting a main course remains a cost-effective option (most servers are happy to do this); ordering a child's portion is worth considering, too (don't be afraid to do it – Susan often opts for a 'kids' meal in the parks, knowing the quantity is usually sufficient for a 'grown-up' appetite). Finally, try to do much of your souvenir shopping at the discount outlets shops rather than the Disney and Universal parks – you can save big bucks.

Otherwise, just go and have fun – it's all here waiting for you!

(downtown Orlando), Lakefront Park (Kissimmee), Mount Dora, Celebration and Winter Park, plus most of the theme parks.

Oktoberfest: 7–8 Oct. A one-of-kind German-themed street party, with music, food, drink and other festivities in the heart of the town of Celebration (**celebrationtowncenter. com**).

Biketoberfest: 20–23 Oct. Another Daytona festival, like its Bike Week cousin celebrating all things 2-wheeled (**officialbikeweek.com**).

Mount Dora 27th Annual Craft Fair: 22–23 Oct (TBC). Some of the best national crafters line up for this annual competition featuring a huge range of arts and crafts (**mountdora.com**).

Orlando Film Festival: 3–7 Nov (TBC). This free festival of films and film-makers highlights the downtown Orlando scene with viewings, live music and discussions, based at the Plaza Cinema (**orlandofilmfest.com**).

Fall Fiesta In the Park: 5–6 Nov. The autumn version of downtown Orlando's big Lake Eola Park festival, drawing up to 250,000 visitors (**fiestaintheparkorlando.org**).

What's new?

Orlando is constantly changing and updating, so here's a quick look at what's new in town.

Walt Disney World: Never one to stand still, Disney has embarked on its biggest overhaul of the Magic Kingdom since it opened in 1971, with a comprehensive rebuild of the **Fantasyland** area, incorporating the former Mickey's Toontown Fair into one much larger and more dramatic 'Land.' This immense project will eventually unveil six new subsections:

Beauty and the Beast (including the Be Our Guest restaurant and a Belle meet-and-greet area); The Little Mermaid (including a terrific new ride, Ariel's Adventure, and a character greeting area); Cinderella (with a grand chateau location to meet one of Disney's most beloved princesses); Aurora's Cottage (and another high-quality character meet-n-greet); Dumbo (a circus-themed area with 2 new versions of the kid-friendly – but slow-loading – ride); and Pixie Hollow (more character greetings plus a new ride for the young 'uns). Other parts of Fantasyland will benefit from a forest-themed makeover, including the Winnie The Pooh ride and play area; the Mad Tea Party; and Goofy's Barnstormer roller-coaster (which will be completely re-themed in a circus/Dumbo style). Sounds good? It certainly will be, but the bad news is it's not scheduled to open until 2012 at the earliest and, in the meantime, this side of Fantasyland will be under major reconstruction, with much of the area either boarded off or shut down, which will certainly impact on the attractions – and crowding. The **Disney Railroad** will also have to close at some stage to allow for rebuilding of the Mickey's Toontown Fair station. The big character meetings in Toontown have been temporarily located to **Exposition Hall** in Town Square at the front of the park while Ariel's Grotto has been moved for the time being to the **Adventureland Veranda**.

The **Epcot** park has just welcomed 2 eye-catching new restaurants – the Via Napoli pizzeria in Italy and the indoor-outdoor La Hacienda (formerly Cantina de San Angel) in Mexico – while it has also seen the long-awaited return of the original groundbreaking 1980s 3-D movie *Captain Eo* starring Michael Jackson. At **Disney's Hollywood Studios**, *Star Wars* fans will be keenly awaiting the reopening of the Star Tours ride in May 2011 as *Star Tours II* with all-new 3-D filming, storyline and special effects, while the *Toy Story Mania* ride has been tweaked with the addition of a new game themed from the *Toy Story 3* movie.

Elsewhere in *Walt Disney World*, there is more to look forward to in the continued redevelopment of the **Pleasure Island** area at *Downtown Disney* (including a proposed lightshow on the lakeside and a new Aquarium Restaurant under consideration) and there should be the first swanky new vacation homes in the five-star **Golden Oak** residential area, part of a massive Four Seasons hotel resort due in 2012.

Universal Orlando: The amazing buzz created by the opening of the **Wizarding World of Harry Potter** in the islands of Adventure park in summer 2010 is still resounding around Orlando as a whole. (NB: it is NOT a theme park in its own right, as some media would have you believe!) This 20-acre/8ha expansion added a truly stunning array of Hogsmeade Village/Hogwarts theming, some unique shopping and dining experiences, and arguably the world's most advanced ride, *Harry Potter and the Forbidden Journey*. Many people flock here just to marvel at the architecture and landscaping and this is sure to carry over into 2011.

Busch Gardens: Not content with its superb Sesame Street Safari of Fun play area for kids in 2010, this ultra family-friendly park should have a BIG new attraction on its hands for summer – 2011. **Cheetaka** will be the latest – and most extensive – coaster in the Busch family and give the Nairobi/ Morocco area a real shot in the arm (once the construction dust has settled).

Legoland Florida: due to open in late autumn 2011 is another BIG development – a whole new park from the renowned Legoland family. On the site of the former Cypress Gardens park in Winter Haven, it will feature a highly kid-friendly mix of 50 rides and other attractions, including their spectacular trademark LEGO models and interactive elements.

Plan your visit

The next few chapters will tell you all you need to know to plan the ideal holiday. Make a rough itinerary and then fine tune it with this book. You can also take advantage of our unique Itinerary Planner Service (see page 49). Now read on and enjoy…

2 Planning and Practicalities

or How to *Almost* Do It All and Live to Tell the Tale

Good planning is the key to your Orlando holiday. This is not a place where you can 'make it up as you go along', and frustration and exhaustion lie in wait for all those without a sound plan of campaign!

This hugely complex and demanding destination can pull you in a dozen different directions at once, with a dazzling array of options for practically *everything*. Nowhere else in the world can be so downright difficult to negotiate, so it is vital to do your 'homework' in advance. Start with WHEN you want to go; WHERE in this vast area is best for you; WHAT sort of holiday you want; WHO you want to book with; and finally HOW MUCH you want to try to do.

When to go

To avoid the worst of the crowds, the best times to go are October to December (but not the Thanksgiving week in November or 20 December to New Year); early January to mid-March (avoiding President's Day in February); and the week after Easter to the end of May.

> **BRIT TIP**
> Thanksgiving is the 4th Thursday in November; George Washington's birthday, or President's Day, is the 3rd Monday in February, and both make for above-average long-weekend crowds.

Orlando is busiest at Easter; from Memorial Day (the last Monday in May, the official start of the summer season) to mid-August (plus the Labor Day weekend at the start of September, the last holiday of summer); and over the Christmas/New Year period. It peaks at the week of Easter itself; the big Fourth of July national holiday; and (massively so) from about 20 Dec–2 Jan. The parks can close to new arrivals by mid-morning at these times. The best combination of good weather and smaller crowds is in April (after Easter) and October. Rain isn't a big factor (although outdoor rides and the water parks will close if lightning threatens), but the crowds will noticeably thin out when it does rain and you can take advantage by bringing waterproofs or buying a cheap plastic poncho (all the parks sell them, but they are even

Downtown Orlando

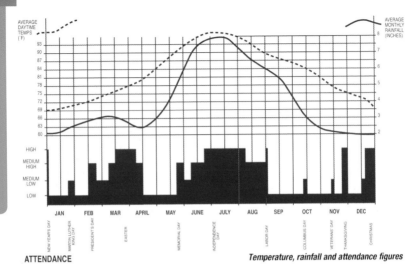

AVERAGE DAYTIME TEMPS (F)

AVERAGE MONTHLY RAINFALL (INCHES)

HIGH
MEDIUM HIGH
MEDIUM LOW
LOW

JAN   FEB   MAR   APRIL   MAY   JUNE   JULY   AUG   SEP   OCT   NOV   DEC

NEW YEAR'S DAY | MARTIN LUTHER KING DAY | PRESIDENT'S DAY | EASTER | MEMORIAL DAY | INDEPENDENCE DAY | LABOR DAY | COLUMBUS DAY | VETERAN'S DAY | THANKSGIVING | CHRISTMAS

ATTENDANCE

Temperature, rainfall and attendance figures

cheaper from Wal-Mart and the other supermarkets). In the colder months, take a few warm layers for early morning queues. Then, when it heats up, leave them in the park lockers. When it gets hot, take advantage of the air-conditioned attractions (and drink LOTS of water).

Where to stay

Where to stay is equally important and, again, there's a huge choice. As a rough guide, 4 main areas make up the great Orlando tourist conglomeration.

Walt Disney World: Some of the most sophisticated, convenient and fun

Rix Lounge at Disney's Coronado Springs

© Disney

places to stay are Disney's own hotels.

The same imagination that created the theme parks also worked on the likes of Disney's Polynesian Resort and Animal Kingdom Lodge. They all feature free transport, a resort ID card (so you can charge purchases to your room and have them delivered to the hotel), free parking and the BIG bonus of **Extra Magic Hours**. This allows Disney resort guests entry to 1 theme park each day, either a full hour before official opening or for 3 hours after closing, meaning you can do many of the attractions with only a fraction of the crowds (though the evenings can still get busy). Many resorts also have great kids' clubs and babysitting services. The drawback is, with the exception of *Disney's All-Star and Pop Century Resorts*, its hotels are among the most expensive, especially to eat in, and are not close to other attractions you may wish to visit. They make a good 1-week base, though.

Lake Buena Vista: Around the eastern fringes of *Walt Disney World* and along Interstate 4 (I-4), this features a good mix of hotels. It is handy for all the Disney fun, with most hotels offering free transport to the parks, plus there is excellent dining and shopping. Still a bit pricey, but its proximity to I-4 makes it pretty convenient.

BRIT TIP

Beware holiday homes (and some hotels) that insist they are 'just minutes from Disney World'. This is often a big exaggeration, and you may be 30 minutes or more from the parks. Try to get the exact address of the property and do a location check on **mapquest.com**.

International Drive: The ribbon development known as I-Drive lies midway between Disney and downtown Orlando and is an excellent central location. Running parallel to I-4, it's about 20 minutes' drive from Disney and close to Universal and SeaWorld. It is also a well-developed tourist area in its own right, with great shops, restaurants and attractions like Wet 'n Wild, Ripley's Believe It Or Not, WonderWorks and iFLY Orlando. The downside is it gets congested in peak times, especially in the evening. But it does represent good value and is one of the few areas with extensive pavements, making it easy to explore on foot. A sub-district off I-Drive is the Universal area of Kirkman Road and Major Boulevard.

Kissimmee: Budget holiday-makers can be found in their greatest numbers along the tourist sprawl of Highway 192 (the Irlo Bronson Memorial Highway), an almost unbroken 20ml/32km strip of hotels, motels, restaurants and shops. It offers some of the best economy accommodation and is handy for Disney, though it is further from Universal and SeaWorld. A car is advisable here, although there is extensive pavement, landscaping, bus shelters and benches, which makes it better for getting around on foot or by bus. **Highway 27** is often referred to as 'Kissimmee' but is actually either in Lake County (on the northern stretch) or Polk County (to the south). This is prime holiday home territory, with

BRIT TIP

A new sub-development of Highway 27 is **Berry Town Center**, a growing area of shops and restaurants, right next to the Highlands Reserve villa community.

numerous developments along its 13ml/21km (and increasing!) extent.

Split holidays

Florida has so much to offer that many people opt to split their holiday by having a week or 2 in Orlando and a week somewhere like the Gulf Coast, Miami or Florida Keys. The Atlantic coast has some great beaches only an hour to the east, the Florida Everglades are 3–4 hours to the south, and there are more wonderful beaches and pleasant coast roads to the west. There's great shopping almost everywhere, while there are stunning golf courses aplenty and opportunities to play or watch tennis, baseball and basketball, go fishing, boating or canoeing. The tour operators all offer a huge variety of packages, plus some popular cruise-and-stay options. If you can afford it, the best option is to have 2 weeks in Orlando then a week relaxing on one of Florida's fabulous beaches. A 2-week, half-and-half split is a regular choice, but can make your time in Orlando rather hectic, unless your additional week is somewhere like Cocoa Beach (near the Kennedy Space Center), which gives you the chance for day trips back to Orlando. Some companies offer a 10-day/4-day Orlando/coast split, which is a better idea for 2 weeks. Fly-drives offer great flexibility, but there is a lot to tempt you and you may find it better to book a 2-centre stay that includes a car and accommodation so you can still travel but avoid too much packing and unpacking (see also Chapter 9, The Twin Centre Option).

Kissimmee at night

Travel companies

There is serious competition for your hard-earned holiday money, but the travel companies work hard to keep Florida costs down, whether you fly-drive, book your own flights or take a package. Shop around to get the best value, but make sure the company you book with has some kind of bonding, either with ABTA in the case of travel agents or ATOL for flights, in case anything goes wrong. There are dozens of operators to choose from, divided roughly into the Big Boys; the Specialists; and the Online Agents.

The Big Boys

British Airways Holidays: BA benefits from its own direct, non-stop scheduled air service (9 Gatwick flights a week to Orlando and 5 to Tampa), offering great flexibility with almost any duration and combination possible, from budget to luxury 5-star accommodation (including its impressive Prestige collection), plus many hotels with 'free night' bonuses. Beach add-ons, 2 centres (a wide selection of both coasts), fly-drives and an extensive choice of villa homes are all available, along with many pre-bookable tours, experiences and excursions. BA also flies twice daily from Heathrow to Miami, opening up more fly-drive and multi-centre possibilities, including the Florida Keys, while its online check-in option can save valuable time at the airport.

Info: 0844 493 0758, **ba.com/florida**. *Airline:* British Airways. *Airports:* Orlando International, Tampa, Miami International.

Artist's impression of the new Dumbo's at the Magic Kingdom

First Choice: A complete programme from 6 UK airports (Birmingham, Bristol, Gatwick, Manchester, Glasgow and Newcastle) using Thomson Airways 6 days a week means First Choice remain a great family-friendly choice. Its flights feature all seat-back entertainment, more leg-room, wider seats and all meals included, plus Premier upgrades with a 92cm/36in pitch and leather seats, a 9in TV screen (with stop/start function), 30 channels to choose from and a choice of meals. First Choice have a great range of accommodation choices, including the highly rated Lake Buena Vista Resort Village & Spa, the excellent value of the new CocoKey Hotel & Water Resort on International Drive and 3 new beach hotels on the Gulf Coast. All kids under 12 also receive a Kids Eat Free card.

Info: 0871 200 4455, **firstchoice.co.uk/ holidays/florida-holidays**. *Airline:* Thomson Airways. *Airport:* Orlando Sanford International.

Monarch Holidays: With a long history in Florida, Monarch (the former Cosmos Holidays) focuses on the key resort areas in Orlando and the Gulf Coast (with an excellent range of properties in Clearwater, St Pete Beach, Sarasota, Newport Richey and Naples). Operating May–Oct with a full range of hotels (including Disney and Universal), suites and villas, it offers 7, 14 and 21-night holidays on a package, fly-drive and flight-only basis, and is well-priced for car hire. There are early booking offers and kids' prices from just £99. Early off-airport check-in is available on I-Drive for £7/person, as is the Royal Palm Lounge at Orlando Sanford International Airport (£10/ adult, £7.50/child).

Info: 0871 423 8568, **monarch.co.uk/florida/ holidays**. *Airline:* Monarch. *Airport:* Orlando Sanford International.

Thomas Cook: This is now the main Florida brand in the Thomas Cook stable (having absorbed the Airtours and Sunset brands in recent years), with a wide range of packages using its own Thomas Cook Airlines (from Gatwick and Manchester from spring-late autumn, plus Belfast and Glasgow in summer). TC Premium upgrades add wider, more comfy leather seats, free bar service and headsets, upgraded menu, dedicated check-in and priority boarding, plus a 30kg luggage allowance instead of 15kg (although an extra 5kg can be pre-booked for £35). With a good range of Disney's Value and Moderate resorts, plus a wide choice on International Drive and in Kissimmee (including many villas, town homes and resorts), this is very much mainstream holiday territory.

Info: 0844 412 5970, **thomascook.com**. *Airline:* Thomas Cook Airlines and Monarch (from Newcastle). *Airport:* Orlando Sanford International.

Thomson: Another of the UK's biggest names, Thomson has a strong emphasis on its Thomson Villas with Pool brand and Disney hotel selection, plus twin-centre International Drive/beach options in Clearwater, Fort Myers and St Pete's Beach. Other great choices include the Platinum-rated Hilton Bonnet Creek Resort and two fly-drive possibilities, while all under-12s receive a free Kids Eat Free card. Thomson offers 6 departure airports (including Newcastle, Glasgow and Manchester), with good in-flight entertainment and attractive kids' packs. Like First Choice, there is a handy day-before check-in service at Gatwick and Manchester. Thomson Airways boast an 84cm/33in standard seat pitch (one of the best anywhere) and great seatback TV in-flight entertainment, as well as options to pre-book seats together and upgrade to its Premium cabin with wider leather seats, improved entertainment choice, priority check-in and disembarkation, free drinks and enhanced meal service.

Info: 0871 230 0900, **thomson.co.uk**. *Airlines:* Thomson Airways. *Airport:* Orlando Sanford International.

Travel City Direct: This popular budget-minded brand was reborn under the Virgin Holidays umbrella in 2008 and now offers its wide range of competitively priced packages with the benefit of Virgin Atlantic flights from Gatwick, Manchester and Glasgow (the latter from April 2011, plus regional flights with other carriers). It still features fly-drives, single and multi-centre stays (including St Pete Beach, Clearwater, Bradenton and Sarasota), a choice of 3, 4 and 5-bed villas with private pool, Disney Resort and Universal Orlando hotels, plus car hire or transfer options and competitive attraction ticket prices. Travel City Direct holidays are all for 14 nights (or more), and offer flexibility to mix and match from a wide choice of accommodation, including affordably priced favourites.

Info: 0844 557 6969, **travelcitydirect.com**. *Airlines:* Virgin Atlantic, plus BA, Delta, US Airways and Continental. *Airport:* Orlando International.

Virgin Holidays: Britain's leading tour operator to Florida – and the Official Holiday Company to Universal Orlando – has a vast variety of combinations, with 150 properties, 2-centre options to Miami, Daytona Beach, Florida Keys and lesser known resorts such as Vero Beach, Crystal Rivers and Singer Island, plus the likes of New York, Jamaica, Barbados, Mexico and Cuba, and cruises with Carnival and Royal Caribbean. With Virgin Atlantic's non-stop scheduled service to Orlando (up to 15 times a week from Gatwick, 9 a week from Manchester and 2 from Glasgow, plus daily Heathrow to Miami), it offers free drinks, kids' packs, meals and games, plus upgrades to Premium

Hollywood Rip Ride Rocket at Universal

© Universal Orlando Resort

Virgin's V-Room

All Virgin Holidays passengers have the option of the V-Room private lounge at Gatwick, a special hideaway that includes a dedicated kids' play area, video games, big-screen TV, internet access, relaxing adults-only area, free snacks, fruit, soft drinks and coffee, and a fast-track security channel. It costs £17 per adult and £10 per child (2-11), but is free with Platinum Collection bookings.

Economy and Upper Class (the latter including the revolutionary fully flat beds), as well as a Twilight day-before check-in service at Gatwick. It has a wide choice of accommodation, including all Disney resorts (plus a free Car Upgrade offer for 7-night stays at any Disney hotel) and a 'favourites' selection offering extra value, location or other benefits, and is popular for fly-drives, flying into Orlando and out of Miami, and vice versa. Its Platinum Collection features deluxe resorts such as Reunion in Orlando and gorgeous Little Palm Island in the Keys. Virgin also has a free Downtown Disney check-in service for return flights, letting guests check in 8.15am–1pm on the day of departure, freeing up the rest of the day to enjoy at leisure. Its car hire choice is the widest around, including 'green' hybrid cars. Airport transfers, shuttle services and 2-centre transfers are all available for non-drivers. Other useful extras include Single Parent and Single Traveller offers, free upgrades to Premium Economy with select accommodations and free Kids

Hagrid's Hut at the new Harry Potter

© 2010 Universal Orlando Resort

Eat Free cards for under-12s at Virgin's in-resort welcome meetings. Virgin's Universal Orlando tie-up also means its bookings also include extra perks to the new **Wizarding World of Harry Potter,** including free breakfast in the Three Broomsticks, free parking and a Potter keepsake. Direct bookings benefit from a unique concierge service to ask questions of Virgin reps in Orlando and tailor-make tours (call 0844 557 3890 after booking or e-mail **orlandorep@fly.virgin.com**), while there are free kids' places for early bookers. Platinum accommodation selections also include free access to Virgin's V-Room lounge at Gatwick Airport.

Info: 0844 557 4000, **virginholidays.co.uk**. *Airline:* Virgin Atlantic, plus regional options with Continental, US Airways and Delta. *Airports:* Orlando International, Miami.

> ### BRITTIP
> Virgin Holidays introduced a price guarantee in 2011. If customers find a lower price for the following year by 21 April, Virgin will match any of its holidays, flying with Virgin Atlantic, against any ABTA/ATOL tour operator.

The specialists

Continental Airlines Vacations: An established airline brand with flights to 11 destinations in Florida from 7 UK airports, offering daily scheduled services for great flexibility. Its Glasgow and Edinburgh routes are particularly popular, while it also features a huge range of multi-centre options, including a New York stopover.

Info: 0844 557 4040, **covacations.co.uk**. *Airline:* Continental. *Airport:* Orlando International.

Funway Holidays: The sister company of America's largest tour operator and a leading US specialist, Funway offers a tailor-made service to match Orlando with any option, providing total flexibility from 13 UK airports. Its private villas are a big feature, but it also serves up a wide array of accommodation, including the 3 Universal resorts and all the Disney hotels, plus the latest fly-drive deals and competitively priced attraction tickets.

Dining Plan options

Most tour operators offer the Disney Dining Plan as an optional extra with Disney hotel packages and it can be good value if you spend ALL your time in Walt Disney World, where there are few cheap dining outlets. But, because ALL members of the family must be included for the FULL length of your stay, even the Quick Service plan adds around £890 for a family of four (with children 3-9) staying for two weeks; the Dining Plan would be £1,232; and the Deluxe Plan a whopping £1,792. You can certainly eat cheaper elsewhere, so consider if this is a good choice before you book. However, the Dining Plan is occasionally offered as a FREE perk by tour operators at quieter times of the year – definitely a BIG bonus.

See more on Disney Dining Plan on page 66.

Info: 0844 557 3333, **funwayholidays.co.uk**.
Airlines: Various scheduled, including Virgin, BA and Continental.
Airport: Orlando International.

Jetsave: This Florida specialist with more than 30 years' experience puts the accent on flexibility, with a wide choice of scheduled airlines, including a Virgin Atlantic upgrade. You have the full selection of hotels and apartments and an exhaustive choice of holiday homes, with simple, accurate star ratings for each property and plenty of mix-and-match two-centre options.

Info: 0871 231 2295, **jetsave.co.uk**. *Airline:* Virgin Atlantic.
Airport: Orlando International.

Ocean Florida: This recent (2003) company has quickly become a reliable source of packages and flight-only options to Florida, as well as providing car hire, airport transfers, cruises and attraction tickets, so it makes a good source for those who want to put together their own holiday. It features several tour operators, such as Thomas Cook and British Airways, and often offers some highly competitive deals.

Info: 0800 804 8430, **ocean-florida.co.uk**.
Airlines: Various scheduled, including BA, plus Thomas Cook, Thomson/First Choice

Complete Orlando

The highly rated Attraction Tickets Direct company now has a full ATOL-bonded travel operator called **Complete Orlando**, which is well worth trying for packages, flights, hotels, car hire and travel insurance. It offers a wide range of accommodation (usually with some great deals on Disney hotels in particular), plus handy online videos, and promises no credit card fees or hidden extras. Info: 0800 294 8844, **completeorlando.co.uk**.

and Monarch charters. *Airports:* Orlando International, Miami, Tampa; Orlando Sanford International (with charters).

Others: Try the high-quality style of **Kuoni** (01306 747002, **kuoni.co.uk**); **USAirtours**, tailor-made US itineraries, many with villas and apartments in Orlando (0800 035 0149, **usairtours.co.uk**); and **Premier Holidays**, more tailor-made choice and seasonal specials (0844 4937 531, **premierholidays.co.uk**).

Online agents

The recent growth of online travel agents has been huge, and you will find some great deals in this group, for packages, flights or accommodation.

eBookers: A big company with a good reputation for flights, hotels, insurance and more (020 3320 3320, **ebookers.com**).

The Flying Fish at Disney's Boardwalk

© Disney

Expedia: One of the biggest companies worldwide, with simple, easy-to-use booking, e-mail updates and a useful Deals section (0871 226 0808, **expedia.co.uk**).

LastMinute: An online company set up purely to offer late deals is now a major mainstream agent, with the full range of holidays, flights, hotels, etc. (0871 222 5952, **lastminute.com**).

Travel Supermarket: A service that instantly searches multiple online travel sites, and gives you the best price match it can find, plus it also has Fare Alert and Bargain Hunters features, weekly e-mails and various travel forums (0845 345 5708, **travelsupermarket.com**).

Others: Trailfinders, the UK's largest independent travel firm and tailor-made specialists (0845 054 6060, **trailfinders.com**); **Travelbag:** (0871 703 4698, **travelbag.co.uk**); **Opodo:** (0871 277 0090, **opodo.co.uk**).

Online search engines

Not travel agents but still worth checking for individual bookings: **Kelkoo** (http://travel.kelkoo.co.uk), **Kayak** (kayak.co.uk) and **Travel Jungle** (traveljungle.co.uk). For flights only: **Flight Centre** (0844 800 8660, **flightcentre.co.uk**), **Dial A Flight** (0844 811 4444, **dialaflight.com**) and **NetFlights** (0844 493 1234, **netflights. com**). For flight price comparison sites: **Sky Scanner** (skyscanner.com), **NowFly** (nowfly.co.uk) and **Cheap Flights** (cheapflights.co.uk) are also worth a visit.

Scheduled flights

Apart from the charter airlines, there are few DIRECT flights to Orlando – only with **Virgin Atlantic** (Gatwick, Manchester and Glasgow), **British Airways** (Gatwick) and **Aer Lingus** (Dublin) – but you can often save money on indirect flights. Choose from **American Airlines** (from Heathrow via New York, Boston, Dallas, Raleigh-Durham, Miami or Chicago; Manchester via New York or Chicago; Dublin or Shannon via Chicago; **americanairlines.co.uk**); **Continental** (Heathrow via New York or Houston; Manchester, Birmingham, Bristol, Belfast, Dublin, Glasgow or Edinburgh via New York; **continental.com**); **Delta/KLM** (Gatwick via Atlanta; Heathrow via Atlanta, Washington, Minneapolis, Detroit or New York; Manchester via New York or Atlanta; or Edinburgh via Atlanta; **delta.com**); **United** (Heathrow via Washington or Chicago; **unitedairlines. co.uk**); and **US Airways** (Gatwick via Charlotte or Philadelphia; Heathrow, Manchester, Glasgow, Dublin or Shannon via Philadelphia; **usairways. com**). The obvious drawback is the extra journey time, and the connecting flight may land you in Orlando late in the evening. However, it does break the journey and places like Detroit and Atlanta often process international passengers quicker than Orlando, meaning less hassle when you arrive in Florida. **Icelandair** (Heathrow, Glasgow and Manchester; 0870 787 4020, **icelandair.co.uk**) also offers a scheduled transatlantic route to Orlando Sanford International Airport via Reykjavik, Iceland.

What to see when

Once you arrive, the temptation is to head for the nearest theme park, then the next, and so on. Except this is the best way to end up exhausted! Some days at the parks are busier than others, while you'll also need a few rest days. So here's what to do.

Using the Planner on pages 360–1 as an example of how to lay out your holiday (or just use the *Brit Guide* Itinerary Planner Service, page 47),

Christmas at Downtown Disney Marketplace

© Disney

Direct flights to Orlando

All flights to Orlando Sanford Airport unless specified; 'Orlando' means Orlando International Airport.

Airline	Flying from	Economy seat pitch	Premium seat pitch	Aircraft used	In-flight entertainment	Baggage allowance
British Airways ba.com or 0844 493 0787	Gatwick (to Orlando and Tampa); Heathrow (to Miami)	31in/ 78.7cm	38in/ 96.5cm (World Traveller Plus); 73in/ 185cm (Club)	Boeing 777	Interactive seatback TVs	2 x 23kg; 3 x 23kg (Club)
Thomson Airways http://flights. thomson.co.uk or 0871 231 4787	Birmingham, Bristol, East Midlands, Gatwick, Glasgow, Manchester, Newcastle	33in/ 83.8cm	36in/ 91.4cm	Boeing 767	Seatback TVs	1 x 20kg; 1 x 23kg in Premier
Monarch monarch.co.uk/ flights or 0870 040 5040	Dublin, Gatwick, Manchester, Newcastle	31in/ 78.7cm	34in/ 86.3cm	Airbus A330, Boeing 767	Seatback TVs in Premium only	1 x 20kg; 1 x 30kg
Thomas Cook Airlines flythomascook.com or 0871 895 0055	Belfast, Gatwick, Glasgow, Manchester	33in/ 83.8cm	35in/ 89cm	Airbus A330	Seatback TVs	1 x 15kg; 1 x 30kg premium cabin
Virgin Atlantic virgin-atlantic.com or 0844 209 7777	Gatwick, Manchester and Glasgow (to Orlando); Heathrow (to Miami)	31in/ 78.7cm (34in pitch available for extra fee at check-in)	38in/ 96.5cm (Premium) and 79.5in/ 202cm (Miami)	Boeing 747 (Orlando) Airbus A340 (Miami)	Seatback TVs	2 x 23kg; 2 x 32kg (Premium) 3 x 32kg (Upper)

make a note of the attractions you want to see over the length of your stay. The most sensible strategy is to plan around the 8 'must-see' parks – *Magic Kingdom Park, Epcot, Disney's Hollywood Studios, Disney's Animal Kingdom Park*, Universal Studios, Islands of Adventure, SeaWorld and Busch Gardens. If you have only a week, drop Busch Gardens and focus on Disney, Universal and SeaWorld. Space fans should also include the Kennedy Space Center, but it often bores young children.

As a basic rule, the *Magic Kingdom* is the biggest hit with children, and families often find it requires 2 days. The same can be said for *Epcot*, but there are fewer rides to amuse the younger ones. Only the most fleet of foot with the benefit of relatively low crowds can negotiate *Epcot* in a day. The *Animal Kingdom* is also a little short on attractions for the youngest visitors but still requires a full day, as does *Disney's Hollywood Studios* (not forgetting the evening Fantasmic! show). SeaWorld occasionally needs rather longer and Universal Studios can be a 2-day park at its busiest. Islands of Adventure also needs at least day now the *Wizarding World of Harry Potter* area is open. Busch Gardens, extremely popular with British families, is another full-day affair, especially as it is 75 minutes away in Tampa to the west. All the attractions are described in detail in Chapters 5–8, so it's best to get an idea of time requirements before you pick up your pencil.

Smaller attractions

Of the other, smaller scale attractions, the nature park of Silver Springs is a full day out as it also involves a near 2-hour drive to get there, but everything else can be fitted around your Big 8 itinerary. The water parks make for a relaxing ½-day, as does the quieter Bok Tower Gardens. Gatorland (requiring a good ½-day) is a unique look at some of Florida's oldest inhabitants and is a good combination with Boggy Creek Airboats. Aviation fans must not miss a trip to Fantasy of Flight (further down I-4) for another novel ½-day experience. Then there are the likes of Ripley's Believe It Or Not museum and the WonderWorks house of fun, both offering several hours' entertainment, the thrills of iFLY Orlando (an indoor 'sky-diving' wind tunnel) and the lure of old-fashioned go-karts and other fairground-type rides at Fun Spot, Magical Midway and Old Town. Many stay open after the major theme parks close.

Disney also has *DisneyQuest*, an imaginative interactive arcade that guarantees several hours of fun (especially for older children) in its *Downtown Disney* area, while each main area is also well served with creatively designed mini-golf courses for that spare hour or two.

Evenings

The evening entertainment features a similarly wide choice. By far the best, and worth at least one evening each, are *Downtown Disney* and Universal's CityWalk – the latter will keep you busy until the early hours! Dinner shows provide a lot of fun; 2-hour cabarets based on themes such as medieval knights, pirates, Arabian Nights, magic shows and murder mysteries that all include a hearty meal.

Shopping

Shopping in Orlando is world class (see Chapter 12). Your battle plan should include at least a day to visit the spectacular malls and discount centres, like the excellent Orlando Premium Outlets or Prime Outlets International, Mall at Millenia and the Florida Mall. These do get busy at weekends, but are handy places if the rain sets in.

What to do when

There are several guidelines for avoiding the worst of the tourist hordes, even in high season. The vast majority are Americans, who often arrive at weekends and head for the main theme parks first. That means Monday is generally a bad time to visit the *Magic Kingdom Park*, as is Sunday, while Tuesday is usually also humming at *Epcot*. New rides like Toy Story Mania (*Disney's Hollywood Studios*) also create longer queues here, too, notably at weekends.

Disney's Extra Magic Hours programme, which allows its hotel guests entry to 1 park a day either 1 hour early or 3 hours after regular closing time, creates bigger crowds, too. So, if you are NOT staying at a Disney hotel, you need to avoid these EMH days. For much of the year, they keep to the following regular weekly

Downtown Disney

© Disney

Our must-do experiences

Soarin' and IllumiNations show (*Epcot*)

Cirque du Soleil® (*Downtown Disney*)

Harry Potter and the Forbidden Journey, plus the Amazing Adventures of Spider-Man and The Hulk rides (Islands of Adventure)

Boggy Creek Airboats (Kissimmee)

Expedition Everest and Festival of The Lion King (*Animal Kingdom*)

Wishes/Nightastic fireworks and Pirates of the Caribbean ride (*Magic Kingdom*)

Fantasmic! show and Star Tours ride (*Disney's Hollywood Studios*)

Shrek 4-D and The Simpsons Ride (Universal Studios)

Shopping!

Believe and Blue Horizons shows (SeaWorld)

Edge of Africa and SheiKra coaster (Busch Gardens)

Shuttle Launch Experience (Kennedy Space Center)

A Disney character meal

A day at a water park

the weekends when locals visit. This often means Monday is quietest at both Universal and Islands of Adventure, getting busier through the week, with the latter being slightly more crowded (especially with the opening of the new Wizarding World of Harry Potter). If *Walt Disney World* is humming early in the week, that makes it a good time to visit SeaWorld, Busch Gardens, Silver Springs or the Kennedy Space Center. Try to avoid Wet 'n Wild and Aquatica at weekends, too.

Getting the most out of your days at the parks is another art form, and there are several options to consider. The opening times seldom vary from 9am but arriving early is highly advisable. Apart from being near the head of the queues (and you will encounter some SERIOUS queues, or 'lines' as the Americans call them), the parks occasionally open earlier than scheduled if the crowds build up quickly. So, you can be a step ahead of the masses by arriving at least 30 minutes before opening time, or an hour early during peak periods. Apart from anything else, you will be better placed to park in the huge car parks and catch the tram to the main gates (anything up to ½ mile away).

BRIT TIP

If your hotel is not far away, take a mid-afternoon break from the park and return for a siesta or a swim. Your car park ticket is valid all day, and the evening is often the best time to be in the parks.

pattern (where you should avoid the parks on those days, unless you are a Disney hotel guest): *Magic Kingdom*, Tues and Thurs in peak season, Thurs only off-peak; *Epcot*, Sun in peak, Tues off-peak; *Disney's Hollywood Studios*, Mon and Fri in peak, Sat off-peak; *Animal Kingdom*, Wed and Sat in peak, Mon off-peak. Be aware EMH days can still change from month to month at short notice, and the *Magic Kingdom* can often have multiple successive days at Easter and Christmas. The *Animal Kingdom* is the hardest to navigate when crowded, while *Epcot* handles the crowds best. *Disney's Blizzard Beach* and *Typhoon Lagoon* water parks hit high tide at weekends, and Thurs and Fri in summer.

At Universal Orlando, the picture is different as there are no early entry days, and the busiest days are usually

Cirque du Soleil

© Cirque du Soleil

Once you've put yourself in pole position, don't waste time on the shops, scenery and other frippery that will lure the unprepared first-timer. Instead, head straight for some of the main rides and get a few big-time thrills under your belt before the main hordes arrive. You will quickly work out where the most popular attractions are as the majority of early birds will flock to them. Use Chapters 5 and 6 to help plan your park strategies. You can also benefit from doing the opposite of what the masses do after the initial rush has subsided. Try not to have all your meals in the parks, too; eating here can be expensive (up to $10/person for even a basic counter-service meal). Eating all you can at a buffet breakfast somewhere like Golden Corral and having a light lunch will save $$$s!

BRIT TIP
The water IS safe to drink in the US but it may not taste great as it's heavily fluoridated. Bottled water is cheap at supermarkets – and you'll save a lot on buying it in the parks.

The spa at Disney's Grand Floridian

© Disney

Pace yourself

Another word of warning: Disney's parks, notably the *Magic Kingdom*, stay open late for the main holidays, until midnight at times, and that can be a *l-o-n-g* day for children. It's vital to pace yourself, especially if you arrive early. There are plenty of options to take time off for a drink or a sit-down somewhere air-conditioned, and you can benefit from the American propensity to take mealtimes seriously by avoiding lunchtime (noon–1.30pm) and dinnertime (5.30–7pm). So, after you've had a couple of hours of park-going, it pays to take an early lunch (before noon), plunge back into it all for another 3 hours or so, have another snack mid-afternoon and then return to the main rides as the crowds ease off a little in late afternoon.

Comfort and clothing

You may feel jetlagged for the first day or two after your arrival, but this can be reduced by avoiding alcohol and coffee on the plane and drinking plenty of water.

BRIT TIP
Don't be tempted to pack a lot of smart or formal clothing – you really won't need it in hot, informal Florida.

The most important part of your holiday wardrobe is your footwear – you'll spend a lot of time on your feet, even at off-peak periods. The smallest park is 'only' 100 acres/40ha, but that is irrelevant to the amount of time you spend queuing. This is not the time to break in new sandals or trainers. Comfortable, well-worn shoes or trainers are essential (many rate Croc-type shoes as ideal park footwear). Otherwise, you need dress only as the climate dictates. T-shirts and shorts are appropriate in all parks and nearly all restaurants will accept casual dress. However, swimwear is not acceptable away from pool areas.

If you feel the need for a change of clothes or a sweater for the evening after a long day, use the handy lockers

Want to see more?

If, like us, you want to make the most of every holiday opportunity, you could travel further afield in America with the help of its efficient low-cost airline system. Orlando is an excellent base from which to explore city destinations such as New York, Chicago, Boston, Dallas, Washington, Baltimore and Memphis, and great states like Georgia, South Carolina, Virginia and Pennsylvania, plus the Caribbean and Mexico, all of which are only 2 hours' flight away; or go even further to glittering Las Vegas, Los Angeles, San Francisco or San Diego. With the benefit of cheap hotel deals (check out **hotels.com** and **orbitz.com**), you can seriously spread your wings (ahem!) by using the likes of **AirTran Airways**, Florida's leading low-cost carrier, which is based at Orlando International Airport and also flies from 9 other Florida airports, including Tampa, Miami, West Palm Beach, Jacksonville and Fort Myers. Skip ahead to page 355 for more on how to extend your holiday. Repeat visitors may like to consider this, and it's only a small additional investment after going all the way to Florida (look up **airtran.com** for its timetable, fares and frequent fare sales).

(unlimited use all day, even if you change parks). All the parks are also well equipped with pushchairs (or 'strollers') for hire, and baby services are located at regular intervals. It is VITAL to use high-factor sun creams at all times, even during the winter when the sun may not feel strong but can still burn. Few things will ruin your holiday like severe sunburn. Orlando has a subtropical climate and you need higher factor creams than in the Mediterranean. Use sun block on sensitive areas like nose and ears, and splash on the after-sun liberally at the end of the day. You'll also need waterproof sun cream for swimming. Skincare products are widely available and usually inexpensive (at the likes of Wal-Mart, Publix and Target). Wear a hat during the day, and avoid alcohol, coffee and fizzy drinks until the evening as they are dehydrating and make you liable to heatstroke. You must increase your fluid intake

BRIT TIP
One of the best ways to keep cool in the sun is to visit a supermarket and buy a simple mist spray fan (about $7.99), which you carry with you and just refill with water.

SIGNIFICANTLY in the summer, but stick to still soft drinks such as Gatorade, an energy squash, and lots of water.

BRIT TIP
Look after your feet and avoid the onset of blisters by buying some moleskin footpads from a supermarket.

Medical aid

Should you require medical treatment, for sunburn or other first aid, consult your tour operator's info about local hospitals and surgeries. In the event of a medical or other emergency, dial 911 as you would 999 in Britain. It cannot be over-stressed, however, that you should take out comprehensive travel insurance (see page 32) for any trip to America, as there is NO National Health Service and ANY form of medical treatment is expensive and must be paid for. Keep all the receipts and put in a claim on your return home.

BRIT TIP
The summer is mosquito time and a spray-on or roll-on insect repellent is highly advisable. Brands to look for locally are Cutter, Repel and Off!

Barrier Island beach

Emergency outpatients: These can be found with Centra Care at Florida Hospital Medical Center in 16 Central Florida locations and can provide hotel in-room services (407 238 2000) and free transport (407 938 0650; **centracare.org**). Open from 8am daily, Centra Care centres are at: 12500 S Apopka-Vineland Road near the Crossroads shopping centre and *Downtown Disney* at Lake Buena Vista (until midnight on weekdays, 8pm Sat and Sun; 407 934 2273); 7848 West Irlo Bronson Memorial Highway (192), in Formosa Gardens Village (until 8pm Mon–Fri, 5pm Sat and Sun; 407 397 7032); 6001 Vineland Road, near Universal Studios (7am–7pm Mon– Fri, 8am–6pm Sat and Sun; 407 351 6682); on Sand Lake Road, between John Young Parkway and Orange Blossom Trail (8am–8pm Mon–Fri, 9am–5pm Sat and Sun; 407 851 6478); and 4320 West Vine Street, near Medieval Times (until 8pm Mon–Fri, 5pm Sat and Sun; 407 390 1888). **Dr P. Phillips Hospital**, 9400 Turkey Lake Road, has an emergency outpatients (407 351 8500). **East Coast Medical Network** (407 648 5252, **themedicalconcierge.com**) makes hotel and villa 'house calls' 24 hours a day.

BRIT TIP

If you take regular prescription drugs, check with your doctor or pharmacist to see if they have a different name in the US. Many do (e.g. adrenaline is known as epinephrine) and it is worth finding out and carrying the drug with both names, in case of an emergency. The US name for paracetamol is acetaminophen.

Chemists: The two largest chemists ('drug stores' in the US) are **Walgreens** (**walgreens.com**) and **CVS** (**cvs.com**), and the Walgreens at 12100 S Apopka-Vineland Road (near Downtown Disney), 5935 W Irlo Bronson Memorial Highway (Highway 192 in Kissimmee), 6201, 8050, 8959 and 12650 International Drive (among others) are open 24 hours a day.

BRIT TIP

Several Walgreens stores have walk-in Take Care Clinics that can treat patients (18 and over) 7 days a week, which can be quicker than visiting a hospital or other medical centre.

Travel insurance

Having said you shouldn't travel without insurance, you shouldn't pay more than you need to either. Your travel agent may imply you need to buy its policy, which might be expensive, but you are certainly free to buy elsewhere. In all cases, you should make sure your policy has:

- Medical cover of at least £2m;

- Personal liability up to £2m (this won't cover driving abroad; you still need Supplementary Liability Insurance with your car hire firm);

- Cancellation or curtailment cover up to £5,000;

- Personal property cover up to £1,500 (but check on expensive items, as most policies limit single articles to £250);

- Cash and document cover, including your passport and tickets;

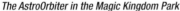

The AstroOrbiter in the Magic Kingdom Park

© Disney

Top things to do for FREE!

While Orlando has a magnificent array of paid-for attractions, there are still many things you can do that don't cost a cent.

Disney's Boardwalk Resort: Free nightly entertainment includes jugglers, comedians and live music. Time your visit to coincide with the 9pm IllumiNations fireworks extravaganza at nearby Epcot. **Fort Christmas Historical Park:** 20ml/32km east of Orlando in the town of Christmas is this replica of an 1837 US Army fort from the Seminole Indian Wars, with tours, exhibits, video presentations and restored homes, and special events during some weekends; 8am–8pm summer, 8am–6pm winter (closed Mon and public holidays; **nbbd.com/godo/FortChristmas**). **Lake Eola Park:** Take a walk on the mild side in downtown Orlando. The kids can play or feed the swans and there is a live rock concert series in summer at the Walt Disney Amphitheater (**cityoforlando.net** and **rockinlakeeola.com**). **Lake Tibet-Butler Preserve:** Just 5 minutes from Disney but light years from the theme park bustle (CR 535, Winter Garden-Vineland Road) is this local nature preserve, with quiet trails, lake overlook and interpretive centre. Open 9am–dusk (not public holidays), it is on the Great Florida Birding Trail and is a minor gem of native wildlife (**http://myfwc.com/Recreation/View_Destinations_site-c07. htm**). **Lakeridge Winery and Vineyards:** Join one of its fun, free wine-tasting tours and you'll know why Lakeridge (in nearby Clermont) has won more than 300 awards. But designate a driver as sample sizes are generous! 10am–5pm Mon–Sat, 11am–5pm Sun (**lakeridgewinery.com**). **Leu Gardens:** Just north of downtown Orlando, this sanctuary of peace and quiet, with wildlife, nature trails and the 1880s' Leu House Museum is free 9am–noon on the first Mon every month (**leugardens.org**). **Morse Museum of American Art:** This superb little museum in tranquil Winter Park, dedicated to American paintings, ceramics and representative arts from the 19th and 20th centuries, is free 4–8pm every Fri Nov–Apr (**morsemuseum.org**). **Old Town, Kissimmee:** The biggest vintage car parade in the US every Sat, with cars on display from 1pm and the parade at 8.30pm, a Friday Night Cruise (classic cars 1975–87) at 9pm and Bike Nites at 6pm every Thurs, with up to 700 motorbikes each week, plus live music nightly (**old-town.com**). **Peabody Duck March:** Turn up at 11am or 5pm at the Peabody Hotel to see its resident mallards get the red carpet treatment as they either arrive or leave their lobby fountain 'home' (**peabodyorlando.com**). **Sanford Museum:** Some quaint local history is well presented through the personal collections of city founder Henry S. Sanford (11am–4pm Tues–Fri, 1–4pm Sat). Combine your visit with a walking tour, including the new Riverwalk (**ci.sanford.fl.us/Museum.aspx**). **Downtown Concert Series:** 4 times a year, local radio station WMMO stages free open-air concerts in front of City Hall with the likes of Joe Cocker and Tears For Fears. Great day out, with festival atmosphere (**wmmo. com/dcs**).

PLUS: Just watching the participants in action at **IFLY Orlando** on International Drive (page 238); watch the NASCAR stock cars and IndyCar machines for free daily at the 1-mile tri-oval of the **Walt Disney World Speedway** (near the Magic Kingdom); the **Cornell Fine Arts Museum** at Rollins College in Winter Park (page 254); and the many hiking trails and scenic points of **Ocala National Forest**, north of Orlando (**stateparks.com/Ocala.html**).

- A 24-hour emergency helpline.

If you want to go horse-riding, check your policy includes **dangerous sports cover**. Shop around at reputable dealers such as: **American Express** (0800 028 7573, **americanexpress.com/uk**); **AA** (0845 092 1677, **aatravelinsurance.com**); **Aviva** (0800 051 3606, **aviva.co.uk**); **Direct Travel** (0845 605 2700, **direct-travel. co.uk**); **Club Direct** (0800 083 2466, **clubdirect.com**); **Columbus** (0870 033 9988, **columbusdirect.com**); **Egg** (0800 519 9931, **http://new.egg.com**); **Worldwide Travel Insurance** (01892 833338, **worldwideinsure.com**). **Money Supermarket** also compares travel insurers at **moneysupermarket.com/ insurance**.

BRIT TIP
Travelling with young children? The new Tiny Tots Away website has travel insurance especially for families, with free cover for youngsters, through Travel Insurance Facilities Group (**tinytotsaway.com** or call 0871 250 7500).

Florida with children

We are often asked what we think is the right age to take children to Orlando, and there is no set answer. Some toddlers take to it instantly, while some 6 or even 7-year-olds are overwhelmed. Very often, the best attractions for young children are the hotel swimming pool or the tram ride to a park's front gates! Some love the Disney characters instantly, while others find them frightening. There is no predicting how they'll react but, at 4½, Simon's oldest boy loved just about every second of his first experience (apart from the fireworks – see page 36) and still talks about it. A 3-year-old may not remember much, but will have fun and provide you with some great memories, photos and videos. Here are some top tips for travelling with youngsters.

The flight: Try to look calm (even if you don't feel it) and relaxed. Small children soon pick up on any anxieties and make them worse. Pack a bag with plenty of little bits for them (comics, sweets, colouring books, small surprise toys, etc.) and keep vital extras such as Calpol (in sachets, if possible), a change of clothes, a small first-aid kit (plasters, antiseptic cream, baby wipes), sunglasses, a hat and sunscreen in your hand luggage.

BRIT TIP
The handy Kids Eat Free card for Orlando offers a free child's meal with every adult meal or entrée purchased for children 11 and under. It costs just £10 per child and features more than 130 local restaurants – from standard choices like Chick-fil-A and Dunkin' Donuts to the upmarket Taverna Opa and Bergamo's – with potential savings of $350. See more at **kidseatfreecard.com** or buy from Attractions Tickets Direct, 0800 975 0002.

Once you're there: Take things slowly and let your children dictate the pace to a large extent. In hot, humid summer, only the most placid

The perfect place for kids

© Disney

Attractions with posted warnings for expectant mothers

Magic Kingdom: Big Thunder Mountain Railroad, Space Mountain, Splash Mountain, Tomorrowland Speedway, The Barnstormer at Goofy's Wiseacre Farm.

Epcot: Soarin', Mission: SPACE, Test Track.

Hollywood Studios: Rock 'n Roller Coaster, Twilight Zone Tower of Terror, Star Tours.

Animal Kingdom: Dinosaur!, Kali River Rapids, Kilimanjaro Safari, Primeval Whirl, Expedition Everest.

Universal Studios: Jimmy Neutron's Nicktoon Blast, Shrek 4-D, Twister-Ride it Out!, Revenge of the Mummy, Disaster!, Jaws, Men in Black Alien Attack, Woody Woodpecker's, Nuthouse Coaster, ET Adventure, Terminator 2: 3-D (stationary seats available).

Islands of Adventure: Cat in the Hat, Dragon Challenge, Flight of the Hippogriff, Harry Potter and the Forbidden Journey, Incredible Hulk Coaster, Jurassic Park River Adventure, Dudley Do-Right's Ripsaw Falls, Popeye and Bluto's Bilge Rat Barges, Storm Force Accelatron, Dr. Doom's Fearfall, The Amazing Adventures of Spider-Man.

SeaWorld: Journey to Atlantis, Kraken, Manta, Jazzie Jellies, Shamu Express, Swishy Fishies, Wild Arctic (ride portion), Rock Wall, Trampoline.

Busch Gardens: SheikRa, Gwazi, Kumba, Montu, Python, Scorpion, Cheetah Chase, Rhino Rally, Stanley Falls Log Flume, Congo River Rapids, Tanganyika Tidal Wave, Sandstorm, Phoenix, Ubanga-Banga Bumper Cars, Crazy Camel.

children (and few under-5s, in our experience) will happily queue for an hour or more at a ride, so use Disney's FastPass system (see pages 106 and 107) judiciously. The heat, in particular, can result in grizzly kids in no time, so take breaks for drinks and splash zones or head for attractions with air-conditioning. Remember to carry your small first-aid kit. Baby wipes always come in handy, and it's a good idea to take spare clothes, which you can leave in the lockers at all the parks. Going back to the hotel for an afternoon snooze is a good idea – you will also dodge the worst of the heat and crowds.

⚡ BRIT TIP

Pushchairs ('strollers') are essential, even if your children are a year or two out of them. The walking wears kids out quickly and a pushchair can save a lot of discomfort. You can take your own, hire them at the parks or, better still, buy one for as little as $20 at a local supermarket.

In the sun: Carry sun cream and sun block at all times and use it often, in queues, on buses, etc. A children's

after-sun lotion is also advisable. And make sure they drink a lot of water or non-fizzy drinks; tiredness and irritability are often the signs of mild dehydration.

Dining out: Look for Kids Eat Free deals in many places, as they can apply to children up to 12, and take advantage of the many buffet options (see Chapter 11, Dining Out) to fill up the family or for picky eaters. Many restaurants do Meals To Go if

Coral Reef restaurant at Epcot

© Disney

you want a quiet meal in your own accommodation without the worry of the kids playing up. And try to let your children get used to the characters (especially the size of them) before you go to one of the many wonderful character meals.

Having fun: Let your children do some of the decision-making and be prepared to go with the flow if they find something unexpected – the many squirt fountains and splash zones in the parks are an example (bring swimsuits and/or a change of clothes!). The Orlando rule of 'You Can't Do It All' applies especially with kids. And be aware the evening fireworks are loud and youngsters can get distressed. The 3 hotels around the Magic Kingdom offer safe ways to view the fireworks at a distance.

Baby centres: All the parks have facilities for nursing mothers and can provide baby food and nappies on request (check the park map for the locations). The centres can even provide spare children's underpants for those little accidents. All Disney hotel gift shops stock baby food and nappies. Expectant mothers are strongly advised not to ride some of the more dynamic attractions and coasters, and there will be clear warnings on park maps and at the rides.

BRIT TIP

Avoid making phone calls from your hotel room – they're hugely expensive. It's cheaper to buy a local phonecard and use a normal payphone. British tri-band mobiles are also costly to use in the US. To call the UK from the US, dial 011 44, then drop the first 0 from the UK area code.

Babysitting: Available through many Disney resorts and some of the bigger hotels elsewhere, while Kids Nite Out is a service providing parents with a chance to have an evening out on their own. It offers in-room sitters or helpers during your stay at a rate of $16/hour for the first child, $18.50 for 2, $21 for 3 and $23.50 for 4 (with an additional $2/hour after 9pm) for children 6 weeks to 12 years. There is a 4-hour minimum and reservations are required (1800 696 8105 or 407 828 0920; **kidsniteout.com**).

Travellers with disabilities

The parks pay close attention to the needs of visitors with disabilities and Florida in general is extremely disabled-friendly (though Americans tend to use the word 'handicapped' as we use 'disabled'). Though there are a few rides that cannot cater for them,

Disabled guests at Kilimanjaro Safaris

© Disney

American-speak

Many words and phrases have a different meaning across the Atlantic. For instance, when Americans say the first floor, they mean the ground floor, the second floor is really the first, and so on. (NB: NEVER ask for a packet of fags; 'fag' is a crude, slang term for a homosexual.) Here are a few everyday words to help you:

American	English	American	English
Appetizer	Starter	Fender	Car bumper
Band aid	Plaster	Freeway	Motorway
Bathroom	Private toilet	Fries	Chips
Biscuit	Savoury scone	Gas	Petrol
Broiled	Grilled	Graham cracker	Digestive biscuit
Cellphone	Mobile phone	Hood	Car bonnet
Check	Bill	Intersection	Junction
Chips	Crisps	Nickel	5 cents
Collect call	Reverse charge phone call	No standing	No parking OR stopping
Cookie	Biscuit	'Pound sign'	The # on a phone keypad
Cot/rollaway	Fold-up bed	Purse	Handbag
Crib	Cot	Quarter	25 cents
Diaper	Nappy	Ramp	Slip road
Dime	10 cents	Restroom	Public toilet
Divided highway	Dual carriageway	Seltzer	Soda water
Eggplant	Aubergine	Shrimp	King prawn
Eggs 'over easy'	Eggs fried on both sides but soft	Soda	Fizzy drink
		Stroller	Pushchair
Eggs 'sunny side up'	Eggs fried on just one side (soft)	Trunk	Car boot
		Turn-out	Lay-by
Entrée	Main course	Yield	Give way
Facecloth/washcloth	Flannel	Zucchini	Courgette
Faucet	Tap		

wheelchair availability and access is usually good. For hearing-impaired guests, there are assistive listening devices and reflective captioning at attractions where a commentary is part of the show. Braille guidebooks are available, plus rest areas for guide dogs. Disney hotels have disabled-accessible rooms (407 939 7807, **disneyworld.com**) and Disney publishes a *Guidebook for Disabled Guests* (as does Universal), available in all 4 main parks (and online). Life-jackets are always on hand at water parks, and there are special tape cassettes for blind guests.

If you require help with queuing or have children with special needs, visit any Disney theme park Guest Relations office, with the person in question, and request a Guest Assistance Card (GAC), which can be tailored to their needs. It doesn't provide front-of-the-line access (which many people believe), but it can make waiting more comfortable. Universal, SeaWorld and Busch Gardens provide similar assistance through their Guest Services offices.

Parking permits: To use any of the plentiful designated disabled parking areas in all public areas (including the parks), UK drivers must obtain a **Temporary Disabled Parking Permit**, which costs $15. You can either go to a local tax collection office, with your UK blue badge and passport when you arrive (but bear in mind most open 8.30am–4pm Mon–Fri only), OR apply by mail at least 4 weeks in advance. You need to send a photocopy of your Blue Badge (both sides), a copy of your passport ID page, and a money order (in US dollars) for $15, or your credit card details (for which there is a $2 surcharge (see below re Visa cards); please do NOT send cash) to: Tag Department, Osceola County Tax Collector, 2501 E Irlo Bronson Memorial Highway, Kissimmee, Florida 34744, USA (407 742 4000 or fax 407 742 3995 8am–4.30pm Mon–Fri). **NB: From Osceola Tax Office: 'Effective May 1, 2009, Visa regulations prohibit us from continuing to accept their credit or debit card.'**

For a list of tax offices in Orange County (for the Orlando area), call 407 836 4145 (**octaxcol.com**, and click on Office Locations); in Osceola County (for Kissimmee), call 407 742 4000 (**osceolataxcollector.com**). The temporary permits are issued for 90 days so it's best to apply no sooner than 5–6 weeks before travelling to ensure it will be valid for your stay. Include an e-mail address when possible for the Tax Office to query any details, plus your UK address and holiday dates. Disney has said it WILL continue to honour the British Blue Badge at its 4 main theme parks, but you cannot count on this elsewhere.

Local company **Suntastic Tours** can help travellers with both physical and mental disabilities in many different ways, including travel, arranging tours of the parks and other accessibility issues (321 284 4507, **suntastictours.**

com). For other local assistance, **Walker Mobility** specialises in 3-wheeled electric scooters and wheelchair rentals, with free delivery and pick-up, even from holiday villas (407 518 6000, **walkermobility.com**). **Rainbow Wheels**, with 3 locations in central Florida, hires out full-size or mini vans equipped for wheelchair users (1800 910 8267 or 407 977 3799 **rainbowwheels.com**). The discussion forums on wdwinfo.com have a board geared to visitors with disabilities, while the excellent **AllEars.Net** website has a big section on advice for a whole range of concerns, from children with ADD to vegetarian and vegan food. Visit **allearsnet.com**, click on Planning, then For Travelers With Special Challenges.

Orlando for grown-ups

You don't need to have kids in tow to enjoy Orlando. There is so much clever detail and imagination, it is usually the grown-ups who get the most out of the holiday experience.

In fact, as many couples and single people visit the parks as do families with children. Certainly, when you look at the entertainment on offer at *Downtown Disney* and CityWalk and the great range of bars and fine restaurants, with a good number of romantic offerings, it is easy to see the attraction for those aged 21 and over. As well as Florida being a key honeymoon destination, its friendly, sociable atmosphere is ideal for singles, while couples without

Orlando is for every age group

© Disney

At-a-glance kids' height requirement for all the parks

Disney's Magic Kingdom

3ft/91cm: The Barnstormer at Goofy's Wiseacre Farm

3ft 4in/101cm: Splash Mountain, Big Thunder Mountain Railroad

3ft 8 in/111cm: Space Mountain

4ft 4in/132cm: Tomorrowland Indy Speedway (for child to drive alone)

Epcot

3ft 4in/101cm: Test Track, Soarin'

3ft 8in/112cm: Mission: SPACE

4ft/122cm: Sum of All Thrills (non-inversion)

4ft 4in/132cm: Sum of All Thrills (with inversion)

Disney's Hollywood Studios

3ft 4in/101cm: Star Tours, The Twilight Zone Tower of Terror

4ft/122cm: Rock 'n' Roller Coaster Starring Aerosmith

Disney's Animal Kingdom

3ft 4in/101cm: DINOSAUR!

3ft 6in/106cm: Kali River Rapids

3ft 8in/115cm: Expedition: Everest

4ft/122cm: Primeval Whirl

Universal Studios

3ft/91cm: Woody Woodpecker's Nuthouse Coaster

3ft 4in/101cm: The Simpsons Ride

3ft 6in/106cm: Men in Black: Alien Attack

4ft/122cm: Islands of Adventure: Forbidden Journey

4ft/122cm: Revenge of the Mummy, Disaster! A Major Motion Picture Ride...Starring YOU (unless accompanied by adult), ET Adventure

4ft 3in/130cm: Hollywood Rip Ride Rockit!

Islands of Adventure

3ft–4ft 8in/91–142cm (must be with a child within that range): Pteranodon Flyers

3ft 4in/101: The Amazing Adventures of Spider-Man

3ft 6in/106cm: Jurassic Park River Adventure

3ft 8in/111cm: Dudley Do-Right's Ripsaw Falls

4ft/122cm: Popeye And Bluto's Bilge-Rat Barges, Flight of the Hippogriff, Harry Potter and the Forbidden Journey

4ft 4in/132cm: Dr Doom's Fearfall

4ft 6in/137cm: The Incredible Hulk Coaster, Dragon Challenge

SeaWorld

3ft 6in/106cm: Journey to Atlantis, Wild Arctic (Polar Express at Christmas)

4ft 6in/137cm: Kraken, Manta

Busch Gardens

3ft 3in/99cm: Rhino Rally (age 3 minimum)

3ft 6in/106cm: The Wild Surge (3ft 2in/96cm with adult), Congo River Rapids, Ubanga-Banga Bumper Cars, Scorpion, Sandstorm, Cheetah Chase (age 6 minimum)

3ft 10in/116cm: Stanley Falls

4ft/122cm: Gwazi, Tanganyika Tidal Wave

4ft 6in/137cm: SheiKra, Kumba, Montu

4ft 8in/145cm: Jungle Flyers

Water Parks

Disney's Typhoon Lagoon: Under 4ft/122cm only: Ketchakiddee Creek; **4ft/122cm:** Crush 'n' Gusher, Humunga Kowabunga. Disney's Blizzard Beach: **2ft 8in/82cm:** Chairlift; **Under 4ft/122cm only:** Tike's Peak; **4ft/122cm:** Summit Plummet, Slush Gusher, Downhill Double Dipper. Wet 'n Wild: **3ft-4ft/92cm-122cm:** The Surge, Bubba Tub, Flyer, Disco H2O; **Under 4ft/122cm only** (with adult): Kids Park; **4ft/122cm:** Bomb Bay, Der Stuka, Black Hole, The Storm, Brain Wash; **4ft 3in/130cm:** Wild One; **4ft 5in/143cm:** Knee Ski Wake-Boarding. **Aquatica: Under 4ft/122cm:** Kata's Kookaburra Cove; **3ft 6in/107cm:** Walhalla Wave, HooRoo Run, Taumata Racer; **4ft/122cm:** Dolphin Plunge, Omaka Rocka.

children can also take advantage of late opening at the parks and clubs like Jellyrolls and Atlantic City Dance Hall at Disney's Boardwalk Resort.

BRIT TIP
If you have a fridge in your hotel, put drink cartons in the freezer overnight and they will be cool for much of the next day in your back-pack. Better still, buy a cheap coolbag, freeze it with some water bottles in, and leave it in the car – great after a day in the parks.

Orlando for seniors

The more mature traveller can also benefit from a healthy dose of the Sunshine State. And, if our parents (all in their senior years) are any guide, they will have just as much fun, within slightly different parameters. For the older person, staying in a Disney hotel is highly recommended as it removes the stress of driving. The extra cost is offset, Simon's parents feel, by the beauty and convenience of their surroundings. They still find plenty to do in the parks, even if they aren't keen on most of the thrill rides – though just watching can be entertainment enough! Both *Epcot* and *Disney's Animal Kingdom* have much to engage the older visitor, while the shows of *Disney's Hollywood Studios* make that a popular choice, too, and the *Magic Kingdom*, while 'probably the noisiest of all the parks',

Orlando is great for older visitors

© Disney

still represents one of the essential experiences.

The *Downtown Disney* area can feel a bit frenetic for the senior crowd, but the *Boardwalk Resort* is popular and the whole of the *Epcot* resort area offers much in the way of fine dining and relaxation. In fact, this is often a prime area for seniors, notably the quieter *Disney's Yacht* and *Beach Club Resorts*, and the superb Swan-Dolphin complex. Simon's parents highlight the following for their age group: Jim Henson's Muppet Vision 3¬D and Fantasmic! at *Disney's Hollywood Studios*; Kilimanjaro Safaris, the Maharajah Jungle Trek and Festival of the Lion King at *Disney's Animal Kingdom Park*; Spaceship Earth, Soarin', Universe of Energy, Test Track and IllumiNations at *Epcot* (plus the superb gardens and architecture); The Haunted Mansion, Jungle Cruise, Pirates of the Caribbean and the monorail ride to the *Magic Kingdom*; watching the children at the many parades and character greetings; dinner at the California Grill in *Disney's Contemporary Resort*; shopping at Orlando Premium Outlets; most of Universal Studios, but less of Islands of Adventure (though, like most, they were wowed by the Amazing Adventures of Spider-Man).

BRIT TIP
Looking for essential travel accessories and useful knick-knacks, like TSA-approved locks, plug adapters and luggage scales (essential for the trip home to avoid excess baggage!)? Check out **tripneeds.com**. Asda supermarkets also sell a good travel range.

In terms of the weather, March was ideal for them, but they wouldn't be keen to visit in summer. Seniors can also take advantage of numerous discounts and special deals for their age group at the attractions, plus many restaurants and hotels. The official Visitor Center on I-Drive (see page 50) publishes a brochure of all the deals.

Hurricane alert?

June-Nov is officially hurricane season, but it is not usually anything to worry about. Even the unprecedented extremes of 2004, when three major storms hit Central Florida, caused no significant damage to the parks and the biggest inconvenience was losing electricity for a few days. In the unlikely event of a major storm, switch your TV to the Weather Channel or local news station WESH 2 and follow its advice.

Measurements

American clothes sizes are smaller than ours, hence a US size 12 dress is a UK 14, or an American jacket sized 42 is a 44. Shoes are the opposite: a US 10 should fit a British size 9 foot. The measuring system is also still imperial, not metric.

You've got mail

Sending postcards and letters home is easy, but the American postal system can be hard to understand. You won't find post boxes in many locations and some post offices don't seem to know the fees for postage to the UK. So here's what you need to know: all the parks have post boxes and you can get stamp books from most stamp machines and City Hall at the *Magic Kingdom*; a standard postcard, birthday or other greetings-type card in an envelope all require a 98c stamp; standard postage within the US is 44c (changing to $1 and 46c in Jan 2011); the main post office for the Disney area is at **10450 Turkey Lake Road** (just north of the junction of Palm Parkway and Central Florida Parkway; 8am–7pm Mon–Fri, 9am–5pm Sat); in Kissimmee, try **2600 Michigan Avenue** (8am–6.30pm Mon–Fri, 9am–4pm Sat) or 1415 W Oak Street (8.30am–5pm Mon–Fri, 9am–2pm Sat). You will also find a post office inside **Mall at Millenia**, off the lower level of the Grand Court.

Wedding bells

Florida is an increasingly popular choice for couples looking to tie the knot (some 20,000 couples a year at the last count). Its almost guaranteed sunshine and lush, natural landscape make it a huge hit as a wedding backdrop. Orlando also has some terrific services, wedding co-ordinators and scenic venues like Magnolia Acres, Winter Park, Leu Gardens and the many resort hotels (like the Buena Vista Palace, Walt

Wedding couple in a Cinderella carriage

© Disney

Disney World Swan and Dolphin, Celebration Hotel and Wyndham Resort) and even the pristine golf courses (like Celebration Golf Club). More unusual ones include getting married at the Hard Rock Café, in a hot-air balloon or a helicopter, on the beach or a luxury yacht, in the pit-lane of the Richard Petty Driving Experience at *Walt Disney World* or even at 145mph/233kph around the speedway itself! All the main tour operators feature wedding options and co-ordinated services and offer a variety of ceremonies, or you can pick a local specialist like **Get Married In Florida** (see opposite). Prices vary from around £300/couple (for a basic civil ceremony) to more than £2,000.

Walt Disney World's Wedding Pavilion: True fairytale romance, with the backdrop of Cinderella Castle, you can opt for traditional elegance in this Victorian setting with up to 260 guests or the full Disney experience, arriving in Cinderella's coach with Mickey and Minnie as guests. Disney's wedding planners can tailor-make the occasion for you (407 828 3400) but at a price – rates START at $3,000/couple for the basic ceremony and can easily top $20,000.

Licence: To obtain a marriage licence you can visit one of the

An Epcot wedding

Disney's Wedding Pavilion

local courthouses, which includes the Osceola County Courthouse, Courthouse Square, Suite 2000, Kissimmee (just off Bryan Street in downtown Kissimmee) 8am–4pm Mon–Fri (407 343 3500); the Orange County Courthouse, 425 North Orange Avenue (downtown Orlando) 7.30am–4pm Mon–Fri (407 836 2067); Clermont Courthouse, 1206 Bowman Street, Clermont (in Sunnyside Plaza) 8.30am–4.30pm (closed noon–1pm; 352 394 2018). All courthouses are closed on US bank holidays. Both parties must be present to apply for the marriage licence, which costs $93.50 (in cash, travellers' cheques or by credit card) and is valid for 60 days, while a ceremony (equivalent to a British register office) can be performed at the same time by the clerk for an extra $20 (times vary according to courthouse). Passports and birth certificates are requested and, if you have been married before, you should bring your decree absolute. After acquiring a licence, a couple can get wed anywhere in Florida. No witnesses or blood tests are necessary and there is no residence qualification. It is also possible to obtain a licence *before* arriving in Florida (see **floridamarriagelicencebypost.com**).

Get Married in Florida: This internet business dedicated to organising

Top 10 romantic restaurants

1 Tchoup Chop, Universal's Royal Pacific Resort

2 California Grill, Disney's Contemporary Resort

3 Todd English's bluezoo, Walt Disney World Dolphin Resort

4 Zen, Omni Orlando Resort at Champions Gate

5 Jiko, Disney's Animal Kingdom Lodge

6 Seasons 52, Sand Lake Rd, Orlando

7 Old Hickory Steakhouse, Gaylord Palms Resort

8 Cala Bella, Shingle Creek Resort

9 Capital Grille, The Pointe Orlando

10 Brio Tuscan Grille, The Mall at Millenia

andreacheesecake.com). Another specialist is harpist **Christine MacPhail**, who can provide an elegant touch to the occasion (407 239 1330, **orlandoharpist. com**). For photographers, try **Abba Photography** (407 672 1121, **abbaphotography.com**) or **Broadway Fotographics** (by Bill Otten, 407 339 5542, **broadwayfoto.com**).

Religious ceremonies: If you would prefer to get married in a church or other place of worship, contact the **Center of Light Church & Spiritual Center** on East Robinson Street (407 228 0101), the **First Baptist Church** on John Young Parkway (407 425 2555), **St Nicholas Catholic Church** on Sand Lake Road (407 351 0133) or **Trinity Lutheran Church** on East Livingston Street downtown (407 422 5704, **trinitydowntown.org**). Another church worth noting for general worship (8.30 and 11am Sun and 7.30pm Thurs) is the **Community Presbyterian Church** in the town of Celebration (near Kissimmee) at 511 Celebration Avenue (407 566 1633, **commpres.com**).

Disney special occasions

Birthday badges: Free badges can be found at City Hall in the *Magic Kingdom Park* and Guest Services at *Epcot, Disney's Hollywood Studios* and *Disney's Animal Kingdom Park*. Cast Members like to make a fuss over children (and adults!) wearing a birthday badge.

Birthday cakes: Contact room service at your resort or Guest Services at one of the parks. All Disney restaurants can offer ready-made 15cm/6in cakes ($21 at each restaurant) or something larger ($32–120) if ordered at least 48 hours in advance on 407 827 2253. If someone in your group has a birthday, be sure to tell the Cast Member at check-in (or when you make your reservation), as well as hostesses and/or servers in restaurants. While not guaranteed, Disney staff often go out of their way to make the day special. If characters know it's a birthday when they sign a child's autograph book, they may add a special birthday wish in it.

Birthday cruise: The IllumiNations Celebration Cruise (to Epcot) provides snacks, drinks, streamers and balloons for a 90-minute tour from Disney's Yacht and Beach Club Resort marina for $344.50 (call 407 939 7529).

The Presidential Suite at Disney's Animal Kingdom Lodge

Birthday parties: *Disney's Polynesian Resort* offers themed birthday parties with lunch options at its Neverland kids' club for ages 4 and over. A themed 2-hour Premium party with cake, pizza, drinks, party activities and one Disney character is $70/person, while the Basic version (without a Disney character) is $35/person (at least one week's notice required on 407 939 7529).

Winter-Summerland Miniature Golf: 2-hour birthday parties for 10 or more, including pizza, soda, cake and a round of mini-golf at $19.95 a head, plus tax (call at least a week in advance on 407 939 7529).

Goofy Party Central: This grand 90-minute experience for up to 12 takes place at Goofy's Candy Company in *Downtown Disney* and offers a choice of Goofy's Scien-Terrific Birthday Bash or the Perfectly Princess Party, each with themed events, games, gifts and treats, plus 2 party hosts for $370 (call 407 939 2329 up to 90 days in advance).

Disney's Pirate Cruise: This 2-hour adventure for kids 4–12 sails (on pontoon boats) from 4 of the resorts (Grand Floridian, Yacht/Beach Club, Port Orleans and Caribbean Beach at 9.30am) to find pirate 'booty' at different ports of call, with a final stop for lunch; $31.95 per child (407 939 7529, up to 180 days in advance).

BRIT TIP
Don't want to take your mobile with you for fear of high charges? Hire a phone for your holiday from Adam Phones and take advantage of its special local rates for the US (0800 123000, **adamphones.com**).

Safety first

While crime is not a serious issue in central Florida, this is still big-city America, so don't leave your common sense at home. International Drive has its own dedicated police unit (the Tourist Oriented Policing Squad, TOPS, a division of the Orlando City Police), with officers patrolling purely this long tourist corridor, arranging crime prevention seminars with local hotels and generally ensuring I-Drive takes good care of its visitors. You will often see these police out on mountain bikes, and they are a polite, helpful bunch should you need assistance. Tourism is such a vital part of the economy, the authorities have a highly safety-conscious attitude. However, it would be foolish to ignore the usual safety guidelines for travelling abroad.

Winter-Summerland Miniature Golf

© Disney

Two-way radio rentals

Two-way radios are popular in Orlando for safety and convenience. Many families buy these 'walkie-talkies' to keep in touch around the parks in preference to mobile phones. You can pick them up locally for as little as $35 in stores including Wal-Mart, Best Buy, Radio Shack, Office Depot and Staples. However, they cannot be used back home as they use the same frequency as UK emergency services.

Emergencies

Emergency services: For police, fire department or ambulance, dial 911 (9-911 from your hotel room). Make sure your children know this number.

General: For smaller-scale crises (e.g. mislaid tickets, lost passports or rescheduled flights), your holiday company should have an emergency contact number in the hotel reception.

Independent travellers: If you run into passport or other problems that need help from the British Consulate, its office is at Suite 2110, Sun Trust Center, 200 South Orange Avenue, Orlando, Florida, 32801, with walk-in visitors' hours 9.30am–noon and 2–4pm, or call 407 254 3300 (**ukinusa.fco. gov.uk/orlando/**).

BRIT TIP

Phonecards, which you need to make a call from a local payphone (much cheaper than using your hotel room phone), are available from most 7–Eleven stores or from your tour rep.

Hotel security

While in your hotel, always use door peepholes and security chains when someone knocks at the door. DON'T open the door to strangers without asking for identification, and check with the hotel desk if you are still not sure. It is stating the obvious, but keep doors and windows locked and always use deadlocks and security chains. Always take cash, credit cards, valuables and car keys when you go out (or put them in the room safe),

and don't leave the door open, even if you just pop down the corridor to the ice machine. Most hotels now have electronic card-locks for extra security and can offer deposit boxes in addition to the standard in-room mini-safes. Don't be afraid to ask reception staff for safety advice for surrounding areas or if you are travelling somewhere you are not sure about.

BRIT TIP

If your room has already been cleaned before you go out for the day, hang the 'Do Not Disturb' sign on the door. Always keep your valuables out of sight, whether in the hotel or the car.

Safety is a major issue for the Central Florida Hotel/Motel Association and hotel staff are usually well briefed to be helpful. A bumbag (Americans say 'fanny pack'!) is a better bet than a handbag or shoulder bag. And try not to look too obviously like a tourist – the map over the steering wheel is a giveaway, but other no-nos are wearing masses of jewellery and carrying lots of camera equipment.

Reunion Resort

© Disney

Private guest room at Disney's Caribbean Beach Resort

The biggest giveaway is leaving a camera or camcorder on view in the car (which the heat may ruin anyway). Finally, and this is VERY strong police advice, in the unlikely event of being confronted by an assailant, DO NOT resist or 'have a go', because this can often make a bad situation worse.

BRIT TIP
For your journey to the US, use a business address rather than your home address on all your luggage. It is less conspicuous and safer should any item be stolen or misplaced

Dining at the Samba Room

© OCVB

Money matters

It is useful to know dollar travellers' cheques can be used as cash almost everywhere (though a few places, like Golden Corral restaurants, no longer accept them) and can be replaced if lost or stolen, so it is not necessary (and not advisable) to carry lots of cash. Sterling travellers' cheques can be cashed only in major banks. You'll need to carry ID in many cases, even for credit card purchases (the new UK driving licence card is useful for this).

BRIT TIP
Want the best exchange rate for your holiday cash? Check out **comparetravelmoney.co.uk** for the best deals on a day-by-day basis.

Having a credit card is almost essential (especially for car hire) as they are accepted everywhere and provide extra buying security. Visa, Mastercard and American Express are all widely accepted. It is worth separating larger notes from smaller ones in your wallet to avoid flashing all your money in view. Losing £300 of travellers' cheques shouldn't ruin your holiday – but losing $600 in cash might. All the theme parks have cash dispensers (called 'ATM machines' in the US) at which you can use a credit

Repeat visitors

Repeat visitors create a large part of the Orlando market and are always on the lookout for something new after they have done all the main parks. To that end, Chapters 8 and 9 (Off The Beaten Track and The Twin Centre Option) are largely designed with them in mind. Listed here are 10 things worth doing once you have Been There and Done That:

1   Behind the scenes tours at the Disney parks.

2   Dolphin watch cruise from Dolphin Landings at St Pete Beach.

3   Wildlife eco-tour with Island Boat Lines at Cocoa Beach.

4   The scenic boat ride and Morse Museum in Winter Park.

5   Bok Tower Gardens and lunch or dinner (plus a visit to the soup cannery!) at the eclectic Chalet Suzanne in Lake Wales.

6   St John's River Cruise in Blue Spring State Park, Seminole County.

7   Boggy Creek Airboats.

8   A zipline ride and buggy tour at Florida EcoSafaris.

9   Merritt Island National Wildlife Refuge at Titusville.

10 A visit to Mount Dora, north-west of Orlando.

card to withdraw cash. Perhaps the best option is the convenient, simple **FairFX card** (**fairfx.com**), a debit card that you charge in advance and use as a credit card to your pre-paid limit. The exchange rate is fixed at loading and you can save 5–10% on High Street currency rates. If you can order well in advance, **Crown Currency Exchange** can often provide a better exchange rate on US dollars ordered 31 or more days ahead (0800 612 7273, **crowncurrencyexchange.com**).

BRIT TIP
Take note: most Orlando prices, both in this book and on every price tag you see, do NOT include the 6–7% Florida Sales Tax. There is also a 4–5% Resort Tax on hotel rooms.

Car safety

With your hire car, it pays to make basic safety checks straight away. Familiarise yourself with the car's controls BEFORE driving away – which button is the air-conditioning, which control operates the indicators, where the windscreen wiper switch is, and so on. Also, try to memorise your route in advance, even if it's

only a case of knowing the road numbers. Most hire firms now give good directions to all the hotels, so check them before you set off (or, better still, hire a GPS system). Make sure the fuel tank is well filled and never let it get near empty. Running out of 'gas' in an unfamiliar area holds obvious hazards. If you stray off your pre-determined route, stick to well-lit areas and ask for directions only from official businesses like hotels and petrol stations or the police.

Guests at Disney's Pop Century Resort

© Disney

Simon and Susan

Apart from the *Brit Guides* to Orlando and Disneyland Paris, we contribute to a wide range of media on a wide range of travel subjects. Find out more about our work at **venesstravelmedia.com**.

BRIT TIP

American banknotes are all the same size and primarily green, with just the occasional splash of colour in the newer notes. The only real difference is the picture of the president and the denomination in each corner.

Sheikra at Busch Gardens

Always try to park close to your destination where there are plenty of lights and DO NOT get out if there are suspicious characters around. Always keep windows closed (and air-conditioning on), and don't hesitate to lock the doors from the inside if you feel threatened (larger cars have doors that lock automatically as you drive off). And don't forget to lock up when you leave the car – not all rental cars have central locking, so double-check! It is comforting to know Orlando does not have any no-go areas in the main tourist parts. The nearest is the portion of the Orange Blossom Trail south of downtown Orlando (a selection of strip clubs

and 'adult bars' that can be downright seedy) and the Parramore area south-west of downtown. For more info on safety, contact the Community Affairs office of Orange County Police (407 836 3720) or the International Drive police team office (407 351 9368).

BRIT TIP

You'll find masses of info on all things Orlando on the fun-packed discussion forums at **attraction-tickets-direct.co.uk**, **thedibb.co.uk** and **wdwinfo.com**, to which we also contribute. They also have great features, theme park info, restaurant advice, news, weather, facts and tips.

Disney's Saragota Springs

Let us plan your holiday...

...with our unique Itinerary Planner Service

In conjunction with the *Brit Guide* website – **britguideorlando.net** – our Itinerary Planner Service (IPS) will help you get the very most out of your time in central Florida. This is a service no one else can offer. We will design an itinerary tailored to your individual plans for the parks and attractions of central Florida. In your planner (which usually runs to 40-plus pages for a 2-week itinerary), we will indicate the best days to visit the parks to avoid the crowds; all the main show and parade times; any rides that may be closed for refurbishment; and provide a detailed touring plan for each park, a shopping guide, updates on new rides, etc., as well as up-to-the-minute advice right from the source of the fun, plus a host of additional Brit Tip Extras and Brit Picks (our special favourites) that we can't fit into this book.

All you have to do is visit the *Brit Guide* website and click on the Itinerary Planner link. Fill out the online form with your travel dates, hotel and family details, the tickets you have bought (or are buying) and what you would like to fit into your visit. Submit the form, along with your payment, and you will receive an acknowledgement of your requirements. A few days before you go, you will receive, by e-mail, your unique Itinerary Planner, which will consist of:

1   An official *Brit Guide* welcome from Simon and Susan Veness.

2   A full day-by-day plan for the length of your holiday.

3   A touring strategy for ALL of the parks, water parks and shopping venues you will visit, avoiding the crowds and taking advantage of the latest developments.

4   An alternative plan in case of bad weather.

5   All the main parade and fireworks times with your daily plans.

6   A note of any rides/shows that are closed during your visit.

7   A special selection of Brit Tip Extras and local advice specifically for you.

8   Our Brit Picks – a guide to a range of personal favourites, from restaurants to shops.

9   The ultimate insider knowledge, as both Simon and Susan are based in the heart of the Orlando magic and are fully up to date on all developments.

10 Our special bonus – an exclusive Platinum VIP Passport for Orlando Premium Outlets (not available to the general public), providing extra savings at select upmarket stores at this fabulous shopping venue (in addition to its free VIP Coupon Book we offer to all readers – see inside back cover).

All in all, it adds up to the most comprehensive package of specialised holiday info anywhere, and it represents the secret to the most fun, in the most hassle-free way, in the most exciting place on earth. What more could you ask for? Just check us out on **britguideorlando.net** and we'll do the rest for you.

Please note: There is a minimum order period, so check the website and apply in good time before your holiday (at least 2 weeks). Password for £20 rate is random and expires on 31 December of the edition's year, no exceptions. We are not a travel agency or ticket service and you MUST know your ticket requirements in advance.

Know before you go

You can contact these organisations for advance info. **Visit Florida** offers a free Vacation Guide and a Map, as well as many online e-brochures (0800 018 6790, **visitflorida.com/uk**). The **Orlando Tourism Bureau** in London has a 24-hour info line, plus a website where you can request or download its free holiday planning pack and Orlando Magicard (0800 018 6790, **orlandoinfo.com/uk/**). You can also visit the **Kissimmee Convention & Visitors Bureau** (**visitkissimmee.com**).

© Universal Orlando Resorts

One Fish, Two Fish, Red Fish, Blue Fish at Islands of Adventure

It's worth checking Orlando's ONLY official **Visitor Center**, 8.30am–6.30pm daily at 8723 International

Christmas fireworks at the Magic Kingdom

© Disney

Drive (407 363 5872 or e-mail **info@orlandocvb.com**) for discounted attraction tickets, free brochures and accommodation advice, free info pamphlets and maps. The **Kissimmee Visitor Center** (8am–5pm Mon–Fri) is at 1925 E Irlo Bronson Memorial Highway, or Highway 192 and also offers free maps, discount coupons and brochures (407 847 5000 or toll-free in the US on 1800 333 5477).

The official sites aren't bad, though Disney's can be hard work: **disneyworld.co.uk** (for opening hours, rides, parades, etc. and bookings). Then see **seaworld.com**, **universalorlando.com** and **buschgardens. com**. The online version of the local paper (**orlandosentinel.com**) is packed with info (especially for shopping, dining and nightlife), while the free *Orlando Weekly* is also worth checking (**orlandoweekly.com**). Among the many fan-based websites, the biggest and best is arguably **thedibb.co.uk** ('Disney with a British accent'), plus **wdisneyw.co.uk** (with more pages for UK visitors), the fully comprehensive **allearsnet.com** (notably for its Disney dining section) and **Orlandorocks.com** (for theme park addicts).

Now, on to the next step of the holiday, your transport…

3 Getting Around

Arriving and driving in Orlando are two of the biggest concerns for visitors, especially first-timers, but there's really no need to worry. Although most people begin their holiday by leaving the airport in a newly acquired, automatic, left-hand-drive hire car on roads that can appear quite bewildering, driving here is a lot easier and more enjoyable than in the UK. Anyone who is familiar with the M25 should find Florida FAR less stressful.

Before you get to your hire car, though, you need to be aware of the arrival process at either Orlando International Airport or Orlando Sanford International Airport.

Orlando International Airport

This is one of the most modern and enjoyable airports in the world, but it can be confusing for newcomers. All flights arrive at one of 4 satellite terminals and you then take a shuttle tram (like a mini monorail) to the main terminal.

International arrivals: If you arrive with British Airways or Virgin Atlantic, you disembark at the satellite for Gates 60–99, where you first need to go through Immigration and Customs. As of 2010, there are now just 2 main queues which feed into the individual immigration kiosks, and you get in either one and just wait for the official to call you to the next open kiosk (like the post office!) which helps to keep the process as smooth and fair as possible. Once through Immigration, collect your baggage from the carousel and go through the Customs check. Then you have a choice: *either* deposit your checked luggage on a second conveyor belt to take it to the main terminal while you go upstairs to the shuttle with your hand luggage only; *or*, if you can manage it all without a trolley, take it with you on the escalator up to the shuttle. If you did the former, once in the main terminal you are on Level 3 and you follow signs down to Baggage Claim **B** (unless you took a Virgin flight, in which case you cross over to Baggage Claim **A**) on Level 2. If you brought all your luggage with you on the shuttle, you can go straight to pick up your transport on Level 1 (or, if a specific driver is meeting you, Level 2). Allow around an hour from landing to ground transportation.

⚡ BRIT TIP
Don't forget you must have filled in your ESTA form and immigration details online before you travel (see page 13). For country of residence put UNITED KINGDOM; for Passport Issuing Country, put UK – BRITISH CITIZEN. And you must give a valid US address for your accommodation.

BRIT TIP

Visit **orlandoairports.net** for a photo preview of the arrival process at Orlando International Airport (click Airport Guide, then Arrivals Guide) and other handy info.

Domestic arrivals: For anyone arriving on a US domestic flight (from another US gateway), you disembark at the satellite terminal and proceed straight to the main terminal on the shuttle to collect your baggage on Level 2 (either A or B side, depending on arrival gate). Once at the main baggage claim, porters can help you to Level 1 (for a $1/bag tip) for all car hire, shuttles and buses. Trolleys need $3 in change (or you can use a credit card) to operate – they are not free as at UK airports.

Transfers: Kerbside pick-up is just outside the doors on Level 2. If a driver is meeting you, he or she will wait on Level 2, either at the bottom of the escalators or by your baggage reclaim. Several tour operators have helpdesks here, too, while Virgin has a big reception desk on Level 1. The public bus system, Lynx (see page 54), operates ONLY from the A side of Level 1 (from 6am–10.30pm; 9.30pm on Sundays and public holidays), in spaces 38–41. Links 11, 41 and 51 depart every ½ hour (less often on Sundays and bank holidays) for Orlando city centre (about 45 minutes away), while Link 42 serves International Drive (about a 1-hour journey) and Link 111 goes to *Walt Disney World* (Hotel Plaza Boulevard and the Transportation & Ticket Center) via the Florida Mall and I-Drive (Canadian Court). Fares are $2 ($4 to Disney).

Car hire: All the main hire companies are now right on site at the airport after a major rebuild was completed in 2010 (no more having to get a shuttle bus to an off-airport location). The 11 to choose from include Dollar, National, L&M, Hertz, Avis and, of course, *Brit Guide* partners **Alamo**, and all offer a full service (look out for Alamo's new automated self-service kiosks, as these are being introduced

at its busier locations and can save queuing time). Dollar is used for packages with Thomson, Travel City and First Choice; Alamo is the main client for Funway, Jetsave, Kuoni, BA Holidays, Virgin and Thomas Cook. After completing your paperwork, simply walk out of Level 1, across the road to the multi-storey car park to collect your car. If you arrive late, consider staying overnight at the **Hyatt Regency** hotel inside the airport itself rather than driving tired. You will be far more ready to drive next day (and the car hire queues will be shorter). Several tour operators also offer an arrival-day transfer, with car hire pick-up arranged the next day, and this is worth asking about.

BRIT TIP

If you are hiring a car from one of the on-airport companies, save time by sending the driver to complete the paperwork BEFORE collecting your luggage on Level 2.

Leaving the airport: When you drive out of the airport, DON'T follow signs to 'Orlando'. The main tourist areas are south and west of the city proper, so follow the respective signs for your accommodation. For International Drive (or I-Drive), take the **North Exit** and the Beachline Expressway (Route 528) west until it crosses I-Drive just north of SeaWorld (you will need $1.75 in toll fees). Most hotels on I-Drive are to the north, so keep right at the exit.

BRIT TIP

The Martin Andersen Beachline (formerly Beeline) Expressway (528) and Greeneway (417) are both toll roads, so make sure you have some US currency before leaving the airport. Toll booths hate to change notes above $20, while some auto-tolls take ONLY coins.

For Kissimmee, Disney and villas in Clermont/Davenport, take the **South Exit** for 3ml/5km and pick up the Central Florida Greeneway (Highway 417) west. For most Disney resorts, take exit 6 and follow the signs; for *Animal Kingdom* resorts, use exit 3 and take Osceola Parkway west. For eastern Kissimmee, come off Highway 417 at exit 11, the Orange Blossom Trail (Highway 17/92), and go south. For west Kissimmee and Clermont/Davenport (Highway 27), take exit 2, turn right on Celebration Avenue and left (west) on Highway 192 all the way to Highway 27 (you will need $1.75–$2.75 in toll fees).

Orlando Sanford International Airport

Arriving at Sanford (in Seminole County) couldn't be easier. The list of airlines visiting this easy-to-use airport currently includes Thomson Airways, Monarch, Thomas Cook Airlines and Icelandair. It generally takes only 30–40 minutes from arrival to leaving the baggage hall, but there may be delays in peak season when several planes arrive at once, as its handling capacity is limited. It's a short walk from the plane to the immigration hall (where there are just 2 queues that feed through to the kiosks); you then collect your baggage, pass through Customs and walk straight out to car hire, shuttle or taxi pick-up.

BRIT TIP
Don't want to drive? Consider a multi-centre stay within Orlando itself, staying first at, say, I-Drive or Universal Orlando and then a Disney resort, to get the best of the free or cheap transport options.

Car hire: You will find the tour operator welcome desks and Dollar car hire offices immediately in front of you, while our *Brit Guide* partner **Alamo** has a large welcome centre via a covered walkway and boardwalk behind this, and its British-dedicated operation is pretty smooth. Avis, Budget, Enterprise, Thrifty and Hertz are also on-airport (turn right out of Customs then take the first door on the right). Look up more on **orlandosanfordairport.com**.

Leaving the airport: It may be 35ml/56km to the north and involve more driving (and taxis and shuttles are much more expensive – a town car service would be around $120 one-way to *Walt Disney World* and a taxi $95), but you usually save time by your quicker exit. There is just one main road out, on to Lake Mary Boulevard, and you then take Seminole Expressway (Highway 417, which becomes Central Florida Greeneway in Orange County) south. The slip road to this toll motorway is just under the flyover on your LEFT, and you need $6.25 to reach Disney or Kissimmee or $5.25 for I-Drive (via the Beachline Expressway). You can avoid the tolls by staying on Lake Mary Blvd for 6ml/10km until you get to I-4, but you're likely to hit heavy traffic through the city centre. The Expressway/Greeneway is an excellent, easy-driving introduction to Orlando, even if it does cost a few dollars. For traffic news and reports, tune to 660AM (WORL) or 580AM (WDBO). Dial 511 on a tri-band mobile phone for traffic info on I-4.

BRIT TIP
If you suspect you may need more boot space in your hire car, it pays to upgrade when you book at home as it is usually more expensive to upgrade when you arrive.

Disney's Old Key West Resort

© Disney

ORLANDO WITHOUT A CAR

Although being mobile is advisable, it is certainly possible to survive without a car. However, few attractions are within walking distance of hotels, and taxis can be expensive. You also need to plan with greater precision to allow for extra travelling time (and with children, taking buses can be tiring). For non-drivers, your best base is either *Walt Disney World* itself (free transport throughout, but harder to get to the rest of Orlando) or International Drive for its location, 'walkability' and the great I-Ride Trolley. Many hotels have free shuttles to some of the parks or a cheap, regular mini-bus service. There are 4 main options: public transport; shuttle services; town cars and limousines; and taxis.

Public transport

Lynx bus system: Reliable and cheap but slightly plodding, it covers much of metro Orlando. Its online system map shows all its routes (or 'links') and the main attractions (407 841 5969, golynx.com). Worth noting are **Link 42** from Orlando International Airport to I-Drive; **Link 56** from Kissimmee to Disney (from Osceola Square Mall, along Highway 192 via Old Town and Celebration to Disney's Transportation & Ticket Center (TTC) by the *Magic Kingdom*); **Link 304** to Disney from the top of I-Drive (Oak Ridge Road to *Downtown Disney*, via Sand Lake Drive); **Link 18** from Kissimmee to downtown Orlando (from Osceola Square Mall, east on Highway 192 and north on Boggy Creek Road, Buenaventura Boulevard and Orange Avenue); **Link 55**, Kissimmee's Highway 192 from Osceola Square Mall west to Four Corners via the Summer Bay Resort; **Link 38**, I-Drive to downtown Orlando (from the Convention Center via Wet 'n Wild, Kirkman Road and I¬4); and **Link 50** (from the TTC via SeaWorld and I-4) and **Link 300** (from *Downtown Disney* via I-4), from Disney to downtown Orlando.

BRIT TIP

Lynx buses use the Downtown Disney West Side Transfer Center as their Disney hub, with Links 301, 302 and 303 spreading out from there to the theme parks and resorts.

Lynx fares are $2 a ride (transfers are free) or $16 for a weekly pass (children 6 and under go free with a full-fare passenger). The service is every 30 minutes in the main areas, every 15 minutes 6–9am and 3.30–6.30pm, but you must have the right change. Lynx stops are marked by pink paw-print signs and all buses are wheelchair accessible. There can be long queues for buses at Disney at closing time, so you could take Disney transport to *Downtown Disney* (via one of the resorts or the TTC), then get a taxi back to your hotel (about $25 to I-Drive).

I-Ride Trolley: Great-value service for the I-Drive area, it operates 2 routes along a 14ml/23km stretch of this tourist corridor. The Main/Red Line (77 stops) runs from the new-look Prime Outlets International shopping centre at the top of I-Drive, to SeaWorld and Aquatica via Westwood Boulevard and Sea Harbor Drive, and on to Orlando Premium Outlets. The Green Line (33 stops) goes from the Universal resort area (Windhover Drive and Major Boulevard) south to Orlando Premium Outlets Boulevard via Universal Boulevard, the Convention Center and SeaWorld. Running every day, 8am–10.30pm at roughly 20-minute intervals (30 minutes on the Green Line), it costs $1.25/trip (25c for seniors) – please have the right change – or you can buy Unlimited Ride Passes for 1, 3, 5, 7 or 14 days at $4, $6, $8, $10, $17. If you need to transfer between routes, ask for a transfer coupon when you board (not required with Unlimited Ride Passes). Kids 12 and under go free with an adult, and all trolleys have hydraulic lifts for wheelchairs. Passes are sold at more than 100 locations in the I-Drive area, including the Official Visitor Center and most hotel desks but NOT on the trolleys themselves (407 248 9590 or US freephone 1866 243 7483, **iridetrolley.com**).

BRIT TIP

Cheapest way to get from I-Drive to Disney? Take the $2 Lynx bus Link 50 from SeaWorld – 6600 Sea Harbor Drive – to the Transportation & Ticket Center next to the Magic Kingdom Park. All Disney transport then operates from here. You can use the I-Ride Trolley to get to SeaWorld.

Busch Shuttle Express: Another regular service worth noting is from SeaWorld to Busch Gardens in Tampa, with 7 departure points, 8.15–9.40am daily. It costs $10/person but is FREE if you have Busch tickets in advance (included in the FlexTicket Plus or 3-Park Ticket with SeaWorld and Aquatica). For more info, call 1800 221 1339 toll-free.

Shuttle services

An alternative to public transport are the well-organised firms offering set-fee shuttles to the attractions that pick up at hotels. There are more than a dozen, with everything from stretch Hummer limos to buses.

Mears: The most comprehensive service, with a 1,000-vehicle fleet from limousines to town cars and coaches. Typical round-trip shuttle fares would be: airport to *Walt Disney World*, round-trip $33 adults, $26 under-12s, under-4s free ($20 and $16 one way); airport to I-Drive, $29 and $23 ($18 and $14 one way); airport to Highway 192 in Kissimmee $45 and $36 ($26 and $21 one way); *Walt Disney World* to Universal Orlando, $18 round trip; I-Drive to *Walt Disney World*, $18; I-Drive or *Walt Disney World* to Kennedy Space Center, $34. You can book a shuttle on arrival at one of Mears' desks in the luggage halls, but be aware it can be a longish journey if it has a full van stopping at several hotels before yours (407 423 5566, **mearstransportation.com**). You can also try **Maingate Transportation** from the Highway 192 area ($15 round-trip to Universal or Wet 'n Wild, $12 to SeaWorld and $11 to Disney parks;

407 870 5553, **maingatetaxi.com**) or **MagicCity National Transportation** to all the main attractions (e.g. $12 each for a family of 4 from I-Drive to Walt Disney World; $9.94 each for 4 from I-Drive to Orlando International Airport; 407 678 8888, **magiccitynationaltransportation.com**). For groups of 7–10, consider **Mira Tours** for personal shuttle service from most hotels (1800 468 6063, **orlandodisneytransport.com**).

Several shopping malls also have their own shuttle service:

- **Lake Buena Vista Factory Stores:** Collects guests free each day from 54 hotels in the Orlando and Kissimmee areas. Ask at your hotel (407 363 1093, or **lbvfs.com**).

- **Orlando Premium Outlets:** Provides a free shuttle from 15 Lake Buena Vista area hotels or for $10 a round trip from Kissimmee hotels (call at least 2 hours in advance on 407 390 0000).

There are also excursion services offered by the likes of *Brit Guide* partners **Florida Dolphin Tours** (407 352 5151, **floridadolphintours.com**) and **Gator Tours** (see page 270).

Town cars and limousines

When it comes to limousine, town car and other transport services, there is again a huge choice (more than 150 at the last count!). The following all earn a *Brit Guide* recommendation:

BRIT TIP

A 'town car' is an American term for a deluxe saloon, such as a Cadillac or Lincoln.

Quick Transportation: A good bet for airport transfers and tailor-made transport packages, its town cars comfortably cope with a family of 4, while luxury vans cater for larger parties and all offer a ½-hour grocery stop, if required, for an extra $20. Luxury van rates (for up to 7) one-way from the airport range from $54.75 to the I-Drive area up to $81.50 for the farthest parts of *Walt Disney World*. Up to 11 can use a van for a small additional fee per person. Larger parties may need a luggage trailer for $20 extra each way. Town car rates are $110 from the airport to anywhere in Greater Orlando and $215 for a round trip, while stretch limos are $185 and $360. It serves all the parks and attractions and offers online quotes for all services, while it can also supply vehicles for the disabled and will quote for Orlando Sanford International Airport pick-ups, too (407 354 2456 or 1888 784 2522, **quicktransportation.com**).

Skyy Limousine: This company has one of the largest selections of vehicles in Orlando, from Lincoln town cars and executive vans to the amazing Hummer limo. One-way airport transfers from $65 (plus a 20% driver gratuity), and vehicles can also be hired by the hour from $50/hour. Other options cover much of central Florida, offering cruise transfers, a night-on-the-town, all-day services, beach trips, concerts and tailor-made excursions (407 352 4644, **skyylimousine.com**).

FL Tours: This well-established and popular company specialises in both airport–Disney routes and Port Canaveral transfers. One-way trips start from $60 and round trips from $109 ($119 and $229 from Orlando Sanford International Airport), plus gratuity; it also offers a free ½-hour grocery stop, free kids' booster and car seats, 24-hour online reservation access, and no extra charge for late pick-ups (407 857 9606, **fltours.com**).

Look up the full airport list at **orlandoairports.net/transport/vfh.htm**.

Taxis

For groups of 4 or 5, taxis can be more cost-effective than the shuttles. Orlando International Airport to I-Drive would be around $35 (plus tip); $40–50 for the Kissimmee area; $55 to *Magic Kingdom* resorts and $50 for the Epcot resort area; $10–15 from I-Drive to Universal Orlando; and $20 from I-Drive to *Downtown Disney*. You will find plenty of taxis waiting in ranks at the parks, hotels and shopping centres, but they don't cruise around looking for fares, so it is often best to book one in advance. You also need to ensure you choose a reliable, fully insured company. Check the name and phone number of the cab company is clearly displayed on the side, the driver's ID and insurance are visible and the rates are shown on the window or inside the car. Some drivers look for fares in the airport baggage hall, which is strictly illegal; all legitimate taxis should be in the rank on Level 1.

Mears: A group of 3 firms – Checker Cabs, Yellow Cabs and City Cabs (407 422 2222) – all of which are reliable. Mears is the main taxi company for Orlando Sanford International Airport, and you can pre-book cabs for around $80 to I-Drive, $100 to Lake Buena Vista and $105 to Disney hotels. Most taxis are metered but it is also acceptable to ask in advance what the fare will be.

Other reputable firms: Ace Metro/Luxury Cab (407 855 1111), Star Taxis (407 857 9999) and Diamond Cab Co (407 523 3333). Several hotels have town cars at their ranks, and these will not have meters, so you can either ask for the fare or call one of the companies listed above.

THE CAR

Ultimately, having a car is the key to being in charge of your holiday and, on a weekly basis, car hire tends to work out quite reasonable.

BRIT TIP
Your first call for car hire should be to *Brit Guide* partners Alamo. See inside the front cover for our special offer.

Weekly rental rates can be as low as $100 for the smallest car, an **Economy** (or sub-compact), usually a Vauxhall Corsa-sized hatchback; next up is the **Compact**, a small family saloon like a Ford Focus; the **Midsize** (or Intermediate) is a more spacious 4-door, 5-seater like a Mondeo; and the **Fullsize** would be a larger-style executive car like a Peugeot 407.

BRITTIP

Double check you have your driving licence BEFORE you leave home (both parts of it with the new photo-card type). You will simply NOT be given a hire car without it.

You can go up the scale further, with **Premium**, **Luxury** and **Convertible**, plus the **Minivan** (a Ford Galaxy or Renault Espace type). The car models, will, of course, be mainly American – Chevrolet, Dodge, Pontiac, Buick, Chrysler, Ford, Mercury and Lincoln. But beware of the low starting rates – there are essential insurances, taxes and surcharges that can take the weekly rate above $300. However, all the big rental companies now offer all-inclusive rates, which can work out cheaper if booked in advance in the UK, and you also benefit from easier processing in Orlando, making the whole business quicker.

BRITTIP

Be firm with the car hire company check-in clerk. Some can push you into having extras, like car upgrades, you simply won't need.

The scale of the car hire operation is huge, with as many as 1,000 visitors arriving at a time. Most holiday companies offer 'free car hire', but that doesn't mean it won't cost you anything. Only the rental cost is free and you must still pay the insurances and taxes (which makes the all-inclusive packages more attractive).

BRITTIP

The boot (trunk) size of American cars tends to be slightly smaller than the British equivalent. You will not get 7 adults PLUS all their luggage in a 7-seat people carrier ('van')!

Car rental companies: Alamo is our *Brit Guide* partner and offers excellent rates and service (see inside front cover). You also benefit with Alamo from being able to choose your own car from the different ranges – Compact, Intermediate, etc. – where the other companies assign you

a specific car. For alternatives, try **Dollar** (0808 234 2474), **Avis** (0844 581 0147), **Budget** (0844 544 3439) or **Thrifty** (01494 751 500).

BRITTIP

Unless you have accepted the SunPass pre-pay auto-toll option from the car rental firm, you cannot drive through the toll booths marked 'Sunpass' or 'E-Pass' only. You must stop at the booths marked 'Change Given' (in green) or 'Exact Change Only' (in blue).

Insurance: Having a credit card is essential, and there are two main kinds of insurance, the most important being the Loss or Collision Damage Waiver (LDW or CDW). This costs $24–26/day and covers you for any damage to your hire car. You can do without it, but the hire company will insist on a deposit in the order of $1,500 on your credit card (and you are liable for ANY damage). You will also be offered Supplemental Liability Insurance (SLI) or Extended Protection at around $13-15 a day, which is not essential but does cover you against being sued by any litigious American you may bump into. Relatively new and again optional is the Underinsured Motorists Protection (in case somebody with only minimal cover runs into you) at around $7 a day. Drivers must be at least 21, and those under 25 have to pay an extra $25 a day. Other costs include local and Florida state taxes, which can add $25-30 a week to your bill. Many

Disney's Coronado Springs Resort

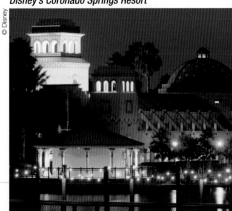

© Disney

companies also offer a Roadside Plus (around $5/day), which covers breakdowns, flat tyres, running out of fuel or locking your keys in the car, but this is again totally optional.

Then there is **fuel**, though this is much cheaper than in the UK. You can either *pre-pay* for a full tank (so you bring it back empty; the charge is usually slightly under the local rate/gallon for this); *fill it up yourself* so you have a full tank on return; or pay a *fuel surcharge* at the end for the company to refill the tank (the most expensive option).

You can also opt for the new SunPass auto-pay system (Dollar calls it Pass24) for the area's toll roads, so you don't have to stop at the toll booths (where some serious queues can build up) but just drive through; all your tolls are auto-recorded for payment when you return the car (plus a $2/day 'convenience fee').

Those on a budget can cut costs by taking travel insurance through specialists like **Extrasure** (01242 518300, **extrasureonline.co.uk**), whose DriveSure policy offers both LDW and SLI at around £14 a day. You may still need to leave a credit card imprint with the hire firm, but it should accept these policies (check in advance).

Controls

Most people soon find driving in America is a pleasure, mainly because nearly all hire cars are automatics and nearly new. And, because speed limits are lower (and rigidly enforced), you won't often be rushed into taking a wrong turn. Keep your foot on the brake when you are stationary as automatics tend to creep forward, and always put the gear lever on to 'P' (for Park) when switching off. All cars have air-conditioning, which is essential for most of the year. Turn on the fan with the A/C button or it won't work! Don't worry if a small pool of liquid forms under the car – it's condensation from the A/C unit. Power steering is also universal and larger cars have cruise control, which lets you set the desired speed

and take your foot off the accelerator. There will be 2 buttons on the steering wheel, one to switch on cruise control, the other to set the desired speed. To cancel cruise control, either press the first button again or simply touch the brake. The handbrake may also be different. Some cars have an extra pedal to the left of the brake, and you need to push this to engage the handbrake. To release it, you pull the tab just above it, if there is one, or give a second push on the pedal. The car probably won't start unless the gear lever is in 'P'. To put the car in 'D' for Drive, depress the brake pedal. D1 and D2 are extra gears for steep hills (none in Florida!). Not all cars have central locking, though, so make sure you lock ALL the doors before leaving it.

BRIT TIP
With an automatic, you won't be able to take the keys out of the ignition unless you put the gear lever in the 'Park' position first.

Finding your way

Your car hire company should provide you with a basic map of Orlando, plus directions to your hotel. Insist it gives you these, as all the hire companies make a big point of this in their literature. Try to familiarise yourself with the main roads in advance and learn to navigate by road numbers (as it's mainly those that are given on the signposts) and exit numbers of the main roads.

BRIT TIP
Be organised – get your directions in advance off the internet at sites like **mapquest.com** or use Google Earth to source maps, directions and even check out the lie of the land in advance. Download it free from its website at **http://earth.google.com**.

The signposting and road-naming systems can be confusing. For instance, you can't fail to find the main attractions, but retracing your steps can be tricky as the exit road may be different from the way in. It's vital to learn the road numbers (and directions, east–west or north–south) around the attractions so you know where you're heading, and if you want I-4 east or west or 192 as you exit *Walt Disney World*. Exits off motorways can be on EITHER side of the carriageway, not just on the right, but you can overtake in ANY lane on multi-lane highways. Therefore, you can sit in the middle lane until you see your exit. You don't get much advance notice of turn-offs, though.

Orlando has yet to come up with a comprehensive tourist map of its streets, and the maps supplied by the car rental companies are pretty basic. It helps that none of the main attractions is off the beaten track, but the support of a front-seat navigator can be useful. Around town, road names are displayed at every junction, hung underneath the traffic lights but suspended ABOVE the road. This road name is NOT the road you are on, but the one you are CROSSING. Once again there is little advance notice of each junction and the road names can be hard to read as you approach, especially at night, so keep your speed down if you think you are close to your turn-off to allow time to get into the correct lane. If you do miss a turning, most roads are on a grid system, so it's easy to work back.

Occasionally you will meet a crossroads where no right of way is obvious. This is a 4-way Stop, and the priority goes in order of arrival. So, when it's your turn, just indicate and pull out slowly (America doesn't have many roundabouts, so this may be the closest you get to one).

> **BRIT TIP**
> Disney is notoriously poor at signposting to help find your way out. Ask for a copy of its Transportation Guide/Map from Guest Services.

Tolls and traffic lights

For the toll roads, have some change handy in amounts from 25c to $2. They all give change (in the GREEN lanes), but you will get through quicker if you have the correct money (in the BLUE lanes). On minor exits of Osceola Parkway and the Greeneway, there are auto-toll machines only, so keep some loose change in the car.

> **BRIT TIP**
> On nearly all toll roads these days (notably the 417, 429 and 528), at the manned toll booths you have to pull in to a slip road on the right to pay. It is SunPass/E-Pass only on the main carriageway. This can catch you out, especially when you have just left the airport.

As well as the obvious difference of driving on the 'wrong' side of the road, there are several differences in procedure. The most frequent British errors occur at traffic lights (which are hung above the road, not on posts). At a red light, you can still turn RIGHT, providing there is no traffic coming from the left and no pedestrians crossing, unless otherwise specified (signs that indicate 'No turn on red'). Turning left at the lights, you have the right of way with a green ARROW but must give way to traffic from the other direction on a SOLID green.

The majority of accidents involving overseas visitors take place on left turns, so take extra care here. There is also no amber light from red to green, but there IS from green to red. A flashing amber light at a junction means proceed but watch for traffic joining the carriageway, while a flashing red light indicates it is OK to turn if the carriageway is clear.

Disney's Grand Floridian Resort and Spa

© Disney

BRIT TIP

The Osceola Parkway toll road (522) that runs parallel to Highway 192 is a better route in to *Walt Disney World* from eastern Kissimmee and costs only $1.75. Use Sherberth Road for Disney access from west 192 or the new Western Beltway (Highway 429).

Restrictions

Speed limits are always well marked with black numbering on white signs and the police are pretty hot on speeding, with steep on-the-spot fines. There are varying limits of 55–70mph (88–113kph) on the Interstates, where there is also a 40mph (64kph) minimum speed limit, to just 15–25mph (24–40kph) in built-up areas. Seat belts are compulsory for all passengers, while child seats must be used for under-4s and can be hired from the car companies at $10–15 a day (better still, bring your own or buy one locally for $70–80). Children aged 4 or 5 must use a seat belt, in the front or back, or have a child seat fitted.

It is illegal to park within 3m/10ft of a fire hydrant or a lowered kerb, and never park in front of a yellow-painted kerb – they are stopping points for emergency vehicles and you will be towed away. Never park ON a kerb, either. Park bonnet first – reverse parking is frowned upon because number plates are only on the rear of cars and police then can't see them. If you park parallel to the kerb, you must face the direction of traffic. Flashing orange lights over the road indicate a school zone; school buses must NOT be overtaken in either direction when they are unloading and have their hazard lights on. U-turns are forbidden in built-up areas and where there is a solid line down the middle of the road. You must pull to the side of the road to allow emergency vehicles to pass, in either direction, when they have lights and/or sirens going. Also, on multi-lane highways in Florida, the Move Over law means you must pull into an adjacent lane if you see a police car on the hard shoulder, or slow down if you can't move over. And you must put on your lights in the rain.

BRIT TIP

Just after exit 34, the Greeneway (417) heading south appears to split into two where it meets Highway 408. Keep RIGHT to stay southbound.

Finally, DON'T drink and drive. Florida has strict laws, with penalties of up to 6 months in prison for first-time offenders. The blood-alcohol limit is lower than in Britain, so it is safer not to drink at all if you are driving. It is also illegal to carry open containers of alcohol in the car.

Bonus for AA members: Your membership is recognised by the equivalent AAA in the US and you benefit from various special offers. Take your AA card and, where you see the AAA 'Show & Save' signs in hotels, shops and restaurants, just produce it to enjoy the same money-saving benefits as the locals. Visit **aaasouth. com** and click on AAA Discounts for the full range (use the zip code 32819 when prompted).

BRIT TIP

You won't encounter any fixed speed cameras like those in the UK, but police cars will often be stationed in busy areas with hand-held cameras (notably on Sherberth Rd in Kissimmee). But there are now cameras on many traffic lights to catch red-light runners, so try not to take any risks here.

Accidents

In the unlikely event of an accident, no matter how minor, you must contact the police before the cars can be moved (except on the busy I-4). Car hire firms will insist on a full police report for the insurance. If you break down, there should be an emergency number for the hire company in its literature or, if you are on a main highway, raise the bonnet and wait for one of the frequent police patrol cars to stop (or dial *FHP on your mobile). Always carry your driving licence (both parts with the new card type) and car hire forms in case you are stopped by the police.

The satnav solution

Of course, the best way to navigate these days is by a GPS or SatNav system. All car hire companies now offer this as an extra (at around $70/week), or you can bring your own. If your system has only the base-level (i.e. UK) maps loaded, you can download the necessary maps for south-east USA for around £35. If you are thinking of buying a GPS system, the likes of Wal-Mart offer new systems, fully loaded for the US, for less than $200.

Key routes

Interstate 4: I-4 is the main route through Orlando, a 4-, 6- or 8-lane motorway linking the coasts. Interstates are always indicated on blue shield-shaped signs. For most of its length, I-4 travels east–west but, around Orlando, it swings north–south, though directions are still given east (for north) or west (for south). All main motorways are prefixed I, the even numbers going east–west and odd numbers north–south. Federal Highways are the next grade down, numbered with black numerals on white shields, while state roads are called Routeways and are prefixed SR (black numbers on white circular or rectangular signs). All the attractions of *Walt Disney World*, plus SeaWorld and Universal Orlando are well signposted from I-4. Lake Wales and Bok Tower Gardens are a 45-minute drive from Orlando west (south) on I-4 and Highway 27, while Busch Gardens is 75–90 minutes down I-4 to Tampa. Be aware I-4 can be packed with traffic for long sections in the morning and evening rush hours. You can check for major roadworks on **trans4mation.org**.

All American motorways have their junctions numbered in mileage terms, which makes it easy to calculate journey distances. I-4 starts at exit 1 in Tampa and goes all the way to exit 132 at Daytona, 132 miles away. In Orlando, the main junctions run from exit 55, at Highway 27, to exit 83 (downtown Orlando) and exit 101, for the Seminole Expressway

(417) and Orlando Sanford International Airport.

International Drive: I-Drive is the second key local roadway, linking a 14½ml/24km ribbon of hotels, shops, restaurants and attractions like Wet 'n Wild, The Pointe Orlando and Festival Bay (I-Drive South, from Highway 192 in Kissimmee north to Route 535, is NOT the main stretch and the 2 sections are linked via Route 535 and World Center Drive). From I-4, take exits 71, 72, 74A or 75A going east (north), or 75B, 74A or 72 going west (south). To the north, I-Drive runs into Oak Ridge Road and the South Orange Blossom Trail, which leads to downtown Orlando (junctions 82C–84 off I-4). I-Drive is also bisected by Sand Lake Road and runs into World Center Drive (536), to the south, also convenient for Disney. I-Drive is a major tourist centre and makes an excellent base, especially around the Sand Lake Road junction, as it is fully pedestrian-friendly. It's a 20-minute drive to Disney and 10 minutes from Universal. However, at peak times, heavy traffic means it's best to avoid the stretch from the Convention Center north. Use Universal Boulevard instead.

◀▶ BRIT TIP
Watch out for the major roadworks at the junction of Osceola Parkway and John Young Parkway in Kissimmee. These will continue until May 2011 and are best avoided, if possible.

Kissimmee: The other main tourist area, south of Orlando and south-east of Disney, its features are grouped along a 20ml/32km stretch of the Irlo Bronson Memorial Highway (192), which intersects I-4 at junction 64B, and is close to *Walt Disney World* (though a good 20–25 minutes from SeaWorld and Universal). The downtown area of Kissimmee is off Main Street, Broadway and Emmett Street and is ideal for walking. A handy visual along Highway 192 is the Marker Series from Formosa Gardens (number 4) to just past Medieval Times (number 15). These highly visible signs are good locators for hotels, restaurants and attractions, and much of this stretch is also walkable (though few places are close together). The unique Disney-inspired town of **Celebration** is also here (just south of *Walt Disney World*). Try to avoid the area of the 192 east of Marker 15, though, it is becoming increasingly run-down and unappealing. If you're heading to downtown Kissimmee (which we DO recommend) use the Osceola Parkway and S Orange Blossom Trail (441).

At the west end of **Highway 192**, you find **Highway 27**, which runs north to Clermont and south to Davenport (and Haines City). Highway 27 is a major area of holiday villa developments that are, generally, quite convenient for Disney. However, many home owners claim they are only '5 minutes from Disney', which is extremely misleading. It is usually a good 15 minutes from Highway 27 to the edge of Disney property. The area is also starting to add shops and restaurants, notably in the Cagan Crossings junction (just north of where 192 meets 27), where there is also a large Wal-Mart, and Berry Town Center (to the south).

Western Beltway: The new 429 provides a western Orlando 'by-pass', avoiding the often-crowded I-4 and linking with the Florida Turnpike and Apopka to the north. More importantly, it offers an alternative west gateway to *Walt Disney World* at Exit 8 (Western Way), which is handy for the Davenport/Clermont areas. This junction is also set to see much new development in the next 4 years in an area called Flamingo Crossings at the junction of the 429 and Western Way (**flamingocrossings.com**).

Fuel

All local petrol ('gas') stations are self-service and most require you to pay before filling up. However, the pumps should allow you to pay by credit card without having to visit the cashier (some stations ask for a local zip code with a credit card swipe, and this means you DO need to go inside). To activate the petrol pump, you may need first to lift the lever underneath the pump nozzle. RaceTrac and Hess petrol stations are often the cheapest. The 2 Hess stations in *Walt Disney World* are, surprisingly, among the cheapest in the area, while the Wal-Mart on SR535 (Vineland Road) is also a cheap option. Petrol stations in Lake Buena Vista just outside Disney are the MOST expensive.

Local maps

The best of the free maps is the bright orange *Welcome Guide Map* (also full of discount coupons), available in the main tourist areas, and the pull-out map inside the *Kissimmee-St Cloud Visitors' Guide* (from the Official Visitor Center on East Highway 192, 407 847 5000). AA members are also well catered for (see page 60).

Enter: Mapman

By far the best and most up-to-date area map is a British production, created by Disney fan and carto-grapher Steve Munns. It is superbly detailed for the I-4 corridor, Highway 192 and Walt Disney World, with special sections on I-Drive and villa locations. All the main attractions, hotels and even many restaurants are clearly indicated and there is accompanying text and photos, while the website adds updates and other insider tips. The latest edition is also ultra hard-wearing. We think it's the perfect companion to the *Brit Guide* and you won't go wrong with it at only £7.40 (plus 78p p&p). Just visit **orlandomaps.co.uk** (online orders only). It's also available as a new iPhone/iPod Touch/iPad App from the iTunes App store for £2.99. Called iOrlando Tourist Map, it is offline so there are no roaming charges, but it does include a searchable database to find places quickly. Even better, Steve is also now our resident 'mapman' for the *Brit Guide*.

Now, let's go on to the next vital step – your holiday accommodation…

Metro Orlando has the second highest concentration of hotels in the world (after Las Vegas) and more are being built all the time. There are currently 115,000 rooms, and counting, not to mention 26,000 villas for rent. Therefore, what follows is only a general guide to the various types, plus our recommendations and favourites.

The main choice is between a traditional **hotel** option and one of the many (and rapidly proliferating) **self-catering types** of accommodation, which can be villas/ vacation homes, townhomes or condos.

HOTELS

Many American hotels, particularly in the tourist areas, tend towards the motel type, where everything is not necessarily located in one main building. Your room may be in one of several blocks sited round the pool, restaurant or other amenities. Room size rarely alters, even from 2 to 4-star hotels; their amenities and services form the basis of their star ratings. A standard room usually has 2 double beds and will accommodate a family of 4 (couples should ask for a king room, with an extra-size bed). All hotels should offer non-smoking rooms. Motel-type accommodation can also lack a restaurant as they operate on a room-only basis, so

you may have to drive to the nearest restaurant (many are within walking distance on International Drive). Check out the dining facilities before you book.

Most hotels are big, clean, efficient and great value. You'll find plenty of soft-drink and ice machines (though it's cheaper to buy drinks from a supermarket), with ice buckets in all rooms. All accommodation will be air-conditioned and, when it is hot, you have to live with the drone of the A/C unit at night. If you need a more spacious room, look for one of the many suite hotels, which provide sitting rooms and mini-kitchens, as well as 1, 2 or even 3 bedrooms.

BRIT TIP
Hotels are expensive places from which to make phone calls. Most add a 45–70% surcharge (Disney resorts even add a connection fee), while you can be charged for an unanswered call if it rings 5 or more times. Buy a phonecard instead (see pages 36 and 44).

Hotel prices are always per *room* (not per person) and they will be cheaper out of the main holiday periods, with special deals at times. Always ask for rates if you book directly and check if special rates apply during your visit (don't be afraid to ask for their 'best rate' at off-peak times, which can be lower than published or 'rack' rates). There may be an additional charge ($5–15/person) for more than 2 adults sharing the same room, plus there is state tax and, sometimes, a resort fee that can add $10–20/day to the rate.

BRIT TIP

Buy soft drinks at the supermarket, and a polystyrene cooler for about $5 that you can fill from your hotel ice machine to keep drinks cold.

If you've just arrived and need a hotel, visit one of the official Visitor Centers: I-Drive just north of Pointe Orlando (on the corner of Austrian Court; 8.30am–6.30pm daily; 407 363 5872); or on east Highway 192 in Kissimmee (8am–5pm Mon–Fri; 407 847 5000), where they have brochures on all current deals. If you're keen on auction websites like **priceline.co.uk**, you may land a bargain. Other agents are **Expedia** (0871 226 0808, **expedia. co. uk**), **Hotel Anywhere** (01444 410555, **hotelanywhere.co.uk**), **Travel Supermarket** (**travelsupermarket.com**), **Hotels.com** (0203 027 81 46; **hotels. com**), **Orbitz** (1888 656 4546 in the US or 001 312 416 0018 from the UK, **orbitz.com**) and **Hotwire** (**hotwire.com**).

There is no widely accepted star rating, so (with the exception of Disney's resorts), we group hotels into 4 ranges: *Budget, Value, Moderate* and *Deluxe*, where the (rough) price groups/night will be:

- Budget = up to $50
- Value = $51–99
- Moderate = $100–160
- Deluxe = $161 plus

The main factor is the extra facilities. Thus, a Deluxe rating will include the

Disney's Beach Club Resort

© Disney

highest level of facilities and service, while a Budget will be a basic motel-type. A key pricing factor is location (the closer to Disney and other parks, the higher the price), so you can save if you don't mind a longer journey.

Disney hotels

Our review of Orlando's hotels starts with *Walt Disney World*. Sited conveniently for all its attractions – and linked by an excellent free transport system of monorail, buses and boats – Disney's hotels, suites and campsites are all magnificently appointed and maintained. It also groups them into 5 types: *Value, Moderate* and *Deluxe Resorts*, then the *Deluxe Villas* (which are just Disney's timeshare properties) and the *Campground* of Fort Wilderness (with a strong element of self-catering for the latter two). They range from the swanky Grand Floridian Resort & Spa to the more basic but still fun style of the Pop Century Resort. And Disney's imagination and attention to detail here are as good as at the parks. There are more than 22,000 rooms, while Fort Wilderness has 1,195 campsites and cabins.

Grand accommodation comes at a price, though. A regular room at the Grand Floridian can be $700 a night in high season (suites can top $2,000) and even the Moderate Caribbean Beach Resort can be $160 a night. Dining at resort hotels is not cheap either, and you'll find few fast-food outlets on site. However, staying with the Mouse is one of the great thrills, for the style, service and extras. The 21 resorts offer a superb array of facilities that children especially love. The benefits are:

- Resort ID card: Every guest receives a card with which to charge almost all on-site purchases.

- Package delivery: Park purchases can be sent to your hotel gift shop.

- Free parking: With your ID card, there is no charge at any of the Disney car parks.

- Refillable mugs: All Disney resorts sell collectable drinking mugs, which are well worth buying ($13

Suite things

Suites hotels, virtually unknown in the UK, provide a combination of hotel and apartment, with extra value for large families or groups. Typically, a suites room gives you a living room and kitchenette, including microwave, coffee-maker, fridge, cutlery and crockery, while many offer a complimentary continental breakfast (or better). All have pools and grocery stores or snack bars and several have restaurants. They vary only in the number of bedrooms and can usually sleep 6–10.

each) as you can then get free refills at their self-service cafés.

- Dining priority: Many Disney restaurants hold tables for resort guests, while you can also book 180 days in advance *plus* the length of your stay (i.e. 194 days if you're going for 2 weeks). Call 407 939 3463 or press the Dining button on your resort phone (non-Disney hotel guests can book only 180 days in advance).

- Priority golf: The best tee times are reserved for resort guests and can be booked 90 days in advance on 407 939 4653.

- Children's services: All resorts have in-room or group babysitting (subject to availability, so book in advance on 407 827 5444) and 8 of the 9 Deluxe resorts have supervised activity centres and dinner clubs (around $12/child per hour), usually open until midnight.

- Mickey on call: What better way to wake than with an alarm call from the Mouse himself?

- Extra Magic Hours: This is the BIG bonus, the chance to get into one of the parks each day either 1 hour early or for 3 hours after regular park closing, and enjoy many rides with reduced crowds.

- Disney's Magical Express Service: The free airport transfer service for guests at Disney hotels. Book at least 10 days before arrival through **disneyworld.com** or a travel agent.

Value resorts

Disney's All-Star Resorts: Disney's first foray into more modestly priced market in 1994, here you can stay in one of the 5 *Sports*-themed blocks (surfing, basketball, tennis, baseball and American football) centred around a massive food court, 2 swimming pools, a games arcade and shops; the *Music*-themed version (Jazz, Rock, Broadway, Calypso and Country); or the *Movies* complex (Mighty Ducks, 101 Dalmatians, Fantasia, Love Bug and Toy Story). The latter is possibly the most imaginative, with its Fantasia pool and kids' play areas, and the most popular blocks are Toy Story and 101 Dalmatians (both non-smoking). All 3 centres, with 5,568 rooms, have pool bars, shops, laundry facilities, video games rooms and a pizza delivery service. The All Star Music Resort (Jazz and Calypso buildings) also has 192 impressive 2-room *Family Suites* (converted by combining 2 standard rooms) that sleep up to 6. Each suite has 2 bathrooms, a well-stocked kitchenette, a lounge and private master bedroom, making the space much more flexible. Standard rooms are bright and compact (read 'tight' for families with older children), but well designed for those who want the Disney convenience but not the price

Disney's All-Star Movies Resort

© Disney

Disney Dining Plan

One other possible perk of staying onsite with Disney is its Dining Plan. This allows its hotel guests to pre-pay most meals during their stay at a set fee per day. There are three different Plans to choose from: (prices shown as of summer 2010):

Quick Service Dining Plan: Provides 2 Counter Service meals and 2 snacks a day, plus 1 refillable resort mug/person. Counter Service meals are defined as 1 entrée or combo meal, plus 1 dessert and 1 (non-alcoholic) drink for lunch or dinner, and 1 juice, 1 entrée or combo meal and 1 drink for breakfast. Snacks can be any item under $4 such as an ice-cream, popcorn, a piece of fruit, a bag of crisps, a bottled drink, a medium soda or tea/coffee. Cost: $31.99/day for adults, $9.99 for 3–9s (children must also order off the Children's Menu).

Disney Dining Plan: Provides 1 Table Service meal, 1 Counter Service and 1 snack per person per day. Table Service meals are 1 appetiser, 1 entrée, 1 dessert and 1 (non-alcoholic) drink, or 1 juice, 1 entrée and 1 drink OR a full buffet for breakfast. Cost: $41.99 and $11.99/day. *NB: At peak season, Disney increases the price to $46.99 and $12.99.*

Deluxe Dining Plan: Provides 3 meals (either Table or Counter Service) and 2 snacks per person per day, plus 1 refillable resort mug per person. Cost: $71.99 and $20.99/day.

All meals do NOT have to be used per day and can be spread over the full duration of your stay; i.e. you can miss a Table Service meal one day and then use 2 Table Service credits another day for a Signature Restaurant or Dinner show. Gratuities are NOT included, though. When you check in at a Disney hotel, you're given a 'Key to the World' card you then use for all your Dining Plan meals and that monitors your daily usage. The Dining Plans CAN be used for Character Meals, when 1 Table Service meal is required per person (2 at ultra-popular Cinderella's Royal Table in *Magic Kingdom*), and for the 8 Signature Restaurants in *Walt Disney World* (notably Jiko at Animal Kingdom Lodge, California Grill at the Contemporary Resort and Citricos at the Grand Floridian Resort), which all require 2 Table Service meals. They can even be used at Disney's Dinner Shows (see pages 306–7), subject to availability, at 2 Table Service meals per person.

However, ALL members of the group must book the Plan for the *full* duration of their stay and inclusive of park tickets. Pre-book (on 407 939 3463) your full-service meals as the sit-down restaurants often book up early. Not all restaurants are on the Plan but you still have 100 options. More info at **disneyworld.co.uk**, where you can now book all table service restaurants online.

tag. Close to the entrance is a large McDonald's if the resort's food court doesn't appeal. All resort transport is provided by an efficient bus service.

BRIT TIP

To make a reservation at any *Walt Disney World* hotel, call 407 934 7639, or visit **disneyworld.co.uk**.

Disney's Pop Century Resort: In a similar vein, themed round the decades of the 2nd half of the 20th century, here are 5 blocks with giant icons – such as yo-yos, Rubik's cubes and juke-boxes – and a riot of period sayings and visual gags. Opened in 2003, it features a pool fashioned like a 10-pin bowling lane (others are shaped like a computer and a flower), a huge table football set-up and open-air Twister mats. Blocks are grouped around a main building housing the check-in area (with a large-screen TV showing Disney films), an imaginative food court, a lounge (with quick-breakfast bar), a Disney store and games arcade. The 177-acre/72ha complex also features a central lake and lots of bright landscaping. It all adds significantly to Disney's budget-orientated offerings and has a well-organised bus service to the parks. The drawbacks? Long queues to check in and a rather hectic feel, even late in the evening. You need to request a hairdryer from reception

Kidsuites = happy families!

Orlando has pioneered a great family accommodation style, worth seeking out if you have kids who enjoy bunk beds. Basically, a kidsuite is a separate area within the hotel room that gives the kids their own 'bedroom' (with bunks), usually also with their own TV and games console.

and rooms are, again, rather small. A 2nd half of the resort was planned but is now being built as Disney's Art of Animation Resort (opening 2012).

Moderate resorts

Disney's Caribbean Beach Resort:
Opened in 1988 with 2,112 rooms spread over 5 Caribbean 'islands' (with an inter-island bus service), rooms are still relatively plain, but comfortably sleep 4, and the Market Street food court, main restaurant Shutters and outdoor activities (with a lakeside recreation area with themed waterfalls, slides, games arcade, bike and boat rentals) are a big hit with children. The 6 Market Street outlets at the Old Port Royale resort hub can get busy in the morning, and the Trinidad South and Barbados 'islands' are a fair walk from the centre. But it is an action-packed resort with some imaginative touches, like Parrot Cay Island with its tropical birds and play area. Transport to all the parks is solely by bus.

Disney's Coronado Springs Resort:
Possibly the best value of this trio (built in 1997), it has slightly more facilities for its 1,921 rooms spread over 125 acres/50ha: 4 pools (including the massive Lost City of Cibola activity pool with waterslide), 2 games arcades, a boating marina, bike rentals, restaurant, food court and café/convenience store, lounge bar, gift shop, beauty salon and health club, business centre and 2 guest launderettes. The chic and upscale Rix Lounge – a bar/nightclub serving unique cocktails and appetisers – gives the Resort another unique claim

to fame. Constructed on a scenic Mexican/Spanish theme in 3 'villages' (Casitas, Ranchos and Cabanas), Coronado is an often-overlooked treasure. Check out the Maya Grill and its New Latino cuisine; sample the many offerings of the tempting Pepper Market food court; or just grab a snack or drink and sit and soak up the splendid lake views from the outdoor terrace. Coronado Springs is also only 5 minutes from *Disney's Animal Kingdom* and is well served by the bus network.

Disney's Port Orleans Resort:
Opened in 1991, this is a 2-part complex (formerly Port Orleans and Dixie Landings) split into the 2,048-room *Riverside* – with a steamboat reception area, a great Riverside Mill food court, Boatwright's full-service restaurant, the River Roost lounge (with live entertainment on certain nights) and an old-fashioned General Store (the gift shop) – and the 1,008-room *French Quarter*, which has the Sassagoula Floatworks and Food Factory court, 2 bars, a games room and shopping arcade. The Riverside includes the magnificent Ol' Man Island, a 3½-acre/1.5ha playground with swimming pool, kids' area and a fishing hole, while the French Quarter has Doubloon Lagoon, with Mardi Gras dragon slide, alligator fountains and a play area. The eye-catching landscaping and design vary from rustic Bayou backwoods to turn-of-the-century New Orleans. Transport for both is by bus to the parks and bus or boat to *Downtown Disney*.

Disney's Coronado Springs Resort

© Disney

BRIT TIP
Disney resort restaurants can (and we think should) be visited even if you aren't staying there. Advance book at any of the parks, call 407 939 3463 or visit **disneyworld.co.uk**.

Deluxe resorts

More than anything, Disney specialises in high-quality hotels with all manner of grand design features, amenities and restaurants. All 9 offer a Concierge level, which adds an exclusive, personalised service, and a private lounge with meals and snacks.

Disney's Animal Kingdom Lodge:
This stunning 'private game lodge' (opened in 2001) is set on a 33-acre/13ha animal-filled savannah, which many rooms overlook. The pervasive African theme is all-encompassing, and the effect of opening your curtains to a vista of giraffes and zebras is immense. All this creativity comes before you consider the amenities: 2 restaurants, café, bar, elaborately themed 'watering-hole' main pool (with waterslide) and kids' pool, massage and fitness centre, large gift shop, children's play area and an awesome 4-storey atrium. The main restaurant, Jiko, is spectacular, but there is also the superb buffet-style Boma, a 'marketplace' restaurant featuring African-tinged dishes from a wood-burning grill and rotisserie for breakfast and dinner. The lavishness and detail are superb, right down to the guides who can tell guests about

Disney's Animal Kingdom Lodge

© Disney

the 200 animals and their habitats, the African folklore stories around the outdoor firepit and the chance for children to become junior safari researchers while Mum and Dad do some wine-tasting (the hotel boasts America's largest collection of South African wines).

BRIT TIP
Jiko at Disney's Animal Kingdom Lodge offers an imaginative New World cuisine menu, attentive service and authentic ambience, and is a wonderfully romantic choice.

Rooms range from standard doubles to 1 and 2-bedroom suites, some of which have bunk beds. Simba's Cubhouse is for 4–12s (4.30pm–midnight), and all transport is by bus (with the *Animal Kingdom* barely 5 minutes away). Part of the main building of the Lodge (now called **Jambo House**) has been converted into studios and 1 and 2-bed villas (the latter boasting full kitchens) for Disney Vacation Club guests, sleeping 4–12, but these are also available to regular guests when not in use for the DVC programme. The new **Kidani Village** wing adds still more (see page 74).

Disney's Boardwalk Inn and Villas:
One of the Crescent Lake resorts next to *Epcot*, opened in 1996, is this 45-acre/18ha extravagant Inn and entertainment 'district'. It features a 512-room hotel, 383 villas, 4 themed restaurants, a TV sports club and 2 nightclubs, plus an array of shops, sports facilities and a huge, free-form swimming pool with a 200ft/60m waterslide, all on a semi-circular boardwalk around the lake. The effect is stunning, and the in-room attention to detail excellent. Highlights are the 'summer cottage' Villas (also part of the Disney Vacation Club), the new Mediterranean-themed restaurant Kouzzina by celebrity chef Cat Cora (breakfast and dinner) and the Big River Grille Brewing Company (lunch and dinner) for some great beers from its own micro-brewery. Top of the lot is the expensive but superb seafood of

the Flying Fish Café (dinner only). You can also try the Boardwalk Bakery for a snack. It's a delightful place to visit for a meal, the nightlife (especially Jellyrolls piano bar and ESPN Club) or just to wander along the boardwalk. Transport is by boat to *Epcot* and *Disney's Hollywood Studios* and by bus to the other parks.

Disney's Contemporary Resort: Situated on the monorail, right next to the *Magic Kingdom*, this 15-storey resort opened with the park in 1971 and boasts 655 remodelled rooms, a cavernous foyer, 5 shops, 4 restaurants, 2 lounges, a real sandy beach, a marina, 2 pools (1 with waterslide), 6 tennis courts, a video games centre and health club – and fabulous views, especially from the superb, hotel-top California Grill (one of the most romantic settings in Orlando; try to get a reservation to coincide with the park's fireworks). Don't miss Chef Mickey's for a breakfast or dinner buffet with your favourite characters, while the monorail runs right *through* the hotel – fascinating for kids. Rooms are some of Disney's largest and were all renovated in 2006, adding elegant new decor, dark-wood furniture and comfy duvets. Ultra-chic restaurant/lounge The Wave features a modern bar and dining area with a highly varied menu and is well worth trying for dinner or just a cocktail (or two!), while the new (in 2009) Contempo Café adds a light meal option 6am–midnight. Within walking distance of the *Magic Kingdom*, transport to other parks is by bus.

Disney's Grand Floridian Resort & Spa: This true 5-star hotel (opened in 1988) is built like an elaborate Victorian mansion, with 867 rooms, an impressive domed foyer and staff in period costume. Again on the monorail, 1 stop from the *Magic Kingdom*, the rooms and facilities are truly luxurious – hence the mega prices, though it's worth a look even if you're not staying. Its 6 restaurants include the top-of-the-range Victoria and Albert's (where the set 6-course dinner with wine costs $185), the chic seafood-based Narcoossee's (one

of our favourites), with its excellent view over Seven Seas Lagoon, and Mediterranean-styled Citricos. There are also 4 bars and impressive sports and relaxation facilities, notably the fabulous Spa and Salon. There's a wonderful second pool area, complete with zero-depth entry and waterslide. The Mouseketeer Club caters for 4–12s (4.30pm–midnight) and the 1900 Park Fare restaurant is hugely popular for character breakfasts and dinners, plus the children's Wonderland Tea Party with Alice and friends (1.30–2.30pm Mon– Fri, $40/child) and Captain's Shipyard Cruise (9.30–11.30am, Mon, Wed, Thurs and Sat, $31.95/child). For young princesses, the Garden View Lounge hosts My Disney Girl's Perfectly Princess Tea Party (10.30am–noon daily except Tues and Wed), featuring Princess Aurora from Sleeping Beauty and with storytelling, singalongs and a princess parade, plus a princess doll and gifts for each child (3–11). The cost for 1 adult and child is a steep $250 ($165 each additional child, plus $85 for an additional adult), but reservations (on 407 939 3463) are still advisable. The Garden View Lounge also serves a variety of traditional Afternoon Teas 2–4.30pm daily, $10.50–25.50/person. Transport to the *Magic Kingdom* is by boat and monorail; by bus to the other parks.

BRIT TIP
Watch out for the free nightly **Electrical Water Pageant** on Bay Lake and Seven Seas Lagoon, on view from all the *Magic Kingdom* resorts.

Disney's Grand Floridian Resort & Spa

© Disney

Disney's Polynesian Resort: The other 1971 original is a South Seas tropical fantasy with modern sophistication and comfort. Beautiful beaches, lush vegetation and architecture are home to 853 rooms built in wooden long-house style, all with balconies and superb views. Also on the monorail line opposite the *Magic Kingdom*, it boasts a lovely 3-storey atrium, with 75 varieties of tropical plants, koi ponds and a waterfall. The Polynesian's large rooms, like those of the Contemporary Resort, have been extensively refurbished to revive the Pacific isles theme, with custom-made furniture, tapestries and warm, earth colours. The resort offers excellent eating: 'Ohana is an entertaining and stylish dinner venue that also offers lively character breakfasts, while the Kona Café is slightly less formal but still with an extensive menu, and Captain Cook's Snack Company offers more basic counter-service fare. Then there are canoe rentals, a beautiful 'Volcano' pool area with waterslide, a games room, shops and children's playground. The Neverland Club caters for 4–12s (4pm–midnight). Catch the monorail or boat to the *Magic Kingdom* and buses to the other parks. The Poly is also home to the *Spirit of Aloha* dinner show (see pages 306–7), which is open to non-resort guests and makes a great evening among the torchlit gardens. The Resort's beach is also a great area from which to view the nightly *Magic Kingdom* fireworks.

Disney's Yacht Club Resort

© Disney

Disney's Wilderness Lodge: Opened in 1994 and one of the most picturesque resorts, this is also a great romantic destination. It is a detailed re-creation of a National Park lodge, from the stream running through the massive wooden balcony-lined atrium into the gardens, past the swimming pool (with hot and cold spas) to a geyser that erupts each hour. Offering authentic backwoods charm with true luxury, the resort is connected to the *Magic Kingdom* by boat and bus (and buses to the other parks). Rooms are all spacious with some lovely furniture, while the Courtyard View rooms are the best of the regular rooms (though at a slight premium). Deluxe rooms sleep up to 6 and the suites (at up to $850 a night) are truly sumptuous. It also has 2 restaurants: the brilliant Artist's Point (lunch and dinner) and the Whispering Canyon Café (lively breakfast and huge all-you-can-eat buffets) – plus a snack bar and pool bar. The Cubs' Den is for 4–12s (4.30pm–midnight). The Villas at Wilderness Lodge is a Disney Vacation Club development of 136 studios and 1 and 2-bed villas. Facilities include living areas, kitchens, private balconies and whirlpool baths. There is a quiet pool area, a spa and health club.

Disney's Yacht and Beach Club Resorts: Disney added more refined quality when this duo opened in 1990 with 630 and 580 nautical-themed rooms respectively. Set around Crescent Lake next to the *Epcot* park, they help to form one massive resort area that is a delight to walk around at any time but especially at night. For dinner, the Yachtsman Steakhouse offers friendly, polished and elegant dining at the Yacht Club, while the sister hotel features Cape May Café for lovely character breakfasts and a nightly New England-style clambake buffet. Beaches & Cream can also be found here, a classic 1950s-style diner for burgers, shakes and sundaes. Both resorts are set along a white-sand beach like a tropical island paradise and share water fun at Stormalong Bay, a superb 2½-acre/1ha recreation area with waterslides and a sandy lagoon. You can go boating or catch a water-shuttle to *Epcot* or *Disney's Hollywood Studios*; other park transport is by bus. The Sand Castle Club here caters for youngsters aged 4–12 (4.30pm–midnight).

> ### ⊞ BRIT TIP
> Look out for the nightly Disney film shows on the big outdoor movie screen by the beach at the Yacht and Beach Club Resorts.

Walt Disney World Swan and Dolphin Resort: These unmistakable twin hotels also went up on Crescent Lake in 1989 and, while not actually owned by Disney, they conform to the same high standards. They have some of the most extensive facilities, a wonderful location, fab restaurants and a night-time view second to none, while they are usually slightly cheaper than most Deluxe resorts. They're within walking distance of *Epcot* and *Disney's Hollywood Studios*, *Disney's Boardwalk Resort* and the Fantasia Gardens Miniature Golf Courses, but also have a boat service to both parks (and bus to the others). The unique architecture is extensive, with the Swan topped by a 45ft/14m statue, as well as 756 large rooms (including 55 suites), while the Dolphin (1,509 rooms, 112 suites) is crowned by 2 even bigger statues. Both have been extensively refurbished to include the Westin Heavenly Bed® and high-speed wi-fi. The Dolphin also boasts the Balinese-inspired Mandara Spa, with a relaxing tea garden and authentic Meru Temple. This resort has 17 restaurants and lounges, 4 tennis courts, 5 pools (1 an amazing grotto pool with hidden alcoves and waterslide), a kids' pool and white-sand beach, 2 health clubs, bike and paddle boat rentals, a great range of shops, a video arcade and the Camp Dolphin centre for 4–12s (5.30pm– 11pm, $10/hour per child). Even for non-guests, Shula's Steak House and celebrity chef Todd English's bluezoo (both Dolphin) are worth seeking out, along with Il Mulino Trattoria, New York's top Italian restaurant (in the Swan). Fresh, the Dolphin's Mediterranean-

style market, serves breakfast and lunch, featuring all made-to-order menu items and both à la carte and tableside dining. The decor and atmosphere at the Swan's Garden Grove Café is inspired by the gardens of Central Park, and it serves à la carte or buffet breakfasts, with Disney characters, at the weekend. Those who like authentic sushi will enjoy the intimate ambience of Kimonos, in the Swan, which also features a karaoke bar. Picabu Buffeteria in the Dolphin is open 24 hours with all-American favourites. With its ideal location and amenities, this is very nearly the perfect resort (407 934 3000, **swandolphin.com**).

Campground and Cabins

Disney's Fort Wilderness Resort & Campground: Opened in 1971, possibly the best value of all the Disney properties can be found here. Situated on Bay Lake across from the *Magic Kingdom*, it offers impressive camping facilities and chalet-style cabins housing up to 6 in a 750-acre/304ha spread of Florida countryside. Two 'trading posts' supply fresh groceries and there are 2 bars and cafés plus a range of on-site activities, including 2 swimming pools, the thrice-nightly Hoop-Dee-Doo Musical Revue, Mickey's Backyard Barbecue (a seasonal character buffet dinner), campfire programme, open-air films, sports, games and a prime position to view the nightly Electrical Water Pageant. You can rent bikes or boats or take

Disney's Fort Wilderness Campground

horse rides around the country trails, while the Tri-Circle D ranch has a small petting zoo. There is even a Segway Tour (the amazing 2-wheeled personal transports), the *Wilderness Back Trail Adventure*, which provides a unique 2-hour trundle around the many trails of the resort ($85/person, Tues, Fri and Sat, over-15s only). The Trails End restaurant (sit-down and takeaway) offers a great value buffet breakfast, lunch and dinner, while Crockett's Tavern serves pizza and appetisers (dinner only). Buses and boats link the resort with other areas (and the short boat ride to the Magic Kingdom is a great start to the day). If you need a lunch or afternoon break from the Magic Kingdom, hop on the boat to Disney's Fort Wilderness Resort and try the family-friendly Trail's End Buffet – only $16.99 for adults and $9.99 for 3–9s.

BRIT TIP

Most Disney hotel rooms will accommodate only 4, with the exception of Port Orleans Riverside (which can take an extra child on a trundle bed). For larger groups, consider Old Key West, Saratoga Springs, the Boardwalk Villas, the villas at Animal Kingdom Lodge, Wilderness Lodge Villas, Fort Wilderness cabins or 2-room suites at the All Star Music Resort.

Disney's Old Key West Resort

© Disney

Disney Vacation Club resorts

Disney's Old Key West Resort: Disney's first Vacation Club resort in 1992, this is primarily a 5-star holiday ownership scheme (one of 8 such 'timeshare' properties), but the 1, 2 or 3-bed studios in a Key West setting can also be rented nightly when not in use by members. Facilities include 4 pools, tennis courts, a games room, shops and a fitness centre, plus the lovely Olivia's restaurant. Transport to all parks is by bus.

Disney's Saratoga Springs Resort & Spa: The most extensive member of the DVC line-up, this 65-acre/26ha apartment complex is opposite Downtown Disney, has some wonderful views over the lake and is next to scenic Lake Buena Vista Golf Course. It boasts 828 units, from standard 2-bed hotel-style studio rooms to massive 2-storey, 3-bed apartments sleeping 12. The first phase opened in 2004 and the theme is the 1880s' New York resort of the same name, with a peaceful, gracious look and a great array of facilities, from the free-form, zero-depth entry main pool (with waterslide and squirt-fountains), a smaller quiet pool, the health-conscious dining room (the Artist's Palette, offering breakfast, lunch and dinner, plus groceries), a large video arcade, tennis courts and a wonderful full-service spa and gym. All but the hotel-style studios have a kitchen (with dishwasher and microwave), washer-dryer, whirlpool bath and DVD player, with TVs in the living room and each bedroom. The resort includes room service, babysitting and childminding services plus a water taxi to the shops and entertainment at *Downtown Disney*. Rates for the 3-bed villas top $1,000 a night, but the 1-bed units are more modestly priced and, although it is a Vacation Club property, rooms are usually available to the public. New in June 2009 were the 3-bed **Treehouse Villas**, 60 beautiful chalets raised 10ft/3m off the ground on pedestals and beams and set among a heavily wooded part of the

Walt Disney World and Lake Buena Vista Accommodation

Big Sand Lake

PALM PARKWAY

Hilton Garden Inn
Residence Inn
Embassy Suites
Hampton Inn
Quality Suites Lake Buena Vista
Garton Inn
Floridays

Hilton Grand Vacations Club (I-Drive)

Toll road

Extended Stay America Deluxe
Hawthorn Suites
Celebrity R...
Courtyard Orlando L...
Holiday Inn Express

APOPKA - VINELAND ROAD

Crossroads Center
Radisson Lake Buena Vista
Courtyard by Marriott, Fairfield Inn, Springhill Suites

Holiday Inn Sunspree
Blue Heron Beach Resort
Caribe Royale

Bryan's Spanish Cove
Embassy Vacation Resort
Buena Vista Suites

APOPKA - VINELAND ROAD

Cypress Pointe Resort

Staybridge Suites
Country Inn & Suites
Sheraton Safari

Hyatt Regency Grand Cypress

Orlando Vista
Doubletree Guest Suites
Best Western LBV
Regal Sun Resort
Holiday Inn

LBV

Marriott Village
Royal Plaza Resort

BUENA VISTA DRIVE

Hilton Orlando Resort

Marriott Vacation Club

Vistana Resort

Orlando World Center Marriott Resort
Nickelodeon Family Suites

WORLD CENTER DRIVE

INTERNATIONAL DRIVE SOUTH

Perri House Bed & Breakfast

Four Seasons Hotel Resort and Disney's Golden Oak Villas (opening 2011/12)

Port Orleans Riverside Resort
Port Orleans French Quarter Resort

Buena Vista Palace
Saratoga Springs Resort & Spa, & Treehouse Villas

Old Key West Resort

DOWNTOWN DISNEY

Typhoon Lagoon

EPCOT CENTER DRIVE

BUENA VISTA DRIVE

Waldorf-Astoria and Hilton Orlando Bonnet Creek

Pop Century Resort

OSCEOLA PARKWAY

© Steve Munns 2010

Fort Wilderness Resort & Campground

Walt Disney World

Car Park

Caribbean Beach Resort

Epcot

EPCOT CENTER DRIVE

Beach Club
Yacht Club
Dolphin
Swan
Boardwalk

BUENA VISTA DRIVE

Car Park

Disney's Hollywood Studios

VICTORY WAY

Magic Kingdom

Contemporary Resort, & Bay Lake Tower
Wilderness Lodge

Bay Lake

monorail

Transportation & Ticket Center
Car Park

WORLD DRIVE

WORLD DRIVE

Blizzard Beach

Coronado Springs Resort

BUENA VISTA DRIVE

Seven Seas Lagoon

Grand Floridian Resort & Spa
Polynesian Resort

BAY LAKE

WESTERN WAY

All-Star Resorts

OSCEOLA PARKWAY

N

Animal Kingdom

Animal Kingdom Lodge Resort & Kidani Village

Resort next to Sassagoula River. Sleeping up to 9, they feature some sumptuous furnishings, including granite counter-tops and flatscreen TVs, as well as 2 full bathrooms, airy ceiling spaces and outdoor barbecue grills. They also have their own leisure pool and whirlpool spa. Transport to all parks is by bus.

Bay Lake Tower at Disney's Contemporary Resort: This resort is linked to the Contemporary Resort by a 5th-floor bridge and features its own pool, waterslide and whirlpool spa, plus kids' water-play area, shuffleboard and bocce courts. The 14-storey, 295-room Tower offers fabulous modern decor throughout, including the studio rooms and spacious 1, 2 and 3-bed villas. The studios (sleeping up to 4) all have small fridges, microwaves and coffee-makers, while the villas (sleeping up to 12) have full kitchens and laundry facilities. The Tower superbly complements its neighbour Resort and affords wonderful views over the Magic Kingdom and nightly fireworks, notably from its exclusive rooftop lounge and viewing deck (DVC members only). There is also a gourmet coffee bar and easy access to the restaurants of the Contemporary Resort. Transport by monorail or bus (or just on foot to *Magic Kingdom*!).

Disney's Animal Kingdom Lodge – Kidani Village: This new (in May 2009) DVC resort adds some superb extras to the Animal Kingdom Lodge line-up. Like Saratoga Springs and Bay Lake Tower, the accommodation is divided into hotel-room studios (sleeping up to 4) and 1, 2 and 3-bed villas (sleeping 5, 9 or 12), all of which feature full kitchens and laundry facilities. The low-rise architecture and decor continue the resort's African theme in eye-catching style and the grand 3-bed villas are magnificently spacious. There is a separate 46-acre wildlife preserve in 4 animal savannah areas, a fabulous pool and kids' play area, and another excellent restaurant,

Sanaa, which continues the Lodge's reputation for fine dining. The stunning Samawati Springs – a 4,700sq ft/437sq m, zero-depth entry pool – is also open to guests at the Lodge, while children will certainly make a beeline for Uwanja Camp, a 3-part interactive water playground (for ages 4 and under, 5–7s, and 8 and over). Other amenities include a video arcade, games centre, basketball court, fitness centre, gift shop and animal programmes, from flamingo-feeding to campfire story-telling. Transport to all parks is by bus.

Disney Hotel Plaza

If Disney's hotel prices are just out of your range, consider the 7 'guest' hotels that are still on site but come with a less hefty price-tag, on Hotel Plaza Boulevard right on the doorstep of *Downtown Disney*. There's a free regular bus service at 30-minute intervals to the parks, guaranteed admission (even on the busiest days), and you can make reservations for shows and restaurants before the general public. The convenience of being able to walk to *Downtown Disney* and the Crossroads shopping plaza is also worth a lot.

Best Western Lake Buena Vista: This 18-storey, tropically themed hotel has 325 rooms (all with high-speed internet access) with views over the Marketplace, in-room coffee-makers and hairdryers, while the huge top-floor suites are magnificent. Garden-themed Traders Island Grill is pleasant for breakfast or dinner, plus there is a Pizza Hut Express and the deli-style Parakeet Internet Cafe, as well as a large pool, video arcade and small gym, with a Garden Gazebo for special occasions, including weddings (407 828 2424; *Value*).

Buena Vista Palace Hotel & Spa: Arguably the outstanding property here, this has been extensively renovated recently, with an all-new lobby area, including bar and lounge, totally remodelled rooms

'Green' hotels

Being environmentally friendly is a key concern these days, and it is good to know many Florida hotels take the issue seriously. Orlando boasts over 50 resorts that submit to the **Florida Green Lodging Certification Program**, which covers various initiatives to protect and preserve the local environment. The programme highlights hotels that demonstrate water and energy conservation, waste reduction, recycling and pollution prevention.

All Disney hotels are signed up to the FGLCP, as are those of Universal Orlando and the Give Kids The World Village in Kissimmee. Other 'green' lodgings are the Rosen trio of the Plaza, Centre and Shingle Creek hotels, the Grande Lakes Resort, the local Marriott and Renaissance hotels, the Embassy and Hawthorn Suites, the Buena Vista Palace and Gaylord Palms. Additionally, the new 'Hiltons at Midtown' – Hilton Garden Inn and Homewood Suites – just off Palm Parkway in Lake Buena Vista, conform to the highest standards for eco-friendly hotels. See more at **dep.state.fl.us/greenlodging/**. For info on all environmental travel options, see **greentravelhub.com**.

(with chic decor, flatscreen TVs, ergonomic chairs, new bathrooms and plush bedding) and extra amenities. The elegant 27-storey cluster offers 1,012 rooms and suites (in 8 categories, many with a view over much of *Walt Disney World*), plus a blissful European-style spa, 3 heated pools, a tennis court, jogging track, basketball and sand volleyball court and no fewer than 5 restaurants. The ultra-spacious 1 and 2-bed Island Suites offer great family style with upgraded design and amenities. The Australian-themed Outback Restaurant (not part of the Outback Steakhouse chain) is an ideal venue for a memorable meal, while Kook Sports Bar has a network of 38 TVs. The smart Watercress Café offers a lovely lake view, breakfast buffet and Sunday breakfast with Disney characters (407 827 2727; *Moderate*).

Doubletree Guest Suites: For extra spacious rooms, this modern choice offers 229 family suites with every convenience, from in-room safe to cookies, high-speed internet, wet bar, 2 TVs, fridge and microwave. There are excellent kids' facilities, with their own check-in area, pool, playground and video arcade, and a casual restaurant, the Evergreen Café & Lounge, plus a large main pool (though right next to noisy I-4), an exercise room and tennis court (407 934 1000; *Moderate*).

Hilton Orlando Resort: Another high-quality choice is this 10-storey, 814-room hotel, with 2 excellent pools, 7 restaurants and lounges and a state-of-the-art health club. It is the only 'outside' hotel to enjoy Disney's Extra Magic Hours feature, while there's a babysitting service and Disney character breakfast on Sundays. The ultra-plush rooms all have high-speed wi-fi. Dining choices feature the superior Benihana restaurant for sushi, sashimi, chicken and great steaks; Covington Mill for a casual breakfast and lunch; Andiamo Italian Bistro; the 24-hour Mainstreet Market deli; a pool bar and grill; and a coffee/wine bar (407 827 4000; *Moderate*).

Holiday Inn: This 323-room, 14-storey hotel reopened in 2010 after a dramatic $35m rebuild to give it a fresh Miami South Beach vibe. Rooms have been comprehensively upgraded

Andiamo at the Hilton Orlando

with fresh décor, flatscreen TVs, mini-fridges, room safes and wi-fi, while there is a fabulous new tropical pool area with an eye-catching zero-depth entry pool and whirlpool. The Palm Breezes Restaurant offers all-day dining, from a breakfast buffet to an elegant dinner, while the chic Aqua Luna restaurant and bar is the lunch and dinner alternative adjacent to the pool. There is then a Grab & Go snack shop and a Kids Eat Free programme for 2–12s. A state-of-the-art gym, business centre and Disney gift shop complete the amenities of a stylish hotel that offers real competition to the next door Hilton but at slightly less than their prices (407 828 8888; *Moderate*).

BRIT TIP
Coffee-makers are standard in almost all hotel rooms but tea-making facilities are rare. Consider bringing your own tea-bags or visit the British Supermarket on Vineland Rd just north of Universal (407 370 2023, **britishsupermarket.com**).

Regal Sun Resort: The former Grosvenor Resort, this has 619 rooms and 7 suites, all with modern decor. There are 2 main pools, a large hot tub and a children's pool with playground, as well as a fitness centre and volleyball, tennis and basketball courts. There is a Disney character breakfast Tues, Thurs and Sat at the graceful LakeView Restaurant, plus a lobby bar, poolside bar and grill and 24-hour café, Sundial 24/7. (407 828 4444; *Moderate*).

Royal Plaza Resort: This spacious 394-room hotel (in 5 categories of rooms and suites accommodating up to 5) features the plush new Royal Beds and excellent personal amenities. There is a full-service diner-restaurant (the Giraffe Café and Lounge, with an excellent breakfast buffet; free for under-11s), Grab 'n Go deli-café, landscaped pool area and pool bar, 4 tennis courts, a health club and fitness centre and Disney gift shop. Standard rooms have a sitting area and balcony, and the magnificent 2-room suites boast oversized private patios (407 828 2828; *Moderate*).

For more info on these 7 hotels, go to **downtowndisneyhotels.com**.

Beyond Disney
Once you move away from *Walt Disney World*, your hotel choice becomes more diverse. The Budget and Value types are most common, and the area you stay in also has an effect on price: the further you go from Disney on Kissimmee's Highway 192, the cheaper (and more basic) the hotel/motel, while parts of International Drive are more expensive than others (north of Sand Lake Road is usually cheaper). Facilities vary little and what you see is usually what you get. All the chain hotels can be found here, with rates as low as $30/room off-peak (but remember the local sales tax). Some also have rooms with a kitchenette (an 'efficiency'). Be prepared to shop around, especially on Highway 192, where many hotels advertise their rates on billboards, and feel free to ask to see a room before you book. Looking from the price perspective, here is a guide to the main options.

Budget Hotels
Chain hotels can be found at their most numerous in this category and you'll find few frills. All have pools but not many have restaurants, bars or lounges (though some provide a free continental breakfast). Many offer fridges and microwaves that add value, though.

Choose from: The **Days Inn** chain, which varies widely from tatty older hotels to smart relatively recent ones, and with free continental breakfast (1800 329 7466, **daysinn.com**); **Econo Lodge**, also with free wi-fi and continental breakfast (1877 424 6423, **econolodge.com**); **Howard Johnson**, which tends to have older properties, many with a 'kids eat free' option and free breakfast, but rooms are often more spacious (1800 446 4656, **hojo.com**); **Knights Inn**, a smarter choice in this area (1800 843 5644, **knightsinn.com**); **Masters Inn**, another to offer a

Our Budget recommendations

The ones we rate among the best include the **Magic Castle Inn & Suites** Maingate in Kissimmee (good range of amenities – free continental breakfast, free Disney transport, in-room fridge, microwave, safe, kids' playground and guest laundry; 1800 446 5669, **magicorlando.com**); the **Inn at Summer Bay** at the Clermont end of Highway 192 (the budget part of the big Summer Bay timeshare complex, just across the Highway, but still benefiting from the many facilities; 1863 420 8282, **summerbayresort.com/inn.html**); **Howard Johnson Enchanted Land** offers some fun frills for kids with their 'treehouse' rooms, plus free transport to all the parks and a hot breakfast (407 396 4343, **enchanted resort.net**); the **Super 8 Kissimmee/Orlando Area** is above average for that low-cost chain and gets great customer feedback (407 396 88883, **super8.com**); the one-off **Champions World Resort** (a converted Howard Johnson on west Highway 192) is a sound budget choice with free Disney transport and wi-fi (1800 638 7829, **championsworldresort.com**); and **Econo Lodge Inn & Suites International Drive** is another above-average example, with free wi-fi and free shuttles to Universal and SeaWorld (407 345 8195, **econolodge.com**). The smart **Ramada Gateway Hotel** in Kissimmee was also exceptional value in 2010 for this brand (407 396 4400, **ramadagateway.com**).

free continental breakfast, plus lower rates for a week or more (1800 633 3434, **masters inn.com**); the **Microtel Inn & Suites** chain, which offers newer properties, plus free wi-fi and breakfast (1800 771 7171, **microtelinn.com**); the bargain basement **Motel 6** (1800 466 8356, **motel6.com**); **Red Roof Inn**, which has several newly renovated properties in Orlando, plus free wi-fi (1800 733 7663, **redroof.com**); the **Rodeway Inn** chain has slipped from Value to more Budget territory in recent years but, still offers a free breakfast (1877 424 6423, **rodewayinn.com**); the **Super 8 Motel** chain varies a lot but has several newer motels (notably on American Way, just off I-Drive) and all offering free breakfast (1800 800 8000, **super8.com**; look for its 'Pride' hotels, which are all above average); and **Travelodge**, also with a excellent property on American Way, plus free breakfast and wi-fi (1800 578 7878, **travelodge.com**).

There are also dozens of smaller, independent outfits that offer special rates periodically, especially a battery of cheap and cheerful motels along Highway 192 in Kissimmee (but try to stay west of Marker 14).

BRITTIP
Hotels designated Maingate East or Maingate West should be close to Disney's main entrance on Highway 192, though it is wise to check.

Value Hotels

At first glance there may not seem much difference here, as some of these are still in motel territory. They should have smarter facilities, but not all have their own restaurant. Again, they are dominated by the big chains: highly worthwhile is **Baymont Inn & Suites** group, which boasts several new properties in the area, all featuring free breakfast and wi-fi (1877 229 6668, **baymontinns.com**); the **Comfort Inn** chain is of the bland, identikit variety but offers a valuable free breakfast, while sister brand **Comfort Suites** has some smart, newer properties, and the **Clarion Inn** (and Suites), also in the Choice Hotels group, often includes restaurants, though properties vary considerably in age (all 3, 1877 424

Royal Plaza Resort

Kissimmee Accommodation

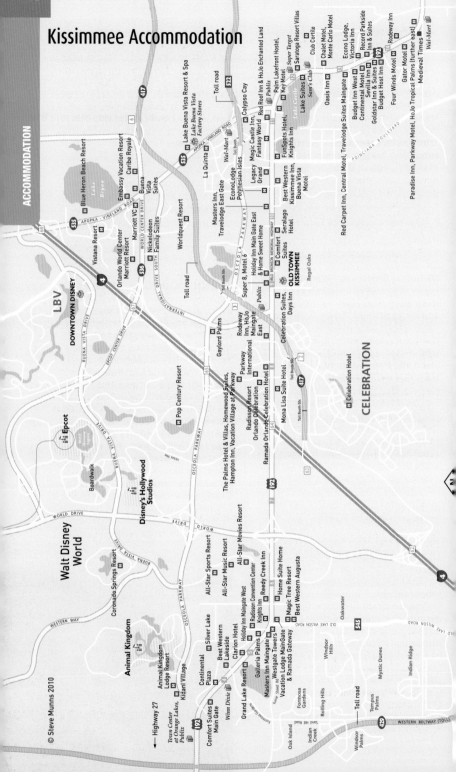

© Steve Munns 2010

6423, **choicehotels.com**); for pure no-frills, clean and consistent chains with more space than many in this category (and fully equipped kitchens), look for **Extended Stay America**, which also has **Extended Stay Deluxe** properties; sister brand **Homestead Studio Suites** offers extra facilities (all 3, 1800 804 3724, **extendedstayamerica.com**); **Fairfield Inns** is the budget version of the Marriott chain and usually has newer hotels, many with gyms and most with free breakfast (1800 1927 1927 in the UK, 1888 236 2427 in the US, **marriott.com**); **Hampton Inns** (and Suites) are also usually above average in this category, with free wi-fi, hot breakfast and tea/coffee in the lobby 24 hours a day (1800 426 7866, **hamptoninn.com**); **Ramada** hotels represent good value at this level as many have free wi-fi and breakfast or a restaurant (1800 272 6232, **ramada. com**); and **Quality Inns** are a popular choice, with a reputation for value, while some hotels boast an exercise room and free continental breakfast (1877 424 6423, **choicehotels.com**).

BRIT TIP
Not all hotels provide hairdryers, though they can often be ordered from the front desk. For your own, you will need a US plug adaptor (with 2 flat pins). Their voltage is 110–120AC (ours is 220) so UK appliances will work sluggishly.

At the upper end of the category, the **Best Western** group has good, family-orientated facilities (0800 393 130 in the UK, 1800 780 7234 in the US, **bestwestern.com**); the **Holiday Inn** (and **Holiday Inn Express**) chain has invested in a big rebrand to go more upmarket but you may still find some great-value (and well-equipped) hotels in Value/Moderate territory as kids eat free (with their parents) at all properties and many include sophisticated pools and extra facilities like games rooms (0800 405060 from the UK, 1888 465 4329 in the US, **holidayinn.com**); the smart **La Quinta Inn** (and Suites), which has some notable hotels in Orlando (1800 753 3757, **lq.com**); and the modern

Wingate Inn chain, with gyms, free breakfast and wi-fi (1800 228 1000, **wingatehotels.com**). Possibly the best overall value here, though, is provided by the **Radisson** group, which has some excellently priced hotels in the area, all with above-average amenities and services, free wi-fi and well situated for the parks (1800 395 7046, **radisson.com**).

There are also a handful of individuals in this category. Look out in particular for the **Seralago Inn Hotel and Suites Maingate East**, which boasts deluxe suites, 2-room suites and kidsuites, plus great pools and kids' facilities (including free films in their own cinema), making it an outstanding family resort. Its proximity to Old Town is also handy, while under-11s eat breakfast free when accompanied by their parents (407 396 4488, **seralago hotel.com**). The reliable 1 and 2-bed **Enclave Suites** (excellent location on Carrier Drive, just off I-Drive) are excellent value as 'kids eat free' with parents, there's free breakfast and free transport to Universal and SeaWorld as well as a good array of facilities (407 351 1155, **enclavesuites.com**). Similarly, the **Palms Hotel & Villas** just off Highway 192 in Kissimmee (close to I-4) features spacious 1 and 2-room condo-style suites with fully equipped kitchens, 2 large pools and kiddie pool, picnic area, sports court, free shuttle to the Disney parks and free breakfast (407

Radisson Lake Buena Vista

396 2229, **thepalmshotelandvillas.com**). Need more space but for no more money? Consider the **Celebration Suites at Old Town** (formerly the Comfort Suites), which offers good value for money in this ideal location for a lively Kissimmee stay, with spacious 1 and 2-bed suites that sleep 4–8, handy kitchen-diners and free shuttle to the Disney parks (1800 327 9126, **suitesatoldtown.com**).

> **BRIT TIP**
> It is usual to tip hotel chambermaids by leaving $1/adult each day before your room is made up.

Moderate Hotels

This is a category with fewer of each brand, so we highlight a few worthy individuals as well as the chain details. All properties provide a good pool (often with extra facilities like a waterslide, kids' pool and/or playground), at least 1 restaurant, bar and café, and extra in-room amenities, such as tea/coffee-makers.

Main chains: The **Country Inn & Suites** are a smart choice, with spacious rooms and a pleasant country-house lobby, serving an extensive free breakfast (1888 201 1746, **countryinns.com**); **Hyatt Place** is the newest name in the area, a chic, contemporary choice with superbly stylish and comfortable rooms, a free continental breakfast (or hot breakfast upgrade), 24-hour café and evening bar service, plus free

Crowne Plaza Orlando Universal

wi-fi (1888 492 8847, **hyatt.com/hyatt/place**); **Residence Inns** also tend to be smart and feature free breakfast and exercise rooms but still with microwave, fridge and tea/coffee-making facilities; the **Springhill Suites** (part of the Marriott group, along with the more upmarket Courtyard hotels) also offer reliable, comfortable value for money in this range (1888 236 2427 in the US, 0800 221 222 in the UK, **marriott.com**).

More upmarket: Here you have **Crowne Plaza Hotels**, which has some eye-catching properties featuring great pool areas, smart restaurants, fitness centres and ultra-comfy rooms (**ichotelsgroup.com**). The **Crowne Plaza Orlando Universal** is a fine example, with 398 rooms and suites in 2 stylish blocks and a spectacular circular atrium. Two restaurants, a cocktail lounge, guest laundry and fitness centre, plus a huge heated pool add up to quality and value in an ideal location on Universal Boulevard's junction with Sand Lake Road (407 355 0550, **cporlando.com**). **Doubletree** hotels are a contemporary upscale choice with fewer frills but spacious, ultra-comfy rooms featuring their Sweet Dreams sleep experience and signature welcome cookies, plus a rare Bed & Breakfast option (1800 445 8667, **doubletree.com**). The recently remodelled **Doubletree Resort Orlando-International Drive** (formerly the Sheraton World Resort and International Plaza Resort) is just off the main I-Drive area and makes a good choice. Set in 28 acres/11ha, it offers 3 pools, 2 kids' pools, a playground and mini-golf, well-furnished rooms and extra-large suites. Dining options are more limited, but the tropical grounds give it an upmarket feel (407 352 1100). The Hilton chain is notable for its **Hilton Garden Inn** brand, with a number of attractive, modern hotels (1877 7829 444, **hiltongardeninn.com**). The **Hyatt** group is rare in tourist territory, but one prime example is the **Hyatt Regency at Orlando International Airport**, especially if you arrive late and could benefit from a first-night

Our Value recommendations

Standout properties in this range include the **Extended Stay Deluxe Orlando-Universal Studios**, a high-quality example of this chain in a great location for Universal Orlando and I-Drive (407 370 4428, **extendedstayhotels.com**); **Galleria Palms Hotel** in Kissimmee at Maingate West, just off Highway 192, has a smart, contemporary look, ultra-comfy rooms, a great location close to Disney, free shuttle to the parks, free buffet breakfast and wi-fi, and a relaxing pool area (there is no restaurant but plenty nearby; 407 396 6300, **galleriakissimmeehotel.com**); **Holiday Inn Maingate East** in Kissimmee (between Markers 8 and 9), which offers 446 well-maintained rooms (including kidsuites) in 2 high-rise towers, plus an oversized pool, kids' pool, waterslides, gym, children's theatre, food court and lobby lounge, plus a 'kids eat free' programme (407 396 4222, **holidayinnmge.com**); equally, the **Holiday Inn Sunspree** in Lake Buena Vista is a great family choice after a big rebuild in 2009 to convert its outdoor-style corridors into fully internal ones for extra comfort and security, with both standard rooms and kidsuites, all with kitchenettes, plus a full-service restaurant, convenience store, pool bar and sports lounge. The pool and kids activities are top-notch, too (407 239 4500, **hisunspreelbv.com**); **Ramada Inn International Drive Lakefront** is a great value-for-money choice in a good I-Drive location with a free continental breakfast, wi-fi and Disney transport, plus oversized rooms all with fridge, microwave and coffee-maker (407 345 5340, **michotel.com**; the great value **Radisson Resort Orlando-Celebration** in Kissimmee (on Parkway Boulevard, close to the Highway 192 junction with I-4), in 20 tropical acres/8ha and with 3 landscaped swimming pools, a state-of-the-art fitness centre, comfy rooms and great dining choices, all in an ideal location (407 396 7000, **radisson.com/kissimmeefl**); the fun-styled **Orlando Vista Hotel** on Apopka-Vineland Road in Lake Buena Vista, at the entrance to Downtown Disney, which features great kidsuites, a pleasant bar and café, large pool deck and spacious, airy rooms, with free breakfast, wi-fi and transport to the Disney parks, making this something of a bargain (407 239 4646, **orlandovistahotel.com**); and the **Wyndham Orlando Resort**, in the heart of I-Drive, with a great range of facilities (3 pools, 2 restaurants, 3 bars, a deli and ice-cream shop, tennis courts, a kids' club and games arcade, and a health club) in landscaped grounds but without the high price tag you might expect. The resort covers 42 acres/17ha and takes some getting around, but is a good all-round choice (407 351 2420; **wyndham.com**).

rest. It has 2 excellent restaurants and a smart pool deck, plus a fitness room, lounge and business centre. Rooms are ultra-spacious, particularly the corner rooms, and many feature internal balconies overlooking the airport atrium. Surprisingly, there is no noticeable aircraft noise and none of the bustle you expect at an airport hotel. Staying there gives the distinct advantage of collecting your hire car in the morning rather than straight after a long flight (407 825 1234, **http:// orlandoairport.hyatt.com**).

BRITTIP

Need a hotel to keep kids amused but not break the bank? Consider the new **CoCo Key Hotel and Water Resort** (page 82). One of the most thoughtful and family-friendly hotels we've seen in ages.

Marriott is another well-represented group here, with some of the smartest hotels in this category, often providing extra facilities and more landscaped grounds, with a choice of restaurants and some of the largest standard rooms. Features include its signature Revive beds for a guaranteed good night's sleep. The **Orlando Airport Marriott** is a great choice for either your first night (especially if you are arriving late) or the final day, letting you relax around the tropical indoor/outdoor pool area and indulge in some fine dining at its excellent steakhouse, Porterhouse (1800 380 6751, **marriott. com**); **Sheraton** hotels are well represented in Orlando and boast a smart, revamped look in recent years. Several are themed and feature extra facilities and good dining (1888 625 5144, **starwoodhotels.com**), like the Africa-themed **Sheraton Safari Hotel** in Lake Buena Vista, which offers a waterslide, heated pool, kids' pool, free transport to Disney parks and 'kids eat free' with parents. Its rooms are large and well equipped, and there's plenty of restaurant and shop choice nearby (407 239 0444, **sheratonsafari.com**).

Notable individuals: There are only a few non-chain properties in the Moderate category. The **Monumental Hotel** is a converted Crowne Plaza property and still ultra-stylish, with an Old Key West theme, 94 spacious, well-equipped rooms, beautiful pool area and Pineapple Grill Restaurant (1877 239 1222, **monumentalhotelorlando.com**). Brand new on I-Drive is the **CoCo Key Hotel & Water Resort Orlando**, an ultra-family-friendly option with excellent amenities, notably the 5,700sq m/ 62,000sq ft water park. Formerly the Ramada Inn and Grand Legacy Resort, it has been transformed in every respect, from the chic new lobby area to the 391 rooms (all now with flatscreen TVs, smart bedding and furniture, coffee-maker and free wi-fi). There is a quiet adults pool, with fountain and Jacuzzi, buffet breakfast room (Tradewinds), food court (Callaloo Grill, featuring Pizza Hut), indoor sports bar and outdoor Tiki Bar overlooking the Key West-themed water park, which has a canopy roof to protect from the worst of the Florida sun (although there is also an uncovered play area and terrace). There is a fitness centre, extensive games arcade, gift shop and convenience store, plus private rooms for birthday parties and a kids' club. The water park is a marvel in itself, with 4 areas: Parrot's Perch, an interactive jungle-gym; Minnow Lagoon, for the youngest children,

Coming Up Rosen

One notable non-chain operator in Orlando is the **Rosen Hotels & Resorts** group, with a good variety of 7 well-run, value-conscious properties. Four are budget-minded, the Brit-popular **Rosen Inn at Pointe Orlando** (formerly the Quality Inn Plaza), **Quality Inn International** and **Rosen Inn** (ex Rodeway Inn) on I-Drive, and the **Clarion Inn Lake Buena Vista**. All have been impressively refurbished and offer standard amenities but thoughtful touches, like family-style buffet restaurants, kids facilities, plenty of pool choice and free wi-fi. The other hotels are the flagship Deluxe **Rosen Shingle Creek Resort**, and the Moderate pair of **Rosen Centre Hotel** (page 83) and **Rosen Plaza Hotel**, a distinctive 800-room property with excellent resort facilities – including 2 restaurants, a pizza shop, deli, fitness centre and nightclub – and spacious, recently redecorated accommodation (1800 627 8258, **rosenplaza.com**).

featuring a zero-depth entry pool and water cannons with mini-slides and other small-scale fun for pre-school kids (with life-jackets provided, plus life-guards on duty); Coral Reef Cove, the teen activity pool, with the Cyclone body-slide; and the outdoor Water-Park, with nine different slides, including the Over The Falls and Surfer Splash body-slides and Boomerango double-rider tube slide. There is a fee for daily use of the whole water park area, but at $19/room, it isn't unreasonable. Day guests are also allowed when the resort is not full, at $19.95/person. This is easily one of the most imaginative resorts in the area and really enhances this part of I-Drive (1877 875 4681, **cocokeywater resort.com**).

Deluxe hotels

When it comes to the best hotels, it is largely a question of individuals. The growing selection of genuinely deluxe properties in this area are all highly distinctive, with excellent facilities, outstanding service and, usually, at least one 5-star restaurant. We detailed Disney's luxury offerings on pages 64–74, so we'll continue here with Universal Orlando.

The deluxe Hard Rock Hotel

© Disney

The Sky's the limit

For a good cross-section of 7 contrasting properties (6 in Orlando, 1 in Daytona Beach), from Value hotels to villas and community resorts, try **Sky Hotels & Resorts**, a specialist management company. Its one-stop shop includes the reliable Enclave Suites just off I-Drive (page 79), 2 Hawthorn Suites properties, the excellent Lake Buena Vista Resort Village & Spa (page 94) and the highly-rated **Coral Cay Resort** in Kissimmee, a well-designed gated development of 3 and 4-bed town-homes (terraced villas), plus the spectacular views of the three-star **Hawaiian Inn Beach Resort** at Daytona Beach. Arguably its crown jewel, though, is the smart new **Palisades Resort** at the western end of Highway 192 in Kissimmee, one of the newest, most upmarket and quality-conscious self-catering resorts in the area, with 2 and 3-bed condos (page 96). Look up more at staysky.com or call 1866 455 4062.

Our Moderate recommendations

The **Embassy Suites International Drive South** consistently gets good reader feedback and is exceedingly smart, with excellent service and spacious rooms (either standard 2-room suites sleeping 4 or double-doubles for 6) providing 2 TVs, coffee-maker, fridge and microwave. There's a great outdoor pool deck, kids' splash pool and indoor pool, plus a sauna and gym. The Fisheye Grill, with its smart bar area and outdoor patio, gives it a real edge in dining options along with its free breakfast option. It is rare in this area in offering a free shuttle service to both Disney and Universal (407 352 1400, **embassysuitesorlando. com**). The 21-storey **Four Points Sheraton Studio City Hotel** is an I-Drive icon near Universal Orlando and features a heated tropical outdoor pool and paddling pool, games room, mini-golf, fitness room and free shuttle to Disney and Universal. All 301 well-appointed rooms have coffee-makers, Nintendo games and free wi-fi, plus superb views over the surrounding area (ask for a Universal view if possible). The Tropical Palms restaurant is a minor gem, with a fun ambience for breakfast, lunch or dinner, and an imaginative dinner menu, while you can also grab a drink at the Oasis Lounge or Tropical Breezes patio pool bar (407 351 2100, **starwoodhotels.com**). **Hyatt Place Orlando/Lake Mary** was the first newly built example of this chain (many others are converted from AmeriSuites) and is a great choice in the Seminole County area (just off I-4 at Exit 98, close to Orlando Sanford International Airport), with 128 rooms, each with the signature Hyatt Grand Bed and 42-in flatscreen TVs, plus the smart Bakery Café (407 995 5555, **lakemary.place.hyatt.com**). **Radisson Hotel Lake Buena Vista** is a dramatically remodelled property extremely convenient for Disney and the Crossroads area, with some sleek rooms and furnishings, the stylish Liquid Bar & Grill (serving Starbucks coffee), small gym and free wi-fi. The extra-spacious rooms all feature a fridge and microwave as well as coffee-maker, large, flatscreen TV and the signature ultra-comfy Sleep Number bed (407 597 3400, **radisson.com/lakebuenavistafl**). Finally, the spectacular 24-storey **Rosen Centre Hotel** is a real star property and one of the area's largest. It caters mainly for the convention trade (it's next door to the massive Convention Center), but also offers excellent facilities with 1,334 rooms and 80 suites. It has a huge swimming grotto, tennis courts, an exercise centre, high-quality restaurants (the excellent steak-and-seafood- orientated Everglades and casual Café Gauguin, a handy 24-hour deli) and the chic Banshoo Sushi bar – superb sushi, sashimi and ceviche – and 2 smart bars. The overall style is distinctly luxurious, yet the prices aren't (1800 204 7234, **rosencenter.com**). We also rate the newly-renovated **Holiday Inn at Walt Disney World** (see pages 75–6) highly in this category.

Universal teamed up with the Loews group to create its fine threesome, and they come with a rare bonus – *Universal Express*, front-of-line access to the main attractions of both parks just by showing your key card. Universal resort guests also benefit from other privileges, like a resort ID card (for buying food, merchandise and other items throughout Universal Orlando), priority seating at most restaurants (show your room key card), package delivery to your room, special golf privileges at 4 nearby courses and the chance to buy a *Length of Stay* pass (for unlimited park access while you're at the resort). All 3 feature excellent kids' activity centres with a meal option (for 4–14s; 5–11.30pm Sun–Thurs, to midnight

Fri and Sat; $15/hour per child, plus $15 for meal). For all Universal hotels, call 1888 273 1311 or visit **universalorlando.com**.

Hard Rock Hotel: Possibly the coolest hotel in Orlando, this icon of rock chic is themed as a former rock star's home, with 650 rooms and suites in California mission style. High ceilings, wooden beams, marble floors and eclectic artwork give an eye-catching style, with a rock-star theme to most public areas, music memorabilia, black-suited foyer staff and fairly constant music. The 14-acre/6ha site includes 3 bars (including the ultra-cool Velvet Bar), 2 restaurants (the full-service The Kitchen and the 5-star, dinner-only Palm Restaurant), plus a takeaway café, fitness centre, gift shop and games room. The lido area features a huge, free-form pool and 240ft/73m waterslide, 2 Jacuzzis, a beach volleyball court, shuffleboard and life-size chess and draughts. The pool even has an underwater sound system! The 650 rooms (including 12 kidsuites and 10 king suites) are big, beautifully furnished in the hotel's chic style and superbly comfortable.

> **BRIT TIP**
> Hard Rock Hotel guests – and music fans – should make a note of the monthly **Velvet Sessions** at the hotel, live gigs by well-known bands ('rock 'n roll cocktail parties' as they like to call them), on the last Thurs of each month. As well as the music, there are free drinks and finger foods. Request tickets online at **velvetsessions.com**.

Orchid Court at Royal Pacific Resort

> **BRIT TIP**
> For some wonderful gift shopping, check out the Portofino Bay's **Galleria Portofino** where you'll find magnificent art and jewellery.

Portofino Bay Hotel: The jewel in Universal's crown is a splendid re-creation of the famous Italian port and a stunning resort with every facility. The elaborate porticos, trompe l'oeil painting, harbourside piazza and faithful ornamentation of the waterfront make it one of Florida's most memorable settings. The 750 rooms are impeccably appointed, with lashings of Italian style. Standard rooms are sumptuous, with huge beds, spacious bathrooms, mini-bar and coffee facilities, ironing board and hairdryer, while the 94 Club Rooms feature concierge service with private lounge, extra room amenities and free entry to the Mandara Spa fitness centre. There are 18 kidsuites (including 6 amazing Dr Seuss-themed suites that are truly wacky and distinctive) with separate bedrooms that each have their own TV. The resort facilities are equally breathtaking – a Roman aqueduct-style pool with waterslide (and poolside films on Saturday evenings), an enclosed kids' play area and wading pool, a separate quiet pool, Jacuzzis, the beautiful Mandara Spa, business centre, a fabulous array of gift shops and a video games room. The Portofino also has an amazing 8 restaurants and lounges, including the 5-star (and very romantic) Bice Ristorante, the boisterous Trattoria del Porto (with themed character dinners on Fridays 6.30–9.30pm), Mama Della's, an authentic Italian family dining experience (watch out for Mama herself!), an aromatic deli, a pizzeria, gelateria and swanky Bar American. It is only a short boat ride to the parks, but is lightyears away in terms of its tranquil ambience.

Royal Pacific Resort: This 53-acre/21ha, 1,000-room resort has an exotic South Seas feel, transporting you back to a 1930s hotel in the tropics, and you really feel as if you have

Suite choice

To our mind the best suites hotels here are the **Embassy Suites**, with smart interior courtyards, good restaurants and relaxing pool areas (1800 362 2779, **http://embassysuites1.hilton.com**). But other worthwhile choices include the **Homewood Suites**, which provide extra room for larger families in 1 and 2-bed suites with full kitchens, a free hot breakfast daily and a more upmarket feel with mid-range pricing (1800 222 4663, **homewoodsuites.com**). Equally, **Hawthorn Suites by Wyndham** and **Staybridge Suites** both feature spacious 1 and 2-bed suites that sleep up to 6 and fully fitted kitchens, plus a hearty free breakfast, wi-fi and free local phone calls (1800 527 1133, **hawthorn.com** or 1877 238 8889, **staybridge.com**). For a more individual choice, try the well-appointed **Buena Vista Suites** (1800 537 7737, **bvsuites.com**) or stylish sister resort **Caribe Royale Resort** (1800 823 8300, **cariberoyale.com**), both on World Center Drive just off the lower end of I-Drive. The former is the more basic type, with spacious 2-room suites, a free full breakfast, heated pool, whirlpool, tennis courts, gift shop, mini-market and the Vista Bistro. The Caribe Royale is more luxurious, with a choice of 1-bed suites and 2-bed villas, a tropical pool area with waterslide, tennis courts and 2 fitness rooms. Its award-winning Venetian Room is a real treat for lovers of fine continental cuisine, and there are 4 other cafés and lounges. Finally, not so much a hotel as a theme park resort, **Nickelodeon Family Suites** on I-Drive South provides a striking, kid-friendly choice. Characters from Nickelodeon TV adorn strategic points and there is plenty of live interaction (notably at breakfast). Activities include scavenger hunts and arcade tournaments, while Studio Nick stages shows in its mini-theatre and a daily **Birthday Celebration** with Spongebob and Team Nick (plus a host of birthday upgrades involving slime, cake, slime, video games, slime, face painting, slime, karaoke and more slime), open to children with birthdays within 30 days of their stay. The 4-D Experience is an interactive 3-D cinema and there is even a Kids' Spa, with manicures and hair wraps for girls and temporary tattoos for boys. There is even an evening 'Sleepover' programme and babysitting to allow parents some free time. Suites come with bunks or twin beds and a TV and video console. The water features form 2 huge play areas, complete with all manner of sprays, slides and flumes, and there are poolside games, video arcade, mini-golf and various shops. Rooms come in 1-bed kitchen suites and 2 and 3-bed kidsuites, with living room and bathroom, microwave and fridge (and full kitchen with some). Nicktoons Café offers buffet dining (plus à la carte in the evening), while the popular character breakfast costs $10.95 for under-13s and $19.95 for adults. Plus there is a food court, pool bar and grill, and adult-friendly Nick@Nite Lounge. It all adds up to a striking (if somewhat raucous) holiday base in an excellent location close to Disney (1866 462 6425; **nickhotel.com**).

stepped into another world as you cross the bamboo bridge into the elegant lobby, faced by the splendid Orchid Garden courtyard. Extensive use of rich, dark woods, cool stone floors and masses of greenery (58,000 plants and 2,500 trees) give the place an opulent, colonial feel, while the rooms and facilities are equally impressive. Standard rooms feature hand-carved Balinese furniture and bamboo-screen accents among many refined touches, and there is also a Club level, with separate lounge and extended facilities, and 51 superlative suites – including 8 new Jurassic Park-themed kidsuites (dinosaurs not included!). The Islands Dining Room offers breakfast, lunch and dinner in a setting of oriental simplicity (children have their own buffet area with TV screen, plus character dining on select nights), while fine dining is taken to a new dimension by a magnificent restaurant run by celebrity chef Emeril Lagasse called Tchoup Chop (possibly the best in Orlando, see page 336). There's a pool snack bar and luau garden area, with the Wantilan Luau Sat and Tues from 6pm, plus Fri in summer, featuring an eye-catching Polynesian feast and dinner show ($58 adults, $32 under-13s; 407 503 3463 to book). The huge freeform pool is ideal for kids, with zero-depth entry at one end and a boat-shaped interactive play area of squirting fountains. Add a health club (with Jacuzzi, sauna and gym), kids' club (with computer games, TVs and

International Drive Accommodation

© Steve Munns 2010

organised activities), video arcade and 2 shops and you have superb value, even at this end of the scale.

International Drive

Stepping back outside Universal, there are a number of excellent offerings on I-Drive.

Hilton Orlando: New in late 2009, this impressive 1,400-room hotel on I-Drive next to the big Convention Center and set in 26 acres/10.5ha boasts some superb leisure facilities. It features an upscale steakhouse (Spencer's), along with David's Club bar and grill, casual dining at The Bistro, a 24-hour Marketplace and an inviting pool bar and grill. A full-service Spa, a large state-of-the- art fitness centre, 2 pools, lazy river (in a wonderful 'tropical island' setting), tennis, volleyball and basketball courts, and a neat 9-hole putting golf course complete the impressive amenities. The Resort pool boasts a waterslide and kids' fountain, while the Quiet pool has several Jacuzzis, and both have cabanas, with fridges and TVs, for hire. Rooms feature the latest Hilton 'Serenity' bedding, 37in LCD HD TVs and high-quality bathroom toiletries, while an executive level adds a superb private lounge and extra services (407 313 4300, **thehiltonorlando.com**).

> **BRIT TIP**
> Spencer's restaurant at the Hilton Orlando offers some of the best dry-aged steaks in Florida, and a unique monthly cooking class with Chef John O'Leary, including wine pairings from its exclusive cellar.

Peabody Orlando: Classy and conventional, this luxurious double-tower icon on I-Drive was due to open its stunning $450 expansion in late 2010, adding even more to the extensive amenities and convention facilities on offer. The original 891-room tower has an Olympic-size pool, health club, 4 tennis courts and some superb restaurants, notably the gourmet Dux, classy Italian of Capriccio and the amazing B-Line

> **BRIT TIP**
> The opening of the Peabody's massive new tower block extension adds a state-of-the-art 22,000sq ft/2044sq m Spa to the hotel, featuring an innovative aquatic therapy called Watsu, a full-service nail and hair salon and gift store.

Diner (with its signature Sunday brunch; see also page 327), which has also been refurbished as part of the rebuild process. Service is superb and the style is a cut above normal tourist fare – just check out the Royal Duck Palace! Larger-than-average rooms and huge suites add to the quality, but conference business can make it a bit hectic. Proper afternoon tea is served Mon–Fri 3–4.30pm. The new 34-storey tower adds a dash of cutting-edge sophistication with another 1,641 luxurious rooms; a lushly-landscaped 3-acre recreation area with 3 pools (notably a tranquil grotto pool) each with pool bar and cabanas; a Napa Valley wine-themed restaurant; grab-and-go Café; new lobby coffee bar; stylish Spa & Athletic Club; and a 7-storey car park for 2,100 cars. All the new rooms (and 193 massive suites) come with LED motion-censored night lights, 42in LCD TVs, iPod docking stations, a Peabody Dream Bed®, premium cable TV, fridges, cordless phones and even mini LCD TVs in bathroom mirrors! (407 352 4000, **peabodyorlando.com**).

> **BRIT TIP**
> Don't miss Peabody's twice-daily red-carpet Duck March at 11am and 5pm, when its trademark ducks take up residence in the lobby fountain.

Peabody Orlando

The largest Marriott on earth!

A firm *Brit Guide* Deluxe favourite over the years that never seems to lose its lustre is **Orlando World Center Marriott**, a hugely impressive landmark on Disney's outskirts, set in 200 landscaped acres/810ha and surrounded by a beautiful golf course. With 2,000 spacious rooms and suites (most boasting fabulous views up to 28 storeys high), 9 restaurants and 6 pools (including 2 kids' pools and a superb freeform main pool that together hold more than a million gallons of water), it is a monumental prospect, set among landscaped tropical foliage and with fabulous facilities, including a Bill Madonna Golf Academy, tennis courts, volleyball, basketball, spa and state-of-the-art gym. Highlights are the Mikado Japanese Steakhouse, Hawk's Landing Steakhouse, Ristorante Tuscany and High Velocity Sports Bar, while there are also excellent children's amenities and programmes – plus the whizziest glass-fronted lifts in Orlando! It gets busy with convention business, but the picturesque pool complex offers true relaxation bliss (407 239 4200, **marriottworldcenter.com**).

Renaissance Orlando Resort: This superb resort (788 rooms on Sea Harbor Drive, behind SeaWorld) is notable for its style, service and genuine hospitality. It boasts a massive 10-storey atrium lobby and some equally enormous rooms and suites, an extensive pool area with bar and grill, tennis courts, fitness centre with sauna and steam room, plus kids' play areas and activities. All rooms have been renovated to a high standard, with extra bathroom amenities, flatscreen TVs and the Marriott company's Revive bedding. The dining line-up consists of Mist Sushi & Spirits, Boardwalk Sports Bar, the upscale but casual Tradewinds for breakfast, lunch and dinner, Palms Pool Bar & Grill and a Starbucks café. The hotel offers some great packages in conjunction with SeaWorld, which is a 2-minute walk across the car park, and its rates are often the best in the Deluxe category (1800 327 6677, **marriott.com**).

Orlando World Center Marriott

© OCVB

Rosen Shingle Creek Hotel: This 230-acre/93ha resort ranks among the grandest for its location, quality and style. In the middle of the award-winning Shingle Creek Golf Club (and acclaimed Brad Brewer Golf Academy) on lower Universal Boulevard, it boasts 1,500 rooms and suites, all with immaculate furnishings and comfort, as well as a full-service spa and fitness centre. Rooms vary from standard doubles to presidential suites, but all with fabulous flatscreen TVs, Wi-Fi, fridges and first-class toiletries. Amenities include 5 restaurants, 4 bars, a lounge, coffee house, deli and ice-creamery, plus 3 outdoor pools, tennis, basketball and volleyball courts and nature trails. There is also a shopping gallery and babysitting service. The whole resort is built in a 1900s Spanish revival style, and it provides immaculate service (especially at concierge level). Don't miss A Land Remembered, its upscale steakhouse (one of the best in the state and named after a famous Florida novel) in the Golf Clubhouse, and Cala Bella, a fine-dining Italian restaurant, with heavenly desserts from its renowned pastry chef (407 996 9939, **shinglecreekresort.com**).

Westin Imagine Orlando: Also on Universal Boulevard, this chic condo-hotel property features 315 king rooms and 1 and 2-bed suites, with either kitchenettes or full kitchens, and the trademark Westin Heavenly bed and bath, plus other distinctive

Condo-hotels

One of the newer developments here is the condo-hotel, a cross between a villa and a hotel. Instead of a villa, people buy 'rooms' in these big properties (which, to all intents and purposes, look like regular resort hotels), which they then own – unlike timeshare, where you just 'own' a time period for a resort. All the rooms are identically furnished, unlike villas, and feature 1, 2 or 3 bedrooms, living/dining room and kitchen or kitchenette. They are then rented out by a management company on behalf of the owners. For guests, they are booked as you would for any hotel. Some are owned by hotel groups such as Starwood and Four Seasons, while others are just managed by hotel specialists to ensure they maintain the right standards. They are usually built in tower blocks around communal facilities like the Clubhouse check-in and swimming pool (often with elaborate water features), and can also include restaurants, fitness centres and even grand spas.

decor and furnishing touches like flatscreen TVs and marble-topped desks. Signature Italian restaurant Fiorella's Cucina Toscana features delicious but casual lunches and upscale dinners surrounded by unique decorative glass designs, with the option of al fresco dining. The bar area is equally distinguished and then there is a huge South Beach-style pool with Tiki Bar and a modern fitness centre to complete a very fresh and modern offering (407 233 2200, **starwoodhotels.com**).

BRIT TIP
Try lunch at Fiorella's Cucina Toscana and sample some real upscale cuisine at very modest prices.

Lake Buena Vista

Moving to the next major resort area, there is a growing range of Deluxe choice here, too.

Hilton at Bonnet Creek Resort: new in October 2009, this rare and extensive development in a unique position inside *Walt Disney World* but privately owned (the only piece of land Walt was unable to buy from the original landowners back in 1966). It is part of a 482-acre/194ha resort complex with the Waldorf-Astoria (see opposite) and shares some of the same facilities. The Hilton features 1,000 rooms, 4 restaurants, a lagoon pool complex with lazy river and waterslide, 18-hole golf course, tennis courts and the adjoining full-service European spa and fitness centre.

Fine dining is provided by the chic modern Italian-themed La Luce restaurant, while the Harvest Bistro offers the main alternative (with kids 12 and under eating free with a full-paying adult), along with the Muse grab-and-go deli (with coffee bar), Zeta bar/lounge and Beech Pool Bar and Grill. One of its prime draws, though, is that it is just minutes from the Disney parks, and benefits from the full Hilton package of stylish accommodation and excellent kids' activity programmes, as well as some blissfully comfy rooms (407 597 3600, **hilton.com**).

Hyatt Regency Grand Cypress: The area's first genuine Deluxe resort is also still one of the best. Opened in 1984, it is a mature 1,500-acre/608ha resort with a unique mix of facilities, including a rare 9-hole pitch-and-putt golf course, 27 holes of regular golf (designed by Jack Nicklaus), a golf academy, boating lake and superb

Hyatt Regency Grand Cypress

pool complex. It underwent a $50m refurbishment in 2009 that added significantly to its upmarket appeal. The elegant lobby boasts all-new Zen-inspired décor with some very relaxing touches, while all 750 rooms have been thoroughly renovated and given a bright, contemporary finish, with large, flatscreen TVs, larger shower units and elaborate lighting. The dining choice is still among the best of any Orlando resort, and the location remains ideal, almost on the doorstep of Disney yet blissfully self contained (on Winter Garden-Vineland Road, just around the corner from the Crossroads area). The huge freeform swimming pool comes complete with Jacuzzis, waterfalls and slide, while the white sand beach and magnificent array of restaurants make for a sumptuous stay, especially Hemingway's, its Key West-styled dinner spot, and La Coquina, with a novel Chef's Table inside the kitchen on Sat and a sensational Sunday Brunch (not in summer). There is also the stylish White Horse sports bar and grill; pool bar and deli-style café; an inviting lobby lounge and sushi bar; and an eye-catching new art gallery. Watersports and other activities like tennis and bike rentals are covered by the one-off resort fee, meaning there is no additional charge to go boating, kayaking or fishing on scenic Lake Windsong, which also offers a white-sand beach. And, once among its richly landscaped grounds, you could easily be light years from the theme-park hustle-bustle (407 239 1234, **http://grandcypress.hyatt.com**).

The town of Celebration

Waldorf-Astoria: The second part of the 480-acre/194ha Hilton Bonnet Creek development, this 497-room hotel is the first US Waldorf outside New York and added a new level of luxury to the Orlando scene when it opened in 2009. Stately, distinguished and serene, the historic hotel features 313 standard rooms with Italian marble bathrooms and high-def flat-screen TVs, plus 185 suites ranging from 945sq ft/88sq m to a vast 3,300sq ft/306sq m, with a grand foyer, 2 bathrooms and butler service. The zero-entry pool boasts cabanas and waiter service, while the dining choice is superb, from the poolside grille and Bull & Bear Steakhouse to the small-plate cuisine of Peacock Alley, gourmet style of signature Oscar's brasserie and private club atmosphere of Harry's Lounge. The Spa by Guerlain is also unashamedly 5-star in its scope. Other amenities include floodlit basketball and tennis, jogging trails, bike rentals, a state-of-the-art fitness centre (with personal trainers), yoga and aerobics classes and a range of boutique shops on a par with the Waldorf's luxury cachet. Even children are not forgotten, with the WA Kids Club providing active and creative fun for 5-12s (10am–9pm, $15/hour per child) and the After Dark programme with dinner and activities from 7–10pm at $75/child (407 597 5500, **waldorfastoriaorlando.com**).

Kissimmee

The more budget-oriented area of Osceola County also now has its share of upmarket properties.

Celebration Hotel: In the Disney-inspired town of Celebration just off Highway 192, this unique hotel offers refreshing small-town America style that is a long way from the usual tourist hurly-burly. With just 115 rooms in its 1920s' wood-frame design, it has a classy ambience and a wealth of high-quality touches, notably in the ultra-comfy rooms. These come in a choice of an attic-like Retreat, Traditional (with either a king or 2 queen-size beds), Studio or a 2-room suite and are all beautifully furnished. Lovely artwork, courteous staff and a good array of facilities

– pool, Jacuzzi and fitness centre, plus the highly-regarded Bohemian Bar & Grill (excellent for breakfast, it becomes a signature Steakhouse at night) – mark out this hotel as a real gem. In addition, it is within a short stroll of the town's shops, restaurants and lakeside walks and makes a great romantic choice (407 566 6000, **celebrationhotel.com**).

Gaylord Palms Resort: One of the most dramatic hotels, with 1,406 rooms, is on the junction of I-Drive South and Osceola Parkway (ideal for Disney). A cross between a convention centre and a vast turn-of-the-century Florida mansion, it features 4½ acres/2ha of indoor gardens, fountains and 'landscaped' waters under a glass dome, with live entertainment nightly. Three themed indoor areas bear witness to great creativity and the resort offers every creature comfort, with an array of restaurants and bars, full-service spa, children's centre and 10 shops. Its imaginative Clearwater Cove water play area has a huge zero-entry pool, waterfall, octopus waterslide and kids' splash area, while the sophisticated adults-only area, Coquina Dunes Recreation Park, offers a quiet pool, bocce court, volleyball, croquet lawn and a realistic 9-hole putting challenge. Standard rooms are some of the smartest and most spacious in the area, while the suites are enormous. The central Emerald Bay offers an even more upmarket room choice with concierge. One area is landscaped like the Everglades (with alligator feeding at 6.30pm on Tues, Thurs and Sat); another copies St Augustine's old-world charm, with a replica Spanish fort; and the third reproduces eclectic Key West, with a mock-up marina and sailboat. To walk into the resort's marbled lobby and cavernous interior at night is like entering a future world. Then there is the resort's signature fine dining, with the choice of Old Hickory Steakhouse, Sunset Sam's (fine seafood) and the Mediterranean buffet-style Villa de Flora (with an excellent Sunday brunch), plus a Sushi Bar. The Relâche Spa is one of the area's largest, with

25 treatment rooms, fitness centre and beauty salon. There are 13 shops, plus the Java Coast coffee shop, Auggie's Jammin' Piano Bar and H2O Sports Bar and Grille. The hotel stages regular special events and is also a great venue for weddings (407 586 2000, **gaylordhotels.com**).

> **BRIT TIP**
> The Gaylord Palms features the truly stunning Christmas celebration ICE!, a wonderland of ice sculptures, snow scenery and ice slides, plus skating and other festive touches. Early Nov–3 Jan, tickets $20-28 adults, $17 over-55s and $12 4–12s, or combo tickets (ICE! plus skating) for $30, $20 and $14.

Mona Lisa Suite Hotel: Another of the area's condo-hotels, on Highway 192 at the entrance to Celebration, this is a luxury 5-storey, 240-unit property set around a spectacular 'vanishing edge' swimming pool and boasting up-scale dining at The Galerie Restaurant & Bistro (breakfast and lunch, plus their Eden Cuisine menu at night). The 1 and 2-bed suites feature beautifully furnished living areas, full kitchens and ultra-comfy bedrooms, with Egyptian cotton linens, down pillows, duvets and L'Occitane toiletries. Balconies overlook the infinity pool or lush landscaping. There is a complimentary shuttle service to Disney's parks and privileged use of the Celebration Day Spa and Golf Club (1866 404 6662; http://**monalisasuitehotel.com**).

Gaylord Palms Resort

BRIT TIP

Don't miss the signature flatbreads at The Galerie Restaurant at the Mona Lisa Hotel. In fact, the Bistro is a wonderful tropical hangout in which to enjoy a drink, snack or sample its Eden Cuisine – fresh creations of traditional dishes in a thoroughly inviting ambience.

Further afield

Beyond the main tourist areas you'll find more high-quality offerings.

Grand Bohemian Hotel: Sister property to the Celebration, this adds a touch of class to the downtown scene. It features an early 20th-century Austrian theme, with the accent on fine art, fine dining and good service. Its 14 storeys make it a major landmark and it boasts the wonderful Boheme restaurant and über-stylish Bösendorfer Lounge – with great live entertainment nightly – plus a 14th-floor concierge suite, heated pool, spa, fitness centre and Gallery of Fine Art. The Sunday Jazz Brunch is another outstanding feature. Rooms are superbly appointed, with wi-fi, mini-bars, CD players and interactive TVs, plus there are 36 superb suites. Every room features the ultra-comfy Sumptuous Bed (407 313 9000, **grandbohemianhotel.com**).

Grande Lakes Orlando: You'll find extensive luxury at this 500-acre/200ha combination of a 584-room, 5-star Ritz-Carlton Hotel, a 1,000-room JW Marriott Hotel, grand Spa, 18-hole Greg Norman-designed golf course, tennis centre and an upscale range of shops and restaurants, like the outstanding Norman's, featuring the 'new world' cuisine of celebrity chef Norman Van Aken. Located on the edge of a forestry preserve, it feels secluded and remote – quite a feat in this area. It is slightly off the beaten track – at the junction of John Young and Central Florida Parkway – yet is only 10 miles/16km from Disney and Orlando International Airport.

JW Marriott: This flagship hotel of the Marriott group has Spanish-Moorish design, a formal restaurant featuring fresh, organic produce, an American brasserie, Starbucks coffee lounge, Sushi Bar and a pool bar and grill. It also has a wonderful 'lazy river' mini-water park, plus a kids' pool and splash fountain. And, while the Marriott is convention-orientated, it is still well geared for families with all its facilities, plus the option to use the Ritz Kids programme and dining options next door. Rooms are plush and ultra-comfortable; 70% have balconies and there are 64 grand suites.

Ritz-Carlton: This offers a wonderful blend of scale and detail, with lush gardens, abundant lakes and streams, Venetian-inspired architecture and a wealth of genuine antiques. It has a large, sloped-entry pool, kids' pool, 3 floodlit tennis courts, a signature shop and 5 dining choices, plus a separate children's check-in and the excellent Ritz Kids Club (5–12s), while all the restaurants offer child menus. Apart from highly rated Norman's, the restaurants include The Vineyard Grill steakhouse (try its excellent Sunday champagne brunch at $65 for adults and $29 for children), Fairways Pub and Bleu pool bar and grill. The rooms are beautifully furnished, with high-quality products in the marbled bathrooms, plasma-screen TVs, radio/CD, mini-bar, slippers and robes, and all have balconies. There are 66 spacious suites and 92 Club rooms on the top 2 floors, with concierge and butler service, food and drink presentations in the Club Lounge and Bvlgari amenities. Two immaculate kidsuites feature a

Grand Bohemian Hotel

Our Deluxe recommendations

It's hard to go wrong in this category, but our Top 5 would be:

Waldorf Astoria

Rosen Shingle Creek Resort

Hyatt Grand Cypress

Gaylord Palms

Portofino Bay Hotel

separate bedroom and bathroom, with toys, games, TV and video games for 100% child appeal. The golf course is immaculate and offers a Caddie Concierge programme for the ultimate in on-course service. The beautiful citrus-tinged Spa boasts a huge fitness centre and aerobics studio, lap pool (all free to guests at both hotels), lovely spa-cuisine restaurant and a huge array of massages and therapies.

BRIT TIP
Head for the Ritz-Carlton's lobby lounge for afternoon tea or drinks in style with a magnificent view, especially at sunset.

The Resort's pricing is suitably upscale, but it is a rare holiday treat (407 206 2300/2400, **grandelakes.com**).

Omni Orlando Resort at Champions Gate: A real golfing paradise, this offers 720 rooms and suites overlooking a superb golf set-up with 2 Greg Norman-designed courses. An imposing hotel with impressive facilities, including the HQ of the renowned David Leadbetter golf academy, main swimming pool and activity pool (including a 'lazy river' feature, fountains and waterslide), 4 restaurants (notably the superb Asian cuisine of Zen and the chic David's Club bar-restaurant), coffee bar, deli, 3 lounge bars, state-of-the-art health club and full service spa. Just 10 minutes south of Disney and right off I-4, this is well situated yet slightly off the beaten track for those (especially golfers) looking for something

different. Set in 1,500 landscaped acres/607ha and with a magnificent vista as you walk in the front doors, it suits both business travellers and leisure-seekers. It also has 59 superb 2 and 3-bed villas, affording a more private stay, with full kitchens and an amazing array of specialised services in addition to opulent furnishings (407 390 6664, **omnihotels.com**).

SELF-CATERING

Once you venture beyond pure hotel territory, your choice varies through a range of 'Resorts' to timeshares, villa communities, studios and condos, all of which are essentially self-catering (although some still boast restaurants and other hotel-type amenities). They all tend to be further away from the theme parks, but they represent a highly flexible option, especially for larger families and groups.

Bahama Bay Resort: A wonderful location on Lake Davenport in Davenport (west on Highway 192, then south on Highway 27 to Florence Villa Grove Rd, or via Westside Rd), this is spread over 70 acres/28ha, with 498 condos in 38 2 and 3-storey buildings. The community is woven with tropical landscaping that includes water features, a recreation centre and clubhouse, restaurant and snack bar, internet café, fitness centre, sauna and spa (the fabulous Eleuthera Spa & Salon), tennis, basketball and volleyball, 4 heated pools and kiddie pools. You can fish in the lake, which has a sandy beach, plus there is a video arcade and small

Bahama Bay Resort

cinema. A shuttle goes to and from the theme parks for a small charge. The 4 types of condo offer 2-bed, 2-bath (sleeping 6, with a sofa-bed in the lounge) and 3-bed, 2-bath (sleeping 8, again with sofa-bed), with fitted kitchen, laundry room/washer-dryer, living room and dining area. The Grand Bahama 3-bed condo has 1,739sq ft/162sq m of space and is one of the most elegant (1877 299 4481 or **bahamabay.com**).

Barefoot'n in the Keys: This boutique little timeshare development of 40 1-bed condos is nicely tucked away next to Old Town in Kissimmee and was dramatically enhanced in 2009 with another 42 1 and 2-bed units. Onsite are a main pool, kids' pool and whirlpool, children's play area, volleyball and BBQ stations. (407 589 2127, **barefootn.com**).

Blue Heron Beach Resort: A superb high-rise complex of 2 high-rise towers (16 and 21 storeys) right on Apopka-Vineland Rd (Highway 535) in Lake Buena Vista, this features 283 beautifully furnished 1 and 2-bed condos, all with 2 bathrooms, a balcony and fully equipped kitchen, including washer-dryer. Imaginatively, there are bunk beds for kids in the wonderfully spacious 1 and 2-bed units, which can comfortably sleep 6–8. All master bedrooms also include a whirlpool tub in their en-suite bathrooms. One side of the towers has a Disney view

Blue Heron Beach Resort

Our definitions

There is some confusion over the terminology for much self-catering accommodation these days, with some tour operators even calling apartment-style condos 'villas', which is completely misleading. Here's what should be the case (and we advise checking with the operator for the exact type if it's not clear):

Villa: a detached vacation home, usually with its own screened-in pool, in self-contained residential communities.

Townhome: a 2-storey terraced-style house, rarely with its own pool; found in many Resorts.

Condo: a 1, 2 or 3-bed apartment-style unit, usually in a low-rise block but sometimes 10 or more storeys.

Studio: a 1-room accommodation unit that includes kitchen facilities.

Resort: a collection of condos (or townhomes) built around central features like pools, recreation facilities and (sometimes) a restaurant/bar or two.

(including the fireworks at night) while the other overlooks scenic Lake Bryan. There is then a superb lido deck, featuring a large freeform pool, kids' pool and hot tub, plus a boardwalk fronting the lake and watersports (jetskis and water-skiing), for an extra charge), while the 36-hole Hawaiian Rumble mini-golf course is right outside. There is a video games room and 2 fitness centres, but no restaurant (though there are plenty nearby, including a CiCi's Pizza, Starbucks and Dunkin' Donuts in front, plus a handy supermarket). As a self-catering resort, daily house-keeping is available only for a charge, but there is a free daily shuttle to all the theme parks (407 387 2200, **blueheronbeachresort.com**).

BRIT TIP
If you prefer a tranquil Lake View room at the Blue Heron Beach Resort, you can still get a view of Disney's fireworks at night from the outdoor corridor/terrace on each floor.

Floridays Resort Orlando: One of the smartest of the area's condo-hotels, this is extremely well situated in a quieter part of I-Drive, but close to Orlando Premium Outlets and with a free shuttle service to the parks. The full site consists of 6 condo blocks (each with 72 rooms), 2 pools (including the elaborate main zero-depth entry pool and water-play area), a pool bar and grill, fitness centre, stylish Welcome Center, kids' activity centre and games room, plus a small grocery store. With concierge services, business centre and meeting facilities, it is highly versatile, while the water-play area will probably keep kids amused for hours! The 2 and 3-bed grand suites are beautifully furnished and will sleep 6–10, and have either a balcony or patio. Living rooms include large-screen plasma TVs, high-speed internet, games console and stereos, while each bedroom also has a TV. And, if you don't fancy cooking, you can use the delivery service from the Marketplace, which also serves Starbucks coffee. All rooms are wheelchair-accessible and some are specifically adapted for the disabled with roll-in showers (1866 797 0022, **floridaysresortorlando.com**).

Fountains Resort: This high-quality timeshare set-up is on a quieter stretch of International Drive (south of SeaWorld). With superb 2-bed, 2-bath condos, all with full kitchens, and the resort's outstanding 75,000sq ft/7,000sq m pool area with waterslides and poolside bar, it offers all the comforts of home in a beautiful tropical environment, complete with the large Clubhouse boasting a games room, kids' activity centre, bar and coffee lounge (1800 456 0000, **bluegreenrentals.com**).

Hapimag Resort: An unusual combination of vacation home and resort, this is the Swiss timeshare operator's only US property (albeit with NO timeshare solicitation), and it sits inside the mature Lake Berkley villa community in Kissimmee (almost behind Medieval Times). The Resort basically encompasses a self-contained circle of 2 and 3-bed town-homes, grouped around a busy clubhouse with pool, volleyball court, small fitness centre and gift shop. There are also a handful of fully furnished 4-bed villas elsewhere in the Lake Berkley community, which also boasts its own clubhouse and smart pool area with kids' pool, plus another gym, games room and internet room. There is then a scenic walkway around the lake, with white-sand beaches in 2 places (407 390 9083, **orlando-hapimag.com**).

Lake Buena Vista Resort Village & Spa: This stylish condo-hotel currently features 5 tower blocks (there will eventually be 15) of 2, 3 and 4-bed condos, right next to Lake Buena Vista Factory Stores on Highway 535. The current phase includes a superb freeform swimming pool, complete with pirate play-ship, a second quiet pool, a state-of-the-art fitness centre, video games room and Kids Club. There is a convenience store and gift shop, a Pizza Hut Express, specialist bar-restaurant Frankie Farrell's Irish Pub & Grille, and a 5-star Spa, as well as a free shuttle to the main theme parks. The rooms (all with full kitchens, Jacuzzi tubs, digital TVs and internet) are comfortable and stylish, with the 4-bed condos incredibly spacious. The Reflections Spa & Salon is a blissful facility, offering some wonderfully relaxing treatments (407 956 6103, **lbvorlandoresort.com** or **staysky.com**).

BRIT TIP
Visiting Lake Buena Vista Factory Stores? Relieve aching limbs by popping next door to the Resort Village & Spa for a soothing pedicure, massage or other spa treatment (407 597 1695).

Hapimag Resort

Liki Tiki Village: On the western fringe of Highway 192, this timeshare set-up often has good-value condos to rent on a weekly basis. Its newest blocks offer huge 1-bed and 2-bed units, with well-equipped kitchens (all with coffee and ice-makers), while the 64-acre/26ha complex boasts 2 pools, a mini water park, tennis courts, paddle boats, bikes, pool-bar and grill and free continental breakfast Mon–Fri (407 239 5000, **LikiTiki.com**).

Mystic Dunes Resort & Golf Club: Tucked away in a quiet corner of Kissimmee is this holiday ownership property that also offers hotel rentals, often at terrific rates. It is a truly luxurious resort with just about every facility, plus an impressive array of beautiful 1, 2 and 3-bed villas that sleep up to 12 (1877 747 4747, **mystic-dunes-resort.com**).

Orange Lake Resort: This vast resort on west Highway 192 offers a mixture of well-furnished 1, 2 and 3-bed condos (NB: Orange Lake refers to them as 'villas' but they are definitely apartment-type) and studios that sleep 4–12, plus golf, watersports and cinema. Then there are kids' activities, exercise classes, tennis, racquetball, mini-golf and a Marketplace of general store, pizzeria and golf shop. The amazing 12-acre/4.8ha River Island water park boasts a lazy river, 2 zero-depth entry pools, mini-golf, whirlpool tubs, waterfalls and a clubhouse, arcade and fitness centre, while the new Water's Edge beach Club adds a restaurant, pool bar, cabañas, stage

Mystic Dunes Resort & Golf Club

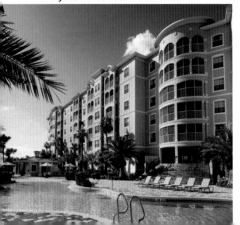

and gift shop, plus an Olympic-size pool with feature beach-style entry. There is also a Publix supermarket at the entrance to the Resort (407 239 0000, **orangelake.com**).

Palisades Resort: A real find out at the rural western end of Highway 192 in Kissimmee, this smart new condo-hotel features wonderfully spacious 1, 2 and 3-bed condos that sleep 4–8, with fully equipped kitchens, including washer-dryers, and private balconies. Each unit offers generous living and dining areas, two bathrooms (master bed with oversized bath) and flatscreen TVs. The tropical lido deck has a large outdoor pool in lush surroundings, while there is also a sauna, cinema, fitness centre, video games room and free wi-fi. It is also close enough to benefit from the shops and restaurants along Highway 192 (and be just 10 minutes from Disney), but secluded enough on Avalon Rd to be wonderfully quiet and tranquil. There are free pastries, coffee and tea at breakfast and, at busier times of the year, spa facilities. There is currently no bar or restaurant, but the Publix supermarket is only 5 minutes away and its rates in 2010 ($89/night for a 3-bed condo) were quite phenomenal (321 250 3030, **palisadesresortorlando. com** or **staysky.com**).

Regal Oaks at Old Town: New in 2008 was this mix of luxury town-homes, from 3-bed, 2-bath units to grand 4-bed, 3-bath villas. It follows the successful blueprint of accommodations set around an elaborate clubhouse, with fabulous water features (zero-entry pool, waterslide, whirlpool and lazy river), Tiki Bar and other facilities. Situated right next to all the fun and shopping of Old Town in Kissimmee, it offers terrific value (407 997 1000, **regaloaksresort.com**).

Regal Palms Resort & Spa: Next door to the serene Highlands Reserve villa community on Highway 27 is this pleasing mix of 3 and 4-bed townhomes and 4–6-bed vacation homes, all set around a beautiful Clubhouse that includes a mini water park (with lazy river and waterslides), pools, Jacuzzis and extensive sun terraces. The sister resort to Regal Oaks, it also features a pub that shows live UK sports, a business centre, gym and gift shop/grocery store, plus an indulgent Spa & Health Club (863 424 6141, **regalpalmsorlando.com**).

Reunion Resort & Club: Arguably the grandest of all the resorts, this will be of keen interest to golfers who appreciate the 5-star touch. On Highway 532 in Kissimmee (just off exit 58 of I-4 south of Disney), this fledgling 'community' boasts a vast line-up of condos, townhomes and luxury villas set around 3 superb golf courses (designed by Arnold Palmer, Tom Watson and Jack Nicklaus). The choice is truly deluxe: immaculate 1, 2 and 3-bed condos (many with stunning golf course views); a range of private homes, from modest 3-beds to mansion-style 8-beds; a stylish golf clubhouse with excellent bar and restaurant; a full-service Spa, with a superb array of treatments; the scenic Seven Eagles pool, complete with Pavilion Bar & Grille, Jacuzzis, fitness room and kids' play centre; floodlit tennis courts; an amazing water park consisting of lazy river, slides, pools, waterfalls and interactive kids' area; and miles of biking and hiking trails. High-rise condo the Reunion Grande features 82 luxurious 1 and 2-bed suites, magnificent fine-dining chophouse Forte, a state-of-the-art fitness facility and ultra-chic rooftop pool and bar, Eleven, offering tapas, cocktails and panoramic views. It all comes with concierge service and even private in-room dining that marks this out as one of Florida's most upmarket resorts. Only those staying here or members can play on the courses, but the scale and imagination of the resort are superb (407 662 1000, **reunionresort.com**). Reunion is also home to the state-of-the-art ANNIKA Academy, created under the direction of top golfer Annika Sorenstam.

Sheraton Vistana Resort: This sprawling family-friendly timeshare set-up in Lake Buena Vista, close to *Walt Disney World*, is a wonderfully

mature development of roomy 1 and 2-bed/2-bath condos (sleeping 4–8; again, they are called 'villas' but are definitely apartment-type) with fully equipped kitchens and magnificent resort facilities. Furnishings and facilities are all modern, with multiple TVs, DVD player and a screened-in private patio or balcony, plus large washer-dryers, which all serves to underline the great self-catering value of this type of accommodation. There are 7 giant pools, 9 floodlit tennis courts, smart Marketplace deli (with Starbucks coffee), Food Court (with KFC, Pizza Hut and A&W), Zimmie's Casual Eatery & Sports Bar and 3 pool bars, plus massage treatments and even a Tues evening 'picnic in the park' session with live music. There is free scheduled transport to the Disney parks and lots of family-orientated activities, including cookouts and storytelling (407 239 3100, **sheraton.com/vistanaresort**).

BRITTIP
At both Sheraton Vistana properties, for a nominal fee, you can arrange to have your condo pre-stocked with groceries and laundry products.

Sheraton Vistana Villages: The sister, newer property, located on International Drive south of SeaWorld, this upscale family resort offers spacious 1 and 2-bed/2-bath condos with fully equipped kitchen or kitchenette, dining area, washer/dryer and more, all in 5 and 6-storey blocks and all set around scenic landscaping or eye-catching pool areas. The beautiful lobby area opens on to a stunning main pool boasting waterfalls, Jacuzzis and children's play areas, while there is also the

Palisades Resort

smart Flagler Station Bar & Grill for breakfast, lunch and dinner. Less than 6mls/10km from Disney, guests enjoy extensive resort amenities like free scheduled transport to the theme parks, 3 more pool areas, a state-of-the-art fitness centre, games room, basketball and tennis courts and a grocery store – although there is also a big Publix supermarket nearby (407 238 5000, **sheraton.com/vistavillages**).

◀◀▶ BRIT TIP

As the Sheraton Vistana resorts are both timeshare properties, you may well be asked if you'd like to take their property tour at some stage, but there is no pressure to sign up or hard-sell if you do.

Summer Bay Resort: Out on west Highway 192 is a mix of Budget motel (The Inn at Summer Bay), Standard hotel (Holiday Inn Express), some 3-bed vacation homes and new 1, 2 and 3-bed timeshare condos. The 700 rooms spread over 64 acres/26ha are all smart, while the facilities include outdoor heated pools and kiddie pools, an elaborate children's water-play area, mini-golf, clubhouse with volleyball, tennis, basketball, shuffleboard and fitness room, video arcade, gift shop and snack bar. The lake provides jet-skis, paddleboats, waterskiing and more, plus daily kids' activities and organised sports. Even those in The Inn and Holiday Inn (which has its own pool and breakfast area) benefit from the clubhouse facilities, while next door is a Denny's

Vista Cay Resort

diner and Publix supermarket. (1888 742 1100, **summerbayresort.com**).

Tuscana: This Mediterranean-inspired condo-resort bordering the Champions Gate golf courses offers 288 elegant, oversized 2 and 3-bed condos, each with 2 full baths, balcony, fully equipped kitchen, washer and dryer. The excellent clubhouse boasts the Tuscana Tavern bar and grill, tiki snack bar, elegant pool, kiddie pool, cabanas, fitness centre and a 24-seat movie theatre (407 787 4800, **tuscana.net**).

Villas at Grand Cypress: Arguably Orlando's top golf resort, this is also a wonderfully upscale option in general terms, in a beautiful setting just behind *Walt Disney World*. It boasts 186 single-room club suites and 1, 2, 3 and 4-bed condo-style villas, all luxuriously furnished, with fully equipped kitchens and patios or balconies. There is a blissful Villa Pool, with poolside saunas and bar, bike rentals and 2 restaurants (The Club sports bar and fine-dining Nine18 overlooking the superb North-South golf course), plus 24-hour room service, for those who prefer not to cook for themselves. Villa guests also get full use of all the amenities of the nearby Hyatt Grand Cypress (page 89), a 5-minute ride on the free on-demand shuttle service (407 239 4700, **grandcypress.com**).

Vista Cay Resort: This recent timeshare development offers some of the most extensive resort facilities in the I-Drive/Universal Boulevard area (just behind the Convention Center North). Convenient for all the attractions, but away from the main hustle-bustle, it has beautiful accommodation (2 and 3-bed executive suites and 3-bed townhomes), plus a large clubhouse with a dazzling pool set in lush, tropical landscaping; whirlpool spa, kids' pool and basketball court; games room, business centre and fitness centre. Apartments range from 1,500sq ft/140sq m to 2,300sq ft/214sq m and offer fully equipped kitchens, large HD TVs with DVD players and Sony PlayStations, dining

Rental Accommodation

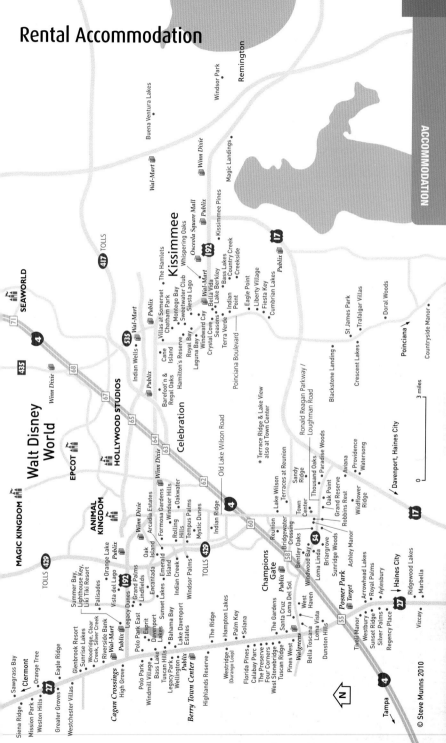

Remington

Windsor Park

Buena Ventura Lakes

Wal-Mart

Magic Landings

Winn Dixie

Kissimmee Pines

Osceola Square Mall

Publix

Whispering Oaks

Kissimmee

The Hamlets

Chatham Park

Montego Bay

Sweetwater Club

Siesta Lago

Villas at Somerset

Publix

Indian Wells

Wal-Mart

Wal-Mart

Bella Vida

Lake Berkley

Seasons

Windward Cay

Crystal Cove

Terra Verde

Royal Bay

Laguna Bay

Hamilton's Reserve

Cane Island

Barefoot 'n &
Regal Oaks

Indian
Point

Bass Lakes

Country Creek

Creekside

Eagle Point

Liberty Village

Fiesta Key

Cumbrian Lakes

Poinciana Boulevard

417 TOLLS

535

Publix

Doral Woods

St James Park

Trafalgar Villas

Countryside Manor

Poinciana

Blackstone Landing

Crescent Lakes

SEAWORLD

71

4

435

Winn Dixie

68

67

Walt Disney World

MAGIC KINGDOM

EPCOT

HOLLYWOOD STUDIOS

65

64

Celebration

Old Lake Wilson Road

* Terrace Ridge & Lake View
also at Town Center

Ronald Reagan Parkway /
Loughman Road

Davenport, Haines City

Providence

Watersong

Aviana

Paradise Woods

Grand Reserve

Wildflower
Ridge

Oak Point

Sandy
Ridge

Thousand Oaks

Town
Center

Robbins Rest

Lake Wilson

Terraces at Reunion

0   3 miles

62

4

60

ANIMAL KINGDOM

Winn Dixie

Arcadia Estates

Formosa Gardens

Windsor Hills

Rolling
Hills

Oakwater

Tempus Palms

Mystic Dunes

Indian Ridge

Oak
Island

Emerald
Island

Indian Palms

Windsor Palms

Publix

Orange Lake

Vista del Lago

Summer Bay,
Lighthouse Key,
Liki Tiki Resort

Palisades

Woodridge, Clear
Creek, Silver Creek

Riverside Bank

Wal-Mart

Publix

Glenbrook Resort

Sunrise Lakes

Cagan Crossings

High Grove

Berry Town Center

TOLLS 429

58

Reunion

Bridgewater
Crossing

Bentley Oaks

Windwood Bay

Loma Linda

Briargrove

Sunridge Woods

Ashley Manor

54

Champions
Gate

Publix

Santa Cruz

Loma Del Sol

West
Haven

Loma Vista

Dunston Hills

The Gardens

Bella Toscana

Pines West

Tuscan Ridge

West Stonebridge

Four Corners

The Preserve

Calabay Parc

Florida Pines

Highlands Reserve

The Ridge

Westridge
(Durango Loop)

Hampton Lakes

Palm Key

Solana

Polo Park

Windmill Village

Bass Lake

Tuscan Hills

Legacy Park

Wellington

Polo Park East

Esprit

Davenport
Lakes

Bahama Bay

Lake Davenport
Estates

Grand Palms

Lindfields

Sunset Lakes

Encantada

Legacy Dunes

Publix

192

Eagle Ridge

Greater Groves

Westchester Villas

Siena Ridge

Mission Park

Weston Hills

Clermont

Orange Tree

Sawgrass Bay

27

Posner Park

Target

Tioli Manor

Westbury

Sunset Ridge

Silver Palms

Regency Place

Arrowhead Lakes

Royal Palms

Aylesbury

Haines City

Ridgewood Lakes

Marbella

Vizcay

Walgreens

55

27

4

17

N

Tampa

© Steve Munns 2010

rooms, master bedrooms (with separate Roman tubs and showers), private balconies and free wi-fi (407 996 4647, **vistacayholidays.com**).

Windsor Palms Resort: Just off west Highway 192 in Kissimmee, this popular gated community has a mix of 2-bed condos, 2 and 3-bed townhomes, and 3 to 6-bed private pool villas. Amenities include a large clubhouse and fitness centre, tennis courts, an Olympic-sized pool, a kiddie pool and spa, basketball, billiard room, volleyball court, video arcade, playground and a 58-seat cinema showing recent films. Similarly, the (slightly newer) sister resort of **Windsor Hills Resort** on Old Lake Wilson Road offers the same spread of accommodation choice and impressive amenities, like its huge lagoon-style pool with waterslide and state-of-the-art fitness centre and is even closer to the Disney parks (1888 426 0427, **globalresorthomes.com**).

HOLIDAY HOMES

This is in many ways the biggest area of accommodation in Orlando, especially for UK visitors, as there has been a huge development of holiday homes, or villas, in the last 20 years. Generally speaking, holiday homes provide a valuable way for large families and groups to stay together and cut costs by self-catering. The homes, whether individual houses, collections of houses, full residential communities or townhomes, sometimes have access to other communal facilities like large pools

Advantage Vacation Homes

and recreation areas, and are always equipped with microwaves, multiple TVs and washer-dryers. For these, a hire car is usually essential, but the savings can be significant. Prices can be as low as $450/week off-peak, but expect to pay at least $1,500/week for a 5 or 6-bed villa in high season. A word of warning, though: once you've experienced pool-at-home life, you may never go back to a hotel!

Holiday homes to rent are big business in central Florida and now account for a huge slice of the European market as they are ideal for repeat visitors, large groups and those who like their privacy and own facilities. They tend to be grouped in newly built estates and some are gated communities for added security. Nearly all offer a private pool and the largest can sleep 16. Some are classed as 'executive' homes, and this usually means more facilities (games rooms, barbeques, Jacuzzis, etc.) rather than an increase in size.

If you book independently, there are several key questions to ask: Do you need to go to an office some way away to pick up the keys or is there a combination lockbox at the house? Is there a local contact if anything goes wrong (most owners do not live in Florida) and is the property maintained by a local company? Does it offer a secure bonding for your booking, and is it a member of a reputable organisation, such as the Better Business Bureau of Central Florida? In winter, is the pool heated, and what is the charge for heating? Finally, is it as close to Disney as it says (some homes can be down in Polk County, more than 30 minutes away)?

There are some 26,000 villas on offer, spread right across Kissimmee and out in Polk and Lake Counties to the west and south-west of Disney. A few still suffer from ongoing construction but most are now well established and mature (Highlands Reserve is a good example). Be aware that homes within a particular community can still vary in quality depending on the care and attention of owners and/or property managers, hence just being in, say, stylish Cumbrian Lakes, is not a guarantee of executive quality status. You can rent either direct from the owners (on sites such as **vrbo.com**, **lastminutevillas.net** and **thedibb.co.uk**) or from a property management company, which will look after multiple villas. Ironically, there are increasing numbers of townhomes (so developers can fit in more); for a 'detached' house, ask for a 'single family home'. The bottom line is you must do your homework, shop around as you would for any significant purchase, and check with organisations like the Central Florida Vacation Rental Managers Association. This is the only widely acknowledged umbrella organisation for the holiday home business and helps to provide a level of credibility.

The following companies all pass the *Brit Guide* credibility test.

Advantage Vacation Homes: In the villa rental business for 20 years and one of the largest companies, few of its 2–6 bed homes (the majority are on west Highway 192 and Highway 27 in Clermont and Davenport) are more than 8 years old, while many are 4–5 years at most. It also manages an increasing portfolio of condos (in the Bahama Bay and Sun Lake resorts) and townhomes. It offers 24-hour management, with courteous and efficient staff at its office just off west Highway 192 (plus an attraction ticket service), open 9am–10pm daily. Its holiday homes are rated Silver, Gold or Platinum, with the difference measured in the extras rather than size (larger-screen or plasma TVs, tiled floors rather than carpeting, a Jacuzzi or games room), although some of the more exclusive villas might be situated on a golfing community or have tennis courts (0871 711 9531 in the UK, 1866 544 5301 in the US, **advantagevacationhomes.com**).

Alexander Holiday Homes: Family-owned Alexander manages more than 200 properties in Kissimmee, from standard 2, 3 and 4-bed condo-villas to luxury 7-bed executive homes sleeping 14, all with pools and immaculately furnished, within 15–20 minutes of Disney, including some of the closest to the parks. This company was the first of its kind in Orlando (in 1981) and still offers a personable, efficient service. It was only the third management company to earn the distinguished AAA (American Automobile Association) 3 Diamond rating and definitely gets our approval. It shows prices in UK and US currency and even offers an airport meet-and-greet service to ensure you get to your home, as well as arrival grocery packages, gas barbeque rentals, scooter and wheelchair hire. Its informative website provides photo tours of all its homes as well as some informative blogs and other features (0871 711 5371 in the UK, 1800 621 7888 in the **US, floridasunshine.com**).

Florida Choice Vacation Homes: Provides townhouses (3 or 4-bed with communal pools and recreation facilities), standard and executive homes (3–7 bed private properties) in Orlando and Naples, some with heated pools and with free local phone calls. There is optional maid service and cot and highchair rentals (407 397 3013, **floridachoice.com**).

Florida Leisure Vacation Homes: Another company we know well and can recommend, it is British-owned and pays great attention to detail. With 100 homes (3–7 beds) in the Kissimmee area, most just a few years old and many in the highly regarded Cumbrian Lakes community, it prides itself on a personal touch (even down to providing personal chef, massage and concierge services) and offers some of the biggest and newest properties, as well as a full online booking system. Many are in

Florida Choice Vacation Homes

the Executive range, with the fullest array of amenities in addition to their private, screened pools, and often in gated communities. All properties have lockboxes, so you don't need to visit the management office to check in. You can see all its homes online (in extended photo and video) plus lots of local info, especially for restaurants and golf, while its new testimonial sections provide first-hand feedback. The website also includes a regular blog, free Newsletter and other useful features. Its office is handily placed on Highway 192 in Kissimmee, at the junction with Apopka-Vineland Road, SR 535 (407 870 1600; **floridaleisure.com**).

Florida Vacation Shop: Another local British specialist, it features a select range of new homes in some of the smartest local developments. Options include Formosa Garden Estates, Emerald Island Resorts, Legacy Park and Crescent Lakes, plus the Regal Oaks resort. Its concierge service offers the chance to arrange other services in advance (like dining), while there are optional maid services, Welcome Packs and Tailor-Made Shopping (specific goods delivered to your villa prior to arrival). Pushchairs, cots, high-chairs and BBQ grills can all be hired on a weekly basis. Its website has a useful Vacation Guide and downloadable handbooks for the various accommodations (1866 394 2583; **floridavacationshop.com**).

Loyalty Homes: For a luxury touch, all these homes (2–6 bedrooms) are no

Park Square Homes, Bella Vida

Check them out!

The Central Florida Vacation Rental Managers Association has a website designed to promote villa rentals and make booking easier. Look it up at **vacationwithconfidence.com**. Another general website that sets out the advantages is **discovervacationhomes.com**.

more than 4mls/6.5 km from Disney and all offer the true 'executive' style, with the likes of digital door locks (so no key collection required), cable TV and many with games rooms. The website offers video tours, too (call 0121 468 0016 in the UK or 407 397 7475 in the US, **loyaltyusa.com**).

Park Square Homes: This operation is actually operated by the home builder, hence it features the complete resort communities of Encantada and Bella Vida, both just off Highway 192 in Kissimmee, with a series of well-built and beautifully furnished 3 and 4-bed townhomes, plus larger villas at Bella Vida, all with private pools. The 2 tropically styled resorts benefit from a central clubhouse, with a large pool, cyber café, exercise room and lakefront gazebo, while Encantada also has a video games room and cafe (1866 930 0444, **bellavidavacationhomes.com** and **encantadaresorthomes.com**).

Premier Vacation Homes: A good range of spacious properties with 2–6 beds, sleeping up to 14, in secure residential communities within a 15-20-minute drive of Disney. All are privately owned and have been purchased and furnished as holiday homes, with screened pools, 2 TVs, fully equipped kitchens (including dishwasher, washer-dryer, microwave and coffee-maker), at least 1 king or queen bed, and free local phone calls. Maid service can be added for a fee. The Luxury homes (2–4 beds) are the standard accommodation, while Executive homes (3–6 beds) are bigger, with an extra TV, VCR and barbecue, and there is also a townhome and condo choice (407 396 2401, **pr-vacation.com**).

Prestige Vacations Direct: Another British-owned and run company, this agency specialises purely in renting out a wide variety of 3–6 bed vacation homes, most just a short drive from Disney. It can provide special monthly rates and even UK sterling prices, as well as having periodic special offers, and features as many as 26 different villa communities, from Windsor Palms to Westridge and Highlands Reserve out on Highway 27 (1877 462 4424, **prestigevacationsdirect.com**).

✚ BRIT TIP

You'll find Marmite, Ribena, McVities and a handful of other British groceries at Publix and Winn-Dixie supermarkets, plus most Wal-Marts (in the 'International' aisle), but your best bet for a full 'taste of home' is the British Supermarket on Vineland Rd (1 block east of its Kirkman Rd junction, just north of Universal; see also page 352).

Villa Direct: Another major Orlando specialist, and one of the biggest, with an extensive range of properties in the area, from 2-bed condos to luxury 7-bed villas, and a good user-friendly website, plus an excellent range of guest services, including arrival groceries and even mobility equipment rental. Its welcome centre is easily found on west Highway 192 in Kissimmee while the head office is close by in Celebration, just off I-4 (407 397 1210, **villadirect.com**).

Buying a holiday home

The quality of life, an attractive 'buyer's market' and fabulous weather are all compelling reasons to consider buying a vacation home, for holidays, investment, a winter retreat or as a retirement home. But, apart from the fact it's easy to be starry-eyed on holiday, there are companies willing to exploit tourists and investors, so be sure to do your homework, especially to understand US property-buying terminology. If you look in the window of a 'realtor' (a US estate agent), you'll notice a BIG price difference with the UK. New homes are still popular, but there are

an increasing number of resales on the market that can represent great value, plus bank resales of foreclosed properties, often at huge markdowns. In summer 2010, prices were still at a near 10-year low, representing a total buyer's market.

Useful home-buying info can be found from Alexander Holiday Homes (**floridasunshine.com**) and Florida Leisure (**floridaleisure.com**), a registered realtor, while UK magazines *International Homes* (**international-homes.com**) and *Homes Overseas* (**homes overseas.co.uk**) have Florida sections and are worth picking up.

✚ BRIT TIP

The British-run *Vacation Homes Magazine* is a handy source of info for both those wanting to buy and existing owners. The quarterly publication has an impressive 'experts panel' and offers a wide range of features and news. Best of all, it is FREE to subscribers. Look up **vacationhomepublications.com**.

Owning a piece of the magic is tempting, but you *must* get all the facts first, both to get the best out of the current Buyer's market and, equally importantly, to avoid the many pitfalls (like under-budgeted or non-operating Home Owners associations, an increasing problem these days). You should also look for a company that specialises in assisting British buyers. Many firms primarily offer vacation-style properties, and several deal mainly with the British. Consider investigating one that enables you to fund your mortgage in sterling, dollars or euros through a UK bank, rather than a US one. If you live in the UK, dealing with a US lender can be costly and inconvenient. For instance, US mortgage companies often 'sell' new mortgages to another lender after closing a loan, making it hard to track. Repayment of a dollar mortgage with sterling can also be hit by exchange rates. In this instance, a company we have been happy to recommend for 10 years now, is **British Homes Group Florida** (**britishhomesgroup.com**). Its British-staffed, Orlando-based team has its finger firmly on the pulse of current sales trends and can offer a range of mortgages tailor-made for UK buyers.

BRIT TIP

Good legal advice for house-buying, business and (especially) immigration matters is essential. Contact Orlando firm **LaVigne, Coton & Associates** (407 316 9988, **lavignelaw.us**) for the best service.

One example allows Brits to purchase buy-to-let villas and second homes using the Florida property (rather than the buyer's UK home) as security for the mortgage (irrespective of currency chosen), which removes the potential of putting the primary UK home at risk and still provides the interest deduction on US tax returns. **British Home Sales Florida**, the group's estate agency, has relationships with the some of the state's top builders and developers and can help search for the ideal property anywhere from the Keys to the Panhandle, and with online access to more than 20,000 properties in Central Florida alone, there is a lot to choose from. Add in BHG's useful Florida Advisory Panel, free Florida rental booking and listing services, and a Florida Blog for the latest local info, and it makes for a great one-stop-shop for British investors. For those wanting to emigrate to Florida, there is a new Visa Advisory Service (see **eb5investmentvisas.com**) offering the **EB-5 Investment Visa** with a guaranteed Green Card (for a fixed high-investment value in excess of $500,000).

British Homes Group's Orlando office can provide an immediate starting point for your property search, an evaluation of a proposed purchase or

Five basic buying tips

1 Get references from UK owners and check management company references.

2 Try to stay in the community on holiday before you buy. Walk through it and talk to people there.

3 Make sure the home meets requirements for short-term rentals, such as pool security fence, emergency exit lighting, smoke detectors and a keyed, locked owners' closet.

4 Ensure the builder offers a warranty and the property regulations allow you to let on a short-term basis.

5 Make sure you have all the proper US fees, registrations and taxes.

an assessment of existing mortgage position, all free and without obligation (see inside back cover for current promotion). Call 407 396 9914, email **info@britishhomesgroup. com** or visit it at 2960 Vineland Rd, Kissimmee, above the Edwin Watts Golf Shop at the junction of Routes 535 and 192, just minutes from *Walt Disney World*.

But, whoever you go with, ensure they can refer you to experts in UK and US taxation, immigration, hazard insurance, structural warranties and other issues essential for hassle-free ownership in Florida. Property in Orlando increased in value dramatically during 2003–08, and then subsided steeply, hence there are no guarantees, but experts believe it will rebound healthily in the near future.

OK, that's enough accommodation advice. Now it's on to the parks…

Dinner at sunset

5 The Theme Parks: Disney's Fab Four

or Spending the Day with Mickey and the Gang

By now you should be prepared to deal with the main business of any visit to Orlando: *Walt Disney World.* This is the heart of all the excitement and fun in store (along with the other theme parks of Universal Orlando, SeaWorld and Busch Gardens).

In our opinion, 2 weeks is barely enough to see all that this vast resort has in store. So, when you add in the other 4 theme parks and the array of smaller-scale attractions, you start to realise the awesome scope of an Orlando holiday!

BRIT TIP
Make a photocopy of the back of your park passes, and of your passport, before leaving home. If your tickets are lost during your holiday you will need the information on the back of each ticket to have them replaced. A copy of your passport will suffice as photo ID in the parks, or if your passport becomes lost.

Buying your tickets in advance is highly advisable (it often adds up to better value and saves time), but work out your requirements first – you wouldn't get full use out of, say, a 7-day Premium ticket AND an Orlando Flex Ticket Plus in just a fortnight. Once you're ready to buy, check what measure of security the ticket outlet offers (ABTA bonding, etc.) and what it does in case of tickets lost or stolen during shipping

or during your holiday. Try to use your credit card for all purchases – there is built-in additional security (for our list of recommended ticket outlets, see pages 9 and 10).

You will also find a welter of **discount coupons** for many of the smaller attractions in tourist publications distributed in Orlando (or from the Guest Services desk at your hotel – it's often worth asking), while the tour operators' welcome meetings usually have special offers and tickets for the latest excursions.

BRIT TIP
Offers of 'free' Disney tickets usually mean timeshare firms, which also claim to have 'official' visitor centres. I-Drive has the only genuine Official Visitor Center.

The **Official Visitor Center** at 8723 International Drive in the Gala Center on the corner of Austrian Row (407 363 5872, **orlandoinfo.com/uk**, see map on page 86) is also worth

Guests at the Magic Kingdom

© Disney

checking out for discounts. Equally, the Universal Attractions booths at several shopping malls have great deals (3 days for the price of 2, 2-for-1 drinks etc.) from time to time. Yes, it IS possible to bag free tickets by attending timeshare presentations, but they can easily take half a day of your precious holiday and do you really want the hard-sell hassle?

BRITTIP

If you DO want to check out timeshare options, look first at **Disney Vacation Club** for the guaranteed way to secure memorable holidays. A tour (for which you will be picked up) will take around 3 hours, but you will be given some Disney FastPasses in return to save time back at the parks. Call 407 566 3300, 1800 500 3990 or visit **http://dvc. disney.go.com/dvc/index**.

Ratings

We judge all the rides and shows on a unique rating system that splits them into **thrill rides** and **scenic rides**. Thrill rides earn T ratings out of 5 (hence a TTTTT is as exciting as they get) and scenic rides get A ratings out of 5 (an AA ride is likely to be twee and missable). Obviously, it is a matter of opinion to a certain extent, but you can be sure a T or A ride is not worth your time, a TT or AA is worth seeing only if there is

no queue, a TTT or AAA should be seen if you have time, but you won't miss much if you don't, a TTTT or AAAA ride is a big time attraction that should be high on your 'must do' list, and a TTTTT or AAAAA attraction should not be missed! The latter will have the longest queues, so you should plan your visit around them. Some rides have height restrictions and are not advisable for people with back, neck or heart problems or for expectant mothers. Where this is the case we say, for example, 'Restrictions: 3ft 6in/106cm'. Height restrictions (strictly enforced) are based on the average 5-year-old being 3ft 6in/106cm tall, those aged 6 being 3ft 9in/114cm and 9s being 4ft 4in/132cm. You can also refer to our **At A Glance Height Restriction Guide** on page 39.

BRITTIP

Smoking is not permitted in the parks, apart from in a handful of designated areas. Check park maps for their exact locations. All restaurants are strictly non-smoking.

Disney's FastPass

One essential aid to queuing is **Disney's FastPass** system. Most of the main attractions have this wonderful service that allows you to roam while you wait for an allotted

Space Mountain

© Disney

Character dining

Having a meal with Mickey and Co (or Winnie the Pooh, Cinderella or Mary Poppins) is one of the great Disney experiences – even if you don't have children! It is also often the best way to meet your favourite characters without a wait, as they come to YOU. All reservations can be arranged up to 180 days in advance by phoning 407 WDW DINE (939 3463), calling at any Guest Services desk in a hotel, or by touching *88 on any Disney pay phone or 55 from a Disney resort room phone.

Some meals are difficult to get. Breakfast at Cinderella's Royal Table at the *Magic Kingdom* usually sells out within minutes of the 90-day window being open. Chef Mickey's and the Princess Storybook meals also go quickly. If you cannot book in advance, try calling the day you'd like to dine or, as a last resort, show up to see if there have been any cancellations. You must check in at the podium 10 minutes prior to your time and you will be given the next available table. Some characters don't enter the restaurant so, if they are in the lobby, you'll want to meet them before you are seated. Dining is all-you-can-eat, served buffet, pre-plated or family-style. Inside the restaurant, characters circulate among the tables giving attention to each group (particularly when children are holding the camera!). Character interaction is top-notch, especially if you dine off-hours when the restaurant is quieter. Be sure to bring your autograph book, a fat pen or marker (easier for the characters to hold) and plenty of film or an extra digital card for your camera. Some characters are huge, and children may be put off by them. If you aren't sure how they'll react, see how they are with the characters in the park before booking a character meal. Price range: breakfast $18.99-47.23 adults, $10.99-31.04 children; lunch $20.99-50.96 and $11.99-32.09; dinner $27.99-57.19 and $13.99-34.78 (NB: beware the peak season price rises – Disney has started the dubious practice of raising its restaurant rates in high season).

time to ride. How it works: insert your main park entrance ticket into the FastPass (FP) machine (to the side of the attraction's entrance) and you get another ticket giving you a period of time in which to return for your ride with only a minimal wait (NB: you need a FP ticket for every person who wants to ride, not just 1 per group). You can hold only 1 FP ticket per 2-hour period, though once you've used it you can get immediately another. If you start by going to one of the FP rides, collecting your ticket and returning later, you can by-pass a lot of standing in queues. You can also get another FP as soon as your 'window' opens: if your time slot for Space Mountain in *Magic Kingdom Park* is 10–11am, you could get another FP for, say, Buzz Lightyear's Space Ranger Spin at 10.01 and then go and ride Space Mountain! Many people still miss out on this, but it is FREE (FastPass rides are indicated by FP in descriptions). If you miss your FP 'window', you will still be allowed to ride, but you cannot ride *before* your time period.

BRIT TIP
Purchase a lanyard for your park tickets if you plan to use FastPass often. This keeps your tickets together and easily accessible.

Cinderella Castle

© Disney

With young ones

All Disney's parks offer pushchair ('stroller') hire, and you can save money by purchasing a multi-day rental at your first park. Children of ALL ages seem to get a big thrill from collecting autographs from the various Disney characters, and most shops sell handy **autograph books**.

PhotoPass

This unique and worthwhile scheme is available in all Disney's parks and (occasionally) in *Downtown Disney*. Disney photographers take photos of guests and, instead of receiving a paper claim ticket, they receive a *Disney PhotoPass* that links together all their photos on one online account for easy viewing. There is no charge for obtaining a *PhotoPass* or for viewing or sharing photos online (though there is if you want to download and print them), while each photo can be enhanced with Disney characters and special borders. Guests typically have 30 days after their photos were taken to decide if they want their photos (visit **disneyphotopass.com**), or you can view them at one of 3 PhotoPass shops – at the *Magic Kingdom*, the *Epcot* park or *Disney's Grand Floridian Resort.* Collect as many as you want (up to 300!) and have them all burned on to one CD for a bargain $149.95. There are also a huge range of other products you can have your photos transferred on to, including mugs, mouse pads, T-shirts and calendars!

Kids love meeting the cast

Cast Members

Disney employees are called Cast Members or CMs (never 'staff' as they all play a 'role' in the entertainment) and they are renowned for their helpful and cheerful style, always willing to assist, offer advice or just stop and chat. Interaction with CMs often provides some of the best memories of a visit. So, if you've had exceptional service or a CM has gone out of their way to help, let Disney know as it values such feedback (plus CMs get credit for it). Call in at Guest Relations (or City Hall at the *Magic Kingdom Park*) to record your thanks.

Child Swap

Where families have small children, but Mum and Dad still want to try a ride with height restrictions, you DON'T have to queue twice. When you reach the entrance to the queue, tell the operator you want to do a

Use the child swap for smaller guests

Character Dining: the meals

MAGIC KINGDOM: Crystal Palace for breakfast, lunch or dinner with Winnie the Pooh and Co – especially good for smaller children; and **Cinderella's Royal Table** for the (expensive) *Once Upon A Breakfast*, with Cinderella and her Princess Friends; *Fairytale Lunch* (Cinderella and Friends); and *Dreams Come True Dinner* (Fairy Godmother only). Breakfast is $32 adults, $22 children; lunch $53 adults, $33 children; dinner $60 adults, $36 children. Payment in full on your credit card is required to book, $10/person may be charged for no-shows (photo package included in price, additional photos available for a fee).

EPCOT: Garden Grill for lunch or dinner with Farmer Mickey, Pluto, Chip and Dale; **Princess Storybook Dining** for breakfast, lunch and dinner; an alternative to Cinderella's, with some of Belle, Jasmine, Snow White, Pocahontas, Mulan, Sleeping Beauty and Mary Poppins (but NOT Cinderella). Breakfast $30 adults, $18 children; lunch $31 and $19; dinner $36 and $21. Credit card needed to book, $10/person charged for no-shows.

DISNEY'S HOLLYWOOD STUDIOS: Hollywood & Vine for breakfast or lunch with the Playhouse Disney Pals, including JoJo and Goliath from JoJo's Circus and June and Leo from Little Einsteins.

DISNEY'S ANIMAL KINGDOM: Donald's Safari Breakfast at Tusker House with Donald, Goofy, Pluto and sometimes Mickey.

DISNEY RESORTS: Chef Mickey's at *Contemporary Resort*; breakfast or dinner with Mickey, Minnie, Goofy, Pluto, Chip and Dale – peak times book up quickly; **1900 Park Fare** at *Grand Floridian*; breakfast with Alice, Mary Poppins and Mad Hatter; dinner with Cinderella, Anastasia, Drizella, Lady Tremaine and, sometimes, Prince Charming – again, book early; **Wonderland Tea Party** at *Grand Floridian*; 1.30–2.30pm Mon-Fri, 4-12s only, $28.17, lunch, activities and storytelling with Alice and friends ($10 no-show); **Perfectly Princess Tea Party** with Princess Aurora at *Grand Floridian*; 10.30am–12pm, ages 3–11 with an adult, $250 for 1 adult and 1 child. Lunch (tea, cake, finger sandwiches), singalong, story time, My Disney Girl doll, bracelet, tiara, scrapbook page, and Best Friend certificate. **'Ohana** at *Polynesian Resort*; breakfast with Lilo, Stitch, Pluto and Mickey; **Cape May Café** at *Beach Club Resort*; breakfast with Goofy, Minnie and Donald; **Mickey's Backyard Barbecue** at *Fort Wilderness*; $44.99 and $26.99, games, storytelling, live entertainment, music and dancing with Mickey, Minnie and Co; chicken, hot dogs, ribs, beer, wine, iced tea and lemonade (6.30pm, Mar–Dec); **Garden Grove Café** at W*alt Disney World Swan*; Sat and Sun breakfast with Goofy and Pluto; dinner nightly with Timon and Rafiki or Goofy and Pluto.

Child Swap. This means Mum can ride while Dad looks after junior in a quiet area and, on her return, Dad can have his go. At some attractions you may be given a Child Swap ticket while you wait.

Park security

All visitors with bags are required to go through a security bag-check before reaching the turnstiles at all parks. This is a fairly cursory (but compulsory) inspection and there is a separate lane for those without bags. When you put your ticket through the turnstile, you are also required to give a finger scan (which stops others from using your ticket).

Jungle Cruise

© Disney

Magic Kingdom Park

The starting point for any visit has to be the *Magic Kingdom*, the park that best embodies the genuine enchantment Disney bestows on its visitors. It's the original development that sparked the Orlando tourist boom in 1971. In comparative terms, the *Magic Kingdom* is similar to the *Disneyland Park* at *Disneyland Resort Paris®* and *Disneyland California*. Outside those, it has no equal as a captivating day out for all the family. However, although superficially some rides are the same as those in Paris or Los Angeles, there are key differences, notably on Pirates of the Caribbean, Big Thunder Mountain Railroad and Haunted Mansion. And Space Mountain is a completely different ride from the one in Paris. And, even if a couple of attractions are closed for refurbishment, you won't be short of things to do! We will now attempt to steer you through a typical day at the park, with a guide to the main rides, shows and places to eat; how to park, how to avoid the worst of the crowds and how much you should expect to pay. The *Magic Kingdom* takes up just 107 acres/43ha of Disney's near 31,000 acres/12,555ha but attracts almost as many visitors as the rest put together. It has 6 separate 'lands', like slices of a cake, centred on Florida's most famous landmark, Cinderella Castle. More than 40 attractions are packed into the park, not to mention numerous shops and restaurants (though the eating opportunities are less impressive than in *Epcot* and *Disney's Hollywood Studios*). It's easy to get overwhelmed by it all, especially as it gets so busy (even the fast-food restaurants have big queues in high season), so plan around what most takes your fancy.

Magic Kingdom Park at a glance

Location	Off World Drive, Walt Disney World
Size	107 acres/43ha in 6 'lands'
Hours	9am–7pm off peak; 9am–10pm President's Day (see BritTip, page 19), spring school holidays; 9am–11pm high season (Easter, summer holidays, Thanksgiving and Christmas)
Admission	Under-3s free; 3–9 $74 (1-day base ticket), $322 (5-day Premium), $332 (7-day Premium); adult (10+) $82, $345, $355. Prices do not include tax.
Parking	$14
Lockers	Next to stroller and wheelchair hire $12 small; $14 large ($5 deposit)
Pushchairs	$15 and $31 (Stroller Shop to right of main entrance); length-of-stay, $13 per day single, $27 per day double
Wheelchairs	$12 or $70 ($20 deposit refunded) at Main Ticket Centre
Top attractions	Splash Mountain, Space Mountain, Mickey's PhilharMagic, Big Thunder Mountain Railroad, Pirates of the Caribbean, most rides in Fantasyland
Don't miss	Celebrate A Dream Come True Parade, Main Street Electrical Parade or SpectroMagic (certain nights) and Wishes fireworks (most nights)
Hidden costs	**Meals** Burger, chips and coke $8.78 3-course dinner (Tony's Town Square) $26.99–44.47 Kids' counter service meal $4.99 **T-shirts** $14.95-34.95 **Souvenirs** $1-25,000 **Sundries** Chalk colour portraits $17.95-35.95, or silhouettes $8, with oval frame $15.95

Location

The *Magic Kingdom* is situated at the innermost end of *Walt Disney World*, with its entrance Toll Plaza ¾ of the way along World Drive, the main entrance off Highway 192. World Drive runs north–south, while the Interstate 4 (I-4) entrance, Epcot Drive, runs east–west. Unless you are staying at a Disney resort, you must pay the $14 parking fee at the Toll Plaza to bring you into the massive car park.

BRIT TIP

For the smoothest entry by road from Highway 192, take Seralago Boulevard opposite the Seralago Hotel & Suites next to Old Town, turn left on to a non-toll stretch of Osceola Parkway and follow the signs to your chosen park. On West 192, turn off on Sherberth Road, go north to the first traffic lights and turn right, then pick up the Disney signs.

The majority arrive between 9.30 and 11.30am, so the car parks are busiest then, which is another good reason to get here EARLY. If you can't make it by 9am during peak periods, you might want to wait until after 1pm, or even later when the park is open as late as 11pm. Remember to note exactly where you park, e.g. Mickey, Row 30; otherwise you'll be struggling, because many hire cars look the same!

A motorised tram takes you from the car park to the Transportation and Ticket Center at the heart of the operation. Unless you already have your ticket (which will save you valuable time), you have to queue up at the ticket booths. From here, the monorail or ferryboat will bring you to the doorstep of the *Magic Kingdom* itself. The monorail (straight ahead) is quicker if there isn't a queue, otherwise bear left and take a slower ferryboat. If you are staying at a Disney hotel, the resort buses deliver you almost to the park's front door (or the monorail or boat will if you are staying at one of the *Magic Kingdom* resorts). Finally, the *Magic Kingdom* is the only 'dry' park – that is, there's NO alcohol on sale.

BRIT TIP

An easy way to remember where you parked is to take a picture of the Section and Row number on your digital camera or phone. Then simply delete it when you get back to your car.

Main Street USA

Right, we've finally reached the park itself… but not quite. Hopefully, you've arrived early and are among the leading hordes aiming to swarm through the main entrance. The published opening time may say 9am, but the gates can open up to 45 minutes earlier.

This is the first of the 7 'lands' and, at opening time, there is an informal Welcome Parade, with costumed singers and dancers, and the Character Train then arrives at Main Street Station to bring a variety of characters for a meet and greet in Town Square (get those autograph books ready!). A family is then chosen at random to sprinkle some 'pixie dust' to open the park officially for the day. Immediately on your right is **Exposition Hall**, the temporary meet-and-greet location for the pixies and princesses formerly holding court in Toontown. On your left is **City Hall**, where you can pick up a park map and daily schedule (if you haven't been given them at the Toll Plaza) and make bookings for restaurants (highly advisable at peak periods). You can also find out where and when the characters will appear. Ahead of you is **Town Square**, where you can

Main Street USA

© Disney

ADVENTURELAND

1 Swiss Family Treehouse
2 Jungle Cruise
3 Magic Carpets of Aladdin
4 The Enchanted Tiki Room (under new management)
5 Pirates of the Caribbean

FRONTIERLAND

6 Splash Mountain
7 Big Thunder Mountain Railroad
8 Country Bear Jamboree
9 Raft to Tom Sawyer Island

LIBERTY SQUARE

10 Liberty Tree Tavern
11 Liberty Square Riverboat
12 The Haunted Mansion
13 The Hall of Presidents

FANTASYLAND

14 'it's a small world'
15 Prince Charming Regal Carrousel
16 Mad Tea Party
17 The Many Adventures of Winnie The Pooh
18 Snow White's Scary Adventures
19 Dumbo The Flying Elephant
20 Mickey's PhilharMagic
21 Peter Pan's Flight
22 Castle Forecourt Stage
23 Cinderella's Royal Table
24 Fairytale Garden (Storytime with Belle)

MICKEY'S TOONTOWN FAIR (Closing 2010–11)

25 Mickey's Country House
26 Minnie's Country House
27 Toontown Hall of Fame
28 The Barnstormer at Goofy's Wiseacre Farm
29 Donald's Boat

TOMORROWLAND

30 Space Mountain
31 Tomorrowland Indy Speedway
32 Tomorrowland Transit Authority
33 Walt Disney's Carousel of Progress
34 Astro Orbiter
35 Stitch's Great Escape!
36 Buzz Lightyear's Space Ranger Spin
37 Monsters Inc. Laugh Floor
38 Galaxy Palace Theater
39 Club 626 Dance Party

TRANSPORT

40 Walt Disney World Railroad
41 Boat Dock
42 Monorail Station
43 Bus Station

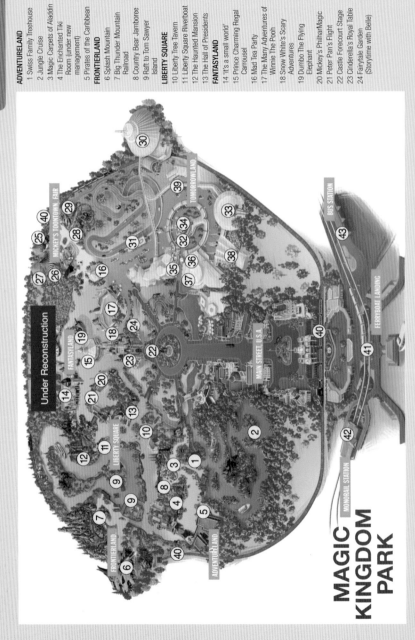

Under Reconstruction

MAGIC
KINGDOM
PARK

take a 1-way ride on a horse-drawn bus or fire engine, or visit the **Car Barn** mini museum. The Street itself houses the park's best shopping (check out the massive Emporium), and the **Walt Disney World Railroad** (AAA), a Western-themed steam train that circles the park and is one of the better attractions when queues are long elsewhere (though Town Square station is often the busiest).

Dining: The Italian-style **Tony's Town Square Restaurant** serves lunch and dinner, **The Plaza Restaurant** offers salads and sandwiches (lunch and dinner), and **The Crystal Palace** (breakfast $24.99 adult, $13.99 ages 3–9; lunch $26.99 and $14.99; dinner $36.99 and $17.99) is buffet-style food with Winnie the Pooh and Co. Quick bites can be bought from **Casey's Corner** (hot dogs, chips and soft drinks), **Main Street Bakery** (coffee and pastries), **Main Street Cinema** and **Main Street Confectionery** (chocolate and sweets) and the **Plaza Ice Cream Parlor**. Disney characters also appear periodically throughout the Square.

Look out for the **Guest Information Board** at the top of Main Street (on the left) as it gives waiting times for all the attractions. The Baby Center (for nursing mothers) is also at the top of Main Street, to the left next to Crystal Palace, along with the park's **First Aid** station.

BRIT TIP

Can't find Mickey and Co? This is often one of the main laments of those who arrive unprepared. Check in at City Hall and they can tell you where all the characters can be found. In fact, City Hall is your best friend for a variety of queries, from the location of baby facilities to meal bookings (but there are NO baby facilities at City Hall). Character meet-and-greets are also shown on all park maps with a 'Mickey glove' icon.

Unless you are a late arrival, give Main Street no more than a passing glance and head for the end of the street to the real entrance to the park. This is where you await the official

opening hour for the famous **'Rope Drop'**, and you should adopt 1 of 3 tactics here, each aimed at doing some of the most popular rides before the queues become substantial (wait times of 2 hours for Splash Mountain are not unknown). 1: If you fancy the 5-star, log-flume ride Splash Mountain, keep left in front of the Crystal Palace with the majority of the crowd, who will head for the same place. 2: If you have young children who can't wait to have a ride on Cinderella's Golden Carrousel or the other Fantasyland rides, stay in the middle and pass around the Castle. 3: If the thrills of indoor roller-coaster Space Mountain appeal first, move to the right by The Plaza Restaurant and you'll get straight into Tomorrowland. Now you'll be in pole position for the initial rush (and it will be a rush; take care with children).

BRIT TIP

The **Move It! Shake It! Celebrate It! Street Party** begins in Town Square, but the real action takes place around the Hub. Stake out a spot well in advance if you want an up-front view.

Other entertainment: Watch out for the **Move It! Shake It! Celebrate It! Street Party** up to 3 times daily, from Town Square, along Main Street, ending up in the Hub area as Disney characters, stilt walkers and energetic dancers lead guests in a high-energy interactive street party. The fun barbershop quartet the **Dapper Dans** and brass band **Main Street Philharmonic** add more lively musical interludes throughout the day.

Mad Hatter's Tea Cups

© Disney

Adventureland

If you head to the left (effectively going clockwise around the park), you will enter Adventureland. If you're going to Splash Mountain first, you pass the Swiss Family Treehouse on your left and bear right through an archway (with toilets on your right) into Frontierland, where you turn left and Splash Mountain is right in front of you. However, stopping in Adventureland, these are the attractions.

Swiss Family Treehouse: This imitation banyan tree is a clever replica of the treehouse from Disney's 1960 film *Swiss Family Robinson*. It's a walk-through attraction where the queues (rarely long) move steadily if not quickly, providing a fascinating glimpse of the ultimate treehouse, complete with kitchen, rope bridges and running water! AA.

Jungle Cruise: It's not so much the scenic, geographically suspect boat ride (where the Nile suddenly becomes the Amazon) that is so amusing here as the patter of your boat's captain, who spins a non-stop yarn about your adventure that features wild animals, tropical plants, hidden temples and sudden waterfalls. Great detail but long queues, so visit either early morning (opens 10am) or late afternoon (evening queues are shortest, but you'll miss some of the detail in the dark). AAAA (FP).

Magic Carpets of Aladdin

BRIT TIP
Look for the special deal on autograph book and fat pen combo, which can be cheaper than purchasing them separately.

Pirates of the Caribbean: One of Disney's most impressive attractions that involves its pioneering work in audio-animatronics, life-size figures that move, talk and, in this instance, lay siege to a Caribbean island! Your 8-minute underground boat ride takes you through a typical pirate adventure and into the world of Captain Jack Sparrow and his nemesis Captain Barbossa as they search for buried treasure. It's terrific family fun (though perhaps a bit spooky for young children, with one small drop in the dark) and the 2006 addition of the *Pirates of the Caribbean* film characters and some new special effects means this is again highly popular. Queues are longest from late morning to mid-afternoon. AAAAA.

The Enchanted Tiki Room: A bird-laden, audio-animatronics show, Iago (from *Aladdin*) and Zazu (from *The Lion King*) lead a colourful 16-minute revue that will especially appeal to younger children. Queues are rare (and it is air-conditioned!). AAA.

Magic Carpets of Aladdin: Here, in an Agrabah-themed area, this ride spins you up, down and around as you try to dodge the spitting camel! Your 'flying carpet' tilts as well as levitates, but it is basically simple stuff geared for younger children (virtually identical to the Magic Carpets of Agrabah in the *Walt Disney Studios* in *Disneyland® Resort Paris*). TT (TTTT under-5s).

Shrunken Ned's Junior Jungle Boats: This costs an extra $2 for kids to try their hand at steering rather tame toy boats. T.

Other entertainment: Outside the Pirates of the Caribbean ride (and a must for young swashbucklers), **Captain Jack Sparrow's Pirate Tutorial** runs up to 7 times daily. Captain Jack and his sidekick Mack invite youngsters to join them in sword fights and treasure hunting, ending with the Pirate Oath as children become honorary buccaneers. **Disney characters** also turn up near Pirates of the Caribbean and Magic Carpets rides and on the Adventureland Veranda. Ariel the Little Mermaid will also make this her temporary home while *Fantasyland* is being refurbished.

Shopping and dining: The best shopping is in the **Pirates Bazaar**. Here, the **Pirates League** (9am–4pm) offers a macho version of the Bibbidi Bobbidi Boutique that lets young swashbucklers transform into fully fledged pirates. Choose from 2 packages ($29.95): *First Mate* includes face painting, an official pirate name, participation in Adventureland Pirate Parade and swearing of the official Pirate Oath; the *Empress Package* is the same but with 'shimmering' face paint and nail polish. Accessories, including bandanas, earrings, eye patches, swords, removable teeth (!), coin necklaces, temporary tattoo and photos, are sold separately. For food, you have **Aloha Isle** (yoghurt and ice-cream), **Sunshine Tree Terrace** (fruit, snacks, yoghurt, tea and coffee), and the more substantial tacos, empanadas and taco salads of **El Pirata y el Perico Restaurante**.

Frontierland
This Western- themed area is one of the busiest and is best avoided from late morning to late afternoon.

Splash Mountain: Based on the 1946 classic Disney cartoon *Song of the South*, this is a watery journey into the world of Brer Rabbit, Brer Fox and Brer Bear. The first part is all jolly cartoon scenery and fun with the main characters and a couple of minor swoops in your 8-passenger log boat. The conclusion, a 5-storey plummet at 45° into a mist-shrouded pool, seems like you are falling off the edge of the world! A huge adrenalin rush, but busy almost all day (try it first thing or during one of the parades to avoid the longest queues). You also get VERY wet! Restrictions: 3ft 4in/101cm. TTTTT (FP).

Big Thunder Mountain Railroad: When Disney does a roller-coaster it will be one of the classiest, and here it is – a runaway mine train that swoops, tilts and plunges through a mock abandoned mine filled with clever scenery. You have to ride it at least twice to appreciate all the detail, but again queues are heavy, so go first thing (after Splash Mountain) or late in the day. Restrictions: 3ft 4in/101cm. TTTT (FP).

Country Bear Jamboree: Now here's a novelty: a 16-minute musical revue presented by audio-animatronic bears! It's great family fun with plenty of novel touches (watch for the talking moose head). Crowds are rare here, so it's a good one when it's busy elsewhere. AAA.

Frontierland Shootin' Arcade: The other of the two attractions in the park that cost extra ($1 for 35 shots), as you take aim at a series of animated targets. TT.

Tom Sawyer Island: Take a raft over to an overgrown playground of mysterious caves, grottos and mazes, rope bridges and Fort Sam Clemens, where you can fire air guns at passing boats (opens 10am). A good getaway in the early afternoon when the crowds are at their biggest, while **Aunt Polly's Dockside Inn** is a refuge within a refuge for snacks and drinks. TT.

Big Thunder Mountain

© Disney

Other entertainment: Musical interludes are provided by the comic trio of The **Notorious Banjo Brothers and Bob**, and the **Frontierland Hoedown**, with the **Country Bears**.

Shopping and dining: Frontierland shops sell cowboy hats, guns and badges as well as Native American and Mexican crafts. Look out for the nicely themed **Briar Patch** and **Prairie Outpost** for interesting gifts. For food, try **Pecos Bill Tall Tale Inn & Café** (salads, sandwiches and burgers), **Golden Oak Outpost** (chicken nuggets, chicken flatbread, fries and drinks) or **Turkey Leg Cart** (massive, smoke-grilled turkey legs).

Liberty Square

Continuing the clockwise tour brings you next to a homage to post-independence America. A lot of the historical content will go over the heads of British visitors, but it still has some great attractions.

Liberty Square Riverboat: Cruise America's 'rivers' on an authentic paddle steamer, be menaced by Native Americans and thrill to the stories of How the West Was Won (opens 10am). This is also a good ride at the busiest times of the day, especially early afternoon. AAA.

The Haunted Mansion: A clever delve into the world of Master Gracey's ghostly bride that is neither too scary for most kids nor too twee for adults. Not so much a thrill ride as a scenic adventure. Watch out for the fun touch at the end when your car picks up an extra 'passenger'. Longish queues for much of the day, however, so try to visit late on. AAAA (TTTT under-6s).

The Hall of Presidents: This is the attraction likely to mean least to us, a 2-part show that is first a film about the Constitution and then an audio-animatronic parade of all 44 US presidents (opens 10am). Technically it's impressive, especially with the new President Obama, but it may bore young 'uns (though it is air-conditioned). AAA.

Shopping and dining: Shopping here includes **Ye Olde Christmas Shoppe** and **The Yankee Trader**; eating options are the full-service **Liberty Tree Tavern** (hearty soups, steaks and traditional dishes like meatloaf and pot roast, plus dinner with Mickey and Co), **Columbia Harbor House** (counter-service fried chicken or fish and some excellent soups, salads and sandwiches, notably for vegetarians) and **Sleepy Hollow** (a picnic area serving snacks, fruit and drinks).

Fantasyland

Leaving Liberty Square, you walk past Cinderella Castle and come into the park's spiritual heart, the area with which young children are most enchanted. The attractions are designed with kids in mind, but the shops are pretty sophisticated.

BRIT TIP

Get more value for your money at the parks by ordering sodas 'without ice' to get a full cup.

'It's a Small World': This could almost be Disney's theme ride, a family boat trip through the different continents, each represented by hundreds of dancing, singing audio-animatronic dolls in delightful set-piece pageants. If it sounds twee, it actually creates a surprisingly striking effect, accompanied by an annoyingly catchy theme song that young children adore. Crowds peak in early afternoon. AAAA.

Hall of Presidents

© Disney

Simon and Susan say…

The entire Fantasyland area is undergoing an extensive refurbishment due to be complete in 2012, and some attractions could be closed temporarily or moved to a new location. The current confusion will lead to a greatly expanded Fantasyland, eventually encompassing all of Toontown, but for now, expect a lot of boarding and the possibility of closed attractions.

Prince Charming's Regal Carrousel: The Fantasyland centrepiece shouldn't need any more explanation other than it is a vintage carousel that kids love. Long queues for much of the day, though. T (TTT under-5s).

Mad Tea Party: The kids will insist you take them in these spinning, oversized tea cups that have their own 'steering wheel' to add to the whirling effect. Actually, they're just a heavily disguised fairground ride. Again, go early or expect crowds. Characters from *Alice in Wonderland* also visit periodically. TT (TTTT under-5s).

The Many Adventures of Winnie the Pooh: Building on the timeless popularity of Pooh, Piglet and Co, this family ride offers a musical jaunt through Hundred Acre Wood with some clever effects (get ready to 'bounce' with Tigger!) and another original soundtrack. AAA (AAAAA under-5s) (FP).

Snow White's Scary Adventures: This lively indoor ride tells the cartoon story of Snow White with a few ghost train effects that may scare young children. Good fun, though, for parents and kids. Again, you need to go early or late (or during the main parade) to beat the queues. TTT (TTTTT under-5s).

Dumbo the Flying Elephant: Parents hate it but kids love it and all want to do this 2-minute ride on the back of a flying elephant that swoops in best Dumbo style (even if the ears don't flap). Ride early or expect a long queue. TT (TTTT under-5s).

Mickey's PhilharMagic: This utterly fun-tastic 10-minute 3-D film show has a host of in-theatre special effects as Donald tries to conduct the Enchanted Orchestra – to comic effect. It features a 150ft/46m wide screen to immerse guests in the 3-D world of *Beauty and the Beast*, *The Little Mermaid*, *The Lion King*, *Peter Pan* and *Aladdin*, with hapless Donald surviving a string of adventures before Mickey brings him back to earth. The lavish theatre, artistic new animation, special effects (you can 'smell' the food!) and all-round family entertainment add up to one of the most enjoyable attractions. There is no scare factor here (though the sudden plunge into darkness at one point and noise of the 'orchestra' can spook young children), while you'll be enchanted when Tinker Bell seems to fly out of the screen in front of you. AAAAA (FP).

'it's a small world'

Peter Pan's Flight: Don't be fooled by the long queues; this is a rather tame ride, though still a big hit with kids. Its novel effect of flying with Peter Pan quickly wears off, but there's a lot of clever detail as your ship sails over London to Neverland. AA (AAAAA under-6s; FP).

Other entertainment: The superb **Dream Along With Mickey** show is staged up to 6 times a day on the Castle Forecourt Stage, a 20-minute fantasy featuring Donald, Mickey, Minnie, Goofy and various Princesses and their Princes. Peter Pan and Wendy join the battle against the evil Maleficent and Captain Hook to help Donald remember the power of believing in your dreams (AAA). The **Fantasyland Woodwind Society** plays up to 5 times daily, while the **Fairy Godmother at Cinderella's Fountain Meet and Greet** happens twice a day. Another worthwhile character experience is **Storytime with Belle** in the Fairytale Garden, on the corner of the Castle facing Tomorrowland.

Shopping and dining: Shop at **Tinker Bell's Treasures** and **Castle Couture**, the excellent **Sir Mickey's**, **Fantasy Faire** and **Pooh's Thotful Shop**. There is also an outlet of the **Bibbidi Bobbidi Boutique** here (the other is in *Downtown Disney*), where 'little princesses' who are over 3 can choose from 3 makeover packages ($49.95-239.95), and three different hairstyles – the Disney Diva, Pop Princess or Fairytale Princess. The salon is open 9am–7pm. Eating opportunities are at **The Pinocchio Village Haus** (pizza,

Bibbidi Bobbidi Boutique

© Disney

chicken nuggets and salads), the **Enchanted Grove** (iced drinks and juices), **Friar's Nook** (hot dogs, French fries, carrot cake, apple dippers and drinks), and **Mrs Potts' Cupboard** (for ice-creams and sundaes). **Cinderella's Royal Table** is a fine setting for the hugely popular character breakfast and lunch (dinner is also served, but with the Fairy Godmother only). The majestic hall, waitresses in costume and well-presented food – salads, seafood, roast beef, prime rib and chicken – provide a memorable experience. It's pricey, though ($164 for a family of 4 for breakfast; $172 for lunch and a massive $192 for dinner).

Mickey's Toontown Fair

In the top corner of Fantasyland (just past the Mad Tea Party) is the shrub-lined entrance to **Mickey's Toontown Fair** (opens 10am). It is easy to miss, but it does have a station on the railroad. Its primary appeal is to young children as they can meet their favourite characters. Exceptionally kid-friendly and well landscaped, there is also the **Toon Park** playground to give youngsters the chance to let off some steam.

Mickey's Country House: Here is a walk-through opportunity to see Mickey at home and have your picture taken with him in the Judge's Tent. AAA (plus TTTTT for the photo opportunity!).

Minnie's Country House: This is a chance to view Minnie's home and unique memorabilia, all designed in a country and western style. AAA.

Toontown Hall of Fame: Meet the Disney Princesses and the Disney Fairies in their own magical settings.

TTTTT. *(Note: relocating to Exposition Hall in Town Square, Main Street USA, late in 2010.)*

The Barnstormer at Goofy's Wiseacre Farm: A mini roller-coaster just for the young 'uns, its masterful design features a swoop right through the barn itself (though it is a pretty short ride after the slow-moving queue). Restrictions: 3ft/91cm. TTT (TTTTT 4–8s).

Donald's Boat: Parents beware, youngsters get seriously wet here! If you've seen the pavement fountains at *Epcot*, prepare for more watery delights as this boat-themed playground spouts off in all sorts of wonderful ways. Ideally, bring a change of clothes or swimsuit for kids. It's also a great place to revitalise tired or irritable children. AAAA under-10s.

Shopping and dining: The huge merchandise area of **County Bounty** will test your wallet; **Toontown Farmers Market** offers fruit, snacks and drinks.

Tomorrowland
The last of the 'lands', this has a cartoon-like space-age appearance that has guaranteed appeal for youngsters, while it also boasts some original shops.

Space Mountain: After a 2010 lighting and special effects refurbishment, Space Mountain is even more atmospheric (and darker!) than before. One of the 3 most popular attractions in the park, its reputation is deserved. Launching from Starport 75, this is a high-thrills, tight-turning roller-coaster, completely in the dark save for occasional flashes as you whiz through the galaxy. Don't do this on a full stomach! The only way to beat the crowds is to go either first thing, late in the day or during one of the parades (or, of course, get a FastPass). Ride photos are available for $18.95 (8x10) up to $32.95. Restrictions: 3ft 8in/111cm. TTTTT (FP). Children are also likely to gravitate towards the **Tomorrowland Arcade** as you exit.

Tomorrowland Indy Speedway: Despite the long queues, this is a rather tame ride on supposed race tracks that just putt-putts along on rails with little real steering required (children must be 4ft 4in/132cm to drive alone). T (TTTT under-6s).

Astro Orbiter: A jazzed-up version of Dumbo in Fantasyland, this ride is a bit faster and higher and features rockets. Large, slow-moving queues are another reason to give this a miss unless you have young children. TT (TTTT under-10s).

Walt Disney's Carousel of Progress: This will surprise, entertain and amuse. It is a journey through 20th-century technology with audio-animatronics in a revolving theatre that reveals different periods in history. Its 22-minute duration is rarely threatened by crowds (open only at peak periods). AAA.

Tomorrowland Transit Authority: A neat 'future transport system', this offers an elevated view of the area, including a glimpse inside Space Mountain, in electro-magnetic cars. Queues are usually short. AAA (TTT under-8s).

Stitch's Great Escape!: This 15-minute experience receives mixed reviews – some like it for the audio-animatronic prequel to Disney's *Lilo & Stitch*, with visitors being recruited into the madcap Galactic Federation prison service (where things go hilariously wrong as Stitch arrives and proceeds to cause havoc), while others find it rather puzzling and, ultimately,

Stitch's Great Escape!

© Disney

surprisingly lame. Young children can also be scared by the complete darkness at times. There are 2 pre-show areas before recruits are ushered into the sit-down chamber (with shoulder restraints) where Stitch is let loose to bounce, dribble and even belch over the unwary audience. Restrictions: 3ft 2in/101cm. AA (FP).

Buzz Lightyear's Space Ranger Spin: Kids won't want to miss joining the great *Toy Story* character in his battle against evil Emperor Zurg. Ride into action against the robot army – and shoot them with laser cannons! A sure-fire family winner, especially as you get to keep score. TTT (TTTTT under-8s) (FP).

Monsters Inc Laugh Floor: This innovative show is based on the hit Pixar film *Monsters Inc*. With 'live' animation, special effects and high-tech voice links, guests can meet and match wits with the likes of Mike, Sulley and Roz and be entertained by their patter and amusing antics. Billy Boil opens the show, introducing various comedians (including 2-headed jokester Sam-n-Ella), with the objective of capturing the audience's laughter. Guest interaction is an integral part of the show. Watch the screen – you may be featured! AAA.

Other entertainment: Stitch fans should enjoy the new **Club 626 Dance Party** (evenings in high season), a chance to bop along with a live VJ and various Disney characters, led by the mischievous alien. Live music with school bands is featured at **The Galaxy Palace Theater** periodically, while **PUSH, the Talking Trashcan**

Buzz Lightyear's Space Ranger Spin

© Disney

makes hilarious regular appearances. **Disney characters** are often on hand by the Galaxy Palace Theater and Carousel of Progress.

Shopping and dining: Shopping highlights are provided by **Mickey's Star Traders** and **Merchant of Venus**. For food, try the amusing **Cosmic Ray's Starlight Café** (burgers, chicken, pasta, soups and salads), the **Plaza Pavilion** (pizza, subs and salads), **Auntie Gravity's Galactic Goodies** (ice-cream and juices), the **Lunching Pad** (smoked turkey legs, snacks and drinks) or **Tomorrowland Terrace Noodle Station** (a healthier line-up of Asian stir-fry, soup and vegetarian dishes; open seasonally).

Having come full circle, you are now back at Main Street USA and it's best to return here in early afternoon to avoid the crowds and have a closer look at the impressive array of shops.

Disney Parades

If there is one thing Disney knows how to do well, it's a parade. Coupled with its range of special seasonal events, there is always much more to look forward to than just the rides.

BRIT TIP
To watch a parade, sit on the left side of Main Street USA (facing the Castle) to stay in the shade if it's hot. People start staking out the best spots an HOUR in advance.

Celebrate A Dream Come True Parade: This truly enchanting multi-float presentation featuring all the favourite characters is the daily highlight. With clever themes, lively music and non-stop (and hard-working!) dancers, the parade halts at regular intervals to reveal some eye-catching special effects. Mickey, Minnie and a host of Disney Princesses all make an appearance, plus some of the classic villains, and it is sure to captivate the whole family (though it is especially popular with children). At Easter and Christmas, the parade takes on seasonal charm with appearances by the Easter Bunny and Father Christmas. AAAAA.

MAGIC KINGDOM PARK with children

Here is a rough guide to the attractions that appeal to different age groups (height restrictions have been taken into account):

Under-5s

Buzz Lightyear's Space Ranger Spin, Cinderella's Golden Carrousel, Country Bear Jamboree, Donald's Boat, Dream Along With Mickey, Dumbo the Flying Elephant, The Enchanted Tiki Room, 'It's a Small World', Jungle Cruise, Liberty Square Riverboat, Main Street Vehicles, Many Adventures of Winnie the Pooh, Mickey's Country House, Mickey's PhilharMagic, Monsters Inc Laugh Floor, Move It! Shake It! Celebrate It! Street Party, Peter Pan's Flight, Tomorrowland Indy Speedway (with a parent), Tomorrowland Transit Authority, Walt Disney World Railroad, Main Street Electrical Parade.

5–8s

Astro Orbiter, The Barnstormer at Goofy's Wiseacre Farm, Big Thunder Mountain Railroad, Buzz Lightyear's Space Ranger Spin, Country Bear Jamboree, Donald's Boat, Dream Along With Mickey, The Enchanted Tiki Room, Haunted Mansion, Jungle Cruise, Liberty Square Riverboat, Mad Tea Party, Magic Carpets of Aladdin, Many Adventures of Winnie the Pooh, Mickey's Country House, Mickey's PhilharMagic, Monsters Inc Laugh Floor, Move It! Shake It! Celebrate It! Street Party, Pirates of the Caribbean, Snow White's Scary Adventures, Space Mountain (with parental discretion), Splash Mountain, Stitch's Great Escape!, Swiss Family Treehouse, Tom Sawyer Island, Tomorrowland Indy Speedway (with a parent), Tomorrowland Transit Authority, Walt Disney World Railroad, Walt Disney's Carousel of Progress, Main Street Electrical Parade.

9–12s

Astro Orbiter, The Barnstormer at Goofy's Wiseacre Farm, Big Thunder Mountain Railroad, Buzz Lightyear's Space Ranger Spin, Country Bear Jamboree, The Haunted Mansion, Mad Tea Party, Mickey's PhilharMagic, Monsters Inc. Laugh Floor, Move It! Shake It! Celebrate It! Street Party, Pirates of the Caribbean, Space Mountain, Splash Mountain, Stitch's Great Escape!, Tomorrowland Indy Speedway (without a parent), Main Street Electrical Parade.

Over–12s

Astro Orbiter, Big Thunder Mountain Railroad, Buzz Lightyear's Space Ranger Spin, Haunted Mansion, Mad Tea Party, Mickey's PhilharMagic, Move It! Shake It! Celebrate It! Street Party, Pirates of the Caribbean, Space Mountain, Splash Mountain, Stitch's Great Escape!, Main Street Electrical Parade.

Move It! Shake It! Celebrate It! Street Party: Up to 3 times daily, with 5 floats featuring Mickey and Friends, characters from *Aladdin, Beauty and the Beast, Toy Story, The Little Mermaid* and *The Incredibles*. Heavy on guest participation, it's a song and dance fest around the Hub that will have you moving, shaking and celebrating!

Main Street Electrical Parade/ SpectroMagic: These 2 sparkling night-time parades alternated in 2010 and it wasn't clear if both would see time in 2011. SpectroMagic is a mind-boggling light and sound festival full of glitter and razzamatazz, with the Disney characters at the centre of

a multitude of sparkling lights and fibre-optic effect floats. The much-loved – and original – Main Street

SpectroMagic parade

© Disney

Electrical Parade replaced Spectro during the *Summer Nightastic!* programme from June to mid-August. It is classic Disney at its best, spruced up with the latest technology to enhance the heart-tugging impact of this cavalcade of sparkling lights. Tinker Bell leads the procession, with each successive float a visual and audio treat, with the music a real highlight. Truly a must-see ending to your Magic Kingdom day. When the park is open late (during peak periods and weekends), there are 2 showings per night, and the second is usually less crowded. AAAAA.

> **BRIT TIP**
> Main Street USA closes 30 minutes after the rest of the park, so you can avoid the inevitable mad rush for the car parks by lingering here to shop or enjoy an ice-cream.

Wishes: Most nights also finish with this stunning fireworks show over the Castle. With a clever soundtrack narrated by Jiminy Cricket and featuring memorable moments from various Disney classics, it is magnificently choreographed and culminates in a sequence of pyrotechnic explosions (many designed especially for this show), which truly dazzle the eyes. Starting with an appearance by Tinker Bell

(from the Castle's top turret), it continues for 12 minutes of typical Disney emotional appeal; the perfect pixie-dust farewell to a memorable day. In 2010, Wishes was replaced by **Summer Nightastic!** for a 10-week season, featuring an enhanced new fireworks show, and it seems likely this will happen again in 2011. AAAAA.

Wishes Cruises: If you prefer not to fight the crowds for a fabulous view of Wishes, book one of 3 speciality cruises to view the fireworks from Seven Seas Lagoon. The *Basic Cruise* holds up to 8 guests onboard a 21ft pontoon boat and costs $266 (includes water, soft drinks and snacks); the *Premium Cruise* holds up to 10 on a 25ft pontoon boat (for $319), including water, soft drinks, snacks and an audio feed to the Wishes music; or splash out for the *Celebration Cruise*, which adds special occasion decorations to the Basic Cruise for a total of $291 and the Premium Cruise for $344. All can be booked 90 days in advance.

> **BRIT TIP**
> After the fireworks crowd exits, you are often allowed to take the Resort Only monorail back to the Transportation & Ticket Center, rather than queue for the main monorail.

Wishes

© Disney

Pirate and Pals Fireworks Voyage:
This kid-friendly Wishes cruise includes meeting Mr Smee and Captain Hook before cruising the Seven Seas Lagoon for a viewing of the Electrical Water Pageant and Wishes fireworks. Snacks and drinks are provided while you enjoy a retelling of the Peter Pan story, then meet Pan himself at the end of your voyage ($53.99/adult, $30.99/3–9; can be booked 180 days in advance).

When it comes to leaving, the monorail is quicker than the ferry but it can still take up to an hour to get back to your car. Also, if the crowds get too heavy during the day, you can escape by leaving in the early afternoon (your car park ticket is valid all day) and returning to your hotel for a few hours' rest or a dip in the pool. Alternatively, catch a boat to one of the Disney resorts. *Fort Wilderness* is especially fun for kids and boasts the great value **Trails End Buffet** for lunch or dinner.

Halloween & Christmas
Two additional annual events in the *Magic Kingdom* provide a separate, party-style ticketed event 7pm–midnight, with most of the rides open and extra themed fun and games.

Mickey's Not So Scary Halloween Party: Sept–Oct sees many visitors dress up for the typical American trick-or-treat fun, with plenty of treats for youngsters along the way. With special music, storytelling, parades and the HalloWishes fireworks (plus some wonderful lighting effects), tickets go on sale about 5 months in advance and sell out quickly.

Mickey's Very Merry Christmas Party: The Christmas party (Nov–Dec) sees 'snow' on Main Street and an array of magnificent festive decorations and theming. There is free hot chocolate and cookies, as well as a special parade and more fireworks. The atmosphere is truly enchanting, though the evening can be prone to unfriendly weather.

Park tours: Finally, one of the park's little-known secrets is the **Keys to the Kingdom**, a 4–5-hour guided tour of many backstage areas, including the service tunnel under the park, and entertainment production buildings. It's an extra $65 (including lunch; not available for under-16s) but is a superb journey into the park's creation. **Disney's Family Magic Tour** is a 2-hour guided adventure that takes you on a search for clues throughout the park at $30/person, or you can experience the 3-hour **Steam Trains Tour** ($45/person; no under-10s) as you join the crew that prepares the park's trains each day. **Mickey's Magical Milestones Tours** is a 2-hour journey to discover the full story of the world's most famous mouse ($25/person; no under-10s; 407 939 8687 for more info).

Halloween make-up

© Disney

Epcot

Epcot actually stands for 'Experimental Prototype Community of Tomorrow', but it might be more accurate to say Every Person Comes Out Tired. For this is a BIG park, with a lot to see and do, and much legwork required to cover its 300-acre/122ha extent. Actually, it is not so much a vision of the future as a look at the world and technology of today, with a strong educational and environmental message. At almost 3 times the size of the *Magic Kingdom Park*, it is more likely to require a 2-day visit (though under-5s might find it less entertaining) and your feet in particular will notice the difference!

Location

Epcot opened in October 1982 and its giant car park can hold 9,000 vehicles, so a tram takes you from your car to the main entrance (though if you are staying at a Disney hotel you can catch the monorail, boat or bus service to the gates; International Gateway is a separate entrance for guests at the *Epcot* resort hotels). Don't forget to note where you have parked (e.g. Create, row 78). Once you have your ticket, you pass through the turnstiles and wait in the immediate entrance plaza for Rope Drop, which is signalled by Mickey and Co arriving to greet guests.

Epcot is divided into 2 distinct parts arranged in a figure of 8 and there are 2 tactics to help you avoid the worst of the crowds. The first or lower half of the '8' consists of **Future World**, with 6 different pavilions arranged around Spaceship Earth (which dominates the *Epcot* skyline) and the 2 Innoventions centres. The second part, or top of the '8', is **World Showcase**, a potted journey around

Epcot at a glance

Location	Off Epcot Drive, Walt Disney World
Size	300 acres/122ha in Future World and World Showcase
Hours	9am–7pm Future World (except Test Track, Mission: SPACE, Soarin'™, 9am–9pm), 11am–9pm (World Showcase)
Admission	Under-3s free; 3-9 $74 (1-day base ticket), $322 (5-day Premium), $332 (7-day Premium); adult (10+) $82, $345, $355. Prices do not include tax.
Parking	$14
Lockers	Through the main entrance to the right hand side and at International Gateway $12 small; $14 large ($5 deposit)
Pushchairs	$15 and $31 to the left after the main entrance and at International Gateway; length of stay $13 per day single, $27 per day double
Wheelchairs	$12 or $70 ($20 deposit refunded) with pushchairs
Top attractions	Mission: SPACE, Test Track, Spaceship Earth, Soarin'™, Captain EO, Maelstrom, Universe of Energy, American Adventure
Don't miss	IllumiNations: Reflections of Earth, Disney Character Spot, live entertainment (including Off Kilter in Canada, JAMMitors in Innoventions plaza, Miyuki in Japan and Voices of Liberty in America), and dinner at any of the World Showcase pavilions
Hidden costs	**Meals**	Burger, chips and coke $9.31 3-course dinner $41.97 (Le Cellier, Canada) Kids' meal $4.99
	T-shirts	$18.95-34.95
	Souvenirs	$1-9,888
	Sundries	Epcot 'Passport' $9.95

the world via 11 internationally presented pavilions that feature a taste of each country's culture, history, entertainment, shopping and cuisine. Once through the entrance plaza, you should aim to get the 3 big-time rides – Test Track, Mission: Space and Soarin'™ – under your belt first, then move into World Showcase for its 11am opening time. Continue around World Showcase until 4 or 5pm, then return to Future World to catch up on the other attractions there, as the majority will have moved on (apart from at the 3 main rides). As a general tactic, head first for the magnificent **Soarin'**, then go across to the other side of Future World and grab a FastPass for **Test Track**. While you wait for your ride time, you can queue for **Mission: SPACE** and perhaps even take in **Universe of Energy**. Alternatively, if the rides don't appeal quite so much as a visit to such diverse cultures as Japan and Morocco, spend your first couple of hours in the Innoventions centres (busy from mid-morning), then head into World Showcase at 11am and you'll be ahead of the crowds for several hours. The other thing you should do early on is book lunch or dinner at one of the fine restaurants around World Showcase (Mexico, Canada and Japan are all highly recommended). The best reservations go fast, but check in at Guest Relations (on the left after Spaceship Earth) for advice and bookings.

Planning your visit

If you plan a 2-day visit, it makes sense to spend the first day in World Showcase, arriving by 11am and going straight there while the majority stay in Future World, booking your evening meal for around 5.30pm, then lingering around the lagoon for the evening entertainment. For your second visit, try arriving in mid-afternoon and then doing Future World in a more leisurely fashion. Queues at most of the pavilions are almost non-existent for rides like Universe of Energy, Spaceship Earth and Journey into Imagination, though Test Track, Soarin'™ and Mission:

Space stay busy all day. You CAN do *Epcot* in a day – if you arrive early, put in some speedy legwork and give some of the detail a miss. But, of all the parks, it is a shame to hurry this one. In the shops (almost 70 in all), try to save your browsing for the times when the rides are busiest.

Kidcot Fun Stops: At 12 activity centres around Epcot (each country in World Showcase, plus the Land and Seas pavilions), children can play games and collect a special Epcot Passport to get stamped as they visit each Stop. Kids will also want to pick up **Goofy's Epcot Guide** at the main entrance, which asks them to answer various questions around World Showcase and solve Goofy's dilemma.

Future World

Here's what you'll find in the first part of your Epcot adventure.

Universe of Energy: There is just the one attraction here but it is a stunner. **Ellen's Energy Adventure** is a 35-minute show-and-ride with comedienne Ellen DeGeneres and Bill Nye the Science Guy exploring the creation of fuels from the age of dinosaurs to their modern-day usages. The film elements convince you that you are in a conventional theatre, but then your seats rearrange themselves into 96-person solar-powered cars and you are off on a journey through the prehistoric era, with some realistic dinosaurs! Queues are steady but not overwhelming from mid-morning. AAAAA.

Honey I Shrunk the Audience

© Disney

Future World

1 Universe of Energy
2 Mission: SPACE
3 Test Track
4 Odyssey Center
5 Imagination! (including Captain Eo)
6 The Land (including Soarin'™)
7 The Seas with Nemo and Friends
8 Spaceship Earth
9 Innoventions West
10 Innoventions East

World Showcase

11 Mexico
12 Norway
13 China
14 The Outpost
15 Germany
16 Italy
17 The American Adventure
18 Japan
19 Morocco
20 France
21 International Gateway (to Epcot resort hotels)
22 United Kingdom
23 Canada
24 Friendship Boats to Italy and Morocco
25 America Gardens Theater
26 Showcase Plaza
27 Monorail Station
K Kidcot Fun Stops

EPCOT

Mission: SPACE: This is more high-tech Disney imagination at work, a journey into the future to join the International Space Training Center. The space-age building prepares you for a major adventure as you enter through Planetary Plaza, with its giant replica planets (check out the model showing the moon landings). At the main entrance you have a choice of 4 queues – FastPass Collection, Standby (the main queue), Single Riders and FastPass Return, and the clever organisation keeps queues to a minimum. As you enter the training facility, there are some superb models and graphics (like the giant revolving Gravity Wheel) to look at while you queue to reach Team Dispatch. Here, the 4 ready rooms form you into teams of 4 for the ride itself, and you will be either Navigator, Engineer, Pilot or Commander, each with different functions to perform. You also have the choice of either the full, dynamic version of the ride (the 'orange' version) or a toned-down alternative that avoids the 'spinning' effect (the 'green' version). Once briefed (by actor Gary Sinise), you enter the Preparation Room to learn your mission – a flight to Mars. And then it's into the ride vehicle – capsules that close down tightly with outer doors, shoulder restraints and screens that move forward to just 18in/46cm from your face (this is NOT a good ride for those with claustrophobia). The sense of realism, with the control consoles, individual speakers and countdown is magnificent. For those on the full version of the ride, the blast-off feels VERY real as you experience some of the genuine forces of a rocket launch (thanks to its huge centrifuge, which is part-ride and part-simulator). Each member of the team has to perform their duties on cue (Sinise will prompt you) and you experience a simulated sling-shot around the moon and on to Mars, where the landing is an adventure in itself. It's a truly original, aggressive ride, but you should heed the advice to keep your head still and look straight into the screen or you WILL feel sick (unless you are on the tamer version, where the capsules just tilt and turn). We think the full-on experience is much too intense for young children, and there is no backing out once you blast off (parents could try it first to check it out), while it is definitely not for expectant mothers. Restrictions: 3ft 8in/112cm. TTTTT+ (FP).

> ### BRIT TIP
> Even if you don't ride Mission: Space, you (and your children) should visit the post-ride area of games and fun. Just enter through the Cargo Bay gift shop to the left of the pavilion.

As you exit the ride, there is an elaborate post-show and activities. **Space Base** is an excellent play area for children who can't ride (and those who just like to climb, slide and crawl); **Space Race** is a great game for 2 teams of 60 players to propel a rocket back to Earth via a series of on-screen challenges; **Expedition Mars** is a computer game to rescue

Mission: SPACE

© Disney

stranded astronauts; and **Postcards from Space** can email a 'space video' to friends and family. There is then the inevitable (and well-stocked) gift shop. All in all, it's a mind-boggling experience and a real taste of space exploration without leaving the building!

Test Track: Another big production – a 5½-minute whirl along Disney's longest and fastest track. It starts with an elaborate queue line that demonstrates car-testing techniques and quality control, and prepares riders for a taste of the ride to come. The way the cars whiz around the outside of the building (at up to 65mph/104kph) provides a glimpse of what's in store. The reality is pretty good, too, as you are taken on a tour of a proving ground, including a hill climb test, suspension test (hold on to those fillings), brake test, environment chamber, barrier test (beware the crash test dummies!) and the steeply banked, high-speed finale. Along with a smart gift store and ride photo opportunity, it makes for an extremely involving exhibit. The downside is its HUGE queues, topping 2 hours at times, while the available FP service often runs out by late morning in peak season. Head straight here when it opens or come back in the evening to keep your queuing to bearable levels. If you are on your own, save time by using the Single Rider Queue. Restrictions: 3ft 4in/101cm. TTTT (TTT teens) (FP).

Test Track

© Disney

BRIT TIP
Innoventions East and West are good places in which to spend time if you need to cool down, or if it's raining.

The Odyssey Center: Next door are baby-care and first-aid facilities, telephones and restrooms.

Imagination!: The 2-part attraction here starts with **Journey into Imagination with Figment**, an uneven but quirky ride into experiments with imagination in the company of Eric Idle (as Dr Nigel Channing of the Imagination Institute) and the cartoon dragon Figment. The sight laboratory sees Figment having fun with a vision chart, the sound lab is a symphony of imaginative melodies and Figment's house is a truly topsy-turvy world (and watch out for the skunk in the smell lab!). It's gentle fun and rarely draws a crowd. AAA. You exit into **Image Works – The Kodak 'What If' Labs**, an interactive playground of sights and sounds, which will probably amuse children more than adults (though you might be tempted to buy various cartoon images and select-your-own CDs). **Captain EO:** Come out of the building and turn right for an encore presentation of this fun 3-D musical film show starring Michael Jackson, which originally debuted in Epcot in 1986 but was replaced by *Honey I Shrunk The Audience* in 1994. Now back after the film has been digitally remastered and sound enhanced, it is a 17-minute romp through space as Captain EO (Jackson) and his band of ragtag renegades set out to save the universe by bringing a special gift to the evil Supreme Leader: the key to unlocking the 'beauty within.' Jackson's signature 'synchronised dancing' and the show's *We Are Here To Change The World* message keep the tone upbeat and engaging, but some of the darker thematic elements may frighten young children. It's a visually thrilling trip down memory lane for Disney fans, as good conquers evil (naturally!) in this carefully revived version. AAAA (FP).

Outside, kids are always fascinated by the Jellyfish and Serpentine Fountains that send water squirting from pond to pond. Have your cameras and camcorders ready!

The Land: This pavilion combines 3 elements to make a highly entertaining but educational experience on food and nutrition – plus the spectacular Soarin'™ ride, which is a pure thrill and a huge draw. **Living with the Land** is an informative 14-minute boat ride well worth the usually long queue. A journey through various types of food production may sound dull, but it is informative and enjoyable, with plenty to make children of all ages sit up and take notice through the 3 ecological communities, especially the greenhouse finale. AAAA (FP). Having ridden the ride, you can also take the **Behind the Seeds** 1-hour guided tour through the greenhouse complex and learn even more about Disney's horticultural projects ($16 adults, $12 3–9s).

The Circle of Life: This is a 15-minute combined live-action and animation story, featuring characters from the film *The Lion King*, which explains environmental concerns and is easily digestible for kids. Queues are not a problem here. AAA.

Soarin'™: *Epcot*'s latest and greatest, this hugely imaginative 'flight simulator' offers an exhilarating ride for all ages. A copy of the Soarin' Over California simulator ride in *Disney's California Adventure* in Los Angeles, it features a breathtaking swoop over the notable landmarks of California, complete with 'aromavision' (smell those orange groves!). An elaborate queuing area leads through to the 'departure lounge', with passengers embarking on rows of seats that are then hoisted into the air over a giant screen. The feeling is somewhat akin to taking a hang-glider ride as the special film, sounds and scents become all-encompassing. Feet dangling, you soar over the Golden Gate Bridge, sweep through a redwood forest and glide above Napa Valley with the wind in your hair. The finale includes a close encounter with a certain Disney theme park in LA! The ride's realism, magnificent music and superb technology ensure a 5-star experience – but also some serious, slow-moving queues. FastPasses often run out by 11am, so visit early and use FP for a second ride. Restrictions: 3ft 4in/101cm. AAAAA (FP).

Dining: The **Sunshine Season Food Fair** offers the chance to eat some of Disney's home-grown produce, and provides healthy alternatives to the usual fast-food fare, while the **Garden Grill** restaurant is a slowly revolving platform that offers more traditional food, including roast meats, pasta, seafood and a vegetarian selection, all in the company of Mickey, Goofy, Pluto and Chip 'n' Dale.

The Seas with Nemo & Friends: This pavilion does for the oceans what The Land does for terra firma, in the company of the characters from the Pixar film *Finding Nemo*. You start with the signature ride, **The Seas With Nemo and Friends**, which takes riders on an underwater journey in 'clamobiles' to meet Nemo and Co (who are brilliantly interwoven into the huge aquarium – to all intents and purposes swimming with the real fish!). Nemo has gone missing (again), hence the ride becomes a quest to reunite him with teacher Mr Ray and the rest of the fishy class in a rousing musical finale. AAAA. You exit into **Sea Base Alpha**, a 2-level development offering 6 modules presenting stories of

Soarin'™

© Disney

undersea exploration and marine life, including a research centre that provides a close encounter with the endangered manatee. Plenty of interactive elements and educational touch-screens are on offer, plus additional fish tanks displaying Caribbean reef fish, jellyfish and the intriguing cuttlefish, while there is also an excellent demonstration of a diving chamber. Crowds are steady, but queues rarely get too long – with one exception. **Turtle Talk With Crush** is a splendidly interactive and original meet and greet with the cartoon surfer dude turtle and his friend Dory, inspired by the film *Finding Nemo*. Crush is literally the star of the show as he swims up and engages children in the audience with some genuinely fun banter. AAAA. Next door, **Bruce's Sub House** is a fun kids' play area including some great photo opportunities with more of the *Finding Nemo* characters, like friendly shark Bruce (TTT under-6s). **Nemo and Friends** is more hands-on fun for kids, while **Mr Ray's Lagoon** showcases some real stingrays.

Dining: The pavilion also includes the highly recommended **Coral Reef Restaurant** that serves magnificent seafood, as well as providing diners with a grandstand view of the massive aquarium. Dinner for 2 will be around $50 (starter and entrée) up to $100, depending on your choices, which isn't cheap, but the food is first class.

Turtle Talk with Crush

© Disney

Spaceship Earth: Spiralling up 18 storeys, this attraction is a convincing time-travel story into various technologies narrated by Dame Judi Dench. From cave paintings to the internet (with a superb depiction of Michelangelo's Sistine Chapel along the way), the gentle ride unfolds in highly imaginative historical stages, culminating in an interactive finale that invites riders to 'predict' the future. Sponsor Siemens (the electronics giant) has added a post-show interactive demonstration area (including predictive surgery and a driving challenge), which makes for an entertaining diversion after the 15-minute ride. Queues are heavy all morning, but almost non-existent late in the day. AAAA.

Innoventions: These 2 centres of hands-on exhibits and computer games – subtitled **The Road to Tomorrow** – include a glimpse of Disney's latest work with virtual reality entertainment and other demonstrations of current and future technologies, especially the internet and computers, presented by the likes of IBM, Underwriters Laboratories and Liberty Mutual. Both sides are routed like a journey into the future and will reward enquiring minds.

Innoventions East: Don't miss the new **The Sum of All Thrills** interactive experience, where budding mathematicians and engineers can design and create their own ride using physics principles and touch-screen technology. Then, hop aboard the motion simulator for a hair-raising, breathtaking ride! Restrictions: 4ft/121cm for non-inversion ride, 4ft 4in/132cm with inversions. TTT. Other novelties include **Test the Limits Lab** and **Don't Waste It** (a recycling challenge), **House of Innoventions** (a 15-minute walking tour through new home technologies) and **Storm Struck** (experience a violent storm from a special viewing theatre). You can also take a look at the latest transport – the wonderful 2-wheeled Segway Human Transporter (which you can also pay to ride – see page 137).

Innoventions West: Kids gravitate to **Smarter Planet**, where they're quizzed on ways to save the planet before creating a personalised avatar for a fun romp through their own video game world! Worth waiting for are the 20-minute **Where's The Fire?**, an interactive game exploring home fire hazards; the **Thinkplace**, presented by IBM and featuring a demonstration of voice recognition technology and the chance to send a 'video-card' to family and friends; and the amusing **Slap Stick Studios** (shows every ½ hour) presented by Velcro. For those who are concerned about their finances, the humorous **Great Piggy Bank Adventure** teaches the importance of setting financial goals and saving money.

Other entertainment: Both Innoventions pavilions feature a **Team Possible Recruitment Center** (11am–8pm) where you can sign up for super secret agent missions as part of the family-friendly *Disney's Kim Possible World Showcase Adventure* interactive programme, which sends guests on special tasks around World Showcase. Some of the 'missions' – using your handy Kim-unicator – are genuinely challenging and we think this is WAY too good just for kids! Live fun is also provided periodically in the Innoventions plaza with the unique **JAMMitors** percussion group, while the **Epcot Character Spot** (across from Innoventions West, 9am–5.30pm) offers a meet and greet with a variety of favourite Disney characters. The majestic **Plaza Fountain** choreographs to musical performances every 15 minutes.

Dining and shopping: Food outlets include the counter-service **Electric Umbrella Restaurant** for lunch and dinner (sandwiches, pizza, burgers and salads) and the **Fountain View Ice Cream** for Edy's ice-cream and drinks. Look out also for **Club Cool** presented by Coca-Cola®, where you can check out the latest Coke-inspired products and souvenirs, along with various free soft-drink tastes from around the world (beware The Beverly!). For shopping, **Mouse Gear** in Innoventions East features a massive variety of Epcot and Disney merchandise (and don't forget to check out the wacky ceiling architecture!).

World Showcase

If you found Future World amazing, prepare to be astounded by the equally imaginative pavilions around the World Showcase Lagoon. Each features a glimpse of a different country in dramatic settings. Several have rides or films to showcase their main features, while the restaurants offer some outstanding fare. There is also a third **Team Possible Recruitment Center** on the bridge from Future World to World Showcase, while many Disney character meet 'n' greets can be found in each country (check the daily *Times Guide* for locations and timings).

Mexico: Starting at the bottom left of the circular tour of the lagoon and moving clockwise, your first encounter is inside the spectacular pyramid of Mexico. Here you have the amusing boat ride **Gran Fiesta Tour Starring The Three Caballeros**, a 9-minute journey through the people and history of the country with Donald Duck, Panchito and José Carioca as your guides. Queues build up in mid-afternoon but are usually light otherwise. AAA.

Other entertainment: As in all of the World Showcase pavilions, there is live entertainment, with periodic 25-minute music shows from **Mariachi Cobre**, while Donald Duck puts in character appearances.

Spaceship Earth

© Disney

Dining and shopping: Much of the pavilion comprises market-style gift shops, while the **San Angel Inn** is a romantic restaurant offering typical Mexican fare and **La Cava del Tequila** has tempting cocktails, light bites and signature tequilas. Outside, choose from the revamped counter service Cantina de San Angel (open air lunch from 11am, serving tacos, nachos and tortillas) and all-new full-service **Hacienda de San Angel** (dinner from 4pm, serving a richer variety of Mexican fare), a grand lagoon view with a grandstand view of the nightly IllumiNations show.

Norway: Next up is the best ride in World Showcase, the Viking-themed **Maelstrom**. This 10-minute longboat journey through Norway's history and scenery features a short waterfall drop and a North Sea storm. It attracts longish queues from early afternoon, so the best tactic is to go soon after World Showcase's 11am opening. TTT (FP). There are periodic Norwegian-themed exhibits in the reconstructed **Stave Church** and twice-daily guided tours (sign up at the Tourism desk). The pavilion also contains a clever reproduction of Oslo's Akershus Fortress.

Dining and shopping: The **Akershus Royal Banquet Hall** offers the Princess Storybook dining for breakfast, lunch and dinner, complete with a host of Disney Princesses, and the **Kringla Bakeri Og Kafé** serves

China Pavilion

© Disney

sandwiches, pastries and drinks. The **Puffins Roost** is a large gift shop for all things Norwegian.

China: The spectacular landscapes of China are well served by the main attraction of this pavilion, the stunning **Reflections of China**, a 360° film in the circular Temple of Heaven. Here you are surrounded by the sights and sounds of one of the world's most enigmatic countries in an eye-catching special cinematic production. Queues build up to ½ hour during the main part of the day (but the waiting area is fully air-conditioned). AAAA.

Other entertainment: Don't miss the periodic shows from classical Chinese musicians **Si Xian** and the stunning **Dragon Legend Acrobats** on the plaza in front of the temple. **Disney characters** from *Mulan* also appear in the afternoon.

Dining and shopping: Two restaurants, the **Nine Dragons** and the counter-service **Lotus Blossom Café** offer tastes of the Orient, while **Yong Feng Shangdian Dept Store** is a warehouse of Chinese gifts and artefacts.

The **Outpost** between China and Germany features hut-style shops and snacks, with entertainment from Africa and the Caribbean.

Germany: This provides more in the way of shopping and eating than entertainment, though you still find strolling players and a magnificent recreation of a Bavarian **Biergarten**, with lively Oktoberfest shows featuring the resident **Musikanten** brass band at regular intervals. It also offers hearty portions of German sausage, sauerkraut and rotisserie chicken. The **Sommerfest** is fast food German-style (bratwurst and strudel), while there are more shops (8 in all) than anywhere else in Epcot, including chocolates, wines, crystal, porcelain, toys and cuckoo clocks.

Other entertainment: An elaborate outdoor model railway is popular with children, and look out for **character appearances** from Snow White and Dopey.

Italy: Similarly, Italy has pretty, authentic architecture, including a superb reproduction of Venice's St Mark's Square, 3 tempting gift shops (including wine, chocolates, Armani collectables, fine crystal, porcelain and Venetian masks). Its full-service restaurant, **Tutto Italia**, is a temporary cover for an upscale themed restaurant slated to open as one component of a big dining expansion in late 2010/early 2011. The first addition (opening in October 2010) will be **Via Napoli**, a delightful full-service pizzeria, featuring wood-burning ovens and genuine Neapolitan style, with 300 seats, including an outdoor terrace. This will be followed by a complete refurbishment and re-branding of Tutto Italia.

Other entertainment: Watch out for the fun entertainment of **Sergio**, a madcap juggler who loves to involve his audience, and the live comedy of the **World Showcase Players** (with audience participation!).

The American Adventure: At the top of the lagoon and dominating World Showcase is this huge edifice, not so much a pavilion as a celebration of the country's history and Constitution. A colonial Fife & Drum Corps and the wonderful singing group add authentic sounds to the 18th-century setting, overlooked by a faithful reproduction of Philadelphia's Liberty Hall. Inside, you have the **American Adventure** show, a magnificent ½-hour film and audio-animatronic production that details the country's founding, its struggles and triumphs, presidents, statesmen and heroes. It's a glossy, patriotic display, featuring some truly outstanding technology and, while some of it will leave foreign visitors fairly cold, it's difficult not to be impressed. Avoid in early afternoon because of the queues. AAAA. If you have some time to spare, check out the special exhibitions in the **American Heritage Gallery**.

Other entertainment: The **America Gardens Theater**, facing the lagoon, presents concerts from international artists, during the Flower & Garden Festival, Sounds Like Summer series and the Food & Wine Festival. Superb *a capella* group **Voices of Liberty** appear several times a day, as do the **Spirit of America Fife & Drum Corps**.

Dining and shopping: Antiques and handcarts provide touches of nostalgia, along with the **Heritage Manor Gifts** store, while **Liberty Inn** offers fast-food lunch and dinner.

Japan: Next up on the clockwise tour, you are introduced to typical Japanese style and architecture, including the breathtaking Chi Nien Tien, a round ½-scale reproduction of a temple, some magnificent art exhibits (notably in the **Bijutsu-kan Gallery**, featuring images by celebrated photographer Kazuyoshi Miyoshi), a tranquil Bonsai garden (complete with carp pond) and landmark Torii gate.

Other entertainment: Live shows are key here, with periodic presentations from the superb **Matsuriza** *taiko* drummers and the eye-catching artistry of child-friendly **Miyuki**, a lovely lady who spins amazing candy creations out of toffee sugar, plus **Honobono Minwa**, a folk story-teller.

Dining and shopping: Great food is a real highlight, and the restaurant line-up consists of the wonderful fine dining of **Teppan Edo** (formerly the Teppanyaki Rooms, and still with its traditional chefs at each table) and **Tokyo Dining**, a new venue featuring typical cuisine and ingredients, showcasing sushi and innovative

Japan Pavilion

presentation. **Yakitori House** is its fast-food equivalent, with great soups, teriyaki and tempura dishes. The huge **Mitsukoshi** store adds some fascinating shopping opportunities, from traditional calligraphy, tea kettles and wind chimes to Hello Kitty souvenirs.

Morocco: As you would expect, this is another real shopping experience, with bazaars, alleyways and stalls selling a well-priced array of carpets, leather goods, clothing, brass ornaments, pottery and antiques. All of the building materials were faithfully imported for the pavilion, which was hand-built to give Morocco a greater degree of authenticity, even by World Showcase's high standards. Ask about its daily (free) 45-minute walking tours of the whole pavilion. **The Gallery of Arts and History** offers more historical and cultural insight into the country, while the **Fez House** depicts the style of a typical Moroccan home.

Other entertainment: Characters from Disney's *Aladdin* appear from time to time, while live musical show **MoRockin'** presents a variety of Arabic rhythms in fun style, including an eye-catching belly-dancer!

Dining: Restaurant Marrakesh provides a full dining experience, complete with traditional musicians and their own belly dancer. It's rather pricey ($42.95/person for the Taste of Morocco Marrakesh Royal Feast; 3 other samplers are available for $35.95 or $36.95), but the lively

atmosphere is entertaining. However, better value can be had at **Tangierine Café**, with a healthy array of foods (roast lamb, hummus, tabbouleh, couscous, lentil salad and Moroccan breads) at more down-to-earth prices ($8.99–13.99; kids' meals $7.99).

BRIT TIP
The Tangierine Café in Morocco is a peaceful haven in which to enjoy a quiet, healthy lunch, especially if you are vegetarian, while there is also a tempting coffee and pastry counter.

France: Predictably overlooked by a replica Eiffel Tower, this is a clean and cheerful pre-World War I Paris, with comedy street theatre adding to the rather dreamy atmosphere and pleasant gardens, plus some stylish shopping. Don't miss **Impressions de France**, another big-film production that serves up all the grandest sights of the country, accompanied by the music of Offenbach, Debussy, Saint-Saëns and Satie. Crowds get quite heavy from mid-day. AAAA.

Other entertainment: Look out for the visual comedy and amazing balancing act of **Serveur Amusant** for some eye-catching antics (not when it's too windy), while Princess Aurora makes regular appearances, along with *Beauty and the Beast* characters.

Dining and shopping: This is also the pavilion for a gastronomic experience provided by 3 restaurants, of which **Les Chefs de France** (where Remy from the movie *Ratatouille* appears

Morocco Pavilion

© Disney

4 times daily) and **Bistro de Paris** are major discoveries. The former is an award-winning, full-service (but expensive) establishment featuring top-quality cuisine created by French chefs on a daily basis, while the latter, upstairs, offers more intimate bistro dining, still with an individual touch (and, if anything, slightly more expensive) and plenty of style (starters $12–16, main courses $34–42, Bistro 4 Course Tasting Menu $54, with wine pairings $89). The Bistro books only 30 days in advance. Alternatively, the **Boulangerie Patisserie** is a sidewalk café offering more modest fare (and wonderful pastries, as you'd expect). Shopping is also suitably chic, with an authentic Wine Shop and elegant **Guerlain** perfumery (ask about its free perfume tour during the *Flower and Garden Festival*).

United Kingdom: The least inspiring of all the pavilions, and certainly with little to entertain those who have ever visited a pub or shopped for Royal Doulton or Burberry goods, it is partly offset by some good live entertainment and pleasant gardens, but that is about it.

Other entertainment: Excellent Beatles tribute band the **British Invasion**, who appear in various 20-minute guises of the Fab Four (plus songs by Herman's Hermits, the Hollies and other '60s classics) are well worth seeing, while **The Hat Lady** is the pub pianist and the **World Showcase Players** add periodic street theatre. Disney characters can also be found here in the shape of Mary Poppins, Winnie the Pooh, Alice in Wonderland and Friends.

Dining and shopping: The **Rose and Crown Pub** is antiseptically authentic (complete with pub pianist), but you can get better elsewhere at these prices (grilled pork loin $21.99, bangers and mash or fish and chips $15.99, and a pint of Bass, Harp Lager or Guinness for a whopping $8). There is also a takeaway **Harry Ramsden's** fish and chippie. The standout shops are the **Tea Caddy,** the **Magic of Wales,** the **Queen's Table,**

Crown and Crest (perfumes and heraldry) and **Toy Soldier** (traditional games and toys), but prices are WAY above what you'd pay back home.

Canada: Completing the World Showcase circle, the main features here are **Victoria Gardens,** based on the world-famous Butchart Gardens on Vancouver Island, some spectacular Rocky Mountain scenery, a replica French gothic mansion, the Hôtel de Canada, and another stunning 360° film, **O Canada!** As with China and France, this showcases the country's sights and scenery in a terrific, 17-minute advert for the Canadian Tourist Board led by comedian Martin Short. It's at its busiest in late afternoon. AAA.

Other entertainment: Resident band **Off Kilter** are also one of the most entertaining acts we've seen anywhere and they perform 30-minute sets up to 5 times a day. Want to hear rock 'n' roll bagpipes? This is the group for you!

> **BRIT TIP**
> Best way to tour World Showcase? Start in Canada and continue anticlockwise or jump on the Friendship Boats and go straight to Italy or Morocco.

Dining and shopping: Le Cellier Steakhouse is an excellent dining room, offering great steaks, prime rib, seafood, chicken and several vegetarian dishes for lunch and dinner. **The Trading Post** and **Northwest Mercantile** provide a range of Canadian clothing and souvenir, notably wonderful glass ornaments, Deauville perfume – and Off Kilter CDs!

Epcot World Showcase

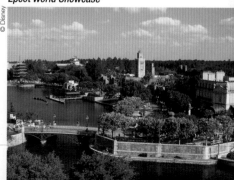

© Disney

IllumiNations: Reflections of Earth

The day's big finale and an absolute show-stopper, this firework and special-effects extravaganza is awesome even by Disney standards. British composer Gavin Greenaway provided the original music for a 15-minute performance of vivid brilliance. Some 2,800 firework shells are launched as a celestial backdrop to a series of fire-and-water effects on the World Showcase Lagoon. The central icon is a 28ft/9m video globe of Earth that opens in a spectacular climax of choreographed pyrotechnics. Truly magnificent. However, people start staking out the best lagoon-side spots up to 2 HOURS in advance. The ultimate way to view IllumiNations is by private boat on one of 3 **speciality cruises** from *Disney's Boardwalk* or *Yacht and Beach Club Resorts* (for non-residents, too). The price range is $319–344 per boat (holding 4–10 guests) and can be used for special celebrations. The *Basic Cruise* costs $319 and the pontoon boat holds up to 10. It includes water, soft drinks and snacks. The *Celebration Cruise* costs $344 and adds a range of occasion decorations. The classic motorboat *Breathless* costs $308 (up to 6 adults; call 407 939 7529 up to 90 days in advance to book). Be aware cruises launch regardless of whether fireworks are taking place.

Behind-the-scenes tours

Epcot also has a big range of behind-the-scenes tours. **Dolphins in Depth** ($194, with refreshments, souvenir photo and T-shirt) is a 3-hour dip into the research areas of The Seas pavilion, including a chance to meet the resident dolphins (13–17s must be accompanied by an adult). **Undiscovered Future World** is a 4½-hour journey into the creation of *Epcot*, Walt's vision for the resort and backstage areas like IllumiNations ($55). **Behind the Seeds**, a 1-hour tour every 45 minutes from 9.45am–4.30pm at The Land pavilion, looks at Disney's innovative gardening practices ($16 adults, $12 3–9s). **Dive Quest** ($175/person, 10 and over) is a 3-hour experience, with a 40-minute dive into the Seas aquarium, plus a backstage look at the facility at 4.30pm and 5.30pm daily, T-shirt and certificate for all participants. Must have scuba certification, park admission not required. The **Seas Aqua Tour** ($140/person, 8 and over; under-18s must be accompanied by an adult is similar but without the scuba diving element (daily at 12.30pm). **Around the World at Epcot** will appeal to those who enjoy new technology, with a World Showcase tour 4 times each morning on the innovative 2-wheeled **Segway Human Transporter**. It costs $99/person (not including park admission; minimum age 16) but the 2-hour tour includes instruction and plenty of travel

Christmas fireworks at Epcot

© Disney

EPCOT with children

Here is our rough guide to the attractions that appeal to different age groups:

Under-5s

Circle of Life, Gran Fiesta Tour Starring The Three Caballeros, Journey into Imagination with Figment, Kidcot stops, Living with the Land, The Seas with Nemo and Friends, Soarin'™ (if tall enough), Spaceship Earth, Turtle Talk with Crush, Universe of Energy.

5–8s

All the above, plus The American Adventure, Captain EO (with parental discretion), Image Works, Innoventions, JAMMitors, Maelstrom, Miyuki the Candy Lady, Test Track, Kim Possible World Showcase Adventure.

9–12s

All the above, plus Dragon Legend Acrobats, Impressions de France, Matsuriza Drummers, Mission: SPACE, O Canada!, Sergio, Le Serveur Amusant, Reflections of China.

Over-12s

Living with the Land, The Seas with Nemo and Friends, Soarin'™, Spaceship Earth, Universe of Energy, The American Adventure, Captain EO, Innoventions, JAMMitors, Maelstrom, Test Track, Dragon Legend Acrobats, Impressions de France, Matsuriza Drummers, Mission: SPACE, O Canada!, Reflections of China, Bijutsu-kan Gallery, British Invasion (UK), Off Kilter (Canada).

time on these amazing machines. **Simply Segway** is then a 1-hour class (mainly indoor) just on riding and controlling the 'Human Transporter' ($35/person; at 11.30am daily). The new **Nature-Inspired Design** tour, going backstage at the Land and Seas pavilions, including a detailed look at the Soarin' ride and greenhouses, plus an off-road experience on a Segway ($124/person; 8.15am Tue, Wed, Thur and Sat). The most comprehensive tour, **Backstage Magic** ($224, 16 and over), going behind the scenes of *Epcot*, *Magic Kingdom* and *Disney's Hollywood Studios* on a 7-hour foray into little-seen aspects, such as the backstage areas of the Studios and the tunnels below *Magic Kingdom*. Book all tours on 407 939 8687.

Annual festivals

There are 2 other annual *Epcot* events to watch out for. The **International Flower and Garden Festival** literally puts the whole park in full bloom with an amazing series of set-pieces, seminars and mini-exhibitions from early March through mid-May. All the exhibits and lectures are free and they add a beautiful aspect to an already scenic park. The **Food and Wine Festival** runs from 1 October through mid-November and showcases national and regional cuisines, wines and beers, with the chance to attend grand Winemakers' Dinners and Tasting Events, or just sample the offerings of more than 20 food booths dotted around World Showcase. One of our favourites! Both also offer free concerts several times a day at the America Gardens Theater.

Soarin'

© Disney

Disney's Hollywood Studios

Welcome to a journey into the world of film and TV, an epic voyage of adventure, creation – and fun. Here you will learn plenty of tricks of the trade; movie-making secrets and behind-the-scenes glimpses that have been cleverly turned into rides, shows and other attractions with guaranteed entertainment appeal. Rather bigger than the *Magic Kingdom* at 154 acres/62ha but smaller than *Epcot, Disney's Hollywood Studios* is a different experience yet again with its rather chaotic combination of attractions, street entertainment, film sets and smart gift shops. Like the *Magic Kingdom*, the food on offer may not win awards, but some of the restaurants (notably the Sci-Fi Dine-in Theater and 50s Prime Time Café) have imaginative settings. The park also has rather more to occupy smaller children than *Epcot*, but you can still easily see most of it in a day unless the crowds are heavy.

Location

The entrance arrangements will be fairly familiar if you have already visited the other parks. *Disney's Hollywood Studios* is located on Buena Vista Drive (which runs between World Drive and Epcot Drive) and parking is $14. Remember to make a note of where you park before you catch the tram to the main gates, where you must wait for the official opening time. If the queues build up quickly, the gates will open early, so be ready for a running start.

Once through, you are into Hollywood Boulevard, a street of gift shops, and you have to decide which of the main attractions to head for first, as these are the ones where the

Disney's Hollywood Studios at a glance

Location	Off Buena Vista Drive or World Drive, Walt Disney World	
Size	154 acres/62ha	
Hours	9am–7pm off peak; 9am–10pm high season (Easter, summer holidays, Thanksgiving and Christmas)	
Admission	Under-3s free; 3-9 $74 (1-day base ticket), $322 (5-day Premium), $332 (7-day Premium); adult (10+) $82, $345, $355. Prices do not include tax.	
Parking	$14	
Lockers	From the Crossroads kiosk through the main entrance; $12 small, $14 large	
Pushchairs	$15 and $31 Oscar's Super Service Station; length of stay $13 per day single, $27 per day double	
Wheelchairs	$12 or $70 ($20 deposit refunded), from Oscar's	
Top attractions	Toy Story Mania, Twilight Zone™ Tower of Terror, Rock 'n' Roller Coaster Starring Aerosmith, Star Tours II, The Great Movie Ride, Voyage of the Little Mermaid, Jim Henson's Muppet*Vision 3-D, Lights, Motors, Action!™ Extreme Stunt Show	
Don't miss	Block Party Bash, Indiana Jones™ Epic Stunt Spectacular, American Idol Experience, Fantasmic!	
Hidden costs	Meals	Burger, chips and coke $8.88 3-course lunch $22.17–42.97 (Mama Melrose's) Beer $5.50–6.25 Kids' meal $4.99
	T-shirts	$14.95–38.95
	Souvenirs	$1.95–2,350
	Sundries	Temporary tattoo $5–10

queues will be heaviest nearly all day. Try to ignore the lure of the shops as it is better to browse in the early afternoon when the attractions are at their busiest.

Incidentally, if you thought Disney had elevated queuing to an art form in its other parks, wait until you see how cleverly arranged it is here. Just when you think you have reached the ride itself, there is another twist to the queue you hadn't seen or an extra element to the ride that holds you up. The latter are holding pens, which are an ingenious way of making it seem you are being entertained instead of queuing. Look out for them in particular at the Great Movie Ride, Twilight Zone™ Tower of Terror and Jim Henson's Muppet*Vision 3-D.

An up-to-the-minute check on queue times at the attractions is kept on a **Guest Information Board** on Hollywood Boulevard, just past its junction with Sunset Boulevard, where you can also book the restaurants. The **Baby Center** here is located just inside the main gates on the left, next to Guest Relations, along with **First Aid**. The park is laid out in a rather more confusing fashion than its counterparts, which have neatly packaged 'lands', so you will need to consult your map often to keep your bearings in the 7 different areas.

The main attractions
The opening-gate crowds will all surge in one of 3 directions, which will give you a pretty good idea of where you want to go. By far the biggest attraction here is the **Twilight Zone™ Tower of Terror**, a magnificent haunted hotel ride that ends in a 13-storey drop in a lift, where queues hit 2 hours at peak periods. So, if the Tower appeals to you, do it first! Head straight up Hollywood Boulevard, turn right into Sunset Boulevard and you'll see it at the end, looming ominously over the park. It's a FastPass (FP) ride (see pages 106 and 107), as is another huge draw, the **Rock 'n' Roller Coaster Starring Aerosmith** (at the end of Sunset Boulevard on the left), so you can get an FP for one and ride the other.

Star Tours II, the newly remodelled *Star Wars™* simulator ride, and **Toy Story Mania** are also serious queue-builders and FP attractions. If you are not up for the really big thrills, grab a FP for Toy Story Mania (straight up Hollywood Boulevard, pass right of the giant Mickey Hat and into the new Pixar Place area), then head for Star Tours (back across the main square past the Indiana Jones™ show). After Star Tours and Toy Story Mania, another gentler experience (and also worth doing early on) is the hysterical **Muppet*Vision 3-D** show,

Photo opportunity at Disney's Hollywood Studios

© Disney

1   Parade Route
    Block Party Bash
2   The Great Movie
    Ride
3   American Idol Live!
4   ABC Sound Studio
    'Sounds Dangerous'
    starring Drew Carey
5   Indiana Jones™
    Epic Stunt
    Spectacular
6   Star Tours II
    (opening May 2011)
7   Jim Henson's
    Muppet*Vision 3-D
8   Honey, I Shrunk
    the Kids Movie Set
    Adventure
9   Catastrophe
    Canyon on Disney's
    Hollywood Studios
    Backlot Tour
10 Studio Backlot Tour
11 Meet Mickey Mouse
12 Toy Story Mania
13 Walt Disney: One
    Man's Dream
14 Voyage of the Little
    Mermaid
15 The Magic of Disney
    Animation

16 Playhouse Disney –
    Live on Stage!
17 Rock 'n' Roller
    Coaster Starring
    Aerosmith
18 The Twilight Zone™
    Tower of Terror
19 Beauty and the
    Beast — Live on
    Stage
20 Fantasmic!
21 Guest Information
    Board
22 Toy Story Pizza
    Planet
23 Lights, Motors,
    Action!™ Extreme
    Stunt Show
24 Premier Theater
25 '50s Prime Time
    Café
26 Hollywood and Vine
27 Hollywood Brown
    Derby
28 Mama Melrose's
29 Sunset Ranch
    Market
30 Sci-Fi Dine-in
    Theater Restaurant
31 Journey into Narnia:
    Prince Caspian

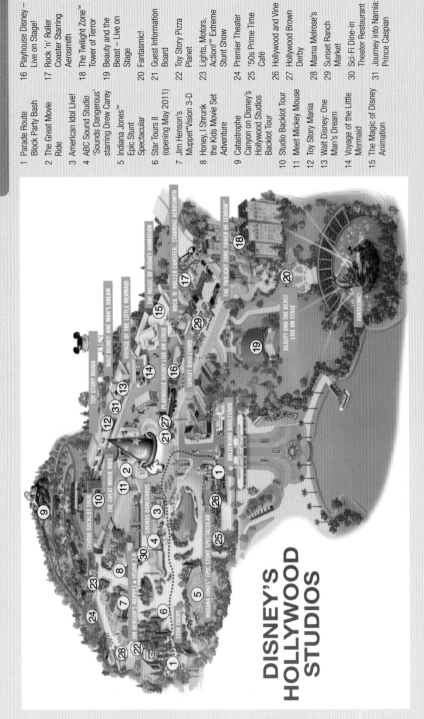

DISNEY'S
HOLLYWOOD
STUDIOS

which is another big draw later in the day. It has the benefit of being air-conditioned, too, for when you need a rest. The park's big stunt show, **Lights, Motors, Action!™ Extreme Stunt Show**, plays 2–5 times a day and is also hugely popular, so this is another one to try to get a FP for.

> 🎌 **BRIT TIP**
>
> People begin queuing for the Lights, Motors, Action!™ Extreme Stunt Show a good ½ hour before seating, and the midday shows are usually full. Go for the first performance, or wait until later.

Hollywood Boulevard

Moving around the park in a (roughly) clockwise direction, you start in the Hollywood Boulevard area. As with the *Magic Kingdom*, your entry here is along a street of shops and services that are best visited in early afternoon when it's busiest elsewhere. Immediately to the left through the turnstiles are the **Guest Relations** and **First Aid** offices, plus the **Baby Care** centre. To the right is Oscar's Station for pushchair and wheelchair hire, while locker hire is obtained at the Crossroads kiosk right in front of you.

The Great Movie Ride: This faces you (behind the Hat icon) as you walk in along Hollywood Boulevard and is a good place to start if the crowds are not too serious. An all-star audio-animatronics cast re-creates a number of box office smashes, including Jimmy Cagney's *Public Enemy*, Julie Andrews in *Mary Poppins*, Gene Kelly in *Singin' in the Rain* and many more masterful set-pieces as you undertake your conducted tour. Small children may find the menace of *The Alien* too strong, but otherwise the ride has universal appeal and features some clever live twists (there are 2 variations on this ride, a cowboy and a gangster version – ask a Cast Member if there's one you especially want to do). AAAA.

Other entertainment: Showing up to 6 times daily in front of the Sorcerer's Hat, **High School Musical 3: Senior Year – Right Here! Right Now!** is a 20-minute song and dance act from the hit Disney TV film series. With the cheerleaders and basketball players from East High putting on an energetic display, it is sure to thrill fans of the *High School Musical* films (AAA). A series of **Streetmosphere** acts also enliven Hollywood Boulevard throughout the day, staging impromptu movie shoots, casting calls or even detective investigations. Have fun with them – you just might end up the star of the show! Also by the Hat, look out for favourite Disney characters during the morning.

Shopping and dining: Hollywood Boulevard has the best of the park's shopping (9 of the 21 stores), including **Sid Caheunga's One-of-a-Kind** (rare movie and TV items, including many celebrity autographs), **Keystone Clothiers** (some of the best apparel), **Mickey's of Hollywood** (all your souvenirs and gift items) and **The Darkroom** (for camera sales, rental, film and accessories). **The Brown Derby** is the park's signature restaurant, offering fine dining in best vintage Hollywood style (reservations usually necessary).

Echo Lake

Turn left out of Hollywood Boulevard and you find another area that pays homage to the movie world of the 1930s and '40s.

American Idol Experience: An exciting audience participation show based on the famous TV reality series. Guest performers undergo the

The Sorcerer's Hat

© Disney

full Idol experience, from audition to preparation (with a vocal coach and hair and make-up artists) to the performance, with those who score highest returning for an end-of-day Grand Finale show and the chance to win a 'front of the queue' pass at any American Idol audition nationwide. The show features 3 contestants with varying degrees of talent (from 'exceptional' to 'good sport'), prompting an empathetic feel-it-in-your-gut anticipation as each singer prepares to dazzle the audience. While the judge's critiques are a bit canned, the experience is suitably realistic, though it will probably appeal most to die-hard Idol fans. AAA.

ABC Sound Studio 'Sounds Dangerous' Starring Drew Carey:
A sound FX special that features American comedian Drew Carey in an instalment of a spoof undercover police show *Sounds Dangerous*. Most of the 12-minute show is in the dark – which upsets some children – and is centred on your special headphones as Carey's stakeout goes wildly wrong. Clever and amusing – if a bit tame for older children – you exit into the Sound Works Studio to try out some well-known sound effects. AAA.

Indiana Jones™ Epic Stunt Spectacular:
Consult your park *Times Guide* for the various times this rip-roaring stunt cavalcade hits the stage. A special movie set creates 3 different backdrops for Indiana Jones'™ stunt people to put on a dazzling array of scenes and special effects from

Honey I Shrunk the Kids Movie Set Adventure

© Disney

the Harrison Ford films. Audience participation is an element and there are some amusing sub-plots. Queues for the 30-minute show begin up to ½ an hour beforehand, but the auditorium holds more than 2,000 so everyone usually gets in. TTTT (FP).

Star Tours II: Due to open in May 2011, the popular *Star Wars*™ simulator ride is undergoing a complete revamp, returns as fully 3D Star Tours II. Climb into your StarSpeeder for a stunning high-speed journey through the worlds created by George Lucas in his award winning films, including trips to Coruscant and Tatooine, where riders blast into the Boonta Eve Classic Podrace with convincing and dramatic results. While the original Star Tours featured the first three films and the Death Star, the latest version highlights the second trio, so expect to meet the likes of Jar Jar Binks and Master Yoda – and with the option to change the story at various points, making for multiple ride options. The realism of entering the *Star Wars*™ world, from the queuing area to the post-ride gift shop, is brilliantly realistic, and lots of fun, with squabbling droids R2-D2 and C-3PO among the entertainment. Restrictions: 3ft 4in/101cm, no under-3s. TTTT (plus AAAAA; FP).

Other entertainment: Kids should make a beeline for the **Jedi Training Academy**, on the stage outside the Star Tours ride up to 8 times a day. Here, young Jedi hopefuls get to try their light sabre technique under the eyes of a Jedi master, before taking on Darth Vader himself. Great fun just to watch, too (TTTT for under-12s).

Shopping and dining: Shop for *Star Wars*™ goods at **Tatooine Traders** (at the exit to Star Tours) and Indiana Jones souvenirs at the **Indy Truck** and **Adventure Outpost**. There are also 3 good dining choices: the **'50s Prime Time Café** is a fun experience as you sit in mock stage sets from American TV sitcoms and eat meals 'just like Mom used to make' (the waiters all claim to be your aunt, uncle or cousin and warn you to take your elbows off the table – good fun!); the **Backlot Express** features superb burgers, hot dogs and sandwiches, while a varied buffet dinner is served up at **Hollywood & Vine** in addition to the **Play 'n Dine** character meal with the Playhouse Disney Pals, available from 8am–2.25pm ($26.99 adults, $16.99 3–9s).

Streets of America

Three of the park's bigger attractions can all be found here, along with an often-overlooked gem of a restaurant.

Muppet*Vision 3-D: The 3-D is crossed out here and 4-D substituted in its place, so be warned strange things are about to happen! A wonderful 10-minute holding-pen pre-show takes you into the Muppet Theater for a 20-minute experience with all of the Muppets, 3-D special effects and more – when Fozzie Bear points his squirty flower at you, prepare to get wet! It's a gem, and the kids love it. Queues build up through the main parts of the day, but Disney's queuing expertise makes them seem shorter. AAAAA (FP).

Honey, I Shrunk the Kids Movie Set Adventure: This adventure playground gives youngsters the chance to tackle massive blades of grass that turn out to be slides, crawl through caves, investigate giant mushrooms and more. There can be long queues here, too, so arrive early if the kids demand it (and bring plenty of film or a spare memory card). TTTT under-10s.

Premier Theater: This fully enclosed theatre is used for the *Star Wars*™ Weekend meet and greets and other set-piece special events.

 BRIT TIP

If you have young children, be aware there is some (loud) mock gunfire in the Lights, Motors, Action!™ Extreme Stunt Show, which can upset sensitive ears, while the motorbike scene includes a rider catching fire, which can be frightening for them, too.

Lights, Motors, Action!™ Extreme Stunt Show: A direct import from the Walt Disney Studios in Paris, this is a truly amazing live stunt spectacular, featuring cars, motorbikes, jet-skis and stuntmen of all kinds. It is one of the most remarkable shows you will see anywhere, full of genuine high-risk stunts that will leave you shaking your head in amazement. Seating starts 30 minutes prior to a show, and there is some amusing pre-show chat before the serious stuff starts. The set is based on a Mediterranean village and is magnificently crafted. Once the preliminaries are completed, you are treated to a 33-minute extravaganza of daredevil stunts, with a Car Ballet sequence, a Motorbike Chase and a Grand Finale that features some surprise pyrotechnics to complete an awesome presentation (keep your eyes on the windows below the video screen at the end). Each scene – featuring a secret-agent and various baddies – is explained by a

Lights, Motors, Action!

© Disney

movie director and the results of each shoot are played back on screen to show how the effects were created. All the cars were specially built for the show by Vauxhall, and there are some extra tricks between the main scenes. It was all designed by Frenchman Rémy Julienne, the doyen of film car stunt sequences from James Bond films *Goldeneye* and *Licence to Kill* and other action epics like *The Rock, Gone in 60 Seconds* and *Enemy of the State*. The exit can be quite a scrum, though, as 5,000 people have to leave together, and it can take 15 minutes to clear the auditorium, hence if you can sit towards the front, you will be out quicker. Because it involves so much genuine, live co-ordination it makes for a truly thrilling experience and you may well want to see it more than once – another reason to see it early on. TTTTT.

BRIT TIP

Don't queue for the Backlot Tour when Lights, Motors, Action! has just ended – it will be far too crowded.

Studio Backlot Tour: Before you board the special trams for a look at the off-limits part of the studios in this 35-minute walk-and-ride tour, you are treated to some special effects (involving an amusing water tank

with a mock Pearl Harbor attack). The tram takes you round the production backlot and then to **Catastrophe Canyon** for a demonstration of special effects that try both to drown you and to blow you up! AAA (plus TTTT). You exit into the **American Film Institute** showcase of costumes and props from recent films.

Other entertainment: Live music is provided periodically on the main street by the comedy rock band **Mulch, Sweat and Shears** (AAA), while this is also a great place to meet various Disney characters – look for *Cars* friends Lightning McQueen and Tow Mater at **Luigi's Garage** in front of the Backlot Tour, and *Monsters INC.* in the building to the right of Lights, Motors, Action! Show.

Shopping and dining: Shop for Christmas items at **It's A Wonderful Shop**, **Stage 1 Company Store** for Muppet and *Sesame Street* souvenirs and **Writer's Stop** for books and speciality coffees. **Mama Melrose's Ristorante Italiano** is a wonderful table-service Italian option (one of our favourites), while there are also the counter-service offerings of **Toy Story Pizza Planet** (pizza, salads and drinks) and **Studio Catering Co. Flatbread Grill** (healthier wraps, salads, grilled chicken, barbecue pulled pork and its own bar).

Catastrophe Canyon

© Disney

Enjoying the sunshine

Commissary Lane

This is just a small link between the Streets of America and the central plaza by the Sorcerer's Hat, and contains only 2 eating opportunities. **The Sci-Fi Dine-In Theater Restaurant** is a big hit with kids as you dine in a mock drive-in cinema, with cars as tables, car-hop waitresses and a big film screen showing old black-and-white science-fiction movie clips. The menu has also been overhauled (now featuring gourmet burgers, ribs, chicken, pasta and sandwiches, as well as the signature milkshakes and sodas; $27.97 for 3-course lunch, $8.99 kids' meal). The counter-service option **ABC Commissary** serves up a multi-ethnic choice that includes a chicken curry, Cuban sandwich and Asian salad.

Pixar Place

This area has undergone a complete transformation from the old Mickey Avenue to the new-look Pixar Studios (styled after the Pixar Film Studios in California) after the opening of the Toy Story Mania ride.

Toy Story Mania: A real family fun fiesta, a 3-D ride into a fantasy fairground of games with the *Toy Story* characters. To start with you are 'shrunk' to toy-size and board special carnival vehicles (each equipped with individual spring-action shooters) to go through Andy's Bedroom, where the toys have set up a Midway Games Play Set with 5 challenges, plus a practice round. Thanks to a pair of 3D glasses, riders can 'see' everything their shooter fires at the sequence of targets (while, with the magic of Disney's special effects, they might also 'feel' objects whirring past as they burst out of the screens; and, if you hit a water balloon, watch out!). Throw virtual eggs at barnyard targets, launch darts at prehistoric balloon targets, break plates with baseballs, land rings on Buzz Lightyear's alien friends and finish up in Woody's Rootin' Tootin' Shootin' Gallery (with a bonus roundup) before totting up your scores and comparing with fellow riders. All the while, the *Toy Story* characters cheer you on (and pass on hints to boost your score, so it works for all abilities) and provide some amusing commentary. At times it is a touch raucous and chaotic, but kids are sure to love the shooting game element and the whole family can enjoy the amusing ride through the toys' world. Even the queuing area is fun, with a huge animatronic Mr Potato Head acting as a fairground barker to entertain while you wait (AAA + TTTT; FP). As a recent ride, it draws some HUGE queues, so you should use the FastPass option here early on.

Other entertainment: Look out for the *Toy Story* characters meet-and-greet here, plus the new audio-animatronic **Luxo Jr** – the amusing lamp character from all Pixar films – who makes regular appearances on a courtyard balcony.

Toy Story Mania

Shopping and dining: For souvenirs and gifts from your favourite Pixar films visit the **Camera Dept**, while **Hey Howdy Hey Take Away** offers counter-service ice-cream, snacks and drinks.

Animation Courtyard

Get ready for a series of wonderful family-friendly shows in this area of the park, starting with **Voyage of the Little Mermaid**, a 17-minute live performance that is primarily for children who have seen the Disney cartoon. It brings together a mix of actors, animation and puppetry to recreate the film's highlights. Parents will still enjoy the special effects, but queues tend to be long, so go early or late. Those in the first few rows may also get a little wet. AAA (AAAAA under-9s; FP).

Journey into Narnia: Prince Caspian: This walk-through experience features a dramatic entryway that leads into a Narnian fantasy world and multimedia show. Set in Aslan's stone temple chamber, it tells the story of the second Narnia film and provides a couple of neat special effects touches to various re-created scenes from the Prince Caspian saga. You then exit into an exhibit of original art, props and costumes from the film itself. AA.

Playhouse Disney – Live on Stage!

© Disney

BRIT TIP

Try to sit at least halfway back in the Mermaid Theatre, especially if you are with young children, as the stage front is a bit high.

Walt Disney: One Man's Dream: This interactive show-and-tell exhibit chronicles Walt himself and his lifetime of accomplishments. From archive school records to a model of the Nautilus from *20,000 Leagues Under the Sea*, the story of the man behind the Mouse comes to vivid life. The homage ends with a preview of Disney's future developments, plus a 10-minute film encapsulating all Walt achieved and dreamed about. AAAA.

The Magic of Disney Animation: An amusing and entertaining 30-minute show-and-tour through the making of cartoons. It starts with a special theatrical performance by Mushu, the Eddie Murphy-voiced dragon from the animated film *Mulan*. From there you exit into a hands-on area of interactive fun (especially for children); *Ink & Paint* is a colouring challenge; at *Sound Stage* you can try a voiceover; and *You're a Character* will tell you which Disney character you most resemble. From there, you have the choice of joining the Animation Academy for a tutored class in cartoon art or stopping for a meet and greet with various Disney characters, including Sorcerer Mickey. You exit via the **Animation Gallery**, which has some fabulous gifts. Queues are rarely serious, so it's a good afternoon choice. AAAA.

Playhouse Disney – Live on Stage!: Straight out of several popular kids' TV series comes this 20-minute live show with pre-school favourites like *Mickey Mouse Clubhouse*, *JoJo's Circus*, *Rolie Polie Olie*, *The Little Einsteins* and *Handy Manny*. It's colourful and entertaining and children of the right age just love it. AAA (AAAAA under-5s).

Other entertainment: Look for the Playhouse Disney characters outside the Live On Stage! show, whilst the latest Pixar characters can be found inside the Magic of Disney Animation.

Rock 'n' Roller Coaster Starring Aerosmith

Sunset Boulevard

The final part of the park contains the 2 high-thrill rides, and the big night-time finale, but it's also the busiest area from midday onwards, so try to visit here first or leave it until the last couple of hours.

Rock 'n' Roller Coaster Starring Aerosmith: Disney's first big-thrill inverted coaster is a sure-fire draw for the adrenalin ride addicts, with a magnificent indoor setting and nerve-jangling ride. It features a clever 3-D film show starring rock group Aerosmith in their recording studio. That leads to the real fun, set to specially recorded tracks from the band itself and with outrageous speaker systems, as riders climb aboard Cadillac cars for a memorable whiz through a mock Los Angeles (watch out for a close encounter with the Hollywood sign!). The high-speed launch and inversions ensure an up-to-the-minute coaster experience. Go first thing or expect serious queues. Restrictions: 4ft/124cm. TTTTT (FP).

The Twilight Zone™ Tower of Terror: This 199ft/60m landmark invites you to experience another dimension in the strange Hollywood Tower Hotel that time forgot. The exterior is intriguing, the interior is fascinating, the ride is scintillating and the queues are huge! Just when you think you are through to the ride, there's another queue, so spend your time inspecting the superb detail. There's a lot more to this than just the big 13-storey drop, however, as the 'Twilight Zone' theme adds a real element of curiosity and invention. Your elevator car twists and turns unexpectedly before it is time to 'drop in', and the random drop sequence provides many hair-raising thrills before you exit! Restrictions: 3ft 4in/101cm. TTTTT (FP).

Twilight Zone Tower of Terror

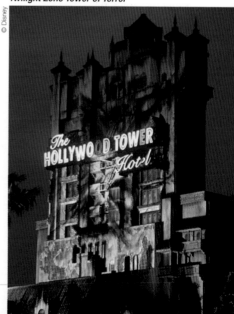

Beauty and the Beast – Live on Stage: An enchanting live musical song and dance performance of the highlights of this Disney classic will entertain the whole family for 30 minutes in the nearby Theater of the Stars. Check the daily schedule for show times, which are up to 5 times a day, usually starting at 11.30am. AAA.

Fantasmic!: This special-effects spectacular is simply not to be missed. Staged every night (at peak periods; twice a week off-peak) in a 6,900-seat amphitheatre, it features the dreams of Mickey, portrayed as the Sorcerer's Apprentice, through films such as *Pocahontas*, *The Lion King* and *Snow White*, but hijacked by the Disney villains, leading to an epic battle with Our Hero emerging triumphant. Dancing waters, shooting comets, animated fountains, swirling stars and balls of fire combine in a breathtaking presentation – but beware of the giant, fire-breathing dragon! The 25-minute show begins seating up to 2 hours in advance and it's best to head there at least 30 minutes before (watch out for the splash zones!). AAAAA.

Other entertainment: Sunset Boulevard is also home to more of the park's **Streetmosphere** characters.

Shopping and dining: The best shopping here is provided by **Legends of Hollywood**, **Planet Hollywood Super Store** and the **Sunset Boulevard** shops (for limited edition watches, clothing and other collectibles). **Rosie's All-American Café** (chicken, burgers and salads) and **Catalina Eddie's** (pizza) are the best of Sunset Boulevard's series of 5 market-style eateries.

Daily parade

In keeping with the park's energetic style, **Block Party Bash**, direct from *Disney's California Adventure* park in Anaheim, is a high-energy cavalcade featuring 60 singers, dancers, gymnasts and Pixar movie characters – from *The Incredibles, Toy Story* and *Toy Story 3, A Bug's Life and Monsters Inc.* – in a street party that stops periodically to interact with guests. Lively music, vibrant costumes and some notable aerial acrobatics make it guaranteed to captivate and amuse. AAAA.

BRIT TIP — Yes, you can get a plain burger without all the bells and whistles at Backlot Express and Rosie's. Just ask when you reach the cashier. It's not on the menu, but it is available.

Studios at Christmas

At Christmas (late Nov–1 Jan), one of the most amazing spectacles anywhere is the **Osborne Family Lights,** which are switched on every evening in the Streets of America area. This simply stunning display of 5 million twinkling, themed fairy lights draws huge crowds all evening (go during a Fantasmic! performance to avoid the worst of the throngs).

Fantasmic!

© Disney

DISNEY'S HOLLYWOOD STUDIOS with children

Here is our guide to the attractions that appeal to the different age groups in this park:

Under-5s

Beauty and the Beast – Live on Stage, Block Party Bash, Fantasmic!, Honey I Shrunk the Kids Movie Set Adventure, The Magic of Disney Animation, Playhouse Disney – Live On Stage!, Voyage of the Little Mermaid.

5–8s

Beauty and the Beast – Live On Stage, Block Party Bash, Fantasmic!, Honey I Shrunk the Kids Movie Set Adventure, Indiana Jones™ Epic Stunt Spectacular, Journey Into Narnia: Prince Caspian, Lights, Motors, Action!™ Extreme Stunt Show, The Magic of Disney Animation, Muppet* Vision 3-D, 'Sounds Dangerous' Starring Drew Carey, Studio Backlot Tour, Toy Story Mania, Voyage of the Little Mermaid.

9–12s

American Idol Experience, Beauty and the Beast – Live on Stage, Fantasmic!, The Great Movie Ride, Indiana Jones™ Epic Stunt Spectacular, Journey into Narnia: Prince Caspian, Lights, Motors, Action!™ Extreme Stunt Show, The Magic of Disney Animation, Muppet*Vision 3-D, Rock 'n' Roller Coaster Starring Aerosmith, 'Sounds Dangerous' Starring Drew Carey, Star Tours, Studio Backlot Tour, Twilight Zone™ Tower of Terror, Toy Story Mania.

Over-12s

American Idol Experience, Fantasmic!, The Great Movie Ride, Indiana Jones™ Epic Stunt Spectacular, Lights, Motors, Action!™ Extreme Stunt Show, The Magic of Disney Animation, Muppet*Vision 3-D, Rock 'n' Roller Coaster Starring Aerosmith, Star Tours, Studio Backlot Tour, Toy Story Mania, Twilight Zone™ Tower of Terror, Walt Disney: One Man's Dream.

Skywalker and Co

Star Wars™ film fans will want to make a beeline for the Studios during weekends in late May and early June when the park becomes a playground for characters, film stars, photo-opportunities, competitions and other memorabilia based on anything to do with Luke Skywalker and Co. Much of the event is scheduled in and around the Premier Theater in the Streets of America area. There is no additional fee to rub shoulders with (and get autographs from) various *Star Wars*™ personalities, and the Studios take on an extra (space) dimension each weekend (though the park is also at its most crowded).

Park tours

New in 2010 was **Inspiration: Through Walt's Eyes**, giving insight into how Walt Disney influenced film making, and how ideas are transformed into the elements, large and small, that we see in the parks.

Tour Hollywood Studio's Sunset Boulevard, go backstage to see Event and Decorating Support, then visit the famous utilidoors in Magic Kingdom (9am Mon, Fri, Sun; $99 per person, no under 16s).

Osborne family lights

© Disney

Disney's Animal Kingdom Theme Park

Disney's newest and smartest theme park opened in 1998 representing a completely different experience. With an emphasis on conservation and nature, it largely eschews the non-stop thrills and attractions of the other parks and instead offers a change of pace, a more relaxing motif, as well as Disney's usual seamless entertainment style, but still with some excellent rides, including one of its very best. The attractions are relatively few, with just 6 out-and-out rides, but there are then 2 elaborate wildlife trails, 4 shows (including 2 that are almost worth the admission price alone), an extravagant adventure playground, conservation station and petting zoo, and a Disney character greeting area. It's a far cry from the hustle-bustle of the *Magic Kingdom*, but its serious environmental message aims to create a greater understanding of many of the world's ecological problems. There are plenty of animal encounters along the way and the overall style is so creative, it positively demands you slow down to appreciate the artistry involved.

It is also outrageously scenic, notably with the 145ft/44m Tree of Life, the Kilimanjaro Safaris and the Asian village of Serka Zong (home to the gigantic Expedition: Everest™ ride), but it won't overwhelm you with Disney's usual grand fantasy. Rather, it is a chance to explore and experience; to learn and understand; and to soak up the gentler ambience of nature at its finest. It is not a zoo in the conventional sense, but it is home to 200-plus species of birds and animals (in some wonderfully naturalistic settings). The educational tone is fairly strong, but children in particular may pick up easily on the essential conservation undertones

Disney's Animal Kingdom Theme Park at a glance

Location	Directly off Osceola Parkway, also via World Drive and Buena Vista Drive
Size	500 acres/203ha divided into 6 'lands'
Hours	9am–5 or 6pm off peak; 8am–7pm in high season
Admission	Under-3s free; 3–9 $74 (1–day base ticket), $322 (5–day Premium), $332 (7-day Premium); adult (10+) $82, $345, $355. Prices do not include tax.
Parking	$14
Lockers	Either side of Entrance Plaza; $12 small; $14 large ($5 deposit)
Pushchairs	$15 and $31 at Garden Gate Gifts, through entrance on right; length of stay $13 per day single, $27 per day double
Wheelchairs	$12 or $70 ($20 deposit refunded) with pushchairs
Top attractions	DINOSAUR!, Kilimanjaro Safaris, It's Tough To Be A Bug!, Kali River Rapids, Festival Of The Lion King, Finding Nemo – The Musical, Expedition: Everest™
Don't miss	Pangani Forest Exploration Trail, Maharajah Jungle Trek, Rafiki's Planet Watch, Mickey's Jammin' Jungle Parade, dining at Rainforest Café
Hidden costs	**Meals** Burger, chips and coke $9.31 3-course meal at Yak & Yeti $35.48 (kid's entrée and dessert ($9.48) Beer $5.50 and $6.25 Kids' meal $4.99 **T-shirts** $19.95-34.95 **Souvenirs** $1-20,000 **Sundries** Face painting $10–15

of things like Kilimanjaro Safaris and Maharajah Jungle Trek. However, the park does get crowded, the walkways can be congested and there are also fewer places to cool down. It is definitely a good idea to be here on time and use FastPass (FP) to minimise queuing.

Getting there

If you are staying in the Kissimmee area, *Disney's Animal Kingdom* is the easiest of the parks to find. Just get on the (toll) Osceola Parkway and follow it all the way to the toll booths. Alternatively, coming down I-4, take exit 65 on to Osceola Parkway. From West Highway 192, come in on Sherberth Road and turn right at the first traffic lights. If you arrive early (which is advisable), you can walk to the Entrance Plaza. Otherwise, the usual tram system takes you in, so make a note of the row you park in (e.g. Unicorn, 67). The entrance plaza is overlooked by the **Rainforest Café**, with its 65ft/20m waterfall, which is open for breakfast, lunch and dinner (but is busy 12.30–3.30pm and an hour before closing). With Orlando so hot in the summer, you need to be at the park as early as possible to see the animals before they take cover in the shade.

BRIT TIP
An early start is especially advised for Kilimanjaro Safaris. You will see far more animals in the first few cooler hours of the day than during the hotter afternoon when they seek the shade.

For the early birds, here is your best plan of campaign. Once through the gates, animal lovers should head first for Kilimanjaro Safaris, through the Oasis, Discovery Island and Africa. After the Safari, go straight to Pangani Forest Exploration Trail and you will have experienced 2 of the park's best animal encounters before it gets too hot. Alternatively, thrill-seekers should walk straight through Discovery Island for Asia, where the Expedition: Everest™ ride is the big draw. With that one safely under your belt, head to Kilimanjaro Safaris or the nearby Kali River Rapids raft ride, followed by the scenic Maharajah Jungle Trek. The best combination for the first arrivals is to get a FastPass for Expedition: Everest™, then ride Kilimanjaro Safaris and, once you have done that (and depending on your FP time), either do your Everest ride or go straight to Kali River Rapids. Check your show schedule for Festival of the Lion King and try to catch one of the first 2 performances, as the later ones draw sizeable queues. The wait time board at the entrance to Discovery Island is helpful. Early birds can also enjoy **The Adventure Begins**, the park's official opening, featuring a welcome from Rafiki and other favourite Disney characters. Cast Members are also on hand with a variety of small critters (some furry, some not so!) as you enter through the turnstiles. Those are your main tactics – here is the full rundown.

Primeval Whirl®

© Disney

The Oasis

1 The Oasis Tropical Garden

Discovery Island

2 The Tree of Life
3 It's Tough To Be A Bug
4 Discovery Island Trails
5 Flame Tree Barbecue
6 Pizzafari

Camp Minnie-Mickey

7 Character Greeting Trails
8 Festival Of The Lion King

Dinoland USA

9 DINOSAUR!
10 The Boneyard
11 Finding Nemo – The Musical

12 Chester And Hester's Dino-Rama!
13 TriceraTOP Spin
14 Primeval Whirl
15 Restaurantosaurus

Africa

16 Harambe
17 Kilimanjaro Safaris
18 Pangani Forest Exploration
19 Rafiki's Planet Watch
20 Tusker House Restaurant

Asia

21 Flights Of Wonder
22 Kali River Rapids
23 Maharajah Jungle Trek
24 Expedition: Everest™
25 Yak 'n Yeti Restaurant
26 Rainforest Café

DISNEY'S ANIMAL KINGDOM

Rafiki's Planet Watch

Asia

Discovery Island

Africa

Camp Minnie-Mickey

Oasis

ENTRANCE

Dinoland U.S.A.

The Oasis

The **Tropical Garden** is a gentle, walk-through introduction to the park, a rocky, tree-covered area featuring animal habitats and studded with streams, waterfalls and lush plant life. Here you meet miniature deer, a giant anteater, exotic boars, macaws, sloths, iguanas and kangaroos in a brilliantly understated environment that leads you across a stone bridge to the main park area. This is a good place to visit in early afternoon when many of the rides are busy. AAA.

Other entertainment: Look out for a host of **Disney characters** here throughout the morning and late afternoon, plus the amusing **Wes Palm** – a potted palm with attitude!

Shopping and dining: Stop at **Garden Gate Gifts** (on the right) for pushchair, wheelchair and locker hire, while **Guest Relations** is on the left. The fun **Rainforest Café** also has an entrance inside the park here. If you haven't seen the one at *Downtown Disney*, you should definitely call in to view the amazing jungle interior with its audio-animatronic animals, waterfalls, thunderstorms and aquariums. A 3-course meal costs anywhere from $30-$62, but the setting alone is worth it and the food is above average. Try breakfast or an early dinner here to avoid the crowds.

Discovery Island

This colourful village is the park hub, themed as a tropical artists' colony, with animal-inspired artwork, nature trails, 4 main shops and 2 eateries. You will also find the **First Aid** station here (look for the 'ladybird' lights) and the **Baby Center**.

The Tree of Life: This arboreal edifice is the park centre-piece, an awesome creation that seems to have a different perspective from wherever you view it. The trunk and roots are covered in 325 carvings representing the Circle of Life, from the dolphin to the lion. **Trails** lead round the tree, interspersed with habitats for flamingos, otters, ring-tailed lemurs, macaws, axis deer, cranes, storks, ducks and tortoises. The tree canopy spreads 160ft/49m, the trunk is 50ft/15m wide and the diameter of the roots is 170ft/52m. It has 103,000 leaves (all attached by hand) on more than 8,000 branches! AAAA.

It's Tough To Be A Bug!: Winding down among the Tree's roots brings you 'underground' to a 430-seat theatre and another example of Disney's artistry in 3-D films and special effects. This hysterical 10-minute show, in the company of Flick from the Pixar film *A Bug's Life*, is a homage to 80% of the animal world, featuring grasshoppers,

It's Tough To Be A Bug!

© Disney

beetles, spiders, stink bugs and termites (beware the 'acid' spray!) as well as several tricks we couldn't possibly reveal. Sit towards the back in the middle (allow a good number of people in first as the rows are filled up from the far side) to get the best of the 3-D effects. Queues build up from midday, but they do move quite steadily. Don't miss the 'forthcoming attractions' posters in the foyer for some excruciating bug puns on famous films. AAAAA (FP).

BRIT TIP

The dark, special effects and mock creepy-crawlies in It's Tough To Be A Bug! can be extremely scary for young 'uns. Use caution.

Other entertainment: The Island is home to live music from percussion group **Village Beatniks** and the South American sounds of **Inka Sikuri**. **Disney characters** are also on hand – Winnie the Pooh and friends at Character Landing (opposite Flame Tree Barbecue) and Lilo and Stitch next to Island Mercantile. Keep an eye (and camera) on the surrounding river for **The Adventure Continues**, a musical character boat featuring Mickey, Goofy and Co.

Shopping and dining: This is where you will find a huge range of merchandise, souvenirs and gifts, most notably in **Disney Outfitters** (unique artwork and collectables) and **Island Mercantile**. Counter-service restaurants **Pizzafari** (pizza, salads

The Tree of Life

Disney's Animal Kingdom Lodge

and sandwiches) and **Flame Tree Barbecue** (barbecued ribs, beef and pork, chicken sandwiches and salads) are both good choices. If it's not too hot, the Flame Tree is a relaxing and picturesque option, set among some pretty gardens and fountains on the bank of Discovery River; the air-conditioned Pizzafari is better in summer months.

Camp Minnie-Mickey

This is a woodland retreat featuring winding paths and more of Disney's clever scenery, plus 2 excellent and highly family-friendly shows, as well as a real character fest, plus the ever-popular (with kids!) squirt fountains.

Character Greeting Trails: A series of trails lead to 4 different pavilions that are home to a variety of jungle encounters with Disney characters such as Mickey and Minnie (naturally), Winnie the Pooh and friends plus, occasionally, Jungle Book and Lion King characters. AAAAA (for kids).

Festival of the Lion King: Not to be missed, this high-powered 25-minute production (up to 8 times a day at peak periods; 5 a day at others) brings the hit animated film to life in truly spectacular fashion, with giant moving stages, huge animated figures, singers, dancers, acrobats and stilt-walkers, plus some fun audience participation. All the well-known songs are given an airing in a fiesta of colour and sound, and it serves to underline the quality Disney brings

© Disney

Kilimanjaro Safaris

to its live shows. However, queuing often begins a good 45 minutes in advance of each high-energy show for the 1,000-seat (air-conditioned) theatre, so it is usually best to try to take in one of the earlier shows of the day. AAAAA.

Other entertainment: The kids' favourite animal songs periodically get an airing with **Gi-Tar Dan**.

Africa

The largest land in the park, it recreates magnificently the forests, grasslands and rocky homelands of East Africa's most fascinating residents in a richly landscaped setting that is part rundown port town and part savannah. The central area, **Harambe Village**, is a superb Imagineer's eye-view of a Kenyan port town, complete with white coral walls and thatched roofs and is the starting point of your adventure. The Arab-influenced Swahili culture is also depicted in the native tribal costumes and architecture.

BRIT TIP

The best (i.e. the most jolting) ride with the Kilimanjaro Safaris is at the back of the truck. There is much less to see from midday to late afternoon when many of the animals take a siesta.

Kilimanjaro Safaris: The queuing area alone earns high marks for authenticity, preparing you for the sights and sounds of the 110-acre/45ha savannah beyond. You board a 32-passenger truck, with your driver/guide relaying information about the flora and fauna on view and a bush ranger/pilot overhead relaying facts and figures on the wildlife, including the dangers threatening them in the real world. Scores of animals are spread out in various habitats, with no fences in sight (the ditches and barriers are all well concealed) as you splash through fords and cross rickety bridges, and you should get good close-ups of lions, rhinos, elephants, giraffes, antelope, zebras, hippos, baboons

Kilimanjaro Safaris

© Disney

and ostriches. Once again, the authentic nature of all you see (okay, some of the tyre 'ruts' and termite mounds are concrete and the baobab trees are fake) is truly breathtaking, with the spread of the vegetation and landscaping, and the only drawback is the lack of a photo stop or two along the way, as the ride is pretty bumpy. The animals also roam over a wide area and can disappear from view. Not recommended for expectant mothers or anyone with back or neck problems. AAAAA (FP).

Pangani Forest Exploration Trail: As you leave the Safari, you turn on to a serious nature trail that showcases gorillas, hippos, meerkats and rare tropical birds. You wander the trail at your own pace and visit 'research' stations to learn more about the animals on display, including the underwater view of the hippos (check out the size of a hippo skull and those teeth!) and the savannah overlook, where giraffes and antelope graze and the amusing meerkats frolic. The walk-through aviary gives you the chance to meet the carmine bee-eater, pygmy goose, African green pigeon, ibis and brimstone canary, among others, but the real centre-piece is the silverback gorilla habitat (in fact, 2 of them). The family group is often just inches away

Rafiki's Planet Watch

from the plate-glass window, while the bachelor group further along can prove more elusive. Again, the natural aspect of the trail is fabulous and it provides a host of photo opportunities. Do this early or save it for late in the day and most of the crowds will have moved on. AAAAA.

Rafiki's Planet Watch: This subsection of Africa involves a rustic train ride, with a peek into some of the backstage areas, as a preamble to the park's interactive and educational exhibits (especially for children). The 3-part journey starts with **Habitat Habit!**, where you can see cotton-top tamarins and learn how conservation begins in your own back garden. **Conservation Station** offers a series

Pagani Forest Exploration Trail

Festival of the Lion King

of exhibits, shows and information stations about the environment and threats to its ecology. Look out for *Sounds of the Rain Forest*, the story of endangered species, at the Mermaid Tales Theater and the Eco-Heroes (who can be quizzed on-screen) trying to redress the balance, then observe the park's veterinary treatment centre, hatchery and neonatal care. You can easily spend an hour absorbing the information here, inspired by **Disney's Worldwide Conservation Fund**. Finally, the **Affection Section** petting zoo consists of a herd of friendly goats and a rather shy calf. AAA.

Other entertainment: There's plenty more to enjoy here, with the splendid percussion of **Mor Thiam**, the pageantry and rhythms of **Tam Tam's of Congo**. With luck you'll also spot the wonderful **DiVine**, a 'moving' part of the foliage! **Disney characters** can be found in Harambe and Rafiki's Planet Watch.

Shopping and dining: Harambe is home to the **Mombasa Marketplace/Ziwani Traders**, where you can suit up safari-style, while Rafiki's Planet Watch has **Out of the Wild** for more

gifts and souvenirs. **Tusker House Restaurant** (featuring *Donald's Safari Breakfast* at $24.99 adults, $13.99 children, and non-character buffets at lunch and dinner) is one of the best diners in the park, with a mouth-watering array of salads, a hot carvery, rotisserie chicken, stews and vegetarian dishes ($25.99 adults, $13.99 children for lunch; $32.99 and $15.99 for dinner). There are also 4 snack and drink bars, most notably the **Kusafiri Coffee Shop & Bakery**, while a light breakfast (bagel sandwich or French toast slices) is offered at **Tamu Tamu Refreshments** (burgers, sandwiches, salads and drinks).

Tamu Tamu Refreshments

Asia

The next 'land' is elaborately themed as the gateway to the imaginary south-east Asian city of Anandapur, with temples, ruined forts, landscape and wildlife. The element of reality is again quite startling and the architecture is full of faithful representations of genuine locations.

Flights of Wonder: Another wildlife show, this portrays the talents and traits of the park's avian inhabitants, built into a production of amusing proportions. A trainer showcases the behaviours of various birds, including macaws and hawks, before being interrupted by a bumbling tour guide – Guano Joe (groan) – who needs to be reminded of key conservation issues. This is the cue for some frolics with our feathered friends, including vultures, eagles, toucans and singing parrot Gaucho. The Caravan Stage is not air-conditioned, though, and is fiendishly hot in summer. AAA.

Maharajah Jungle Trek

Kali River Rapids: Part thrill-ride, part scenic journey, this bouncy raft ride will get you pretty wet (not great for early morning in winter). It starts out in tropical forest territory before launching into a scene of logging devastation, warning of the dangers of clear-cut burning. Your raft then plunges down a waterfall (and one unlucky soul – usually the one with their back to the drop – gets seriously damp) before you finish more sedately. Queues can be long through the main part of the day, so use FastPass here. Restrictions: 3ft 6in/106cm (a few rafts have adult-and-child seats allowing smaller children to ride). TTT (plus AAAA; FP).

Maharajah Jungle Trek: Asia's version of the wildlife trail is another picturesque walk past decaying temple ruins and animal encounters. Playful gibbons, tapirs, Komodo dragons and a bat enclosure (including the flying fox bat, the world's largest) lead to the main viewing area, the 5-acre/2ha Tiger Range, whose pool and fountains are a popular playground early in the day for these magnificent big cats. An antelope enclosure and walk-through aviary complete this truly breathtaking trek (which rarely draws heavy crowds). AAAAA.

Kali River Rapids

© Disney

Expedition Everest

Expedition: Everest: A major attraction, this wonderfully clever roller-coaster takes you deep into the Himalayas for an encounter with the mythical Yeti. The queuing area alone will convince you of its authentic location (try to do the main queue at least once rather than FastPass to appreciate all the fine detail) as it delivers you to an old abandoned tea plantation railway station. Here you undertake the ride to the foothills of Mount Everest, but you must first brave the perils of the Forbidden Mountain – lair of the Yeti – to get there. Will the beast be in evidence? You bet! The ride becomes a typically fast-paced whiz (though with no inversions), forwards AND backwards, as you attempt to escape the creature's domain. The final encounter with a massive audio-animatronic Yeti is truly jaw-dropping and underlines the splendidly creative nature of this massive ride. It has proved to be a fabulous attraction, but it draws equally impressive crowds all day, so make it one of the first things you do. You can also take advantage of a Single Rider queue here (at the FP entrance) if you don't mind your group being split up. Restrictions: 3ft 8in/115cm. TTTTT (FP).

BRIT TIP

Although Expedition: Everest™ is a FastPass ride, its popularity means FastPasses often run out, so don't leave it too late to visit here.

Flights of Wonder

© Disney

Shopping and dining: The retail options are pretty limited in Asia (just 2 minor kiosks), but it is also home to the fab **Yak and Yeti** combination diner. Outside is the counter-service **Local Foods Café** (honey chicken, chow mein, egg rolls, chicken salad and sweet and sour pork), while inside the 2-storey structure is the full **Restaurant**. This latter offers some of the most imaginative cuisine in any of the parks, from a Dim Sum basket to Maple Tamarind Chicken and a superb spicy Vietnamese Pho, as well as more standard Asian-fusion dishes. A good range of drinks and cocktails complement this outstanding eatery.

DinoLand USA

The final area of the park is somewhat at odds with the natural theming of the rest, a full-scale palaeontology exercise, with the accent on a 'university fossil dig'. Energetically tongue-in-cheek (the students who work the area have the motto 'Been there, dug that', while you enter under a mock brachiosaurus skeleton, the 'Oldengate Bridge' – groan!), it still features some glimpses into genuine dino research and artefacts.

DINOSAUR!: Renamed after Disney's big animated film (it was initially called *Countdown to Extinction*), this is a herky-jerky ride experience, rather dark and intense (and often too scary for young children). It is also a wonderfully realistic journey back to the end of the Cretaceous period, when a giant meteor put paid to dinosaur life. You enter the high-

DINOSAUR!

The Boneyard

tech Dino Institute for a multimedia history show that leads to a briefing room for your 'mission' 65 million years in the past. However, one of the Institute's scientists hijacks your trip to capture a dinosaur, and you career back to a prehistoric jungle in a 12-passenger 'Time Rover'. The threat of a carnotaurus (quite frightening for children; try to sit them on the inside of the car) and the impending doom of the meteor add up to a breathtaking whiz through a menacing environment. You will need to ride at least twice to appreciate all the detail, but queues build up quickly, so go either first thing or late in the day. Restrictions: 3ft 4in/101cm. TTTT plus AAAA (FP).

The Boneyard: A hugely imaginative adventure playground, it offers kids the chance to slip, slide and climb through the 'fossilised' remains of triceratops and brontosaurs, explore caves, dig for bones and splash through a mini waterfall. The amusing signage will be wasted on most kids, but it's ideal for parents to let their young 'uns loose for up to an hour (though not just after the neighbouring Finding Nemo show has finished). TTTT (kids only).

Finding Nemo – The Musical: This lovely show is a first for Disney entertainment, taking a non-musical animated feature and turning it into a fully fledged all-singing extravaganza. The show combines colourful puppets, dancers, acrobats and animated backdrops with innovative

DISNEY'S ANIMAL KINGDOM PARK with children

Here is our guide to the attractions that appeal to the different age groups in this park:

Under-5s

Affection Section, The Boneyard, Character Greetings Trails, Discovery Island Trails, Festival of the Lion King, Finding Nemo – The Musical, Kilimanjaro Safaris, Maharajah Jungle Trek, Pangani Forest Exploration Trail, TriceraTOP Spin, Mickey's Jammin' Jungle Parade.

5–8s

All the above, plus Conservation Station, DINOSAUR! (with parental discretion), Flights Of Wonder, Habitat Habit!, It's Tough To Be A Bug (with parental discretion), Kali River Rapids, Primeval Whirl.

9–12s

All the above, plus Expedition: Everest™.

Over-12s

DINOSAUR!, Expedition: Everest™, Festival of the Lion King, Flights Of Wonder, It's Tough To Be A Bug!, Kali River Rapids, Kilimanjaro Safaris, Maharajah Jungle Trek, Pangani Forest Exploration Trail, Primeval Whirl, Mickey's Jammin' Jungle Parade

---

lighting, sound and special effects. The basic idea remains faithful to the story of Nemo, his dad Marlin and friends Dory and Crush and features larger-than-life puppetry, plus rod, bunraku and shadow puppets, all designed by Michael Curry, who created the award-winning Broadway version of Disney's *The Lion King* show. It's a spectacular combination of music and grand staging, and performs up to 5 times a day. AAAA.

BRIT TIP
Finding Nemo – The Musical is a popular addition, but although it draws long queues, the theatre seats 1,500, so most people usually get in.

Chester & Hester's Dino-Rama!: This mini-land of rides, fairground games and stalls adds a rather garish element to the park. Its main icon is a towering concretosaurus (!), and it is designed to have a quirky, tongue-in-cheek style reminiscent of 1950s' American roadside attractions. The rides are: **TriceraTOP Spin:** another version of the Dumbo/Aladdin rides in the *Magic Kingdom*, where a flying, twirling, spinning top bounces you up and down with a surprise at the top. AA (TTTT under-5s); and **Primeval Whirl:** coaster fans will get a laugh out of this wacky offering that sends its riders through a maze of curves, hills and (quite sharp) drops that make it seem faster than it actually is. It's basically a lampoon of the DINOSAUR! ride, a mock journey 'way back in time', with plenty of cartoon frippery. Extra fun is provided by the fact that the cars spin, which gives an unpredictable element to each 3-minute ride. The queuing area is a riot of visual gags, but the ride is not recommended for anyone with back or neck problems. Restrictions: 4ft/122cm. TTTT (FP).

TriceraTOP Spin

© Disney

Other entertainment: Dino-Rama also features the **Fossil Fun Games**, 6 fairground-type stalls (each costing a rather hefty $2.50-5) designed to tempt you into trying to win a large cuddly dinosaur. Comic trio **Smear, Splat and Dip** perform up to 6 times a day with their brand of madcap juggling and acrobatics, while the highly entertaining percussion band **Village Beatniks** can also be found here, along with a new **Disney character** meet-and-greet featuring Goofy and Pluto.

Shopping and dining: Chester and Hester's Dinosaur Treasures (the 'Fossiliferous Gift Store' – groan!) offers a wide range of dino-related souvenirs. You can get a counter-service meal at the (you've guessed it!) **Restaurantosaurus** (burgers, hot dogs and salad) or grab a snack at **PetriFries**.

Parades and tours

Mickey's Jammin' Jungle Parade: The daily highlight is a tour de force in which the Imagineers have created a series of fanciful 'Expedition Rovers' that give various Disney characters the chance to celebrate all the animals that live here. The parade is enhanced by stilt-walkers, puppets, mobile sculptures and different 'party animals', plus live percussionists as

Mickey's Jammin' Jungle Parade

it snakes down a narrow path from Harambe, around Discovery Island and back. With memorable musical backing, it sounds as good as it looks, while 25 park guests are chosen to take part every day, travelling on the back of amusingly designed rickshaws that follow each of the character jeeps. AAAAA.

Tours: Finally, for a behind-the-scenes look at the park, **Backstage Safari** is a wonderful 3-hour journey into the handling and care of all the animals ($70, no under-16s), while **Wild By Design** offers a 3-hour tour of the park's art, architecture and history and how it was all created ($60, no under-14s). Book on 407 939 8687.

That's the full Disney theme park story, but there is still PLENTY more in store…

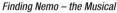
Finding Nemo – the Musical

6 Five More of the Best

or Expanding Orlando's Universe

It's time to leave the wonderful world of Disney now, and venture out into the rest of Central Florida's great tourist attractions. And, believe us, there's still a terrific amount in store.

For a start, they don't come much more ambitious than **Universal Orlando**. The area that used to consist of just 1 theme park, Universal Studios Florida, is now a fully fledged resort in its own right. Second park Islands of Adventure opened in 1999, as well as the CityWalk entertainment district. The first hotel, Portofino Bay, also opened in 1999, followed by the Hard Rock Hotel and Royal Pacific Resort in 2000 and 2002 respectively. Other recent additions include **Blue Man Group** in 2007 (see page 301), the amazing **Hollywood Rip Ride Rockit** coaster in 2009, and the biggest thing to hit Orlando in more than 10 years, 2010's **The Wizarding World of Harry Potter**.

A waterway network connects the hotels to the CityWalk hub, while the multi-storey car parks, for more than 20,000 vehicles, have done away with the need for any other transport system, as it is easy to move between parks. The Orlando FlexTicket tie-up with SeaWorld and

Hogwarts Castle at the Wizarding World of Harry Potter

Shrek-4D

Busch Gardens, plus the purchase of the Wet 'n Wild water park, has also proved a success – not to mention great value. It's certainly a multi-day experience these days and there are periodic special ticket deals. In 2010, UK ticket outlets featured a Universal 2-Park Bonus ticket with unlimited admission for 14 days for little more than the cost of two 1-day tickets and a 3-Park Bonus (with Wet 'n Wild) also valid for unlimited admission over 2 weeks. Sadly, Universal does

Jimmy Neutron

© OCVB

not offer a free system like Disney's FastPass, only the paid-for **Universal Express Plus**, a day pass providing 1-time access to all their rides (with the exception of Pteranodon Flyers in Islands of Adventure) with minimal queuing – for an extra $20–60 ($26–70 for both parks) per person, depending on time of year. A limited number go on sale an hour after park opening and are snapped up, but they can also be bought online for a specific day at **universalorlando.com** or in the parks themselves for another day. The new **Park to Park VIP Ticket** provides park admission AND unlimited **Express Plus** front-of-queue access for 1, 2, 3, 4 or 7 days, for $180-382/adult, $170-362/child (online only). It does save time, but at quieter times of the year it can be unnecessary. Universal hotel guests benefit from Express ride priority ALL DAY by producing their room key. In addition, some rides have Single Rider queues, which save time if you want to go by yourself or don't mind splitting up your group. Once again, height/health restrictions are noted in ride descriptions.

Universal Studios Florida®

Universal opened its first Florida park in June 1990 (its original Los Angeles movie site opened to the public in 1917!) and quickly became a serious rival to Disney. For the visitor, it means a consistently high standard and good value (though the choice can be bewildering), but there are few similarities to the LA Studios. Universal is also a different proposition to Disney, with a more in-your-face style that appeals especially to teens. Younger children are still well catered for, though. Universal parks can also need more than a full day in high season. Strategies are the same, though: arrive EARLY (up to 30 minutes before opening), do the big rides first, avoid main meal times and take time out for an afternoon break (try shopping, dining or visiting the cinemas at CityWalk) if it gets too crowded.

Location

Universal Studios Florida® is subdivided into 6 main areas, set around a huge, manmade lagoon, but there are no great distinguishing features, so you'll need your map. The main resort entrance is just off Interstate 4 (I-4 eastbound take exit 75A; westbound take exit 74B) or via Universal Boulevard from International Drive by Wet 'n Wild. Parking is in its massive multi-storey car park and there is quite a walk (with moving walkways) to the front gates. Once through, your best bet is to turn right on to Rodeo Drive, along Hollywood Boulevard and Sunset Boulevard and into World Expo for The Simpsons, followed by Men In Black – Alien Attack. From there, head across the bridge to Jaws, then go back along the Embarcadero

Universal Studios Florida® at a glance

Location	Off exits 75A and 74B from I-4; Universal Boulevard and Kirkman Road		
Size	110 acres/45ha in 7 themed areas		
Hours	9am–6pm or 7pm off peak; 9am–10pm high season (Washington's birthday, Easter, summer holidays, Thanksgiving, Christmas)		
Admission	Under-3s free; 3–9 $69 (1-day Ticket), $121.99 (2 Day Park to Park Ticket), $239.95 (FlexTicket), $279.95 (FlexTicket Plus); adult (10+) $79, $134.99, $259.95, $299.95. Prices do not include tax.		
Parking	$14 (preferred parking $18; valet parking $22)		
Lockers	Immediately to left in Front Lot $8		
Pushchairs	$14 and $19, kiddie cars $17.99 and $22.99 next to locker hire		
Wheelchairs	$12 and $50 (with photo ID as deposit), with pushchairs		
Top attractions	Revenge of the Mummy, Men in Black, Jaws, ET Adventure, Shrek 4-D, The Simpsons, Terminator 2: 3-D, Hollywood Rip, Ride Rockit!		
Don't miss	Universal 360: A Cinesphere Spectacular (peak season only), Curious George Playground (for kids), The Blues Brothers		
Hidden costs	Meals	Burger, chips and coke $8.68 3-course dinner $27.97 (Lombard's) Kids' meal $5.49 ($4.99–7.99 in Finnegan's)	
	T-shirts	$19.95-28.95	
	Souvenirs	95c-$1,500	
	Sundries	Hair braiding $25 no beads, $30 with beads	

Production Central

1 Main Entrance
2 Shrek 4-D
3 Jimmy Neutron's Nicktoon Blast
4 Hollywood Rip, Ride, Rockit!
5 Donkey's Photo Finish
6 Monsters Café

New York

7 Twister
8 Revenge Of The Mummy
9 The Blues Brothers
10 Alley Climb
11 Finnegan's Bar and Grill
12 Louie's Italian Restaurant

San Francisco/Amity

13 Disaster! A Major Motion Picture Ride ... starring YOU
14 Jaws
15 Beetlejuice's Graveyard Revue
16 Central Lagoon
17 Lombard's Seafood Grille
18 Fear Factor Live

World Expo

19 The Simpsons Ride
20 Men In Black – Alien Attack

Woody Woodpecker's Zidzone

21 Animal Actors On Location!
22 Fievel's Playland
23 A Day In The Park With Barney
24 ET Adventure
25 Woody Woodpecker's Nuthouse Coaster
26 Curious George Goes To Town

Hollywood

27 Universal's Horror Make-Up Show
28 Terminator 2: 3-D Battle Across Time
29 Lucy: A Tribute
30 Guest Services
31 Mel's Drive-In
32 Café La Bamba

for Disaster! and into New York for Revenge Of The Mummy. This will get most of the main rides under your belt before the crowds build, and you can then take it a bit easier by seeing some of the shows. Alternatively, try to be among the early birds flocking to the Shrek 4-D film show in Production Central and Revenge Of The Mummy in New York to avoid the queues that build up here, then visit the likes of The Simpsons and Men in Black. Thrill-ride seekers should head first for the tremendous Hollywood Rip Ride Rockit, which opened in 2009 and quickly became the must-try for coaster fans. Here's a full blow-by-blow guide to the Studios (for CityWalk, see Chapter 10, Orlando by Night). Watch out for the helpful mobile electronic **Wait Times** boards placed around both parks, too.

Production Central

Coming straight through the gates brings you immediately into the administrative centre, with a couple of large gift stores (have a look at these in mid-afternoon) plus **Studio Sweets**. Call at **Guest Services** here for guides for disabled visitors, TDD and assisted listening devices, and to make restaurant bookings, which can also be made at a kiosk to the right after the turnstiles, next to the Beverly Hills Boulangerie. **First aid** is available here (and on Canal Street between New York and San Francisco), while there are

facilities for nursing mothers at **Family Services** by the bank through the gates on the right. In addition, Universal Studios hosts **Total Non Stop Action Wrestling** (specific dates April–July), with tickets available on a first-come, first-served basis (call 407 224 6000 for more details). Coming to the top of the Plaza of the Stars brings you to the business end of the park.

Shrek 4-D: This adds a whole new dimension to the genre of 3-D films as the original cast of the Oscar-winning *Shrek* movies (Mike Myers, Eddie Murphy, Cameron Diaz and John Lithgow) return for a 13-minute prequel to *Shrek 2*. The evil but vertically challenged Lord Farquaad is back in ghost form to welcome visitors to his dungeons and ruin the honeymoon of Shrek and Princess Fiona. The amusing 7-minute pre-show leads into the 500-seat main theatre, where you don your Ogre Vision 3-D glasses and prepare to enter a new world. The film is funny enough as Shrek and Donkey rescue the Princess, but the special effects (watch out for the spiders!) and moving seats add a startling extra element that is hugely entertaining. State-of-the-art digital projection and audio systems, lighting effects and smoke (plus a hilarious finale featuring an out-of-control Tinker Bell) ensure a real laugh-fest. A major draw, so try to go first thing or expect waits of over an hour. AAAAA+.

Production Central

Jimmy Neutron's Nicktoon Blast:
Anyone not familiar with the cartoon antics of Jimmy Neutron (Boy Genius) and other members of the Nicktoon stable (Rugrats, the Fairly Odd Parents and SpongeBob SquarePants) might feel bemused by this rather noisy simulator ride. It revolves around Jimmy tangling with the evil (but hapless) Emperor Ooblar and battling to save the world with the help of his zany inventions and cartoon friends. It's great for kids and the ride is quite dynamic. It quickly draws a queue as it is one of the first you encounter through the gates. There is no height restriction as long as a child can sit unaided, but those with heart, neck or back problems should ask for the stationary seats. TTT (TTTTT, under-10s).

Hollywood Rip Ride Rockit!: This iconic ride is a high-tech colossus, a roller-coaster packed with unique features and audio-visual gizmos that allow you to select your own ride music – then take home the DVD afterwards. The dimensions alone are daunting – at 167ft/51m it is Orlando's highest coaster and, at almost 70mph/113kph, it is also the fastest. You can't miss it as it loops out of the front of the park by the Blue Man Group theatre in CityWalk and runs to the back of the park, too, curling around and through the buildings of

Hollywood Rip Ride Rockit!

the New York area – a vivid red steel beast that dares you to ride it! It starts with a video presentation while you queue that reveals 5 music choices (Rap/Hip Hop, Country, Classic Rock/Metal, Pop/Disco and Club Electronica), with 6 tracks in each category. You're then strapped into an open-sided car that goes straight up a vertical lift-hill 17-storeys high. Breathless yet? You soon will be – the ride goes into a steep dive and then the signature Double Take, the world's first non-inverted loop (you don't actually go upside-down but it feels like it!). Two more first-of-a-kind features follow – the Treble Clef (a twisting manoeuvre shaped like the musical symbol) and Jump Cut (a spiralling zero-gravity roll that feels like a corkscrew but again without an inversion) – with another 3 breathtaking manoeuvres before you return to the station. You will soar over the heads of other people in the queue, dive below ground level and fly around a 150° banked turn, all in the course of the 1-min 40-sec ride along 3,800ft/1,158m of track. The innovative open cars make the whole experience feel even faster and more dynamic than it actually is, while the mix of pounding music (from your headrest and speakers along the track) and eye-catching concert-style lighting (flashy enough during the day, stunning at night) ensure this is a ride that rocks you to the core. You can then opt to buy the ride video, complete with your musical selection that is captured by multiple cameras both in your car and along the track (for $25). In truth, it *looks* more frightening than it actually is, and it is truly exhilarating. Restrictions: 4ft 3in/130cm. TTTTT+ (see all your music options, and more, at **hollywoodripriderockit.com**. Our choice? *Bring Me To Life* by Evanescence in the Rock/Metal category. Kicking!).

BRIT TIP
If you don't empty your pockets before riding Rip Ride Rockit!, you'll find them empty by the end of the ride! Put ALL loose times in the free lockers.

Twister

Other entertainment: Meet Shrek, Fiona and Donkey on 8th Avenue for **Donkey's Photo Finish**, well worth catching for the amusing patter. And look for a **SpongeBob** photo opportunity in the Nickstuff Store.

Shopping and dining: You'll find some of the best of the shops here, including **On Location** (film, apparel, sundries and 2-way radio rentals), **Nickstuff** (Toon merchandise with Jimmy Neutron, SpongeBob SquarePants and Dora the Explorer), the massive **Universal Studios Store** (the full range of gifts) and **It's A Wrap** (discounted items). The main eating outlet is the wonderful **Monsters Café**, offering salads, pasta, ribs, pizza and chicken (peak season only). The counter-service area is themed like Frankenstein's lab, with the dining areas subdivided into Swamp, Space, Crypt and Mansion Dining, all accompanied by old black-and-white horror film clips.

New York

From Production Central, you head to New York and some impressive scene-setting architecture and detail. It's too clean to be authentic, but the façades are first class.

Twister: This experience, based on the hit film, brings audiences 'up close and personal' with the awesome destructive forces of a tornado. The 5-storey terror shatters everything in its path (OK, it's pretty tame compared to the real thing), building to a shattering climax of destruction

(watch for the flying cow!). The noise can be a bit much for young children, so parental discretion is advised for under-10s. The pre-show area is a work of art in itself but do it early or late in the day. TTT.

Revenge Of The Mummy: This superb offering in Orlando's roller-coaster catalogue is a high-thrill, high-fun journey into the world of *The Mummy* film series. It features an indoor spin into Ancient Egypt, fusing coaster technology with space-age robotics and special effects. It starts out as a dark ride (a slow journey through the shadowy, curse-ridden interior of Hamunaptra, The City of the Dead) but soon evolves into something far more dynamic – with a breathtaking launch.

BRIT TIP

For the best ride experience on Revenge Of The Mummy, try to get a back row seat. You are not allowed to carry anything on the ride – loose items must be left in the (free) lockers provided.

Revenge of the Mummy

The basic premise of the film studio becoming a full archaeological discovery is a good one, and the transition from dark ride to coaster is ingenious, with a host of special effects and audio-animatronics as you brave the Mummy's realm. The high-speed whiz in the dark (backwards to start with) doesn't involve inversions but is still a thrill with its tight turns and dips, while there are several clever twists (the front row may get slightly damp!). It is a hugely immersive experience and, with the elaborate queuing area, is a real 5-star attraction. However, it is probably too scary for under-8s. Be sure to preview your ride photos ($19.95–29.95) as you enter the gift shop. Restrictions: 4ft/122cm. TTTT½.

The Blues Brothers: Fans of the film will not want to miss this live show as Jake and Elwood Blues (or pretty good doubles anyway) put on a stormin' performance on New York's Delancey Street several times a day. They cruise up in their Bluesmobile and go through a series of the film's hits before heading off into the sunset, stopping only for autographs. AAAA.

Other entertainment: The energetic can try the **Alley Climb** (rock wall) on 5th Avenue ($5). New York also boasts the inevitable amusement arcade.

Disaster!

© OCVB

Shopping and dining: Check out **Sahara Traders** for Mummy souvenirs, as well as jewellery and toys, **Rosie's Irish Shop** for all things Irish and **Aftermath** for Twister souvenirs. For dining, you have 2 main restaurants: **Finnegan's Bar and Grill** offers shepherd's pie, fish and chips, corned beef and cabbage, along with steak, burgers, fries and a good range of beers, plus Irish-tinged entertainment and Happy Hour 4–7pm ($3.50 Bud and Bud Light; $4.50 imported beers), while **Louie's Italian Restaurant** has counter-service pizza and pasta, ice-cream and tiramisu. You will also find a **Ben and Jerry's** store for delicious ice-cream and smoothies, and a **Starbucks** for coffee and pastries.

San Francisco/Amity

Crossing Canal Street brings you right across America to San Francisco/ Amity and 2 more serious queues.

Disaster! A Major Motion Picture Ride… Starring YOU: This hugely funny 3-part adventure (which replaced the Earthquake attraction in 2008) gets busy from mid-morning until late afternoon and goes behind the scenes into film special effects in the mythical Disaster Studios. You go first into the Screening Room, where your tour host interacts with a creative projection of actor Christopher Walken (playing Studios boss Frank Kincaid in high style) to set the scene for the Sound Stage (a sequence of amusing set-pieces using audience volunteers) and then the Disaster Set – an underground train ride into a San Francisco earthquake, with YOU as the 'extras'. Tremble as walls and ceilings collapse, trains collide, fire erupts and a tidal wave of water pours in. Finally, check out how you did on the screen at the end, which reveals some hilarious results! It's probably a touch scary for small children, while those with bad backs or necks or expectant mothers should not ride the final scene. Restrictions: 4ft/122cm (unless accompanied by an adult, with parental discretion). AAAA and TTT.

Jaws

Jaws: The technical wizardry alone will amaze you here, and queues of an hour are common as you head out into the waters of this mini 'Amity'. This is no ordinary ride, and its 6-minute duration will seem a lot longer as your hapless boat guide steers you through a spectacular series of stunts, explosions and menace from the Great White. You WILL be impressed – and just a little scared. It can also be a wet experience for those sitting on the right! TTTT.

Beetlejuice's Graveyard Revue: Disney's Hollywood Studios has *Beauty and the Beast* and *The Little Mermaid*: Universal goes for *Dracula, Frankenstein, The Wolfman* and *Frankenstein's Bride* in this 20-minute 'shock 'n' roll' extravaganza, compèred by Beetlejuice himself. The raucous concert shuns the twee prettiness of Disney's attractions yet still comes up with a fun family show, as the graveyard characters perform specially adapted rock and pop anthems (like Dancing in the Dark and Jump) with a mock-horror theme in a great setting. AAAA.

Fear Factor Live (high season only): This live action version of the reality TV show asks audience volunteers to take part in some hair-raising (and stomach-churning!) challenges, with a head-to-head competition to find the biggest daredevil. Auditions take place 70 minutes before each show, and the audience then gets to see the chosen few battle it out, with clips from the TV show interspersed with live action. Some of the stunts are distinctly off-colour (anyone for a maggot milkshake?) and may not be good for young children (or anyone of a weak disposition!), but it is a well-staged production. TTT.

Other entertainment: A **Boardwalk** of fairground games (which cost $2–5 to play) includes an amusing Guess Your Weight stall.

Shopping and dining: Visit **Quint's Surf Shack** (beach apparel and other clothing), **Oakley** (sunglasses and accessories), **Amazing Pictures** (have your photo superimposed on a variety of film backgrounds; $29– 49.99) and the **San Francisco Candy Factory** (great pick-n-mix!). This area also has the park's best dining choices, with **Lombard's Seafood Grill** the highlight (high season only; reservations accepted). Great seafood, pasta and sandwiches are accompanied by a good view over the Central Lagoon. **San Francisco Pastry Co** offers desserts and coffee, **Richter's Burger Co** has some tempting burger options and **Midway Grill** provides hot dogs and fries.

World Expo

Crossing the bridge from Amity brings you to a rather nondescript area, but home to 2 of the park's most amusing attractions.

The Simpsons Ride: This replaced the old Back To The Future ride in 2008, bringing the world of Springfield to vibrant life in a hugely colourful and amusing production, even if you're

Universal Studios

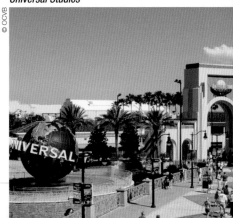

Men in Black – Alien Attack

not fans of the cartoon family. It is themed as Krustyland amusement park, brainchild of irascible Krusty the Clown, a bizarre funfair that is the setting for a hectic, breathtaking ride in the company of Homer, Bart, Lisa, Marge and Maggie. A wicked sound system and state-of-the-art motion simulator technology ensure a frantic race through outlandish attractions (watch out for the Tooth Chipper!) with the Simpsons by your side. The feel of the 'ride' is truly amazing and the huge domed screen ensures a sensory experience that is both breathtaking and outrageously comical. All the characters have been voiced by the original stars of the TV show and even the queuing area is a riot of gags and visual hilarity. However, this can also be the park's biggest draw, hence you need to do this early or expect a LONG queue. Restrictions: 3ft 4in/101cm. TTTTT.

Amity

© OCVB

Men in Black – Alien Attack: This combination thrill/dark ride takes up where the hit films, starring Will Smith, left off. Visitors are secretly introduced to the MIB Institute in an inventive mock-futuristic setting and enrolled as trainees for a battle around the streets of New York with a horde of escaped aliens. Your 6-person car is equipped with laser zappers for an interactive shoot-out that is like a real-life arcade game, as the aliens can also shoot back to send your car spinning. The finale features a close encounter with a 30ft/9m bug that is all mouth. Will you survive? Only your collective shooting skills can save the day, and there are numerous ride variations according to your accuracy. Will Smith and Rip Torn are your on-screen hosts, and Will returns at the end to reveal if your score makes you Galaxy Defenders, Cosmically Average or Bug Bait! Fast, frantic and a bit confusing, you'll want to come back until you can top 250,000 (for Defender status). Restrictions: 3ft 6in/106cm. TTTT.

> **BRIT TIP**
> For a big score in Men In Black, when you meet the Big Bug – push the big red button!

Shopping and dining: To complete the Springfield effect, visit the **Kwik-E-Mart** for a range of Simpsons souvenirs (plus more trademark humour), while **MIB Gear** has more themed gifts and clothing. The

International Food and Film Festival is a food court offering Italian, American, Asian and salads (in air-conditioned comfort), while **Expo Eats** offers drinks and snacks.

BRIT TIP
Along the lagoon in the World Expo/ KidZone area is East Green, a quiet spot where you can stop to take a break for a while.

KidZone

This is great place to let the kids loose for a while, but it does also feature several great family attractions.

Animal Actors On Location!: An amusing mix of video, animal performance and audience interaction, several children are invited to help present some unlikely feats and stunts featuring a range of wildlife, from a raccoon to a snake, and on to cats and dogs. Many have been rescued from animal shelters and gone on to feature in films before finding a home at Universal. The theatre also provides an escape from the queues. AAAA.

Fievel's Playland: Strictly for kids, this playground, based on the enlarged world of the cartoon mouse, offers the chance to bounce under a 1,000-gallon hat, crawl through a giant boot, climb a 30ft/9m spider's web and shoot the rapids (a 200ft/61m waterslide) in Fievel's sardine can. TTTT (young 'uns only!).

A Day in the Park with Barney: Again strictly for the younger set (2–5), the purple dinosaur from kids' TV is brought to super-dee-duper life in a large arena that features a pre-show before the 15-minute main event, plus an interactive post-show area. Parents will cringe but the youngsters love it. NB: Check out the amazing loos! AA (AAAAA under-5s).

ET Adventure: This is as glorious as scenic rides come, with a picturesque queuing area from the film and then a spectacular leap on the trademark flying bicycles to save ET's home planet. Steven Spielberg has added some special effects and characters, and you have an individual ET greeting at the end. The masses often overlook this corner of the park, hence it is worth saving for later in the day. There is a height restriction of 4ft/122cm to ride alone, but smaller children can ride with parents. AAAAA.

Woody Woodpecker's Nuthouse Coaster: Anchoring the excellent under-10s adventure land is this child-sized but still quite racy roller-coaster. The ride reaches only 28ft/8m high and 22mph, but it seems the real deal to young 'uns. However, there is still a height restriction of 3ft/91cm. TTTT (juniors only).

Curious George Goes To Town: Kids of all ages love this amazing adventure playground and huge range of activities – with plenty of

Curious George Interactive Playground

© OCVB

Terminator 2

ways to get wet. It combines toddler play, water-based play stations and a huge interactive ball pool, and is a real bonus for harassed parents. The town theme includes buildings to climb, pumps and hoses to spray water, a ball factory in which to shoot, dump and blast thousands of foam balls and – the tour de force – 2 huge buckets of water that dump their contents on the street below at regular intervals. TTTTT (under-12s). Curious George himself roams the KidZone from time to time, while other characters make regular appearances.

BRIT TIP

If you want to let your youngsters loose in the Curious George playground, it is advisable to bring swimsuits or a change of clothing.

Woody Woodpecker in the Kid Zone

© OCVB

Other entertainment: Check out the **Star Toons Show** up to 6 times a day, with music and dance from the 1980s, and a **Madagascar** meet-and-greet with the stars of the cartoon films.

Shopping and dining: Shop at the **Cartoon Store**, **Barney Store** or **ET's Toy Closet and Photo Spot**. For a quick bite, **Kidzone Pizza Company** offers snacks such as pizza and chicken fingers.

Hollywood

Finally, your circular tour of Universal returns you to the main entrance via Hollywood (where else?).

Universal's Horror Make-Up Show: Not recommended for under-12s, this demonstrates some of the often amusing ways in which films have attempted to terrorise us, with clips from modern additions to the genre like *Van Helsing*. It's a 20-minute show, queues are rarely long and the special effects secrets are well worth discovering. AAA

Terminator 2: 3-D Battle Across Time: Another first-of-its-kind attraction, this is hard to describe. Part film, part show, part experience but all action, it usually leaves its audience in awe. The 'Wow!' factor works overtime as you go through a 10-minute pre-show representing a trip to the Cyberdyne Systems company from the *Terminator* films and then into a 700-seat theatre for

UNIVERSAL STUDIOS with children

Our guide to the attractions that generally appeal to the different age groups:

Under-5s

Animal Actors On Location!, Curious George Goes To Town, A Day In The Park With Barney, ET Adventure, Fievel's Playland.

5–8s

All the above (minus Barney), plus Disaster! (with parental discretion), Jimmy Neutron's Nicktoon Blast, Men In Black, Shrek 4-D, The Simpsons and Woody Woodpecker's Nuthouse Coaster.

9–12s

All the above, plus Hollywood Rip Ride Rockit, Beetlejuice's Graveyard Revue, Fear Factor Live!, Jaws, Revenge Of The Mummy, Terminator 2: 3-D Battle Across Time, Twister, Universal 360: A Cinesphere Spectacular.

Over-12s

Hollywood Rip Ride Rockit, Beetlejuice's Graveyard Revue, The Blues Brothers, Disaster!, ET Adventure, Fear Factor Live, Jaws, Jimmy Neutron's Nicktoon Blast, Men In Black – Alien Attack, Revenge Of The Mummy, Shrek 4-D, The Simpsons, Terminator 2: 3-D Battle Across Time, Twister, Universal 360: A Cinesphere Spectacular, Universal's Horror Make-Up Show.

a 'presentation' on its latest robot creations. The show is interrupted, though, by John and Sarah Connor and mayhem ensues, with the audience subjected to a huge array of (loud) special effects, including real actors interacting with the screen and the audience, indoor pyrotechnics and a climactic 3-D film finale that takes the Terminator story a step further. Arnold Schwarzenegger and other members of the original cast all collaborated on the 12-minute movie and the overall effect is dazzling, but you need to arrive early or expect queues of over an hour (parental discretion for under-12s). TTTTT.

Lucy: A Tribute: The last attraction (or first, depending on which way you go round) will mean little to all but devoted fans of the late Lucille Ball and her 1960s TV comedy *The Lucy Show*. Classic shows, home movies, costumes and scripts are paraded, but youngsters will find it tedious. AA.

Other entertainment: The **Hollywood Character Zone** provides numerous character appearances throughout the day along Hollywood Boulevard, from Scooby Do and Shaggy to Dudley Do-Right, The Flintstones and Lucille Ball.

> ### BRIT TIP
> Budding magicians should make a bee-line for the small Theater Magic shop next to Mel's Drive-In, with merchandise and some terrific small-scale magic shows several times daily.

Shopping and dining: Look for Terminator gifts and clothing in **Cyber Image**, all manner of headgear in **The Brown Derby**, Hollywood legends' jewellery in **Studio Styles** and movie memorabilia in Silver **Screen Collectibles**. If you haven't eaten by now, there are 4 contrasting eateries: **Mel's Drive-In**, a re-creation

The Simpsons Ride

© 2010 Universal Orlando Resort

from the film *American Graffiti*, serving all manner of burgers and hot dogs (though Richter's has better burgers); **Café La Bamba** for rotisserie chicken, ribs, salad and burgers, plus margaritas and beer (Happy Hour 3–5pm; high season only); **Schwab's Pharmacy**, with traditional ice-cream, milkshakes and sundaes; and **Beverly Hills Boulangerie** for a range of sandwiches, cheesecake, pastries, juices and Seattle's Best coffee.

Special programmes

Universal Studios features some brilliant extra seasonal entertainment for **Mardi Gras**, with a hectic, bead-throwing parade, plus music, street entertainment and authentic New Orleans food each Saturday at 6pm from mid-Feb to late May (and free with normal park admission). The evening culminates in a live concert with well-known acts (like Aretha Franklin, 3 Doors Down, Chicago and Sheryl Crow in 2010), but it does draw HUGE crowds. Universal also throws a major party for the **4th July**, when the park presents a stunning fireworks spectacular, while the **Summer Concert Series** runs on Saturdays in June and July, with the likes of Earth, Wind and Fire, Counting Crows and Train (in 2010).

And finally, **Universal 360: A Cinesphere Spectacular** brings down the curtain each night in peak season and at special events with a blaze of fireworks and 4 gigantic 'cinespheres' that allow for cinema projection. The overall effect places guests in the middle of their favourite films, with an all-new musical score (on 300 outdoor speakers), lasers and other pyrotechnics, using the spheres as video screens. It's a stunning performance, so check your park map to see if it's showing during your visit.

Mardi Gras

Islands of Adventure

You could be forgiven for calling this Harry Potter Land since 2010. The much-heralded opening of the Wizarding World gave Universal's second park a huge shot in the arm and massive public appeal (although it has always been one of our favourites). The Islands of Adventure opened in 1999 under the supervision of Universal's creative consultant, Steven Spielberg, and it provided one of the most complete and thrilling theme parks you could imagine; brilliantly conceived and executed, containing a wonderfully upbeat collection of high-adrenalin rides, shows and other entertainment (not to mention some fine dining). And then The Wizarding World of Harry Potter opened in June 2010, adding a whole new land and a world of excitement unlike anything Orlando had seen in many years.

Islands of Adventure has a full range of attractions, from the real adrenaline overloads to pure family entertainment, and it even sounds good – with some 40 pieces of original music, you can buy the CD of the theme park! OK, so they aren't really islands (the areas form a chain around the central lagoon), but that's the only illusion. And you get a lot for your money here, unless you have extremely timid children or under-5s. Seuss Landing will usually keep preschoolers amused for several hours, while Camp Jurassic is a clever adventure playground for the 5–12s, but the rest of the park, with its 8 5-star thrill rides and other standout attractions, is primarily geared to kids of 8 and over, their parents and especially teenagers. There are 6 elements that look truly alarming, but don't be put off – they

Islands of Adventure at a glance

Location	Off exits 75A and 74B from I-4; Universal Boulevard and Kirkman Road
Size	110 acres/45ha in 6 'islands'
Hours	9am–7pm off peak; 9am–10pm high season (Washington's birthday, Easter, summer holidays, Thanksgiving, Christmas)
Admission	Under-3s free; 3–9 $69 (1-day Ticket), $121.99 (2-day Park to Park Ticket), $239.95 (FlexTicket), $279.95 (FlexTicket Plus); adult (10+) $79, $134.99, $259.95, $299.95. Prices do not include tax.
Parking	$14 (preferred parking $18; valet parking $22)
Lockers	Immediately to left through main gates; $8
Pushchairs	$14.99 and $19.99; next to locker hire.
Wheelchairs	$12 and $50 (with photo ID as deposit)
Top attractions	Harry Potter and the Forbidden Journey, Amazing Adventures Of Spider-Man, Dragon Challenge, Incredible Hulk Coaster, Jurassic Park River Adventure, Dudley Do-Right's Ripsaw Falls, The Cat In The Hat
Don't miss	Eighth Voyage Of Sindbad, Jurassic Park Discovery Centre, If I Ran The Zoo playground (for toddlers), Three Broomsticks restaurant and Ollivander's Wand Shop
Hidden costs	**Meals** Burger, chips and coke $8.68 3-course lunch $29.94 (Confisco Grill) Kids' meal $5.49–6.49 (drink not included) **T-shirts** $18.95-26.95 **Souvenirs** 95c-$4,995 **Sundries** Caricature drawings $15–36 (black and white and airbrush colour); Butterbeer $2.99

Port of Entry
1 Ocean Trader Market
2 Confisco Grille

Marvel Super-Hero Island
3 Incredible Hulk Coaster
4 Dr Doom's Fearfall
5 Café 4
6 Captain America Diner
7 The Amazing Adventures Of Spider-Man
8 Storm Force Accelatron

Toon Lagoon
9 Popeye And Bluto's Bilge-Rat Barges
10 Dudley Do-Right's Ripsaw Falls
11 Me Ship, The Olive
12 Comic Strip Café
13 Toon Lagoon Amphitheater

Jurassic Park
14 Jurassic Park River Adventure
15 Pteranodon Flyers
16 Camp Jurassic
17 Discovery Center
18 Thunder Falls Terrace

The Wizarding World of Harry Potter
19 Harry Potter and the Forbidden Journey
20 Filch's Emporium
21 Flight of the Hippogriff
22 Dervish and Banges
23 Olivander's
24 Three Broomsticks
25 Zonko's

The Lost Continent
26 Dragon Challenge
27 Mythos Restaurant
28 Mystic Fountain
29 The Eighth Voyage of Sindbad
30 Poseidon's Fury

Seuss Landing
31 Seuss Landing Dining
32 High In The Sky Seuss Trolley Train Ride
33 Caro-Seuss-el
34 If I Ran The Zoo
35 The Cat In The Hat
36 One Fish, Two Fish, Red Fish, Blue Fish

Main Entrance

ISLANDS OF ADVENTURE

all deliver immense fun as well as terrific spectator value! If any one ride sums up IoA, it is Harry Potter and the Forbidden Journey, which took theme park ride technology to a whole new level. Its jaw-dropping special effects are sure to leave you in awe and admiration.

Private nursing facilities, an open area for feeding and resting (with high chairs) and nappy-changing stations, can be found at the **Family Service Facility** at Guest Services (to the right inside the main gates), while ALL restrooms throughout the park are equipped with **nappy-changing** facilities. **First aid** is provided in Sindbad's Village in the Lost Continent, just across from Oasis Coolers, and in Port of Entry.

Port of Entry

You arrive for IoA as you do for Universal Studios, in the big multi-storey car parks off I-4 and Universal Boulevard and pass right through the CityWalk area, where you come to the main entrance plaza (head for the huge Pharos Lighthouse). As with Universal Studios, you can purchase the **Universal Express Plus** pass for Marvel Super-Hero Island $20-60 (depending on time of year) at various locations throughout the park, and at Guest Services. Once through the gates, the lockers, pushchair and wheelchair hire are all on your left as the Port of Entry opens up before you. This elaborate 'village' consists of shops and eateries, so push straight on until you hit the main lagoon. Later in the day, return to check out the extensive retail experience at places like **IoA Trading Company** and **Ocean Trader Market**. Enjoy a snack at **Cinnabon** (cinnamon rolls and pastries) or **Croissant Moon Bakery** (excellent coffee, croissants and sandwiches), or chill out with a soft drink or ice-cream from **Arctic Express**. Alternatively, sit down for lunch or dinner (steak, pasta, fish, pizza, burgers and salads) at **Confisco Grille** and grab a beverage or snack at the **Backwater Bar** (Happy Hour 4–7pm). There is also a **Character Breakfast** at Confisco

Grille (9–10.30am Thurs and Sun) with various Universal characters like Spider-Man and The Cat In The Hat, plus The Grinch at Christmas ($17.95 adults, $11.95 children; 407 224 4012 for reservations). Above all, take in the wonderful architecture, which borrows from Middle East, Far East and African themes and uses bric-a-brac from all over the world. At the end of the street, you will need to decide which way to head first as there are 9 attractions where the queues build up quickly and remain that way most of the day. If you are among the majority lured by the massively popular **Wizarding World of Harry Potter** and its outstanding Forbidden Journey and Dragon Challenge rides, turn right (through Seuss Landing and The Lost Continent). If you're after the big thrill rides, turn left into **Marvel Super-Hero Island** and head straight to Spider-Man, then do Dr Doom's Fearfall and the Incredible Hulk Coaster.

> **BRIT TIP**
> There are 2 entrances to the Wizarding World of Harry Potter: from Jurassic Park and The Lost Continent. The latter is much more dramatic and offers the full Hogsmeade Village panorama.

Dr Doom's Fearfall

© 2010 Universal Orlando Resort

Dinosaur fans should head straight around the lagoon (turn left) to Jurassic Park, where you can do the River Adventure before the majority arrive. Once you are nice and wet, go back to Toon Lagoon for Ripsaw Falls and the Bilge-Rat Barges. Or, if you have younger children, turn right into the multicoloured world of Seuss Landing and enjoy The Cat In The Hat and High In The Sky Seuss Trolley Train Ride prior to the main crowd build-up.

Turning right, in an anti-clockwise direction, here's what you find.

Seuss Landing

There is not a straight line to be seen in this vivid 3-D working of the books of Dr Seuss. The characters may not mean much to those unfamiliar with the children's stories, but everyone can relate to the fun here (though queues build up quickly). There is so much clever detail, from squirt ponds to beach scenes, it can be easy to miss something, so take your time.

Caro-Seuss-el: This intricate carousel ride on some of the Seuss characters – cowfish, elephant-birds and dog-a-lopes, for example – has rider-activated features that are a big hit with children. AA (AAAA under-5s).

One Fish, Two Fish, Red Fish, Blue Fish: A fairground ride with a twist as you pilot these Seussian fish up and down according to the rhyme that plays while you ride. Get it wrong and you get squirted! More fun for the younger set. TTT (TTTTT under-5s).

The Cat in the Hat: Prepare for a ride with a difference as you board these

Seuss Landing

crazy 6-passenger 'couches' to meet the world's most adventurous cat and friends Thing One and Thing Two. You literally go for a spin through this storybook world, and it may be a bit much for very young children. The slow-moving queues are a bit of a drag, so try to get here early or leave it until later in the day. AAAA/TTT.

If I Ran the Zoo: Interactive playgrounds don't get much better for the pre-school brigade than with these different Seuss character scenarios, some of which can be pretty wet! Hugely imaginative and great fun to watch. TTTTT (under-5s).

The High in the Sky Seuss Trolley Train Ride: This fun family adventure high above Seuss Landing has terrific appeal to youngsters as you board a special trolley to journey into the world of the Sneetches, visiting the Inking and Stamping Room, the Star Wash Room and a tour inside the Circus McGurkus Café Stoo-pendous. It is slow-paced, scenic and eye-catching, but it does draw slow-moving queues, so head here early on if your children are the right age (2–8). AAAA.

Other entertainment: Look out for **character appearances** by The Cat In The Hat, Thing One and Thing Two and The Grinch outside the Circus McGurkus, and the character-filled celebration of the new **Oh! The Stories You'll Hear** street show.

Shopping and dining: If you have been captivated by the land, you can buy the books at **Dr Seuss' All The Books You Can Read Store**, Christmas-themed merchandise at **Honk Honker's**, or a full variety of character merchandise at the **Mulberry Street Store**. Snookers and Snookers Sweet Candy Cookers is a super sweet shop, while snacks and drinks can be had at **Hop On Pop Ice Cream Shop**, **Moose Juice Goose Juice** and **Green Eggs and Ham Café** (sandwiches and burgers). The **Circus McGurkus Café Stoo-pendous** is a mind-boggling eatery for fried chicken, lasagne, spaghetti and pizza – with clowns and pipe organs.

Mythos Restaurant

The Lost Continent

This land underwent a rather drastic reduction to accommodate Harry Potter. However, it still offers some great attractions.

The Eighth Voyage of Sindbad: This stunt and special effects show is fun for both elaborate staging and performance. Mythical adventurer Sindbad and sidekick Kabob tackle evil witch Miseria in a bid to rescue Princess Amoura, and the action springs up in surprising places. There are several loud bangs that could scare young children, but otherwise it's good family fun. There is also a great post-show feature where the cast reappears for photos and autographs. TTT/AAAA.

Poseidon's Fury: A walk-through show that puts its audience at the heart of the action as a journey in the company of a hapless young archaeologist takes a turn for the worse in the lost temple of Poseidon. You pass through an amazing water vortex before your expedition unexpectedly awakens an ancient demon. There is an element of suspense, but the special effects showdown between Poseidon and the demon is amazing. Queuing is tedious, but it is inside. TTT.

Other entertainment: For an extra $5–10, try the **Pitch and Skill Games** or a bit of mystic manipulation with **Psychic Readers**. But beware **The Mystic Fountain**; it can strike up a conversation – and then soak you!

Shopping and dining: Find some original souvenirs at **The Coin Mint** (watch coins forged and struck) and **Historic Families** (explore the history of your family name and coat of arms), **Tangles of Truth** (hand-crafted jewellery), **The Pearl Factory** (pick an oyster) and **The Dragon's Keep** (dragon apparel, games and toys). Food options include **The Fire-Eater's Grill** (sausages, chips and drinks) and **Frozen Desert** (sundaes and sodas). The elaborate **Mythos Restaurant** provides the best dining in IoA; the food (seafood, salads, grills, pizza and pasta) is first class, but the setting (inside a dormant volcano with streams, fountains and clever lighting) is a real attraction (3-course meal around $25, kids' meals $5.99–10.99).

The Eighth Voyage of Sindbad

Wizarding World of Harry Potter

This 'Island' is now THE big draw in Orlando and has significantly boosted the park's attendance since it opened in June 2010. The magnificent edifice of Hogwarts Castle looms large over the 20-acre spread of the famous Wizarding World but *everything* you see here takes you fully inside this incredible creation, which owes much to the design genius of the film series but is also 100% faithful to the books. Entering from The Lost Continent area provides the grand view, through Hogsmeade and with Hogwarts seemingly towering above (the use of masterful architectural perspective is stunning), and you are drawn into an all-encompassing realm where chimneys smoke, icicles glitter, owls roost, visitors are warned to 'Observe the spell limits' and Butterbeer is real!

Hogsmeade Village: Walk through the grand archway into the Wizarding World and a powerful sense of realism envelops you. This is a shimmering, ancient, snow-covered extravaganza, a fully immersive and interactive version of the magical settlement Harry, Ron and Hermione inhabit. It is the shopping and dining heart of the Wizarding World, but is so brilliantly executed it is an attraction in itself. Here you will also find the **Hogwarts Express**, puffing and steaming as it 'awaits its passengers', and, while you can't board Engine 5972, it makes a wonderful photo opportunity. Nearly all the windows feature clever 'wizardly' animatronic

Hogsmeade Village

© 2010 Universal Orlando Resort

Hogwarts Express

touches, the **Owl Clock** comes to life every 15 minutes, the wooden-raftered **Owlery** is a work of art and you may just encounter Moaning Myrtle in the loos! Numerous other clever effects and design touches all help to transform this corner of Florida into J K Rowling's authentic creation (see also Shopping and dining). AAAAA+

Dragon Challenge: Formerly the Dueling Dragons coaster, this sees riders delving into the *Goblet of Fire* story involving the big contest between the 3 wizarding schools of Hogwarts, Durmstrang and Beauxbatons, represented by the billowing banners at the entrance. The long, elaborate queuing area (we LOVE the Corridor of Candles!) sets the scene for your 'flight' on either a Chinese Fireball or Hungarian Horntail dragon, with perils aplenty to avoid. You choose which dragon to ride (the tracks differ slightly), and this is a suspended coaster, so your legs dangle free. The initial drop is therefore like going into free-fall! Coaster aficionados reckon the best ride is in the back of the Hungarian (blue) dragon, but both offer an awesome experience. The coaster features a 100ft/30m drop, multiple loops, twists and 3 near-miss encounters at almost 60mph/96kph. Restrictions: 4ft 6in/137cm; all loose items must be left in the lockers by the entrance. TTTTT+.

BRIT TIP

The lockers for Dragon Challenge are in the Hogsmeade train station, but are free only for the duration of your ride. Make a note of your locker number!

Simon & Susan say...

We were lucky enough to get a long and detailed look at the Wizarding World of Harry Potter before it opened and were absolutely astounded at the look and 'feel' of J K Rowling's epic work of fiction. The large-scale nature of the design is almost overwhelming but the attention to detail is truly extraordinary, with a multitude of features that are sure to thrill Potter aficionados, but will also ensure those not familiar with Harry and Co are still captivated. Led by award-winning film designer Stuart Craig, art director Alan Gilmore and Universal Orlando producer Paul Daurio, a literal cast of thousands set out to create a permanent, fully 3-D home for the mystical, magical wizard and his pals. We think they succeeded far beyond expectations with THE most amazing theme park creation we have ever seen.

The Flight of The Hippogriff: This junior-sized coaster (formerly the Flying Unicorn) is aimed primarily at youngsters and features a journey into Hagrid's realm, where his love of outlandish creatures, and especially the mythical Hippogriff, gives rise to this swooping ride. Hagrid offers instructions and warnings as you wind through the queue, and you may even hear Fang barking from inside Hagrid's hut. There are no big drops on this ride, but it delivers a surprisingly fast-paced whirl. Be sure to bow to the Hippogriff at the start of the ride, though! TTT (TTTT for 6–12s Restrictions: 3ft 4in/92cm).

Harry Potter and the Forbidden Journey: This is the Big One as far as the Wizarding World is concerned, a trip inside the legendary halls of Hogwarts – and a breathtaking plunge on a state-of-the-art ride, Quidditch and all. The basic premise is that 'muggles' (non-wizarding types, i.e. you!) have been invited to tour the school for the first time and you get to see much of the castle's interior. The queuing area is part discovery, part story-telling, part entertainment – and wholly mind-blowing (especially as it winds through, out, around and back in again for some 400 metres before you even get to the ride!). Be ready for a LONG time on your feet as you traverse the corridors, traipse through the greenhouse, tiptoe along the Portrait Hall (where the paintings of the 4 founders of Hogwarts come to life in magical fashion) and tread the stone floors of the Gryffindor common room.

Harry Potter and the Forbidden Journey

Along the way, you will be greeted by Professor Dumbledore in his study (complete with more talking portraits), be accosted by the Fat Lady (another painting-come-to-life) and enter the Defence Against the Dark Arts classroom. Here, Harry, Ron and Hermione appear to urge visitors to abandon their 'boring' tour and come to the Quidditch match instead (with the aid of a magic spell).

BRIT TIP

Once again, this is an unpredictable, dynamic ride, with sudden twists, turns and tilts. You are **strongly** advised to leave all loose items in the free-to-use lockers just inside the castle.

Finally, you reach the Room of Requirement (past the Sorting Hat), where your mode of transport to the match is revealed – magical flying benches. With some pre-ride warnings ('It flies like a dragon with its tail on fire!'), you are then strapped in to your 'bench' and (with the aid of some Floo-powder) are up, up and away. Only things don't quite go as planned and, before you can say 'Expecto Patronum,' you are on a crazy dash through some of the young wizard's most dangerous adventures. Your unique ride vehicle – which moves on a giant robotic arm – sweeps you through a series of dramatic settings that combine clever film technology with full-scale, all-encompassing scenery, creating a totally convincing effect as you move up, down, backwards, forwards and even sideways.

Harry Potter and the Forbidden Journey

© 2010 Universal Orlando Resort

A close encounter with a fire-breathing dragon sends you off course into the Forbidden Forest, where an army of giant spiders lays in wait before Ron comes to the rescue, via a narrow escape with the clutches of the Whomping Willow. That only paves the way for a battle with the Dementors, who try to grab you and deliver their deadly Kiss in a spooky underground cavern. Naturally, Harry is there to save the day and bring you safely back to Hogwarts for a warm welcome from all the main characters. The 4-minute whirl will seem a LOT longer as the ride's breathtaking sequence of special effects make this an eye-popping extravaganza of sound, movement and high-tech dynamics. It is genuinely one of the most astounding theme park experiences anywhere in the world but it WILL scare small children (and anyone with arachnophobia!), and it draws HUGE queues – in excess of 4 hours at times in summer 2010 – so you are strongly advised to do this early in the day. Restrictions: 4ft/122cm. TTTTT+ You exit through **Filch's Emporium of Confiscated Goods**, where you'll find plush Hedwig owls, Crookshank cats, Scabbers rats and 3-Headed Dogs (watch out, he growls!), plus a range of tempting Azkaban and House-related clothing and gifts. You also pick up your ride photos here ($16.99–35.99).

BRIT TIP

Look out for the Marauders Map in Filch's Emporium, plus other clever Hogwarts signature gadgets and gizmos among the merchandise.

Other entertainment: Hogwarts' students work in the shops and restaurant, and wander the streets, but the real entertainment in Hogsmeade is the **TriWizard Spirit Rally**, celebrating the upcoming tournament. Witches from the Beauxbatons Academy of Magic perform ribbon dances and wizards from Durmstrang Institute pose mock staff-fighting challenges. Hogwarts is represented by the **Frog Choir** (4 students and 2 enormous, hilarious frogs!), an ensemble whose unique vocal talents result in an immensely entertaining show.

Shopping and dining: As with all things in the Wizarding World of Harry Potter, the level of detail given to shopping and dining locations is so intricate they are really attractions in their own right. Many items can be found only here in Hogsmeade, but whether you pull your wallet out or not, be sure to have a wander through each to soak up the atmosphere.

The Hogsmeade Arch

Zonko's

supplies 'students' with Quidditch gear and school related clothing and robes, Luna Lovegood's 3-D Quibbler, and even the Nimbus and Nimbus 2001 broomsticks. **Owl Post**: Purchase your wand here after visiting Ollivander's, and don't miss sending a letter by owl! Your mail will receive 1 of 4 different Hogsmeade postmarks, a wonderful little detail friends and family back home can enjoy. Also here are stationery and owl-related gifts. Every wizard needs a wand, and incredible **Ollivander's** has 13 varieties to choose from. Here, 'the wand also chooses the wizard,' with surprising special effects similar to those Harry experienced when choosing his wand. Because the environment is interactive and the shop is small, a limited number of

Honeydukes at the new Harry Potter

When shopping, be sure to visit, **Zonko's**, George and Fred Weasley's favourite stomping ground, which predictably sells novelty items and joke gifts, such as the Sneakoscope, Extendable Ears and Screaming YoYo. Sweetshop **Honeydukes** is the place for Cauldron Cakes, Bertie Bott's Every Flavour Beans and Chocolate Frogs! Find 136 varieties of sweets, many from the Harry Potter films or well-known British favourites (including jelly babies, humbugs and sherbet lemons). **Dervish and Banges**, Hogsmeade's general store, guests are allowed inside for each 'show'. AAAAA.

There is only one sit-down dining location here, but it's a corker. A 'Cathedral to Butterbeer', **The Three Broomsticks** menu features British favourites such as shepherd's pie, fish and chips and Cornish pasties, along with the Great Feast, a family-style dinner of salad, ribs, chicken, roast potatoes and corn on the cob ($49.99 party of 4; $12.99 per extra person). Entrées range from $7.99 to $13.49, with desserts $3.49–3.99, including strawberry and peanut-butter ice cream, found only in the Wizarding World. Next door is the **Hogs Head Pub** where you'll find Hogs Head Brew ($6.50), created especially for the Wizarding World, and complete with animatronic boar's head!

◀✈▶ BRIT TIP

Of all the buildings, The Three Broomsticks is a must-see experience of dramatic interior design and special effects. Look up in the rafters for arriving owls, magical maids and Dobby the House Elf!

All in all, it's an immense collection of vivid and charming elements (witness the animated *Prisoner of Azkaban* poster in Hogsmeade) that add up to a masterful portrayal of J K Rowling's work. You don't need to be a fan to enjoy the Wizarding World and the only snags are the crowds it draws for much

Ollivander's

© 2010 Universal Orlando Resort

of the day, as most of the shops are quite small and quickly feel crowded. Arriving early is highly advisable, but you should also try to see it after dark, when the lighting effects make it even more dramatic. But just take your time and wander the area, and we're sure you'll feel quite, well, *magical.*

Jurassic Park

Leaving the comic-book lands behind, you travel back to the Cretaceous age and the make-believe dinosaur film world. Again, the immersive style is first class and the extravagant scenery will have you looking over your shoulder for stray dinos.

Jurassic Park River Adventure: From scenic splendour, the mood changes to hidden menace as your journey into this magnificent waterborne realm brings you up close and personal with some seriously realistic dinosaurs. Inevitably, your passage is diverted from the safe to the hazardous, and the danger increases as the 16-person raft climbs into the heights of the main building – with raptors loose everywhere. You are aware of something large lurking in the shadows – will you fall prey to the T-Rex, or will your boat take the 85ft/26m plunge to safety (plus a good soaking, down the longest water descent in the world)? Queues usually move briskly but will top an hour in mid-afternoon. Restrictions: 3ft 6in/106cm. TTTT. The ride photo comes in various packages ($26.95-$34.95).

◀✈▶ BRIT TIP

Automobile Association members receive a 10% discount on all ride photos at Universal Orlando.

Pteranodon Flyers: The slow-moving queues are a major turn-off, especially for a fairly average ride, which glides gently over much of Jurassic Park (though it reaches a height of almost 30ft/9m at one point). It is designed mainly for kids, though, and the height range of 3ft–4ft 8in/91–142cm requires anyone

Jurassic Park River Adventure

OVER the upper limit (usually 11 or older) to be accompanied by a child of the right height. TT (TTTT under-9s).

Camp Jurassic: More excellent kids' fare here with the mountainous jungle giving way to an 'active' volcano for youngsters to explore, climb and slide down. Squirt guns and spitter dinosaurs add to the fun. TTTT (for kids, but parents can explore!).

Discovery Center: This indoor centre offers various interactive options, including creating a dinosaur through DNA sequencing, mixing your own DNA with a dino via a touch-screen, seeing through the eyes of various large reptiles and even handling 'dino eggs', plus other fun hands-on exhibits. Being air-conditioned, this is a good place to visit when it's hot (10am–5pm, 7pm peak season). AAA.

Other entertainment: The more adventurous can try the **Rock Climbing Wall** (just outside River Adventure) for an extra $5.

Shopping and dining: Visit **Discovery Center** for the best shopping, while you can eat at the **Burger Digs** (some huge burger platters), **Pizza Predattoria**, **Thunder Falls Terrace** (counter service for rotisserie chicken and salads, plus a great view of the River Adventure) or the **Watering Hole** bar (Happy Hour 3–5pm).

Toon Lagoon

The thrills continue here with a watery theme and more comic-book elements as the (US) newspaper cartoon characters take a bow. Children will also love the fountains, squirt pools and overflowing fire hydrants!

Popeye And Bluto's Bilge-Rat Barges: Every park seems to have a variation on the white-water raft ride, but this is one of the wettest! Fast, bouncy and unpredictable, it has water coming at you from every direction, a couple of sizeable drops and a whirl through the Octoplus Grotto that adds to the fun. If you don't want to get wet, don't ride, because there is no escaping the deluge here. This is also one of the top 5 for long queues (at least when it's hot), but it's definitely worth the wait. Restrictions: 4ft/122cm. TTTTT. You can also try the Water Blasters (for 25c) on the bridge at the start of the ride to give riders a wet start!

BRIT TIP
A change of clothes is often advisable after the Barges, unless it's so hot you need to cool down in a hurry. Bring a waterproof bag for your valuables or leave them in a locker.

Dudley Do-Right's Ripsaw Falls: Universal's designers also hit the jackpot with this flume ride that sends its passengers on a wild (and precipitous!) journey in the company

Popeye And Bluto's Bilge-Rat Barges

of guileless Mounties Dudley Do-Right, bidding to save girlfriend Nell from the evil Snidely Whiplash. The action builds to an explosive finale at the top of a 75ft/27m abyss that drops you through the roof of a ramshackle dynamite shack to the lagoon below. Just awesome – as are the queues from mid-morning to late afternoon. Wet? You bet! Restrictions: 3ft 8in/111cm. TTTTT. There are more Water Blasters here (25c) on the bridge overlooking the final drop to get riders even wetter.

Me Ship, The Olive: This purpose-built kids' playland is designed as a 3-storey boat full of interactive fun and games, including water cannons, bells and slides (ideal for squirting riders on the Bilge-Rat Barges below), in best Popeye style. TTTT (for youngsters).

Other entertainment: The **Toon Lagoon Amphitheatre** stages seasonal live shows (like the high-flying skateboard, roller-blade and BMX bike stunts of **Mat Hoffman's Aggro Circus** in summer 2010), while the **Toon Character Zone**, on King's Row and Comic Strip Lane, is the place to meet the area's many characters like Beetle Bailey, Hagar the Horrible, Krazy Kat, Blondie, Popeye, The Flintstones and Dudley Do-Right.

The Incredible Hulk Coaster

© 2010 Universal Orlando Resort

Toon Lagoon

Shopping and dining: There is the usual array of character shops, like **Gasoline Alley**, **Boop Oop A Doop** and **Toon Extra**, while you can grab a humongous sandwich at **Blondie's** (home of the Dagwood), a trademark burger or chicken wrap at **Wimpy's**, sample the food court of **Comic Strip Café** (Mexican, Chinese, American and Italian), something cool at **Cathy's Ice Cream** or a cold beverage at **Ale To The Chief**.

Marvel Super-Hero Island

Finally, you arrive in the elaborate comic-book pages of the super-heroes. As with all the islands, the experience is total immersion. The amazing façades of this world surround you with an utterly credible alternative reality that is one of the park's triumphs – and that's before you have tried the rides.

The Incredible Hulk Coaster: Roller-coasters don't come much more dramatic than this giant green edifice that soars over the lagoon, blasting 0–40mph/64kph in 2 seconds, and reaching a top speed of 65mph/105kph. It looks awesome, sounds stunning and rides like a demon as you enter the gamma-ray world of Dr David Banner, aka the Incredible Hulk, and zoom into a weightless inversion 100ft/30m up.

BRIT TIP
At the Hulk Coaster, keep left where the queue splits up and you will be in line for the front car for an even more extreme Hulk experience.

© 2010 Universal Orlando Resort

ISLANDS OF ADVENTURE with children

Our guide to the attractions that generally appeal to the different age groups:

Under-5s

Caro-Seuss-el, The Cat In The Hat, High In The Sky Seuss Trolley Train Ride, If I Ran The Zoo, Jurassic Park Discovery Center, Me Ship, The Olive, One Fish, Two Fish, Red Fish, Blue Fish.

5–8s

All the above, plus Amazing Adventures Of Spider-Man, Camp Jurassic, Eighth Voyage of Sindbad, Flight of the Hippogriff, Jurassic Park River Adventure (with parental discretion), Pteranodon Flyers, Storm Force Accelatron, Harry Potter and the Forbidden Journey (if tall enough).

9–12s

Amazing Adventures Of Spider-Man, Camp Jurassic, The Cat In The Hat, Dr Doom's Fearfall, Dudley Do-Right's Ripsaw Falls, Dragon Challenge, Eighth Voyage Of Sindbad, Flight of the Hippogriff, Harry Potter and the Forbidden Journey, Incredible Hulk Coaster, Jurassic Park Discovery Center, Jurassic Park River Adventure, Popeye And Bluto's Bilge-Rat Barges, Pteranodon Flyers, Storm Force Accelatron.

Over-12s

Amazing Adventures Of Spider-Man, Dr Doom's Fearfall, Dudley Do-Right's Ripsaw Falls, Dragon Challenge, Eighth Voyage Of Sindbad, Harry Potter and the Forbidden Journey, Incredible Hulk Coaster, Jurassic Park Discovery Center, Jurassic Park River Adventure, Popeye And Bluto's Bilge-Rat Barges, Storm Force Accelatron.

Just watching is mind-boggling, and the effects are distinctly brain-scrambling! You will need to deposit ANY loose articles in the lockers at the front of the building as the ride is guaranteed to shake anything out of your pockets. Crowds build up rapidly but queues move reasonably quickly. Restrictions: 4ft 6in/137cm. TTTTT+. You can also buy the DVD of your ride for $24.95, with extra park footage.

Dr Doom's Fearfall: This is where, oh hapless visitor, you wander into the lair of the evil Dr Doom – arch-enemy of the Fantastic Four – and his sinister cohorts. His latest creation is the Fearfall, a device for sucking every iota of fear out of his victims, and YOU are about to test it as 16 riders at a time are strapped into chairs at the bottom of a 200ft/60m tower. The dry ice rolls, and whoosh! Up you go at breakneck speed, only to plummet back seemingly even faster, with an amazing split second in between when you feel suspended in mid-air. Summon up the courage to do this and we promise an astonishing (if brief!) experience. There are

substantial queues from mid-day. Restrictions: 4ft 4in/132cm. TTTTT+.

The Amazing Adventures Of Spider-Man: Just queuing is a novel experience as your visit to the Daily Bugle, home of ace reporter Peter Parker (aka Spider-Man), turns into a reporting assignment in one of the 'Scoop' vehicles. Prepare for an audio¬visual extravaganza as the blend of 3-D and motion simulator takes you into a battle between Spidey and arch-villains like Dr Octopus with

The Amazing Adventures Of Spider-Man

his anti-gravity gun, culminating in a convincing 'drop' off a skyscraper as the contest literally hots up. There are lots of eye-popping special effects and you'll need to do it at least twice to appreciate all the detail. Ride early on or leave it until late in the day – the queues often top an hour from mid-morning. Restrictions: 3ft 4in/101cm. TTTTT+. NB: You can beat some of the queues on the Spider-Man ride at busy times by opting for the Single Rider line.

Storm Force Accelatron: This ride, primarily for kids, puts you in the middle of a whirling battle between X-Men heroine Storm and arch-nemesis Magneto. It's basically an updated spinning-cup ride, but with some neat twists (there is a 3-way rotation where the cars look set to collide). TTT (TTTTT under-12s).

BRIT TIP
For some of the park's best shopping bargains, visit Port Provisions right by the exit gates (to the left as you come through) where all the merchandise is 30–50% off.

Dueling Dragons

Other entertainment: The **Marvel Super-Heroes** appear here periodically for photos and autographs, while **Spider-Man** has his own meet 'n' greet booth at The Marvel Alterniverse Store. A high-energy **video arcade** can be found at the exit to Dr Doom's Fearfall.

Shopping and dining: Each ride has its own character merchandise, while the **Comic Book Shop** and **Marvel Alterniverse Shop** sell other souvenirs. For a bite to eat, try the Italian buffeteria **Café 4** (pizza, spaghetti, sandwiches and salads) or a burger, chicken fingers or salad at the **Captain America Diner**.

And that, folks, is the full low-down on arguably the world's most thrilling and complete theme park. Not to be missed!

Marvel Super-Heroes

SeaWorld

SeaWorld is firmly established with British visitors as one of the most popular parks for its more peaceful and naturalistic aspect, the change of pace it offers and the general lack of substantial queues. Like Disney's Epcot park, it is large enough to handle big crowds well (though it still gets busy in peak season) and is a big hit with families in particular, but it has some dramatic rides and imaginative attractions too, including the park's coaster Manta, new in 2009. It is also one of the SeaWorld Parks & Entertainment group, along with sister parks **Busch Gardens** in Tampa, with its emphasis on animal encounters (see pages 207–18), **Discovery Cove**, an exotic tropical 'island' with dolphin, stingray and snorkelling adventures (see pages 203–6) and **Aquatica** (see pages 250–2). These latter have added huge appeal in this area, along with new 2 and 3-day tickets and Discovery Cove's Ultimate Ticket, which includes all 4 parks. SeaWorld's recent new shows and other enhancements mean this remains a wonderfully fresh and invigorating place to visit.

Happily, this is still a park where you can proceed at a relatively leisurely pace, see what you want without too much jostling and yet feel you have been well entertained (even if the restaurants get crowded at mealtimes). SeaWorld is a good starting point if this is your first Orlando visit as it gives you the hang of negotiating the vast areas, navigating by the various maps and learning to plan around the

SeaWorld at a glance

Location	7007 SeaWorld Drive, off Central Florida Parkway (Junctions 71 and 72 off I-4)
Size	More than 200 acres/81ha, incorporating 26 attractions
Hours	9am–6pm off peak; 9am–10pm high season (Easter, summer holidays, Thanksgiving, Christmas)
Admission	Under-3s free; 3–9 $68.95 (1-day Ticket), $99.95 (2-Park Ticket, w/Aquatica or Busch Gardens), $139.95 (3-Park Ticket inc Aquatica and Busch Gardens), $239.95 (Orlando FlexTicket), $279.95 (Orlando FlexTicket Plus); adult (10+) $78.95, $109.95, $149.95, $259.95, $299.95
Parking	$12, $20 preferred parking
Lockers	Inside Entrance Plaza (next to Sweet Sailin' Candy), $7 and $10 (rent from Pushchair and Wheelchair location)
Pushchairs	$14 and $19, to right of Guest Services inside park
Wheelchairs	$12 and $45; with pushchairs
Top attractions	Believe at Shamu Stadium, Shark Encounter, Journey To Atlantis, Kraken, Manta, Wild Arctic, Blue Horizons
Don't miss	Reflections (high season), Manatee Rescue, behind-the-scenes tours, A'Lure Call of the Ocean show, dining at Sharks Underwater Grill
Hidden costs	**Meals** Burger, chips and coke $11.28 3-course lunch $39.00 (Sharks Underwater Grill) Kids' meal $7.29, including souvenir Shamu lunchbox; $8–10 at Sharks Underwater Grill **T-shirts** $16.99–26.99 **Souvenirs** $1.99–$1,599 **Sundries** Manta ride photo $19.99, combo with Kraken $24.99

1 Entrance plaza
2 Key West at SeaWorld
3 Stingray Lagoon
4 Turtle Point
5 Dolphin Cove
6 Blue Horizons
7 Garden of Discovery
8 Manatee Rescue
9 Journey To Atlantis
10 Kraken
11 The Manta
12 Penguin Encounter
13 Pacific Point Preserve
14 Sea Lion and Otter Stadium
15 Xtreme Zone
16 The Waterfront
17 Seaport Theater

18 Seafire Inn/ Makahiki Luau
19 Sky Tower
20 Dolphin Nursery
21 Voyager's Smokehouse
22 Shark Encounter
23 Nautilus Theater – A'lure
24 Sharks Underwater Grill
25 The Terrace
26 Shamu Stadium
27 Shamu's Happy Harbor
28 Wild Arctic
29 Mango Joe's Café
30 Atlantis Bayside Stadium

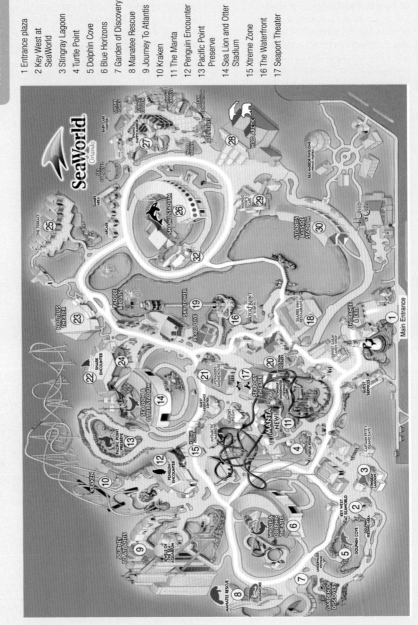

show times. This park has a strong educational and environmental message, plus some behind-the-scenes tours that provide great insight into SeaWorld's conservation and research programmes, as well as its entertainment resources. There are special offers for booking online at **seaworld.com**, where you can print your tickets to save waiting in line, plus a website for UK visitors – **seaworldparks.co.uk**.

Their 7 backstage programmes are as follows (book in advance online, call 1800 406 2244, or visit the Guided Tours counter first thing when you arrive): the 7-hour **VIP Tour**, with individual tour guide and back-door access to rides, shows, lunch and animal feeding ($125/adult, $100 3–9s;); the **Elite VIP Tour**, similar but just for your family or group, and including a penguin meeting and lunch at Sharks Underwater Grill ($275/person); the 1-hour **Dolphins Up-Close Tour,** a fascinating glimpse backstage at the training and care of the stars of the Blue Horizons show, as well as a look into the extensive dolphin-care facilities, finishing with a Q&A session with one of the trainers at Dolphin Cove and the chance to touch one of the residents ($50 adults, $40 3–9s); the 1-hour **Penguins Up-Close Tour**, highlighting penguin and puffin care, including limited encounters with these delightful birds ($40 and $30); the new (in 2010) **Sea Lions Up-Close Tour**, a 90-minute walking tour focusing on the care and training of the stars of the Clyde & Seamore show, including a photo with the 'stars' and a chance to feed the Pacific Point Preserve sea lions ($40 and $30); the 90-minute **Behind The Scenes Tour**, providing a look at what goes on in the turtle and manatee rescue areas, with the chance to meet a small shark, check out a polar bear den and touch one of the penguins ($30 and $20); and the **Family Fun Tour**, a 4-hour guided walking tour of the top children's attractions, feeding dolphins and sea lions, touching a penguin, reserved seats at the Believe show, a light meal and select rides in Shamu's Happy Harbor, finishing

with an exclusive meet 'n' greet with the park's cuddly Shamu character and a special gift ($65 and $50). There are then 3 interactive programmes: **Marine Mammal Keeper Experience**, taking 2 visitors daily to discover the care necessary to rehabilitate injured manatees, plus bottle-feed some of them, meet the seals and walruses and prepare meals for the beluga whales (starts at 6.30am and lasts around 8 hours; $399/person including lunch, T-shirt, special book, souvenir photo and 7-day SeaWorld pass; must be 13 or older); **Sharks Deep Dive**, a chance to suit up and dive in a specially constructed cage in the huge shark aquarium, spending a ½-hour up close and personal with these creatures and with an educational induction into the world of sharks and what makes them tick. You are equipped for the dive with wetsuit (the water is COLD), gloves, dive belt and a special underwater helmet (no scuba gear needed) in the reinforced steel cage that glides slowly through the long tank for an astounding fish-eye view of these creatures – and you won't tire of the underwater panorama, which includes waving to people in the shark tunnel! ($149/person, including souvenir T-shirt and shark book; must be 10 or older); and the **Beluga Interactive Program**, a unique

Dolphin Spotlight Tour

chance to meet some of the park's biggest but most benign denizens in their own environment. Swimming isn't necessary but guests must be comfortable in the water as touching, feeding and using hand signals are all part of this informative tour ($99-149/person, including a book on whales; no expectant mothers; must be 10 or older).

Location

SeaWorld is located off Central Florida Parkway, between I-4 (exit 71 going east or 72 heading west) and I-Drive, and parking is $12 ($20 for preferred parking, closer to the entrance). It is still best to arrive a bit before the official opening time so you're in a good position to book one of the backstage tours, dash to one of the few attractions that draws a crowd, like Manta, or purchase Quick Queue, the park's queue-beating, paid-for pass that entitles bearers to the unlimited access to Manta, Kraken, Journey to Atlantis, and Wild Arctic, plus unlimited use of the Skytower and paddle boats (pricing is seasonal at $14.95-$24.95, quantities limited).

The park covers more than 200 acres/81ha, with 6 shows (7 with the splendid nightly **Makahiki Luau**

Beluga Interactive Program

Shamu Stadium

dinner show at the Seafire Inn, a 2-hour South Seas extravaganza with island music, songs, great costumes and the eye-opening fore-dance, as well as a huge feast; $46 adults, $29 3–9s; nightly, times vary, call 407 351 3600 or book online), 4 major rides, 10 large-scale continuous viewing attractions and 7 smaller ones, plus a smart range of shops and restaurants (a notable feature of the SeaWorld group). As in the other parks, try to eat before midday or after 2.30pm for a crowd-free lunch, and before 5.30pm if you want a leisurely dinner (better still, book Sharks Underwater Grill). Pre-school children may also want to try **Breakfast with Elmo & Friends** (daily at the Seafire Inn at 8.30 or 10.30am), a big buffet meal featuring the stars of Sesame Street like Big Bird, Cookie Monster and Elmo himself ($18 adults, $16 3–9s; book in advance online or 407 351 3600). Non-drivers should note the special daily bus service from SeaWorld (and other points on I-Drive) direct to sister park **Busch Gardens** (see pages 207–18), which you can book at Guest Relations.

SeaWorld is not organised into neat 'lands' like the others, though, and it often requires much to-ing and fro-ing to catch the various shows, which can be wearing. Keep a close grip on your map and entertainment schedule and try to establish a programme to allow regular breaks. Going in a clockwise direction, here's what you find.

Entrance plaza
Coming through the turnstiles brings you to the park's main business area, including the **Guest Information** kiosk, **Lost & Found**, **Behind The Scenes** tour desk, lockers and pushchair and wheelchair rental. You will also find some good shopping and snack options here. Look for the large **Shamu Emporium** for the full range of SeaWorld souvenirs, while **Keyhole Photos** provides all your park pictures taken by the SeaWorld photographers. You can grab a quick breakfast (tasty pastries and coffee) at **Cypress Bakery** or something colder from the **Polar Parlor Ice Cream**. This is also the place to find a photo opportunity with **Shamu and friends**.

Key West at SeaWorld
A whole collection of exhibits is grouped together here under the clever Key West theme. S**tingray Lagoon**, where you can feed (for $5) and touch fully grown rays, includes a nursery for newborn rays, while the park's rescued and rehabilitated sea turtles can be seen at **Turtle Point**. The centre-piece, the 2.1-acre/0.8ha **Dolphin Cove**, is a more spectacular, naturalistic development and offers the chance to feed this community of frisky Atlantic bottlenose dolphins (for $7 at specified periods through the day). There is also an excellent underwater viewing area, and park photographers are ready to snap you at play with the dolphins (a 6 x 8 photo will set you back $19.99; frames are $12 and $20).

BRIT TIP
If you drop your fish on the ground when feeding the dolphins, seals or sea lions you are asked to throw it away, for the animals' health and safety.

Garden of Discovery: A lovely, semi-secluded walk-through nature cove, with bench seats, just right for some time off your feet. Occasional small animal encounters occur here, adding to the delightfully relaxing atmosphere.

The whole Key West area is designed in the eclectic, tropical flavour of America's most southerly city, but it also underlines the environmental message of conservation through interactive graphics and video displays adjacent to the animal habitats, and children will find it a fun, educational experience. AAAA.

Shopping and dining: There are 5 gift shops and kiosks here, the best being **Coconut Bay Trader** (apparel and soft toys) and **Sandcastle Toys 'n Treats**. You can grab a hot dog or chicken tenders at **Captain Pete's Island Eats**.

BRIT TIP
Seek out Gulliver's store in Key West for a range of heavily discounted SeaWorld and Discovery Cove apparel and gifts.

Whale & dolphin theatre
The first large-scale encounter is the setting for a magnificent show, plus the Manatee rescue exhibit.

Blue Horizons: This wonderful production serves up a big helping of dramatic animal behaviour in best Broadway style. It features dolphins, false killer whales and exotic birds (including an Andean condor), but a lot more besides as the general (and rather abstract) theme of a girl's dream about maritime wildlife is brought to life. The elaborate set design is eye-catching, with a 40ft/12m sea-meets-sky backdrop that also conceals the setting for a host of additional performers, from

Blue Horizons

high divers to bungee jumpers and trapeze-like aerialists. There is no obvious interaction between trainers and animals as the show moves from one scene to the next, both above and below the water, but there is plenty to admire as the stage is filled with graceful and daring action. The complex staging and vivid costuming (all created by Broadway designers) is also underpinned by a stirring original score by the Seattle Symphony Orchestra and it adds up to a magnificent 25 minutes that often draws a huge ovation. AAAAA.

Manatee Rescue: Next door is an exhibit to tug at your heartstrings as you learn the plight of this endangered species of Florida's waterways. Watch these lazy-looking creatures (half-walrus, half-cow?) lounge in their man-made lagoon, then walk down the ramp to the circular theatre where a 5-minute film with 3-D effects reveals the dangers facing the harmless manatee. Pass on into the underwater viewing section, with hands-on TV screens offering more information. It's a magnificent exhibit and should invoke a strong sense of animal conservation. Try to avoid going just after a Blue Horizons show as it can get congested. AAA½.

Shopping and dining: Look to **Manatee Cove** for a kids' wonderland of cuddly toys, while there are also 2 drinks carts.

Ride central

Continue past Whale & Dolphin Theatre and you come to the park's serious thrill quotient.

Journey to Atlantis: Unique in Orlando, this terrific water-coaster gave SeaWorld its first 5-star thrill attraction in 1998. The combination of extra elements here ultimately makes it a one-off, with some illusory special effects giving way to a high-speed water ride that becomes a runaway roller-coaster. The discovery of Atlantis in your 8-passenger 'fishing boat' starts gently through the lost city. But evil spirit Allura takes over and riders plunge into a dash through Atlantis, dodging gushing fountains and water cannons, with hundreds of dazzling holographic and laser-generated illusions before the 60ft/18m drop, which is merely the entry to the roller-coaster finale back in the candle-filled catacombs. Be ready to get soaked, which is great in summer but not so clever first thing on a winter morning. Restrictions: 3ft 6in/106cm. TTTTT.

Kraken: This member of the coaster family is one of Florida's most breathtaking. Based on the mythical sea monster, Kraken is an innovative pedestal ride (you are effectively sitting in a chair without a floor – pretty exposed!) that plunges an initial 144ft/44m, hits 65mph/105kph,

Kraken

Journey to Atlantis

dives underground 3 times, adds 7 inversions (including a vertical loop, a diving loop, a zero-gravity roll and a cobra roll) and a flat spin before riders escape the beast's lair. The ride from the front row, especially down an opening drop at an angle best described as ludicrous, is positively blood-curdling, and sitting in the rear is thrilling, too. Restrictions: 4ft 6in/137cm. TTTTT+.

Manta: This ride (new in 2009) is a triumph of the designer's art, turning a high-tech coaster into a unique mixture of ride and animal encounter. The elaborate queuing area winds through cool, rocky caverns, passing waterfalls and floor-to-ceiling windows showcasing some 300 rays and thousands of fish, which lead through to the 'undersea world' of the manta ray. Themed like a giant ray, riders are strapped into a face-down position before being launched into an exhilarating series of 4 inversions along 3,359ft/1,024m of track, reaching nearly 60mph/96kph and 140ft/43m high as well as skimming the surface of the lagoon. The 'flying' nature of the coaster and smooth ride vehicles make this a true original. Restrictions, 54in/137cm. TTTTT. It is a visual treat and a breathtaking ride, and even non-riders can enjoy the nearby walk-though aquarium with its own entry. Lockers located near the queue entry are available for use during your ride (50c).

Shopping and dining: Don't miss the **Sea Aquarium Gallery** as you exit Journey to Atlantis, a combination gift shop and aquarium full of tropical fish (remember to look upwards), while there are more animal-orientated souvenirs in **Kraken Gifts**. **Manta Market** and **High Seas Market**, each near their namesake coaster, offer convenient grab-and-go snacks and drinks.

Penguins and sea lions
Getting back to the animal side of the park brings you to 2 more outstanding natural habitats, and a hilarious show.

Penguin Encounter: Always a hit with families (and one of the more crowded exhibits), the ever-comical penguins are brilliantly presented in this chilly showpiece. You have the choice of going close and using the moving walkway along the display or standing back and watching from a non-moving position. Both afford fascinating views both above and below the water of the 17 different species. The 5 or so daily feeding times are also popular, so arrive early if you want a prime spot. There is a Q&A session at 2pm every day – the winner gets to pet a penguin! AAAA.

Pacific Point Preserve: This carefully re-created rocky coast habitat shows the park's seals and sea lions at their most natural. A hidden wave machine adds the perfect touch, while park attendants provide informative talks. You can also buy packs of smelt ($5

Top of the drop on Manta

per tray or 5 trays for $20) to throw to these ever-hungry mammals. AAA.

Sea Lion and Otter Stadium: The venue for a wonderful show, *Clyde And Seamore Take Pirate Island*, it features the resident sea lions who, with their pals the otter and walrus (plus a couple of humans as the fall guys), put on a hilarious 25-minute performance of watery stunts and gags. Arrive early for some first-class audience mickey-taking from the resident pirate 'mime'. AAAA.

Other entertainment: Xtreme Zone offers a 2-minute Trampoline Jump for an extra $8 (reservations required).

Shopping and dining: Pets Ahoy Gifts is the best of the shops here, along with the large **Friends of the Wild**. Grab a meal at **Mama's Kitchen** (a good range of fresh sandwiches, salads and chilli) or the **Seaport Pizza** (cheese and pepperoni pizza), while there are also 3 drinks carts and an ice-cream counter.

The waterfront

Backtracking slightly (or turning right after the Entrance Plaza area) brings you to this beautiful 5-acre/2ha seafront 'village' of restaurants and shops, which is a great place to spend some time when other parts are busy, especially for lunch or dinner.

Pets Ahoy!: Just inside the Waterfront is the air-conditioned haven (during the hottest part of the day) of the Seaport Theater, which hosts this cute 25-minute giggle featuring the unlikely talents of a menagerie of dogs, cats, birds, rats, pot-bellied pigs

and others, the majority of which have come from local animal rescue shelters. AAA.

Other entertainment: The Tower is the centrepiece of the Waterfront, with a 400ft/122m landmark offering (at an extra $4) slowly rotating rides for a bird's-eye view of the park and surrounding areas. The **Dolphin Nursery** provides close-up views with some of the park's younger dolphins.

Shopping and dining: This has some of the best in SeaWorld, starting with 4 interlinked boutique-style shops that offer a stylish range of souvenirs and other gift items (check out **Allura's Treasure Trove** and **Artisans Hall**, as well as the brand name fashions at **Currents**). The unique **Oyster's Secret** shop features resident pearl divers who can be viewed underwater as they collect the pearl-bearing oysters on request, to be incorporated into jewellery pieces by the shop's artisans. The 3 excellent eateries are: **Seafire Inn** (gourmet burgers, salads, Cuban sandwich and fish and chips); **Voyagers** (smoked chicken, barbecue ribs, salad, children's menu with chicken tenders, hot dog, or macaroni and cheese); and **The Spice Mill** (offering flame-grilled burgers and grilled chicken sandwiches with a range of seasonings). There are also 3 snack bars: **Café de Mar** for pastries, coffees, smoothies and soft drinks; **Smugglers Feast** for smoked turkey legs; and **Freezas** for frozen yoghurt and other drinks. The **SandBar** is a water's edge cocktail bar, serving snacks and speciality drinks – the place to watch the sun go down!

Clyde and Seamore Take Pirate Island

Sharks and co

Continuing the clockwise tour brings you towards the back of the park (which usually doesn't open until 11am). Here you find more animal encounters – and a wonderful show.

> **BRIT TIP**
> Grab an evening meal at The Spice Mill, then head out on to its open-air terrace for one of the best seats in the house to experience the Reflections summer nightly finale.

Shark Encounter: Top of the bill, the world's largest collection of dangerous sea creatures can be found here, brought dramatically to life by the walk-through tubes that surround you with more than 50 prowling sharks (including sand tigers, black tips, nurse sharks and sand bars), sawfish, tropical fish and gigantic groupers. It's an eerie experience (and perhaps too intense for young children), but brilliantly presented and, again, highly informative. You can also watch the intrepid Sharks Deep Dive cage as it traverses the aquarium (see page 193). Queues build up here at peak times, though. AAAA or TTTT.

A'Lure, the Call of the Ocean: This imaginative 30-minute show in the Nautilus Theater features creative acrobatic feats, engaging live music, yo-yo artists, clever lighting and in-theatre special effects. The show tells the stylised story of a fisherman who is pulled into the ocean and finds himself in an undersea world ruled by a tyrant queen. He becomes the unwilling pawn in her battle against a beautiful Siren for control of the ocean kingdom. AAAA. The theatre is also home to various weekend events throughout the year, notably **Jack Hanna's Animal Adventure**, the **Bud and BBQ Country Music Festival**, and the **Viva La Musica** Latin weekends.

Other entertainment: The flamingo pedal-boats on the lagoon rent for $5 per 20 minutes (for 2 people). You can also **feed the sharks** and stingrays outside Shark Encounter ($5 per tray).

> **BRIT TIP**
> Looking for a quiet spot for a break from the hectic pace? Seek out the terrace along the lagoon (with tables and chairs) situated directly behind Fins gift shop and across from Sharks Underwater Grill.

Shopping and dining: The 3 shops here (**Ocean Treasures**, **Shark Photo** and **Gulf Breeze Trader**) are relatively small-scale but, at the entrance to Shark Encounter is the top dining choice, **Sharks Underwater Grill**. Not only do you have an amazing backdrop for your meal in a clever, subterranean environment (check out the incredible bar, which is a mini-aquarium), but also the upscale menu features appetising 'Floribbean' cuisine, blending local and spicy Caribbean fare. The emphasis is on seafood – and wonderful creations with scallops, jumbo shrimp (king prawns), grouper and sea bass – plus

Sharks Underwater Grill

pasta, filet mignon, chicken and pork – and desserts to die for. Some refreshing (non-alcoholic) cocktails and menus for under-10s and teens complete the picture; it's a real treat on a hot day. Open from 11am to park closing, it's busy at lunch but quieter in late afternoon, so we advise booking (at the restaurant itself) as soon as you arrive. The Terrace Café (formerly Hospitality House), now offers deli sandwiches, salad, beef stew, bratwurst and hot dogs, while the Terrace Bar has a selection of American and imported beers. Sadly, it no longer offers free tastes of the Anheuser-Busch products.

Shamu central

The other main area of the park features the iconic Shamu Stadium and a fabulous play area to entertain the kids, plus another engaging ride/animal attraction.

> **BRIT TIP**
> The first 14 rows at Shamu Stadium get VERY wet (watch out for your cameras) – when a killer whale leaps into the air in front of you, it displaces a LOT of water on landing. In fact, the Splash Zones should be renamed the Soak Zones!

Shamu Stadium: SeaWorld has long outgrown its tag as just the place to see killer whales, but the **Believe** show is still one of its most amazing sights. Watch the killer whales and their trainers pull off some spectacular stunts, all set within the story of a young boy's dream of interacting with these creatures of the deep. The basic message of needing to believe in your dreams is a touch schmaltzy, but there is no doubting the brilliant choreography as animals and trainers put on a seamless display – apparently without any commands. Some dramatic staging and an original music score by the Prague National Symphony Orchestra are combined with high-tech video screens that slide and rotate in eye-catching fashion to create a truly majestic extravaganza that is way beyond usual animal shows. And, if you think it looks good during the day, return in the evening (in high season) for an even more dramatic presentation under the lights, with the video screens coming into their own. As it is the park's signature element, Shamu Stadium is extremely popular, hence you should try to take in one of the early shows. AAAAA+. All guests can then enjoy the backstage **Underwater Viewing** area.

Shamu's Happy Harbor: 4 acres/1.6ha of brilliantly designed adventure playground and rides await youngsters of all ages here. Activities include a 4-storey net climb, 2 tented ball rooms to wade through, a giant trampoline tent, a mock pirate ship

Believe

SEAWORLD with children

The following gives a general idea of the appeal of the attractions to the different age groups:

Under-5s

Believe, Blue Horizons, Clyde And Seamore Take Pirate Island, Clydesdale Hamlet, Elmo Show, Manatee Rescue, A'Lure, the Call of the Ocean, Pacific Point Preserve, Penguin Encounter, Pets Ahoy!, Shamu's Happy Harbor, Waterfront entertainment, Wild Arctic (without the ride).

5–8s

All the above, plus Reflections, Shark Encounter, Wild Arctic (with the ride).

9–12s

All the above, plus Journey to Atlantis, The Manta and Kraken.

Over-12s

Believe, Blue Horizons, Clyde And Seamore Take Pirate Island, Journey To Atlantis, The Manta, Kraken, Reflections, A'Lure, Shark Encounter, Wild Arctic.

and a splashy water play area, **Water Works** (great on a hot day). The signature junior-sized coaster **Shamu Express** offers mild thrills over more than 800ft/245m of track. The **Jazzy Jellies** is a jellyfish-themed samba tower ride that lifts and spins, while **Swishy Fishes** features oversized seats that spin round a giant waterspout. **Flying Fiddler** (a 20ft/6.1m tower ride on a jumping giant crab), **Ocean Commotion** (a rocking tug ride) and **Sea Carousel** (a traditional carousel featuring 65 sea creatures) complete the line-up. The area gets busy from midday, but the kids seem to love it at any time. Next door is the arcade and **Games Area**, a series of fairground-type stalls ranging from $1–10 a time. TTTT. At the back of the Harbor is a well equipped, comfortable **Baby Care Center** and the park's **First Aid** station.

Wild Arctic: This interactive ride-and-view experience provides a realistic environment that is both educational and thrilling. It's an exciting simulator jet helicopter journey into the white wilderness, arriving at 'Base Station Wild Arctic' where passengers disembark into a frozen wonderland to see polar bears, beluga whales and walruses. This one is not to be missed (but avoid just after Believe when the hordes descend). Restrictions: 3ft 6in/106cm. TTTT/AAAAA. Those who don't want to do the (quite dynamic) ride can walk through to the Base Station.

Shopping and dining: The **Wild Arctic Gift Shop** is the best of the 3 stores here. For dining, **Mango Joe's Café** offers grilled fajitas, speciality salads and sandwiches, while **Coconut Cove** offers drinks and snacks in Shamu's Happy Harbor, but weary parents will enjoy the convenience of Harbor Market grab-and-go snacks and drinks.

Sea Lion and Otter Stadium

BRIT TIP

Any purchases can be forwarded to Package Pick-up in Shamu's Emporium to collect on your way out, provided you give them at least an hour's notice.

Dine with Shamu: A VIP experience 'backstage' with the killer whales and their trainers. A huge all-you-can-eat buffet on a covered terrace by the main pool allows the trainers to display their unique bond with and care for the animals (you may also get a little wet). Offered daily (times vary) but book in advance online or on 1888 800 5447 *(Note: Dine with Shamu experience was suspended in 2010, but may return without prior notice. Be sure to call in advance to check availability).* The **All Day Dining Deal** is a set fee for a special wristband that gives unlimited visits to 6 restaurants (Spice Mill, Voyager's Terrace Café, Mango Joe's, Seaport Pizza and Seafire Inn), claiming an entrée, side dish and drink each time ($29.99 and $14.99).

Atlantis Bayside Stadium

The final part of SeaWorld is this large outdoor arena facing the central Lagoon. It's home to an array of seasonal entertainment but is most susceptible to any bad weather.

Elmo and Abby's Treasure Hunt: Each summer sees a special *Sesame Street* live show on stage here, from late May to 1 Sept. Guaranteed to appeal to the pre-school set, the musical presentation features Elmo, Cookie Monster, Rosita, Grover, Abby Cadabby and others in a 25-minute song and dance fest, encouraging youngsters to use their imagination in a mock treasure hunt. There is also a post-show character meet and greet. AA (or AAAA, depending on age).

Summer extras

During the official summer season, SeaWorld has extended hours to 10pm and offers an array of extra live entertainment as part of its **AfterDark** programme. The 'rock 'n' roll' party atmosphere is generated by live DJs and other entertainers and features extra shows, notably **Shamu Rocks**, which adds a more high-energy, free-form version of the main show, including live music and dramatic lighting. Then, over at Sea Lion & Otter Stadium, there is a second evening show, **Sea Lions Tonite**, which serves up a fun parody of other SeaWorld shows.

BRIT TIP

Learn more about SeaWorld's conservation and environmental efforts at **seaworld.org**.

It all leads up to the big **Reflections** finale on the Waterfront lagoon. This is a neat mix of pyrotechnics and special effects, with towering fountains (up to 100ft/30m high), mist sprays, unique fireworks and an epic soundtrack. View from the Waterfront, or arrive early for seating at the Bayside Stadium. AAAA.

Dine with Shamu

Discovery Cove

Fancy a day in your own tropical paradise, with the chance to swim with dolphins, encounter sharks, snorkel in a coral reef and dive through a waterfall into a tropical aviary? Well, Discovery Cove is all that and more. The only drawback is the price. This mini theme park comes at a premium because it is restricted to just 1,000 guests a day, creating an exclusive experience that is reflected in the admission fee.

The weather can get distinctly cool in the winter, but the water is always heated (apart from the dolphin lagoon, which remains at 72ºF/22ºC) and full wetsuits are available to keep out the chill. The attention to detail is superb, guest satisfaction ratings are extremely high and it is hugely popular with British visitors. However, if any element falls below expectations, it's worth bringing it to the attention of a manager as they are always keen to rectify any oversights.

The costs

In 2010, the flat-rate entrance fee was $199–299, depending on season. The only reduction is $100 off for those not wishing to do the Dolphin Swim, and under-3s (free). So, just what do you get for your money? Well, as you would expect, it's a supremely personal park. You check in at the beautiful entrance lobby as you would for a hotel rather than a theme park, and you have a guide to take you in and get you set. All your basic requirements – towel, mask, snorkel, wet-jacket, lockers, beach umbrellas, food and drink – are included, and the level of service is excellent. A pass for SeaWorld, Aquatica, or Busch Gardens is also included (valid for 14 consecutive days before or after your Discovery Cove visit), or you can upgrade to the **Ultimate Experience,** which provides 14 days at SeaWorld, Aquatica AND Busch Gardens for an extra $80 (superb value). Continental breakfast, snacks, beverages (including Anheuser-Busch products) and an excellent buffet

at the **Laguna Grill** are all included. But gift shop and photo prices reflect the entry fee – expensive. It is also an extra $100-$200 (seasonally) to hire one of their swanky **cabañas** for the day (which include tables, chairs, loungers, towels and drinks service). In addition to the basic cabaña, Pool view cabañas are available for $125-225, Premium cabaña (with upgraded furniture and concierge service) $175-275. Ultimate cabañas are also available for $600 (year round), available only by advance reservation.

Therefore, for all its style and dolphin appeal, Discovery Cove will take a BIG bite out of your holiday budget. A family of 4, with children old enough to do the Dolphin Swim, would pay $1,196 in peak season. Even with a free SeaWorld pass, it's a big outlay. The charge for ages 3–5 is also pretty steep, in our opinion. Your sundries can add up, too. A 6x8 photo is $20; then there are various photo packages at $60, $139 and $219, while the DVD of your experience (which includes 30 minutes of park highlights) costs $50 and the Ultimate Package (7 6x8 photos, 1 4x6 photo, 2 key chains, digital photo CD, Interaction video, photo album, 16x24 poster) is $219. Poster-size photos (24x36) are available for $25. However, despite the costs, the feedback we get is almost unfailingly positive and most people are totally captivated by the experience. One handy free perk,

Dolphin Swim

A close encounter at Discovery Cove

though, is the **Horticulture Tour**, twice a day, which takes guests through the care and maintenance of the park's rich tropical plant and tree life.

There is also an additional programme that adds a great deal of appeal to the basic day, but at more cost. **Trainer for a Day** is an exciting opportunity to go behind the scenes into the park's training, feeding and welfare. You get to work with the experts as they interact with dolphins, birds, sharks, stingrays and tropical fish, including a behavioural training class, the chance to experience a double-foot push (ride on the front

Trainer for a Day

of 2 dolphins), a souvenir shirt, dolphin book and waterproof camera. Participants must be at least 6 and in good health, and it costs $389–$488 (seasonally). For all Discovery Cove bookings, call 407 370 1280 (freephone 0800 3344 1818 in the UK) or visit **discoverycove.com**.

Location

Situated on Central Florida Parkway, almost opposite the SeaWorld entrance (open year-round 9am–5.30pm; parking free), the whole 30-acre/12ha park is magnificently landscaped, with thatched buildings, palm trees, lush vegetation, white-sand beaches, gurgling streams – even hammocks to chill out in. The overall effect is of being transported to a tropical paradise. The usual tourist hurly-burly is left far behind. The 5-star resort feel is enhanced by a high staff-to-guest ratio, there are no queues (though the restaurant may get busy at lunchtime), and the highlight Dolphin Encounter is world class. Visitors with disabilities are well catered for, with special wheelchairs that can move in sand and shallow water, and an area of the Dolphin Lagoon that allows those who can't enter the water still to touch a dolphin.

Discovery Cove

The essence of a day here involves close encounters with all the animals and the ultimate feeling is total relaxation, a holiday from your holiday.

The main attractions

Tropical Reef: A huge rocky pool, filled with several thousand tropical fish, offers the most amazing man-made snorkelling experience you'll find. The water teems with angelfish, silverjacks and yellowtail snapper and, even if the 'coral' is hand-painted concrete, it's a clever environment. Some of the larger rays inhabiting the bottom are fascinating to watch. Swimmers also come within inches of sharks and barracuda – all behind a Plexiglass partition – which adds another novel element. If you stay reasonably still in the water, many of the tropical fish will crowd around to inspect their latest pool-mate! AAAA. **New for 2011** will be an additional Tropical Reef section where you can wade, swim or snorkel freely through a vibrant undersea world and safely share the water with exotic eels, lionfish and sharks, plus explore water-side trails and bridges to one of the reef's many islands.

Ray Lagoon: Another carefully sculpted pool provides the opportunity to paddle among several dozen southern and cownose rays – harmless, but with a hint of menace added to the fascination. AAAA.

Wind-away River: This 800yd/732m circuit of gently flowing bath-warm water is a variation on the lazy river feature of many of the water parks, though with a far more naturalistic aspect and none of the inner tubes. It is primarily designed for snorkellers and features rocky lagoons, caves, a beach section, a tropical forest segment, sunken ruins and an underwater viewing window into the Coral Reef. The lack of fish makes it seem a bit bland after the Coral Reef and Ray Lagoon, but it is as much about relaxing as having fun. It is up to 8ft/2.4m deep at points, so non-swimmers are advised to use a flotation vest. It finishes in the freeform **Serenity Bay Pool**, which provides more idyllic relaxation. AAA.

Explorer's Aviary: This 3-part adventure is both an area in its own right and a 120ft/37m section of the Tropical River. You can walk in off the beach or swim in through the waterfall from the Tropical River, which is a beautifully scenic touch and fun for snorkellers. Some 250 tropical birds (plus tiny muntjak deer) fill the main enclosure and, if you stand still, they are likely to use you as a perch. There is a small-bird sanctuary – full of finches, honeycreepers and hummingbirds – and a large-bird enclosure, featuring toucans and the red-legged seriema. Guides will introduce you to specific birds (which you can hand-feed) and tell you about their habitats and conservation issues. AAAAA.

Ray Lagoon

Dolphin Swim: The park's headline attraction is the encounter with the park's Atlantic bottlenose dolphin community. A 20-minute orientation programme in one of the beach cabañas, with a film and instruction from 2 of the animal trainers, sets you up for this thrilling experience. Groups of 6–8 go into the lagoon with supervision from the trainers and, starting off standing in the waist-deep (slightly chilly) water as one of the dolphins comes over, you gradually become more adventurous until you are swimming with them. Timid swimmers are well catered for and there are flotation vests for those who need them. The lagoon is up to 12ft/3.6m deep so there is a real feeling of being in the dolphins' environment. You learn how trainers use hand signals and positive reinforcement to communicate, and get the chance to stroke, feed and even kiss your dolphin. The encounter concludes dramatically as you are towed ashore by one of these awesome animals (which weigh up to 600lb/272kg), though the activities vary according to the dolphins' attention span. You spend around 30 minutes in the water and it is totally unforgettable. Under-6s are not allowed in the lagoon. TTTTT+.

Dolphin Swim

Discovery Cove 'extras'

This isn't a cheap day out, but the extra quality is everywhere. The **Laguna Grill** lunch is excellent and you can visit as often as you want, while a Calypso band adds to the tropical paradise feel. **Conservation Cabaña** allows guests to meet a neat selection of the park's small mammals (like an anteater and tree sloth); **parking** is free and you also receive an 8 x 6 **welcome photo**. And, while official opening time is 9am, they will check you in as early as 8am to take advantage of the free breakfast!

Special occasions

For that special birthday or anniversary, or for somewhere different to propose marriage, Discovery Cove has a range of options that involve dolphin interaction and private beach cabañas. The **Platinum Ring** (an extra $489/couple) includes sharing your special moment with a dolphin, who delivers a specialised message buoy, 6x8 photo, frame, private cabaña, a bottle of champagne with souvenir champagne chiller and 2 crystal flutes, a dozen roses, chocolate truffles, private cabaña, animal meet-and-greet and a video of the occasion; the **Golden Ring Package** ($249/couple) includes personalised buoy, video, photo, frame, private cabaña, champagne and chocolate truffles; the **Sweetheart Package** ($149) includes personalised buoy, photo, frame and video; the **Birthday Package** ($89) includes 6x8 photo, frame, bag, T-shirt and souvenir buoy, while a Premium version ($229) adds a disposable underwater camera, bag, T-shirt, a video of the occasion and a private cabaña.

You are advised to book at least 3 months in advance as these special packages do sell out in peak periods. There is also a 10% advance discount periodically for online bookings. See more at **discoverycove.com**.

Busch Gardens

When is a zoo not a zoo? When it is also a theme park like 335-acre/136ha Busch Gardens in Tampa. The sister park to SeaWorld, it started as a mini-menagerie for the wildlife collection of the brewery-owning Busch family (makers of Budweiser). In 1959, it opened a small, tropical-themed hospitality centre next to the brewery and now it is a major, multi-faceted family attraction, the biggest on Florida's west coast and just an hour from Orlando. It is rated among the top 4 zoos in America, with more than 2,700 animals representing over 320 species of mammals, birds, reptiles, amphibians and spiders. But that's just the start. It boasts a safari-like section of Africa spread over 65 acres/26ha of grassy veldt, with special tours to hand-feed some of the animals. Interspersed among the animals are more than 20 bona fide theme park rides, including the mind-numbing roller-coasters **Kumba**, **SheiKra**, **Montu** and **Gwazi**, with guaranteed fun for coaster addicts (and the new Cheetaka to come in summer 2011), plus plenty of scaled-down rides for children. Then there are the animal shows, musicians, strolling players and big-stage show productions.

The overall theme is Africa, hence the park is divided into areas like Nairobi and Congo, and dining and shopping are equal to most of the other theme parks. It doesn't quite have the pizzazz of Epcot or Universal, and the staff are a bit more laid back, but it has guaranteed, 5-star family appeal, especially with its selection of rides just for kids, and it is a big hit with British visitors. In a way, it is like the big brother of Chessington World of Adventures in Surrey, though

Busch Gardens at a glance

Location	Busch Blvd, Tampa; 75–90 minutes' drive from Orlando		
Size	335 acres/136ha in 11 themed areas		
Hours	9 or 10am–6 or 7pm off peak; 9am–8pm Easter, Thanksgiving, Christmas; 9 or 9.30am–10.30pm summer		
Admission	Under-3s free; 3–9 $64.95 (1-day Ticket), $79.95 (2-Park Ticket inc Adventure Island water park), $99.95 (2-Park Ticket inc SeaWorld), $139.95 (3-Park Ticket inc Aquatica and SeaWorld), $279.95 (Orlando FlexTicket Plus); adult (10+) $74.95, $89.95, $109.95, $149.95, $299.95.		
Parking	$12, $18 preferred, $24 valet		
Lockers	$6, in Morocco, Congo, Egypt and Stanleyville		
Pushchairs	$14 and $19		
Wheelchairs	$15 and $45, with pushchairs		
Top attractions	Congo River Rapids, Gwazi, Kumba, Montu, Rhino Rally, SheiKra, Tanganyika Tidal Wave, Cheetaka (2011)		
Don't miss	Jungala, Edge of Africa, Animal Keeper talks, Myombe Reserve, Mystic Sheikhs band		
Hidden costs	**Meals**	Burger, chips and Pepsi $9.58 3-course meal $17.99–24.95, family-style diner $14.95 and $8.45 (Crown Colony House) Kids' meal $7.79	
	T-shirts	$15.92-32.00	
	Souvenirs	95c-$1,400	
	Sundries	Ride photos $14.99–17.99; ride DVD $26.99	

Morocco
1 Marrakesh Theater
2 Moroccan Palace Theater
3 Gwazi
4 Myombi Reserve

Egypt
5 Edge of Africa
6 Animal Connections
7 Skyride Station and Cheetaka (opening 2011)
8 Montu
9 Tut's Tomb

Nairobi
10 Curiosity Caverns
11 Elephant Habitat
12 Rhino Rally
13 Jambo Junction

Timbuktu
14 Scorpion
15 Cheetah Chase
16 Phoenix
17 Carousel Caravan
18 Timbuktu Theater – Lights, Camera, Imagination!

Congo
19 Kumba
20 Congo River Rapids
21 Ubanga-Banga Bumper Cars

Jungala
22 Jungle Flyers
23 The Wild Surge
24 Treetop Trails
25 Tiger Lodge
26 Orang Overlook

Stanleyville
27 Stanley Log Falls and Plume
28 Tanganika Tidal Wave
29 SheiKra
30 Stanleyville Theater
31 Skyride Station
32 Zambia Smokehouse

Sesame Street Safari of Fun
33 Air Grover
34 123-Smile With Me
35 Sunny Day Theater

Bird Gardens
36 Garden Theatre
37 Lory Landing
38 Aviary
39 Walkabout Way
40 Gwazi Pavilion

on a grander scale (and in a better climate). Busch Gardens is the only park to offer 1-day Tickets with a rain guarantee, which means if you get rained out on your visit, you can return FREE within 7 days. Look for self-serve ticket machines to the right of the park entrance to save time at ticket booths.

BRIT TIP

Want to avoid the queues? Like SeaWorld, Busch Gardens offers Quick Queue, for priority entry into shows and front-of-queue access to rides. Price varies from $24.95 for One-time use, $34.95 for Unlimited use.

All Day Dining Deal: For just $29.99 ($14.99 3–9s) you can enjoy all-you-care-to-eat-and-drink privileges at 7 restaurants throughout the park. With your special wristband, choose 1 entrée, 1 side or dessert and a soft drink each time you pass through the dining queue (child's price valid for kids' meal only; baby back ribs excluded).

Look out also for the many **Meet The Keeper** sessions around the park, where the animal handlers come out to explain various features of the park's animal husbandry, notably with the gorillas, elephants and hippos. You will find them at the Alligator Habitat, Myombe Reserve, Edge of Africa, Jungala, Elephant and Rhinoceros Habitats and Jambo Junction (where they feature various small-animal encounters).

Location

Busch Gardens can be a hard place to locate on the sketchy local maps as the signposting is not as sharp as it could be but, from Orlando, the directions are pretty simple. Head west on I-4 for almost an hour (it is 55mls/88km from I-4's junction with Highway 192) until you hit the intersecting motorway I-75. Take I-75 north for 3½mls/5.5km until you see the exit for Fowler Avenue (Highway 582). Continue west on Fowler for another 3½mls/5.5km, then, just past the University of South Florida on

your right, turn LEFT into McKinley Drive. A mile/1.6km down McKinley Drive, Busch Gardens' car park is on your left, where it costs $12 to park.

Those without a car can use the **Busch Gardens Shuttle Express** bus, which makes several $10 round trips a day from Orlando (FREE if you have a multi-day ticket). You board at SeaWorld, Orlando Premium Outlets, Universal Studios, Ramada Maingate West, Best Western Lakeside or Old Town in Kissimmee and pick-up times range from 8.30 to 9.40am, returning at 6 or 7pm. Book at the **Guest Services** window at SeaWorld or call 1800 221 1339.

You may think you've left the crowds behind in Orlando but, unfortunately, in high season you'd be wrong. It's still advisable to be here at opening time, if only to be first in line to ride the dazzling roller-coasters, which all draw big queues (especially SheiKra). The Congo River Rapids, Stanley Falls Log Flume ride and Tanganyika Tidal Wave (all opportunities to get wet), and the off-road Rhino Rally adventure are also prime draws in peak season. But queues take longer to build here, so for the first few hours you can enjoy a relatively crowd-free experience.

On your left through the main gates is the **Adventure Tour Centre**, and you should go there straight away (better still, book in advance on 1888 800 5447 or online at **buschgardens. com**) if you'd like to do the wonderful Serengeti Safari or one of its other Adventure Tours (see page 217). Busch Gardens is divided into 11 main sections, with the major rides all a bit of a hike from the main entrance. Check your park map for times and locations of various small-animal encounters throughout the park – then watch out for passing flamingos as they take the first of their twice-daily promenades in the main courtyard!

Rhino Rally, which opened in 2001, is one of the prime attractions, so you should head here first (especially as the animals are more evident early in the day). Bear right through Morocco, turn left into Nairobi, pass the train station, and the Rally entrance is next to the elephant habitat. Coaster fans flock in serious numbers to **SheiKra**, the world's highest and fastest dive coaster, and queues can hit 2 HOURS by mid-afternoon in peak season. So, if you are tempted by this first, bear left through Morocco past the Zagora Café, through the Bird Gardens and up into Stanleyville. **Gwazi**, the rattlin' wooden coaster, is another to draw a crowd quickly, and you could do this en route. Then continue through Stanleyville to Congo for **Kumba**, and retrace your steps to do **Congo River Rapids** and the other 2 water rides. Here is the full layout of the park in a clockwise direction (usually the optimum route). When **Cheetaka** opens in summer 2011, this is likely to draw some serious queues, so head here first for the latest coaster experience (turn right, into Egypt).

Morocco

Coming through the main gates brings you into the home of all the guest services and a lot of good shops. *Epcot's* Moroccan pavilion sets the scene better, but the architecture is still impressive and this version won't tax your wallet as much as Disney's does! Turning the corner brings you to the first animal encounter, the alligator pen. Morocco is also home to 2 of the park's biggest shows.

Marrakesh Theater: In summer 2010, this live venue presented **Rock A Doo Wop**, a song and dance show offering a host of rock 'n roll classics from the

Bolingo in the Myombe Reserve

1950s and 60s, with period costumes and lively singalong numbers. With faithful reproductions of numbers by the likes of Frankie Valli, Johnny Rivers, Frankie Lymon and The Coasters, it's a musical walk down memory lane. AAA.

Moroccan Palace Theater: The former home of lavish stage show KaTonga, this will now showcase an all-new **Ice Show** in 2011, with eye-catching costumes and special effects to maintain the park's standards for high-quality live productions. AAAA (expected).

Myombe Reserve: One of the largest and most realistic habitats for the threatened highland gorillas and chimpanzees of Central Africa, this 3-acre/1.2ha walk-through has a superb tropical setting where the temperature is kept high and convincing with the aid of lush forest landscaping and water mist sprays. Take your time, especially as there are good, seated vantage points, and be patient to catch these magnificent creatures on their daily routine. It is also highly informative, with attendants on hand to answer any questions. AAAAA.

Gwazi: Busch's second largest roller-coaster is a massive 'duelling' wooden creation in the classic style (i.e. no going upside-down). The 2 sets of cars, the Gwazi Lion and Gwazi Tiger, each top 50mph/80kph and generate a G-force of up to 3.5 as they career around nearly 7,000ft/2,134m of track with 6 fly-by encounters. You get to choose your ride in the intricately themed 8-acre/3ha village plaza and then you are off up the 90ft/27m lift for a breathtaking 2½ minutes. The shake, rattle 'n' roll effect of a classic wooden coaster is much in evidence and the Lion and Tiger rides are slightly different, so you should try both. Restrictions: 4ft/122cm. TTTTT.

Gwazi Gliders: This gentle circling 'hang-gliding' ride is purely for the pre-school crowd. T (TTT under-6s).

Other entertainment: The great fun of the marching, dancing, 8-piece brass band **Mystic Sheikhs** can be found in Morocco at regular intervals, along with **Men of Note**, a strolling 4-piece a cappella group with Motown specialities, and **park characters** like TJ the Tiger, Gina the Giraffe and Hilda Hippo. Basketball fans can try the Hoops Challenge ($3 for a 3-point shoot out, $5 for 2 tries, $10 for 5 tries) next to Gwazi.

Shopping and dining: Choose from 7 different shops, with **The Emporium** and **Marrakesh Market** the pick of the bunch. For a quick meal, try **Zagora Café**, especially at breakfast. Alternatively, the enticing **Sultan's Sweets** serves coffee and pastries.

Bird Gardens

The most peaceful area and the original starting point of the park in 1959, it is possible to unwind here from the usual theme-park hurly-burly. The exhibits and shows are all family-orientated, too, with live shows, an elaborate kids' playground and more animal exhibits.

BRIT TIP
The Bird Gardens area is a good place to visit in mid-afternoon when most of the rides are busy.

Garden Theater: This hosts the amusing 25-minute **Critter Castaways**, a show featuring numerous animals (almost 80 in all) in a light-hearted desert island romp. Dogs, cats, birds and even kangaroos all get in on the act with their human co-stars. AAA.

Lory Landing: Walk through this tropical aviary featuring lorikeets, hornbills, parrots and more, with the chance to become a human perch and feed the friendly lorikeets. A cup of nectar costs $5, but makes for a great photo opportunity. AAA.

Walkabout Way: brand new in 2010 was this charming Australia-themed area with a chance to feed the free-roaming kangaroos and wallabies and meet other Down Under denizens, like the Kookaburra. AAA. Other encounters include the lush, walk-through **Aviary**, **Flamingo Island**, the

Living Dragons and **Eagle Canyon**, plus the **Backyard Wildlife Habitat**.

Other entertainment: stop by the outdoor terrace next to **Garden Gate Café** for an array of songs from the resident piano player, while **Gwazi Park** is home to the seasonal live entertainment during summer and other special events.

Shopping and dining: A real novelty here is the eye-catching **Xcursions** eco-friendly gift shop. Its live frog and gecko displays and conservation info on interactive touch-screens make it worth visiting whether you buy or not (but all proceeds contribute to the Busch Gardens Conservation Fund). **Garden Gate** is another imaginative shop. Pizza, salads and sandwiches are on offer at the pleasant **Garden Gate Café**.

Sesame Street Safari of Fun

Formerly the Land of the Dragons, this children's interactive play area underwent an extensive re-theme in 2010 and is now the impressive 'home away from home' for much-loved *Sesame Street* characters, dressed in best African Safari finery. You will be hard pressed to get pre-schoolers away when they catch sight of this land's 7 rides (including a junior-sized coaster, a gentle flume ride and character-themed fairground style rides), entertaining stage show and the wonderfully extensive water play and climb-and-slide areas. The huge treehouse climb, ball pools and

Air Grover

adventure play structures alone will keep most kids busy for hours! But there's more:

Air Grover: A whizzy little dip-and-turn coaster packing plenty of junior-sized thrills, piloted by everyone's favourite blue guy, Grover. Restrictions: 2ft 9in/97cm accompanied; 3ft 5in/104cm unaccompanied.

Sunny Day Theater: Elmo, Abby, Zoe, Grover and Cookie Monster star in *A is for Africa*, a delightfully zany stage show that brings tales of adventure to life, with a gently uplifting message. Children (and adults!) can't help but sing and clap along, and it is a great photo opportunity as the characters arrive and then come out for a meet-and-greet afterwards.

BRIT TIP
Arrive early and find a seat in the first 5 rows for an unobstructed view at the Sunny Day Theater. Seat children on the ends for the best character interaction.

Big Bird's 123-Smile with Me: Big Bird and various friends have their own meet-and-greet area, near Air Grover. The big bonus here is one-on-one time with the character in a quiet, air conditioned room (photo $16.99, frame $7-$15; add a special background for $7).

Bert and Ernie's Watering Hole: Thoughtfully designed with even the smallest guests in mind, this gentle water-play area is filled with bubblers, water jets, dump buckets, geysers

Dine with Elmo, Bert and Ernie

and splash tubs. Swimwear and sun block are available at nearby Cookie Monster's Trading Post if you forget yours. Convenient seating surrounds the Watering Hole. Be aware, seating and play area are not covered from the sun. TTTTT (young 'uns only!).

BRIT TIP
Early birds get $10 off *Sesame Street* character meet 'n' greet 6x8 photos before noon.

Shopping and dining: In **Safari of Fun** look for **Abby Cadabby's Treasure Hut** and **Cookie Monster's Trading Post**. For a quick bite here, try **Snack-n-Getti Tribal Treats**. The big opportunity, though, is **Dine with Elmo & Friends**, where visitors can enjoy breakfast or lunch with Elmo and his chums in an outdoor covered dining area. A kid-friendly buffet along with a character song-and-dance show make this a delight for the younger set, with loads of time to meet their favourite *Sesame Street* characters (breakfast $18 adults, $15 children; lunch $23 and $17; both include 6x8 photo per family).

BRIT TIP
Dine with Elmo has a great Birthday Package option, with birthday photo, decorated table and special Happy Birthday song, Muppet-style. Call 1888 800 5447 or visit **SesameStreetSafariofFun.com**.

Stanleyville

This brings you back into true ride territory, with the park's biggest coaster, as well as several water rides and shows. You will also find one of the 3 **Train Stations** here (next to SheiKra), for the gentle 35-minute journey around the park.

SheiKra: The park's outstanding big-thrill attraction is the giant steel structure of this monstrous coaster. A world first at 200ft/62m tall and hitting 70mph/112kph, this is the ride to put Alton Towers' fearsome Oblivion in the shade. Higher, longer and faster, it features an initial drop at an angle as near vertical as makes no difference (with a delicious moment of stop-go balance as you teeter on the edge!), a second drop of 138ft/42m into an underground tunnel, an Immelman loop (an exhilarating rolling manoeuvre) and a water splashdown over 0.6mls/1km of smooth-as-silk track. As if all that isn't enough, a 2007 modification removed the coaster's *floor*, so there is nothing between you and track but air! The whole ride lasts less than 3 minutes and is almost as much fun (or terror, depending on your point of view) to watch as to ride. It also draws massive crowds, so get here early or expect a long wait (or use the paid-for Quick Queue system). You can buy the video of your ride for $26.99, or a 6 x 8 photo for $14.99. Restrictions: 4ft 6in/137cm. TTTTT+.

Stanley Falls: Almost identical to Log Flume rides at Chessington, Legoland, Thorpe Park and Alton Towers, this guarantees a good soaking at the final 40ft/12m drop. Restrictions: 3ft 10in/116cm. TTT.

Tanganyika Tidal Wave: A distinctly more scenic ride, this takes you on a journey along 'uncharted' African waters before tipping you down a 2-stage drop that really does land with tidal-wave force. Restrictions: 4ft/122cm. TTTT.

BRIT TIP
Don't stand on the bridge by Tanganyika Tidal Wave or by the SheiKra splashdown unless you want to get seriously wet!

Stanleyville Theater: A good place to put your feet up as you watch the resident entertainers turn on the style. This varies seasonally and includes musical acts, acrobats and family-style comedy, plus occasional animal encounters. AAA½.

Skyride: Take the one-way cable-car ride from here back to Egypt (by Crown Colony House) to save a long walk back to the park exit. However, it closes when it's windy and has long queues late in the day. AA. *(NB: This may well close for a while in 2010/11 as part of the big Cheetaka development).*

Other entertainment: Test your skills at **Bahati Hoops** (next to SheiKra); $3 for 1 ball, $5 for 2 balls, $10 for 5 balls.

Shopping and dining: The **Kariba Marketplace** has the best of the shopping, while, for a hearty meal (and a great view of SheiKra), try the **Zambia Smokehouse**, where its wood-smoked ribs platter is a delight among a heavily barbecue-orientated menu (also with salads, sandwiches and kids' meals).

Jungala

One of the park's biggest expansions, this 4-acre/1.6ha land opened in 2008 adding a couple of small-scale rides, some superb animal habitats and a hugely elaborate children's play area, designed with older children in mind (where Sesame Street Safari of Fun is primarily for under-6s). It also gets busy quite quickly, so visit either early on or late in the day.

Jungle Flyers: This kids' ride (6–13s) is a junior-sized zip line journey over part of the Jungala area, a 1-seat there-and-back trip from the upper level of Treetop Trails. Great fun for kids, but a rather short ride, and queues build up quickly and move slowly for much of the day. Maximum height 4ft 8in/145cm. TTT.

The Wild Surge: Get ready to 'surge' 4 storeys into the air on this tower ride from inside a giant waterfall providing a (brief!) glimpse over Jungala before bouncing back down again. Queues are also long and slow-moving as the ride takes just 14 at a

Jungala stilt walkers

time. Restrictions, 3ft 6in/106cm to ride solo (3ft 2in/96cm with a parent). TTT (TTTTT under-12s).

Treetop Trails: Climbing nets, elaborate bridges, crawl tubes and a multi-level maze are the basis of this fab 3-storey playground for children of all ages, with smaller-scale adventures at ground level, including squirt fountains and other watery fun (swimsuits or a change of clothes are advisable!). It is also cleverly mixed in with 2 different animal habitats, for the fun-loving gibbons, flying fox-bats and the rare tomistoma (an Asian crocodile). TTTT (young 'uns only).

◀❖▶ BRIT TIP

It's worth knowing for parents with younger children that the toddler play area in Treetop Trails is very thoughtfully in the shade.

Tiger Habitat: One of the park's most creative animal environments is this multi-level tiger exhibit (including its rare white tigers). It is divided into **Tiger Lodge**, an air-conditioned overlook including conservation info and issues, and **Tiger Trail**, a walkthrough section with various close-up opportunities, including a unique pop-up turret (which has a separate queue) in the main enclosure and a rope-pull for guests to 'test their strength' (periodically) against the big cats. Huge windows provide maximum viewing of the animals at play, especially in their plunge pool. AAAA.

Tiger Habitat

Orang Outpost: Another brilliant animal habitat, this showcases the park's orang-utans, who love to look in on guests, viewing them as much as vice versa. A series of close-up windows (including a glass floor over the hammock play area and a kids' tunnel) provide superb observation of the specially designed forest canopy environment. AAAA.

Other entertainment: Look out for colourful **stilt-walkers** around the village area periodically.

Shopping and dining: Shop for gifts at **Tiger Treasures** (organic cotton T-shirts and conservation-related items) and **Cubs Closet** (kids' clothing), and then stop to eat at **Bengal Bistro** (fish, smoked turkey, veggie wraps, salads and sandwiches) or the more snack-orientated **Orang Café** (chicken strips, sandwiches and cookies).

Congo

As you continue into the Congo, this is primarily about just 3 rides, plus a stop on the Serengeti Railway.

Kumba: Another of the park's signature coasters, with this unmistakable giant turquoise structure looming over the area. It's one of the largest and fastest in south-east USA and, at 60mph/97kph, features 3 high-thrill elements: a diving loop plunging a full 110ft/33m; a camel-back, with a 360° spiral; and a 108ft/33m vertical loop. For good measure, it dives underground! It looks terrifying close up but is absolutely exhilarating, even for non-coaster fans. Restrictions: 4ft 6in/137cm. TTTTT.

Congo River Rapids: These look pretty tame after Kumba, but don't be fooled. The giant rubber rafts will bounce you down some of the most convincing rapids outside of the Rockies, and you will end up with a fair soaking for good measure. Restrictions: 3ft 6in/106cm. TTTT.

Ubanga-Banga Bumper Cars: Fairly typical fairground dodgems, you won't miss anything if you pass by (restrictions: 3ft 6in/106cm). TT.

Shopping and dining: There is just the **Congo River Rapids** gift shop here, plus 3 refreshment kiosks.

Timbuktu

Passing through Congo brings you to another heavily ride-dominated area. Here in a North African desert setting you will find many typical funfair elements, with a couple of brain-scrambling rides and 2 good shows.

Sesame Street presents Lights, Camera, Imagination!: Brand new in late spring 2010 this delightful show is a vivid 3-D film romp with all the TV series characters as they try to save the Sesame Street Film Festival. It all goes wrong when the films unravel, cuing a multitude of in-theatre special effects, visual gags and sensory surprises, so be ready to get wet (beware Grover the fireman!) and even tickled. Wind, bubbles and stampeding vermin are all part of the '4-D' experience, which is sure to thrill pre-schoolers, but is also lively enough to engage older children and adults, particularly those who grew up with Big Bird, Elmo and Cookie Monster. AAA (TTTT for under 6s).

BRIT TIP
Water effects during Lights, Camera, Imagination! are rather more than just a light misting. Ladies in light coloured tops beware (and children at eye-level with the chair-backs)!

Cheetah Chase: This family-orientated 'Crazy Mouse' style coaster is surprisingly energetic, rising as it does some 46ft/14m and adding tight turns and swift drops. Top speed is only 22mph/35kph, but it seems faster and will thrill younger kids. TTT (TTTTT under-10s).

The Phoenix: A positively evil invention that involves sitting in a gigantic, boat-shaped swing that eventually performs a 360° rotation in dramatic, slow-motion style. Don't eat just before this one! Restrictions: 4ft/122cm. TTTT.

Scorpion: A 50mph/80kph roller-coaster, this features a 62ft/19m drop and a 360° loop that is guaranteed

to dial D for dizzy for a while! It lasts just 120 seconds, but *seems* longer. Queues build here from late morning, and you must be at least 3ft 6in/106cm to ride. TTTT.

Sandstorm: A fairly routine whirligig contraption that spins and levitates at high speed (hold on to your stomach). Restrictions: 3ft 6in/106cm. TTT.

Carousel Caravan: This offers the opportunity to ride a genuine Mary Poppins-type carousel. TT.

Other entertainment: As well as the big rides, there are scaled-down Kiddie Rides geared to under-10s. The **Sultan's Arcade** and **Games Area** offers sideshows and stalls that require a few extra dollars ($1–10), or buy the Games Pass (it can be loaded in the Games Area) and simply swipe your card to play. The **Desert Grill Theater** is also home to regular live musical entertainment in air-conditioned comfort (a lively song-and-dance cabaret that changes on a regular basis). In 2010 it was **Let's Dance**, a Broadway-style international dance festival.

Shopping and dining: Desert Grill is an excellent themed café-diner (serving great sandwiches, salads, pasta and kids' meals in souvenir buckets), while Timbuktu also has 2 snack kiosks.

Nairobi

It's back to the animals as we enter this area, with 5 different habitats, plus one of the park's top rides, which also includes an animal adventure.

Rhino Rally: This dramatic and scenic ride is an imaginative off-road jeep safari that has been extended to include even more animal encounters in 2011 (although the original water-raft part of the ride has been scrapped). The 8-minute whirl through the wilds of Africa encounters elephants, rhinos, crocodiles, antelope and more, as the safari nature of the ride is just about as real as they can make it. Your driver adds to the fun with some amusing spiel about the rally and your Land-Rover vehicle, but it does draw some big, slow-moving queues from mid-day on, so try to arrive early to beat the crowds. Restrictions: 3ft 3in/99cm. AAAA.

Serengeti Plain: A 49-acre/20ha spread of African savannah, this is home to buffalo, antelope, zebras, giraffes, wildebeest, ostriches, hippos, rhinos and many exotic birds, and can be viewed for much of the journey on the Serengeti Express, a full-size, open-car steam train that chugs slowly from its main station in Nairobi to the Congo, Stanleyville and back. AAA.

BRIT TIP
Take the Serengeti Railway from Nairobi (or Congo or Stanleyville) in mid-afternoon to give your feet a rest when it's busy elsewhere.

Jambo Junction: The park's field hospital and nursery is an interesting animal encounter, with some friendly flamingos and a series of small critters (lemurs, sloths, possums and various babies needing extra care) on view through the large windows. Some animal interaction is encouraged periodically, with feeding, lessons in husbandry and behaviour training as part of the Meet The keeper sessions. AA.

Other entertainment: Look out here for the **Elephant Habitat** and periodic sessions with animal staff (notably for the afternoon Elephant Wash), while you can see more of the park's inhabitants at the **Reptile House**, **Curiosity Caverns** (nocturnal animals) and **Tortoise Habitat**.

Shopping and dining: Caravan Crossing (safari apparel and hats) has the best shopping here while **Kenya Kanteen** offers drinks and snacks.

Egypt
The final area of Busch Gardens is somewhat tucked away, so it's best visited either first thing or late in the day (sooner rather than later if you want to ride Cheetaka). It sits in the park's bottom right corner and much of it is carefully re-created pharaoh country, dominated by

roller-coaster Montu, named after an ancient Egyptian warrior god. You can also take the **Skyride** cable car to Stanleyville (providing a great look at Rhino Rally en route).

Cheetaka: Due to open in summer 2011, this combined ride and extensive animal habitat is another major development and promises to be a must-see as well as must-ride experience (although visitors in late 2010/early 2011 should also expect some construction disruption in the area). It incorporates the park's **Edge of Africa** area, a 15-acre/6ha 'safari experience' that guarantees a close-up almost like the real thing. The walk-through attraction puts you in an authentic setting of native wilds and villages from which you can view giraffes, lions, baboons, meerkats, crocodiles, hyenas and vultures, and even an underwater inspection of a hippo habitat. Look out for the abandoned jeep – you can sit in the cab while the lions lounge in the back! Wandering naturalists offer informal talks, and the attention to detail is superb. The feature new habitat is for the cheetahs (hence the ride name), with a vivid setting for these graceful animals. There is a separate entrance so those not keen on the ride can just walk through to view.

BRIT TIP
Edge of Africa offers some fantastic photo opportunities but, in the hot months, come here early in the day as many animals seek refuge from the heat later.

The ride itself is intricately interwoven with the animal habitats, providing great viewing while you queue – and a terrific build-up to this immense, high-speed coaster. At more than 4,500ft/1,400m long and with 2 fast-launch sections, this will be the park's new signature attraction. Unlike many, it is not designed for great height, but it will feature a series of low-level (and even underground) elements that accentuate the fast-paced nature of a ride that stretches out to the Rhino Rally area and then zooms back over (and through) Edge of Africa. The initial launch

(0–50mph/80kmph in 2 seconds) is the starting point for a tight-turning journey with no inversions but a lot of fast bends and sudden camel-back effects, while a second relaunch brings you back to the station almost as quickly! This is sure to be a BIG hit with coaster fans and gives the park another completely novel element to its ride collection. TTTTT (expected).

Tut's Tomb: This re-creation of the Tutankhamen discovery by archaeologist Howard Carter is now missing most of its clever lighting and audio effects, hence is pretty unremarkable. A.

Montu: You cannot miss the area's other main attraction, another breathtaking inverted coaster, covering nearly 4,000ft/1,219m of track at up to 60mph/97kph and peaking with a G-force of 3.85! Like Kumba, it looks terrifying but really is an absolute 5-star thrill as it leaves your legs dangling and twists and dives (underground at 2 points) for almost 3 minutes of brain-scrambling fun. Restrictions: 4ft 6in/137cm. TTTTT.

Other entertainment: Youngsters can make their own excavations in the **Shifting Sands**, a neat sand play area. The whole family can also have fun with the imaginative new **Animal Connections** (in the former Clydesdale stables), a chance to be a wildlife TV 'presenter' complete with lemur (or owl monkey, macaw, marmoset or bush baby). There is a preparation studio, make-up room and green-screen camera to record your efforts, with the DVD to take home, all for $29.95.

Shopping and dining: The high-quality **Golden Scarab** offers hand-blown glass items and authentic cartouche paintings, while you can grab more souvenirs at **Edge of Africa Gift Shop** and **Montu Gifts**. For dining, the **Crown Colony Restaurant**, a large Victorian-style building overlooking the Serengeti Plain, offers counter-service salads, sandwiches and pizzas downstairs or a full-service restaurant upstairs, with magnificent views of the animals. For

a memorable meal (11.30am until an hour before park closing), head here for lunch (it doesn't take bookings) or, even better, come back for dinner in the early evening and see the animals come down to the waterhole.

Special tours

Busch Gardens features a wide range of behind-the-scenes animal tours and adventure expeditions that add an extra dimension to the park. For all tours, book at the Adventure Tour Center in Morocco or, better still, book in advance on 1888 800 5447 or online at **buschgardens.com**.

Serengeti Safari: A 30-minute excursion (5 times a day, taking 20 people at a time) aboard flat-bed trucks, takes you to meet some of the Serengeti Plain's residents and hand-feed the beautiful giraffes while learning more about the park's environmental efforts. It tends to fill up quickly and costs $33.95/person (children must be at least 5, and 5–15s must be accompanied by an adult); the Sunrise Safari adds a continental breakfast to this experience at park opening ($39.95); the **Guided Adventure Tour** takes just 15 at a time on a 5-hour VIP trek, with your own guide, reserved seating at the Moroccan Palace Theater, front-of-line access for the major rides like Gwazi and Rhino Rally, counter-service lunch at one of the restaurants and close encounters with many of the animals, including the Serengeti Safari ($94.99 adults, $84.99 children); **Elite Adventure Tour** is a personal,

Montu

exclusive park tour with front-of-line access to all rides, the Serengeti Safari, reserved seating at shows, free bottled water throughout and lunch at Crown Colony ($199.99/person, 5 and over); **Endangered Species Safari** is a 45-minute meet and greet with various animal specialists (notably getting close-up with the rhinos), learning about their work and conservation issues, including how Busch Gardens is involved with various wildlife projects worldwide ($39.95; no under-5s); the 45-minute **Sunset Safari** begins at the Crown Colony, then heads out on the Serengeti Plain to hand-feed giraffes, meet the wildlife and enjoying a beer or 2 as you tour ($39.99/person, 21 and over only, with valid photo ID); **Keeper for a Day** is an exclusive 6-hour behind-the-scenes tour where you join the keepers as they feed, train and care for giraffes and antelope, then move on to assist the Avian team on the Serengeti ($249.95/person, including park admission; 13 and over only); the **Tiger and Orang-utan Keeper Experience** is a private 90-minute backstage tour for up to 6 guests into the care and health of the animals in the Jungala area ($199.95 for group of up to 6); the **Elephant Keeper Experience** is a similar 90-minute opportunity with the park's elephants ($199.95 for up to 6; no under 10s, sturdy footwear required); **Elephant Insider** is a 45-minute group walking tour behind the scenes with the elephant handlers and their charges ($19.95/person); **Roller Coaster Insider** offers a unique 45-minute look at how the park builds and maintains its amazing

Jungala Insider

array of rides, with front-row seats for Montu to finish with (14 and over only, $19.95/person); finally, **Jungala Insider** is a fascinating 45-minute group visit behind the scenes in the Jungala area to meet the keepers, see how they care for the magnificent tigers (you might even help to weigh one!) and orang-utans, and learn a few zoo husbandry secrets ($19.95/person). There is even a Serengeti Night Safari (park admission not required) for a 2-hour after-dark excursion into the Serengeti Plain, with appetisers and hot and cold drinks provided ($60/person, 21 and over only)

Special programmes

Busch Gardens is open until 10pm for the **Summer Nights** programme (June–Aug), which features outdoor food and drink, live entertainment (notably at the Desert Grill Theater), music and DJs, plus some clever lighting effects on coasters like SheiKra. In 2010, it also introduced a new high-energy nightly finale show, **Kinetix**, bringing together live musicians, singers, dancers and original artists for a 30-minute contemporary rock experience enhanced by innovative lighting effects. There is also a huge **fireworks spectacular** 2–4 July.

For a full family day out, you can combine Busch Gardens with sister water park **Adventure Island** (on McKinley Drive), which is blissful when it hots up. The 25 acres/10ha of watery fun, in a Key West theme, offer a full range of slides and rides, such as the **Wahoo Run** raft ride, a 210ft/64m plunge on the body slide **Gulf Scream**, the exciting 4-lane mat slide **Riptide** and spiralling tube ride **Calypso Coaster**. Adventure Island is open mid-Mar to late Oct (weekends only Sept and Oct) 10am–5pm (8pm in summer). Tickets are $39.95 (adults) and $35.95 (3–9s), while a Busch Gardens-Adventure Island combo is $89.95 and $79.95.

Well, that's the low-down on all the main theme parks, but there is still MUCH more to discover…

The Other Attractions

If you think you can 'do' Orlando just by sticking to the main theme parks, think again! There is still a LOT more to discover, starting with Kennedy Space Center, which we rate as an essential place to visit these days. It will easily demand a day of your attention.

Then there are Silver Springs and Bok Tower Gardens, which offer a taste of the more natural Florida, while Gatorland provides another great-value experience with its alligators and shows. Then you have fun venues like WonderWorks, Orlando Science Center and Ripley's Believe It Or Not. For more individual attractions, there is the unique aviation museum

Fantasy of Flight, the amazing 'skydive' experience of iFLY Orlando, plus some magnificent water parks. The choice is yours, but it's an immense selection. Let's start with One Giant Leap for Mankind.

Kennedy Space Center

Welcome to the past, present and future of NASA's space programme, and one of the most enjoyable, fun and downright fascinating places in Florida. The KSC has undergone huge redevelopment in recent years, culminating in 2007 with the opening of the stunning **Shuttle Launch Experience**, part of a complete overhaul of the main Visitor Complex. This has really put the KSC among the front rank of local

Sulcata tortoise at Aquatica

Orlando's Other Attractions

✈ Sanford International Airport

Sanford Airport via Interstate 4 has no tolls, but can be far busier, especially during rush-ho...

Sanford Airport via 417 has a few tolls, but is much quiete...

↖ Mount Dora

Daytona

ALTAMONTE SPRINGS

Sanford-Rivership Romance, Central Florida Zoo ↑

436

Toll road (from 25c to $4.50)

Lake Apopka

429

OCOEE

WINTER GARDEN

Winter Park ■

Black Hammock Fish Camp ↑

Leu Gardens ■

417

50

WEST COLONIAL DRIVE

50

EAST - WEST EXPRESSWAY

Amway Center ■   Downtown Orlando ■
                  Lake Eola ■

408

Citrus Bowl Stadium ■

FLORIDA TURNPIKE

KIRKMAN RD

WINDERMERE

429

441

SEMORAN BOULEVARD

Universal Studios ■

Islands of Adventure ■

Cocoa Beach

Port Canaveral ←

Pirates Dinner Adventure ■

SAND LAKE RD

528

BEACHLINE

Sleuth's Mystery Dinner Shows

INTERNATIONAL DRIVE

Orlando Watersports Complex ■

✈ Orlando International Airport

Mickey's Backyard Barbecue, Hoop-Dee-Doo Musical Revue

535   435

SeaWorld ■

BOGGY CREEK ROAD

Magic Kingdom ■

Richard Petty Driving Experience

Lake Buena Vista

4

423

Nick Faldo Golf Institute ■

ORANGE BLOSSOM TRAIL

JOHN YOUNG PARKWAY

CENTRAL FLORIDA GREENEW...

WESTERN BELTWAY

Epcot ■

Disney's Hollywood Studios ■

Fantasia Gdns Mini-golf

Buena Vista Watersports ■

Animal Kingdom ■

Winter-Summerland Mini-golf

417

MainGate West

Arabian Nights ■

OLD LAKE WILSON ROAD

WORLD DRIVE

EPCOT DRIVE

Osceola Parkway   ─ Toll road

FLORIDA TURNPIKE

BOGGY CREEK ROAD

Celebration

KISSIMMEE

Capone's Dinner Show ■

Medieval Times ■

192   IRLO BRONSON

Silver Spurs Arena ■

East Lake Tohopekaliga

Osceola County Pioneer Museum ■

Warbird Adventures & Museum ■

Kissimmee Airport

MEMORIAL HIGHWAY

Champions Gate

Green Meadows Petting Farm ■

Kissimmee Scenic Lake Tours ■

17

Florida Eco-Safaris, Reptile World Serpentarium

↖ Dinosaur World

ST CLOUD

Tampa, Clearwater, Gulf Coast

Horse World Riding Stables, Disney's Wilderness Preserve, Boggy Creek Airboat Rides

Lake Tohopekaliga

Miami

© Steve Munns 2010

0   5 miles

N

Kennedy Space Center at a glance

Location	Off State Road 405 in Titusville
Size	Visitor Complex 70 acres/28.3ha
Hours	9am–5 or 6pm) year-round (except Christmas Day or launch days)
Admission	Under-3s free; 3–11 $28; adult (12+) $38. Prices do not include tax but include admission to US Astronaut Hall of Fame.
Parking	Free
Lockers	No
Pushchairs	Available on a complimentary basis (with photo ID as deposit) inside the Information Center
Wheelchairs	Available on a complimentary basis (with photo ID as deposit) inside the Information Center
Top attractions	Shuttle Launch Experience; IMAX films; Astronaut Encounter; KSC Bus Tours
Don't miss	Apollo-Saturn V Center on Bus Tours; Astronaut Memorial; Rocket Garden; Space Shuttle Plaza
Hidden costs	**Meals** Burger, chips and coke $9.78 / Kids' meal $6.29 **T-shirts** $14.99-21.99 **Souvenirs** 69c-$29,999! **Sundries** Lunch with an Astronaut $16.99 children, $24.37 adults

attractions and there is even more now to justify an all-day visit. There are 5 continually running shows (including 2 splendid IMAX films and a live theatre presentation for kids), 6 static showcases, a children's play area, an art gallery, the captivating Astronaut Encounter and moving Astronaut Memorial, and a bus tour of the Space Center, which add up to great value. Plus there are 2 additional programmes, the **Astronaut Training Experience** and **Family Astronaut Experience** that provide outstanding extras.

You enter through the futuristic ticket plaza and can spend several hours just wandering around the exhibits and presentations of the Visitor Complex itself. But, with the huge draw of its latest attraction, you should head here first and save your meandering for later on.

Shuttle Launch Experience: This is the BIG one in every sense, a dramatic presentation into a real-life shuttle launch – with you on board! You enter the huge building along

a life-like gantry and there is then a clever pre-show, with dry ice (for launch 'smoke'), atmospheric lighting and some clever sound and vibration effects to provide the feel of a launch. Then you enter the high-tech 'ready room' to prepare for your own blast-off into space. There are 4 'capsules' of 44 passengers each, designed to look like crew cabins in the cargo hold of the Shuttle, and, once aboard you go through the full launch procedure as the vehicle moves into a near-

Shuttle launch

vertical position for take-off. On the command 'Go for engine start' the fun really begins as you are at the heart of an awesome 5-minute simulation that provides all the features of a realistic launch, with the use of massive vibration generators, sound effects, cabin and seat movements and screen visuals. You get a real taste of the G-forces involved, the Rocket Booster and External Tank separations, and a moment of 'weightlessness' as you enter the earth's orbit. Finally, the cargo hold doors open above you to provide a truly awe-inspiring view. To make sure you don't get your breath back for a while, you exit the Shuttle to 'walk' back to earth via a spiral walkway surrounded by the stars and more satellite views of the planet.

Don't miss the plaques to mark every Shuttle flight – and the memorials to the tragic Challenger and Columbia missions. Even the Gift Shop is a cut above average! TTT and AAAAA.

◀▶ BRIT TIP

All of the Shuttle Launch Experience is fully wheelchair-accessible, and there is a seat outside for potential riders to test their comfort level. For anyone wary of the full ride experience, there is a customised bypass room where you can experience the attraction without the motion.

Bus tours: The KSC's signature air-conditioned coaches depart every 15 minutes from 10am and are fully narrated throughout to provide the full overview of the Space Center.

Shuttle Launch Experience

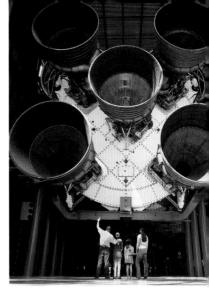

Apollo Saturn V rocket

They make 3 important stops in addition to driving around much of the working areas (including the massive Vehicle Assembly Building). The first stop is the **LC39 Observation Gantry**, just 1ml/1.6km from shuttle launch pad 39A, a combination 4-storey observation deck and exhibition centre. The exhibits consist of a 10-minute launch preparation film, models and videos of a countdown and touch-screen info on the shuttle programme. Next up is the **International Space Station Center**, where you can discover the full story of this orbiting station and the many experiments being conducted there, as well as see new components being put together. A brief film tells the story of the ISSC to date, and you can walk through some full-scale replicas of the modules to feel how it is to live and work in space. Finally, you stop at the **Apollo/Saturn V Center**, one of the KSC's great exhibits, where you can easily spend 90 minutes. It highlights the Apollo missions and first moon landing with 2 impressive theatrical presentations on the risks and triumphs, a full-size 363ft/111m Saturn V rocket and a hands-on gallery that brings space exploration into sharp focus. Allow 2–3 hours to do the tour justice, but be aware that the last bus leaves the Visitor Center at 2.20 or 2.50pm, depending on time of year. AAAAA.

Lunch with an astronaut

For another fully engrossing feature at the Kennedy Space Center, book its special Lunch With An Astronaut, where a small group gets to dine with the star of the daily Astronaut Encounter. The featured person gives their own special briefing, adding extra insight into their space missions, plus answers individual questions, gives autographs and poses for photos. It is $24.37 for adults and $16.95 for children at 12.15pm daily, and tickets may be bought online or by calling 321 449 4400. It's a highly worthwhile opportunity and one we strongly recommend. The buffet-style lunch is pretty good, too!

IMAX films: Back at the Visitor Complex are the IMAX cinemas – 55ft/17m screens that give the impression of sitting on top of the action. The 40-minute film **Magnificent Desolation: Walking on the Moon**, features rare NASA footage and is narrated by Tom Hanks, taking the audience to the lunar surface to walk alongside the astronauts. **Hubble 3-D** (narrated by Leonardo DiCaprio) is a breathtaking new 43-minute journey through the universe as seen by the Hubble Space Telescope. Float beside astronauts as they adjust and repair Hubble, marvel at the sensation of moving through galaxies, wonder at the magnificence of star 'nurseries' and experience the profound tranquillity of a dynamic cosmos. This presentation truly dazzles with the spirit of human achievement and you may feel the urge to stand up and cheer at the end! AAAA. At one end of the IMAX building you'll find *Eye on the Universe: The Hubble Telescope Exhibit*, featuring still images taken by Hubble.

Astronaut Encounter: This engaging feature is a daily talk and Q&A session, along with personal observations and anecdotes from various veterans of the Mercury, Gemini and Apollo programmes, plus several Space Shuttle astronauts. It is an insightful and engrossing programme, up to 3 times a day at the Astronaut Encounter Theater. AAAA.

Robot Scouts: This walk-through display-and-show is done in the company of Starquester 2000, your 'robot host', who explains the history of NASA's unmanned space probes in a surprising and amusing style. AAA.

Shuttle Explorer: This exhibit allows you to inspect a full-scale replica Space Shuttle, while the recently renovated **Launch Status Center** displays shuttle and rocket history boards and rocket scale models, plus live mission briefings of upcoming launches. Free tours are available several times a day. AA.

Early Space Exploration: A clever and coherent walk-through trip into the space programme's recent past, including the Hall of Discovery, the Mercury Mission Control Room – the original consoles from America's first manned space flights – and the Hall of History. AAA.

Exploration Space: A new interactive exhibit and showcase featuring the Explorers Wanted show, an engaging NASA presentation geared toward children. Check out the computer photo stations for a neat souvenir. AAA.

Star Trek Live: Showing 5 times daily in the Astronaut Encounter Theater, this 30-minute interactive stage show encourages audience members to become Starfleet cadets experiencing their first day of training at the Academy. Living and working in

Astronaut Encounter

space, space travel, communication, and technology are among the challenges cadets must deal with, all under the threat of intergalactic chaos when a pesky Romulan launches an attack on Earth. Captain Kirk and Mr Spock make on-screen appearances and cutting edge special effects add to the excitement, with science and (of course!) logic being the keys to success. AAA

Other exhibits: Try **Nature and Technology** (which showcases the unique balance the Center maintains with the local environment), the **Center for Space Education** (an interactive learning and teacher resource centre), the **Space Walk of Honor** and **NASA Art Gallery** (space exhibits and artwork).

Youngsters have their own playground, the covered **Children's Play Dome**, which has also been upgraded recently with a range of climbing/crawling/sliding elements. Finally, head out to see some of the hardware of space flight in the completely revamped **Rocket Garden**, which has a kids' splash fountain and an Apollo space capsule gantry, to give you the feel of that last earthbound walk before the astronauts boarded the Saturn V rocket. Free guided tours are given twice a day (9.30am and 10.30am). Don't forget to stop at the **Astronaut Memorial**, a sombre but moving tribute to the men and women who have died in the cause of the space programme. AAA.

Astronaut Training Experience

Shopping and dining: The Visitor Complex has an excellent **Space Shop** (the world's largest store for space memorabilia and gifts – enter at your peril!), the smaller **Space Shop II** by the main exit and **The Right Stuff Shop** at the Apollo/Saturn V Center. Stop for a bite to eat at the newly enhanced **Orbit Food Court**, a cafeteria-style diner serving a fresh range of salads, burgers, pasta, pizza and sandwiches. Quick bites can be found at **G-Force Grill** (hot dogs, turkey legs, fries, drinks) plus **Shuttle Plaza Snacks** and various kiosks for light snacks and drinks. You will also find the **Moon Rock Café** at the Apollo/Saturn V Center on the bus tour. The Center then has 2 optional extra tours and its Astronaut Training feature.

Cape Canaveral: Then and Now: If you want to learn more about NASA past and present, here is a 2-hour-plus guided journey (daily at noon) into the early days of space exploration around the older part of the facility. Highlights include the Air Force Space and Missile Museum, Mercury launch sites and Memorial, original astronaut training facility and several active launch pads, all of which are otherwise off-limits. Photo ID is required for all visitors on this tour ($21 adult/$15 3–11s).

Discover Kennedy Space Center: Today & Tomorrow: The 2-hour guided tour (tours depart between 10am and 1.50pm daily) takes visitors as close to the launch pad as it is possible to get, in the company of an expert guide. Tour the Shuttle Landing Facility, view the launch area, and make a stop outside the Vehicle Assembly Building ($21 for adults, $15 3–11s; all tours require Space Center admission. Book online or call 321 449 4400.

Astronaut Training Experience (ATX): Away from the main attractions, you have the choice of the thrilling, full-day programme into the training required for a Shuttle mission. You progress through a sequence of simulated and hands-on preparations, with the input of

Kennedy Space Center

various NASA veterans. The training provides a range of activities, from the multi-axis trainer and one-sixth gravity chair, to operating a full-scale Shuttle mock-up and taking the helm in Mission Control. The ATX Half-Day Core experience (morning or afternoon sessions) is limited to a few participants each day and you must be at least 14 (under-18s must be accompanied by a parent). Hard-wearing clothes and athletic shoes are advised, and 'recruits' should be free of neck and back injuries. It costs $145/person (including ATX gear), but it guarantees a memorable day for 'space cadets'.

BRIT TIP

Reader Les Watson advises: 'Head to Port Canaveral, and there is a recreation area called Jetty Park. It has a wooden jetty about 100yd/91m long, brilliant for watching Shuttle launches. What an experience.'

Family Astronaut Training Experience: A chance for children as young as 7, with a parent, to participate in a half-day course. The morning session is spent building and launching rockets, riding realistic simulators, meeting an veteran NASA Astronaut and working together on a realistic shuttle mission to the International Space Station in the full-scale orbiter mock-up and Mission Control. It's $145 per person and includes an ATX t-shirt and cap. Book in advance on 321 449 4400 or online (see opposite).

Getting there: Take the Beachline Expressway out of Orlando (Route 528, and a toll road, see map on page 220) for about 45 minutes, bear left on SR 407 (don't follow the signs to Cape Canaveral or Cocoa Beach at this point) and turn right at the T-junction on to SR 405. The Visitor Complex is located 9mls/14km along on the right. The tours and IMAX presentations start at 10am (**Kennedy SpaceCenter.com**).

US Astronaut Hall of Fame

While the Space Center tells you primarily about the machinery of putting men and women in space, the US Astronaut Hall of Fame (on SR 405, just before the main entrance to the KSC) gives you the low-down on the people involved, with fascinating memorabilia, exhibits and engaging explanations. A chronological approach divides it into 5 sections. The **Entry Experience** introduces the visions of space flight, with an 8-minute video of the astronauts as modern explorers, and leads into **Race to the Moon**, the stories of the *Mercury, Gemini* and *Apollo* missions (where you can see how incredibly small the first space capsules were). The Museum's heart and soul is the **Space Shuttle: The Astronaut Experience** exhibit, a unique collection of astronaut testimonials, personal experiences and authentic artefacts, which create a personal connection for visitors with the enduring stories and endeavours of the Space Shuttle men and women

Astronaut Hall of Fame

US Astronaut Hall of Fame

honoured in the Hall of Fame. The **Astronaut Adventure** room then features space-walk 'chairs', a G-force simulator, moon exploration, interactive computers (try to 'land' a Shuttle) and Mars Mission experience. **Science on a Sphere:** New in 2010, this fascinating 3-D exhibit explores the Earth, the moon, and the planets in our solar system as if you are viewing them from space. Watch hurricanes form, see how ocean currents move and weather patterns change, and learn about space technology's role in understanding global climate trends.

Admission: Included with Kennedy Space Center, or $17 adults, $13 3–11s on its own. Open 9am–6 or 7pm (depending on season). If you enjoyed the KSC, try to spend a couple of hours here (it is busiest towards the end of the day). AAA1

Bok Tower Gardens

Bok Tower Gardens

For those wishing to experience the genuine peace, tranquillity and floral ambience of Florida, there is no better recommendation than this national monument and natural garden centre at Lake Wales, 50mls/80km to the south-west of Orlando (go west on I-4, then south on Highway 27). With one of the most extraordinary attractions in the state – a majestic 205ft/62.5m pink-and-grey marble carillon tower – set in 250 acres/101ha of unique parkland, this is a feast for the eyes and soul. Called the Singing Tower, the 1920s-built carillon is the centrepiece of the Gardens and concerts are given every day at 1pm and 3pm. A carillon is a series of cast bronze bells played by a keyboard or clavier. There are only around 500 in the world, and this one consists of 60 bells (crafted in Loughborough, UK) ranging from 16lb/7.2kg to nearly 12 tons. The Gardens has its own resident player, or carillonneur, and his daily concerts are a real highlight. The Tower is also a work of art, a neo-Gothic and art deco mix crafted from coquina stone and marble, with some stunning sculptures. It is wonderfully photogenic and quite stunning on a cloudless day.

Gardens: Around the Tower are a wide moat, a pond and semi-formal gardens. At one of the highest points on Florida's peninsula (all of 298ft/90m above sea level), the view is inspiring and uncluttered, and retains an inherent peace and solitude that persuaded the founder, philanthropist Edward Bok, to grant the estate to the community in 1929. The gardens also provide a wildlife observatory (the **Window by the Pond**, where you can often see up to 126 species of birds, plus reptiles, butterflies, squirrels, turtles, rabbits and armadillos, as well as the endangered gopher tortoise), nature trails, an endangered plant exhibit, butterfly and woodland gardens and pine forests. The acres of ferns, palms, oaks and pines create a lush backdrop for the seasonal bursts of azaleas, camellias, magnolias and other flowering shrubs. There is even a children's play area, plus brass rubbing and art classes.

Education and Visitor Center: The award-winning centre illustrates the story of Edward Bok (don't miss the orientation film about him and his impact on American society), his vision for the gardens, the carillon and architecture (with a close-up of the bells themselves), the landscape design and the ecology of Florida. The **Blue Palmetto Café** adds a pleasant opportunity for a light lunch and snacks (in the open air when it's not too hot – and there's often a pleasant breeze here), while the **Tower & Garden Gift Shop** offers gift and souvenir items.

Pinewood Estate: For an additional fee ($6 adults, $5 5–12s, noon and 2pm daily), you can tour one of the finest examples of Mediterranean-style architecture in Florida. The 20-room mansion was built as a winter retreat for a Pennsylvania steel tycoon in the early 1930s, and has been lovingly maintained to show a slice of period opulence.

Getting there: Located off US Highway 27 on Burns Avenue. Take I-4 west to exit 55, then go south on US 27 for 25mls/40km, turn left on Mountain Lake Cutoff Road (2 traffic lights past Eagle Ridge Mall) and follow the signs. **Admission:** $10 adults, $3 5–12s (under-5s free), apart from occasional specially ticketed events (mainly carillon festivals and recitals). Open 8am–6pm daily (last entry 5pm; Visitor Center 9am–5pm only; 863 676 1408, **boktowergardens. org**). AAA½.

Lake Wales

Continue on around the Lake Wales area after Bok Tower Gardens and you encounter some other local gems.

Chalet Suzanne: A wonderfully eclectic yet classy country inn and restaurant, quietly famous throughout Florida, this family-run (since 1931) delight is a 100-acre/40.5ha estate featuring 30 individual and quite charming guest rooms, a tropical sunken wedding garden, a swimming pool and private lake, plus – wait for it – a soup cannery (which sent its produce to the moon)! In fact, the Chalet is such a sought-after hideaway, it has its own airstrip. Its other claim to fame is its restaurant, voted one of Florida's Top 20 for more than 30 years, and a truly amazing venue. Made up of various cast-off buildings (a wing of stable here, a chicken house there), lovingly restored and melded together, the dining rooms are built on no fewer than 14 levels! The food is another highlight – gourmet cuisine but with a semi-set menu, with specialities including broiled grapefruit, baked sugar-cured ham, Chicken Suzanne, and its own Romaine Soup – such a favourite of Apollo 15 pilot James Irwin that he persuaded NASA to take it on the mission with them, hence it became known as Moon Soup. The à la carte lunch varies from $8–42 per

Bok Tower Gardens

main course, while dinner can be à la carte or the signature set meal from $59–78, depending on main course selection, which includes Duck Confit a l'Orange Chalet Suzanne and Maine Lobster Newburg. Even if you don't dine or stay in one of its remarkable Swiss-style cottage rooms ($149–209/night), it's well worth a visit for the unique charm and to learn the story of the Hinshaw family.

Getting there: Chalet Suzanne can be found just outside Lake Wales, off Highway 27 on Chalet Suzanne Road. Call 1800 433 6011 to book (always essential) or visit **chaletsuzanne.com**.

Lake Wales: Head into the quaint town of Lake Wales itself and you will discover **Spook Hill** (where cars mysteriously roll uphill!), **Grove House Visitor Center** (home of Florida's natural fruit juice products – as fresh as it gets; 10am–5pm Mon–Fri; 10am–2pm Sat, seasonally. Closed Memorial Day-end of September) and the quaint **Museum and Cultural Center** (set in a restored 1928 Atlantic Coast Line railroad station; 9am–5pm Mon–Fri, 10am–4pm Sat). The **National Historic District** of the downtown area is also being restored, building by building, to its original 1920s appearance, while you can check out the exhibitions and workshops of the **Lake Wales Arts Council**, which is set in a beautiful Mission-style 1920s church. This is also known as the world's sky-diving capital, from Lake Wales airport, with every kind of parachuting known to man. For more info, call Lake Wales Chamber of Commerce on 863 676 3445 or visit **lakewaleschamber.com**.

Chalet Suzanne

Legoland (autumn 2011)

Looking ahead, with Merlin Entertainments Group's purchase of the former Cypress Gardens in 2010, Europe's biggest attraction operator plans to open **Legoland Florida** by late autumn 2011. This will be Merlin's second Legoland park in North America, and its largest, and will feature its trademark range of rides and attractions geared primarily for the 2–12 age group, all with a unique Floridian flair. The park in Winter Haven (south-west of Disney and Kissimmee) will include some 50 rides, shows and attractions, plus their wonderfully creative Lego models and interactive elements. Not only will the care of Cypress Gardens' much-loved gardens and the popular water park (formerly Splash Island) remain, but Merlin also plans to establish an entire resort area, complete with accommodation and additional Merlin-branded attractions. Look up more details and opening date at **legolandfloridaresort.com**.

Silver Springs

Continuing the theme of natural attractions, we have Silver Springs, just under 2 hours' drive to the north of Orlando. This peaceful 350-acre/142ha nature park surrounds the headwaters of the crystal-clear Silver River. Glass-bottomed boats take you to watch the world's largest artesian springs, along with plenty of wildlife.

> **BRIT TIP**
> Silver Springs and Wild Waters are both busy at weekends, but you shouldn't encounter many queues on weekdays, especially in summer. NB: The park continues to experiment with its autumn/winter hours, closing Mon–Thurs at times. Check **silversprings.com** for the full opening hours.

Expect close encounters with alligators, turtles, raccoons and lots of waterfowl, while the park also has a collection of more exotic animals such as bears, panthers and giraffes. Five animal shows, an alligator and crocodile encounter, a large bear exhibit, a petting zoo, kids' adventure playground, a tower ride and a white alligator exhibit complete the attractions. To destroy a few more illusions of the film industry, this was also the setting for the 1930s and '40s Tarzan films starring Johnny Weissmuller (a long way from Africa!). In all, you'd probably want at least ½ a day here.

Tours and shows: The park's main attraction (dating back to 1878) is the **Glass-bottomed Boat Ride**, a 20-minute tour that goes down well with all the family and gives a first-class view of the 7 different springs and a host of water life. Similarly, the **Lost River Voyage** is another 20-minute boat trip down one of the unspoilt stretches of the Silver River, with a visit to the park's wildlife outpost. The 3rd boat trip, the **Fort King River Cruise**, takes you back to pioneer Florida, the Seminole wars and a reconstruction of Fort King. With sightings of native wildlife, an archaeological dig, movie set and Florida Cracker Farm, it is another gentle 20-minute historical perspective, with some storytelling from the boat captain as a bonus. The **Wilderness Trail** features a tram ride towed behind a Wrangler Jeep into a wilderness area populated by assorted local wildlife (including gators!). Then there are the 2 **Ross Allen Island Animal Shows**, each lasting 15 minutes and featuring an entertaining – and occasionally hair-raising – look at the worlds of reptiles and non-venomous snakes and **Wings of the Springs**, a 25-minute bird show, with dramatic free-flight demonstrations that showcase a diverse collection of parrots, ducks, hawks, owls, falcons and vultures.

Animal Attractions: On Ross Allen Island, take time to wander the **Crocodile Encounter** and **Big Gator Lagoon** in a cypress swamp habitat, viewed from a raised boardwalk. See the largest American crocodile in captivity, the 2,000lb/900kg Sobek, as well as a collection of alligators, turtles and Galapagos tortoises (with gator feeding daily at 2.30pm). The

Florida Natives attraction features snakes, turtles, spiders, otters and other local denizens. Other large-scale exhibits are the **World of Bears**, an educational presentation including conservation information in a 2-acre/0.8ha spread devoted to bears of all kinds, from grizzly to spectacled and black bears; **Panther Prowl**, with a unique look at the endangered Florida panther and Western cougar; and the **White Gator** exhibit, which shows why these creatures are known as swamp ghosts. All 3 also have educational presentations several times daily. Petting zoo **Kritter Korral** (with sheep, rabbits, donkeys, llamas, pot-bellied pigs, ponies, turkeys and goats) is a big draw for the little 'uns, while the Giraffe enclosure allows close-up encounters with these gentle giants, plus a feeding option (for a small fee).

Rides: In addition to its boat tours, Silver Springs also boasts a child-friendly **Carousel**, next to the imaginative **Kids Ahoy** playland, with its centrepiece riverboat featuring slides, rides, air bounce, ball crawl, 3D net maze, bumper boats and games. Older children will gravitate to the **Lighthouse Ride**, a combined carousel and gondola lift rising almost 100ft/30m above the park (and magnificently lit at night). By contrast, the **Floral Gardens** provide a peaceful haven in which to sit and watch the world go by.

Shopping and dining: Springside Mall provides an array of shops and eateries, with the **Deli** offering some pleasant sandwich choices and the

Glass-bottomed boat

Springside Café also above average, while **Swampy's Emporium** and the **Silver Bells Holiday Store** are the best of the shopping.

Special events: Silver Springs also offers a regular concert series at the **Twin Oaks Mansion** stage (included with admission) through the spring and autumn, with artists like Blue Oyster Cult, Foreigner and a variety of well-known country and western acts. Other special events include 4th of July celebrations, themed weekends (like the Ocala Scottish Highland Games in October) and Halloween **Fright Nights** (on specific dates throughout October), with haunted houses and the Gatorman River Cruise. The Christmas **Festival of Lights** (late Nov–30 Dec, dusk–8.30pm), features a huge light display through the park and other festive touches.

Wild Waters: Worth at least a couple of hours, the neighbouring 9-acre/4ha water park offers slides such as the Alligator Ambush (a daring tube ride into a 35ft/10.7m bowl with water-spraying gator!), Bunyan's Bend (a winding body slide), the 220ft/67m Silver Bullet and the helter-skelter Osceola's Revenge, as well as a 400ft/122m tube ride on the turbocharged Hurricane, a huge wave pool, and various kid-sized fun in Cool Kids Cove and Tad Pool for tots.

Bunyan's Bend at Wild Waters

© OCVB

> **BRITTIP**
> Check Silver Springs' website for current discounted admission offers, or buy an annual (Silver) pass for multiple visits for less than the cost of 2 days' admission.

Getting there: On SR40 in Ocala, 72mls/116km north of Orlando. Take the Florida Turnpike (a toll road, see map on page 8) until it turns into I-75. 28mls/45km further north, go east on SR40 for 10mls/16km, just past Wild Waters on your right. Admission: $29.99 adults and seniors (55+), $24.99 3–10s (under-3s free); parking $7; 10am–5pm most days, Mar–July; closed some Mon and Tues in Aug and Sept (Oct–Jan hours vary; check the website before visiting). Wild Waters is $29.99 adults and $22.99 3-10s. (under 48in/122cm). A joint Silver Springs/Wild Waters ticket is $44.99 (352 236 2121, **silversprings. com**). AAA½.

Gatorland

For another taste of 'real' Florida wildlife, this is as authentic as it gets and is popular with children of all ages. The 'Alligator Capital of the World' was founded in 1949 and is still family-owned, so it possesses a home-spun charm and naturalism few of its big-name rivals can match. And, when the wildlife consists of several thousand menacing alligators and crocodiles in various natural habitats and 4 fascinating shows – plus a fabulous new Zip Line attraction – you know you're in for a different experience. Overall, Gatorland is something you're unlikely to get anywhere else, though encounters with these living dinosaurs may not be everyone's cup of tea. features a huge light display

> **BRITTIP**
> If you have an evening flight home from Orlando International Airport, Gatorland is handy to visit on your final day. Conveniently located about 20 minutes' drive from the airport, it is the ideal place to soak up half a day.

throughout the park, plus other festive shows and touches.

Tours and attractions: Start by taking the 15-minute **Gatorland Express** railway around the park to get an idea of its 110-acre/45ha expanse. This costs an extra $2 but is good for multiple rides, is fully narrated (usually in amusing style) and is especially fun for kids. You also get a good look at the native animal habitat, which features whitetail deer, wild turkey and quail. Wander the natural beauty of the 2,000ft/610m **Swamp Walk**, as well as the **Alligator Breeding Marsh Walkway**, where a 3-storey observation tower gives a close-up view of these reptiles. Ask yourself: are they hanging around the walkway in the hope someone might 'drop in' for lunch?

◀▶ BRIT TIP

If you are at Gatorland first thing in the morning, take the Swamp Walk straight away. There will be far more wildlife activity then and the peaceful ambience is quite invigorating.

Breeding pens, baby alligator nurseries and rearing ponds are also situated throughout the park to provide an idea of the growth cycle of the gator and enhance the overall feeling that it is the visitor behind bars here, not the animals. **Jungle Crocs** features some of the deadliest animals of Egypt, Australia and Cuba, with authentic lairs and brilliant presentation (look out for Sultan and his 'harem' of lady crocs from the Nile). Many of the small-scale attractions have been designed with kids in mind and there is plenty to keep everyone amused. **Allie's Barnyard** is a petting zoo, while you can feed some friendly lorikeets at the **Very Merry Aviary**, and view the pink inhabitants of **Flamingo Lagoon**.

Don't miss the **White Gator Swamp**, showcasing 4 extremely rare and completely white alligators. They are leucistic (without pigment), hence they have startling blue eyes, not pink like albinos. A truly remarkable exhibit and superbly presented. Other animals to see include bats, iguanas, turtles, turkey vultures, tortoises, snakes, emus, deer and 2 cute tree porcupines from South America. The park is also home to hundreds of wading birds, providing a fascinating close-up of the nests during Mar–Aug. However, the gators and crocs are the main attraction and the shows are the real draw (though you will never find yourself on the end of a queue here).

Shows: The 800-seat **Wrestling Stadium** sets the scene for some real cracker-style feats (a 'cracker' is a Florida cowboy) as Gatorland's resident 'wranglers' catch themselves a medium-sized gator and proceed to point out the animal's features, with the aid of some daredevil stunts that will have you questioning their sanity. The **Gator Jumparoo** is another eye-opening spectacle as some of the park's biggest creatures use their tails to 'jump' out of the water and be hand-fed tasty morsels, like whole chickens! **Upclose Animal Encounters** is another amusing showcase of various creatures, from the expected snakes to less obvious cockroaches and scorpions. Great photo opportunities for brave children! **Critters On The Go** (new in 2010) features Ms Vera, trail boss Gabe and other Gatorland entertainers who host Orlando's cuddliest character meet-and-greet, with the chance to stroke some of the park's furrier residents. Watch out for these small animal encounters as they crop up around the park.

Gatorland

© OCVB

Gator Gully: This superb little water park features numerous ways for kids to cool down, get wet and generally have lots of fun. The ½-acre/0.2ha park features 5 different elements, including a giant jalopy with water jets for spokes and a fountain radiator, an old shack that 'explodes' with water, and giant gators with squirt guns. The neighbouring dry play area and chairs and tables allow parents to sit back and watch their offspring expend some energy, perhaps with a drink from one of the kiosks.

But wait…that's not all!

Eco Zip Line: As of autumn 2010, Gatorland fixed its eyes firmly on the brave of heart, introducing a first-of-its-kind zip line experience, with 4 zips soaring high above the park's most notorious residents. At 1,200ft long and up to 56ft high, the zip lines afford spectacular views of jumping Cuban Crocodiles and the scenic Alligator Breeding Marsh. The 45-minute experience includes orientation, a nature walk through the swamp, the zip line and a trek across a thrilling swinging bridge. There is a separate fee for this, but at $60/person, it includes all-day admission to the park.

Shopping and dining: In addition to 3 different gift stores around the park and the amusing **Gator & Snake photo opportunity**, you should visit the **Gift Shop** complex (rebuilt after a 2006 fire) at the entrance, which incorporates the trademark Gator

Gator Gully

Mouth entryway. You can grab a bite or drink at 3 snack bars, try **Gator Jake's Fudge Kitchen** or dine on smoked gator ribs and fried gator nuggets (as well as burgers and hot dogs) at **Pearl's Smokehouse**, with excellent kids' meals at $4.99.

Special events: Three unique options if you really want to get to know your gators are: **Trainer for a Day**, with the chance to work behind the scenes at the park 8am–10am, finding out what it takes to handle such dangerous animals, behavioural training and novice gator wrangling ($125 for 12s and over, max 5 people; includes park admission); **Gator Night Shine**, which takes guests into the Breeding Marsh after dark for a 1-hour tour with one of the park's senior gator experts, with torches and gator food to lure the local denizens. You can then marvel at how gator eyes shine like red beacons in the torchlight and learn more about the habits of these amazing animals – a real family treat, which kids seem to love (8.15pm summer, 6.30pm autumn and winter; $19 all ages; bug spray provided; reservations required); and **Adventure Hour**, a chance to go truly 'behind-the-scenes' in the Breeding Marsh to feed and pose for photos with the gators here ($10/person). **Rookie Wrestling** is every kid's chance to show their bravery and have the picture to prove it ($10 to kneel over a gator's back, extra for the photo).

Getting there: Gatorland is on the South Orange Blossom Trail, 2mls/3km south of the Central Florida Greeneway and 3mls/5km north of Highway 192 (see map on page 14). **Admission:** $22.99 adults, $14.99 3–12s, 9am–5pm (6pm summer), parking free. Annual passes are only $43.99 and $29.99 if you plan more than one visit (407 855 5496, **gatorland.com**). AAAA.

⊞ BRITTIP

For photographers and bird-watchers there is a special Single Day Photo Pass for entry to the Boardwalk rookery section of Gatorland from 7.30am to dusk.

Fantasy of Flight

Fantasy of Flight

Another wonderful and fresh alternative on the central Florida scene – voted No 1 'Best Kept Secret' by the locals – is this aviation attraction, which offers a 5-part adventure featuring the world's largest private collection of vintage aircraft. Even those not usually interested in aviation or the glamour of the golden age of flying should be fascinated.

You start by entering the **History of Flight**, a series of expertly re-created 'immersion experiences' into memorable moments in aviation history. The entrance alone is eye-opening – along the fuselage of a DC-3 Dakota as if for a parachute drop, stepping out into a moonlit night. Then you visit set-pieces that include a dogfight over the trenches in World War I and a bomber mission with a Flying Fortress in World War II. The latter includes a walk-through of an actual B-17 as it prepares for its bombing run! Audio-visual effects and film clips enhance the experience and give everything an awe-inspiring feeling of authenticity. You exit into the Vintage Aircraft displays in 2 huge hangars, with the exhibits ranging from a replica *Spirit of St Louis* to a Ford Tri-Motor, a Mk-XVI Spitfire and the world's only fully airworthy Short

Sunderland flying boat, which you can actually board. One aircraft is selected from the collection of more than 40 vintage planes each day for an **Aerial Demonstration** (weather permitting), with the pilot holding a Q&A session about that plane before going on to perform a series of manoeuvres over Fantasy of Flight.

More family-orientated entertainment is provided by **Fun with Flight**, a hands-on interactive area where guests can test their paper aeroplane-making skills in The Fly Zone and learn about the principles of lift with Bernoulli's Ball. Kids will want to try out the hang-glide simulator while the mock balloon flight is also great fun. Other special exhibits include **They Dared To Fly**, a tribute to the Tuskegee airmen of World War II. A variety of **guided tours** is given each day, with a tram tour of the restricted areas (including the Maintenance Hangar and Wood Shop, where specialists restore and rebuild wooden aircraft), a walking tour of the Backlot, and a visit to the Restoration Shop, highlighting in detail what it takes to restore and maintain these magnificent machines. Finally, **Fightertown** features 8 realistic fighter simulators that take you on a World War II aerial battle. You get a pre-flight briefing on how to handle your 'plane' (a Vought Corsair), and then climb into the enclosed cockpit to do battle with the Japanese Air Force. It's difficult, absorbing, fun and totally addictive. The whole experience is crafted in

Fantasy of Flight

1930s art deco style and includes a full-service diner (the excellent **Compass Rose**; 11am–3pm) and an original gift shop. There is strong Brit appeal, too, with the exhibits of both World Wars. Then there is Fantasy of Flight's 3-hour balloon ride for $175 (up to 4 passengers; seasonal operations and reservations required). Want a private flight for two? Opt for the Exclusivity For Two **balloon flight** ($475 per couple).

Fantasy of Flight is the brainchild of American entrepreneur and aviation whiz Kermit Weeks – who still shows off his pilot skills occasionally for the aerial demonstration – and we have yet to encounter an attraction put together with more genuine affection. In fact, it is as much a work of art as a tourist attraction, and the masses have yet to discover it.

Getting there: 20 minutes west of Walt Disney World on I-4 at exit 44 (Polk City), turn first right, then left on SR 559 for ½ml/800m to the entrance on the left. Admission: $28.95 adults, $14.95 6–15s (under-6s free); 10am–5pm (parking free; closed Thanksgiving and Christmas Day),

(863 984 3500, **fantasyofflight.com**). AAAA.

Waldo Wright's Flying Service

Flying daily from the Fantasy of Flight airfield is this wonderfully authentic biplane experience. If you ever fancied yourself as a silk-scarf-and-leather-jacket-wearing flying ace, this is definitely the place for you (even if you don't, try it anyway – it's terrific fun). There are 2 distinct rides: in an open-cockpit 1929 **New Standard D25** biplane (where the front seats can hold up to 4) for $69.95/person; or the more daring, hands-on, 2-seater 1942 **Boeing Stearman PT-17** biplane trainer, where your pilot takes you up and then lets you take the controls! The 30-minute experience costs $229. Both rides are fairly gentle (and just a little thrilling) as you get a slow, bird's-eye view of this pretty part of central Florida. The way the planes seem able to turn on a wingtip gives you a deep respect for the pilots of these wonderful machines (863 873 1339, **waldowrights.com**).

Simon and Susan at Waldo Wright's

INTERNATIONAL DRIVE

The 14½ml/23km tourist corridor of I-Drive (see maps pages 86, 220 and 340) continues to be an ever-changing source of hotels, restaurants, shopping and, more importantly, fun. There are more than 33,000 hotel rooms, 150 restaurants and 500-plus shops, as well as 14 attractions, including 6 mini-golf courses. The **I-Ride Trolley** links it together in transport terms and **International DriveOrlando.com** highlights all the options. Its Official Visitors Guide has an I-Ride map and valuable money-off coupons, which you can download to get you started. There is also a hotel booking facility.

Here's a look at the area's top attractions (see also Chapter 10, Orlando By Night, and Chapter 12, Shopping, to get the complete picture).

BRIT TIP

Ripley's, Festival Bay and WonderWorks are all handy retreats to keep in mind for a rainy day.

Ripley's Believe It Or Not

You can't miss this particular attraction and its extraordinary tilted appearance as it's designed to appear as though it's falling into a Florida 'sinkhole'. However, once inside you soon get back on the level and, for an hour or two, you can wander through this quirky museum dedicated to the weird and wonderful. Robert L. Ripley was an eccentric explorer and collector (a real-life Indiana Jones) who for 40 years travelled the world in his bid to assemble a collection of the greatest oddities known to man. The Orlando branch of this chain features 8,900sq ft/830sq m of displays, including authentic artefacts, interactive exhibits, illusions, video presentations and music. The elaborate re-creation of an Egyptian tomb showcases a mummy and 3 rare mummified animals, while the Primitive Gallery contains artefacts (some quite gruesome) from tribal societies around the world.

There are then Human and Animal Oddities, Big and Little galleries, Illusions and Dinosaurs, plus extra interactive elements. The collection of miniatures includes the world's smallest violin and a single grain of rice hand-painted with a tropical sunset. Larger-scale exhibits include a portion of the Berlin Wall, a ⅔-scale 1907 Rolls-Royce built in matchsticks and a 26ft/8m tall 'painting' of Van Gogh made out of postcards!

Admission: $18.95 adults, $11.95 4– 12s; 9.0am–12am daily (last admission 11pm; 407 363 4418, **ripleysorlando.com**). AAA.

Titanic – The Experience

Go back in time at this fascinating attraction just north of Sand Lake Road. Weave through the re-designed Experience featuring full-scale re-creations of the *Titanic*'s famous rooms, including her grand staircase, first class parlour suite, Veranda Café and the newly added Marconi Room, third class cabin and bridge. Actors in period costume portray such notables as Captain Smith and Molly Brown, sharing stories of passengers and crew during a 1-hour guided journey of the famous ship. The 18-room attraction features an interactive Underwater Room, including a 15ft/4.5m 'iceberg' and a detailed replica of the vessel as she appears on the bottom of the Atlantic today. More than 200 artefacts and treasures, including memorabilia from James Cameron's blockbuster movie *Titanic* are also on display here.

Ripley's Believe It Or Not

Admission: $21.95 adults, $12.95 4–12s (under-4s free); 10am–9 pm daily (**titanictheexperience.com**). AAAA.

New in July 2009 was the exclusive **Titanic Dinner Event** (Fri and Sat only), a set-piece theatre/dining occasion with the impressive cast of the Experience. Starring Molly Brown, Captain Smith and Thomas Andrews, it offers each table a front row seat for the whole Titanic story, setting the scene and delivering a dinner party with a difference, all in period style. A sumptuous 3-course meal, featuring roast sirloin and chicken, is served, along with tea, coffee and soft drinks, and the ambience is one of genuine maritime splendour. The 3-hour performance costs $64.95 for adults, $39.95 for 6–11s (not recommended for under-6s) and must be booked in advance on 407 248 1166.

Fun Spot Action Park
Here's another choice for full-scale, family-sized fun, just off I-Drive on Del Verde Way (look for the 100ft/31m Big Wheel past the junction with Kirkman Road). The main focus is the go-karts, with 4 challenging tracks, including the max thrills of the 1,600ft/488m **Quad Helix**, the 1,000ft/305m **Conquest**, with its triple level corkscrew, the fiendish 800ft/244m **Thrasher** and the multi-level **Commander**. Then there are also bumper cars and boats, 4 daring fairground-type rides (including the whizzy **Scrambler** and **Paratrooper**), an impressive 2-storey video arcade (one of the largest in Florida), 7 Kid Spot rides and a Cadet track for the little ones. This 4.7-acre/2ha park promises hours of fun! The Oasis

Star Trucks at Fun Spot Action Park

Snack Bar serves hot dogs, pizza, nachos, popcorn and ice-cream and the arcade games include some of the latest. Passes are geared around children's height (above and below 4ft 4in/1.32m), with younger children getting free run of all the rides (and as a passenger on the 2-seater go-karts with an adult) and older children (and grown-ups!) having unlimited access to all the rides, go-karts and games.

Admission: Free; then Go-Kart Armband (all day on all 4 tracks, plus all rides and unlimited Free Play arcade) $34.95; Rides Armband (all day on all rides plus unlimited Free Play arcade) $24.95; Kid Spot Armband (all day on Kid Spot rides plus unlimited Free Play arcade) $14.95; and Free Play Armband (unlimited play in upstairs Free Play arcade) $4.95. Go-kart rides $6, ride tickets $3. Height requirements: over 4ft 4in/1.32m for Quad Helix, Conquest and Commander; 4ft 6in/1.37m for Thrasher. Open daily 10am–midnight, noon–midnight Mon–Fri in low season (407 363 3867, **fun-spot. com**). TTTT.

Magical Midway
In a similar vein, **Magical Midway** back on I-Drive (just north of Sand Lake Road) offers more go-karts, games and thrill rides, including the **Space Blast Tower** (0–180ft/55m in 3 seconds!) and the amazing **StarFlyer**, a 230ft/70m tower with chair swings that lift and rotate up the full height for a dizzying view of the surrounding area at 54mph (the only ride of its kind in America). The 2 elevated kart tracks, the double uphill corkscrew of **The Avalanche** and the sharply banked **Alpine Jump** are its signature rides (you must be at least 12 and 4ft 8in/147cm tall to drive, at least 16 to drive a passenger, and at least 5 and 3ft/91cm to be a passenger). **Fast Track**, a flat concrete track with a 25° bank turn (riders must be 12 and 4ft 8in/147cm to drive; single cars only) complete the line-up. There are also bumper cars, bumper boats, 3 more fairground-type rides, a large arcade, a pizza parlour and ice-cream counter.

Admission: Free, then 3-hour Armband (unlimited go-karts and midway rides for 3 hours, not SlingShot) $25; Package 1: SlingShot or Starflyer plus t-shirt and DVD, $50; Package 2: SlingShot and Starflyer, plus DVD and t-shirt $75. Individual ride tickets are $25 SlingShot or $7 Starflyer (ride DVD $15), $7 for go-karts, and $3 for other rides; must be 4ft/121cm for Space Shot, and Bumper Cars, and 3ft 6in/106cm for Bumper Boats and Kiddie Track. 2–10pm Mon–Tues, 2pm–midnight Wed-Fri, 10am–midnight Sat-Sun (407 370 5353, **magicalmidway.com**). TTTT.

WonderWorks

This interactive entertainment centre is I-Drive's most unmistakable landmark, a 3-storey chamber of family fun with a host of novel elements. Unmistakable? How many upside-down buildings do you know? That's right, all the 82ft/25m edifice is constructed from the roof up! The basic premise (working on the theory that every attraction must have a story behind it) is that WonderWorks is a secret research facility into unexplained phenomena that was uprooted by a tornado experiment and dumped in topsy-turvy fashion in the heart of this busy tourist district (yeah, right!). Well, you have to give full marks for imagination and, with various enhancements since it opened in 1998, there's a lot here, especially for 6–12s.

✚ BRIT TIP

WonderWorks, Fun Spot and Magical Midway are open until midnight in high season, long after most theme parks are shut, so you can have a day at the park, then let the kids loose here for a while to tire them out!

You enter through an 'inversion tunnel' that orientates you the same way round as the building (look out of the window to check!) and then progress to various chambers of entertaining and mildly educational hands-on experiences that demand several hours to explore fully. Without

ever using the words 'science' or 'museum', WonderWorks steers you through various 'labs' of interactive activities, including **natural disasters** (earthquakes, hurricanes, famous disasters and the new Global VR – a virtual reality trek into the Desert War); **physical challenges** (virtual basketball and soccer, virtual 'swim with the sharks', Bed of Nails and the chance to make an impression of your entire body in 40,000 plastic nails at Wonderwall!); **illusions** (with a computer ageing process and 'elastic surgery', ethnicity changer and a 'couple's morph' that combines 2 faces to see what the resulting children would look like!); and **The Control Room**, where you have **Jet Fighters** (virtual reality F18 fighter jet), **Shuttle Landers** (your chance to pilot the Discovery Space Shuttle), a Mercury capsule mock-up, an astronaut spacesuit and **Wonder Coaster** (a pair of enclosed 'pods' that let you design and ride your own coaster). Recent additions include biofeedback game of Mindball, a 3-storey indoor rope climbing structure with 20 obstacles, and the new **XD Theater 4-D Extreme Motion Experience** simulator ride. Plus there is the **WonderWorks Gift Shop and Café**. A **Lazer Tag** game on the top floor adds even more appeal for youngsters. If you have already seen DisneyQuest, WonderWorks may seem tame, while it isn't as educational as the Orlando Science Center, but it also offers a fun dinner-show option, The **Outta Control Magic Comedy Dinner Show** (see page 310), with a good value combo ticket.

WonderWorks

Admission: $19.95 adults, $14.95 seniors (55+) and 4–12s; $4.95 for Lazer Tag; $24.95 and $16.95 for The Outta Control Dinner Show; $38.95 and $28.95 for WonderWorks/dinner show combo; $22.95 and $17.95 for WonderWorks/Lazer Tag combo; $39.95 and $29.95 for all 3; 9am– midnight (407 351 8800, **wonderworksonline.com**). AAA/TTT.

iFLY Orlando

At the junction with I-Drive and Kirkman Road is this unmistakable blue and yellow funnel that houses one of the most fun 'rides' in town. Formerly SkyVenture, now iFLY Orlando, it is billed as a 'free-fall skydiving adventure' but it is much more than that – a fun, addictive, difficult but exhilarating 'flying' experience, with the bonus of being a great spectator sport! The basic premise is it's a huge vertical wind tunnel, which provides the feeling of a freefall parachute jump without the hassle of having to leap out of a plane, wrestle with a parachute and possibly hit the ground too hard. The standard 1-hour programme provides a full briefing of this kind of skydiving, with a fully qualified instructor to get you suitably inspired. Then you are provided with all the

iFLY Orlando

equipment, including helmet, pads, goggles, earplugs and flight suit, and your group of 8–12 returns to the flight deck, where you get 2 1-minute 'flights' (which seem a lot longer!) with your instructor helping you all the way. Just watching makes it seem all too easy but, as soon as you hit the tunnel, you discover how fiendishly tough it is to just 'hang' in this 125mph/200kph column of air. However, before long it becomes an immensely fun and absorbing experience and it's almost guaranteed to make you want to try again. There is no fee for non-participating members of your group to watch from the observation deck, and you can also just turn up to see for yourself at any time (you might even get to see sky-dive groups practising at this popular venue).

Admission: Standard flight, which includes a special certificate, is $49.95/person; add a DVD and photo CD of your flight for $19.99. Discount coupons and gift certificates can be found on its website, with $8 off if you register online. Try a Family Package for up to 5 flyers at $239.95 or a Spread Your Wings Package (double your flight time) for $89.95. 10am– 9pm Sun–Thurs, 10am–10pm Fri and Sat; reservations recommended (407 903 1150, **iflyorlando.com**). TTTT.

Helicopter rides

These are another local staple, and you can go for any one of 9 tours with **Air Florida Helicopters** at 8990 International Drive (just north of the big Convention Center). A minimum of 2 people are required, and then it's just a question of whether you want the local 8ml/12.87m tour, a trip over Universal and SeaWorld, the chance to see Disney from the air, a birds-eye view of Downtown Orlando, or a mega 30ml/48km grand journey that includes flying over Windermere and homes of the rich and famous (such as Tiger Woods). Prices vary from $25 for the short flight to $335 for the longest ($20–325 for children). No need to book; you just turn up and go. They fly 9.30am–7pm daily (407 354 1400, **airfloridahelicopter.com**).

© OOVB

Super Shot

Mini-golf

For those in need of more holiday fun, don't miss the 6 mini-golf outlets along International Drive (see page 274).

Old Town, Kissimmee

In the heart of tourist Highway 192 in Kissimmee is the shopping and entertainment attraction of **Old Town**. The shopping part is covered in Chapter 12, but there are many associated attractions worth noting. Old Town itself features 14 out-and-out rides, from the standard and rather tame **Happy Days** bumper cars, Happy Days go-karts and large **Ferris Wheel** to the **Windstorm** roller-coaster, the **Super Shot** (a free-fall-style ride of over 140ft/43m), and the **Bull**. There is a **Fun Town** area of junior rides, plus a **Laser Tag** game, and tickets are sold separately for most rides ($2 each), but if you plan to do several, go for the Valuepak at $20 for 22 tickets, $30 for 35, or $50 for 60. There are also 3 All You Can Ride Wristbands, the Mega Saver at $35 (14 rides plus bumper cars, go karts and laser tag), the $25 Super Saver (14 rides plus bumper cars), or the Tiny Tyke (all $2 rides plus bumper car passenger ride with paying adult). There are also two Family Day Sunday Wristbands (noon–6pm Sun): Mega Saver for $25 and Super Saver for $15. There are separate fees for bumper cars ($5), The Bull ($10 adults, $7 children), Laser Tag ($5) and go-karts ($6). For a different kind

of fun, you can also try the 2-storey **Grimm Haunted House** ($10 adults, $6.75 children). The Old Town rides are open noon–11pm (later at peak periods; 407 396 4888, old-town.com). TTTT. at $35 (14 rides plus bumper cars, go karts and laser tag), the $25 Super Saver (14 rides plus bumper cars), or the Tiny Tyke (all $2 rides plus bumper car passenger ride with paying adult). There are also two Family Day Sunday Wristbands (noon–6pm Sun): Mega Saver for $25 and Super Saver for $15. There are separate fees for bumper cars ($5), The Bull ($10 adults, $7 children), Laser Tag ($5) and go-karts ($6). For a different kind of fun, you can also try the 2-storey Grimm Haunted House ($10 adults, $6.75 children). The Old Town rides are open noon–11pm (later at peak periods; 407 396 4888, **old-town.com**). TTTT.

> **BRIT TIP**
> Old Town offers a Birthday Party package for up to 10 children at a time, consisting of 2 or 3 hours of unlimited rides, meal vouchers for any of their restaurants and use of its party room for 2 hours. E-mail **aharvey@old-town. com** for more info.

Fun Spot USA

Right next door to Old Town (but not connected in any way) is another area of rides and fun owned by Fun Spot of International Drive. There are 19 rides (a good selection of thrill rides, a Kid Spot of junior-sized rides and 2 high-adrenalin signature rides, which

Sky Coaster

are real one-offs) and 4 go-kart tracks. **Galaxy Spin**, a coaster formerly in Cypress Gardens, was due to arrive in December 2010. Top of the lot is the amazing **SkyCoaster**, a 300ft/90m tower that sends up to 3 riders at a time on a free-fall plunge (for the first 120ft/37m) that turns into a giant swing – at 85mph/136kph! The more down-to-earth rides consist of 2 flat concrete go-kart tracks, **Slick** and **Road Course**, and 2 multi-level concrete tracks, the labyrinthine **Chaos** and the **Vortex**, with its hugely challenging banked bowl section. The other rides are almost as much fun – check out the **Extraordinary Bike** (pedal your way upside-down!), the **Double Ferris Wheel**, the more fairground style of **Flying Bobs** and the **Paratrooper**, the giant swing of the **Hot Seat** and the tower-ride **Screamer**. Also part of Fun Spot USA is the indoor **Full Speed Race & Golf**. The Race features 6 full-motion NASCAR motor-racing simulators, while the latter is a racing-themed, and quite challenging, 18-hole black-light mini-golf course. There is a well-stocked **Snack Bar** (with free soft drinks) in the outdoor rides section, drinks and snacks at **SkyCoaster** and a shop for gifts and snacks at **Full Speed Race & Golf**, plus pizza, hot dog and candy floss kiosks throughout the park. Oh, and look out for race cars from the former Race Rock restaurant, and the giant-wheeled **Bigfoot 7** truck – it featured in the films *Road House* (Patrick Swayzee) and T*ango & Cash* (Sylvester Stallone and Kurt Russell).

Admission: Free, then Go-Kart Armband $34.95 (unlimited go-karts and other rides), Rides Armband (unlimited rides) $24.95, Kid Spot Rides Armband $14.94 and Track Sampler $20 (4 goes on go-karts or rides); regular tickets $3 each or 15 for $40 (Go-Karts 2 or 3 tickets each). The SkyCoaster is $40 for 1 rider, $70 for 2, $90 for 3. Full Speed Race $9.95, $6.95 Race Again, $4.95 passenger; Golf, $9.95 adults, $7.95 under-13s, $4.95 Play Again; All-Day Race & Golf $19.95; 10am–midnight; (407 397 2509, **fun-spotusa.com**). There is also a special 2-park Armband for Fun Spot and Fun Spot USA at $54.95.

BRIT TIP
Visit **fun-spotusa.com** for discount coupons off Fun Spot USA's Ride Armband, or save your armband from one Fun Spot location for 20% off the other.

Skyline Tour of Downtown Orlando

DOWNTOWN ORLANDO

The last few years have seen a major revamp of Orlando's city centre (the 'downtown' area), with new offices, apartments, shops and restaurants. This has also enhanced some notable tourist attractions and is well served by the new **Information Center** on Orange Avenue (9am–6pm, Mon–Fri; 407 254 4636, **downtownorlando. com** – click the *Visit Downtown* tab). Start here to get a full overview, with interactive info kiosks, a 3-D city model and ultra-helpful staff (plus free internet). They can provide free maps of the area, a Historic Walking Tour guide and info on riding the free **Lymmo** bus service around downtown. There is also a free guided tour twice a month with local historian Richard Forbes (not June–Sept). The other must-try opportunity is the free **Skyline Tours** (a guided rooftop-view of the city) with one of its tourist Volunteers, who can provide essential city history and other info while pointing out the main sights from the top of one of the city's high-rise buildings. These are provided daily, usually on a turn-up-and-go basis (although it is best to call in advance – 407 254 4636 – if you plan to visit) and are a real 'high'-light of any downtown visit!

✚ BRIT TIP

Visiting the downtown Orlando Information Center? Take exit 82B off I-4 and there are 4 multi-storey car parks nearby, the best being the Library park (take 4th right on Central Boulevard).

Want more? Try the **Orlando Ghost Tours**, a 2-hour walking tour downtown most evenings at 8pm (not Sun). Although largely modern, parts of the city date back to the 1880s, including the Greenwood Cemetery, and there is a lot of history involved, as well as the tour's 'paranormal investigations.' Haunted? Maybe. Fascinating? You bet ($25 adults, $20 students and seniors, $15 7-12s, under 7 free; 407 247 0452, **hauntedorlando.com**).

Orange County History Center

This smart, modern addition to the downtown scene offers an imaginative journey into central Florida history, from the wildlife and Native Americans to today's tourist issues and space programme. Again, the accent is on the interactive, with hands-on exhibits and audiovisual presentations, and it is very much a journey through time, starting outside in renovated Heritage Square, complete with cypress trees and fountains. The Center itself is in the former 1927 Orange County Courthouse, with the foyer converted into a dome featuring more than 150 icons unique to central Florida (see how many you can identify before and after your tour).

The 4-storey adventure starts at the top with the **Orientation Theater**'s 14-minute multimedia presentation as you sit in rocking chairs on the 'front porch'. Then you visit the **Natural Environment** and **First Peoples** exhibits (12,000 years ago), before First Contact brings in the European element. Jump into the 1800s and visit a Seminole settlement, a pioneer cracker (the first true cowboy) home, hear tales of the old ranching days, the Seminole wars and learn about the citrus industry. The story of tourism in Orlando before Walt Disney World Is showcased in *Destination Florida. Walt Disney World* picks up where Destination Florida leaves off, highlighting Orlando's changes once the Mouse showed up.

Orange County History Center

Aviation explores transportation's history, from World War II bombers to the outer reaches of space. From there, you move on to the beautifully restored **Courtroom B** for some more real-life Orlando history.

◀ BRIT TIP

Combine a visit to the History Center with lunch at the wonderfully eclectic Globe restaurant on the corner of Heritage Square nearby.

Finally, you reach the newest permanent exhibit, **Orlando Remembered** – a journey from the 19th century to the edge of the 21st. This tells the story beyond the theme parks and is an inclusive history of Orlando's people, uncovering secrets of the past, including significant artefacts from the Historical Society of Central Florida. Find out about events like the Big Freeze of the 1890s and the area's contribution to World War II (with a replica Flying Fortress). An exhibit on African American history, featuring the achievements and tragedies of central Florida's African American community, and a series of travelling exhibits (like **The Highwayman**, **Seminole Wars** and **Florida in the Civil War**) round things off, while a visit to the **Historium** gift shop completes your visit. Special large-scale exhibits scheduled for 2011 include *The Story of Harness Racing by Currier & Ives* (27 Aug–17 Oct), a collection of more than 30 original lithographs.

Downtown Orlando

Orange Blossom Special outside the station

Getting there: Off Central Boulevard and Magnolia Avenue downtown (exit 83A off I-4, Amelia Street; turn right on to Amelia, 1st right on to N. Orange, then 5th left on to E. Central Blvd; see also map on page 220). Park at the Public Library multi-storey car park on Central Boulevard (History Center admission includes 2 hours' free parking if you show your ticket). Admission: $12 adults, $9 seniors (60+), $7 5–12s; 10am–5pm daily (407 836 8500, **thehistorycenter.org**). AAA.

Theatre and more

Staying downtown, the free **Lymmo** bus service connects the central area along Magnolia Avenue, from South Street to the stunning new **Amway Center** for sports and concerts on W Church Street and up to the Centroplex area, with the old Amway Arena, and **Bob Carr Performing Arts Center** (to be replaced by the Orlando Performing Arts Center in 2012). Try **SAK Comedy Lab** at Eola Capital Loft on Orange Avenue, with fun improv comedy on Tues–Sat (7.30, 9, 9.30 or 11.30pm, $2-$15; 407 648 0001, **sak.com**). Also here is **City Arts Factory**, (11am–6pm Tues–Sat), with a huge collective of galleries under one roof from a wide range of local and national artists, plus art classes and a city-wide Gallery Hop on the third Thurs of each month (407 648 7060, **cityartsfactory.com**). The **Plaza** is the new multiplex in the heart of downtown, boasting a state-of-the-art 12-screen cinema,

2 café bars, with a full menu and extensive beer and wine selections, and 2 Downtown Arts District galleries (321 558 2878, **plazacinemacafe.com**), while it also plays home to the annual **Orlando Film Festival** each November (**orlandofilmfest.com**). The restaurant/bar choice is also pretty good here, too. Take your pick from a smart **Urban Flats** café bar (look out for their Wine Down Wednesdays!), **Corona Cigar Co** (fine bar and cigar emporium), **The Globe** (an eclectic lounge/café in front of the History Center, open late Thur-Sat), **Wall Street Plaza** (a lively collection of bars and lounges that are the heart of downtown nightlife) and **Church Street Station**, the remains of the old entertainment district, which still includes a cluster of fine restaurants and bars, notably the stylish Spanish cuisine of **Ceviche**, the elegant boutique style of **The Dessert Lady** and **Hamburger Mary's Bar & Grille**. Live music fans should make a beeline for **The Social**, one of Orlando's trendiest small-scale venues (407 246 1419, **thesocial.org**), while the artistic **Mad Cow Theatre** offers a variety of high-quality stage productions featuring highly-lauded local talent.

BRIT TIP

In party mode? Head for Wall Street Plaza, between Orange Ave and N Court Ave, on any Thurs, Fri or Sat night and bar-hop with the locals all night long! (**wallstreetplaza.net**)

Once you have sampled the heart of downtown, head out to wander the neighbouring **Lake Eola** area, with more restaurants and shops, plus a beautiful lakeside walk, children's play area, Swan paddleboats and a peaceful ambience. Children can feed the birds, fish and turtles or take a paddleboat ride, while there are regular open-air concerts and storytelling at the Disney Amphitheater. The **Sunday Farmers Market** (around Lake Eola, 10am–4pm) is another major focal point, with vendors now including local artists as well as wonderful fresh produce. Stop for a great meal, with a view, at either of **310 Lakeside** (407 373 0301, **310lakeside.net**) or **Spice Modern Steakhouse** (407 481 9533, **spicesteakhouse.com**). Continue on to the **Thornton Park** area and enjoy the most happening part of Orlando, with Thornton Park Central (at the junction of Summerlin Avenue and Central Boulevard, just south-east of Lake Eola) offering a mix of unique boutiques and trendy restaurants. **Hue** is consistently rated one of Orlando's top restaurants and is as stylish as they come (407 849 1800, **huerestaurant.com**), **Cityfish** is a more casual seafood café/bar alternative (407 849 9779, **cityfishorlando.com**), **Anthony's Pizzeria** is a great upscale pizza restaurant (407 648 0009, **anthonyspizza.com**) and **Wildside BBQ** is a lively locals' hangout (407 872 8665, **wildsidebbq.com**).

Ceviche

BRIT TIP

Don't miss the annual **Spring** and **Fall Fiestas** around Lake Eola, with hundreds of vendors, live entertainment and special fun for kids, every April and November (see also page 16–17).

Loch Haven Park

Continue north out of downtown and you travel the 'Cultural Corridor' to Loch Haven Park and the area's fine collection of theatres, museums and the Orlando Science Center. The **Dr Phillips Performing Arts Center** is home to the Orlando Opera and Orlando Ballet. The 34-year-old **Orlando Ballet** is central Florida's only full-time ballet company, with national and international dancers, plus a Family Series that accommodates children (407 426 1739, **orlandoballet.org**). Also here are the extensive **Orlando Museum of Art** (407 896 4231, **omart.com**), the superbly diverse **Mennello Museum of American Art**, with a permanent collection by painter Earl Cunningham (407 246 4278, **mennellomuseum.com**), the **Orlando Philharmonic Orchestra** (407 896 6700, **orlandophil.org**) and the **Orlando Shakespeare Theater** (407 447 1700, **orlandoshakes.org**). Parents should also make a note of the **Orlando Rep**, a fabulous company specialising in family theatre and with youth academies and summer camps for kids. Their 2011 season includes *Anne Frank And Me* and *Disney's My Son Pinocchio* (407 896 7365, **orlandorep. com**). Highly recommended.

NatureWorks

© OCVB

Orlando Science Center

Orlando Science Center: Because this is Orlando, there is no such thing as a simple museum or science centre. Everything must be all-singing, all-dancing just to compete. Hence, the Orlando Science Center is more than a mere museum and far more fun than the average science centre. Here you are given a series of hands-on experiences and habitats that entertain as well as inform, and school-age children in particular will benefit greatly from it. It has 9 main permanent exhibits, a night sky observatory, an inviting café and a giant screen cinema.

NatureWorks is an immersion-style exhibit creating 6 typical Florida habitats, complete with native plants and animals (with field stations such as how sea turtles make their nests and a live beehive); **KidsTown** is for those a bit too young for the educational element, with plenty of junior-sized fun and games for under-6s (you'll be amazed at how much they can learn while having fun!); **DinoDigs** was a gift from the Walt Disney Company of its former Dinosaur Jubilee exhibit in *Disney's Animal Kingdom*, re-created in the OSC as a palaeontological excavation site, complete with 8 full skeleton replicas and some genuine fossils; **TechWorks** is a hands-on adventure into the worlds of physical science and technology, including a hurricane simulator and Dr Dare's Laboratory; and **Xperience Factory** offers a variety of different live science shows (notably **Cool Science** – fun with frigid temperatures and chemical reactions). Preschoolers will appreciate **All Aboard**, with child-sized trains, planes, and automobiles. The newest exhibits (in summer 2010) were **Careers for Life**, focusing on careers in health care, **Science on a Sphere** (show times vary) exploring Earth's landscape and the cosmos, and **H2NOW**, a miniature city powered by hydrogen. You will also find a handy **Café** and a large **Science Store** here. In addition, the centre has 2 separate programmes in **Dr Phillips CineDome**, a 310-seat cinema that almost surrounds its audience with large-format films and digital planetarium shows. It also boasts a 28,000-watt digital sound system that makes the experience unforgettable.

BRIT TIP
Visit the Crosby Observatory (selected times only; be sure to call in advance) on top of the Science Center to gaze through the region's largest publicly accessible refractor telescope.

Getting there: On Princeton Street in downtown Orlando, just off exit 85 of I-4 (go east on Princeton, the Center is on your left but the multi-storey car park is on the RIGHT, see map on page 220). **Admission:** $17 adults, $16 seniors (55+), $16 Student with ID, $12 3–11s; parking $5. 10am–5pm daily (closed Easter Sunday, Thanksgiving, Christmas Eve and Christmas Day; **osc.org**) AAA.

THE WATER PARKS

Florida specialises in elaborate water parks, and Orlando boasts the very best. Predictably, Disney has the 2 most sophisticated ones, but the opening of SeaWorld's Aquatica park in 2008 provided some real competition, while Universal-owned Wet 'n Wild is also adept at providing hours of watery fun. They adopt a variety of styles that owe much to the flair of the theme park creators, and are truly imaginative for both the rides and the imagery around them. All require at least ½ a day of splashing, sliding and riding to get full value from their rather high prices. Lockers are provided for valuables and you can hire towels.

BRIT TIP
Want a day of watery fun but don't want to purchase an extra pass for a water park? Consider **CocoKey Water Resort** on International Drive. You can purchase a day pass for under $20; it's great for the pre-school to 10-year-old crowd, and it's covered, to protect kids from the harsh Florida sun (**cocokeywaterresort.com**).

Typhoon Lagoon

Disney's Typhoon Lagoon Water Park

When *Typhoon Lagoon* opened in 1989, it was the biggest and finest of Florida's water parks. And, although it has since been superseded, in high season it is still the busiest, so be prepared for more queues. *You should definitely arrive ½ an hour early if possible as entry often begins before the official opening hour.* The park's 56 acres/23ha are spread out around the 2½/1ha lagoon fringed with palm trees and white-sand beaches. It is extravagantly landscaped and the walk up Mount Mayday, for instance, provides a terrific overview as well as adding scenic touches such as rope bridges and tropical flowers. Sun loungers, chairs, picnic tables and even hammocks are provided to add to the comfort and convenience of restful areas like Getaway Glen. However, you need to arrive early to bag a decent spot. Or, for $40 extra (!!) you can reserve 2 beach loungers, 2 towels, an umbrella and a small table by stopping in at High 'n Dry Rentals. Same day only, first come first served. Really want to splash out? Opt for a **Beachcomber Shack** (cabaña), which includes a locker, drinks mug, cooler with ice, bottled water, towels, loungers and table, and waiter service. Full day rental for up to 6 guests will set you back $250 (admission not included). Reserve in advance on 407 939 7529 (we're fans of arriving early and getting your loungers for free!).

Crush 'n' Gusher

© Disney

© Disney

Shark Reef at Typhoon Lagoon

BRIT TIP
While water parks provide a great way of cooling down, it is easy to pick up a 5-star case of sunburn. So don't forget the high-factor waterproof suncream, and reapply often.

To avoid the worst of the summer crowds (when the park's 7,200 capacity is often reached), Mon morning is the best time (steer clear of weekends at all costs) and, on other days, arrive either before opening or in mid-afternoon, when many decide to dodge the daily rainstorm. Early evening is also pleasant when the park lights up. The park is overlooked by Mount Mayday, on top of which is perched the luckless *Miss Tilly*, a shrimp boat that legend has it landed here during the typhoon that gave the park its name. Watch out for the water fountains that shoot from *Miss Tilly's* funnel at regular intervals, accompanied by the ship's hooter, which signal another round of 6ft/1.8m waves in the **Surf Pool** (hire inner tubes to bob around on or just try body-surfing). Circling the lagoon is **Castaway Creek**, a 3ft/1m deep, lazy flowing river offering the chance to float idly along on rubber tyres.

BRIT TIP
Want to learn to surf? Typhoon Lagoon offers Surfing School 2 hours before park opening every day. Call 407 939 7529 in advance to book at $150/person.

Slides and rides: These are all clustered around Mount Mayday and vary from the breathtaking body slides of **Humunga Kowabunga**, which drop you 214ft/65m at up to 30mph/48kph down some pretty steep inclines (make sure your swimming costume is securely fastened!) to **Ketchakiddee Creek**, which offers a selection of slides and pools for youngsters under 4ft/122cm. In between, you have the 3 **Storm Slides**, body slides that twist and turn through caves, tunnels and waterfalls, **Mayday Falls**, a wild 460ft/140m single-rider inner-tube flume down a series of banked drops, **Keelhaul Falls**, a more sedate tube ride that takes slightly longer, and **Gangplank Falls**, a family ride inside rafts that take up to 4 people down 300ft/90m of mock rapids.

The fun **Crush 'n' Gusher** is a fabulous trio of 'water-coaster' tube rides, plus a large heated pool with zero-depth entry (great for toddlers). It also has an extensive sandy beach, which makes it a great place to bag a spot in the sun. The 3 different slides feature tubes for 2 or 3 riders at a time that whoosh you down and UP several inclines before dropping you into the pool with a significant splash. This is also busy from midday on. The imaginative (but chilly) **Shark Reef** is an upturned wreck and coral reef that you can snorkel through among 4,000 tropical fish and a number of real, but harmless, nurse sharks. Those who aren't brave enough to get in can still get a close-up through the underwater portholes of the sunken ship. The Reef is closed during the coldest months. Substantial queues build up from late morning, so do this early.

BRIT TIP
'Buy a disposable waterproof camera to tie around your wrist when you visit the water parks. We bought one cheap at Wal-Mart and have some lovely photos from Typhoon Lagoon,' says reader Judith Bingham.

Keeping out of the sun can also be a problem as there's not much shade, but a quick plunge into Castaway Creek usually prevents overheating. There are health and 4ft/122cm height restrictions on Humunga Kowabunga and Crush 'n' Gusher (not suitable for anyone with a bad back or neck, or expectant mothers).

Shopping and dining: If you have forgotten a sunhat or bucket and spade for the kids, or even your swimsuit, they are all available at **Singapore Sal's**. You CAN'T bring your own snorkels, inner tubes or rafts, but snorkels are provided at Shark Reef and you can hire inner tubes for the lagoon. For snacks and meals, **Lowtide Lou's** and **Let's Go Slurpin'** both offer a bite to eat and drinks, while **Typhoon Tilly's** and **Leaning Palms** serve a decent mix of sandwiches, burgers, salads and ice-cream. Avoid main mealtimes here if you want to eat in relative comfort. You can bring your own picnic (unlike the main theme parks), which you can eat in special scenic areas (but no alcohol or glass).

BRIT TIP
As the busiest of the water parks, Typhoon Lagoon can hit capacity quite early in the day in summer. Call 407 824 4321 in advance to check on the crowds.

Getting there: On Buena Vista Drive, ½ml/800m from Downtown Disney (see map on page 73). Admission: $46 adults, $40 3–9s (under-3s free); included with Premium and Ultimate tickets; parking free; 9am (10am off season)–dusk daily. TTTT/AAAAA.

Crush 'n' Gusher

© Disney

Disney's Blizzard Beach Water Park

Ever imagined a skiing resort in the middle of Florida? Well, Disney has, and this is the wonderful result. This park opened in 1995 and is still the largest, with all 66 acres/27ha arranged as if it were in the Rocky Mountains rather than the subtropics! That means snow-effect scenery, Christmas trees and waterslides cunningly converted to look like skiing pistes and toboggan runs. The same 'premium' offer at Typhoon Lagoon applies here: if the price doesn't scare you off completely, you can hire a **Polar Patio** (cabaña), which includes a locker, drinks mug, cooler with ice, bottled water, towels, loungers and table, and waiter service. Full day rental for up to 6 guests is $250 (admission not included). Reserve in advance on 407 939 7529 (once again, we're fans of arriving early and getting your loungers for free).

Slides and rides: Main features are **Mount Gushmore**, a 90ft/27m mountain down which all the main slides run. A ski chair-lift operates to the top, providing a magnificent view of the park and surrounding areas. Don't miss the outstanding rides here, including the world's tallest free-fall speed slide, the terrifying 120ft/37m **Summit Plummet**, which rockets you down a 'ski jump' at up to 60mph/97kph. For those not quite up to the big drop, the brilliantly named **Slush Gusher** is a slightly

Summit Plummet

less terrifying body slide. Then there is **Teamboat Springs**, a wild family inner-tube adventure and arguably the best of all the water rides; **Runoff Rapids**, a choice of 3 tube plunges; **Snow Stormers**, a daring head-first 'toboggan' run; and **Toboggan Racers**, the chance to speed down the 'slopes' against 7 other head-first daredevils. All 4 provide good-sized thrills without overdoing the scare factor. The 2 side-by-side slides of **Downhill Double Dipper** send you down 230ft/70m tubes in a race timed on a big clock at the bottom, with a real jolt half-way down!

Tike's Peak is a kiddie-sized version of the park's slides and a mock snow-beach, and **Ski-Patrol Training Camp** is a series of challenges and slides for pre-teens. **Melt-Away Bay** is a 1-acre/0.4ha pool fed by 'melting snow' (actually blissfully warm), and **Cross Country Creek** is a lazy-flowing 1½ml/800m river round the whole park that also floats guests through a chilly 'ice cave' (look out for the ice-water waterfalls!).

Shopping and dining: There is a 'village' area with a **Beach Haus** shop and **Lottawatta Lodge** fast-food restaurant (pizzas, burgers, salads and sandwiches), offering diners a grandstand view of Mount Gushmore. Snacks are also available at **Avalunch** (ouch!), the **Warming Hut**, **Polar Pub** and **Frostbite Freddie's Frozen Refreshments**.

Slush Gusher

Adjacent to Blizzard Beach are the amazing **Winter Summerland Miniature Golf Courses** (where Santa's elves hang out!), with 2 wonderfully elaborate courses that are a great diversion for children. Watch out for a riot of visual gags, as well as some tricky golf.

Getting there: Just north of *Disney's All-Star Resorts* off Buena Vista Drive (see map on page 73). **Admission:** $46 adults, $40 3–9s (under-3s free); included with Premium and Ultimate tickets; parking free; 9am (10am off-season) to dusk daily. TTTTT/AAAAA.

Wet 'n Wild

If Disney scores highest for scenic content, Wet 'n Wild, the world's first water park in 1977, goes full tilt for thrills and spills of the highest quality, with its 2 newest rides also being highly sophisticated. This park will certainly test your swimsuit material to the limit!

Wet 'n Wild is one of the best-attended water parks in the country, and its location in the heart of I-Drive makes it a major draw. Consequently, you will encounter some crowds here, though the 15 slides and rides, **Lazy River** attraction, elaborate kids' park (with mini versions of many of the slides), **Surf Lagoon**, restaurant and picnic areas absorb a lot of punters before queues develop. Waits of more than ½ hour at peak times are rare, but it is busy at weekends and throughout July as well.

BRIT TIP

The Kids' Park at Wet 'n Wild was built especially for those under 4ft/122cm tall – right down to having the only junior wave pool in the world.

Slides and rides: You are almost spoilt for choice of main rides, from the highly popular group inner-tube rides of **Surge** and **Bubba Tub**, to the more demanding **The Flyer**, **The Blast** and **Mach 5** (head-first on a mat-slide). For body slides, try the high-energy plunge of **The Storm** and the sheer terror of **Der Stuka** and **Bomb Bay**. The latter duo are definitely not for the faint-hearted. Basically, they are 276ft/23m body slides with drops as near vertical as makes no difference. Der Stuka is the straightforward slide, while Bomb Bay adds the extra terror of being allowed to free-fall on to the top of the slide. Strangely, only a minority of the park's visitors pluck up the courage to try it! There are 4ft/122cm height restrictions on Bomb Bay and Der Stuka, while older kids can enjoy the huge, inflatable **Bubble Up**, which bounces them into 3ft/1m of water. Latest enhancement is to the old Black Hole tube ride, which is now **Black Hole: The Next Generation**, a pulsating 2-person ride down a fully enclosed flume, with the addition of an explosive lighting package and other dynamic special effects.

Our favourites? We like the thrilling toboggan-like **Flyer**, which takes 4 passengers in 8ft/2m in-line tubes down more than 450ft/137m of banked curves and straights, and **The Blast**, with its 1 or 2-passenger tubes that surprise you with sudden twists and turns, explosive pipe bursts and drenching waterspouts, leading to a final waterfall plunge. And don't miss **The Storm**, a pair of identical circular slides billed as 'body coasters' – the enclosed tubes (complete with storm sound and light effects) send the rider plunging into a circular bowl, around which they spin at high speed before landing in the splash-pool below. Possibly the funniest, though, is **Disco H2O**, a superbly themed family raft ride that plunges down an enclosed

Lazy River

tube into a wildly swirling 'disco bowl' (featuring lights and a mirror ball!) before spitting you out through a waterfall. It is all accompanied by 1970s-style music and commentary to add to the fun (big queues from midday to late afternoon). Equally, **Brain Wash** is a 65ft/20m funnel ride that sends riders on 2, 3 or 4-person tubes down a long, enclosed flume into a huge swirling funnel that washes the tube wildly backwards and forwards before setting it up for the final splashdown.

For those under 4ft/122cm, the **Kids' Park** has a full range of junior-sized slides, plus a sandcastle structure with 2 semicircular waterslides and a giant bucket that fills and tips up at regular intervals. Uniquely, the children can use tubes, beach chairs and tables designed specifically for their height. The neighbouring lake is also part of the fun (though not in chilly winter and spring), adding the options for cable-operated **Knee Ski**, **Wake-Skating** and the **Wild One** (large inner tubes tied behind a speedboat). Or take a breather in the slow-flowing **Lazy River** as you float past palms and waterfalls, or abandon the water altogether for one of several picnic areas (though they can be crowded). The energetic can play beach volleyball. Lockers, showers and tube and towel rentals are all available; if you bring your own floating equipment, you must have it checked by the lifeguards.

Brain Wash

Shopping and dining: Sportswear, swimwear, sunglasses, hats and more can all be found at **Breakers Beach Shop**. For food, **Bubba's Bar-B-Q** serves chicken, ribs, fries and drinks, the **Surf Grill** features burgers, hot dogs, chicken and sandwiches, and **Manny's Pizza** has pizza (naturally) and subs. Two additional snack bars offer ice cream, funnel cakes, kettle corn and more. You can also bring your own picnic, but not alcohol or glass containers.

BRIT TIP
For all the water parks, it's a good idea to bring a pair of deck shoes or sandals that can be worn in water. All the local supermarkets sell them cheaply.

Getting there: Wet 'n Wild is ½ mile/ 800m north of I-Drive's junction with Sand Lake Road at the intersection with Universal Boulevard (see map on page 14), and just off exit 75A and 74B of I-4. **Admission:** $47.95 adults, $41.95 seniors (60+) and 3–9s (under-3s free); half price after 5pm (also included with Orlando FlexTicket). Towels $3 ($3 deposit) and lockers $5-8, or $10 ($3 deposit); parking $10; open year-round, 9.30–9pm in summer, 10am–5, 6 or 7pm at other times (**wetnwildorlando.com**). TTTTT/ AAA

Aquatica by SeaWorld

Orlando's newest and most eye-catching water park opened in March 2008 and quickly became a firm family favourite for its wonderful range of children's attractions and facilities. With the benefit of some vivid, colourful styling (inspired by the tropical Pacific cultures of the South Seas), the 59-acre/24ha park, featuring innovative rides, iconic architecture, **small animal encounters** and unique features such as private cabañas and an all-you-can-eat buffet meal option, appeals to the widest possible audience.

Slides and rides: Aquatica's signature attraction is the **Dolphin Plunge**, a twin body slide that sends riders down 300ft/91.5m of tubes and through a lagoon of playful, black-

and-white Commerson's dolphins (it's a touch gimmicky as you catch only the briefest of glimpses of them on the way down, but it is an exhilarating slide). You can then view the **Dolphins** at the end of the ride through the huge lagoon window, where the inhabitants often hang out to look at their human visitors! **Whanau Way** is a quadruple raft ride with 2 distinct variations that twist and turn before landing with a resounding splash, while **Tassie's Twisters** are double bowl rides that send riders down 1 and 2-person tubes into giant bowls before splashing back into the **Loggerhead Lane** lazy river (which also incorporates a cool coral reef viewing section). **Taumata Racer** is a fast-paced mat slide set up like an 8-lane racing toboggan run, partly enclosed and then with a double drop into daylight (queues can look long here but they usually move quickly). Family raft rides **Walhalla Wave** and **HooRoo Run** offer contrasting experiences: the longer Wave features a winding, enclosed section before a big splash finale; the latter is a shorter and straighter ride – with a couple of distinctly sudden drops on the way! New in 2010 was **Omaka Rocka**, 2 high-speed single-rider tube flumes, each with 3 sets of funnels that send you coursing up one side and down the other with a sensational 'feel it in your tummy' weightlessness before final splash-down. That is followed by not 1 but 2 wave pools, side-by-side lagoons that operate independently to create a variety of different wave patterns. **Big Surf Shores** offers the bigger, more dynamic waves, while **Cutback Cove** features gentler rolling surf (and a total of 860,000 gallons of water!). The pools front the huge, wide sandy **Beach**, which offers most of the large array of sun loungers and umbrellas, and the private cabañas (which cost from $100–225/day according to season; a deluxe cabaña is $599). Roa's Island loungers (includes 2 loungers, shade umbrella, towels and locker) can be hired for $40-60, depending on season.

BRIT TIP

Head for the Beach area when you first arrive to stake out a place to base yourselves and try to grab one of the bigger fixed umbrellas that offer the most shade.

As well as the gentle Loggerhead Lane, you will certainly want to try out the distinctly dynamic **Roa's Rapids**, which provides a helter-skelter whirl along this river feature, with a series of fountains, jets and other watery boosts to keep you bobbing along with no effort at all. Free life vests are on offer here and it is worth trying on one for the feeling of floating along in high style! Height restriction for Taumata Racer is 3ft 6in/107cm; for Walhalla Wave and HooRoo Run guests under 4ft/122cm must wear a life vest; Dolphin Plunge 4ft/122cm; Roa's Rapids, under 51in/129cm must wear a life vest, under 4ft/122cm on Loggerhead Lane.

Kids features: The big success of the park, though, is its extensive features for children, from the youngest to young teens. **Kata's Kookaburra Cove** is an exclusive area for those under

Taumata Racer

4ft/1.2m tall, with a whole range of scaled-down slides, rides, pools and fountains to provide a gentler experience for the young 'uns. By contrast, **Walkabout Waters** is a vast and frenzied 60ft/18m-high water play structure with every kind of climb and slide and all manner of water eruptions and outpourings, including 2 giant buckets that fill and dump their contents in spectacular fashion over those below. You may lose the kids in here all day! The park's **small animal encounters** are also designed to appeal to children, so watch out for the resident macaws, kookaburra, tortoises and tamanduas (a type of anteater).

> ### BRIT TIP
> Like the other water parks, Aquatica will close to new arrivals when it reaches capacity, which can be as early as 11am in peak season, and it may not reopen again until 4pm. We advise being here for opening time and chilling out on the beach when it gets busy later on.

Shopping and dining: The imaginative **Kiwi Traders** is the biggest of the 4 shops in the park, but both **Adaptations** and **Beachies** are worth a look. The food offerings are pretty inventive, too. **Waterstone Grill** offers a fine mix of salads and sandwiches, while **Mango Market** is a fresh offering of pizza, chicken tenders and wraps and speciality coffees. Perhaps the most novel feature, though, is the **Banana Beach Cookout**, which serves up a buffet

Walkabout Waters

you can sample on a one-off basis ($13.99 adults, $9.99 3–9s) or with an all-day pass ($19.99 and $11.99) that allows you to visit as often as you like through the day. The food choice is a bit more limited but still features salad, burgers, chicken, hot dogs, macaroni and cheese, fresh fruit, corn on the cob, baked beans and desserts, and non-alcoholic drinks are all included. Add another 4 snack/drinks kiosks and it's a truly impressive spread of watery fun that guarantees a full day out in high style.

> ### BRIT TIP
> Buy Aquatica tickets online for a saving on adult prices and enjoy early entry – an hour before official opening time – in summer months.

The only general drawbacks are a lack of shade in parts of the park (which adds to the value of arriving early) and long, slow-moving queues at Tassie's Twisters and the Dolphin Plunge. Long lines can also develop at the car park entrance at peak times from around 9.30 to 11am. But features like Roa's Rapids and Walkabout Waters give Aquatica elements no other water park currently has. And, if you take advantage of the new 2-park ticket with SeaWorld, it's great value as, in summer, you could spend much of the day in Aquatica and then hop over to SeaWorld for the evening entertainment.

Getting there: Just across the road from SeaWorld on International Drive, exit 71 or 72 off I-4. **Admission:** $47.95 adults, $41.95 3–9s; 2-Park Ticket (with SeaWorld) $109.95 and $99.95; 3-Park Ticket (inc Busch Gardens) $149.95 and $139.95; parking $12, locker rental $10 and $5 (plus refundable $5), towels $4; 9am–10pm (summer season), 9am–7pm (Easter) or 10am–5 or 6pm (407 351 3600, **aquaticabyseaworld.com**) TTTT/AAAAA.

That sums up the large-scale attractions on offer, but let's explore some alternatives to the mass-market experience…

8 Off the Beaten Track

or When You're All Theme-Parked Out

Orlando's main attractions are undoubtedly a lot of fun, but they can also be extremely tiring and you may well need a break from all the hectic theme park activity. Or you may be visiting again and looking for a different experience. If either is the case, this chapter is for you.

Hopefully, you will already have noted the relatively tranquil offerings of Silver Springs and Bok Tower Gardens in the previous chapter, but to enhance your view of the area further, the following are all guaranteed to take you off the beaten tourist track. This chapter could easily be subtitled 'A Taste of the *Real* Florida', as it introduces the towns of Winter Park, Disney-inspired Celebration and Mount Dora, plus the natural delights of Central Florida's different counties, the state parks, day-trips, eco-tours and sports.

ORLANDO/Orange County

Foremost among the 'secret' hideaways is the elegant northern suburb of Winter Park, little more than 20 minutes from the hurly-burly of I-Drive yet a world away from the relentless commercialism. It offers museums and art galleries, boutique shopping, numerous restaurants, walking tours, a delightful 50-minute boat ride around the lakes and, above all, a chance to slow down. You could easily spend a full day here with the attractions on offer. Take exit 87 from I-4, Fairbanks Avenue; turn right on Fairbanks and go east for 2mls/3km and turn left at the junction with Park Avenue.

Albin Polasek Museum and Sculpture Gardens: Worth a look for culture buffs and for the serene setting devoted to this Czech-American artist (10am–4pm Tues–Sat; 1–4pm Sun Sept–June, gardens open 10am–4pm Mon–Fri only, July

Albin Polasek Museum

and Aug; $5 adults, $4 seniors, $3 students, under-12s free; **polasek.org**).

Kraft Azalea Gardens: Another Winter Park highlight is on Alabama Drive (off Palmer Avenue at the north end of Park Avenue), 11 acres/5ha of shaded lakeside walkways, gardens and hundreds of magnificent azaleas. The main focal point, the mock Grecian temple, is a beautiful setting for weddings.

Leu Gardens: Midway between Winter Park and downtown Orlando is this 50-acre/20ha retreat featuring formal gardens, peaceful walks and a boardwalk overlooking Lake Rowena. The Leu House Museum is open 10am–4pm with tours every 30 minutes (last tour 3.30pm). It's on the corner of Forest and Nebraska Avenues, via Mills Avenue and Princeton Street from exit 85 on I-4 (9am–5pm daily; $7 adults, $2 children; free 9am–noon Mon; closed Christmas Day, **leugardens.org**).

Morse Museum of American Art: A must for admirers of American art pottery, American and European glass, furniture and other decorative arts of the late 19th and early 20th centuries, as it includes one of the world's foremost collections of works by Louis Comfort Tiffany. The dazzling chapel restoration from the 1893 Chicago World Expo is now on display in its original form for the first time since the late 19th century and is worth the entrance fee alone It also has special Christmas exhibitions and periodic family programmes

Leu Gardens

(9.30am–4pm Tues–Sat, 1–4pm Sun, also 4pm-8pm Fri only Nov–April; adults $3, students $1, under-12s free; free 4–8pm each Fri Nov–April; **morsemuseum.org**).

Park Avenue: The heart of Winter Park is a classy street of restaurants, fine shops and a wonderfully shaded park. At one end is Rollins College, a small but highly respected arts education centre housing the beautiful Cornell Fine Arts Museum, with the oldest collection of paintings, sculpture and decorative arts in Florida (10am–4pm Tues–Fri, 12am–5pm Sat and Sun, closed Mon and holidays; $5 adults; **rollins.edu/cfam**). You should also take the Park Avenue Walking Tour, with free maps provided by the Chamber of Commerce (on New York Avenue). The shops of Park Avenue are a cut above most and, while you may find the prices equally distinctive, just browsing is an enjoyable experience with the charm of the area highlighted by the friendliness hereabouts. For shops both unique and fun, look for **Park Promenade Jewelers**, T**en Thousand Villages** (international arts and crafts), **Bebe's** (children's clothes), the wonderfully eclectic **Bullfish** (a combination pet shop and gourmet Mediterranean food store), **Siegel's** (men's clothing) and **Jacobsons** (department store), plus **Peterbrooke Chocolatier**. Regular craft fairs and art festivals add splashes of colour to an already inviting scenario, plus live jazz in Central Park once a month on Sundays in summer. Street parking allows 3 hours free, but there is a multi-storey car park on the corner of Comstock and Park Avenue, which is a better ½-day option. Keep an eye out for the *Taste of Winter Park* in Apr and *Autumn Art Festival* in Oct (**winterpark. org** and **parkave-winterpark.com**).

Scenic Boat Tour: Started in 1938, this is located at the east end of Morse Avenue and offers a charming, 12ml/19km narrated tour of this beautiful area. It takes you around the lakes and canals, giving a fascinating glimpse of some stunning homes, boat houses and lakeside gardens (property prices in the area start at around $1m and several top $10m!).

A dining delight

Winter Park boasts some of the best dining in Orlando, with a brilliant array of chic, contemporary choices. The trendy, upmarket range includes French, Italian and even Turkish restaurants, highlighted by the **Park Plaza Gardens**, which specialises in a modern mix of American and Continental cuisines, plus a wonderful Sunday brunch. **Rocco's Italian Grille & Bar** is an exceptional authentic Italian choice, created by well-known restaurateur Rocco Potami, while **310 Park South** offers the epitome of elegant, European café culture. You can also try the pavement bistro of **Briarpatch** or Italian style of **Pannullo's,** while we are also big fans of **Luma on Park**, a 'gastropub' featuring fresh, daily specials from simple burgers to gourmet offerings and a superb wine list (lumaonpark.com). Equally, **The Ravenous Pig** has a similar wide-ranging and upscale pub choice, from its fine micro-brewery to wonderful steaks and seafood. **Palmano's Roastery & Espresso Bar** is a great place to stop just for coffee.

boardwalks where the cypress swamps, freshwater marshes, scrub and pine flatwoods are home to gopher tortoises, turtles, armadillos and especially birds (it is on the Great Florida Birding Trail). Stop by the Visitor Center to pick up a map and see its wildlife exhibits (notably the 'pig-frog'!) and enjoy an hour or two of peace and quiet (10am–5 or 6pm daily, **http://myfwc.com/recreation/ View_Destinations_site-c07.htm**).

MOUNT DORA/ Lake County

Immediately to the west and north of Orlando is this large, rural county that is home to more unspoiled Florida charms and several small-scale attractions, including a notable state park and well-known winery.

Mount Dora: This lovely city (actually, a smallish town) on beautiful Lake Dora is one of Florida's hidden gems; a day here is a genuine breath of fresh air with its unique mix of pleasant shops, restaurants, bars, inns and tours. Mount Dora is also renowned as a festival city, with 17 annual galas. Visit **mountdora.com** to see if there is one during your visit (**4 July** and **Christmas** are especially notable, while the **Sail Boat Regatta** each April is one of Florida's finest). Start with the **Mount Dora Trolley** from the **Lakeside Inn**, a 1-hour narrated trundle around the streets (11am, noon, 1 and 2pm Mon–Fri, $13 adults, $11 2–13s; 352 385 1023), giving you a good feel for one of the

Tours run 10am–4pm daily (closed Christmas) at $12 for adults and $6 for 2–11s, cash only; and this is one of the most relaxing hours you can spend in Orlando (**scenicboattours.com**).

Maitland Art Center: Further north brings you to the city of Maitland and its delightful arts centre, which features periodic travelling exhibitions as well as its own regular displays of modern American art, sculpture gardens and a good range of art classes, notably for children. There is also a guided history tour of the grounds, gardens and exhibitions on the third Mon each month (9am–5.30pm Wed–Sat, noon–5.30pm Sun; adults $3, seniors $2, children free; reservations required; 407 539 2181, **maitlandartcenter.org**).

Lake Tibet-Butler Preserve: For a more natural view of Florida, head to this small reserve just north of Walt Disney World on SR535 (Winter Garden-Vineland Rd). The 440-acre/178ha park features 4mls/6.5km of trails and elevated

Mount Dora Trolley

'Top 100 Great Towns of America', and a former key stop on the now-defunct Florida railroad. Then stroll round the compact centre, which is full of quaint shops, cafés and bars. Antique hunters are spoiled for choice but should definitely visit **Pak Ratz** and the **Village Antique Mall**, with more than 80 vendors. **Uncle Al's Time Capsule** is a must for fans of movie and celebrity memorabilia (owner Al Wittnebert also has regular celebrity signings), while other unique stores include a **Walk in the Woods** (for clothing and Crocs shoes), **Li'l Guys and Dolls** and **Thee Clockmaker Shoppe**. The town even boasts **Ridgeback Winery**, which offers tastings of its hand-crafted fruit wines (Wed–Sun, 11am–5pm). Other stops of interest include **Mount Dora Historic Museum** (the former town jail!), which displays more (free) local history, and the **Museum of Speed**, a constantly changing homage to high-powered American sports cars of yesteryear (plus other memorabilia such as vintage juke boxes and Coca-Cola machines; 10am–5pm Mon–Fri; $9/person, no under-14s; 352 385 1945, **classicdreamcars.com**).

Possibly the best way to see Mount Dora is with the fully narrated Guided Tours of **Segway of Central Florida**. They use unique, state-of-the-art, 2-wheel Segways to take small groups downtown, on to the iconic Mount Dora lighthouse and around scenic Palm Island Park. They pass some of the city's many fine B&Bs (including the award-winning

Lakeside Inn

Magnolia Inn on East 3rd Avenue) and the genteel 125-year-**Lakeside Inn**, on the National Register of Historic Places, where you can stop for a drink in Tremain's Lounge or dine in the Beauclaire Dining Room (great Sunday brunch – look at **lakeside-inn.com**). The Segway is easy to master (after a brief hands-on lesson) and this effortless and exhilarating mode of travel is ideal for the quiet streets. If you enjoy the 1-hour tour, there is a second guided tour of nearby **Dogwood Mountain**. Both cost $48/person and tours run Wed–Sun 10am, noon, and 2pm (reservations advised; 352 383 9900, **segwayofcentralflorida.com**). Riders must be 18 (16 with parent) and no more than 260lb/118kg. This is one of our favourite activities!

You can see more with **Premier Boat Tours** via the *Captain Doolittle* from the Lakeside Inn for a fascinating eco-tour of the lakes and Dora Canal. As well as gators, you may see raccoons, turtles, otters, birds of prey and other nesting birds along this beautiful waterway. There are narrated 2-hour tours daily at 11am and 2pm ($20 adults, $10 children) and 1-hour Sunset Tours $15 (bring your favourite beverages; reservations advised on 352 434 8040, **floridasecrets.com/lake_county_tours.htm**). Pontoon rentals are also available.

Getting there: On US Highway 441 north-east of Orlando, take the (toll) Florida Turnpike to exit 267A for the (toll) Western Beltway (429), and the Beltway north to its junction with 441, from where Mount Dora is 10ml/16km further north. For more info, contact the excellent Mount Dora Chamber of Commerce on 352 383 2165 or **mountdora.com**. The visitor centre is at 341 Alexander Street.

Lake Louisa State Park: Another Lake County gem just off Highway 27 (at the west end of Highway 192), this offers some beautiful countryside, with 6 lakes and rolling hills. There are over 20mls/32km of hiking trails, a picnic pavilion, swimming in Lake Louisa (with lifeguards late May–Aug), plus 20 cabins, sleeping up to 6

Mount Dora dining

You should definitely stop for a meal in Mount Dora, as it offers a wide range of temptations. Try a leisurely lunch at **Palm Tree Grille**, the charming **Goblin Market** or **5th Avenue Café**. **Mount Dora Coffee House** is the place for coffee and the **Windsor Rose** is a genuine English tea-room. For something stronger, **Maggie's Attic** is a fabulous wine bar (and an equally good gift shop) and there are notable pubs like **O'Keefe's Irish Pub** or the Icelandic flavour of **The Frosty Mug**. All the above also offer dinner, but our choice – especially if you arrive before the sun goes down – is **Pisces Rising**, a lovely Key West-themed restaurant, with fresh, stylish decor, a charming outside Tiki-bar, another even more authentic interior bar – and a grandstand view of sunsets over Lake Dora. The food is excellent, too, with fresh Florida seafood and great steaks, plus an impressive wine list (352 385 2669, **piscesrisingdining.com**).

(8am–dusk daily, entry $5/car; 352 394 3969, **floridastateparks.org/lakelouisa**). Further up Highway 27 is the **Citrus Tower**, built in 1956, with panoramic views from its 22-storey glass observation deck (9am–5pm Mon–Sat, $4 adults $2 3–11s; 352 394 4061, **citrustower.com**); and **Lakeridge Winery**, a 127-acre/51ha estate producing some award-winning wines with free tours and tastings (10am–5pm Mon–Sat, 11am–5pm Sun; 1800 768 WINE, **lakeridge winery.com**).

The newest attraction is perfect for the adventurous wanting to see more of the real Florida and anyone with kids of 16+. British-run **Revolution Offroad** is set in 230 acres/93ha of prime countryside with a private lake. They offer 3 off-road experiences – ATV, Jeep and Dune Buggy rides – plus water-sports and fishing. Their purpose-built ATV trail features 2 40-minute sessions of fab driving on these challenging but safe 4-wheel wonders (must be 16+; 12–15 can ride with an instructor). The trails and dirt tracks are all genuine wilderness but groomed for off-road activity, and you WILL get dirty, so wear old clothes (including long trousers and close-toed shoes or trainers). There is a short 'test' to ensure riders are in control, then it's off over the sand-hills and native grasslands. The 4 x 4 Experience (in a Jeep Wrangler) can be driven by anyone with a driving licence and passengers are welcome, but it is primarily about skill and not speed over the steep hills and man-made stairway. The Dune Buggies are open to all with a valid driving licence, under 280lb/127kg and under 1.9m/6ft 3in. Purely and simply, this is one of the best off-road drives in Florida – novel, enjoyable and highly addictive! Booking essential on 352 400 1322 or **revolutionoffroad.com**. ATV is $70/person; ATV & Dune Buggy or ATV & Jeep $100, or all 3 for $150. To get there, take Highway 192 west to Highway 27; go north on 27 for 3 traffic lights; turn left on Highway

Lake County Eco Tour

474 and go west until it hits 33, then go north (right) for 2mls/3km and Revolution Offroad is on the right.

OSCEOLA COUNTY

The Kissimmee area is home to much more than just hotels, motels and Mickey Mouse. You'll find some of Florida's most scenic and nature-orientated attractions here – you just need to know where to look!

Balloon trips

Florida is hugely popular for ballooning and you will often see them up, up and away in Osceola County. It's a majestic experience; the utterly smooth way in which you lift off into the early morning sky is breathtaking, but the peace and quiet, not to mention the stunning views, are awesome. It's not a cheap experience, but it is appealing to all but young children or those with a fear of heights. It can also be a highly personal ride, with basket capacity starting at just 4 people.

BRIT TIP
Dresses are not advisable for balloon trips and hard-wearing shoes for the set-up and landing areas are essential.

Orlando Balloon Rides: The main operator in central Florida, British-run, it flies every day (weather permitting), meeting at **Ramada Orlando Celebration Resort** on Highway 192 (by Marker 4) at

Boggy Creek Airboat Rides

5.30–6.30am depending on season (the best winds are nearly always early) then transferring to the take-off site. Here you can help the friendly crew set up the new, safety-designed balloons (for 4, 8, 10, 12 or 18 passengers) one of which is also disabled-accessible. Then you fly off for 1 hour, floating serenely or sinking to skim the treetops or one of the many lakes. After your flight enjoy a champagne landing ceremony before returning to the hotel for a breakfast buffet and your balloonist's certificate. It all lasts 3–4 hours and costs $175/person (inclusive of tax), $10 discount if booked online. Kids 10 and under fly free with their parents (additional children $95). Hotel pick-up is available at $10/person for the round trip, or for $20 you can be part of the chase crew and just enjoy the champagne landing and breakfast. Book well in advance on 407 894 5040 or **orlandoballoonrides.com**.

BRIT TIP
Susan says: Orlando Balloon Rides has the largest balloons in the US, with 'segmented' baskets that make you feel as if you have your own space. Very comfortable, even for a height-chicken like me!

Thompson Aire: Top local pilot Jeff Thompson, a veteran with more than 30 years' flying, also flies every day (weather permitting), meeting at the **Best Western Lakeside** on Highway 192, and returning there for a hearty buffet breakfast. Fares are $185 ($105 10–15s; 1 child 5–9 can fly free with a paying adult; discounts for 4 or more adults travelling together). Call 407 421 9322 or visit **thompsonaire.com**. Hotel pick-ups can be arranged at $15/person.

Airboat rides

The thrill of airboat rides can be experienced on many of Florida's lakes, rivers and marshes, but especially in Osceola County. An airboat is totally different from any boat ride you will have had – it's more like flying at ground level. As much a thrill as a scenic adventure, it has the bonus of exploring areas otherwise inaccessible to boats. Airboats simply skim over and through the marshes, to give you an alternative, close-up and highly personal view. Travelling at up to 50mph/80kph means it can be loud (hence you will be provided with headphones) and sunglasses are also a good idea to keep stray flies out of your eyes. It is NOT the trip for you, however, if you are spooked by crickets, dragonflies and similar insects that occasionally land in the boat! In summer months, a good insect repellent is essential.

🇬🇧 BRIT TIP

Look out for discounts on Boggy Creek's website, **bcairboats.com**, for either $1.50 off if you book online or for a $1 discount coupon.

Boggy Creek Airboat Rides: Several operations offer airboat rides in the area, from 'you-drive' boats that do barely 5mph/8kph to much bigger ones, but for the most quality-conscious (and downright friendly) operation, our vote goes to Boggy Creek. Its airboats can be found at its main site on Lake Toho at peaceful **Southport Park**, all the way down Poinciana Boulevard, off Highway 192 between markers 10 and 11, and across Pleasant Hill Road into Southport Road – about a 35-minute drive. Boggy Creek's ½-hour ride features the most modern 18-passenger airboats in Florida, skimming over the local wetlands for a close-up of the majestic cypress trees and wildlife including eagles, ospreys, snakes and turtles, as well as the ever-present gators. Southport Park has the feeling of being a million miles away from the main tourist area, and it is likely you'll see a variety of wildlife, especially in spring.

You don't need to book, just turn up, as boats go every ½ hour (9am–5pm daily; $25.95 adults, $19.95 3–10s). Don't forget the sunscreen as you can really burn on the water. It also does a 1-hour Night Tour ($49 adults, $45.95 3–10s, approx 9pm–10pm mid-Mar to mid-Nov only) for a completely different and exhilarating

experience (gator eyes glow red in the dark!), but you must book up to 2 weeks in advance. There's also a 45-minute private tour in a 6-person boat ($54.95 each), which provides an even more personal view of this area while round-trip hotel transport is offered at $50/person (including ½-hour tour). Boggy Creek Airboats make a great ½-day adventure by the time you stop on their covered picnic terrace for a drink or ice-cream (407 344 9550 or **bcairboats.com**).

Powerboat ride

Turbo's Boat Rides: Captain Turbo's motto says it all: 'Get in, sit down, shut up, hold on'! Turbo's 1998 29ft Warlock powerboat is one mean water demon, topping out at 80mph/128kph during an undeniably thrilling 25–30-minute ride across East Lake Toho. The sleek Factory One class racing boat has a specially designed hull for stability, and holds several world championships from her days on the racing circuit. Accommodating 5 guests at a time, each ride is tailored to the rider's comfort, from mild to full-out racing speed. Turbo's powerboat is eco-friendly and feels surprisingly solid and secure for a ride all the family can enjoy. Goggles are available and will fit over your sunglasses. Find Turbo's at East Lake Fish Camp (either take exit 17 off Central Florida Greeneway – 417 – and go 3mls/5km south on Boggy Creek Road, then right into East Lake Fish Camp, or take Osceola Parkway east until it hits Boggy Creek

Turbo's Boat Rides

Road. Go left and then turn right at the Boggy Creek T-junction, then right into East Lake Fish Camp after about 2mls/3km; 1-2 people $55 per person, 3-5 $45 per person; call for reservations on 407 436 4571, **turbosraceboatrides.com**).

East Lake Fish Camp is itself a little gem, offering a variety of boating and fishing options (407 348 2040, **eastlakefishcamp.net**), a pleasant outdoor terrace, as well as the wonderfully authentic rural charm of the restaurant and gift shop (8am–9pm daily). If you're here for a morning powerboat ride, consider arriving early for a huge all-day breakfast at the fish camp, where the more adventurous will want to try the local delicacies – catfish, frogs' legs and gator tail. For another great slice of local eating, the Friday all-you-can-eat catfish dinner is $12.95, or try the weekend breakfast buffet for $8.95.

Celebration

In 1994, the Walt Disney Company set out to build a 'new urban' neighbourhood, a model community with a friendly, welcoming spirit and strong traditional values. The result was Celebration, where picture-perfect Victorian homes mingle with smart, well-kept town-houses with a charming array of shopping, dining and entertainment options. Today, it is a self-sufficient, bustling town with a hospital, schools, cinema and 2 distinctive hotels. Located on Disney's southern border, Celebration is easily found off Highway 192. Enter at the

landmark water tower via Celebration Ave, then follow signs to Celebration Hotel in the town centre.

Once in the downtown area, you are spoiled for choice when it comes to shopping. Market Street shops are open 10am–9pm Mon–Sat, noon–6pm Sun, with delightful boutiques like **Market Street Gallery** (featuring Disney collectables, Swarovski crystal, Lladro, and other fine gifts), **Spot Me Kids** (children's clothing and a fun 'create your own treat' station), **Confetti of Celebration** (speciality and customised gifts) and **Lollipop Cottage** (children's clothing and gifts). Besides having a wonderfully whimsical name, **Soft as a Grape** is the place to find casual wear for the whole family. Other specialists include **Jewel Box** and **Day Dreams** (dolls, bears books). There are miles of bike and walking paths to take advantage of here, with the pretty lakefront setting, children's play area and periodic festivals. A huge event is held on **4 July**, with picnics, entertainment and face-painting plus Disney-inspired fireworks over the lake (parking is laid on at the entrance to Celebration, with a park-and-ride bus for visitors), while the **Christmas** period sees festive events and nightly snow on Market Street (**http://celebrationtowncenter.com**).

Disney's Wilderness Preserve: This authentic slice of Florida is run by the Nature Conservancy (the world's leading private international conservancy group) in Poinciana, south of Kissimmee. The restoration of a 12,000-acre/4,860ha preserve is a work in progress and allows visitors in for various (well-marked) hiking trails. The preserve's pine and scrubby flatwoods, dry and wet prairies, freshwater marshes and forested wetlands are home to more than 300 wildlife species, including bald eagles, Florida scrub-jays and sandhill cranes, Sherman's fox squirrels, eastern indigo snakes and gopher tortoises, plus more than 50 butterfly species. Come here for a chance to unwind and enjoy the peace and quiet of the Florida countryside. Located at the end of Pleasant Hill

Downtown Kissimmee

A cause for Celebration

Dining in Celebration is a real highlight. Try **Market Street Café**, a 50s-style diner serving down-home favourites such as turkey dinners, meatloaf and hearty sandwiches, or try award-winning **Café D'Antonio** for authentic Italian cuisine in a sleek, family-friendly atmosphere (407 566 2233, **antoniosonline. com**); Spanish-Cuban **Columbia** uses unique combinations of authentic ingredients to create mouth-watering dishes (407 566 1505, **columbiarestaurant.com**); **Shannon's of Celebration** offers authentic Irish food in a pretty setting; **Celebration Town Tavern**, a casual ambiance, specialising in New England seafood dishes; **Seito Sushi**, is the place for contemporary sushi and fusion dishes; and the **Imperium Food and Wine** is an excellent option for fine wines and cocktails, plus a tempting light bite menu, including soups, sandwiches, salads and flatbreads (407 566 9054, **imperiumwine room.com**). You should also consider the **Bohemian Bar & Grill** at the Celebration Hotel, a contemporary American steakhouse with old-world Florida charm.

Road (CR531; follow Hoagland or Poinciana Boulevard south off Highway 192, then turn right on Pleasant Hill; open 9am–5pm daily; $3 adults, $2 6–17s). Trails may be closed due to flooding or conservancy work, so call 407 935 0002 or visit **http://nature.org/wherewework/northamerica/states/florida/**.

Florida Eco-Safaris

For our money, this is one of the most outstanding non-theme-park attractions in Florida. Both a 4,700-acre/1,900ha wilderness preserve and working ranch, it offers a close-up of the flora, fauna and conservation issues, plus a real taste of cracker-style life ('crackers' were the original Florida cowboys of the 19th century), which is a fascinating slice of history. Eco-safaris, horseback safaris and nature walks are all on offer, but the real highlight is the new **Zipline Safari**. This 2½-hour adventure starts with a short scenic hike to the launch point, which provides a breathtaking aerial view of the preserve at up to 55ft/16.8m high. The professionally engineered course includes 7 different zip lines, 9 observation platforms and 2 sky-bridges over 3 eco-systems. The longest run is 750ft/229m and riders reach top speeds of 25mph/40kph for a really novel experience. The final zip brings you back to ground level and a visit to its wildlife interaction area, including a Florida panther, alligators and other animals. There are also themed 'party' events on Saturdays, including a Moonlight Safari on select dates, but you must book in advance (1866 854 3837, $85/person; min weight 70lb/32kg, max 275lb/125kg).

BRITTIP
For Celebration, don't stop at the first set of shops and services you come to off Highway 192. Keep going until you find Market Street and the centrepiece lake that lets you know you have found the proper downtown area.

You should certainly start at the magnificent **Cypress Restaurant and Visitor Center**, with its essential 30-minute orientation programme into the preserve's creation. Beginning as a dream of gifted young biologist and ecologist Allen Broussard, it was completed after his death (from complications of Hodgkin's disease) by his parents, Dr William and Margaret Broussard as a non-profit-making memorial to their son. The education element alone is awesome,

Florida Eco-Safaris

and the 2 tours feature a strong conservation message. The 2-hour **Coach Safari** is its stock-in-trade, a tranquil trundle in a large-wheeled, open-sided buggy round much of the woods, swamp and prairie that make up the Crescent J Ranch and Conservancy. Your guide gives the low-down on the fascinating history and environmental issues, as well as some insights into life before the tourists arrived. A boardwalk along Bull Creek affords the chance to get up close with a typical cypress 'dome' and breathe the amazingly pure air it gives out. You are likely to encounter alligators (at a safe distance), turtles, whitetail deer, armadillos and a host of bird life – including bald eagles and wild turkeys – as well as the native cattle and horses, and you'll leave with a good understanding of the *real* Florida. Eco-Safaris cost $28 ($22 6–12s) and depart daily at 10am and 1pm. **Horseback Safaris** are another feature (ages 12 and over; 10 and 11 only with proven riding experience), with the chance to enjoy their Western trail rides for 1, 2 or 3 hours with a native cracker guide. Horseback Safaris cost $40, $60 or $80 (book at least 24 hours in advance on 1866 854 3837).

> ### 🇬🇧 BRIT TIP
> Long trousers and closed-toed shoes are essential for Florida Eco-Safaris' Horse Safaris. An early morning ride here is one of the most enjoyable hours you're likely to spend in Florida.

Green Meadows Petting Farm

Horseback riding

If you want to go further into cowboy country, **Rawhide Round-up** is a ½-day experience with cattle on the Crescent J Ranch, including lunch ($99). The **Horseback Safaris** can also be extended to 2 days ($199), staying in bunk-house accommodation. Forever Florida is a good 80-minute drive out of Orlando, 40mls/64km east on Highway 192, through St Cloud as far as Holopaw, then 7½mls/12km south on Highway 441, but is well worth the journey to experience the charm and tranquillity on offer (1866 854 3837, **floridaeco-safaris.com**).

Green Meadows Petting Farm

From one extreme to another, this is guaranteed fun for kids 2–11 and their parents. It's the ultimate hands-on experience as, on the 2-hour guided tour, kids get to milk a cow, pet a pig, cuddle a chick or duckling, feed goats and sheep, meet a buffalo, chickens, peacocks and donkeys and learn what makes a farm tick. There are pony rides and a play area, tractor-drawn hay rides, and the Green Meadows Express train tour. Don't forget your camera! The shaded areas, free-roaming animals and peaceful aspect all contribute to another pleasant change of pace, especially as Green Meadows is barely 10 minutes from the tourist hurly-burly of Highway 192. Allow 3–4 hours for your visit. Drinks, snacks and gifts are available, but it is also the ideal place to bring a picnic (on Poinciana Boulevard; 9.30am–5.30pm daily, last tour 4pm; $21/person, $17/seniors, under-2s free; 407 846 0770, **greenmeadowsfarm.com**).

Osceola Pioneer Museum

Only just off the beaten track in Kissimmee, but a delightful discovery, is this small-scale homage to 19th-century Florida life, with a preserved 'cracker' homestead portraying how the original settlers lived in the 1890s. This fascinating little museum traces the history of Osceola County, and includes a cattle camp, nature walk, school house, country store and information centre with library. A recent addition is an 1890 citrus-packing operation from nearby Narcoossee, which was originally started by a family from the UK! But the real bonus is the volunteers who take you round, providing a fascinating view of life here more than a century ago (on N Bass Road, just off Highway 192 by the Wal-Mart Supercenter next to Medieval Times between markers 14 and 15. 10am–4pm Thurs–Sun; $5 adults, $2 children, under-5s free; 407 396 8644 **osceolahistory.org**).

Reptile World Serpentarium

Another throwback to an earlier time in Florida is this wonderfully kitsch roadside halt in St Cloud. Florida is actually home to a wide variety of both venomous and non-venomous snakes, and all of them can be seen here. In all, there are more than 60 species of worldwide reptile featured in the clean, indoor exhibits (including the Australian taipan – rated the world's deadliest snake), but the main feature is the twice-daily (noon and 3pm) 'milking' of venom from some of the more hazardous residents (cobras and vipers) for snake research. Snakes are its stock-in-trade, but you will also meet turtles, gators and iguanas (on east Highway 192, past St Cloud; 9am–5.30pm Tues–Sun; $6.75 adult, $4.75 6–17s, $3.75 3–5s; 407 892 6905, **reptileworldserpentarium.com**).

BRIT TIP
If you are brave enough to volunteer during the venom show, you won't actually be asked to help in this dangerous activity, but you will get the chance to stroke a boa.

Scenic Lake Tours

For a more sedate view of the local flora and fauna, try this company in downtown Kissimmee. Under the expert guidance of a local captain, you will head out on to Lake Tohopekaliga for a 1½-hour circuit in its 24ft/7m pontoon boat, taking in Makinson Island and the Shingle Creek waterway (with soft drinks, water and snacks included). Your guide will point out all the wildlife, from gators and turtles to ospreys and eagles, and you will gain a valuable insight into the local ecosystems. Once again, it's an opportunity to step into the real Florida, leaving the tourist version behind. Scenic Tours leaves the Toho Marina dock (on Lakeshore Boulevard; take Ruby Avenue off Broadway in downtown Kissimmee; 10am, noon, 2pm and 4pm Mon–Fri, 9am, 11am, 1pm and 3pm Sat and Sun; $25 adults, $15 ages 12 and under). There is also a special sunset cruise on request, plus a 2-hour Makinson Island Nature Tour, a combined cruise and guided tour of the island, daily ($50 adults, $30 children). Alternatively, try its fishing excursions on Lake Toho, some of the surrounding lakes or even inshore in the Fort Myers-Sanibel Island area. Fishing is from $250 for 2 anglers for

Fishing at Grand Lakes

4 hours to $450 for a full 8-hour day, and inshore saltwater fishing $350–625 (1800 244 9105, **fishingchartersinc. com**).

Warbird Adventures and Kissimmee Air Museum

Anyone even slightly interested in World War II aviation should consider a trip to Warbird Adventures. This is the best ride in town, bar none – guaranteed. Not only do you get to fly in one of its 3 1945 T-6 Harvard fighter-trainers, but also, after a period of getting used to the front seat of this vintage 2-seater… you get to fly it! And you don't just handle the controls; your instructor will get you doing all manner of aerobatics. This is simply the most exhilarating ride we have ever tried, enhanced by in-flight video and wingtip camera to record every moment. It's the only place we know of where, 20 minutes after walking in off the street and with no previous experience, you can be flying a warplane. Roller-coasters? They're for wimps! Mind you, this is not cheap – a 15-minute flight costs $240, a 30-minute trip is $420 and an hour $720. Aerobatics (on 30 or 60-minute flights only) cost $35, while the DVD is $50 and photos $25. Nevertheless, the memory of this would last a lifetime, and just the thought of it is still thrilling. Maximum weight is 18 stone/115kg and minimum height is 4ft/122cm. Or try your hand at piloting a helicopter (15 minutes $125, 30 is $199, 60 $375). Also on site is **Kissimmee Air Museum**, a

Warbird Adventures

combination warplane showcase and restoration centre where you can get up close with the exhibits, which include a Bell 47 helicopter, an open-cockpit Ryan PT-22, a Boeing Stearman biplane, its 3 T-6 Harvards and the amazing one-off Aerocar, plus small-scale offerings like a WWII rifle collection and Luftwaffe memorabilia. New in 2010 were the exhibits of *Air power and Pearl Harbor - the stories behind the events*, beginning with Billy Mitchell's 1924 prediction that Pearl Harbor would be attacked to the actual attack on 7 December, 1941, plus rare photos and artefacts behind the story. In the corner of the main hangar you'll find the incredible Focke-Wulf 190 restoration project (**white1foundation.org**), where the keen-as-mustard volunteer mechanics will happily explain their painstaking work. It can all be found just off Hoagland Boulevard, ½ml/800m south of Highway 192, on the left (Air Museum open 9am–5pm Mon–Sat, Sun 9am–noon; $6/person, ages 6–12 $3, under-5s free; 407 870 7366, **warbirdadventures.com** and **kissimmeeairmuseum.com**).

SEMINOLE COUNTY

You may well have arrived in the heart of Seminole County – with its historic town of Sanford – without realising it if you flew into Orlando Sanford International Airport. But it's worth pointing out the diversions here that get you well off the beaten track. In fact, if you want to finish your holiday with a day or two in the area, there are now many good hotel choices – and you can catch your breath after all the hectic theme-parking!

Altamonte Springs: Seminole County's second city (right off exit 92 of I-4) is now the area's brightest development of shops, restaurants, parks and lakeside walks, highlighted by the chic **Uptown** area. This modern, pedestrian-friendly urban scene is set around Cranes Roost Lake and features numerous small shopping plazas (as well as Altamonte Mall – see page 350), with free concerts at the Eddie Rose Amphitheater, karaoke, children's activities and other live entertainment (Fri and Sat). Some 19 restaurants and bars are added to the overall mix, notably the lively Elephant Bar Restaurant, Bahama Breeze and TooJays. Look up more at **uptownaltamonte.com**.

Black Hammock Fish Camp and Restaurant: One of the most fun and entertaining of the area's airboat rides is found off exit 44 of the Central Florida Greeneway (take SR 434 east, turn left on Deleon Street and left on Black Hammock Road). This quiet backwater on scenic Lake Jessup is home to Captain Joel Martin, a Frenchman who enjoys his Florida boating, and his ½-hour tour takes you into every nook and cranny of either the east or west lake (and this really is a great lake to explore, positively crammed with gators, including some of the biggest in Florida). It's an eye-opening adventure, and Capt Joel even keeps his own gators, large and small, at the Fish Camp. The standard rides leave every ½ hour (no reservation required) and are $23.95 and $19.95 (under-11s), but there are then 1-hour rides ($39.95 and $34.95) and 45-min night rides ($39.95/person, 4 person minimum for which reservations are required. Or try the 45-minute tour, for your party only, at $45/person, 4 person minimum, reservations required. (407 365 1244 ext 101 or 105, **theblackhammock.com**). Then grab lunch or dinner at the **Black Hammock Restaurant** (fine local delicacies, especially the catfish and gator tail, plus other dishes and a kids' menu; 11am–9pm Sun–Thurs, 11am–10pm Fri and Sat; 407 365 2201) or visit the **Lazy Gator Bar** (2pm–11pm Mon–Wed, 2pm–1am Thurs, 2pm–2am Fri, noon–2am Sat and 11am–11pm Sun), with nightly drink specials from 6.30pm–close. You can rent canoes or fishing boats and experience another view of unspoilt Florida.

Bill's Airboat Adventures: This is a 90-minute tour on the St Johns River east of Sanford in the company of river historian and conservationist Captain Bill Daniel for $45 ($30 under-13s) on his 6-person boat. Reservations required, minimum $160, but if you're a smaller party you can be put on a list to combine groups. (407 977 3214, **airboating.com**).

Central Florida Zoological Park: This private, non-profit organisation puts a pleasant, natural accent on the zoo theme, set in a wooded 116 acres/47ha of unspoilt Florida countryside with boardwalks and trails around all the attractions. These include more than 100 species of animal, weekend feeding demonstrations, educational programmes, a picnic area, pony rides and a butterfly garden, plus the Zoofari Outpost gift shop and a new water play area. It's good value at $11.95 for adults, $9.95 for seniors (60+) and $7.95 for 3–12s and is open 9am–5pm daily (not Thanksgiving Day or Christmas Day). Recent updates have enlarged several exhibits and added new habitats, including an Australian section with emus and kangaroos, while the Tropical Splash Ground is a great way for kids to cool down, with animal 'fountains', raining trees, a water tunnel and bucket dump. A big new expansion in 2009 added **ZOOm Air Adventures**, a separate series of eco-friendly rope bridges, zip lines, guide wires and other aerial challenges through the Zoo's treetops. The 2 courses can be taken separately or combined (4ft 6in/137cm to take part), while there are also 2 separate children's courses (for 3–5ft/92–152cm). It costs $22.95

ZOOm Air Adventures

for the Upland course and $14.95 for the kids' versions, while the combo Upland and Rainforest costs $39.95 (off exit 104 of I-4; 407 323 4450, **centralfloridazoo.org**).

> ### BRIT TIP
> Visit Central Florida Zoo at the weekend and you will be offered a series of educational and enjoyable animal encounters (ranging from gators and snakes to hedgehogs).

Rivership Romance: For a lower-key approach, this is a great choice (daily out of downtown Sanford), especially for the lunch cruises on the wildlife-rich St John's River. The old-fashioned steamer can take up to 200 in comfort and adds a fine meal, live entertainment and river narration, as well as providing a relaxing alternative to the tourist rush. Choose from the 3-hour lunch cruise (11am–2pm Mon, Wed, Fri, and Sat; $38/person), 4–hour lunch cruise (11am–3pm Tues and Thurs; $48.50), or Moonlight Dinner Dance (7.30–11pm Sat; $53.75, all drinks extra) or the **Sunday Brunch Cruise**, with live entertainment (11am–2pm, $38). There is an additional $2.50 port charge for every cruise. Its dock can be found off exit 101A of I-4, east into Sanford, then left on Palmetto Ave (407 321 5091, **rivershipromance.com**).

St Johns River Cruise: At Blue Spring State Park, there's an immensely personable 2-hour nature tour of this historic waterway, with interactive narration of the flora, fauna

Fishing in Seminole County

(including manatees in winter) and history. It leaves from Orange City marina at 10am and 1pm daily (not Thanksgiving or Christmas Day). Take Highway 17/92 north from Sanford to French Avenue and head west for 1ml/1.6km ($22 adults, $20 seniors, $16 3–12s; 407 330 1612, **sjrivercruises. com**).

Sanford: The heart of Seminole County, this quaint town on Lake Monroe boasts a historic centre full of brick-paved streets, antique shops and an artist colony regeneration project. It's very much small-town America, having lost the growth battle with Orlando years ago, but it makes a peaceful diversion with some lovely walks, notably along the **Riverwalk**. Head for **Sanford Museum** (520 East 1st Street) for an overview of the city's incorporation – in 1877 under the patronage of pioneering lawyer and diplomat Henry Sanford – as a hub on the St John's River, the 'Nile of America'. The free museum (11am–4pm Tues–Fri, 1–4pm Sat) illustrates the life and times of the city's founder, its growth into the 'celery capital of the world' and modern history as a US naval base. From there, head on to **First Street** and check out the many restored turn-of-the-century buildings, stopping for a bite at **Two Blondes & A Shrimp** or **The Hart Sisters Café, Tea Room and Catering**. It's a pretty setting for a meal, serving sandwiches, salads, quiches and soufflés, as well as afternoon tea, on Park Avenue, 13 blocks out of the town centre (11am–3pm Tues–Fri, 11am–4pm Sat; 407 323 9448, **hartsisters.com**).

State Parks: You could, of course, just head for one of Seminole County's splendid parks and follow the well-marked trails. **Wekiva Springs State Park** offers bike rentals, hiking, canoeing, swimming, picnic areas and shelters, and **Little Big Econ** state forest has 5,048 acres/2,045ha of scenic woodlands and wetlands. **Spring Hammock Preserve** offers 1,500 acres/607ha of wilderness to explore and the **Lake Proctor** area has 6mls/10km of equestrian, hiking and biking adventures. There are more trails along the Econlockhatchee River at the **Econ River Wilderness Area**, while **Chuluota** has 625 acres/253ha and the **Geneva Wilderness Area** 180 acres/73ha, including **Ed Yarborough Nature Center.**

Where to stay: At Altamonte Springs, try the new **Embassy Suites Orlando North** (407 834 2117), while the rapidly-growing Lake Mary area (right off exits 98-101 of I-4, closest to downtown Sanford) offers the **Courtyard by Marriott** (407 444 1000), **La Quinta Inn & Suites** (407 805 9901), **Hampton Inn Suites** (407 995 9000), **Homewood Suites** (407 805 9111), **Candlewood Suites** (407 585 3000) and the smart **Hyatt Place** (407 995 5555). The new jewel in the crown here is the **Westin** (407 531 3555) with **Shula's 347 Grill**, a stylish, casual eatery with exceptional Black Angus steaks, plus gourmet salads, speciality dishes, and full bar. Lake Mary has become a real eco-traveller's delight and a worthwhile family day away from the hectic pace. An overnight stay will reward visitors with a chance to unwind and de-stress amid some of Central Florida's prettiest natural scenery. Also here are **Colonial Town Center,** a new plaza of shops and restaurants, including the Irish pub style of **Liam Fitzpatrick's**, Mexican **Vamonos Taqueria** and **Lake Mary Vineyard Wine Company**, and **Route 46**, an excellent evening entertainment/dining complex (see also page 305).

BRIT TIP
The Visit Seminole website (see below) offers discounts such as a '2nd night free' with many of its hotel bookings, military discounts, and other special offers.

More info: See **visitseminole.com** or go to one of the Visitor Centers at Orlando Sanford International Airport (in the Welcome Center as you exit the main building) or the new office at the Heathrow junction of I-4 (exit 98, go west on Lake Mary Blvd, right on International Parkway and left at AAA Drive; 407 665 2900).

CITRUS COUNTY

If you enjoy the Seminole County experience, you may want to travel a little further, in which case the 2 state park delights of Citrus County, on the Gulf Coast north-west of Orlando, are well worth seeking for a day out.

Crystal River Preserve State Park: Head to this park, just north of Homosassa Springs, to find another wildlife fiesta. The Crystal River is home to the endangered manatee and it is possible to go swimming with these wonderful creatures, either on a self-guided or an organised tour. Winter and spring are ideal times for manatee sightings, but the park offers year-round adventure, with hiking and biking trails, kayaking, canoeing and fishing – or just pack a picnic lunch and enjoy a relaxing afternoon amid the natural beauty.

BRIT TIP
Never touch or disturb a wild manatee. They are protected animals and there are heavy fines, strictly enforced, for harassing them.

Getting there: Take the (toll) Florida Turnpike north to I-75, then, almost immediately, take SR44 west to Crystal River. **Admission:** Free (8am–dusk; 352 563 0450, **floridastateparks. org/crystalriverpreserve**).

Homosassa Springs Wildlife State Park: Another major venture into the wealth of Florida nature, this park also showcases the manatee

Homosassa Springs Wildlife State Park

(via its underwater observatory), plus whooping cranes, deer, bobcats, black bear and even a hippopotamus among an active display of rehabilitating animals. There are daily educational programmes on its wildlife (10.30am, 11.30am, 12.30pm, 1.30pm, 2.30pm and 3.30pm), notably Florida's snakes and birds of prey, plus a hands-on children's education centre. The park's 210 acres/85ha take in some of the state's loveliest landscape as well as the headwaters of the Homosassa River and this is extremely popular in the spring.

Getting there: As for Crystal River, but turn left on to CR490 just after Lecanta on SR44. **Admission:** $13 adults, $5 6–12s (9am–5.30pm, last entry 4pm; 352 628 5343, **homosassasprings.org**).

BREVARD COUNTY

Out on the Atlantic coast you'll find the immense beauty of the Cocoa Beach Thousand Islands. Tranquil canals wind past mangrove stands, wildlife flourishes in the still waters and the Indian River Lagoon Estuary is one of the most biodiverse eco-systems in the world.

Island Boat Lines: This family owned enterprise offers eco-tours, fishing and the wonderful **Indian River Queen** dinner boat, recalling Mark Twain's tales of paddleboats and peaceful gentility. A relaxing 2-hour **In Search of Wildlife Eco-tour** onboard Coast Guard-certified pontoon boats departs from the Banana River Marina, passing some of Cocoa

Island Boat Lines

Beach's most impressive homes before heading into the canals. Here you may spot bottlenose dolphins as they hunt for fish or swim lazily in the warm waters, catch sight of a manatee bobbing just below the surface and marvel at the staggering variety of coastal birds creating a ruckus in the trees along the banks. Knowledgeable tour guides offer a wealth of information about the flora and fauna, encouraging visitors to ask questions and move about the boat for a closer look (no worries about getting the 'scenic' side!). Tours run at 10am and 1pm Mon–Sat, 2pm Sun ($28 adults, $26 seniors and military personnel, $23 2–12s; book in advance on 212 206 3370; **islandboatlines.com**) **Getting there:** Take the Beachline Expressway (Hwy 528) to Hwy 1 south, then Merritt Island Causeway (Hwy 520) east to S Banana River Dr, apx. 1ml/1.6km south, with the marina on the right.

Indian River Queen: Also used for private events, this beautifully appointed triple-deck paddlewheel riverboat is open to the public on weekends, with an elegant **Friday Night Dinner Cruise** featuring live music, themed dinner buffet (varies; Traditional Riverboat BBQ, Southern, Caribbean or Italian) and full bar. Captain Georges and owners Penny and John provide an authentic Southern hospitality that makes your cruise a truly memorable event. Boarding begins at 6.30pm, sailing from 7–9.20pm ($40/person). On Sundays, try the **Jazz Cruise** with live music and 'It's Tea Time' buffet of Southern BBQ pork sandwiches, pasta salad and homemade cookies. Boarding begins at 2pm, sailing from 2.30–5pm ($30/person; reservations required on 321 454 7414 or **indianriverqueen.com/events.cfm**). Film buffs may also recognise the 'Queen' from the movie *Out of Time* starring Denzel Washington. **Getting there:** To reach Cocoa Village Marina, take the Beachline (Hwy 528) east to Hwy 1, go south to Hwy 520, make a slight left at Bee Line, continue to N Cocoa Blvd, turn left at King, then left again at Delannoy.

Brevard Inshore and Nearshore Fishing: Also out of Banana River Marina, Captain Pete offers inshore fishing along the Indian River, Banana River and Sykes Creek, or out of Port Canaveral (summer only) for offshore fishing. Cast a line in for local favourites snook, black drum, redfish and gator trout. The scenery is as exciting as the fishing, with rays and horseshoe crab skittering along the shallow flats and the water so clear you may spot your prey before you feel it on your line. Offshore catches include tarpon, cobia and redfish. Florida native Captain Pete has been fishing here for 15 years and knows all the best spots (inshore 6-hour trip for 1–4 anglers $275-$350; 4-hour trip $225-300; offshore, calm days only, up to 3 anglers, 4-hour $350, 6+ $475; fishing license, tackle, bait and bottled water included; call for reservations on 321 302 0549, **brevardinshore.com**).

Cocoa Beach Sportfishing: Board the fully equipped *Centerfold*, a 33ft/10m Tournament-rigged boat, and get ready for big game fishing! Troll for dolphin (the fish, not the mammal), sailfish, wahoo, kingfish, grouper and more with a crew who boast plenty of experience in finding 'the big one' (Captain Tim has been fishing these waters for 32 years). Captain Tim, along with Captains Beau and Brandon, share their passion for fishing with anglers of all experience levels (novice to pro), and do it with great humour, dedication and professionalism. *Centerfold* offers 9-hour trips at $800, 5-hour trips $600, up to 6 passengers; the 24ft Center Console *Killer Bee* accommodates 1–4 passengers at $550 for 8 hours, $400 for 5 hours, calm weather only (fishing license, tackle, bait, fish cleaning included; reservations on 321 848 2662, **cbsportfishing.com**). For more Cocoa Beach info, see page 284.

Excursion operators

For those without a car (or anyone just looking to put their feet up for a day or two), there is an increasing number of tours and day trips offered in and around Orlando, visiting as far afield as the Everglades, Miami, Florida Keys and even the Bahamas. And, if you are prepared to put up with a long day out (up to 16 hours), you can see a lot this way. However, if the main attraction of a trip to the Everglades is the airboat ride, you are better off going to Boggy Creek Airboats (see page 259) and avoiding the journey.

BRIT TIP
More info on all tours on 407 352 5151 or visit **floridadolphintours. com**. To enjoy our special discount, just call and say: '12½% off with the *Brit Guide*, please!'

Florida Dolphin Tours: Make this first on your list to check as it offers an increasingly diverse range of memorable excursions, notably its swim-with-dolphins trips to the Florida Keys and manatee swim adventure. More to the point, as a *Brit Guide* partner, it offers readers a 12½% discount on all tours (see inside back cover). Choose from: **Cocoa Beach and Airboat**, an excellent-value all-day trip to Cocoa beach for an afternoon of fun in the sun, an exciting airboat ride in search of gators on the St Johns River, all with a wonderful lunch included ($75 adult, $59 3–9s); the **Kennedy Space Center** trip, with transportation to both the Space Center and Astronaut Hall of Fame – ask about options such as including an airboat ride, Lunch with an Astronaut, or even

Inshore fishing at Banana River

the Ultimate Kennedy Experience (from $95 adult, $85 3–11s); **Swim with the Manatees**, another all-day adventure (and the No.1 Florida attraction), featuring breakfast and a 2-hour boat trip on the picturesque Crystal River (with snorkel and mask to check out at close quarters where the manatees swim). There are picnic lunches, airboat rides and trips to Homosassa State Wildlife Park, too, plus an educational briefing on manatees and a chance to see them being fed from the underwater viewing area ($119 adult, $89 3–11s); **Swim with the Dolphins**, its trademark tour, a holiday within a holiday: a 2-day excursion to the beautiful Florida Keys with a 2-hour dolphin programme (and the choice of an organised or unstructured dolphin swim), including transport, accommodation, dolphin swim, buffet-style evening meal, continental breakfast, Everglades airboat ride, (interactive!) alligator and snake-handling show, and ½-day to see Miami with shopping at Bayside or a boat tour along the inland waterways. The dolphin programme includes a full briefing and about 30 minutes in the water, with dolphin contact guaranteed ($199–349; add Star Island boat tour for $30); **American Football**, where high-energy action is up for grabs with an all-day excursion to see the Jacksonville Jaguars of the National Football League ($109/

person, Aug–Dec); **NBA Basketball**, more sporting excitement with the Orlando Magic ($99/person, Nov–Apr; playoff games $179); **Disney limo trips** give you the Grand Floridian character breakfast, Chef Mickey's character dinner buffet or Planet Hollywood VIP (from $79); **Clearwater Paradise**, a day-trip to the Gulf Coast for a beach adventure, including a ride on the huge Sea Screamer powerboat (or other optional boat excursions), lunch, a chance to see the local dolphins in their natural environment AND work on your tan! (from $75 and $65-$90 and $75); and a **Shopping Extravaganza**, an all-day retail adventure with stops at the top Malls and outlets like Super Wal-Mart and Lake Buena Vista Factory Shops, breakfast and lunch included ($45 and $35; floridadolphintours.com).

Gator Tours: This company offers a wide range of more than 30 tours and sight-seeing around Orlando but specialises in day trips to the Kennedy Space Center and Daytona Race Speedway. The company also features Space Shuttle launches and landings, a wide range of sporting events (including golf, Orlando Magic basketball and motorsport), shopping excursions and even a unique **Orlando City Tour** ($65 adults, $49 2–11s). Its **Kennedy Space Center** trips go daily and some include an airboat ride ($95–115 adults, $85–99 2–11s; $55/person for transportation only). It offers a **Shoppers Paradise** ($39 and $29) excursion to Florida Mall and several of the discount outlets. Other tours include transportation to the **Beaches** at Clearwater ($55); an **Everglades and Miami** adventure ($125 and $99); a 1-way or round-trip transport to Miami ($75 and $99); and even transport (with or without tickets) to **Gatorland** ($35–49). For full pricing, call 407 522 5911 or visit gatortours.com.

Of course, a great day-trip can also be had by just jumping into your hire car and heading for the superb Beaches (see Chapter 9, The Twin Centre Option).

Clearwater Beach

© OCVB

SPORT

In addition to virtually every form of entertainment known to man, central Florida is one of the world's biggest sporting playgrounds, with a huge range of opportunities to either watch or play your favourite sport.

Golf

Without doubt, the No.1 sport is golf, with almost 200 courses in the central Florida area. The weather makes it a popular pastime, but some spectacular courses, many designed by legends like Greg Norman, Tom Watson, Arnold Palmer and Jack Nicklaus, add to the attraction, and there are numerous packages for golfers of all abilities. With an 18-hole round, including cart hire and taxes, from as little as $40 (average around $75), it's an attractive proposition and quite different from British courses. If you go in for 36-hole days, it's possible to save up to $30 by replaying the same course, while it is cheaper to play Mon–Thurs than Fri–Sun. Sculpted landscapes, manicured fairways and abundant water features and white-sand bunkers add up to some memorable golf. Winter is the high season, hence more expensive, but many courses are busy year-round. Be aware some courses pair golfers with little thought given to age, handicap etc., so, if 2 of you turn up, you may be paired with 2 strangers.

BRIT TIP
Golf balls are inexpensive in Florida, so there's no need to bring your own. Good-quality clubs are usually available for hire, including top brands.

Virtually every course will offer a driving range to get you started, plus lockers, changing rooms and showers, while the use of golf carts is universal (many include the GPS system, which gives the yardage for every shot). They all feature comforts like iced-water stations and drink carts that circulate the course (don't forget to tip the trolley drivers). Some have swimming pools, and all offer a decent bar and restaurant afterwards!

Your best starting point is visiting one of the 5 **Edwin Watts** golf shops around Orlando for a free copy of the *Golfer's Guide* or the *Guide to Golf* for a handy introduction to most of the courses (and perhaps some new clubs at the Watts National Clearance Center just south of Wet 'n Wild on I-Drive; 407 352 2535, **edwinwatts. com**). **Tee-Times USA** (1888 465 3356, **teetimesusa.com**) offers excellent advice and a reservation service. Daytona Beach has an excellent website, **golfdaytonabeach.com**, devoted to the sport in its area (1800 881 7065), while **Visit Florida** also has its own golf section (**visitflorida.com/golf**).

Professional Golf Guides of Orlando: For a unique and personal touch, you can't beat this all-in-one service, led by owner/operator and PGA member Phillip Jaffe, who is a mine of golf lore and knowledge, as well as great company. The guides take up to 3 at a time around some of the finest courses, and can supply transport and clubs if required. The playing lesson is of the highest quality and includes full on-course instruction, course management strategies, game analysis, improvement suggestions, shot-making demos and a wrap-up lesson to leave you with the skills and knowledge to take your game to the next level. It's an eye-opening experience to play alongside Phillip and his staff of professionals and well worth it for the keen golfer who wishes to improve their game in 1 round. It costs $195 for 1 player, $245 for 2 and $295 for 3, while there are

Disney golf course

© Disney

also driving range lessons at $75/hour or a 3-lesson package at $200 (407 227 9869, **progolfguides.com**). Alternatively, the **Nick Faldo Golf Institute** on the lower portion of I-Drive (1888 463 2536) is a great place to hit a few balls.

Walt Disney World: Quick to attract the golf fanatic, Disney has 4 high-quality courses, including the 7,000yd/6,400m **Palm**, rated by *Golf Digest* in its top 25 (the 18th hole is reputedly one of the toughest in America), plus a 9-hole par-36 course, **Oak Trail**. Fees are $89–135 for Disney resort guests and $99–145 for visitors ($38 at Oak Trail), with a third off after 3pm. Call 407 938 4653 for tee-times. Private and group lessons are available under PGA professional guidance, with video analysis and a range of club rentals.

BRIT TIP

Some of the best tee-times at *Walt Disney World* golf courses are reserved for those staying at a Disney resort.

Champions Gate: Challenging and eye-catching, the 2 magnificent Greg Norman-designed courses to the south of Disney (exit 58 off I-4) are the International (a British-style links course) and the National (a more traditional style). The practice facilities, clubhouse, service and coaching (at the HQ of the renowned David Leadbetter Academy) are world class, and there are stay-and-play packages with the superb Omni Orlando Resort (407 787 4653, **championsgategolf.com**).

Champions Gate

Golf at Walt Disney World

Falcon's Fire: An outstanding course in Kissimmee, featuring the ProShot digital caddy system carts and with some extensive renovations in 2009. Plenty of water around the course assures a testing 18 holes, but it is highly picturesque (407 239 5445, **falconsfire.com**; $69-99).

Grande Lakes Orlando: This wonderful resort complex just off John Young Parkway is another Greg Norman masterpiece, offering 18 holes of Florida nature with a caddie-concierge service (call for rates, 407 206 2400, **grandelakes.com**).

Hawk's Landing: At the Orlando World Center Marriott, this beautiful course boasts extensive practice facilities, an award-winning shop, resort exclusivity and the world-class teaching skills of Bill Madonna's Golf Academy (1888 305 9236, **marriottworldcenter.com**; from $89).

Hyatt Grand Cypress: A luxury experience on Winter Garden-Vineland Road (407 239 1904, grandcypress.com/golf; $120–190), with 3 elegant 9-hole courses and a superb 18-hole links-style offering (all designed by Jack Nicklaus).

Kissimmee Oaks: Some majestic moss-draped oaks as well as 18 holes of memorable lakeside golf, all just 3½mls/6km south of Highway 192 in the Oaks Community off John Young Parkway (407 933 4055, **kissimmeeoaksgolf.com**; $55–85).

Legends Golf and Country Club: Just 25 minutes from Disney on

Highway 27 towards Clermont, this has a pleasant layout with rolling hills (unusual for Florida) in an ultra-peaceful location (352 243 1118, **legendsgolforlando.com**; $71–85).

Magnolia Plantation: Up in Seminole County, this wooded haven feels miles from the theme park world yet is just a ½ hour away up I-4 among the lakes of the Wekiva River basin. Phillip Jaffe rates it a 'must-play' course (407 833 0818, **magnoliaplantationgolfclub.com**; $45–90).

MetroWest Country Club: On South Hiawassee Road, north of Universal Orlando (407 299 1099, **metrowestgolf.com**; $90–130), this is a 7,051yd/6,447m masterpiece designed by Robert Trent Jones Snr, featuring elevated tees and greens, with rolling fairways and expansive bunkers.

Mystic Dunes: Just off Highway 192 near the Disney entrance, this course winds through native oaks and other vegetation and is a real test. There's a wonderful menu at the clubhouse, plus the latest equipment (407 787 5678; **mysticdunesgolf.com**; $55–110).

Orange Lake Country Club: A massive vacation resort just 4mls/6km from Disney. It offers two 18-hole courses, a 9-hole course and a par-3 floodlit 9 (407 239 1050, **orangelake.com**; $60–120).

Reunion Resort and Club: This extravagant club (in Davenport, just south of Disney, exit 54 off I-4) has 3 courses – a Watson, Palmer and Nicklaus collaboration, with 18 holes designed by each. Watson's 7,257yd/6,636m Independence Course is the most challenging, with a style not dissimilar to Augusta National (1888 300 2434, **reunionresort. com**; $50–85). Golf here is restricted to those who own property in the resort or are staying here (see page 97) but, with the 5-star clubhouse, it is well worth it.

Shingle Creek: A beauty from talented local architect Dave Harman, set in dense oaks and pines along historic Shingle Creek. Within a mile of the Convention Center, it is a world-class facility with some amazing features, at the heart of this 5-star resort. The Brad Brewer Golf Academy is highly rated by Golf magazine and features a teaching range with state-of-the-art technology (407 996 3306, **shinglecreekgolf.com**, $65–110).

Sugarloaf Mountain: This new club, the first in Florida from the respected team of Bill Coore and Ben Crenshaw, is carefully sculpted to follow the natural features of the land and offers 18 holes of the finest golf in the state (407 544 1104, **themountain.cc**; from $89).

Timacuan Golf Club: A stunning 7,047yd/6,444m championship course in Lake Mary (near Sanford), the front 9 resembles a Scottish links layout while the back 9 is all pineland and nature (407 321 0014, **golftimacuan.com**; from $85).

Victoria Hills: Rolling and aptly named, you'll find this in DeLand (midway between Orlando and Daytona Beach, exit 116 of I-4). It gets a big thumbs-up from Phillip Jaffe ('A great track, very challenging!'), with a par-72 course and superb practice facilities (386 738 6000, **stjoegolf.com**; $40–80).

There are dozens of others, so this is only a sample. Don't be afraid to ask if green fees are negotiable, as they can often be reduced at quiet times of the year or even on a quiet day. There are also often reductions for seniors. When you book, check on the dress code, as there are differences from club to club. Typically, you need a

Magnolia Plantation

collared shirt, Bermuda shorts and no denim.

Fans: For those just looking to see the stars in action, Orlando has two big annual events. The **Arnold Palmer Invitational** at the Bay Hill Club off Apopka-Vineland Road in west Orlando (21–27 Mar 2011) is a major tournament, with Ernie Els the winner in 2010 (407 876 7774, **arnoldpalmerinvitational.com**). The **Children's Miracle Network Classic** is another big PGA date each Nov, on Disney's superb Palm and Magnolia courses (407 835 2525, **childrensmiraclenetworkclassic.com**).

Mini-golf

Not exactly a sport, but definitely for fun, Orlando's many extravagant mini-golf centres are a big hit with kids and fun for all the family (if you still have the legs after a day at the parks!). Several attractions and parks offer mini-golf as an extra, but for the best, try the self-contained centres, of which there is a large variety. Typically, Disney has some of its own.

Disney's Fantasia Gardens Miniature Golf: Next to the Swan Hotel just off Buena Vista Drive is a 2-course challenge over 36 of the most varied holes of mini-golf you will find. Fountains leap, hippos dance, and broomsticks march on the 18-hole crazy-golf-themed **Fantasia Gardens** – its style is taken from the classic film *Fantasia*, meaning lots of cartoon fun and a riot of visual gags as well as some tricky mini-golf. Watch out for

Pirates Cove Mini-golf

Toccata and Fugue in D Minor, where good shots are rewarded with musical tones, and The Nutcracker Suite, where obstacles include dancing mushrooms! **Fantasia Fairways** is a cunning putting course, complete with rough, water hazards and bunkers to test even the best golfers. The 18 holes range from 40ft/12m to 75ft/23m, and it can take more than an hour to play a full round ($11.75 adults, $9.75 children, 10am–11pm daily).

Winter-Summerland Mini-Golf: You'll find this at the entrance to Blizzard Beach water park. Divided into 2 18-hole courses, these mini works of art feature a 'summer' setting of surf and beach tests (watch out for squirting fish) and a 'winter' variety of snow and ice-crafted holes, all with a welter of visual puns as befits the vacation resort of Santa's elves (yes, that's the theme, and kids love it – you can even see the marks where Santa landed his sleigh!). An adult round is $11.75 ($9.75 3–9s), a double round is half price (10am–11pm; Blizzard Beach admission not required).

International Drive: Mini-golf is a staple part of the scene here, with no fewer than 6 courses in the vicinity. Check out the 18-hole **Congo River** set-up in front of the Sheraton Studio City hotel and its 36-hole course just south of Wet 'n Wild ($10.95 adults, $8.95 under-10s; see **congoriver.com** for money-off coupon; 10am–1pm Sun–Thurs, 10am–midnight Fri and Sat); **Hawaiian Rumble** has 36 holes next to WonderWorks on I-Drive (and in Lake Buena Vista on Apopka-Vineland Ave; 9am–11.30pm Sun–Thurs, 9am–midnight Fri and Sat; $9.95 adults, $7.95 4–10s for 18 holes and $14.95 and $11.95 for 36; see **hawaiianrumbleorlando.com** for a discount coupon); the unusual indoor, glow-in-the-dark 18 holes of the **Putting Edge** at Festival Bay, at the top of I-Drive (10am–9pm Mon–Sat, 11am–7pm Sun; $9.35 adults, $8.35 7–12s, $6.85 5–6s); **Pirates Cove** remains the original I-Drive set-up, with caves, waterfalls and rope bridges to test your skills over twin 18-hole courses (the Captain's Course and harder **Blackbeard's Challenge**; 9am–11.30pm daily; $10.95 adults, $9.95 children, or $16.95 and $14.50 for all 36). There is a near-identical **Pirates Cove** set-up at Lake Buena Vista at the back of the Crossroads shopping plaza. Finally, the extensive **Gator Golf & Adventure Park** is just past Carrier Drive, next to Murphy's Arms Pub. With a free gator show each evening, you can sink your teeth into a round of surprisingly challenging mini-golf (10am–11pm; $9.99/person, $4.99 before 4pm).

Kissimmee: Here you'll find the wonderfully scenic 36-hole **Congo River Golf & Exploration Co** set-up on Highway 192 (by marker 12; $10.95 adults, $8.95 under-10s; 10am–11pm Sun-Thurs, 10am-midnight, Fri-Sat, **congoriver.com**). Then there are the 2 imaginative cowboy-themed mini-golf courses of **Bonanza Golf** (also on Highway 192 by marker 5) 9am–11pm Mon-Fri, 9am-midnight Sat and Sun). **Pirates Cove** is a 36-hole course next to Old Town (behind the Red Lobster restaurant, between markers 9 and 10; 9am–11.30pm); as is **Jungle Golf** (Highway 192 at mile markers 4 and 5; 9am–11.30pm; $8.95 adults, $7.95 4–12s, all-day play for $12.95; a second location is near Celebration at marker 8, **junglegolfminigolf.com**). **Pirates Island Adventure Golf** is just off Highway 192 between marker 14 and 15 (open 9am).

Freshwater fishing

Freshwater fishing on central Florida's abundant rivers and lakes attracts enthusiasts worldwide. In addition, many find a quiet day's angling provides an enjoyable change of pace. The primary draw for most is the opportunity to catch giant Florida bass – which often grow to record sizes in the area's grassy waters – and view some of the wildlife in its natural environment.

To fish in a lake or river you need a Florida Freshwater Fishing License, from the Florida Fish and Wildlife Commission (**http://myfwc.com/License/Index.htm** to purchase online at $2.25 surcharge with a credit card). You'll

be issued with a temporary licence number within minutes, enabling you to fish right away. A permanent licence will be mailed within 48 hours. A 3-day licence costs $17. It's advisable to book at least 2 weeks in advance, especially at peak periods.

AJ's Freelancer Bass Guide Service: This long-running company specialises in trophy bass fishing on Lake Toho in Kissimmee. Toho is rated the best big bass lake in the USA, and AJ's holds the record for largemouth bass – 16lb 10oz/7.5kg! Saltwater trips are also offered. The Freelancer is owned and operated by Captain A James Jackson, one of the top guides in the country, providing a personalised service to both regular and novice fishermen. All guides are experienced, full-time professionals and run trips of 4, 5, 6 and 8 hours. Rates start at $250 for a ½-day (4-hour) guided trip, max 3 clients per boat ($50 for 3rd person). For other services, photos, testimonials and fish reports, visit the excellent website **orlandobass.com**. For reservations call 407 348 8764.

Ultimate Guide Service: Another personal guide and fishing service with 36 years' experience and with trophy bass the principal aim, this is led by Captain Jim Passmore and is great for novices and even better for those seeking a real challenge. The patient captain (or one of his pro guides) will steer you through the full bass-fishing process and ensure you get the best experience on the local waters. It makes for a superb day or

Freshwater fishing

½-day and their attitude is notably one of low-environmental impact and extremely conservation-conscious. It costs $250 for a ½ day (4 hours) of fishing, $300 for ¾ of a day (6 hours) or $350 for a full day, not including fishing licence, lunch and bait. Or just take their 1-hour scenic boat ride to view the local wildlife at $25/person (407 572 5391, **fishcentralfla.com**).

For other opportunities, try **Scenic Lake Tours** (see page 263, or see **visitkissimmee.com**, click on *Visitors*, then *Things To Do* and *Get Outdoors*). Go bass fishing (catch-and-release) at Walt Disney World (from any of 11 of its resort hotels, plus the Marketplace at Downtown Disney) for $230/person or $270 for 2 hours for a boat with up to 5 people. Book 24 hours in advance on 407-939-7529.

Water sports

Florida is mad keen on water sports of all types. So, on any area of water bigger than your average pond, don't be surprised to find the locals water-skiing, jetskiing, knee-boarding, canoeing, paddling, windsurfing, boating or indulging in many other watery pursuits.

Buena Vista Watersports: This is the place to come for jet-skiing ($55 ½ hour, $98/hour), water-skiing, wake-board and tube rides ($50/15 min, $85/30 min, $145/hour) on Little Lake Bryan by the Holiday Inn Sunspree on Highway 535 (407 239 6939, **bvwatersports.com**). **Orlando Watersports Complex:** Just off the Beachline Expressway (528) near Orlando International Airport, this is an elaborate teaching facility featuring wake-boarding and water-skiing, by boat and suspended cable, for both novices and experts. It has a huge range of classes for individuals, groups and birthday parties. (407 251 3100, **orlandowatersports.com**).

Walt Disney World: Disney offers all manner of boats (from catamarans to canoes and pedaloes) and activities (from water-skiing to parasailing) on **Bay Lake**, as well as the smaller **Seven Seas Lagoon**, **Crescent Lake** and **Lake Buena Vista**. Parasailing (from *Disney's Contemporary Resort* – see page 69) comes in 2 price categories: a Regular flight, which goes to 450ft/137m for 8–10 min, and a Premium flight to 600ft/183m for 10–12 min. It costs $95–130 solo or $170-195 tandem, while boat rentals vary from $33/½ hour (21ft pontoon boat) to $125/hour (personal watercraft and wave runners), and can be found at 11 Disney resorts, plus The Marketplace at Downtown Disney. To book, call 407 939 0754.

Horse riding

For a more peaceful and scenic way to see some of Florida, take a tour on horseback. Several locations feature it, and we thoroughly recommend giving it a try.

Horse World Riding Stables: Out in rural Kissimmee, on Poinciana Boulevard (just 12mls/19km south of Highway 192), this gets you out into the wilds and you can spend anything from 1 hour to a full day enjoying the rides and lessons. The 3 main rides through 750 acres/304ha of untouched Florida countryside are the Nature Trail ($43 adults, $16.95 5 and under riding double with parent), a walking-only tour of 1 hour for beginners aged 6 and over; the Intermediate Trail (10 and over) for 1 hour ($52.95); and the Advanced Private Trail, a 1 hour 15 minute-trip with a private guide for advanced riders ($74.95). There is also a picnic area with fishing pond, playing fields and farm animals to pet. Riding

Horse riding at Disney's Fort Wilderness Resort

© Disney

lessons are available (call for prices). Check the website for discount coupon. There is no charge for just looking (9am–5pm daily; 407 847 4343, **horseworldstables.com**).

Rock Springs Riding Ranch: Up in Seminole County, on wilderness property inside the state park, you can try one of 3 different guided trails (1–3 hours, plus half- and full-day treks) or pony rides for under 8s. Your guide will have plenty of insight into Rock Springs Run State Reserve and you will also enjoy the beautiful countryside hereabouts, while all skill levels can be accommodated ($37-$80/person; reservations recommended; 8am-5pm daily; 352 735 6266, **rsrranch.com**). **Florida Eco Safaris** also offers Horseback Safaris, an excellent way to see more of the 'real Florida'. See pages 261–2.

Spectator events
When it comes to spectator events, Orlando isn't as well furnished as some cities, but there's always something for those who'd like to see a local game. There are no top-flight American football or baseball teams, but there is an indoor version of gridiron called Arena Football (the **Orlando Predators** at the Amway Center), plus Spring Training (pre-season) for several baseball teams (**Atlanta** in *Disney's ESPN Wide World of Sports*™ and **Houston** at Osceola County Stadium in Kissimmee).

Basketball: This is the main sport in town, with the **Orlando Magic** of the National Basketball Association (NBA). The season runs Nov–May (with exhibition games in Oct), and the only drawback is the new 18,500-seat **Amway Center** where the team plays (on W Church Street, exit 82B off I-4) can be fully booked. Contact the Magic (407 896 2442, **orlandomagic.com**) to see if there are any tickets, but you'll have to call in person to buy them (from $10 in upper seats to $1,500 courtside), or try TicketMaster on 407 839 1630 for credit card bookings. **Florida Dolphin Tours** (407 356 4646, **floridadolphintours. com**) also offers Orlando Magic packages for $99 (regular season,

$179 playoffs) with transport. More information at **nba.com/magic/**.

American football: For the real thing, the nearest teams in the **National Football League** are **Tampa Bay Buccaneers**, 75mls/120km to the west, **Miami Dolphins**, 3–4 hours' drive south, down the Florida Turnpike, or Jacksonville Jaguars up on the east coast past Daytona, a 3-hour drive on I-4 and I-95. Again, TicketMaster can give you ticket prices ($50–130) and availability (Sept–Dec). **Florida Dolphin Tours** (see pages 269–70) runs a limited number of trips to Jacksonville each year, and these are worth seeking out.

Baseball: For spring training each March, Osceola County Stadium for the Houston Astros is a real experience in local colour. You can book online at **osceolastadium.com**, or TicketMaster (**ticketmaster.com**). However, the best opportunity is to head to St Petersburg on the Gulf Coast where the **Tampa Bay Rays** play at indoor Tropicana Field (Apr–Sept). Tickets are nearly always available and the indoor stadium is superb (see page 287).

✠ BRIT TIP
We rate the local sports highly if you want to experience some real Americana. You don't need to understand the game, just turn up and enjoy the excitement and fan-friendly atmosphere. Sports are a family event here.

Disney's ESPN Wide World of Sports

© Disney

ESPN Wide World of Sports™

Inevitably, the best all-round sports facility in the area is a Disney project, though there are only a handful of genuine spectator events here. ESPN Wide World of Sports™ is a 220-acre/86ha state-of-the-art complex, featuring 30 sports and just wandering round even when there's no game is impressive. The main features are a 9,500-seat baseball stadium, a softball quadraplex, a 10-court tennis complex, 5,000-seat indoor facility, athletics track and extensive sports field.

The Ballpark: Top of the crop for a must-see visit, this is home for spring training of baseball's Atlanta Braves, where the crowds flock for 16 pre-season games 24 Feb –30 Mar (highly recommended; tickets $13–21, 407 839 4263). This is a big deal for American sports fans and games do sell out. The centre's extensive fields also cater for soccer, lacrosse, baseball and softball, and you can often see some keen sporting action just with college and school teams. **Disney's Soccer Showcase** (Sept–Jan) is a fine example of this, with some 400 teams competing under the eye of various scouts. The level of skill is bound to surprise you. Standard admission is $13.50 adults, $10 3–9s, but it is also an option with Premium and Ultimate tickets (excluding special events like baseball). ESPN Wide World of Sports™ is off Osceola Parkway, on Victory Way (**espnwwos.com**).

Disney's ESPN Wide World of Sports

Walt Disney World Marathon: A major annual event, its 16th running will be on 9 Jan 2011. Some 15,000 runners take part – including some of the world's leading athletes – drawing huge crowds and taking in all 4 Disney theme parks. Be aware the parks face some serious disruption but, as with the London Marathon, the Disney version is a great spectacle. The annual **half-marathon** takes place the same weekend.

Rodeo

An all-American pursuit straight out of the Old West, the **Silver Spurs Rodeo** is staged twice a year at the 8,300-seat Silver Spurs Arena. The biggest event of its kind in the south-east, it is held in Feb and early June (check website for 2011 dates). However, it sells out fast so book in advance on 407 677 6336 (**silverspurs rodeo.com**). The event features classic bronco and bull riding and attracts top competitors from as far as Canada. The arena is part of **Osceola Heritage Park**, which includes Osceola County Stadium (for baseball) and the Kissimmee Valley Livestock Show and Fair Pavilion. The **Arena** is a state-of-the-art facility that can be used for concerts too, and there isn't a bad seat in the house.

Motor sport

Richard Petty Driving Experience: For the guaranteed ultimate in high-speed thrills, *Walt Disney World* has its own racetrack (next to the car park for the *Magic Kingdom*). Here on the 1-mile oval, you can experience one of its 650bhp stock cars as either driver or passenger at up to 145mph/233kph, with programmes devised by top NASCAR driver Richard Petty. Choose from the 3-lap **Ride-Along Experience**; the 3-hour **Rookie Experience** (with tuition and 8 laps of the speedway); the **Kings Experience** (tuition plus 18 laps); the Experience of a Lifetime (an intense 30-lap programme) and the ultimate experience of **Speedway Challenge** (50 laps, Ride-Along, shop tour with tech talk, and lunch with instructor and Crew Chief). The Ride-Along

Experience will probably appeal to most (16 and over only) – 3 laps of the circuit with an experienced driver lasting just 37 seconds a lap but an unbelievable blast all the way. Your start from the pit lane takes you from 0–60mph/97kph in a couple of seconds and you are straight into Turn One with your brain some distance behind – it's a bit like flying at ground level! It's hot and noisy and you must wear sensible clothes (you have to climb in through the window), but it is definitely the real thing in ride terms and a huge thrill.

You don't need to book the Ride-Along Experience, which runs daily, and there is no admission fee, so you can come along just to watch (8am–1pm). The 3 driving programmes (not Tues or Thurs; Sun offers Ride-Along only) all require reservations. However, wait for the prices: $99 for Ride-Along; $399–449 (varies by season) for Rookie; $799–849 for Kings; $1,249–1,299 for the Experience of a Lifetime and $2099 for the Speedway Challenge. You must be 18 or over for all but the Ride-Along (min age 16; 407 939 0130, **drivepetty.com**).

Indy Racing Experience: Thrill seekers can also strap into an IndyCar Racing car (that has actually been driven in the Indy 500) for an unforgettable ride! Suit up in an authentic fire suit, helmet, gloves and fire shoes, then slide into the comfortable open-wheel cockpit and discover why Indy racing is a completely different experience to stock car racing. Your F1-style car rides just inches above the track, and the sensation is intense, exhilarating, and undeniably adrenalin inducing!

BRIT TIP

The Indy Racing Experience does not operate in the rain, so book your ride or drive early in your holiday for the best chance of rebooking.

The **Driving Program** includes a classroom session, orientation and 8 laps for $399. Not ready to take the wheel but still want to experience the speed and G-forces? Opt for the Two-Seater Ride, going 3 laps with an experienced driver ($109). Family and spectators are welcome to watch at no cost (4pm–sundown daily; 1888 357 5002; **indyracingexperience.com**).

Daytona International Speedway: Just up the road in Daytona (take I-4 east, then I-95 and Highway 92), race fans will find lots more of big-league thrills. The renowned Speedway hosts more than a dozen weekend events a year, including motorcycle, stock car, sports car and go-karts. Highlights are the **Rolex 24** (a 24-hour sports car event, late Jan), the famous **Daytona 500** (Feb), and **Coke Zero 400** (early July). The big events attract crowds of 200,000-plus and provide some exhilarating sport (800 748 7467, **daytonainternationalspeedway.com**).

And don't forget to visit the fun, interactive **Daytona 500 Experience** attraction as well, and the chance to tour the Speedway (see page 283). The **Richard Petty Driving Experience** is available here, too (but 16 and over only), and the $135 fee for 3 laps of the world-famous, steeply banked 2½ml/4km tri-oval includes entrance to Daytona USA. There is also a Daytona Highbanks 8 ($525, $549 peak season), and Daytona Super 16 ($1,249, $1,299).

OK, that's the local area sorted out; now let's take you further afield…

Daytona USA

© OCVB

9 The Twin Centre Option

or To Orlando – and Beyond!

While Orlando and its surrounding areas continue to get bigger and better year by year, it is equally true there is a LOT more to see in the rest of Florida, with some magnificent twin-centre options. From St Augustine in the north-east to Key West in the extreme south (the 'Floribbean'), it's easy to find wonderful resorts, glorious beaches and more family attractions.

The beaches of the Gulf (west) coast, the Atlantic coast from Ormond Beach all the way down to Miami, and the fabulous Florida Keys all feature some of the best seaside escapes in the world, while cities like West Palm Beach, St Augustine, Daytona, Fort Lauderdale, Tampa, Miami and Key West provide more Sunshine State fascination. Two-centre (or fly-drive) options are common with most tour operators, but it is also easy to arrange your own, be it for a week, 2 weeks or just a night. A cruise-and-stay holiday is also a great choice, with the ports of Tampa, Port Canaveral, Port Everglades (Fort Lauderdale) and Miami all within easy reach.

You can pretty much head out from Orlando in any direction in search of a great twin-centre experience: go **East** to Cocoa Beach, New Smyrna Beach, Ormond Beach and the famous Daytona Beach, all with terrific appeal and barely an hour's drive away. The sea is a degree or so cooler on the Atlantic side, and the surf and currents are more noticeable, hence this is good surfing territory; to the **North-East** you have historic St Augustine about 2 hours away; go **West** for the city of Tampa and miles of pristine sands, from Clearwater Beach all the way south to Naples and lovely Marco Island. This tends to be slightly better for families with younger children, while the Clearwater-St Pete Beach area is a perfect combination with Orlando (about 1½–2 hours' drive); go **South-East** and you hit Vero Beach, West Palm Beach, Fort Lauderdale and Miami (about a 4-hour drive); continue **South** and there are the Keys, a magnificent 110ml/177km chain of islands linked by roads and bridges, culminating in eclectic Key West. So, heading north-east first, here's what you find:

> ### BRIT TIP
> Spanish adventurer Ponce de Leon was searching for the Fountain of Youth when he arrived at the site of St Augustine in 1513. The modern day Archaeological Park tells the story of his arrival and discovery of the continent of America – and offers the chance to drink the famous waters. Visit **fountainofyouthflorida.com**.

BRIT TIP
The Florida Turnpike (toll) is the main route south-east from Orlando, but it is a dull drive. If time is not a factor, take the Beachline Expressway (528) east and then I-95 or, better still, Highway 1, south. The journey will be far more rewarding.

St Augustine

A 2-hour drive up I-4 and then I-95 brings you to America's oldest city.

Founded by Spanish conquistadores in 1565, St Augustine is a genuine historic relic, full of authentic buildings and signs of the original settlement around the imposing Castillo de San Marcos. Much of the original walled city still remains and 'old' is a much-revered term here, as 18th and 19th-century Mediterranean influences are seemingly everywhere. Walk the narrow, uneven streets of the Restoration Area to discover a host of colonial architectural treasures, now home to gift shops, restaurants, pubs, ice-cream parlours, antiques shops, quaint B&Bs and other historic attractions. To see as much as possible, you can hop on a horse-drawn carriage, the St Augustine Sightseeing Train or the Old Town Trolley Tours for a narrated ride round the city. For a spookier experience, walk the streets with Ghost Tours of St Augustine, with your guide in period costume. Other tours reveal St Augustine's rich architectural heritage (also the product of British and colonial American rule). Florida railroad mogul Henry Flagler was another big influence here, building some magnificent hotels for his 'passengers to paradise'. The ornate Lightner Museum, formerly Flagler's Hotel Alcazar, is home to his turn-of-the-century treasures, including Tiffany and other glass works of art. Don't miss the hotel's remarkable indoor swimming pool – considered a wonder in its day. Other attractions include a modern theatre, art galleries, Potter's Wax Museum, Ripley's Believe It Or Not Museum and a local chocolate factory. Restaurants range from The Spanish Bakery and the famous, family-owned Columbia Restaurant, where recipes have been handed down for more than a century, to a modern microbrewery, A1A Ale Works. Golf fans should visit nearby Ponte Vedra for the World Golf Hall of Fame.

BRIT TIP
Festivals are an integral part of St Augustine's routine, from monthly art walk nights to annual costumed torchlight re-enactments of British occupation and the City Birthday on 8 Sept.

Where to stay: The city's premier hotel is historic Casa Monica (904 827 1888, **casamonica.com**), but there are also numerous B&Bs, plus chain hotels like Best Western and Hampton Inn. The boutique St George Inn (904 827 5740; **stgeorge-inn.com**) is also a good choice.

More info: St Augustine Visitors & Convention Bureau, 1800 653 2489, **getaway4florida.com**.

Volusia County

Travel south from St Augustine and you arrive in one of Florida's most famous beach areas.

Daytona Beach: Only 1 hour from Orlando along I-4 east, this area is undergoing a transformation to a more sophisticated seaside resort with all mod cons, including new hotels and restaurants, but still extremely family-friendly (**familybeachbreak.com**). It is busiest in summer (mid-June to mid-Aug) but there is something for everyone, especially in the quieter period around Easter when there are often some good deals to be had here. The prime attraction is the array of good beaches (some of which you can drive on – for a $5 toll, speed

Daytona Lagoon

limit 10mph/16kph). From these open expanses of sands, you can go boating, parasailing, biking, jet-skiing and fishing, while there is also plenty of sightseeing. Base yourself in the Oceanfront area and you are at the heart of all things beach-related, with the Pier, the historic Bandshell, Boardwalk and the shops and restaurants of **Ocean Walk Village**.

BRIT TIP

Look out for Speeding Through Time, a series of memorials and plaques along Daytona's Boardwalk, highlighting the world speed records set on the beaches, including those of Britons Sir Henry Segrave and Sir Malcolm Campbell.

Here you have RC Theatres' Ocean Walk Movies 10 Cineplex, the fun of the Mai Tai Bar, Sloppy Joe's, Johnny Rockets Diner, Santora's Pizza, Quiznos, Starbucks, Ker's Winghouse and unique shopping at Maui Nix Surf Shop, Caribongo and Sunglass Hut. When you want to eat, our recommendation is the film-themed style of Bubba Gump Shrimp Co. (based on the movie *Forrest Gump*). With fun decor, wonderfully casual vibe and an excellent menu (food that lives up to its surroundings), it is ideal for a quick lunch or leisurely dinner (**bubbagump.com** and **oceanwalkshoppes. com**).

BRIT TIP

Spend the day on Daytona Beach, then try some water park fun at Daytona Lagoon after 4pm, when admission is only $11.99.

Right opposite Ocean Walk Village is **Daytona Lagoon**, a combination water park, go-kart track, mini-golf course, arcade and laser tag centre, plus an exciting new thrill ride, **The Phoenix**, which propels riders on a 210° arc to experience 4Gs of force at 55mph/88kph. The water park has a wave pool and lazy river, 10 different flumes and an area purely for toddlers (adults $27.99, children under 4ft/122cm $19.99). The 3 9-hole mini-golf courses ($7 for 18 holes), single and double go-karts ($7–9), laser tag

(must be above 3ft 6in/108cm, $7), The Phoenix ($7–12) and carousel ride ($1) are all separate items. Find out more at **daytonalagoon.com**.

Historic **Downtown Daytona Beach** on Beach Street is the heart of the city, with a museum of local history, restaurants, nightclubs, coffee bars and a performing arts theatre, all in a riverside setting. The **Angell & Phelps Chocolate Factory** (established 1925) is another notable curiosity. Head to the Riverfront in early evening when the street takes on a café society style. There are plenty of worthwhile places to eat, but for something different try the lively **Loggerhead Club & Marina** (right on the river at Ballough Road) or chic **Chez Paul** (on N Beach St with a view of the Halifax River). Similar upmarket choices are **Martini's Chophouse Restaurant** (on S Ridgewood Avenue) and **The Cellar** (on Magnolia Avenue). The new **Vince Carter's** (on LPGA Blvd, co-owned by the Orlando Magic basketball star) is another smart choice, with a chic Dining Room, eye-catching Highlight Zone Sports Grill and relaxing Piano Lounge (**http://vincecarters.com**).

Other local highlights include a variety of ways to enjoy the waterways. Cruising the intra-coastal Halifax river to see the sights, including dolphins at play, is highly worthwhile. Check out a **tiny cruise line** (at Halifax Harbor Marina on S Beach Street; 386 226 2343) for 4 different cruises ($13.61–25.58), which include a lovely Sunset/City Lights tour Apr–Oct. Head south along S Atlantic Avenue and you find even more choice of beaches and attractions, including **Sun Splash Beach**, **Frank Rendon Park** and especially **Lighthouse Point Park**, a 52-acre/21ha stretch of nature trails, fishing, observation deck, swimming and picnicking (8am–9pm; $3.50/vehicle). The tide here can retreat up to 500ft/150m and the beaches, open to the public year-round, tend to be quieter, though there can also be some serious rip-tides. At the southern end of the beaches is the wonderful **Ponce de Leon Inlet Lighthouse**, with a formidable 203 spiralling steps to the top. This well-preserved national monument is a magnificent re-creation of 19th-century Florida maritime life and the view from the top of America's second tallest lighthouse is superb (10am–5 or 6pm; $5 adults, $1.50 children). It also has a lovely gift shop. Ponce Inlet has some great deep-sea fishing, too – see **http://inletharbor.com/fishing.html**.

BRIT TIP
Try lunch or dinner at Lighthouse Landing in Lighthouse Point Park for an eclectic Floridian experience.

More family-orientated fun can be found at the **Marine Science Center** (just round the corner from the lighthouse), which showcases mangrove, manatee and sea turtle exhibits, a seabird sanctuary and a turtle rehab facility. It has a 5,000 gallon/22,750 litre artificial reef aquarium, as well as static and interactive educational displays. A boardwalk and nature trail extend through the Center, which also has a gift shop (10am–4pm Tues–Sat, noon–4pm Sun, closed Mon; $5 adults, $4 seniors, $2 under-13s; **echotourism. com/msc**). One of the most novel tours is the **Aqua Safari**, a combined 4-hour coastal eco-tour and entry to the Marine Science Center and Ponce de Leon Inlet Lighthouse. Climb aboard its red double-decker bus at Daytona Lagoon and head south to pick up its boat for an eco-tour of the Inlet waterway (11am–3pm every Wed). Led by a licensed captain and marine biologist, the tour provides a hands-on overview of the region's ecosystem (pulling up fishing nets and crab traps), with refreshments provided. You are then free to visit the Lighthouse and Marine Center ($50 adults, $30 under-13s, reduced prices available for non-all-inclusive admission; 386 405 3445, **daytonabeachaquasafari.com**).

Of course, one of the biggest draws is the Daytona Speedway (see page 279), while the accompanying **Daytona 500 Experience** is well worth trying even if you're not a race fan. This interactive centre offers a series of hands-on exhibits, rides and films to give you a taste of the high-speed action. Change tyres in the **Chevy 16-Second Pit Stop Challenge**, design and video test a racing car, check out the technology involved, commentate on a race and experience the Daytona 500 film. Other elements include **Acceleration Alley** (for an additional fee), with full-size NASCAR simulators to capture the thrills of head-to-head racing at more than 200mph/322kph, and **Daytona Dream Laps**, another elaborate motion simulator to put riders inside the Daytona 500 itself. The history of speedway is well detailed in **Heritage of Daytona** and there is a good gift shop. A ½-hour **Tram Tour** of the Speedway stops on the track, in Pit Road and Victory Lane, giving a real close-up of this stunning arena. The **Coca-Cola IMAX Theater** features the unique 45-minute NASCAR 3-D: The IMAX Experience (10am–6pm off peak; 9am–7pm peak, not Christmas Day; $24.99 adults, $19.99 seniors and 6–12s, under-6s free with adult; Speedway tour on its own $9/person; 386 947 6800, **daytona500experience.com**).

Continue south on Highway 1 and you come to up-and-coming (but still largely undiscovered) **New Smyrna Beach**, with 13mls/20km of pristine white sands, great surfing, shell collecting and boating at any of the many marinas hereabouts (386 428 1600, **nsbfla.com**).

Where to stay: You'll find some of our favourite resorts in Daytona Beach. The **Wyndham Ocean Walk Resort** is a huge ultra-modern complex right on the beach at Ocean Walk Village, with versatile 1, 2 and 3-bed condos (all with kitchens and fab views).

New Smyrna Beach

With 3 outdoor pools, waterslide and lazy river, plus a kids' water play area, 2 indoor pools, indoor mini-golf, kids' programmes, spa and an excellent lounge and food court, it is hugely family-friendly (386 323 4800, **oceanwalk.com**). The nearby **Hilton Daytona Beach Oceanfront Resort** is another large, recently renovated hotel with wonderfully spacious rooms, beachfront cabañas and suites, plus a terrific dining choice (notably Hyde Park Prime Steakhouse), 2 pools and a modern fitness centre (386 254 8200, **daytonahilton.com**). **Shores Resort & Spa** is a boutique choice on a quieter stretch of the beaches, with an elegant ambience, beautiful rooms, charming bar and fine-dining Azure restaurant. It also boasts an excellent pool, kids' pool and fitness centre, plus a heavenly Spa with a range of Balinese and Thai treatments (386 767 7350, **shoresresort.com**).

More info: Call 01737 643 764 in the UK, 1800 854 1234 in the US or visit **daytonabeach.com**.

Ormond Beach: Immediately to the north is another up-and-coming area where you find more smart resorts and great beaches, notably at **Bicentennial Park** (with a nature walk, fishing dock, tennis courts and playground) and **Birthplace of Speed Park** (which commemorates the first automobile race on the beach here in 1903). Just west of Daytona Beach is **DeLand** and St Johns River Country. Located in the western half of the region, this is home to several nature preserves (**visitwestvolusia.com**).

The Space Coast

Further south on the Atlantic seaboard is the 'Space Coast', so called for its proximity to the Kennedy Space Center (see pages 219–25).

Cocoa Beach

BRIT TIP

For good info on all Kennedy Space Center rocket launches (and any Shuttle missions that may be delayed after Nov 2010), especially good public viewing locations, see **spacecoastlaunches.com**.

Cocoa Beach: Closest to Orlando, barely 50 minutes east (on the Beachline Expressway 528, then south on Highway A1A), this area has 2 excellent public beaches plus trademark shopping at **Ron Jon's Surf Shop**, a massive neon emporium of all things water related. As it's the Atlantic, the sea can be chilly Nov–Apr, but its resort style ensures good facilities (**cocoabeach.com**). Cocoa Beach is also home to the excellent **Astronaut Memorial Planetarium & Observatory**, which holds daily shows in its large-screen cinema and world-class planetarium, plus an exhibition hall, art gallery and gift shop, all on Brevard Community College Campus (321 433 7373, **brevardcc.edu/planet**) – and don't forget Island Boat Lines (see also page 268).

Titusville: Head here for attractions like the **US Space Walk of Fame** (a river walk with displays of memorabilia, plaques and public art depicting America's history in space), **Merritt Island National Wildlife Refuge** (a 6ml/9km driving tour adjacent to the Kennedy Space Center) and the fascinating and rather moving **American Police Hall of Fame & Museum**, with all you ever wanted to know about the history of crime and law enforcement, a tribute to police officers who have died in the line of duty, plus an indoor shooting centre and helicopter rides (see **aphf.org** for $3 off coupon). Aviation fans may want to check out the **Valiant Air Command Warbird Museum**, with more than 35 vintage war planes and guided tours through the history of military aviation (**vacwarbirds.org**). Look out for the 3-day **Warbird Air Show** each March, while Cape Canaveral is host to the new (and fun) **Art of Sand Festival** every Apr (**artofsandus.com**).

Breakfast with a difference!

Just north of DeLand in DeLeon Springs State Park is the unique Old Spanish Sugar Mill grill and griddle house, one of Florida's little restaurant treasures. Famous for its hearty cook-it-yourself breakfasts (9am–4pm; 8am at weekends), each table has an inset griddle, and you choose your ingredients and get cracking. Its speciality is pancakes (pitchers of batter provided), with all manner of fillings, but it also has bacon, eggs, ham, sausage, home-made breads, French toast, sandwiches and salads. You'll struggle to pay more than $10/person and it's great fun, as well as a local institution. However, as it is inside the State Park, there is a $6/car entry fee (386 985 5644, **planetdeland.com/sugarmill**). You can then try the park facilities, which include canoes and kayaks, boat tours and hiking trails (**floridastateparks.com**).

Melbourne: Family-friendly **Brevard Zoo** is well worth a visit here, with almost 500 animals in 4 main themed areas, including the excellent new Cheetah Complex in the Expedition Africa exhibit. Other highlights include Australia/Asia, Wild Florida and Paws On Play, where children can enjoy water play, a petting zoo and explore Seaside Cove and Sea Turtle Beach (9.30am–5pm; $13.50 adults, $12.50 seniors, $10 2–12s; 321 254 9453, **brevardzoo.org**).

BRIT TIP
For top value at Brevard Zoo, consider a Young Explorer's Package (admission, train ride, giraffe and lorikeet feeding at $18, $17 and $14) or Wild Explorer's version (a choice of kayaking in Wild Florida or Expedition Africa, plus giraffe and lorikeet feeding at $20, $19 and $16.50).

Where to stay: Try the lively, surf-themed **Four Points by Sheraton Cocoa Beach** (321 783 8717, **starwoodhotels.com**) or **International Palms Resort** (321 783 2271, **internationalpalms.com**).

More info: Call 321 433 4470 or **space-coast.com**.

Tampa

Going west from Orlando brings you down I-4 to the bright city of Tampa, right on a major sea bay and with some excellent attractions of its own.

Dinosaur World: Right on I-4 as you head to Tampa (and a nice stopping point by exit 17) is this family-run attraction ideal for 3–8s. With more than life-sized dinosaurs in a lush, natural setting, plus walking trails, a picnic area, playground and gift shop, it makes a pleasant diversion for an hour or two. There are no rides or audio-animatronics, just set-piece models with explanatory signs, plus a cave-themed video theatre, small-scale fossil dig, museum and large 'boneyard' sand pit, while the **Skeleton Garden** features 6 replica dino skeletons. It's mildly educational, very laid back and a nice change of pace from the main parks. There is no food service (just drinks machines), but it does have picnic facilities and there are fast-food locations nearby, including a pizza delivery service (9am–6pm; 5pm Nov–Jan; $12.75 adult, $10.75 seniors, $9.75 3–12s, under-3s free; 813 717 9865, **dinoworld.net**).

Florida Aquarium: In the heart of Tampa (right next to the port area) is this superb 6-part journey into Florida's waterways, coast and deep-sea elements, beautifully presented and ultra child-friendly. It starts with the **Wetlands**, then moves on to **Bays & Beaches** (including Sea Turtle Corner), **Dragons Down Under** (the amazing Leafy Sea-dragons), **Coral Reef Ocean Commotion** (full of interactive modules, including touch-screens, videos and podcasts) and the outdoor **Explore A Shore** water-play area, with squirt pools, fountains and pirate ship, plus an excellent tropical-themed Bar & Grill. Highlights include the daily Penguin Promenade (where a pair of the Aquarium's penguins are brought out for a meet-and-greet), the Touch Tank, the amusing River Otters and Shark Bay, where anyone 15 and older who is scuba-certified can join the daily dive into the lagoon ($150/person, reservations required on 813 2713 4015). Other extras include a daily non-scuba 'Swim with the fishes' reef swim ($85/person), a 2-hour Shark Feeding programme every Tues and Sun ($65/person) and a twice-daily Penguins Backstage tour ($25/person). There's also a daily (weather permitting) **Wild Dolphin Eco-Tour** on their new 130-passenger catamaran, leaving from the aquarium to explore the Bay where more than 500 dolphins live, along with the occasional manatee (9.30am–5pm daily, closed Thanksgiving and Christmas Day; parking $6; $19.95 adults, $16.95 seniors, $14.95 under-12s; with Dolphin Eco-Tour, $35.95, $31.95, $27.95; 813 273 4000, **flaquarium.org**).

The Aquarium is right next to the **Channelside Bay Plaza** centre of shops and restaurants, which is well worth exploring for unique stores like Paintings of the World, Lit Cigar Lounge, Surf Down Under, White House Gear and Quachbal Chocolatier and some great entertainment and dining options. Choose from Bennigan's, Hooters, Oishi Sushi, Gallagher's Steakhouse, Tina Tapa's, Howl At The Moon piano bar, Splitsville 10-pin bowling attraction, Thai Tani, Precinct Pizza and Stumps Supper Club, plus Coldstone Creamery (great ice-cream and milkshakes!). Like Ybor City, this is where Tampa parties – hence the restaurants and bars, many featuring live music, are hopping at weekends. You will also find the **Official Tampa Bay Visitor Center** here (**channelsidebayplaza.com**).

Museum of Science and Industry: More family-friendly fun (especially for 4–12s) can be found at this highly entertaining science centre, with 3 floors of education-tinged exhibits, activities and large-screen IMAX films. Highlights include the huge **Kids In Charge** science play area (under-13s), **The Amazing You** (a tour of the human body), **Disasterville** (an interactive look at natural disasters – feel a hurricane in close-up!) and the **High-Wire Bicycle** (ride a bike on a steel cable 30ft/9m up). The permanent exhibits include the **Gulf**

Coast Hurricane and **The Saunders Planetarium**, while the **IMAX® Dome Theatre** offers a range of films daily on its 82ft/25m hemispherical screen and there are periodic travelling exhibits. Outside is the **BioWorks Butterfly Garden** and the **Historic Tree Grove**, providing more insight into Florida's natural wonders (9am–5pm Mon–Fri, 6pm Sat and Sun; $25.95 adults, $22.95 seniors, $19.95 2–12s, includes 1 standard IMAX film; additional films $7.95, $6.95 and $5.95; 813 987 6100, **mosi.org**).

Ybor City: Tampa's other entertainment district can be found in the rejuvenated Cuban quarter of the city, where a fine mix of shops and restaurants provide a lively vibe both by day and at night. Shop at **Wear Me Out**, for signature handbags, jewellery and jackets; **Stogie Castillo's**, where you can see its cigars being made; **Urban Outfitters** for trendy apparel and accessories; **Ybor Ybor** for visitor merchandise; **Sunglass Hut** and more. Then stop for a meal at any of **Fresh Mouth** (tempting burgers), **Rock-N Sports Bar & Bistro**, **Samurai Blue** (fine sushi and sake), or (our favourite) the **Tampa Bay Brewing Co**, a British-run brewpub with an inviting, varied menu, a great range of beers, multiple TV screens and pool table. More fun can be had at **Gameworks**, a huge arcade of games, bars and restaurant, and the **Improv Comedy Theatre**. Again, it is busiest on Fri and Sat but lively most evenings (**centroybor.com**). Start at the **Visitor Information Center & Museum**, which shows a handy film on the fascinating history of the city, then visit the well-presented **Ybor City Museum** on East 9th Avenue for more insight into this eclectic gem (daily 9am–5pm, $4 adults, under-6 free; **ybormuseum.org**).

Much of downtown Tampa, including Ybor City and Channelside, is linked by the handy TECO Line Streetcar, replicas of authentic electric trams, with one-way fares of $2.50 and just $5 for an all-day card.

Where to stay: try the wonderful boutique style of historic **Don Vicente**

Inn in Ybor City, a beautiful period refurbishment of a 19th-century building with just 16 individual rooms (813 241 4545, **donvicenteinn.com**).

BRIT TIP

Make sure you have lunch or dinner at the original Columbia Restaurant in Ybor City. Opened in 1905, it incorporates a whole city block that was gradually absorbed into this Spanish/Cuban bar-diner and is one of Florida's finest. Ask at the host stand if they can give you a tour, with the story of the Gonzmart family (813 248 4961, **columbiarestaurant.com/ybor.asp**).

More info: Call the Visitor Center on 813 223 2752 or **visittampabay.com**.

St Pete/Clearwater

Continue west and you have the gorgeous **Gulf Coast**, a 2-hour drive down I-4 and through Tampa on I-275 south to **St Pete Beach** (105mls/169km) or **Clearwater Beach** (110mls/177km), with a string of beautiful resorts in between, all featuring white-sand beaches, water sports and far fewer crowds than you would think, plus the smart new **Beach Walk** in Clearwater. The sea is a bit warmer and calmer on this side of Florida so is more suitable for small children. The 35ml/56km stretch from St Pete–Clearwater represents the heart of the Sunshine State beach experience and is one of the most popular 2-centre options. It has a wonderful array of attractions and averages 361 days of sun a year.

St Petersburg: This city, just across the Howard Frankland Bridge from Tampa, is a wonderful mix of developments, both recent and historic. Take time here for the world-renowned **Dali Museum** (10am–5.30pm Mon–Wed and Fri and Sat, Thurs 10am–8pm, noon–5.30pm Sun; $17 adults, $14.50 seniors, $12 students, $4 5–9s; **salvadordalimuseum. org**), and the **Bay Walk** complex of restaurants, shops and a Muvico IMAX 20-screen cinema (**yourbaywalk. com**). An additional mix of museums, notably the elegant **Museum of Fine**

Arts, with its new Hazel Hough Wing (**fine-arts.org**), the recently expanded St **Petersburg Museum of History** on the Pier, the exceedingly child-friendly International Museum and fascinating **Great Explorations Children's Museum** (**greatexplorations. org**). Pedestrian-friendly streets and the Pier provide plenty of interest, while fan-friendly Tropicana Field hosts the **Tampa Bay Rays** baseball team (Apr–Sept) for truly terrific local entertainment ($12–300; **http:// tampabay. rays.mlb.com**). For a tour with a difference, you should try the **Bayside Tours** from the Museum of History on the amazing 2-wheeled Segways – 'the ride technology of the future'. They are easy to master and provide a wonderful way to see much of the city's miles of waterfront parks, beaches and residences with your knowledgeable guide. Suitable for ages 12 and over (max 275lb/125kg), choose from its standard downtown tours or the off-road/beach tours at Bilmar Beach Resort on Treasure Island (Mon 12.30, 2.30 and 4.30pm; Tues–Sat 10.30am and 2pm, Sun 12.30 and 2.30pm; 1-hour tour $35, 1½-hour $50; call for reservations on 727 896 3640, **gyroglides.com**).

Weedon Island Preserve: Enjoy the rich cultural history of this 3,700-acre/1,500ha seaside nature park in St Petersburg. Start at the **Natural History Center** (the main entrance, confusingly, is at the back) and learn about the prehistoric and Native American settlements here (plus periodic exhibitions), then go up to the 3rd floor observation deck. There are several miles of boardwalks and trails around these tidal wetlands, which are home to a wide variety of wildlife, including ospreys, turtles, spoonbills, turtles, mangrove crabs, raccoons and gopher tortoises, and guided hikes at 9am on Saturdays (10am–4pm Wed–Sun, free entry; 727 453 6500, **weedonislandcenter.org**). The more energetic may want to try a paddle round the shallow waters with **Sweetwater Kayaks**. This beautifully peaceful close encounter with nature (stingrays, jumping mullet and the occasional manatee) takes 2–3 hours on the self-guided tour (9am and 12.30pm Sat and Sun; $40 for a ½-day single-kayak rental, $56 for double, or $17 and $25 hourly; 727 570 4844 or **sweetwaterkayaks.com**).

BRIT TIP

Insect repellent is essential for any visit to Weedon Island Preserve as it is not sprayed for mosquitoes, and the little pests will feed on tourists!

Beaches: Head out to the beaches themselves and you are spoiled for choice, from the 1,100-acre/445ha **Fort De Soto Park** in the south to stunning **Caladesi Island State Park** in the north (regularly voted in America's Top 10). There is plenty to do, too, with the likes of Treasure Island, Sand Key and St Pete Beach all receiving the Blue Wave Award for cleanliness and safety. Fort De Soto Park offers free walking tours of its Spanish-American War-era fort, while newly renovated **John's Pass Village and Boardwalk** is an eclectic shopping district and marina full of art galleries and restaurants (and home to the fun **Pirate Cruise** – a replica sailing ship offering a 2-hour party cruise; $33 adults, $28 for 65 and over, $23 under-20s, inclusive of beer, wine and soft drinks; 11am, 2pm and sunset Mon–Sat; 727 423 7824). Parasailing, jet-skiing and fishing are also popular (**johnspass.com**).

BRIT TIP

Most public beaches will have toilets, changing facilities and picnic tables, but there is usually a parking fee.

You definitely shouldn't miss **Dolphin Landings** in St Pete Beach, with a pair of 51ft/15.5m yachts that sail on 2-hour trips along the calm inland waterway 3 times a day (usually

Sand Key Park, south of Clearwater Beach

9.30am, noon and 2.15pm) for close-up dolphin-watch cruises and sunset sailings, plus Shell Island day trips and fishing excursions ($35 adults, $25 children; 727 367 4488, **charterboatescape.com**). Further north at Indian Shores is America's largest wild bird hospital, the **Suncoast Seabird Sanctuary**, usually caring for thousands of injured birds including birds of prey, pelicans, spoonbills and egrets. There is no charge to visit this non-profit-making rehabilitation centre, but it does ask for donations (727 391 6211, **seabirdsanctuary.com**).

BRIT TIP

Don't leave Clearwater Beach without visiting the Aquarium's star attraction, a dolphin called **Winter**. Rescued from a crab trap, her tail had to be amputated and she was not expected to survive. Happily, she not only lived but has learned to swim with a prosthetic tail!

Continue north to **Clearwater Beach** for acres of clean, white sands and the **Clearwater Marine Aquarium**, a wonderful non-profit organisation that rescues and rehabilitates injured dolphins, turtles, river otters and more. The dolphins are the star attraction but there are other animal presentations and lively exhibits. Try its VIP behind-the-scenes tour, with access to all the rehab areas and a close-up of the dolphins, or 2-hour **Sea Life Safari** (great for kids) that goes out on the coastal waterway (9am–5pm Mon–Thurs, 9am–7pm Fri and Sat, 10am–5pm Sun; $12.95 adults, $8.95 seniors & 3–12s; add $9/person for VIP tour; admission plus Sea Life Safari $29.95, $28.95 and $21.75; or all 3 for $36.95, $34.95 and $27.75; 727 441 1790, **cmaquarium. org**). The new **Beach Walk** is the heart of this area, a winding beachside promenade of lush landscaping and artistic touches that links a ½-mile stretch of resorts, shops and restaurants (like the fun Frenchy's, Britt's Laguna Grill and Crabby Bill's) to **Pier 60** where the daily sunset celebration (complete with craft stalls and music) is held. Also here is the marina where you can catch the 2-hour **Captain Memo's Pirate Cruise** (10am and 2pm daily; $36 adults, $31 seniors and teens, $26 under-13s) or the Sunset Champagne Cruise (at 4.30, 5, 6 or 7pm, $39, $31, $26; **captainmemo.com**). Going further north brings you to **Caladesi Island** and another of the world's most picturesque beach spots.

For those wishing to take it easy rather than drive, the **Suncoast Beach Trolley** is the perfect transport link (5.05am–10.10pm daily) both along the beaches and into St Petersburg for $1.50 a ride, $4 for an all-day pass and $20 for a week pass (727 530 9911, **psta.net**). The area also boasts 2,000 restaurants, of which the Key West bistro style of **Frenchy's Rockaway Grill** and **Frenchy's South Beach Café** (both in Clearwater Beach), the **Daiquiri Deck/Oceanside Grill** (Madeira Beach), **Crabby Bill's Seafood** (Indian Rocks, Clearwater Beach and St Pete Beach) and the **Moon Under Water** (St Petersburg) are all well worth visiting. The chic **Parkshore Grill** in downtown St Pete is also worth seeking out for a relaxing lunch or elegant dinner (727 896 9463, **parkshoregrill.com**).

Where to stay: There's a wide choice of accommodation here. A range of **Superior Small Lodgings** combine beachfront locations with small-scale, personal service. Weekly rates can be from $800 for a 3-room apartment (727 367 2791, **floridassl. com**). Upmarket hotels include the family-friendly **Tradewinds Island Resorts** on St Pete Beach, a 743-room complex with great facilities and dining in a blissful location (1800 360 4016, **tradewindsresort.com**) and the superb **Soundpearl Resort**, a 4-star choice on Clearwater Beach, with a mix of stylish standard rooms and spacious suites. The pool, bar and grill are a real beachfront sanctuary, while the modern Spa has a fab array of treatments. Caretta on the Gulf offers memorable dining with an inventive fusion cuisine, plus ceviche, sushi and a raw bar (727 441 2425, **sandpearl.com**). **Sunset Vistas Beachfront Suites** on Treasure Island, with 1- and 2-bed suites and fully

equipped kitchens, is another smart choice for a week or more (727 360 1600, **sunsetvistas.com**). However, the jewel in the crown is the new **Hyatt Regency Clearwater Beach Resort & Spa**, an all-suite luxury hotel at the heart of Beach Walk, with sumptuous accommodation. Fantastic pool facilities are superbly picturesque with great Gulf views, while the eco-friendly Sandova Spa is one of Florida's best. A state-of-the-art gym and two wonderful restaurants complete the amenities, along with the excellent Camp Hyatt programmes and activities for kids (727 373 1234, **clearwaterbeachhyatt. com**).

More info: Call 0208 651 4742 in the UK, 727 464 7200 in the US, or see **visitstpeteclearwater.com**.

BRIT TIP
Don't miss the chance to dine at the Hyatt Regency's SHOR Seafood Grill, with its dramatic show kitchen and superb local seafood dishes.

The south-west

Bradenton/Sarasota: Around 2 hours' drive from Orlando is this artsy area (take I-4 then I-75), which features the superb beachfronts of **Anna Maria Island** (charming and secluded beaches), **Longboat Key** and **Venice** ('the shark tooth capital of the world' and great for fossil hunters). Sarasota is year-round home to the **Ringling Circus**, and there are many circus-influenced offerings hereabouts, including the unmissable **Ringling Estate and Museum of Art**, which includes the unique Circus Museum and Tibbals Learning Center (an incredible scale model – the largest in the world – of a classic circus). The Museum of Art features a multi-million dollar collection of Old Masters in a palatial setting while the former Ringling family home, the dazzling Ca d'Zan Mansion, grounds and gardens are also part of the entry fee (daily 10am–5.30pm; $25 adults, $20 seniors, $10 6–17s; **ringling.org**). There is superb shopping at **St Armand's Circle** in Lido Key, and the **Mote Aquarium** is also worthy of note. In Bradenton, look out for the **Village of Arts**, and the sophisticated **South Florida Museum**, which includes the Parker Manatee Aquarium and Bishop Planetarium. The Aquarium is home to Bradenton's mascot, Snooty, the world's oldest living manatee (10am–5pm Mon–Sat, noon–5pm Sun; closed Mon in May, Jun and Aug–Dec; $15.95 adults, $13.95 seniors, $11.95 4–11s; 941 746 4131, **southfloridamuseum.org**). Good food is always on the menu here, and you should try another outlet of the excellent **Columbia Restaurant** in Sarasota (941 388 3987, **columbiarestaurant.com/sarasota. asp**) and lively beachfront **Siesta Key Oyster Bar** (941 346 5443, **skob.com**).

◀🇬🇧▶ **BRIT TIP**
The Londoner Inn in Bradenton also offers an excellent British-style afternoon tea Mon–Sat, 11.30am–3pm.

Where to stay: Anna Maria Island is full of small-scale B&Bs and cute beachfront inns. The **Hyatt Sarasota** is one of the top resorts in the area (941 953 1234, **sarasota. hyatt.com**), while the **Ritz-Carlton** is a Gulf Coast landmark (941 309 2000, **ritzcarlton.com**). The **Londoner** is a sumptuous British-run B&B in Bradenton that features 6 gorgeous, individually decorated rooms, a private 2-bed carriage house and great local hospitality (941 748 5658, **thelondonerinn.com**).

More info: Sarasota, call 941 957 1877 or **sarasotafl.com**; Bradenton (and Anna Maria Island), 941 729 9177 or **floridasgulfislands.com**.

Charlotte Harbor: Go further south (170mls/272km from Orlando) and you have the lower-key destinations of **Punta Gorda**, **Port Charlotte**, **Englewood** and **Boca Grande**. From here, the **Fort Myers/Sanibel** area is only a short drive. This is part of the mini tropical paradise of the **Lee Island Coast**, featuring history- and nature-rich **Fort Myers** and funky **Pine Island**.

Among the many highlights of the barrier islands are bustling family-

Seminole Central

Head west out of Fort Lauderdale to Big Cypress and you find the rewarding **Ah-Tah-Thi-Ki Museum**, home to the Seminole tribe of Florida. Here you can learn about Native American culture, from its customs to the bitter 19th century Seminole Wars and its modern face as 'guardians' of the Everglades. See the Living Village and walk the 1ml/1.6km Boardwalk over the Cypress Swamp. Then try the **Billie Swamp Safari**, a 2,200-acre/1.6ha Cypress Reservation featuring close-ups of the wildlife (including snakes and gators) via its giant-wheeled buggy, airboat rides and swamp critter shows. And you can even stay overnight in its Chickee huts (1800 683 7800, **seminoletribe.com**).

orientated **Fort Myers Beach**; **Sanibel Island**, centred around its famous shell-strewn beaches; the bird-watching Mecca at the **Darling National Wildlife Refuge**; the quirky jumble of shops and restaurants in **Captiva Island**; and **Bonita Beach**, where the **Great Calusa Blueway** paddling trail heads north for 90mls/145km. Sanibel is home to the unique **Bailey-Matthews Shell Museum**, plus a quaint Historical Village & Museum and several wildlife attractions. Canoeing, kayaking and nature tours are all featured among these beautiful beaches.

Where to stay: There is a good mix of vacation homes and cottages in Fort Myers Beach and Sanibel, while the top hotels are **Lovers Key Resort** (239 765 1040, **loverskey.com**) and **Sanibel Harbor Resort & Spa** (1866 283 3273, **sanibel-resort.com**). In downtown Fort Myers, try the smart **Holiday Inn**, which boasts a stylish HI Restaurant for lunch and dinner (239 332 3232, **holidayinn.com/ftmyersdwntn**).

More info: Call 239 338 3500 or **fortmyers-sanibel.com**.

Paradise Coast: Continue south for about 230mls/368km and you have the magnificent 'Paradise Coast' of **Naples** and **Marco Island**, 2 of Florida's lesser-known seaside treasures. Naples is both a fresh, modern city with plenty of attractions (notably the **Museum of Art**, **Naples Nature Center** and **Corkscrew Swamp Sanctuary**, plus ultra-chic shopping) and a major beach destination. Its art-tinged ambience is well-evidenced in its 2 main areas of **Fifth Avenue South**, with boutique shops, sidewalk cafés and art festivals, and **Third Street South**, a mini-downtown with more distinctive stores, galleries and café society atmosphere (try the Old Naples Pub for fine food in a relaxed ambience with an outdoor patio and live music Thurs–Sat). Upscale **Bayfront**, sea-going **Crayton Cove**, eclectic **Tin City** (and its original Waterfront Marketplace), the **Waterside Shops at Pelican Bay** and **Village on Venetian Bay** are other notable shopping districts. The beaches are mere steps away; at the municipal beach, **Naples Pier** juts into placid Gulf waters, while **Lowdermilk Beach** is fully family-friendly, with volleyball and other facilities. Marco Island is the largest of the Ten Thousand Islands, consisting of 2 main communities: **Marco**, known for its wide-coved beach and fine resorts, plus a multitude of fishing charters; and **Goodland**, with its eclectic collection of fish house restaurants, plus fishing charters into the Everglades backwaters.

BRIT TIP

The Naples/Marco Island area is the perfect base from which to explore the amazing Florida Everglades themselves, though you can also reach them from Fort Lauderdale on the east coast.

Where to stay: Take your pick from high-quality resorts like the picturesque **Marco Island Marriott Beach Resort** (239 394 2511, **marcoislandmarriott.com**), **Marco Beach Ocean Resort** (239 393 1400, **marcoresort.com**) and **Naples Grande Resort & Club** (239 597 3232, **naplesgranderesort.com**). We also like the small-scale **Lemon Tree Inn** in Naples, with its Caribbean flair (239 262 1414, **lemontreeinn.com**), and the excellent value of the cosy 1- and 2-bed suites at **Marco Island Lakeside**

Inn (239 394 1161, **marcoislandlakeside. com**).

More info: Call 1800 688 3600 or **paradisecoast.com**.

Treasure Coast

Returning to the Atlantic Coast, heading south on Highway 1 brings you to an often-overlooked Florida jewel, **Vero Beach**. Nicknamed the Treasure Coast (for its history of shipwrecks), it boasts the intriguing **McLarty Treasure Museum** and the **Pelican Island National Wildlife Refuge**. Vero Beach itself is located on the barrier island of North Hutchinson but spreads to the mainland, with an array of art galleries, smart shops, restaurants, small resorts and beach parks, including a boardwalk atop the dunes. Go south for another hour and you reach **Palm Beach** and the mainland city of **West Palm Beach**, foremost among Florida's chic communities. A traditional playground of the rich and famous, Henry Flagler's **Whitehall** mansion is a highlight, while the many upscale restaurants are places to go celebrity-watching. Also here is **Lion Country Safari,** with lions, elephants and giraffes.

Where to stay: Disney's Vero Beach Resort doesn't always have availability (it is a Disney Vacation Club property first and foremost), but it is 71 acres/ 24ha of true Disney fantasy and the perfect family resort on this coast (772 234 2000, **dvcresorts.com**). In Palm Beach there is really only one place to stay (or visit) – the truly opulent **The Breakers**, one of America's legendary resort destinations (561 655 6611, **thebreakers.com**).

More info: Call 561 233 3000 or **palmbeachfl.com**.

The Breakers

Miami and Fort Lauderdale

From Palm Beach, your enjoyable coast drive brings you through increasingly built-up resort territory – Delray Beach, chic Boca Raton, Deerfield Beach, Pompano Beach and **Fort Lauderdale**. This latter has become one of Florida's most upmarket and enjoyable destinations in recent years, with a great mix of resorts, shopping, attractions and a fabulous beachfront. It also has a canal and waterway network that makes it the 'Venice of America', with **water taxis** being more plentiful than the wheeled variety. Top things to see are the **Museum of Discovery & Science** (one of the state's finest), **Bonnet House Museum & Gardens**, **Old Fort Lauderdale Village & Museum** and the unmissable **Las Olas Boulevard**, full of eye-catching shops and mouth-watering restaurants. Shop at **Sawgrass Mills**, Florida's largest mall, which has more than 300 outlet-style stores with some of the big-name designers, plus the Wanadoo City role-playing park for kids. Fort Lauderdale is also a perfect stay for a few days before or after a cruise, as both Port Everglades and Miami are only a short distance away.

Where to stay: Look for their **Superior Small Lodgings** or the many high-class resorts now dotting the beachfront, like **Sheraton Yankee Clipper Hotel** (954 524 5551, **starwoodhotels.com**) and the dramatic 5-star **Ritz-Carlton** (954 465 2300, **ritzcarlton.com**).

More info: Call 954 765 4466 or **sunny. org**.

If you have taken the full 4-hour drive south from Orlando, you will finally arrive in the state's biggest and most glamorous city, **Miami**. With superb high-rise resorts, miles of open, accessible beaches, the ultra-chic South Beach area (with its atmospheric **Art Deco District**), fantastic shopping, great sports, scintillating restaurants and nightlife, and an array of outstanding attractions, you could spend 2 weeks

Miami nice

If you see nothing else in Miami, do spend some time in **South Beach** (or SoBe as it is known) and über-cool Ocean Drive, full of open-air cafés, art galleries and pulsating nightclubs. Tranquil during the day, non-stop at night, this is where the beautiful people hang out, or just cruise in their Ferraris and Hummers. Here the restored Art Deco gems twinkle at night and will use up plenty of film or a spare memory card.

here and still not see it all. The city is actually 5mls/8km from the Beaches area, which runs north for almost 15mls/24km along the sprawling corridor of Collins Avenue, where you have most of the resorts and nightlife. High style is almost everywhere, and a narrated boat tour (from the **Bayside Marketplace**) will show off the mansions of the rich and famous, while you should also tour **Coral Gables** and the older, neater **Coconut Grove** (with its CocoWalk shopping district and superbly ornate **Vizcaya Museum**).

Other attractions include **Miami Seaquarium** on the island of Key Biscayne, the amazing **Venetian Pool** at Coral Gables, and the surprising and hugely entertaining family attraction **Jungle Island**, a combination of zoo, animal shows and gardens with some great up-close encounters (**jungleisland.com**). You are spoiled for choice for shopping, from fashion-conscious **Bal Harbor Shops**, to the massive **Aventura Mall** and funky Lincoln Road in South Beach. Brand new is the **Village of Merrick Park** in Coral Gables, a Mediterranean-style outdoor mall with more designer-label style, including the iconic Nordstrom department store and superb dining, notably at the excellent Italian restaurant Villagio (305 529 0200, **villageofmerrickpark.com**).

Where to stay: There are boutique hotels and dazzling resorts aplenty; the iconic **Fontainebleau** is open again after a $1b renovation (305 538 5000, **Fontainebleau.com**); the beautiful

Mandarin Oriental is about as smart as it gets (305 913 8288, **mandarin oriental.com/miami**); more modest but still decent is the **Best Western Atlantic Beach Resort** (305 673 3337, **bestwesternflorida.com**).

More info: Call 305 539 3000 or **miamiandbeaches.com**.

Florida Keys

Leaving Miami behind on Highway 1 brings you to the unique realm of the Keys, a loose archipelago of 1,700 islands that arc down into the Caribbean. If you thought mainland Florida was easygoing, just try the laid-back 'Conch Republic', where shorts and flip-flops are official wear and the mix of Floridian and Caribbean influences merge into a 'Floribbean' culture. Scuba divers are in their element here, with some of the world's best coral reefs, with renowned **John Pennekamp Coral Reef State Park** the highlight of the many miles of National Marine Sanctuary. Brand new is the **Vandenberg Artificial Reef** off Key West, an old US Navy ship that was intentionally sunk in 2009 to create a man-made reef. The first city you encounter is **Key Largo**, closely followed by **Islamorada**, where you should stop to see **Theater To The Sea**, with its dolphin and sea-lion interaction programmes. If you're looking for fishing, some of the best charters can be found at Islamorada, **Marathon** and **Big Pine Key**.

◆▶ BRIT TIP

Don't miss the opportunity to feed the hungry giant tarpon that hang around the docks by Robbie's boat rentals in Islamorada (**robbies.com**).

Marathon is the starting point of the amazing **Seven Mile Bridge**, the unofficial 8th wonder of the world, which connects the biggest gap between the islands, while Big Pine Key is home to **Bahia Honda State Park**, one of Florida's finest beaches. Finally, the 375ml/600km drive from Orlando brings you to the southernmost city in the US (just 90mls/145km from Cuba). **Key** West is possibly the most eclectic city in the US, a mix of the laid-back and outrageous, with street performers, sidewalk artists, cafes and bars (LOTS of bars!), plus the former home of **Ernest Hemingway**, whose residence and museum are essential viewing. You should also see **Key West Aquarium** and **Shipwreck Historeum**, and the wonderfully diverse array of shops. You must be on the harbour front, though, for the daily **Sunset Celebration**, when Key West's party spirit is in full force. The other great feature of Key West is its myriad of ways to get around – you can try the **Conch Tour Train**, **Old Town Trolley Tours**, **pedicabs** and **bicycles**. Just don't expect your stay to be sedate!

Where to stay: Guest houses, inns and B&Bs are plentiful in the Keys, like **Old Customs House Inn** (305 294 8507, **oldcustomshouse.com**) in Key West's Old Town or the utterly charming **Banyan Resort** (305 296 7786, **thebanyanresort.com**).

More info: Call 1800 352 5397 or visit **fla-keys.com**.

Cruise-and-stay

The options for 2-centre holidays don't end just because Florida does. Taking a cruise is now a popular option with an Orlando stay and you'll see a lot of advertising for these well-priced 3, 4, 5 and 7-day sailings out of Port Canaveral, Tampa, Fort Lauderdale and Miami.

Disney has 2 breathtaking ships, the 83,000-ton *Disney Magic* and *Wonder* but will make it 3 with the sparkling new *Disney Dream* (128,000 tons) in Jan 2011 and sister ship *Disney Fantasy* in 2012, all sailing from a dedicated Port Canaveral cruise terminal (although the original duo will also visit Europe, the Mexican Riviera and Alaska in 2011). Classic design plus the usual Disney Imagineering have produced vessels that incorporate special features for kids, teenagers AND adults. In fact, they are a destination in their own right. With 5 restaurants (one for adults only), a theatre, cinema, nightclub complex, choice of bars and a gorgeous spa, plus superb children's activities and facilities, they sail from Port Canaveral to the Bahamas, Key West, Caribbean and Disney's stunning private island of Castaway Cay, which has an amazing array of beach amenities. It's not a cheap option and the 3 and 4-night cruises can feel a bit frenzied, but there is also a new 5-night option and the 7-night Caribbean voyages offer a genuinely relaxing style that is hard to beat. They boast novel touches with their on-board entertainment, including dazzling theatre shows, original Disney character interaction and wonderful features like an adults-only champagne brunch. Book with many of the tour operators or direct with Disney on 1800 511 9444 (**disneycruise.com**).

Other Port Canaveral options (**portcanaveral.org**) include glitzy **Carnival Cruise Lines** (all-modern hardware, party atmosphere; 1888 2276 4825 in the US or 0845 351 0556 in the UK, **carnivalcruise.co.uk**) with 3 and 4-night Bahamas voyages and 7-night cruises to the east and west Caribbean; **Royal Caribbean International** (also 2 modern, glamorous ships; 0844 493 4005, **royalcaribbean.co.uk**), similar 3 and 4-day trips to Nassau and its private island of Coco Cay and alternating 7-night Caribbean cruises; and **NCL** (1 ship, Oct–Apr only; 0845 201 8912, **ncl.co.uk**) with two 7-night Caribbean itineraries, including its private Bahamian island.

From the port of Tampa (**tampaport. com**), you can choose from Carnival (with 4, 5 and 7-day cruises year-round to Mexico and the Caribbean), Royal Caribbean (4 and 5-day cruises year-round to Mexico), NCL (7-day voyages to Mexico and Central America, Oct–Apr) and upmarket **Holland America** (7 and 14-day cruises to the western Caribbean, Oct–Apr; 1877 724 5425, **hollandamerica.com**). The busy port of Miami (**miamidade.gov/portofmiami**) offers a huge variety, with 3–14 day cruises year-round from Carnival, Royal Caribbean, NCL (including that

A real Dream-boat

The new *Disney Dream* will be a fantastic addition to the cruise world in 2011, with a host of novel features and more of the Disney cruise style that has been such a hit since its debut in 1998. The most remarkable aspect of the new vessel will be the unique AquaDuck 'water-coaster,' a 765ft/233m powered water-tube ride that actually goes OUT over the side of the vessel and features a 4-deck drop! Other highlights are a new adults-only French-themed fine-dining restaurant, Remy; sophisticated sports bar 687 and lounge-bar Pink, designed to look like the inside of champagne bottle; Nemo's Reef splash pool for toddlers; a mini-golf course; and 5 superb kids' clubs.

line's amazing new ship, *Norwegian Epic* Oct–Apr), **Celebrity Cruises** (0844 493 2043, **celebritycruises.co.uk**), upmarket **Oceania Cruises** (1800 531 5658, **oceaniacruises.com**) and 6-star **Crystal Cruises** (020 7287 90401, **crystal cruises.co.uk**). Sail from Fort Lauderdale (**porteverglades.net/ cruising**) and the choice is equally huge, including the 'world's largest ship,' Royal Caribbean's 220,000-ton *Oasis of the Seas* (and sister ship *Allure* in December 2010), offering mainly 7 and 14-day cruises year-round to the Bahamas, Caribbean, Mexico and Central America. Select from Carnival, Celebrity, Holland America, Royal Caribbean, the Italian style of **Costa Cruises** (0845 351 0552, **costacruises.co.uk**), 6-star **Regent Seven Seas Cruises** (023 8068 2280, **rssc.co.uk**), **MSC Italian Cruises** (0844 561 7412, **msccruises.co.uk**) and glamorous **Princess Cruises** (0845 355 5800, **princess.com**).

For more advice, consult *World of Cruising* magazine (0870 429 2686, **worldofcruising.co.uk**) or specialist travel agent **The Cruise Line Ltd** (0800 008 6677, **cruiseline.co.uk**). In Orlando, try **Cruise Planners** on 1877 772 7847 or **gocruiseplanner.com**.

Well, that represents pretty much the full range of holiday choices. Now we need to tell you about how to enjoy all the night-time entertainment…

10 Orlando by Night

If Orlando and the parks are hot during the day, they positively sizzle at night, with yet more diverse and thrilling entertainment, much of it also extremely family friendly. Inevitably, Disney and Universal lead the way, but there is much to enjoy in the live music scene generally.

The full range runs from purpose-built entertainment complexes and an amazing range of dinner shows to a unique array of bars and nightclubs. The choice is suitably widespread and almost always high quality. Disney raised the bar for the big evening entertainment concept in 1987 when it opened Pleasure Island, an inspired range of clubs, discos and restaurants, but the area is quiet now as it goes through a redesign. **Downtown Disney West Side** still has several evening venues worth visiting, while **Disney's BoardWalk Resort**, which opened its doors in 1996, remains a favourite night time option.

> ### BRIT TIP
> Photo ID is essential for most bars and clubs, even if you happen to be the 'wrong' side of 30. No ID equals no alcohol, and there are no exceptions.

I-Drive caught up with this process in 1997 when **Pointe Orlando** opened. Although its prime focus is shopping and restaurants, it now has a strong evening entertainment component with a magnificent array of exceptional restaurants, BB King's Blues Club and the big Regal Cinemas 20+ IMAX multiplex. Finally, Universal Orlando got with the beat in 1998 with the opening of **CityWalk**, possibly the most elaborate and sophisticated centre of the lot. They all represent yet another slick opportunity for you to be dazzled and relieved of your cash all in the name of holiday fun!

Wishes fireworks over Cinderella Castle

© Disney

DOWNTOWN DISNEY

Disney's big shopping, dining and entertainment district remains a 3-part adventure (The Marketplace, West Side and Pleasure Island) but has removed all of the old nightclubs that made up most of Pleasure Island. This latter 'third' is slowly evolving into a more mainstream area of restaurants and shops, with more due to be added through 2011. As things stand at the moment, Downtown Disney's main nightlife attractions are as follows (see also pages 338–41 for Shopping).

Raglan Road: This pub, situated just inside Pleasure Island, features live traditional Irish music in its Grand Room 6pm–midnight Mon–Sat, plus Irish dancing periodically. Enjoy its full bar, highlighted by an ample collection of genuine Irish Whiskey, 10 cool, creamy European beers and bartenders who know how to pull the perfect pint. Full service dining is, of course, available (see page 316) (407 938 0300, **raglanroadirishpub.com**.).

Raglan Road

BRIT TIP
Raglan Road has established itself as one of Orlando's must-do venues, as much for its genuine pub charm as its fabulous food.

Downtown Disney West Side

Paradiso 37: The newest element in Pleasure Island, this expansive, split-level bar-restaurant offers a fine array of food from the Americas (all 37 countries) plus an amazing Tequila Bar featuring – you guessed it – 37 varieties. Live music adds to its picturesque waterfront location (see also page 316).

Bongos Cuban Café: Over on the West Side, the 'big pineapple' restaurant with Latin flair has more to offer than great dining; it also has 3 bars that carry the theme forward with their bright mosaics, bar stools shaped like conga drums, the sultry salsa sound of Havana and a *muy caliente* live band every Fri and Sat night. Ask to sit on the outdoor balcony on a balmy evening (407 828 0999; **bongoscubancafe.com**).

House of Blues: Free live music every night at the Front Porch bar, with top-name bands appearing at the separately accessed music venue next to the restaurant, plus a superbly entertaining Gospel Brunch (at 10.30am and 1pm every Sun). Former headliners include Duran Duran, Cyndi Lauper and Cheap Trick. Most bands are lesser known local artists, but with the level of talent you would expect at a Disney venue. Be aware there are no seats in the music hall, and all concerts are standing room only. Tickets required, no discounts for children ($15–$75 and up; 407 934 2583, **hob.com**).

AMC® Pleasure Island 24 Theaters Complex: With 24 screens and 6,000 seats and inspired by the grand movie theatres of the 1920s, Pleasure Island 24 shows first-run films in state-of-the-art surroundings, with occasional 'unique in-theatre experiences' at extra cost ($8–15 adults, $9-14 seniors, $7-12 2–12s; call 1-888-262-4386 for show times). Disabled accessible; assisted listening devices available at Guest Services.

BRIT TIP
Be aware some films have added features, such as enhanced sound, larger screen, or 3-D, that will increase your ticket price. However, you can save $2 on adult tickets at the AMC® cineplex by visiting before 3.55pm.

DisneyQuest

The most unusual element to Downtown Disney, DisneyQuest is described variously as 'an immersive, interactive entertainment environment', the latest in arcade games, a series of state-of-the-art adventure rides or, as one Cast Member said, 'a theme park in a box'. It houses 11 major adventures, such as **CyberSpace Mountain** (design and ride your own roller-coaster), **Mighty Ducks Pinball Slam** (a fun life-size pinball game), **Ride the Comix!** (a virtual-reality battle, this time with super-villains), **Virtual Jungle Cruise** (shooting the rapids, prehistoric style) and **Aladdin's Magic Carpet** (more virtual-reality fun in best cartoon fashion), a host of old-fashioned video games in **Replay Zone**, the latest sports games, a test of imagination in **Animation Academy** and 2 cafés – **Wonderland Café**, with computers and internet tables, and **Food Quest**, straight out of a space-age comic book.

BRIT TIP
You can buy a combined annual pass for DisneyQuest and Disney's water parks at $129 for adults and $99 for 3–9s that can work out good value for multiple visits.

Two more interactive experiences are **Pirates of the Caribbean: Battle for Buccaneer Gold** (an amazing 3-D immersion in a swashbuckling, cannon-shooting quest for pirate treasure) and **Buzz Lightyear's Astro Blasters** (inter-galactic bumper cars with cannonball action! Restrictions: 4ft 3in/129cm). You enter via the clever Cybrolator to Ventureport and then have 4 main areas to explore: **Score Zone** (for most of the game-playing); **Explore Zone** (a mix of role-playing and virtual-reality games); **Create Zone** (hands-on activities to be your own 'Imagineer'); and **Replay Zone** (a 'moonscape' of classic games and rides). Admission: 11.30am–10pm Sun–Thurs, 11.30am–11pm Fri and Sat. But, if you want to avoid the queues (the building admits only 1,500), go during the day. A 1-day ticket costs $42 ($36 3–9s). It's a bit too elaborate for most youngsters, but teenagers will absolutely love it.

Characters in Flight

This tethered balloon ride (similar to the wonderful Panoramagique balloon in the Disney Village area of *Disneyland Paris*), offers 6-minute 'flights' over the Downtown Disney area (weather permitting) at heights up to 300ft/91.5m, providing a wonderful panorama of much of the huge extent of *Walt Disney World* itself (10.30am–11pm, midnight Fri and Sat). It costs $18 per adult and $12 for 3–9s. Under-12s must be accompanied by an adult.

Characters in Flight

© Disney

Cirque du Soleil® – La Nouba

Saving the best for last here, the most eye-catching part of West Side is home to the greatest show on earth (or at least, the greatest we've seen anywhere) – the Cirque du Soleil® production **La Nouba**™. Twice a day, 5 times a week, the company's purpose-built, 1,671-seat theatre stages the most stupendous combination of dance, circus, acrobatics, comedy and live music in a 90-minute show that involves more than 60 performers. Anyone familiar with the unique styling, outrageous costumes and captivating sounds of the world-famous Cirque company will have an idea of what to expect, but even they will be left in awe by this stunning multi-dimensional assault on the senses.

The show title comes from the French phrase *faire la nouba*, to party or live it up, and this La Nouba does in grand style. It features trampolines, acrobatics, trapezes, juggling and even mountain bikes, woven with comedy (watch out for the inspired clowns), innovative dance routines and spellbinding music, all with the most magnificent staging. Some of the stunts are truly jaw-dropping, notably the Chinese diabolo acrobats, the new world-record juggler Anthony Gatto (a seemingly impossible whirl of balls, clubs and hoops in ever-increasing numbers) and the mind-boggling final act, Power Track/ Trampoline, which alone is worth the entry price. But the overall effect of the constant flow of movement, sublime timing and multitude of different characters (almost to the point where you hardly know where to look at any one time) is a masterpiece of modern theatre. It is a kaleidoscopic explosion of talent that never fails to amaze and astound, and is just as fresh and exciting as when it first opened in 1998.

Words alone do not do it justice – go and see it. It is not cheap, but we believe it is worth every cent and a highlight of any visit to Orlando. Booking is vital and can be done up to 6 months in advance on 407 939 7719 (or **cirquedusoleil.com**). Shows are at 6pm and 9pm Tues–Sat, but try to be early for some excellent pre-show fun. **Admission:** there are 5 pricing groups, Category Front and Center at $124 for adults and $100 for 3–9s; Cat 1 at $108 and $87; Cat 2 at $88 and $71; Cat 3 at $71 and $57 (but there is hardly a bad seat in the house). We've seen it multiple times and still come out absolutely in awe of the talent – and fun – in this show.

La Nouba

© OCVB

The sun sets on Disney's Boardwalk Villas

Disney's BoardWalk

Disney's other big evening entertainment offering is part of its impressive Disney's BoardWalk Resort, where the waterfront entertainment district contains several notable venues (not counting the excellent micro-brewery and restaurant of the Big River Grille and Brewing Works, the thrilling ESPN Club for sports fans and the 5-star Flying Fish Café). **Jellyrolls** is a variation on the duelling piano bar, with the lively pianists conjuring up a humorous and often raucous evening of audience participation songs (7pm–2am; $10 cover charge; 21 and over only). The **Atlantic Dance** club features mainly modern dance music (it started life as a classic 1930s dance club and also moved through a Latin phase) with both house and guest DJs, plus occasional live music, all with a huge dance floor and a great bar service and ambience. It's especially popular on Fri and Sat nights, perhaps because there's no longer a cover charge (9pm–2am; closed Sun and Mon). It's strictly 21 and over, so remember your ID (no ID, no entry here). Disney's BoardWalk Resort also features some amusing stalls and live entertainers, which add to the carnival atmosphere, while the **ESPN Club** features regular celebrity (American) sports guests.

Jellyrolls

UNIVERSAL'S CITYWALK

As part of the big Universal Orlando development – and in direct competition with Downtown Disney – this 30-acre/12ha spread offers just about everything in the world of entertainment. The resort's hub is a busy, bustling expanse of restaurants, snack bars, shops, open-air events and nightclubs. It offers a huge variety of cuisines, from fast food to fine dining, an unusual blend of speciality shops and a truly eclectic nightclub mix, from reggae and rock 'n' roll to salsa, jazz and high-energy disco, plus the Blue Man Group show and a karaoke theatre/bar. There's a $7 entry fee at the 6 clubs but you can buy a **CityWalk Party Pass** ($11.99) or **Party Pass with Movie** (1 free film at the 20-screen **Universal Cineplex**; $15.00) for entry to all of them, while most multi-day tickets include a Party Pass. The area splits into 3, the Main Plaza (shopping and dining), Lagoon Front (dining, live music and theatre) and the Promenade (dining and nightclubs).

BRIT TIP

Park in Universal's multi-storey car park for all CityWalk venues – only $3 after 6pm. For more info, call 407 363 8000 or visit **citywalkorlando.com**.

Universal Studios Store

Fossil

Main plaza

Shopping: Among the most original (and amusing) of the 10 shops are **Endangered Species**, with products designed to raise eco-awareness; **Quiet Flight**, for radical surf and beachwear; the retro-American decor of **Fossil** for leather goods, watches and sunglasses; **Fresh Produce** for swimwear, casual clothing and accessories; **Cigarz**, for cigars, accessories and a full bar; the large **Island Clothing Store** for Tommy Bahama clothing and merchandise; **Katie's Candy Company** sweet shop, and **Hart & Huntington Tattoo Company** with an astonishing array of permanent tattoos, as well as clothing and accessories. New in 2009 was the skate-boarding chic of **Element**, while the huge **Universal Studios Store** stocks all manner of park souvenirs.

Restaurants: Take your pick from a wide dining choice. **Bubba Gump's Shrimp Co.** has a full *Forrest Gump* theme, from the Southern-inspired menu offerings to the decor and the little flip-sign on your table to tell your server whether you need something (Stop Forrest Stop!) or not (Run Forrest Run!). The menu is predictably heavy on seafood – with prawns done every possible way – but also includes chicken, sandwiches, ribs, salads and more, with catchy names like Bubba's After the Storm 'Bucket of Boat Trash'. The gift shop carries Shrimp beanies, Gump Gear clothing, lots of miscellanea and, of course, A Box of Chocolates. Open 11am–12am.

 BRIT TIP
Mention you are celebrating a birthday at Bubba Gump's and you'll find you quickly become the centre of attention!

Emeril's: At the 5-star end of the range, this is a sophisticated and vibrant journey into the cuisine of New Orleans with master chef Emeril Lagasse. Fine wines and a cigar bar both enhance Emeril's Creole-based gourmet creations, and if you don't try the Louisiana oyster stew you'll have missed a real treat (lunch 11.30am–2pm; dinner 5.30–10pm Sun–Thurs, 5.30–11pm Fri and Sat). It books up well in advance at weekends, so try for a weekday (407 224 2424, **emerils.com**).

Jimmy Buffet's Margaritaville: An island homage to Florida's laid-back musical hero, with 'Floribbean' cuisine (a mixture of Key West and Caribbean), live music and 3 bars (11.30am–2am), with the Volcano Bar, which 'erupts' margarita mix (!) when the blender needs filling. There is a cover charge ($7) in the evening when the live band hits the stage.

NASCAR Sports Grill: A must for motor-racing fans (11am–late), with full-size stock cars and racing memorabilia, tableside plasma screens, videos and interactive games while you dine on burgers, steaks, ribs, pasta and grilled shrimp. The interior has been revamped throughout and now has a smart, sophisticated look, with a balcony and patio seating for a taste of the 'Tailgating' experience (that uniquely American 'picnic in the car park' phenomena).

 BRIT TIP
Parents with hungry kids to feed can benefit from the Kids Buffet at Pastamore – just $8.95/child for their 10-item spread. No children? Try the Chef's Table for a special dining experience, seating up to six (must be booked at least 2 days in advance, 407 224 3663).

Pastamore: A delightful indoor/outdoor Italian diner, with the choice of full-service dining (5pm–10pm) for pizza, pasta, grilled chicken and steaks, or try the counter service Marketplace Café for breakfast (breakfast pizza, egg dishes, pastries, until 11am), pastries and snacks.

Lagoon front
Blue Man Group: The newest element of CityWalk - and the most entertaining - descended on the Sharp AQUOS Theatre (the old Nick Studios building) in 2007 with its unique brand of comedy, music and multi-media theatrics, adding something completely novel to the Universal line-up. In the hands (or mouths!) of the Blue Men, mundane items like pipes, paintballs, cereal and even audience members become the instruments of wild creativity with sometimes stunning, occasionally slightly gross but always hilariously gratifying outcomes. There is a strong live music element to the show and it can feel like a rock concert at time – to such an extent one of their acts is all about how to be a proper rock star audience, with suitably comical results. Their penchant for percussion is another recurring theme and their ability to drum up a tune on various bits and pieces is truly amazing. The wild finale, involving the whole theatre, is a real corker, and don't worry if you're seated in the 'poncho section'; the Blue Men will make sure you have adequate protection. Like Cirque du Soleil, words don't

Emeril's

© OCVB

really do it justice (Simon once likened it to entertainment from the Planet Tharg!) but it all adds up to an unforgettable evening of family entertainment starting at $74 adults, $25 3–9s (save $10 per adult ticket by purchasing online). Tickets are available at **universalorlando.com** or from the theatre box office.

Hard Rock Café and Hard Rock Live: Of course, you can't miss the world's largest example of this worldwide chain, with its collection of rock 'n' roll memorabilia (including a pink 1959 Cadillac) and concert venue. It remains hugely popular, so try to get in early for lunch or dinner (11am–midnight) to sample its classic diner fare. Collectors of Hard Rock souvenirs will also find prices in the excellent gift shop friendlier than in the UK. **Hard Rock Live** is the massive mock-Coliseum architecture, a 2,500-seat theatre with high-tech staging and sound. Big-name bands and performers are on stage several times a week (both Backstreet Boys and Crowded House played here in 2010) in this slightly retro rock 'n' roll venue (407 351 LIVE, **hardrock.com**).

NBA City: Across the CityWalk waterway is the 2-storey Lagoon Front location of NBA City, another huge dining experience that is sure to thrill basketball fans with its Cage dining room, interactive playground area and Club lounge where you can watch live and classic games (11am–10.30pm Sun–Thurs; 11am–11.30pm Fri and Sat).

Hard Rock Live

✚ BRIT TIP
CityWalk too crowded? Can't get in any of the restaurants? Jump on one of the boats to the Hard Rock Hotel or Portofino Bay Hotel and you can usually dine without a wait at The Kitchen (Hard Rock), Trattoria del Porto or Mama Della's (Portofino Bay).

Promenade
Finally, you come to the Promenade area, which offers a choice of nightclubs and some more fine dining, plus the ubiquitous **Starbucks** coffee house and a new (in 2010) **Fat Tuesday** bar for its trademark frozen drinks and other signature New Orleans-inspired cocktails.

Bob Marley – A Tribute to Freedom: A clever re-creation of Marley's Jamaica home is turned into a courtyard live music venue, restaurant and bars. The bands are excellent, the atmosphere authentic and the place really comes alive at night (4.30pm–late, 21 and over only after 9pm; cover charge $7 after 8pm).

Latin Quarter: South America is the vibe for this wonderful venue/restaurant that serves up a genuine slice of Latin style in its atmosphere, music, dance, decor and cuisine. The food is outstanding – a combination of beef, fresh fish and poultry with tangy fruit sauces, spicy salsas and mouth-watering marinades (don't miss its version of rack of lamb) – the ambience is mesmerising and the

Bob Marley – A Tribute to Freedom

The Groove

sounds are so wonderfully vibrant and alive, you can't help dancing, even in your seat. Drop in for a meal or just check out the music (open 5–10pm). There's even a Latin Quarter Express dining window if you'd like a quick bite on the go.

Pat O'Brien's: This is a faithful reproduction of the famous New Orleans bar and restaurant (4.30pm–1am), with its Flaming Fountain courtyard, main bar and special duelling piano bar (5pm–2am, with a $7 cover charge; 21 and over only). Excellent Cajun food and world-famous Hurricane cocktails are the order of the day, but if you have too many don't expect to walk back!

Rising Star Karaoke: It's karaoke taken to the next level, with a live band, back-up singers and a host who makes every volunteer singer feel like the latest, greatest star. There is also a full bar with speciality cocktails, appetisers and a large selection of songs from which to choose (21 and over; 18 and over on Thurs only; 8pm–2am nightly; $7 cover charge, no additional charge to sing). Tues–Sat live band, back-up singers and host; back-up singers and host only on Sun and Mon.

Red Coconut Club: This retro dance club has a trendy, tropical vibe. With live music, signature cocktails, tapas-style menu and eclectic South Seas

décor, it is a popular venue (8pm–2am Sun–Thurs; 6pm–2am Fri and Sat; cover charge $7, free admission for ladies on Thurs). DJ daily, live music Thurs–Sat.

The Groove: For club-minded visitors this is high-tech disco entertainment – a vivid, pounding, high-energy dance venue designed like a Victorian theatre but with the latest in club music, lighting and special effects (9pm–2am; 21 and over only; cover charge $7; attire casual chic, no hats, no tank-tops).

Not breathless yet? Well, there's still the 20-screen **Universal Cineplex** with a capacity of 5,000 and the latest in movie comfort. There's also a Meal & Movie Deal for a film and dinner at one of the 8 restaurants for $21.95.

Red Coconut Club

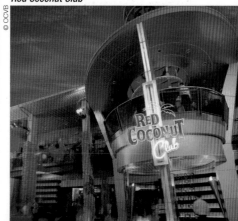

POINTE ORLANDO

This eye-catching development on I-Drive, almost opposite the Convention Center, is a mix of unique shops, cinema multiplex, restaurants, live entertainment and the **WonderWorks** fun centre (with its magic-themed dinner show). The Pointe is open all day but has notable evening appeal. The shops (12pm–10pm Mon–Sat, 12pm–8pm Sun) are all upscale and include some imaginative touches (see pages 343–4). Here is the full choice of night-time entertainment.

Adobe Gila's: On the upper level you have a fine Mexican cantina, home of the 64oz margarita and more than 70 tequilas (!), plus some south-of-the-border dining delicacies – try the signature Gila Wraps. Adobe Gila's is especially popular with locals and is often packed at weekends as it stays open late and features live outdoor music and DJs several days a week.

Cuba Libra

Capital Grille

On Fri and Sat the place should be kicking from 6.30pm: on weekdays, it's more likely to be 8.30pm (407 903 1477; **adobegilas.com**).

BB King's Blues Club: Live jazz and blues make this a fine choice for a meal or drinks and a show in this imaginative venue, which features a main 2-storey concert hall, a variety of bars, an open-air terrace and a gift shop. If what you want is a real party, BB King's takes some beating. A Southern comfort-food menu features items such as Fried Green Tomatoes, Fried Shrimp Po Boy, Lip Smacking Ribs and (Simon's favourite) Southern Fried Catfish, and a full bar is available. There is live music nightly from 7pm with one of its 2 excellent house bands, plus special guest performers (407 370 4550, **bbkingclubs.com**).

Capital Grille: An elegant dining option, with an extensive wine menu, chops, dry-aged steaks, plus seafood and complimentary valet parking (407 370 4392, **thecapitalgrille.com**).

Cuba Libre: This bar/club/restaurant adds a touch of 1940s Havana to the local scene, with Latin floorshows, salsa dancing – and some wicked cocktails! The energetic tropical open-air atmosphere lends itself to the party spirit, with the architecture, music and art to match. It serves up genuine Latin-inspired cuisine, combining beef, pork, seafood and chicken with exotic fruits, vegetables, herbs and seasonings. (5pm-11pm daily, bar open until 2am weekends; **cubalibrerestaurant.com**).

Funky Monkey: New in 2010, their menu is Asian-American fusion, featuring locally grown organic beef, fresh seafoods, and hand-rolled sushi, but the big highlight here is

Maggiano's Little Italy

their extensive wine list. (11am–11pm Mon–Thurs, 11am–midnight Fri and Sat; noon–9pm Sun 407 351 5815; **funkymonkeywine.com**).

Hooters is the local party place, with its famous 'Hooter Girl' waitresses and 'soon to be relatively famous' wings, burgers and seafood; **Johnny Rockets** provides a 1950s diner-style, with an indulgent burger-and-milkshake menu; **Maggiano's Little Italy** is a journey into family-style Italian dining in a relaxed, friendly atmosphere; the **Oceanaire Seafood Room** offers a classic 1930s ocean liner vibe and a heavenly range of fresh fish and shellfish, ideal for a special night out; **Taverna Opa** is a chance to go Greek and enjoy some lively taverna society, where impromptu table dancing may erupt all around you with paper napkins thrown at all and sundry (cheaper than breaking plates!); and **Tommy Bahama's Tropical Café**, a laid-back

Island setting for an impressive array of food, wine and cocktails, for both lunch and dinner (plus a huge emporium of home furnishings, accessories and clothing).

Also here is the **Regal Cinema**, a 21-screen movieplex (one an IMAX) with a vast and cleverly themed entrance foyer, state-of-the-art stadium seating and sound systems, where you can often see a new film several months before it arrives in the UK. Look for the ticket office on the ground level (407 248 9228). For more on Pointe Orlando, call 407 248 2838 or visit **pointeorlando.com**. For more on the restaurant choices, see page 332.

Route 46

Up in Sanford, in Seminole County, is this new purpose-built centre of dining and live entertainment, which is well worth a try for an evening out, especially at the weekend. Designed in eye-catching style like a vintage 1950s roadhouse stop, it consists of two main restaurants, an upscale bar/lounge and a lively music bar, with an outdoor stage for live bands and dancing. **Monroe's** is the classic American steakhouse, serving regional cuisine with a steak-and-seafood bias in historical Southern charm (5-10pm Wed and Thur, 11pm Fri and Sat); **The Smokehouse** is a cabin-style diner offering an array of home-made barbecue favourites from a tempting wood-smoked grill (11am–9pm Mon–Fri, 7am–9pm Sat and Sun); **The Saloon** is a refined bar

Oceanaire Seafood Room

that also offers a full dinner menu in elegant surroundings whether for one of their extensive martini selections or a relaxed dessert (5–10pm Wed and Thur; 11pm Fri and Sat); and the **Garage Bar** is the uptempo, younger hang-out for those in party mood, incorporating hot rods, classic car collectibles and vintage cars with innovative lighting and sound. The outdoor Main Stage provides the live music, with various rock and country bands Fri and Sat, plus a DJ and Ladies Night on Weds (5pm–12am Wed and Thur; 1am Fri and Sat; 407 268 4646, **route-46.com**).

> **BRIT TIP**
> Route 46 features Happy Hour in all its bars from 4–7pm daily, with various drink specials, plus Kids Eat Free with an adult at The Smokehouse on Mon and all-you-can-eat wings Tues & Wed 4–8pm.

DINNER SHOWS

Another source of evening entertainment comes in the many and varied dinner shows that are a major Orlando phenomenon. From murder mysteries to full-scale medieval battles, it's all wonderful, imaginative fun, even if the food is usually quite ordinary. As the name suggests, it is live entertainment coupled with dinner and free wine, beer and soft drinks in a fantasy-type environment, where even the waiters and waitresses are in costume. They have strong family appeal and you are usually seated at large tables where you get to know other people, too, but, at $35–60, they are not cheap (especially with taxes and tips). Be aware, too, of the attempts to extract more dollars from you with photos, souvenirs, upgrades, etc.

> **BRIT TIP**
> American cinema popcorn is invariably of the SALTED variety! Sweet popcorn in the US is usually called Kettle Corn.

Disney shows

Walt Disney World's offerings are often overlooked by visitors unless they are staying at one of the hotel resorts, but they are certainly worth considering.

Disney's Spirit of Aloha: For an excellent night of South Seas entertainment, go to Luau Cove at *Disney's Polynesian Resort*. It's a bit expensive – $59.99 for adults (Category 1 seating, including tax and tip) and $30.99 for under-10s; or Cat 2 $54.99 and $26.99; Cat 3 $50.99 and $25.99 – but good value all the same as the 2-hour show features some splendid entertainment, from the fun to the thrilling (Hawaiian sounds, singers, dancers and other Polynesian acts, including the amazing Samoan fire juggler, all with a strong family story). You need to come hungry as the food is plentiful, with salad, roast chicken, ribs, vegetables and rice, plus a Kilauea Volcano Dessert (or, for kids, peanut butter and

Hoop-Dee-Doo Musical Revue

jam sandwiches, chicken fingers, macaroni cheese and hot dogs). Beer, wine and soft drinks are included, and shows are at 5.15 and 8pm Tues–Sat. You can make reservations up to 180 days in advance, with full payment to be made when booking.

Hoop-Dee-Doo Musical Revue: At Disney's Fort Wilderness Resort & Campground, this is an ever-popular nightly dinner show that maintains the resort's impressive Western theme, and has great food (all-you-can-eat ribs, fried chicken, corn-on-the-cob, baked beans and strawberry shortcake, plus unlimited beer, wine, sangria and soft drinks). Especially loved by children, it features the amusing song and dance of the Pioneer Hall Players in a merry American hoedown-style show. Okay, it's corny and a tad embarrassing to find yourself singing along with the hammy action, but it is performed with great gusto – and you're on holiday, remember! The Revue plays nightly at 5, 7.15 and 9.30pm at the Pioneer Hall, Category 1 seating is $61.99 for adults (inclusive of tax and tip), $31.99 for under-10s; Cat 2 $56.99 and $27.99; Cat 3 $52.00 and $26.99 (under-3s free; Cat 3 pricing is seasonal) and the show lasts almost 2 hours. Reservations are ALWAYS necessary and can be made up to 180 days in advance (full payment due at booking).

Mickey's Backyard Barbecue: If you can't get enough of the Disney characters, try this twice-weekly dinner show, usually Thurs and Sat, Mar–Dec at 6.30pm and 8pm, at Disney's Fort Wilderness resort. It features Mickey and the Gang in a country buffet-style dinner at picnic tables under an open-air pavilion with live music, line dancing, rope tricks and other entertainment, and plenty of character interaction (great for younger children). The all-you-can-eat buffet offers barbecued pork ribs, baked chicken, hot dogs, macaroni cheese, salads, watermelon and ice-cream. Like all Disney dining, this is a no-smoking environment. The show may be cancelled if bad weather threatens ($46.99 adults,

$27.99 3–9s). To book a Disney show, call 407 939 3463.

Electrical Water Pageant: An alternative is the nightly (and free!) pageant that circles Bay Lake and the Seven Seas Lagoon, passing by each of the Magic Kingdom resorts in turn. It lasts just 10 minutes so it's easy to miss, but it's almost a waterborne version of the SpectroMagic parade, with thousands of twinkling lights on a floating cavalcade of boats and mock sea creatures. The usual schedule is 9pm at Disney's Polynesian Resort, 9.15 at Disney's Grand Floridian Resort & Spa (get a grandstand view in Narcoosee's restaurant), 9.35 at Disney's Wilderness Lodge, 9.45 on the shores of Disney's Fort Wilderness Resort and 10.05pm at Disney's Contemporary Resort. It can also be seen from right outside the Magic Kingdom.

> **BRIT TIP**
> Most dinner shows can be quite chilly, especially those with animals like Arabian Nights and Medieval Times, so bring a jacket or sweater to beat the air-conditioning.

Arabian Nights

This lovingly maintained, family-owned attraction, which celebrated its 20th anniversary in 2008, is a real large-scale production and one of the most popular with locals as well as tourists. It's a treat for horse lovers but you don't need to be an equestrian expert to appreciate the spectacular stunts, horsemanship and marvellous costumes as some 70 horses, including Arabians,

Arabian Nights

© OCVB

Andalusians, Belgians and Walter Farley's famous black stallion, perform a 20-act show. The storyline features Abra Kadabra, the sultan's genie, acting as mentor to the brash young Hocus Pocus, genie to the Princess. The show is staged in the huge arena at the centre of this 1,200-seat 'palace'. Daring gypsy acrobats, magical genies, square-dancing cowboys, exotic Latin Garrocha riding, and a thrilling chariot race all add up to a memorable show that kids, especially, adore. A special **Christmas Holiday Show** takes over for the winter season (Nov–Jan), and there is also some impressive pre-show entertainment, featuring star magician Michael Baron. The food is above average too, with a choice of sirloin steak, Black Angus chopped steak with gravy, pork tenderloin with Marsala sauce, grilled chicken breast with steakhouse mashed potatoes, plus salad, seasonal vegetables, and choice of Oreo fudge brownie or cheesecake with strawberry drizzle. Vegetarian lasagne is also available, and children have the option of chicken tenders with macaroni & cheese. Hot tea available on request. Located just ½ml/1km east of I-4 on Highway 192 (on the left, just to the side of the Parkway shopping plaza, at marker 8), Arabian Nights runs every evening at 6 or 8.30pm (often both), with occasional matinees. It lasts almost 2 hours, and you can buy tickets ($63.99 adults, $40 3–11s; VIP experience $79.99 and $45.03) at the box office 8am–10pm or by credit card on 407 239 9223 (visit **arabian-nights.com** for a saving offer or free upgrade or $10 discount per ticket). A 'VIP' upgrade adds a souvenir poster and bracelet, pre-show drink in the VIP area, priority seating (in the first 3 rows), the chance to meet the stars pre-show, a photo op on the back of a horse for under 18s, a special backstage Parade of Breeds featuring many of the show's most distinctive horses, a guided tour, and one lucky child can add their handprint in paint on the horse featured in the Native American Tribute.

Medieval Times

Spain in the 11th century is the entertaining setting for this 2-hour extravaganza of medieval pageantry, sorcery and robust horseback jousts that culminate in furious hand-to-hand combat between 6 knights. It's worth arriving early to appreciate the clever mock castle design and the staff's costumes as you are ushered into the pre-show hall before being taken into the arena itself. The Knights of the Realm show features fast-paced skills tests, loosely centred on a treacherous plot within the king's inner circle. But honour and bravery ultimately prevail, restoring order to the Kingdom, and it's all set to a dramatic musical score by the Prague Symphony Orchestra. The weapons are all real and used with great skill, and there are some neat special effects. You need to be in full audience participation mode as you cheer on your knight and boo the

Medieval Times

Pirates' Dinner Adventure

gruesome dungeon and torture chamber (definitely not for young children!). Stay on after the show (the 2nd show only on busy nights) for **The Knight Club**, with bar service, music, dancing and the chance to meet royalty and knights for autographs and photo opportunities.

Pirates' Dinner Adventure

This show (which has been revamped several times since it opened in 1997) features one of the most spectacular settings, with the Spanish galleon pirate ship centrepiece that is 150ft/46m long, 60ft/18m wide, 70ft/21m tall and 'anchored' in a 300,000 gallon/1,365,000 litre lagoon. It also delivers good value with its pre-show elements, plentiful (if ordinary) food and drink, and the imaginative after-show Buccaneer Bash disco until 10.30pm. Coffee is also served at the Buccaneer Bash, and there are kids' meals (chicken fingers and vegetarian) if the main choice of pork, chicken, and seafood medley, with rice and roasted potato doesn't appeal. The basic premise of wicked pirates 'hijacking' the audience is a clever one, even if the story is sometimes hard to follow. Chaos and mayhem ensue, with the local princess abducted by the villainous crew of Captain Sebastian the Black. Swashbuckling abounds, with sword fights, acrobatics, trapeze artists and boat races. There are plenty of energetic stunts and special effects – plus audience participation, which the kids love ($59.95 adults, $39.95 3–11s; see website for discounts).

others, but kids (not to mention a few adults) get a huge kick out of it and they'll also love eating without cutlery (don't worry, the soup bowls have handles!). The elaborate staging is backed up by an excellent chicken dinner and the serfs and wenches who serve you make it a fun experience. Prices, which include the **Medieval Life** exhibit (see below), are $59.95 for adults and $34.95 for 3–12s. A basic Royalty Package upgrade for $10/person includes preferred seating, knight's cheering banner, commemorative programme and behind-the-scenes souvenir DVD. The King's Royalty Package adds a framed group photo and VIP first-row seating all sections or second row in the centre seating area ($20) and the Celebration Package adds the framed group photo and a slice of cake ($16 more). Doors open 90 minutes prior to show time. Times vary seasonally, so call 1866 543 9637 or visit medieval times.com for reservations and details. The recently-renovated Castle is on Highway 192, 5mls/8km east of the junction with I-4. If you have 45 minutes to spare before the show, the **Medieval Life** exhibit is an interesting diversion. This mock village portrays the life and times of people living 900 years ago, with artisans demonstrating pottery and tool-making, glassblowing, spinning and weaving, plus a wonderfully

BRIT TIP
When there are 2 or more shows of The Pirate's Dinner Adventure in one night, opt for the last one if you want the disco bash afterwards.

There is also a **Governor's VIP Upgrade** (available only by calling in advance or at the ticket window) with an exclusive pre-show lounge and bar, front-row seating, guaranteed audience participation, special appetiser buffet, champagne toast, opportunity to upgrade dinner fare to Filet Mignon or Lobster Tail with shrimp and salmon, and one-on-one cast photo opportunity; **Treasurer's Upgrade,** with enhanced seating (row 2), pirate hat and beads; and **Pirate's Upgrade** row 3 seating, hat and beads. The show is located on Carrier Drive between I-Drive and Universal Boulevard, and runs daily at 6pm, 7.30pm or 8.30pm (additional shows in peak periods), with appetisers served for 45 minutes until it's time to be seated (407 248 0590, **piratesdinneradventure.com**). Parking is $3. There is also a special **Pirates Christmas Dinner Adventure** show, which adds suitably festive themes.

Sleuth's Mystery Dinner Shows

This is a real live version of Cluedo acted out before your eyes in hilarious fashion while you enjoy a substantial meal (with a main course choice of honey-glazed Cornish hen, prime rib or lasagne with or without meatballs) and unlimited beer, wine and soft drinks. You can choose between 3 theatres and no fewer than 14 different plot situations (several of which have amusing British settings), including Joshua's Demise, Roast 'Em & Toast 'Em and Lord Mansfield's Fox

Sleuth's Mystery Dinner Shows

Hunt Banquet (mayhem at an English banquet), that add up to some elaborate murder mysteries. The action takes place all around you and members of the audience can take some cameo roles. The quick-witted cast keep things moving and keep you guessing during the theatrical part of the 2½-hour show, then during the main part of dinner you think up questions for interrogation (but be warned, the real murderer is allowed to lie!). Solve the crime and you win a prize, but that is pretty secondary to the overall enjoyment and this is a show we enjoy a lot, plus it's a terrific choice with teens ($52-56 adults, $24-27 3–11s, price determined by meal choice; times vary; 407 363 1985, **sleuths.com**). There are periodic afternoon children's shows, but you should call in advance to see if one is running during your stay. On the other end of the spectrum is **Sleuths Sizzling Comedy Nights**, for mature audiences only, every Saturday at 10pm ($10, with full bar and light bites). Sleuth's is located in the plaza just past Ripley's Believe It Or Not on International Drive, with 3 different theatres, a smart pre-dinner bar area and gift shop.

WonderWorks: Outta Control Magic Comedy Dinner Show

On a smaller scale but no less fun, this show is at WonderWorks on I-Drive (on one corner of Pointe Orlando) and is a real gem. A novel mixture of improvised comedy and clever, close-up magic, the show is accompanied by all-you-can-eat pizza, salad and dessert, plus beer, wine and coke. Set in the intimate Shazam Theater, it features live music, special lighting effects and some slick magic tricks from illusionist (and all-around funny guy!) Tony Brent. The tricks are fairly routine, but the show is served up in terrific style and involves plenty of audience participation. There are a couple of brilliant running gags throughout the fast-paced show, but beware of sitting too close to the stage – you WILL end up as part of the act! Performed twice nightly at 6pm and 8pm, it costs a reasonable $24.95 for adults and $16.95 for 4–12s and seniors. Alternatively, a Magic Combo ticket for the show and access to WonderWorks afterwards (open until midnight, see pages 237–8) is $38.95/$28.95 (407 351 8800, **wonderworksonline.com**).

Capone's Dinner & Show

The setting is 1930s gangland Chicago and, although prohibition is still in full swing, the drinks flow freely at Al's speakeasy. Enter Capone's comedy show and you enter a mixed-up world of song-and-dance acts loosely fitted around the nefarious dealings of local gangster 'Bugs' Moran and. Ditzy Bunny-June (the real star of the show, with a voice worth paying to hear!) and her new husband, Fingers Salvatorio, keep the snappy one-liners coming and the servers join in at key moments to ensure the momentum never lags. Although it leans slightly toward the risqué, the show still remains in family-friendly territory, and many of the gas are first class (and a big improvement on the previous version of the show prior to 2007). A huge Italian-American buffet offers 3 types of pasta, ham, turkey, pot roast and side dishes; it won't win any awards but usually keeps everyone well fed and happy. Unlimited Bud Light draughts, a selection of wines and cocktails, plus soft drinks, juice, Kiddie Cocktails and Mama Capone's 'dessert surprise' round out the all-you-can-eat-and-drink menu ($50.99 adults, $30.99 4–12s, 3 and under free; 407 397 2378, **alcapones.com**; see the website for money-off coupons).

Live music

Orlando's live music scene is always lively and always changing but several venues can be relied on to provide consistent, quality entertainment. As already noted, the House of Blues and Hard Rock Live provide regular big-name concerts, while international acts appear at the new, state-of-the-art **Amway Center** in downtown (as well as the Orlando Magic and Orlando Predators sports

teams). The Jonas Brothers were the headline act for the venue's opening October 2010, and there are sure to be more in 2011 (**amwaycenter.com**). On a smaller scale but just as engaging, **The Social** is Orlando's premier venue for live music most nights of the week, with a wide range of bands and great bar vibe (on Orange Avenue in downtown). La Roux and The Hold Steady provided two contrasting acts in summer 2010, along with top Country artist Blackberry Smoke. Look up the latest info at **thesocial.org** (or call 407 246 1419).

Sports bars

The Sports Bar is a particularly American invention and is well served hereabouts if you'd like to sample the way the locals follow their sport (American football is usually the biggest on weekends Sept–Jan, but basketball is also popular, along with baseball and ice-hockey). Among the multitude of sports bars are our favourites, the **Orlando Ale House** group, with a fine example on Kirkman Road, opposite Universal Studios (407 248 0000) at Lake Buena Vista on Highway 535 (407 239 1800), on Winter Garden-Vineland near Downtown Disney (407 239 1800) and the newest location, Miller's Ale House on International Drive (407 370 6439). The Ale Houses feature more than 30 TVs (each!), classic American bar food, including their signature spicy 'chicken zingers' and an above-average range of beers. There is no better place to be on game day, and every day is game day at the Ale House! (**millersalehouse.com**).

Capone's Dinner & Show

Another chain worth noting is **Buffalo Wild Wings**, with 3 Orlando locations (notably on I-Drive just south of Wet 'n Wild, 11am–2am daily, 407 351 6200), where masses of chicken-orientated dishes (including signature wings with 14 sauces; watch out for the Blazin' – it's seriously hot!) are served up in a casual, lively atmosphere, highlighted by its Buzztime Trivia System at each table and multiple big-screen TVs (**buffalowildwings.com**).

Walt Disney World boasts the excellent **ESPN Club** at Disney's BoardWalk Resort, a full-service restaurant with sports broadcast facilities, video games, more than 70 TV monitors, giant scoreboards and even a Little League menu for kids. No sports fan should miss it. Equally, Universal CityWalk boasts the **NBA City** (for basketball fans) and **NASCAR Sports Grille** (for motor-racing followers), with more big-screen TV style. The owners of The Social also have **McRaney's Tavern** in Winter Park, a traditional-style pub that is also great for live sport (plus an amazing array of beers! 407 622 4474, **mcraneystavern.com**). The various British-style pubs also offer sports bar style and are great places to watch both American and UK sport. Try the **Cricketers' Arms** in Festival Bay (11am– 2am; **cricketersarmspub. com**), **Orlando George & Dragon** on International Drive next to Wet 'n Wild (**britannia pubs.com**), the football-focused **Best of British Soccer World**, also on I-Drive (**bestofbritishpub.com**) and the **Shamrock Pub & Grille** (**theshamrockpub.net**) on Highway 27 in Davenport. (See more on these 'home-from-home' pubs on pages 326-7).

Howl at the Moon

© OCVB

Icebar

Something different

Icebar: Spend 45 minutes surrounded by 50 tons of carved ice while sipping a chilled vodka beverage, then warm up in Nordic-inspired Fire Lounge, at Orlando's ICEBAR on International Drive, located just north of WonderWorks. Ponchos and gloves are provided (wear a warm shirt as the ponchos don't cover your arms), and entry fee is $19.95, drinks not included (save $5 by booking on line). Open 7pm–midnight, with the first ICEBAR entry time at 7:15pm; ages 8 and up allowed 7:15pm and 8pm time slots only. No cover charge for Fire Lounge, but no children allowed (407 426 7555 or **icebarorlando.com**).

Howl at the Moon: If you're looking for a serious party, look no further than Howl at the Moon on I-Drive, where the live music doesn't stop until the wee hours of the morning and the audience doesn't want to go home! A fresh, energetic piano-playing duo take to the ivories and pound out a rockin' good time, highlighted by 'Showtime', when the whole bar joins in a choreographed dance-fest. Signature cocktails are available by the glass or the bucket (!), with drink specials nightly (21 and over only; 7pm–2am Sun–Thurs, 5pm–2am Fri, 6pm–2am Sat; $10 cover charge, free Sun; cover charge after 8pm Mon-Thurs; 5pm Fri, 6pm Sat; 407 352 5999, **howlatthemoon.com**).

Now you'll want to know a lot more about where, when and how to tackle that other holiday dilemma – where to eat. Read on…

Dining Out

or Man, These Portions are HUGE!

America takes its dining out VERY seriously. Consequently, the restaurant scene is an essential part of any Orlando visit. Going out for meals is second nature in the US and is usually much cheaper and better value than in the UK, while it has an extra element of convenience that is extremely family friendly.

The options for dining out are therefore seemingly omnipresent and large scale, which is excellent news for us Joe Tourists as it means it's impossible to go hungry and easy to feed the family – without breaking the bank.

Variety
The variety, quantity and quality of restaurants, cafés, fast-food chains and snack bars is in keeping with the local tradition of convenience and value. The choice is overwhelming at first glance; just cruising along I-Drive or Highway 192 will reveal a baffling array of eateries.

As a general rule, food is plentiful, relatively cheap, available 24 hours a day, and nearly always appetising and filling. You will encounter an increasing number of fine-dining possibilities, but the basic emphasis is still on value for money. Put simply, portions will be large! Service is also efficient and friendly, and it's usually hard to come by a bad meal. The one real exception is if you like fresh veg. Many restaurants

seem to overlook this staple, but if you look up the vegetarian options or visit outlets like Sweet Tomatoes, you will find a more balanced choice.

Exceptional deals
In keeping with the climate, most restaurants tend towards the informal (T-shirts and shorts are nearly always acceptable) and cater readily for families; you will always find a kids' menu, for example, and many have activity packs. This also leads to 2 great deals for the budget-conscious, especially those with a large tribe. Many hotels and restaurants offer 'kids eat free' deals, provided parents are also dining. The age limits vary from under-10 to under-14, but it does represent good value. The all-you-can-eat buffet is another common feature. This means you can probably eat enough at breakfast to keep you going to dinner! Some places also offer early-bird specials – a discount to dine before 6pm. Be aware that 5.30–7.30pm is peak time for many restaurants, though, and you may have to wait for a table if you arrive between 6 and 8pm.

BRIT TIP
As portions are so large, you can save money by sharing a main course. Your waiter or waitress should be happy to oblige (provided you keep their tip up to the full rate).

Don't be afraid to ask for a doggy bag if you have leftovers (even if you haven't brought the dog!). Just ask for the leftovers 'to go'. Don't hesitate to say if something isn't right: Americans will readily complain if they are not happy, so restaurants are keen to ensure everything is to their diners' satisfaction. And, please, don't forget to tip; the basic wage for waiters and waitresses is low, so they rely heavily on tips as part of their income and are taxed on an assumed level of tips. Unless service really is shoddy (in which case you should mention it), the usual tip rate is 10% of your bill at buffet-style restaurants and 15% at full-service restaurants. It is worth checking to see if service is already added to your bill, though this is not common in the US.

With Orlando such a worldwide holiday favourite, you will encounter a huge array of food types. Florida is renowned for its seafood, which comes much cheaper than in the Mediterranean; crab, lobster, shrimp (what we call king prawns), clams and oysters can all be had at decent prices, as well as several dozen varieties of fish, many of which you might not have tried before (like mahi mahi and grouper). Latin-style cuisines, notably Cuban and Mexican, are common, and the South American influences mean the delicious citrus-marinated seafood called ceviche is often featured. There is also plenty of Asian fare, from Chinese and Indian to Japanese, Thai and Vietnamese. The big shopping malls offer a good choice in their food courts, which are often particularly good value. 'Cracker' cooking is original Floridian fare, and the speciality is alligator, either stewed, barbecued, smoked, sautéed or braised. Fried gator tail 'nuggets' are a local favourite, as are frogs' legs. And you must try key lime pie, a truly wonderful Floridian dessert.

The Californian Grill

© Disney

How to order

Ordering food can be an adventure in itself. The choice for each item is often the cue for an inquisition! You can never order just 'toast' – it has to be white, brown, wholewheat, rye, muffin or bagel; eggs come in a baffling variety (order them 'sunny side up' for a traditional British fried egg; 'over easy' is fried both sides but still soft); an order of tea or coffee often brings the response 'Iced, lemon, green, herbal or English? Regular or decaf?'; and salads have more dressings than the NHS. Ask to see a menu if what you fancy isn't displayed.

BRIT TIP

An excellent section of the All Ears Net website run by Deb Wills lists places that cater for special diets, including veggie, at **allearsnet.com/din/special.htm**.

Vegetarian options

In a country where beef is king, vegetarians often find themselves hard done by. However, there are some bright spots. First, there are several largely veggie restaurants, like the Indian cuisine of **Woodlands** on S Orange Blossom Trail (407 854 3330; **woodlandsusa.com**), the popular Chinese of the **Garden Café** on Highway 50 (407 999 9799, **Black Bean Deli** on S Orlando Ave in Winter Park (try its tamales platter; 406 628 0294) and the trendy **Ethos Vegan Kitchen** on N Orange Ave, just north of downtown (407 228 3898, **ethosvegankitchen.com**). The tapas-style **Café Tu Tu Tango** on I-Drive also serves a good variety of vegetarian dishes. However, most upscale restaurants can offer a veggie option and will be happy for you to ask in advance. In *Walt Disney World*, the **California Grill** (in Disney's Contemporary Resort), **Citricos** (Grand Floridian Resort and Spa), **Le Cellier** (Canada pavilion in Epcot) and **Jiko** (Animal Kingdom Lodge) feature good vegetarian choices, while the seafood-orientated **Flying Fish** (Disney's Boardwalk) and **'Ohana** (Disney's Polynesian Resort) also serve up decent veggie fare if asked. Most full-service restaurants (notably **Bongos Cuban Café™** and **Wolfgang Puck® Café** in Downtown Disney) and even some counter-service outlets can cater for non-menu requests. It's always worth asking.

BRIT TIP
Sweet Tomatoes is a restaurant chain we recommend highly, and you can benefit from its enhanced dinner menu by arriving a little before 4pm but still paying only the lunch buffet price.

However, **Sweet Tomatoes** (with 4 outlets in the area, notably on I-Drive by the Kirkman Road junction and a new location in the Crossroads Plaza at Lake Buena Vista) is notably the most popular vegetarian-friendly regular outlet. A buffet restaurant with some great meal deals, it has an all-you-can-eat lunch for $8.39 ($9.79 at dinner, after 4pm) that includes a vast salad counter, a choice of freshly made soups, pizza, pasta, bread and pastries, plus fruit and frozen yoghurt. The menu as a whole is distinctly health conscious and the quality is consistently first class, while its website lists all the nutrition info. Drinks are $2.69 (refills free) and kids' meals are $3.99 3–9s and $4.99 9–12s (11am–10pm; **soup plantation.com**). **Chamberlin's Market & Café** (with 6 Orlando outlets, notably in the Dr Phillips Plaza just off Sand Lake Rd) is another more enlightened choice, with home-made soups, vegetarian chilli, salads, sandwiches and fruit smoothies (**chamberlins.com**). The **Panera Bread** chain also offers some decent veggie options (plus free wi-fi).

BRIT TIP
American bacon is always streaky and crisp fried, and sausages are chipolata-like and slightly spicy.

Eating 24/7

It's not unusual to find restaurants that never close – you can eat around the clock, or '24/7' as the Americans say. So, for those who can't sleep on their first night in the US (plus those who just like to eat!), here is where you can go for a snack or even a full-scale meal at 4 in the morning. **Chain restaurants:** Denny's, Waffle House, Steak & Shake, some McDonald's. Individuals: B-Line

Diner (Peabody Hotel, I-Drive), Planet Java (Gaylord Palms Resort), Sundial 24-7 (Regal Sun Resort) and Mainstreet Market (Hilton at Walt Disney World Resort).

Drinking

A big complaint from Brits on holiday in the US is about the beer. With the exception of a handful of English-style pubs and micro-breweries, American beer is always lager, either bottled or on draught, and ice cold. It goes down great when it's hot, but is generally weaker and fizzier than our own. Of course, there are exceptions (try Killian's Red, Michelob's Amber Bock, Bare Knuckle Stout or Sam Adams beers for a fuller flavour), but if you are expecting a good, old-fashioned British pint, forget it (though the **Cricketers Arms** at Festival Bay has introduced a new chilling process for some of its ales, which serves them closer to a more familiar temperature). You should also look out for **The Big River Grille** at Disney's BoardWalk Resort and **Orlando Brewing** (on Atlanta Ave, just south of downtown Orlando), an organic micro-brewery with a range of 9 distinctive brews, plus free brewery tours (407 872 1117, **orlandobrewing. com**). Spirits (always called 'liquor' by Americans) come in a typically large selection, but beware of ordering just 'whisky' as you'll get bourbon. Specify if you want Scotch or Irish whiskey and demand it 'straight up' if you don't want it with a mountain of ice. Also, when you order a Coke or similar from a counter-service outlet, ask for 'no ice' or 'light ice' unless you want a drink that is 50% ice.

BRIT TIP
If there are several of you drinking beer, ordering a pitcher will work out cheaper than buying it by the glass.

If you fancy a cocktail, there is a massive choice and most bars and restaurants have lengthy happy hours with good prices. Good-quality Californian wines are better value than European. If you stick to soft drinks ('sodas') or coffee, most bars and restaurants give free refills. You can also run a tab in the majority of bars and pay when you leave. But be aware that US licensing laws are stricter than ours and **you must be 21 or over to drink alcohol in a bar or lounge**. You'll often be asked for proof of age before you are served (or allowed into a club), and this means your passport or photo driving licence. Don't bother to argue – no photo ID, no beer!

Where to eat

That gives you the inside track on HOW to eat and drink like the locals. Now you need to know WHERE, so here's a guide to that profusion of choice. There are 4,000-plus restaurants in greater Orlando, so it would be a tall order to list each one. However, the following selection covers the main areas. We group them into: Fast Food, Family Favourites, International Flavours, Home From Home, Seafood Specials and Deluxe Dining. You'll find the Fast Food and Family Favourite type in all the main areas. We also indicate a budget:

$ = most main courses under $10

$$ = most main courses $10–15

$$$ = most main courses $15–20

$$$$ = most main courses $20–$30

$$$$$ = most main course $30-plus

We also have a special section on each of the three main areas of International Drive, Highway 192/Kissimmee and Lake Buena Vista. But, as ever, we start with the options of *Walt Disney World* itself.

✈ BRIT TIP
Raglan Road is one of Orlando's must-do venues, as much for its genuine pub charm as its fab food. Drop in after 7pm when house band Creel livens things up (Mon–Sat) with its lively blend of rock and traditional Irish music.

DOWNTOWN DISNEY DINING

While the parks and resorts hold their share of dining delights, the heart of Disney dining can be found at Downtown Disney with some 17 different outlets in the 3 main areas.

Belly up to the bar!

If you'd like to sample a restaurant's fare without going to the whole hog of a proper sit-down experience, many places now offer a bar or appetiser menu for those who'd just like a drink and/or snack in their bar area. Some distinctly stylish restaurants offer this opportunity, and you can dine well without breaking the bank. Notable examples include the Capital Grille, Fishbones, Seasons 52, The Oceanaire, McCormick & Schmick's, Luma on Park, Carrabba's, Fulton's Crab House, Fleming's, Samba Room, Old Hickory, Salt Island Chophouse, and Moonfish, plus The Crab House (for its Mon–Fri Happy Hour, 4–7pm), Landry's Seafood House (ditto, 4–6.30pm) and The Palm (5–7pm and 9pm–close).

Pleasure Island

Raglan Road: This Irish-themed pub, with lively music, food to match and a genuine Emerald Isle style, is where you really can enjoy the craic. Much of the restaurant's interior was shipped over from Ireland (including no fewer than 4 reclaimed 130-year-old bars, plus 9 European beers on draft), establishing an authentic backdrop to an original menu created by celebrity master chef Kevin Dundon. Fresh, simple ingredients combined with an imaginative twist make the likes of shepherd's pie, mussels, beef stew, Irish sausages and bread pudding (the best we have tasted!) a real wake-up call for the senses. Stop in at the gift shop for all your souvenirs and be sure to check out Kevin Dundon's Full On Irish cookbook to create a taste of Raglan Road at home ($$–$$$;11am–2am, 407 938 0300, **raglanroadirish pub.com**).

Paradiso 37: New in summer 2009, this 'Taste of the Americas' offers a wide variety of foods, much of it with a Latin-tinged flavour, and live music nightly to bring a bit of much-needed life back to the heart of the Pleasure Island area. A tempting menu includes Argentinean skirt steak, Chilean salmon, Mexican fare, classic burgers, ribs, great salads and a hefty surf & turf platter, plus some equally hefty signature cocktails and an amazing selection of 37 tequilas. Give the Venezuelan Shrimp and Jicama Orange Salad a try for some different flavours. The lively style, split-level restaurant, chic bar area (inside and out), eye-pleasing lakeside setting and outdoor patio mark this out as a relaxing venue for lunch or an upbeat dinner, or just somewhere to kick back with a drink or one of its speciality coffees ($$–$$$$; 11.30am–midnight Sun–Thurs, 1am Fri and Sat; 407 934 3700).

Portobello: Easy to overlook (but don't!) is this Tuscan-country trattoria that underwent a major makeover in 2008. From the complimentary glass of Italian sangria and fresh bread with oven-baked garlic to the family-style menu and full wine list, this is a restaurant to be enjoyed in relaxed style. You can choose from something as simple as pizza or a classic Caesar salad to Mahi Mahi with polenta and zucchini ribbons in a tomato seafood broth, with fine steaks, veal, chicken and fabulous pastas. The Portobello Mushroom is a superb starter, while other signature dishes are ravioli gigante (a heavenly ricotta-and-spinach filled pasta) and black linguine with Florida rock shrimp. A great wine list, speciality beers and seasonal prix fixe menus (at $34.95 for a 3-course dinner) complete an impressive picture here and it all adds up to one of Disney's most enjoyable dining options, with reservations not always necessary ($$–$$$$; 11.30am–11pm; 407 934 8888; **portobellorestaurant.com**).

Fulton's Crab House: Good seafood is not hard to come by, but great seafood is the preserve of a handful – like Fulton's. This mock riverboat has 6 dining rooms (albeit each with the same menu), plus the Stone Crab Lounge, which features a busy raw bar. The interior is filled with nautical props, photos and lithographs, giving it an eclectic, period atmosphere, but the real attraction is the food – some of the freshest and most tempting fish, crab and lobster dishes in Florida. The Alaskan king crab is a rare treat, the steamed crab, snow crab, blue crab cakes and whole Narragansett lobster are as succulent as they come, but there are fresh specials every day, as well as a kid's menu. The Stone Crab Lounge serves lunch and dinner 11.30am–11pm, while the restaurant is open for dinner only ($$$–$$$$$; 4–11pm; 407 394 2628; **fultonscrabhouse.com**).

T-Rex Cafe: It's a 'Prehistoric Adventure' as you enter the latest audio-animatronic world of the people who created the Rainforest Café chain. The vast setting alone is impressive – a series of themed areas like the Ice Cave and Jurassic Forest, which are home to all manner of roaring, menacing dinos, with extra sound effects, meteor strikes and thunderstorms for good measure! The food is fairly straightforward (albeit with fancy names like Woolly Mammoth Chicken and Boneyard Buffet) but portions are suitably large ($$–$$$; 11am–11pm, midnight Fri and Sat, 407 828 8739, **trexcafe.com**).

Other choices: To one side of Raglan Road is **Cooke's of Dublin**, a chippie serving up real chips, beer-battered fish, gourmet battered sausages and 'Do bars' (deep-fried Snickers bars!). **Fuego Cigars by Sosa** is an upscale lounge offering premium cigars and wines.

> **BRIT TIP**
> For reservations at any Disney restaurant, call 407 939 3463 (407 WDW DINE), while you can also book online at **disneyworld.co.uk**.

Paradiso

The Marketplace

While The Marketplace is largely the shopping heart of *Downtown Disney* (see page 338), it also offers some tempting dining.

Rainforest Café: With its safari-style 'adventures' under a volcano-topped exterior, this is the place to entertain the family while they fill up on huge platefuls of chicken, pasta, steak, seafood and burgers, surrounded by audio-animatronic jungle creatures and periodic 'rainstorms', with an excellent kids' menu for 10s and under ($$–$$$; 11.30am–11pm; 407 827 8500, **rainforestcafe.com**).

Cap'n Jack's Restaurant: Head here for great chowder, crab cakes, shrimp and many other fine seafood offerings, as well as its trademark 'fishbowl' margaritas. Open for lunch and dinner, it makes for a more relaxing choice in a busy area with great lake views ($$–$$$$,11.30am–10pm).

Other choices: Ghirardelli Ice Cream & Chocolate Shop is a great location for dessert or just a milkshake while you wander. The **Earl of Sandwich** is an excellently priced café for a quick bite or a lighter meal, while there is also a new **Pollo Campero**, a Latin American chicken-based fast-food restaurant, and a **Wolfgang Puck Express** for quick-service Californian cuisine.

West Side

Back in the more hip night-time district of Downtown Disney are another 5 options.

Planet Hollywood: This is the largest and busiest example of this worldwide chain, hence you get lashings of its film-related fun style, with a widely varied menu (if heavy on American

Wolfgang Puck® Café

diner fare) and some wonderful cocktails ($$–$$$; 11am–1am; 407 827 7827, **planethollywood.com**).

Bongos Cuban Cafe: Co-owned by Gloria and Emilio Estefan, the sights, sounds and tastes of Old Havana come to this imaginative setting, with red-hot Latin music and some excellent Cuban fare ($$–$$$$, 11am–10.30pm, Sun–Thurs 11.30pm Fri and Sat; 407 828 0999, **bongoscubancafe.com**).

House of Blues®: This cavernous combination live music venue and restaurant in backwoods Mississippi style is a must for anyone even vaguely interested in blues, rock 'n' roll, R&B, gospel and jazz – while its trademark Gospel Brunch on Sundays serves up some fab food with a full gospel show (10.30am and 1pm; $33.50 adults, $17.25 3–9s). The 500-seat restaurant (11am–11pm) offers some fine fare, including seafood jambalaya, fresh fish and a host of Cajun delicacies, with live music Thurs–Sat ($$–$$$$; 11.30am–11pm, 1am Thurs–Sat; 407 934 2583, **houseofblues.com**).

Wolfgang Puck® Café: A rich experience from the renowned Californian chef, with no fewer than 4 options: the Café, gourmet food in a casual setting; Wolfgang Puck Express, the fast-food version; the Sushi Bar for seafood, pizzas and micro-brews; and the Dining Room, an upscale restaurant featuring top international cuisine. It caters for just about every taste (the sushi is to die for) and is highly family friendly ($$–$$$$$; 11.30am–11pm, 6–10.30pm in the Dining Room; 407 938 9653, **wolfgangpuck.com**).

Other choices: Grab a snack at **Wetzel's Pretzels**, with the choice of pretzels, hot dogs, lemonade and **Haagen-Dazs** ice-cream.

FAST FOOD

This section is reserved primarily for counter-service fast-food outlets and all will be in the $ category.

The big names: If you are a fan of **McDonald's**, there are around 70 outlets in the area, from small drive-through types to a mega, 24-hour establishment on Sand Lake Road (near

© OCVB

It's McDonald's, Jim, but not as we know it!

McDonald's is not renowned for its healthy options – until you come to Orlando and find the restaurants owned and operated by Oerther Foods, which pioneered the chain's Bistro Gourmet menus. Oerther has 24 McDonald's outlets, with many of them themed and open 24 hours, plus 5 featuring the new Bistro offerings – an amazing deviation from the fast-food norm. As well as the usual burgers and fries, they feature fresh pastas, hand-made pizza, gourmet sandwiches, veggie wraps, salads, gourmet coffees and eye-catching desserts. You order in the normal way, then watch your meal being created for you at the deli counter. Portions are generous, freshly made and quite delicious. Bistro breakfast selections (7am–10.30pm) include eggs Benedict, Belgian waffles and French toast. The themed locations vary from a 1950s theme (at 5890 S Orange Blossom Trail) to Motorbikes (5400 S Kirkman Road) and Hollywood (2500 S Kirkman Road). The finest examples, though, are the Sand Lake Road duo – The World's Largest Entertainment McDonald's & PlayPlace (6875 Sand Lake Road) and European Café (7344 Sand Lake Road), an ultra-modern venue. The former features a huge games arcade and vivid themed areas, plus a Kids' Club and toddler area (bistro hours 7am–11pm Mon–Thurs, to 3 am Fri–Sun; regular McDonald's menu available 24 hours; **mcfun.com**).

the junction with I-Drive) that also has the biggest Play Place for kids of any McDonald's in the world. **Burger King** is well represented, as is that other burger bastion, **Wendy's**. **KFC** also has outlets throughout the area, and you'll find plenty of **Pizza Huts** and **Domino's Pizza**, both of which deliver locally – even to your hotel room.

Local variations

Check out **Checkers** or **Hardees** for burgers, **Popeye's Famous Fried Chicken & Biscuits** or **Chick-fil-A** as a KFC alternative, **Taco Bell** if you'd like the cheap and cheerful Mexican option, or **Arby's** for a range of hot roast beef sandwiches that make a nice change from burgers. **Dairy Queen** offers a mix of burgers, hot dogs, pork sandwiches and ice-cream dishes, while **Papa John's**, **Little Caesar's** and **Hungry Howie's** make a decent alternative to Pizza Hut. The 'sub', or torpedo-roll sandwich, is what they serve at **Subway**, **Sobik's**, **Quiznos** and **Miami Subs**. An even better bet is health-conscious **Tijuana Flats**, which started in central Florida and now has more than 70 outlets in the US, notably in Winter Park and Thornton Park. Its Tex-Mex style (an American version of Mexican cuisine that originated in Texas) is geared around fresh, hand-made products in a lively, convivial atmosphere. Check out its burritos,

quesadillas, enchiladas, tacos and salads – and you'll struggle to spend more than $10 per person (**tijuanaflats. com**). The big up-and-coming brand, though, is the award-winning **Five Guys Burgers & Fries**, with a dozen Orlando outlets and also a more healthy approach. Using only fresh-ground beef (never frozen), peanut oil and no trans fats, they serve up just 4 basic burgers (plus Little Burgers), hotdogs and sandwiches, and allow you to add your own extras from a 16-item toppings bar (**fiveguys.com**).

Drive-through

Many fast food options also have a drive-through, which is fun to try. Simply drive around the side of the building where indicated, choose from the take-away menu and speak your order into the voice box. Carry on around the building (don't wait by the voice box!) and you pay and receive your food at a side window. A neat variation on this theme is **Sonic**, a modern version of the drive-in diner, where you stay in your car and the 'carhop' waiter or waitress comes to take the order. The fare – burgers, hot dogs, wraps, salads and sandwiches – won't win any awards, but the style is fun. Try its I-Drive location just north of Kirkman Road (7am–11pm; **sonicdrivein.com**).

FAMILY FAVOURITES

After all the fast food choices, there is a huge selection that specialises in more regular fare, still with an all-American flavour but with greater variety and ultra family friendly. They vary from the buffet kind to fairly sophisticated, and you'll find them in multiple locations.

The breakfast specialists

Need to start the day by stoking up with a big breakfast? Look no further than this selection.

Cracker Barrel: Delightful old country store style, with mountainous breakfasts, well-balanced lunch and dinner menus, Kid's Stuff choices and an old-fashioned charm that's a nice change from the usual tourist frenzy ($; 6am–10pm Sun–Thurs, 6am–11pm Fri and Sat; **crackerbarrel.com**). **Bob Evans:** Also notable for its friendly, country-style, hearty menus (plus low-carb options) and delicious desserts. It also offers a good takeaway and country store selection ($; 6 or 7am–10pm; **bobevans.com**). **International House of Pancakes (or IHOP) and Waffle House:** You will struggle to spend more than $7 on a full meal, whether on of their huge breakfast platters or a hot sandwich with fries. Waffle Houses are open 24 hours a day ($; wafflehouse. com) and IHOPs 6am–midnight ($; **ihop.com**). **Denny's:** Another traditional 24-hour restaurant, its wide selection makes a traditional bacon-and-egg breakfast seem ordinary, and it does an excellent range of toasted sandwiches and dinner meals, like grilled catfish, as well as a Senior Selections menu, with smaller portions at reduced prices for over-55s ($; **dennys.com**). **Perkins:** Also a great breakfast choice; for a really hearty meal try Perkins Eggs Benedict (2 eggs and bacon on a toasted muffin with hash browns and fresh fruit), while its bread-bowl salads are equally satisfying (some branches open around the clock; **perkinsrestaurants.com**). **Friendlys:** Another cheerful diner, with a typical array of American fare, plus delicious ice-cream-based desserts ($; 7am–11pm; **friendlys.com**). **Village Inn:** massively popular with the tourist crowd is this unassuming outlet of a

national chain on Westwood Boulevard, just off I-Drive north of SeaWorld. Totally unpretentious but fabulous value for breakfast, lunch and dinner, it serves up heaps of basic fare in no-nonsense style with friendly service, plus some of the most decadent desserts in the cosmos (we dare you to try their Boston Cream, French Silk or Key Lime pies!). Huge breakfast plates (all at around $6.59), great kids' menus and excellent salads, sandwiches and burgers all add up to exceptional value ($–$$; 6am–midnight; **villageinn.com**).

Buffet style

The unarguable value of the all-you-can-eat restaurants is very much in evidence here.

Ponderosa Steakhouse and Sizzler: These 2 popular, identikit, consistent but unspectacular big-chain offerings feature huge breakfast, lunch and dinner buffets. You order and pay as you enter and are then seated, before being unleashed on the help-yourself serveries. You'd be hard pushed to tell whose food was whose, but there IS a difference in price depending on location, with I-Drive tending to be a dollar or two dearer than elsewhere. Standard dinner fare includes chicken wings, meatballs, chilli, ribs, steaks (for a small extra supplement) and seafood, while their immense salad bars are also a big draw ($–$$; 7am–late evening, **ponderosasteak houses.com** and **sizzler. com**). **Golden Corral**, **Shoney's** and **CiCi's Pizza:** The buffet theme is served rather better by these 3, where you may pay a bit more but the extra quality is undeniable. Golden Corral impresses for its fresh style and Carver's Choice of roast meats plus an excellent vegetable

Simon's fave

The best value buffets is **CiCi's Pizza**, where its 4 Orlando locations all offer not just a 20-item pizza spread – all made fresh every hour – but also salad and pasta options, and a couple of delicious desserts (the chocolate brownies are to die for!). Or their chefs will make something fresh just for you. Great service and quality, at an unbeatable price.

selection and terrific dessert bar (usually at least 20 choices!). There is a weekend supplement at some outlets as they add steak to the main choices ($–$$; 7.30am–10pm; **goldencorral.com**).

Shoney's: An à la carte menu as well as excellent buffets, all with a Southern accent ($; 7am–11pm; **shoneys.com**).

CiCi's Pizza: A real hit with us, it features an extensive pizza buffet, plus salad and desserts all for a bargain $5.99 ($; under-3s eat free; 11am–10pm; **cicispizza.com**).

BRIT TIP A buffet breakfast at Golden Corral or similar should keep you going until tea-time and is a good way to start a theme-park day.

The big chains

Moving up into the next price and facilities are the following choices.

Applebee's: Self-styled 'neighborhood bar and grill', this offers a rather more health-conscious menu with good salads and weight-watchers' choices as well as a tempting array of steaks and chicken dishes ($–$$; 11am–midnight; **applebees.com**).

Bahama Breeze: Step forward into the Caribbean with this lively chain that boasts food as good as the surroundings. Try West Indies Patties, Calypso Shrimp Linguine or the Jerk Chicken Pasta. Service is in keeping with its personable style, there is a pleasing individual touch and you will struggle to get better value just about anywhere else in Orlando. The decor is refreshing and entertaining, and it's worth just popping in for a drink ($$–$$$$; 4pm–2am Mon–Sat, 4pm–

midnight Sun; **bahamabreeze.com**).

BRIT TIP The Bahama Breeze restaurants don't take reservations and are extremely popular in the evening. Try to arrive before 5.30pm to avoid a wait or try the Lake Buena Vista location, which can be a bit quieter.

Bennigan's: This chain is a *Brit Guide* favourite for its friendly, efficient service, smart decor and tempting menu, especially for lunch. Its bar atmosphere is straight out of TV's *Cheers*, and the Irish flavour comes into its own on St Patrick's Day ($–$$; 11am–2am; **bennigans.com**).

Boston Market: Typical home cooking, café style, they specialise in fresh-carved meats, rotisserie chicken, decent vegetables and excellent value ($–$$; 11am–10pm; **bostonmarket.com**).

Buffalo Wild Wings: A huge sports bar and grill, featuring chicken wings, tenders, wraps, salads, burgers and ribs. Simple but tasty, and very popular with its multiple large-screen TVs ($–$$; 11am–1am Mon–Fri, to 2am Fri and Sat, noon–midnight Sun; **buffalowildwings.com**).

Café Tu Tu Tango: Another original local restaurant (like Bahama Breeze) high on style and quality, the accent is artist-colony Spanish, with an original tapas-style menu, live entertainment and artwork on the walls that changes daily. Vegetarians are well catered for, and you can try some succulent pizzas, seafood, salads and soups plus imaginative Mexican dishes and a well-thought-out kids' menu (11.30am–11am, midnight Fri and Sat; **cafetututango.com**).

Cattleman's Steak House: In 3 locations, all with a neat Western-style Saloon, periodic early bird specials (4–6pm) and good kids' menu, this

Café Tu Tu Tango

goes all-out for the cowboy approach. Steaks are the order of the day, but you can also try chicken, seafood and pork ($$–$$$; 5pm–11pm, 2am in Saloon).

Cheesecake Factory: While its prime feature is desserts (including more than 30 cheesecakes), the rest of the huge menu is impressive in an eclectic, high-tech setting. Mexican dishes jostle with pizza, pasta, seafood, burgers, steaks and salads, plus it offers a great brunch, so come here hungry! ($$–$$$; 11am–11pm; **thecheesecakefactory.com**).

Chevy's: A healthy slice of Mexicana while still providing reassuring American selections, its salsa is fresh-made every hour, and the tortilla chips, guacamole, fajitas and tortillas are delicious ($–$$; 4–11pm Mon–Thurs, 4pm–midnight Fri, 11am–midnight Sat, 11am–11pm Sun; **chevys.com**).

BRIT TIP
Take advantage of Chevy's Kids Eat Free Tuesdays (free kids' meal with any regular entrée purchase). Chevy's also has a 3–7pm Happy Hour in its Cantina bar, with a $3 drink menu and half-price appetisers.

Chili's: Also in Tex-Mex territory, it places the emphasis more on steak and ribs and less on tortillas and spices. Service is usually highly efficient ($–$$; 11am–1am Mon–Sat, 11am–11pm Sun; chilis.com).

Don Pablo's: A fairly elaborate Mexican offering with clever theming, a fun, lively atmosphere (especially round the Cantina bar) and classic, well-explained

Chili's

menus ($$; 11.30am–10pm Sun–Thurs, 11.30am–11pm Fri and Sat; **donpablos. com**).

Fuddruckers: Purely and simply some of the best burgers you'll find, with a huge choice (including veggie and ostrich) and a real kid-friendly style. Make your selection, find a table and wait for your burger to be cooked fresh, or choose from the salad and sandwich options, plus tempting shakes, cookies and desserts ($–$$; 11am–10pm Sun–Fri, 11pm Sat; **fuddruckers.com**).

Hooters: A lively place that makes no bones about its style – 'delightfully tacky yet unrefined' – this is popular with the beach-party crowd – and for the famous Hooter Girl waitresses. The entertaining menu features seafood, salads and burgers, plus Hooters Nearly World Famous Chicken Wings in eight strengths – beware of the Samurai! ($–$$; 11am–midnight Mon–Thurs, 11am–1am Fri, Sat, noon–11pm Sun; **hooters.com**).

Houlihan's: Classic bar-restaurant with plenty of style, cheerful service, an extensive and appetising menu (try its Down Home Pot Roast) – and huge portions (but also a mini-dessert option; $–$$; 11am–1am; **houlihans.com**).

Logan's Roadhouse: A fun and, rustic atmosphere includes masses of peanuts in their shells (which end up all over the wooden floor!), plus a menu featuring burgers, chicken, steaks and ribs, $2.99 kids' meals, plus an express lunch selection ($$; 11am–10pm Sun–Thurs, 11pm Fri and Sat; **logansroadhouse.com**).

Lone Star Steakhouse: Head to Texas for its mesquite-grilled steaks, ribs, chicken and fish, with a friendly welcome and roadhouse ambience (plus huge portions! $–$$; 11am–11pm; **lonestarsteakhouse.com**).

Longhorn Steakhouse: The newer, fancier version of the Texas steakhouse and 'Flavour of the West', this features fresh-grilled steaks, chops and ribs, plus chicken and seafood that is hard to beat at the price, with a good menu for under-10s ($$–$$$; 11am–10pm, 11pm Fri and Sat; **longhornsteakhouse.com**).

Pop into our 'local'

The nearest thing to a typical pub in these parts is the **Orlando/Miller Ale House** chain. Hugely popular with the locals, it features pool tables, multiple TV screens for all the sports action and a friendly, efficient style with a varied menu. Check out its spicy chicken zingers, fish sandwiches and barbecue ribs for some great tastes. It can be rowdy on weekend big-game days, but it's still a great place to hang out with friends, bring the family or just pop in for a drink. The Ale House in Lake Buena Vista on Winter Garden-Vineland Road is also our 'local', and the new-style Miller's Ale House on I-Drive is positively vast ($–$$; 11am–2am; **millersalehouse.com**).

Olive Garden: One of America's big successes, bringing Italian food into budget, mass-market range. The light and airy dining rooms create a relaxing environment and, while it doesn't offer a huge choice, what it does, it does well and in generous portions. Pasta is the speciality, but it also offers chicken, veal, steak, seafood and great salads (with unlimited refills), garlic breadsticks and non-alcoholic drinks ($$–$$$; 11am–10pm Sun–Thurs, 11pm Fri and Sat; **olive garden.com**).

Outback Steakhouse: An Australian slant, some of the best fare – and biggest portions. Its thick, juicy, well-seasoned steaks, ribs and seafood selections are all above average, while its trademark is the Bloomin' Onion, a large fried onion with a dipping sauce. Good kids' menu ($$–$$$; 4–10.30pm Mon–Thurs, 4–11.30pm Fri, 3.30pm–11.30pm Sat, 3.30–10.30pm Sun; **outback.com**).

Smokey Bones: With a rustic, log-cabin touch and some succulent, deep-smoked barbecue, it serves up fire-grilled steaks, salmon, chicken, burgers and salads, but we recommend the barbecue platters and rib combos. Sports fans can also enjoy a huge array of TVs ($–$$$; 11am–11pm Sun–Thurs, midnight Fri and Sat; **smokeybones.com**).

Sonny's Real Pit Bar-B-Q: A national chain with no great pretensions, just masses of food of the slow-cooked barbecue persuasion served up in friendly, let's-get-messy style. The good kids' menu makes it ideal for families, and you should definitely try the ribs and its own-recipe coleslaw ($–$$; 11am–10pm; **sonnysbbq.com**).

TGI Fridays: Lively, eclectic style, Orlando boasts multiple offerings (notably on I-Drive just north of Pointe Orlando). The drinks menu is the size of a book and the main menu is heavy on wings, ribs, burgers and steaks ($–$$; 11am–2am; **tgifridays.com**).

Tony Roma's: 'Famous for ribs', the airy decor and ambience, clever kids' menu, junior meals and melt-in-the-mouth ribs are a winning combo. You can still get chicken, burgers and steaks, but why ignore a dish that's done this well? ($$–$$$; 11am–11pm Sun–Thurs, 11am–midnight Fri and Sat; **tonyromas.com**).

Uno Chicago Grill: The place to go if you're bored with Pizza Hut, it specialises in deep-dish pizzas plus pastas, chicken dishes, steaks and salads, ($–$$; 11.30am–midnight; **unos.com**).

Urban Flats: An upmarket chain of flatbread grills, specialising in creative dips, salads, wraps and a wide variety of tempting toppings for its flatbreads. They offer more than 30 wines by the glass and 100 by the bottle, and their trademark Wine Down Wednesdays offer a range of wines to sample, along with appetisers and flatbreads, from 5-8pm at $20/person. ($–$$; 11am–10pm Sun–Wed, 11am–11pm Thurs–Sat, **urbanflats.net**).

INTERNATIONAL FLAVOURS

Your food choice extends beyond the obvious to an international array, featuring Chinese and Indian, but also Thai, Japanese and Italian. Some are still chains, others are one-offs.

Indian, Chinese and more

There's a wide range of Asian restaurants in Orlando, from ordinary Chinese to five-star Japanese. Take your pick from this recommended selection.

Aashirwad: A decent Indian choice, with an excellent lunch buffet and some seriously spicy Mughlai dishes ($–$$$; 11.30am–3pm and 5.30–10.30pm; 407 370 9830; **aashirwadrestaurant.com**).

Dragon Court Buffet: This locals' Chinese favourite in Lake Buena Vista serves a huge spread of fresh, appetising dishes at a terrific lunch price. With 100 items, including sushi, this is well worth trying ($$–$$$; 11am–11pm; 407 238 9996, **dragoncourtorlando.com**).

India Palace: An unassuming location tucked in a small shopping plaza in Lake Buena Vista, this serves good food in large amounts and with family-friendly service ($–$$$; 11.30am–11pm Tues–Sun, 5–11pm Mon; 407 238 2322).

Kobe: This brings a touch of Americana to its Japanese-themed dining, but still achieves individuality with the chef preparing the food at your table ($$$; 11.30am–11pm; **kobesteakhouse.com**).

Memories of India: A sound Indian on Turkey Lake Rd and a good choice for vegetarians. Its Goan fish curry is a particular speciality, but it also offers a great range of biryanis, tandoori dishes and fresh breads, and a novel Champagne Sunday Brunch ($$; 11.30am–2.30pm and 5.30-10pm, 9pm Sun; 407 370 3277, **memoriesofindiacuisine.com**)

Ming Court: The Rolls-Royce of Chinese is this beautiful place on I-Drive, opposite Pointe Orlando, with its magnificent setting and live music most evenings. The menu is extensive and beautifully presented by friendly servers, who make you feel right at home. Many dishes can be had as a side order rather than a full main course, and there are extensive dim sum and

Ming Court

The cream of America

Orlando boasts outstanding ice-cream parlours. Check out Carvel, Baskin Robbins, Dairy Queen and Marble Slab Creamery. However, for the crème de la crème, try **Cold Stone Creamery** at Winter Garden Village and Blake Boulevard (just off Highway 192 west of I-4). Its amazing range of ice-creams can be combined with a range of wonderful ingredients that are sheer heaven. It also mixes sensational shakes (**coldstonecreamery.com**).

even sushi and sashimi choices, plus an imaginative kids' menu. The basil chicken is one of our all-time favourites ($$–$$$; 11am–2.30pm, 4.30pm–midnight; **ming-court.com**).

BRIT TIP
Check out Ming Court's website for a print-at-home 10% money-off coupon or an Early Bird special (4.30-6.30pm) offering 50% off a 2nd entrée (click 'Menus').

New Punjab: Another fine Indian choice on I-Drive, with great tandoori dishes and extensive vegetable selection ($–$$$; 5–11pm Mon, 11.30am–11pm Tues–Sun; 407 352 7887; **punjabindianrestaurant.com**).

PF Chang's China Bistro: This mixes classic Chinese fare with American bistro style that makes fans of virtually all who sample it. You should try the spicy ground chicken and eggplant (aubergine), Cantonese roasted duck or Oolong marinated sea bass. There is also a good veggie selection ($$–$$$$; 11am–11pm, 10pm Sun; **pfchangs.com**).

Red Bamboo: Wonderfully authentic Thai flavours and clean, contemporary decor. Its soups and curries are to die for, while house speciality Smokey Pot is a stew of marinated prawns, vegetables and glass noodles in chilli ($$–$$$$; 11am–2.30pm and 5–10pm Mon–Fri, noon–10pm Sat, closed Sun; 407 226 8997; **redbamboothai.com**).

Seito Sushi: Another great Japanese offering from this local chain, with a formal sushi bar and a more inviting, small-scale approach ($$–$$$$;

A Florida steak-out

We're often asked where to go to get a good steak in Florida and the answer is, just about anywhere! America serves great steaks and it is usually hard to get a BAD sirloin, T-bone or filet. Many restaurants specialise in steak, but even those that don't can turn out a decent slab of prime beef. For those who really want to indulge, the following (totally unofficial) ranking should help (NB: the US Dept of Agriculture grades its meat quality Standard, Select, Choice and, for the top 2%, Prime).

Standard: Ponderosa, Golden Corral, Sizzler, O'Charley's, Beef O'Brady's, Great Western, Western Sizzlin', Shamrock Pub. **Select:** Black Angus, Bennigan's, Applebee's, TGI Fridays, Cattleman's Steakhouse, Chili's, Logan's Roadhouse, Lone Star, Tony Roma's, Uno Chicago Grill, Cricketer's Arms, Colorado House of Beef, Smoky Bones, Rainforest Café, Chevy's, Ruby Tuesday, Miller's Ale House, Macaroni Grill, Red Lobster, Copper Canyon Grill. **Choice:** Outback, Salt Island Chophouse, Longhorn Steakhouse, Kobe, Shogun, Brio Tuscan Grill, Charley's, Vito's Chophouse, The Oceanaire, J Alexander, Texas de Brazil, The Venetian Room, Palm Restaurant, Le Cellier (Epcot), Jack's Place, Amura's, Carrabba's, Cantina Laredo, Bergamo's, Johnnie's Hideaway. **Prime:** A Land Remembered, Old Hickory, Fleming's, Spencer's, Ruth's Chris, Del Frisco's, Everglades, Morton's, Capital Grille, Antonio's, Christini's, Vito's Chophouse, Timpano's, Porterhouse, Shula's, The Yachtsman (Disney's Yacht Club resort).

11.30am–2.30pm, 5–10pm; 407 644 5050; **seitosushi.com**).

Shogun Steakhouse: This national chain, which is ideal for those a little unsure whether to go for the full Japanese experience, opts for the Teppanyaki-style service, at long, bench-like tables with the chef cooking in front of you. But you can still order a no-nonsense steak or chicken ($$$–$$$$; 6–10pm Sun–Thurs, 6–10.30pm Fri and Sat; 407 352 1607, **shogunorlando.com**).

Sizzling Wok: A cheerful budget-orientated offering on Sand Lake Road (by the Florida Mall), it features a massive Chinese buffet at a reasonable price ($–$$; 11am–10pm Sun–Thurs, 11am–10.30pm Fri and Sat; 407 438-8389).

Tastes of the Med

Some excellent Italian dining chains here, too.

Antonio's: This impressive local chain goes distinctly upmarket, with 3 restaurants (including 1 with a café, deli and superb wine shop) that all feature an individual, exclusive style as well as outstanding cuisine – sensational risottos are a signature dish, while veal and New York strip steak are equally good ($$$–$$$$$; 5–10pm Mon–Sat; **antoniosonline.com**).

Bravo Cucina Italiana: Brand new in Orlando, this fresh, inviting twist on classic Italian fare features home-made pasta, pizza, flatbreads, steaks, chops and seafood in an inviting 'Roman-ruin' decor. Casual and chic, and fun for the grown-up crowd ($$–$$$$; 11am–10pm, to 11pm Fri and Sat; 407 351 5880; **bravoitalian.com**).

Carrabba's: Direct from Sicily, here's casual-but-elegant dining in a warm, festive atmosphere. House specialities include crispy calamari, chicken marsala, pasta and hand-made pizzas. The kids' menu is one of the best and the style is very child friendly ($$–$$$; 4–10pm Sun–Thurs, 3–11pm Fri and Sat; **carrabbas.com**).

La Nuova Cucina: this latest entry to the stylish scene on Sand Lake Road's 'Restaurant Row' is a modern Italian, with a contemporary setting for a delicious menu from local chef Paulo Baroni, that features the amuse-bouche concept. Bold flavours, colours and textures are all part of Paulo's repertoire, plus a highly personal touch. Take your pick from tempting antipasti and salads, rich pastas and risottos, and some superb steaks and chicken dishes, plus daily chef specials. Highlights include the pumpkin soup with grilled shrimp and a touch of curry; lobster raviolini; veal saltimbocca; and mahi-mahi with tomato and saffron sauce. The desserts are another real delight (we recommend the tiramisu and signature chocolate pudding), while there is also an extensive wine list, with an excellent mix of Italian and New World offerings ($$–$$$$, Mon–Thurs 5–10pm, noon–11pm Fri and Sat, noon–9pm Sun; 407 354 4909, **lanuovacucina.com**).

Macaroni Grill: Another wonderful slice of Little Italy, its spacious restaurants are stylish, comfortable and well served, with excellent à la carte and family-style menus (serving 8–10). The pasta and wood-oven pizzas are first class and the wine list is impressive ($$–$$$$; 11.30am–10pm Sun–Thurs, 11.30am–11pm Fri and Sat; **macaroni grill.com**).

Anatolia: For something more exotic, head for the genuine Turkish flavours of Anatolia, a new restaurant in the Dr Phillips Plaza off Sand Lake Road. With a delicious range of authentic breads, hot and cold appetisers, salads, soups, pides (Turkish pizzas), kebabs and regional specialities like moussaka and baklava, you can dine royally without breaking the bank. Try the babaghanoush (chargrilled aubergine puréed with fresh herbs and spices), tabouli, kofte kebab or chicken adana ($–$$; 11am–10pm Sun–Thurs, 11pm Fri and Sat; 407 352 6766, **anatoliaorlando.com**).

HOME FROM HOME
Having extolled the virtues of the all-American choices, there is an array of British-style pubs that should appeal to UK visitors. All offer predictable pub

Simon and Susan at Sherlock's

grub and beers and you can happily take the kids into any of them.

Best of British: This fresh choice (opposite Ripley's Believe It Or Not on I-Drive) goes for a full footy-themed style, with 12 flat-screen TVs, plus a giant theatre-style screen for all the big games. It boasts 8 British beers on tap, plus pool and darts, Curry Nights, a traditional roast on Sundays (noon–5pm), karaoke, live music and even 2 internet terminals, as well as a private meeting room (ideal for football fan club meets). Typical menu items include shepherd's pie, fish 'n' chips, ploughman's, burgers, steak and kidney pies and kids' specials, while its full breakfast really is the Best of British (8am–midnight; 407 264 9189, **bestofbritishpub.com**).

Cricketers Arms: This is the area's oldest-established British pub (having moved to Festival Bay in 2007) and is a favourite haunt of visitors. There are up to 17 beers (including 4 real ales), appetising food, live evening entertainment, stylish indoor and outdoor seating and live Premiership and other domestic matches. It gets busy in the evenings, its live music is usually good and there is Happy Hour 7 days a week 5–7pm, plus free wi-fi ($$–$$$; noon–2am; 407 354 0686, **cricketersarmspub.com**).

Frankie Farrell's: Inside the Lake Buena Vista Resort Village & Spa is this smart pub-style restaurant and bar with an imaginative menu, excellent range of beers and live entertainment ($$–$$$; 9am–2am daily; 407 597 0214).

Hagan O'Reilley's: rather off the beaten track in Winter Garden (about 20 minutes north of Disney) is this genuine Irish pub, boasting good beers, classic fare and traditional evening entertainment most nights. With 15 beers on tap and a daily Happy Hour from 4–7pm, you could easily be in the Emerald isle, although the beer garden is pure Florida! ($–$$$, 11.30am–11pm; 407 905 4782, **haganoreillys.com**).

Orlando George & Dragon: Another all-British operation, this serves a hearty traditional breakfast as well as typical pub fare. It stocks Guinness,

International Drive

The majority of restaurants in this busy tourist area are of the Fast Food or Family Favourite type, but there are several individuals.

The **North** section (from Prime Outlets International to Sand Lake Road) features *Fast Food:* Baskin Robbins, Burger King, Cold Stone Creamery, Dairy Queen, Dunkin' Donuts, Five Guys Burgers & Fries, KFC, McDonald's, Quiznos, Pizza Hut, Popeye's Chicken, Sonic, Starbucks, Subway and Taco Bell. *Family Favourites:* Buffalo Wild Wings, Chili's, CiCi's Pizza, Denny's, Fuddruckers, IHOP, Perkins, Sizzler, Sweet Tomatoes, TGI Fridays. *International Flavours:* Aashirwad, New Punjab Indian Restaurant, Red Bamboo, Shogun Steakhouse. *Home From Home:* Cricketers Arms, Orlando George & Dragon. *Seafood Specials:* Red Lobster. *Deluxe Dining:* Salt Island Chophouse, Texas de Brazil. Plus, **Bergamo's:** at Festival Bay, an Italian restaurant that features fine dining – and singing waiters! Opera and pasta are served up in equal measure and quality, plus great Italian wines ($$$–$$$$$; 5–10pm; 407 352 3805, **bergamos.com**).

The **South** section (from Sand Lake Rd to Orlando Premium Outlets) has *Fast Food:* McDonald's, Pizza Hut, Subway. *Family Favourites:* Bahama Breeze, Café Tu Tu Tango, Cattleman's Steakhouse, Denny's, Don Pablo's, Friendlys, Golden Corral, Houlihan's, IHOP, Miller's Ale House, Olive Garden, Outback Steakhouse, Ponderosa, TGI Fridays, Tony Roma's, Uno Chicago, Village Inn. *International Flavours:* Kobe Steakhouse, Ming Court, *Home From Home:* Best of British Pub. *Seafood Specials:* Boston Lobster Feast, Crab House, Red Lobster. *Deluxe Dining:* Charley's Steakhouse, Everglades, Vito's Chophouse, Spencer's. Plus, **B-Line Diner:** inside the Orlando Peabody Hotel is a fab art deco homage to the traditional 1950s diner. You sit at a long counter or in one of its booths, with a good view of the chefs at work and a rolling menu that changes 4 times a day. The food is way above usual diner standards, but the prices aren't. Desserts are displayed in a huge glass counter and you just can't ignore them! ($$; 24 hours; 407 352 4000; **peabodyorlando.com**).

Stella, Boddingtons, Fosters, Newcastle Brown, Bass, Grolsch and Carlsberg, and also features darts, pool, karaoke, Sky Sports and live entertainment on its outdoor patio. A good option for traditional Christmas dinner, Sunday lunch, and St George's Day on 23 April celebrated in style; $–$$$; 9am–2am; 407 351 3578; **Britanniapubs.com**).

Sherlock's: not to be confused with the former Celebration café/tea room, this bistro-pub at Champions Gate (just off exit 58 of I-4) is a pleasant retreat after the hustle-bustle of the theme parks. Owned and run by a British mother-daughter couple from the north-east, they feature traditional pub fare for lunch and dinner, plus a good range of wines, a daily Happy Hour 3–7pm and special events for the British footie ($$, noon–9pm Sun–Thurs, 10pm Fri and Sat; 863 852 4300).

Stage Door: Another friendly, family-run pub and restaurant, this has also been a local fixture for years and still draws a good crowd of locals and tourists, with typical fare (including a Sunday roast) and a good range of beers, plus live entertainment or karaoke most nights ($–$$; 4pm–1am Tues–Sat, 4pm–midnight Sun; 863 424 8056, **stagedoorpub.com**).

The Shamrock Pub & Grille: (formerly The Pub), on Highway 27 in Davenport (at the junction with I-4, exit 55), this has a great range of beers, excellent food, multiple HD TVs and a genuine family-friendly touch. Its new beer garden offers live karaoke and other entertainment Wed–Sat ($–$$; 11am–2am Mon–Sat, 11am– midnight Sun; 863 424 4242, **theshamrockpub.net**).

BRIT TIP
For some soccer matches, notably England and some cup finals, the bars have to levy a cover charge of $15–20/person as the satellite firms offer them on pay-per-view only.

SEAFOOD SPECIALS

The choice of seafood eateries is equally wide and features some fun chains and excellent individuals.

Big Fin Seafood: Orlando's newest and possibly most imaginative – not to mention quality-conscious – seafood diner, in the new Dellagio complex just off Sand Lake Rd. Classy but casual, refined but relaxed, the owners have created a big-scale experience that also offers that special-occasion atmosphere, from the entrance seafood kitchen to the elegant outdoor bar (the Bar-A-Cuda – *groan!*). The main dining room features a grand salon style, but two smaller rooms offer a more intimate feel, while the Trophy Bar is a fun first stop for a pre-dinner drink. The menu is a fairly dazzling collection of sushi, sashimi, oysters and ceviche; classic salads and chowders; meat, chops and chicken; their exclusive crab and lobster dishes; fresh fish; and tempting pastas. You can push the boat out with the $35 Alaskan king crab dinner, or opt for a modest burger ($10) or grouper sandwich ($14). Stand-out dishes are the signature (and truly succulent) swordfish steak, lobster mac-n-cheese, crab cakes and Bonner's famous fish and chips, plus the chorizo stuffed dates starter. A good kids' menu, delectable desserts (don't miss the bread pudding!) and superb service all add up to a high-quality experience – but without the price tag to go with it in most instances. There are also 2 happy hour periods: 5–7pm and 10pm–closing, with $5 appetisers and select wines and cocktails ($$–$$$$; 5–11pm, **bigfinseafood.com**).

BRIT TIP

Big Fin Seafood has possibly one of the best meal deals in town, with its Monday Lobster Dinner special, featuring a whole Maine lobster at just $16.95.

Bar-A-Cuda at Big Fin Seafood

Bonefish Grill: This chic choice can be found throughout Florida and offers both casual dining and an upscale dinner experience, with some of the freshest fish and a terrific range of martinis and other cocktails (the mojitos are truly superb!). Non-fish fans can also choose from chicken, chops, steak and main-course salads ($$–$$$$; 4–10.30pm Mon–Thurs, 11.30pm Fri and Sat, 10pm Sun; **bonefishgrill.com**).

Boston Lobster Feast: The place for a real blow-out on an unlimited lobster and seafood buffet. There are usually early-bird specials (4–6pm Mon–Fri, 2–4.30pm Sat and Sun), and, while it is not gourmet fare, its 40-item Lobster Feast is guaranteed to stretch the stomach ($$–$$$$; 4–10pm Mon–Fri, 2–10pm Sat and Sun; **bostonlobsterfeast. com**).

The Crab House: Self-explanatory: garlic crabs, steamed crabs, snow crabs… you could try its prime rib, pasta or seafood, but it would be a shame to ignore the house speciality ($$–$$$$; 11.30am–11pm Mon–Sat, noon–11pm Sun; **crabhouseseafood.com**).

Flying Fish: At Disney's BoardWalk Resort, the menu of this superb seafood experience is not overburdened with choice, but what it does is brilliantly presented. Its Chardonnay-steamed mussels starter is a taste sensation. Steak and beef short ribs, plus a vegetarian option, are also available (4–11pm Mon–Sat, 4–10pm Sun; 407 939 3463).

Joe's Crab Shack: Part of Crab House chain but more fun and inventive and less seafood-based (despite the name). Distinctly family friendly with its Sand Lot play area, this is ideal if you don't want the whole shellfish thing ($–$$$; 11am–11pm Sun–Thurs, 11am–midnight Fri and Sat; **joescrabshack. com**).

Landry's Seafood: From the same company but with a more elegant touch, there is a fresh catch of the day, seafood platters and an excellent salad bowl with each dish, while the staff really know the menu ($$–$$$$; 11am–10pm Sun–Thurs, 11am–11pm Fri and Sat; **landrysseafoodhouse.com**).

Sand Lake Road

This area, just off International Drive (west of I-4 and including Dr Phillips Marketplace and the new Dellagio development next door) is dubbed 'Restaurant Row' for good reason.

Fast Food: Coldstone Creamery, Five Guys Burgers & Fries, McDonald's, Panera Bread, Pizza Hut, Starbucks, Subway. *International Flavours:* Anatolia, Antonio's, Bravo Cucina Italiana, La Nuova Cucina; *Seafood Specials:* Big Fin Seafood, Bonefish Grill, Moonfish. *Deluxe Dining:* J Alexander's, Fleming's, Morton's, Roy's, Ruth's Chris Steakhouse, Samba Room, Season's 52, Timpano Chophouse. Plus, **Amura Sushi:** fine dining, Japanese style, with some of the best sushi in Florida ($$$; 11.30am–2.45pm and 5–10.15pm Mon–Fri, 5–10.45pm Sat, noon–2.45pm and 5–10.15pm Sun; 407 370 0007); **Christini's:** a lovely, formal Italian restaurant in the Dr Phillips plaza, with regional specialities as well as prime aged steaks, chops and Maine lobster ($$$$–$$$$$; 6pm–midnight; 407 345 8770, **christinis.com**); **Press 101:** almost next door, this trendy wine bar offers some great light bites, as well as a fuller menu featuring sandwiches, salads and delicious pastries ($$; 11am–10pm Mon–Thurs, 11pm Fri and Sat; 407 351 2101, **press101.com**); **Cantina Laredo:** also new at the Dellagio, its gourmet Mexican style is both casual and refined, using fresh ingredients daily and with some killer margaritas! ($$$–$$$$; 5–11pm; 407 345 0186; **cantinalaredo.com**).

McCormick and Schmick's: Easily one of the most eye-catching of the seafood chains, the chef creates a daily menu based on product, price and availability (with a prominent list of what's fresh). Oysters are a speciality, along with soups and salads, and you will be hard pushed to find better prawns, scallops and salmon ($$–$$$$$; 11am–10pm Mon–Thurs, 11am–11pm Fri and Sat, 11am–9pm Sun; **mccormickandschmicks. com**).

BRIT TIP
For something different, check out Moonfish on its Sushi Sundays, with $4 selections all day long. It also has a Happy Hour Mon–Sat (4.30–6.30pm) with bar specials and half-price sushi.

Moonfish: Another great place for seafood, you could make a feast of its appetisers alone, while its sushi and sashimi are inspired and it has a superb raw bar. Many restaurants that go for the avant-garde look often fail to deliver the goods, but Moonfish doesn't fall into that trap ($$–$$$$; 4.30–10.30pm, 11pm Fri and Sat; 407 363 7262, **talkofthetownrestaurants.com**).

Red Lobster: Part of the Olive Garden chain and for the family market, with a varied menu, lively atmosphere and one of the best kids' menu/activity books. While lobster is the speciality, the wood-fired steaks, chicken, salads and other seafood are equally appetising, and it does a variety of combination platters ($$–$$$$; 11am–10pm Sun–Thurs, 11am–11pm Fri and Sat; r**edlobster.com**).

DELUXE DINING

This is where you can really go to town with your dining choice.

Bohème Restaurant: A magnificent menu can be found in this tucked-away gem at the Grand Bohemian hotel in downtown Orlando. Fine seafood mixes with exquisite lamb, duck and seafood, with some eclectic twists, plus a great Sunday Brunch ($$$–$$$$; 5.30–10pm, 10.30pm Fri and Sat 407 313 9000; **grandbohemianhotel.com**).

Cala Bella: At the stylish Rosen Shingle Creek Resort is this superb Italian-influenced restaurant, with overtones of Tuscany, heavy on pasta and seafood, but with signature dishes like its sensational cala bella lamb, veal piccata and Mediterranean pork. Save room for dessert, too – the pastry chefs are among the finest in America ($$$–$$$$; 5.30–10.30pm; 407 996 3663, **calabellarestaurant.com**).

Charley's Steak Houses: Cooking over a specially built wood-fire pit earns high marks from US meat-lovers. All the meat is specially aged, hand-cut and seasoned, making for a superb array of steaks and chops and, while it also offers fine seafood, you'd be foolish to overlook its stock-in-trade ($$$–$$$$$; 5–11pm; **talkofthetownrestaurants.com**).

Del Frisco's: Locals consistently rate this (on Lee Road in north Orlando) their favourite steakhouse and the more formal dining experience is enhanced by prime steaks and lobster, beautifully cooked and presented ($$$$–$$$$$; 5–10pm, closed Sun; 407 645 4443; **delfriscosorlando.com**).

Everglades: Tucked away inside the Rosen Centre Hotel is this beautiful Florida speciality restaurant, specialising in great steaks and fine seafood. Don't miss the Broiled Florida Grouper and melt-in-the-mouth Filet Key Largo ($$$–$$$$$, 5.30-10.30pm; 407 996 2385, **evergladesrestaurant.com**).

Fleming's: check in here for finest aged prime beef and an inventive array of fresh seafood, chops, generous sides and salads, plus tempting desserts. Its award-winning wine list features 100 wines by the glass and a magnificent Reserve List for the real connoisseur ($$$–$$$$, 5–10pm Sun–Thurs, 11pm Fri and Sat; 407 352 5706, **flemingssteakhouse.com**).

J Alexander's: The chic new venue on Sand Lake Road for a relaxing lunch or upscale dinner, with a varied menu that covers the basics (burgers, salads and sandwiches) and the more gourmet (filet mignon béarnaise, ahi tuna and cilantro shrimp). An excellent wine list and range of hand-crafted martinis add to the quality ($$–$$$$; 11am–10pm,

Shula's 347

11pm Fri and Sat; 407 345 1039; **jalexanders.com**).

Johnnie's Hideaway: Not so much a hideaway as a chic lakefront supper club in the Crossroads plaza at Lake Buena Vista, serving a rich mix of salads, premium seafood, stone crabs, veal and succulent, dry-aged steaks. The menu is colossal, and there is also a raw bar and some of the biggest desserts you've ever seen, along with a charming bar area and outdoor Tiki Deck terrace ($$$–$$$$$, 5-10pm, 11pm Fri and Sat; 407 827 1111, **talkofthetownrestaurants.com**).

Morton's of Chicago: A more upmarket style following a recent refurbishment, with a lively ambience that adds to the enjoyment of its trademark steaks, cooked on an open range. Not cheap, especially as vegetables are extra, but eating here is always memorable ($$$$; 5pm–11pm Mon–Sat, 10pm Sun; **mortons.com**).

BRIT TIP

American restaurant terminology calls a starter an 'appetizer' and a main course an 'entrée'. 'Broiled' also means 'grilled' in European terminology.

Old Hickory Steakhouse: In the Gaylord Palms Resort, the elaborate Everglades theme gives it an extra dimension, but the steak needs few gimmicks as the house speciality of certified prime-aged beef is cooked to perfection. Side dishes are extra, but the attentive service and alternatives such as oven-roasted swordfish and Maine lobster provide a memorable experience ($$$–$$$$$; 5.30–10.30; **gaylordhotels.com**).

Porterhouse: At the Orlando Airport Marriott just off Semoran Boulevard and a hidden gem under British chef Tony Hull, this has a relaxed, intimate ambience that perfectly sets off its prime cuts of beef, chops and grilled seafood, plus a good wine list and dreamy desserts ($$$$; 5.30–10pm Mon–Fri; 407 851 9000).

Roy's: Go upscale Hawaiian at this grand choice, where the Asian-Pacific fusion cuisine is as spectacular as the decor and service. Creator and celebrity chef Roy Yamaguchi displays his sense of grand style ($$$$–$$$$$; 5.30–10pm, 10.30pm Fri and Sat; **roysrestaurant.com**).

Ruth's Chris Steak House: Another major chain, this also offers prime beef in a mouth-watering variety of choices. It isn't cheap, but you'll be hard pushed to get a better steak. Simply seared, seasoned and served, they are the reason it has more than 80 locations worldwide, including in the Sand Lake Road 'restaurant row' ($$$$–$$$$$; 5–10pm Mon–Sat, 9pm Sun; **ruthschris. com**).

Salt Island Chophouse and Fish Market: An unusual place, in the heart of International Drive, from its tiki-torch outdoor terrace to the eclectic aquatic interior decor and live jazz lounge. The extensive wine list superbly offsets the heavily steak and seafood dominated menu, while service is suitably refined. All dishes are well explained and even demonstrated, and it's a tough choice between the oak-grilled steaks and trademark daily seafood specials. Three trendy bars, including an outdoor terrace, add to the atmosphere ($$$–$$$$; 5–11pm; 407 996 7258, **saltislandrestaurant.com**).

Samba Room: Try this if you like a memorable Cuban experience in an elegant lakefront restaurant with a Latin ambience. The menu exhibits a wonderfully exotic touch, with the likes of Argentinean Skirt Steak and Chilean Sea Bass, and its range of cocktails is Cuban-laced. Extremely popular, though a touch pricier than others, so reservations are advised ($$$–$$$$$; 4–10pm Sun–Thurs, 11pm Fri and Sat: 407 266 0550; **sambaroom.net**).

Sanaa: The latest dining experience at *Walt Disney World*, this is in the new Kidani Village resort next to Animal Kingdom Lodge and features a novel take on Indian cuisine, with some imaginative variations, many served as sampler platters and, for once, not the usual huge portions. It also offers great animal savannah views ($$$$; 11.30am–3pm, 5–9pm; 407 939 3463).

Shula's Steak House: Expansive (on your waistline) and expensive, the porterhouse and prime rib steaks are outstanding, and this chain (owned by famous ex-American football coach Don Shula) is highly popular with locals at the Walt Disney World Dolphin Hotel ($$$$$; 5–11pm; 407 934 1362; **donshula. com**). Less formal but equally stylish is the new **Shula's 347** bistro in the swish new Westin Hotel at Lake Mary, near Sanford (right on exit 101A of I-4), a nice balance of casual diner with upscale menu offerings. It still features the signature Shula Cut steaks but also more modest burgers and salads, as well as great fish dishes. As part of the hotel, it is open for breakfast, lunch and dinner and is fun for big sports events with its multiple flatscreen TVs ($$–$$$$, 407 531 3567; 6.30am–midnight).

Spencer's: The new Hilton by the Convention Center on I-Drive is home to this beautiful upscale restaurant that features magnificent steak and chops, plus superb seafood. Side dishes are all extra, but the natural steaks are all pasture-raised without hormones or antibiotics, aged for 21 days and cooked in a special, custom-made grill. The prime porterhouse for 2 is a real highlight, as are the loaded hash browns ($$$$–$$$$$, 5-10.30pm Tues–Sat; 407 313 4300, **thehiltonorlando.com**).

◆ BRIT TIP
Non-Hilton guests who dine at Spencer's Steakhouse benefit from free valet parking. Its monthly Culinary Class, featuring select wine pairings, is worth checking out on the first Sat every month.

Texas de Brazil: An unusual but delicious Brazilian-style steakhouse, or churrascaria, with a wonderfully upscale touch. Its variety of meats – every one carved at the table off sword-like skewers – is quite superb, all beautifully cooked over its open-flame grill ($$$–$$$$$; 5–10pm Mon–Thurs, 5–10.30pm Fri, 4–10.30pm Sat, 4–9.30pm Sun, plus brunch noon–3pm Sat and Sun; 407 355 0355, **texasdebrazil. com**).

The Palm Restaurant: The opening of Universal's Hard Rock Hotel brought with it this upscale nationwide chain. Founded in New York in 1926, it is famous for prime-aged steaks and

Try it all at Pointe Orlando

Dining choice doesn't come more varied than at Pointe Orlando after its 2008/09 rebuild.

Fast Food: **Johnny Rockets** 1950s-style diner for burgers and shakes ($; 11am–9pm Sun–Thurs, 11am–11pm Fri and Sat; 407 903 0762, **johnnyrockets.com**); **Pizza Valdiano**, for café-style pizza, salads, subs and panini ($–$$; 11am–10pm Sun–Thurs, 11pm Fri and Sat; 407 903 5855, **pizzeriavaldiano.com**). *Family Favourites:* **Hooters**; and **Copper Canyon Grill**, which appeals to hearty appetites with its wood-fired rotisserie chicken, hearty chicken pot pie, steaks and succulent barbecued ribs ($$–$$$$; 11am–10.05pm Sun–Thurs, 11.05pm Fri and Sat; 407 363 3933; **ccgrill. com**). *International Flavours:* the lively bar and Mexican-restaurant style of **Adobe Gila's**, with more than 50 tequilas (!) and live music and karaoke most nights of the week, plus happy Hour specials 4–7pm weekdays ($–$$; 11.30am–2am, 11pm Sun; 407 903 1477, **adobegilas.com**). New in 2009 was the **Funky Monkey Wine Company**, a fun-style wine bar and café, featuring tapas-like appetiser plates and some great steaks and seafood, plus stylish Sushi Mondays and a superb wine list, many of them available by the glass ($$–$$$, 407 418 9463, noon–11pm Mon–Thurs, noon–midnight Fri and Sat, 5–11pm Sun, **funkymonkeywine.com**). **Maggianos Little Italy** serves exceptional family-style Italian dining in a relaxed, friendly atmosphere with vintage 1940s Chicago decor and ambience. Portions are huge (even by Orlando standards!). The Bombalina appetiser platter will feed a family of 4, while the Family Style meals feature all-you-can-eat refills – and no one leaves hungry ($$–$$$$; 11am–10pm Mon–Thurs, 11pm Fri and Sat, noon–10pm Sun; 407 241 8660; **maggianos.com**); **Taverna Opa** is a lively Greek option, with a thoroughly traditional and appetising menu, from hot and cold meze to moussaka, souvlaki and stewed lamb, but much more besides, like fine steaks and fresh seafood – plus dancing on the tables and a great ouzo bar! ($$–$$$$; 11am–11pm Sun–Thurs, 2am Fri and Sat; 407 351 8660, **opaorlando.com**). *Deluxe Dining:* **Capital Grille**, a wonderfully upscale and elegant restaurant featuring dry-aged steaks, seafood and tantalising desserts – perfect for that special night out ($$$$–$$$$$; 11.30am–3pm Mon–Fri, 5–10pm Sun–Thurs, 11pm Fri and Sat; 407 370 4392, **thecapitalgrille.com**); **Cuba Libre Restaurant and Rum Bar** is The Pointe's latest dining and entertainment spot, featuring traditional Cuban cuisine with an exciting twist, from tasty ceviche to pan-seared sugarcane-skewered jumbo shrimp. Great cocktails (notably its mojitos and caipiranhas) and smooth service are the perfect complement to the Latin-flavoured menu, and it is tempting just to stop by the bar and graze on its appetisers. The interior setting alone is magnificent, while it also offers live music later in the evening at weekends to match its Old Havana style and ambience ($$$–$$$$$; **cubalibrerestaurant.com**); The **Oceanaire** (see Top 10, page 335); **Tommy Bahama's Tropical Café** offers inspired dining in a laid-back, tropical setting. The menu is refreshing for lunch or dinner, with highlights being its Loki Loki Tuna appetiser and mouth-watering shrimp entrées, plus sandwiches, chicken, fresh fish and fab salads ($$–$$$; 11am–11pm Sun–Thurs, to midnight Fri and Sat; 321 281 5888, **tommybahama.com**).

Other options include **BB King's Blues Club**, with a Louisiana-tinged menu and some excellent chicken, ribs, catfish, Cajun pasta carbonara and steak, as well as standard burgers and salads ($$–$$$$; 4pm–midnight Sun–Fri, 11am–1am Sat; 407 370 4550, **bbkingclubs.com**); and **La Creperia Café**, a charming little bistro and espresso bar, serving sweet and savoury crepes, salads, wraps and panini sandwiches ($–$$, 407 370 0008; 10am–10pm Sun–Thurs, 11pm Fri and Sat, **lacreperia.com**).

jumbo lobsters, served in spacious, elegant surroundings. The house speciality, Jumbo Nova Scotia Lobster, is truly spectacular. All this is reflected in the prices, and vegetables are extra, but non-hotel guests also qualify for free valet parking ($$$$–$$$$$; 5–10pm Mon–Thurs, 11pm Fri and Sat, 9pm Sun; 407 503 7256, **thepalm.com**).

Timpano Italian Chophouse: Step back in time at this richly decorated upscale diner. The dark, elegant interior is bustling and convivial and the 1950s' New York accent is carried through with panache. And, from its trademark Martini Bar to the tiramisu dessert, everything is served with style and taste, with the addition of live music at its baby grand Tues–Sat. Menu highlights include filet mignon, pork chops and Maine lobster ($$$–$$$$; 11.30am–11pm Sun–Wed, midnight Thurs–Sat; 407 248 0429, **timpanochophouse.net**)

Our Top 10

Finally, if you fancy really splashing out, here are some suggestions for venues with that 'something special' element. Fine dining is on the increase in Orlando, and this selection is always popular, so you should certainly book in advance. For a romantic evening out, you also can't go wrong with any of these.

A Land Remembered: Quite simply, this is the best steakhouse we've ever visited. Inside the golf clubhouse of the Rosen Shingle Creek Resort (but open to non-residents), it is a superbly refined venue boasting exquisite service and an outstanding wine list. The menu oozes class from top to bottom and features local specialities like frogs' legs, gator stew, a fresh fish selection and key lime pie. But, while the lamb, chicken and short ribs are outstanding, the steak choice is out of this world (featuring all-natural prime black Angus beef from the Harris Ranch in California). Filet mignon, New York strip, ribeye, porterhouse, prime rib, chateaubriand and a surf & turf (with lobster) are among the most succulent meat dishes you will find anywhere and, while it is suitably pricey, it is worth every cent ($$$$–$$$$$; 5.30–10pm; 407 996 3663; **landrememberedrestaurant.com**).

bluezoo: When it comes to one of the hippest places in town (at the Walt Disney World Dolphin Hotel), bluezoo not only looks the part, but it also serves some of the finest food in the Disney realm. Celebrity chef Todd English has made a splash by creating individual and contrasting restaurant experiences and bluezoo is a real gem. With an undersea theme that benefits from superb lighting (dine later rather than earlier for the full effect), it has

a truly soothing feeling, whether you are just at the bar or in one of the 3 main restaurant areas. Both the service and the waiting staff's knowledge of the cuisine and extensive wine list are impeccable, so feel free to let them steer you around a mouth-watering menu, which includes ceviche and a raw bar. Fish is the signature dish (though rotisserie chicken, beef filet and pork loin are also on offer) and seafood lovers will struggle to narrow down the choice here: miso-glazed black cod, Basque-style tuna, swordfish, Cantonese lobster and more, or just try the Simply Fish – your choice of freshly caught fish, whole-roasted on its Teppenyaki grill with a choice of sauces. There is also a daily fresh pasta selection and a Chef's 5-course Tasting Menu ($$$$–$$$$$; 3.30–11pm; 407 934 1111; **thebluezoo.com**).

Brio Tuscan Grille: With 2 Orlando locations (Mall at Millenia and Winter Park Village, plus another 5 throughout Florida), this stylish Italian offering makes for a superb casual lunch or a great romantic dinner. A mouth-watering menu – featuring delicious flatbreads, luscious salads, superb steaks (including a surf & turf with shrimp and crab cake), creative pastas and regional specialities like chicken limone and gorgonzola lamb chops, plus daily fish specials – is complemented by a well-balanced wine list and superior service. Its weekend Brunch adds another delicious choice that won't break the bank ($9.95–13.95). The Tuscan country villa style adds to the quality-conscious

bluezoo

Kissimmee/Highway 192

The long stretch of this tourist corridor offers the greatest density of restaurants in Central Florida. Here's how they line up, starting with the **East** section from the junction with I-4 to John Young Parkway: *Fast Food:* Arby's, Burger King, Chick-Fil-A, Domino's, Dunkin' Donuts, KFC, McDonald's, Pizza Hut, Quiznos, Subway, Taco Bell, Wendy's. *Family Favourites:* Applebee's, Bennigan's, Bob Evans, Cattleman's Steakhouse, Chevys, Chili's, CiCi's Pizza, Cracker Barrel, Denny's, Friendlys, Golden Corral, IHOP, Logan's Roadhouse, Longhorn Steakhouse, Olive Garden, Perkins, Ponderosa, Ruby Tuesday, Shoney's, Smokey Bones, TGI Fridays, Uno Chicago, Waffle House. *International Flavours:* Kobe Steakhouse, Punjab Indian Restaurant. *Seafood Specials:* Boston Lobster Feast, Joe's Crab Shack, Red Lobster. *Deluxe Dining:* Charley's Steakhouse. Plus, **Pacino's:** a well-established and family-friendly Italian choice, offering suitably healthy portions in a themed setting. Highly traditional and with an emphasis on pasta and seafood, plus some good steaks ($$–$$$$; 4–11pm; 407 396 8022; **pacinos.com**).

In the **West** section (from I-4 all the way to Highway 27) you have: *Fast Food:* Burger King, Chick-Fil-A, Dunkin' Donuts, McDonald's, Pizza Hut, Subway, Taco Bell, Wendy's. *Family Favourites:* Bennigan's, Black Angus, Bob Evans, Carabba's, Cracker Barrel, Denny's, Golden Corral, IHOP, Longhorn Steakhouse, Olive Garden, Outback Steakhouse, Perkins, Ponderosa, Shoney's, Sizzler, TGI Fridays, Waffle House. *International Flavours:* Passage to India. *Home From Home:* Stage Door. *Seafood Specials:* Red Lobster. Plus, **Colorado House of Beef:** an excellent, more budget steakhouse choice but still high on quality, this features a good range of steaks, ribs, veal, prime rib and fresh seafood, plus burgers and a good kids' menu ($$–$$$; 4–11.30pm; 407 396 1170, **coloradohouseofbeef.com**).

ambience and there is even a fresh kids' menu ($$–$$$$; 11am–10pm Mon–Thurs, 11pm Fri and Sat, 10am–10pm Sun; 407 351 8909/622 5611; **brioitalian.com**).

BRIT TIP

At Brio Tuscan Grille, don't miss the melt-in-the-mouth beef carpaccio starter, the bistecca insalata and sensational shrimp and scallop risotto as a superb dinner combination.

Jiko

© Disney

Jiko: This great favourite of ours is at Disney's Animal Kingdom Lodge and is possibly Disney's most imaginative and impressive culinary offering to date. Maintaining the hotel's African theming with its decor and lighting, Jiko ('the cooking place') features twin wood-burning ovens, a masterful menu and an exclusive selection of South African wines. The menu has Indian, Asian and African influences, with dishes like Swahili curry shrimp, Chermoula Tanglewood chicken and maize crusted wreck-fish, plus a couple of excellent vegetarian choices and a cheese plate that can be ordered as a main course or dessert. Its flatbreads are also a speciality and the full dessert selection is truly decadent. The personal service and ethnic ambience underline the adventure of eating here, and it's also the perfect venue for a romantic meal (5–11pm; 407 939 3463).

Luma on Park: Head to Winter Park for this ultra-trendy 'gastropub', where the cuisine can be as simple as a well-cooked burger or pizza or a fabulous filet mignon. The mix of outdoor patio, lounge bar and restaurant makes this a chic and lively venue, with a fresh contemporary cuisine

Lake Buena Vista

The third main tourist area, this features the broadest range of choice. Looking first at the area **East** of I-4: *Fast Food:* Subway, Dunkin' Donuts, Wendy's. *Family Favourites:* Bahama Breeze, Bennigan's, Carraba's, CiCi's Pizza, Golden Corral, Lone Star Steakhouse. *Home From Home:* Frankie Farrell's. *Seafood Specials:* Landry's Seafood.

To the **West** of I-4 (in the Crossroads area, SR 535 and Palm Parkway) there is: *Fast Food:* McDonald's, Pizza Hut, Quiznos, Steak 'n Shake, Subway, Taco Bell. *Family Favourites:* Black Angus, Buffalo Wild Wings, Chevys, CiCi's Pizza, Denny's, Fuddruckers, Hooters, IHOP, Macaroni Grill, Olive Garden, Orlando Ale House, Perkins, Shoney's, Sizzler, Sweet Tomatoes, TGI Fridays, Uno Chicago, Waffle House. *International Flavours:* Dragon Court Buffet, India Palace, Kobe Steakhouse. *Seafood Specials:* Crab House, Joe's Crab Shack. *Deluxe Dining:* Johnnie's Hideaway. Plus: **Giordano's**, a fabulous Chicago-style pizzeria serving some of the best deep-dish pizza pies, plus salads, sandwiches and pasta ($–$$$, 11am-10pm; 407 377 0020, **giordanos.com**).

from chef Brandon McGlamery that is imaginative and constantly changing. Fine lamb, duck and fish are among the highlights, along with a wine cellar that lists almost 190 varieties and serves many by the glass, half-bottle and even half-glass, if you'd like a good sampling! It also features a 3-course prix fixe menu at $35 a head ($45 with wine pairings) Sun–Tues, and a special Chef's Table that should be booked in advance ($$–$$$$$; lounge bar 4.30–midnight, dining room 5.30–10.30pm; 407 599 4111; **lumaonpark.com**).

The Oceanaire: Step back in time at this relaxed and stylish seafood room at Pointe Orlando. The decor, reminiscent of a classic 1930s ocean liner, and mood music lead you into a fish and shellfish wonderland, complete with a superb oyster bar. Shrimp, crab, scallops, clams, lobster and as many as 15 types of fish all jostle for attention on a sumptuous menu that also offers great salads, steaks and chicken (though you'd be crazy to ignore the seafood here). The selection varies daily according to the freshest produce available, but typical examples include 'Black & Bleu' Ecuadorian swordfish, cioppino (a delightful fish and shellfish stew), stuffed Atlantic flounder and stuffed Caribbean lobster tail, as well as a surf & turf option and a dozen types of oyster. Its grand shellfish platter (at $26 per person) is an eye-opening extravaganza of shrimp,

crab, lobster and oysters and it has an equally impressive wine list. Service is top-notch – to match the pricing – but there is also a seasonal 3-course prix fixe menu at a very reasonable $30/person ($$$$–$$$$$; 5–10pm Sun–Thurs, 11pm Fri and Sat; 407 363 4801; **theoceanaire.com**).

Seasons 52: A trendy and growing national chain (in the Plaza Venezia on Sand Lake Road and next to the Altamonte Mall), this presents some of the best fine dining in the state. The name reflects the weekly seasonal, seriously creative menu. It's also highly health conscious, with a balanced approach to carbohydrate and fat content. All appetisers, salads and soups range from 100–250 calories, the majority being either grilled or oven-roasted, and all entrées are less than 475 calories. Its fish and seafood are a real highlight but lamb, chicken and steaks are equally tempting and vegetarians are offered some good choices. The 'mini indulgence' desserts (individual servings in small glasses) are ideal to finish a meal in style but without over-eating. Your server will be able to offer bags of advice – not least with an extensive wine list – while the bar area and outdoor terrace are equally stylish, ideal for a romantic occasion ($$–$$$$; 11.30am–2.30pm and 5–10pm Mon–Fri, 11.30am–11pm Sat, 11.30am–10pm Sun; 407 354 5212; **seasons52.com**).

Wolfgang Puck's: At Downtown Disney, this unusual mix of styles and restaurants – 4 under 1 roof – represents some of the best family dining, with a great upscale option in the **Dining Room**. The main Café is smart enough, but head upstairs and you are in seriously romantic territory, with a great view of Pleasure Island and service to match. The contrast with the fun hubbub below is striking, while the menu is well thought out and varied – try the Chinois-style lamb rack or lobster risotto, or just opt for one of their superb steaks. Fans of fine German cuisine will want to try the signature pork Wiener schnitzel while there are also two fixed-priced menus, a 4-course for $60/head and a 3-course for $50. ($$$–$$$$ Café 11.30am–11pm; $$$$–$$$$$ Dining Room 6–10.30pm; 407 938 9653; **wolfgangpuck.com**).

Tchoup-Chop

© OCVB

Zen: Find a fine hotel and you will find a fine restaurant, and that is true of the Omni Orlando resort at Champions Gate, where Zen is a wonderful Asian-themed restaurant. With a sake bar, sushi bar and its elegant main restaurant, this is an oasis of oriental charm and style. Highlights are the mouth-watering Beijing Spare Ribs and Sautéed Shrimp with Chile Pepper Sauce and Glazed Walnuts, or just opt for the stunning Zen Experience, a multi-course sampler feast. ($$–$$$$, 6–10pm Tues–Sun; 407 390 6664; **omnihotels.com**).

And our No 1...

While it's practically impossible to single out one restaurant from this vast wealth of culinary delight, if pushed we would have to plump for what we consider the most amazing restaurant experience in central Florida, at Universal's Royal Pacific Resort. **Tchoup-Chop** (pronounced 'chop chop'), from the gourmet stable of New Orleans master chef Emeril Lagasse, offers Asian-Pacific fusion cuisine in the most eye-catching setting. Service is a team effort at each table and the superb menu is well presented and explained. And oh, that menu! Blending aromatic and flavoursome elements of Thai, Chinese, Japanese, South Seas and other Pacific Rim cuisines, Lagasse has conjured up a delectable array of dishes. Start with steamed vegetable dumplings (with a sake-soy dipping sauce) or Polynesian crab cake (with mango-habañero butter sauce and caramelised pineapple compote), then graduate to furikake-crusted Atlantic salmon (with coconut purple sticky rice, cucumber namasu and sweet sake yuzu soy jus), Mongolian barbeque grilled pork tenderloin or smoked sea salt grilled filet of beef tenderloin (with garlic potatoes in a green peppercorn sake reduction sauce). The desserts are equally fragrant and mouth-watering and the whole experience is a five-star treat ($$$–$$$$$; 5.30–10.30pm Sun–Thurs, 11pm Fri and Sat; 407 503 2467; **emerils.com**).

And now on to another of our favourite topics – shopping...

12 Shopping

As well as being a theme park wonderland, this vast area of Florida is a shopper's paradise, with a dazzling array of specialist outlets, malls, flea markets and discount retailers. New centres also spring up all the time, from smart malls to cheap gift shops – and you can't go a few paces in the tourist areas without a shop insisting it has the 'best bargains' of one sort or another.

With the exchange rate in recent years being favourable for UK visitors, shopping has become as much of an attraction as the theme parks. The only danger is seriously exceeding your baggage allowance for the flight home – or your duty free allowance. Your limit in the catch-all duty category of 'gifts and souvenirs' is now £390 per person, but it's still easy to exceed that! If you do, you need to keep your receipts and go through the 'goods to declare' channel (though paying the duty and VAT can still be cheaper than buying the same items at home). As of 2009 some items, such as clothing and footwear for children, do not incur a VAT rate. However, restrictions apply to all reduced rate VAT items, so be sure to check details with HM Revenue & Customs.

You pay duty (which varies depending on the item) on the total purchase price (i.e. inclusive of Florida sales tax) once you have exceeded £390, plus VAT at 17.5% You CANNOT pool your allowances to cover one item that exceeds a single allowance. Hence, if you buy a digital camera that costs £400, you have to pay the duty (at 4.9%) on the full £400, taking the total to £419.60 and then VAT on that figure.

Shopping in the World of Disney® store

However, if you have several items that add up to £390, and then another that exceeds that, you pay the duty and VAT only on the excess item (and customs officers usually give you the benefit of the lowest rate on what you pay for). Duty rates are updated regularly and vary from 2.2% (e.g. video games) to 14% (e.g. a computer monitor) bearing in mind VAT rates are subject to change. For more info, contact the Customs and Excise National Advice Service on 0845 010 9000 or visit **hmrc.gov.uk**. Your ordinary duty-free allowances from America include 200 cigarettes and 1 litre of spirits or 2 litres of fortified wine or sparkling wine and 4 litres of still wine. Alligator products, which constitute those of an endangered species (to UK authorities), require an import licence, and you should consult the Global Wildlife Licensing and Registration Service for more info.

BRIT TIP
Pick up the *Orlando Sentinel* newspaper on a Sunday and you will get the full local lowdown on all the great sales for the coming week.

When it comes to the fun part of shopping (and American stores are genuinely fun to just browse, let alone splash out in), you can expect to pay roughly the same in dollars as you do in pounds for items like clothes, books and CDs, and real bargains are to be had in jeans, trainers, shoes, sports equipment and cosmetics. Virtually everywhere offers free, convenient parking, while American shop assistants couldn't be more polite

World of Disney store

© Disney

and helpful. Be aware, though, of the hidden extra costs of shopping. Unlike our VAT, Florida sales tax is NOT part of the displayed purchase price, so you must add on 6% or 7% (it varies by county) for the final price. Also, some shops will ask for photo ID with credit card purchases, so if you have a new UK card driving licence it is useful to have it with you. That's the mechanics of it; here's a rundown of the main shopping fun to be had.

BRIT TIP
Don't buy electrical goods in the US – they won't work in the UK without an adapter. Most games systems (notably X Box, Wii and PS3) are also NOT compatible with UK players. Hand-held games are fine, though.

Downtown Disney
In many ways, the heart of Walt Disney World is its Downtown Disney district, split into 3 linked sections: Disney Marketplace, Pleasure Island and West Side. This is typical Disney, a beautiful location, imaginative architecture and a host of one-off elements that make shopping a pleasure, with no fewer than 48 shops and dining opportunities. A water-taxi links the 3 main elements of this 120-acre/48.5ha plaza, making for easy movement around the whole area.

Downtown Disney can be found off exits 67 and 68 of I-4 and is well signposted (exit 68 can be congested at peak periods). You can also rent boats at **Cap'n Jack's Marina** (Marketplace), including the fun 2-person Sea Raycers ($32 per ½ hour) and the 21ft/6.5m Sun Tracker pontoons, which take up to 10 people ($45 per ½ hour).

Disney Marketplace: When you are here (9.30am–11pm), don't miss the **World of Disney** store, the largest of its kind, which now includes **Bibbidi Bobbidi Boutique** (where young girls can have hair, make-up and nails done in true Princess style, or opt for the Hannah Montana-inspired Disney's Secret Star Makeover), the **Lego Imagination Center** (an interactive playground and shop), the amazing **Art of Disney** and **Team Mickey's Athletic**

Club. **Once Upon A Toy** is a gigantic toy emporium complete with a host of classic games, many with a Disney theme, for kids to try. Other worthwhile one-offs are the blissful Basin (for hand-carved soaps, bubble baths and shampoo bars) and **Disney's Wonderful World of Memories** (for all scrapbook fans, plus the only place to get a Disney postmark for your postcards home!). **Arribas Brothers** is another big, attractive store of gifts (including hand-blown glass) and collectibles. Those keen on the Disney hobby of pin trading should check out **Pin Traders**. Then there is **Disney Design-A-Tee** (exactly what it sounds like!) **Tren-D**, a unique and cutting edge Disney fashion store for women and **Disney's Days of Christmas**. For bargain-hunters, the aisle next to **Goofy's Candy Company** and **Pooh Corner** offers **Mickey's Mart** – everything for $10 or less. Dancing fountains and squirt pools (where kids tend to get seriously wet), the lakeside setting and boating opportunities all add to the appeal here.

> **BRIT TIP**
> Young girls in the princess mood may want to take part in the daily **Princess Parade** from the World of Disney store. Held at 2pm weekdays (noon at weekends) each day, it marches in full pomp from the Princess Hollow end of the store through the Marketplace section of Downtown Disney, finishing at the Carousel, where all children get a free ride. Girls can dress up (or not) as they wish, and there is NO fee to take part.

The restaurants here include the superbly themed **Rainforest Café**, **Pollo Campero** (which replaced McDonalds in 2010), **Wolfgang Puck Express** and the casual waterfront setting of **Cap'n Jack's Restaurant**, while ice-cream and chocolate fans should check out **Ghirardelli's** for cool sundaes and super shakes. For a British touch, opt for one of the range of speciality hot sandwiches and salads at **Earl of Sandwich** (from just $5.95 and some will feed 2!), making them some of Disney's best-priced fare. For an upmarket touch, we rate **Fulton's Crab House** and **Portobello** (see Chapter 11, Dining Out) highly. **T-Rex**

Café is another innovative restaurant from the people who run Rainforest Café, offering dining with dinosaurs and plenty of interactive features! It includes a Build-A-Dino workshop in its gift shop, and an extensive menu featuring the likes of Pterodactyl Wings, Gigantosaurus Burgers, Triassic Tortellini and Paleo Shrimp, along with soups, salads, pizza, sandwiches, chicken and steak. A full kid's menu is available and the desserts are dino-rific (try the Chocolate Extinction – big enough for sharing!).

> **BRIT TIP**
> Parents beware! The Bibbidi Bobbidi Boutique hair and make-up shop is hideously expensive. Packages range from $49 to $240, so you may want to steer your Princess gently away!

Pleasure Island: This area is still being revamped with new shops and restaurants being added to make it lively during the day as well as by night. You can check out the cornerstone **Harley-Davidson** store, as well as **Curl by Sammy Duvall,** a surfing, apparel and accessories shop with the latest trendy clothing, and **Fuego Cigars by Sosa** to enjoy a premium range of cigars. With a beautiful view over Village Lake, **Paradiso 37** restaurant and bar features wonderfully creative North, South and Central American cuisine and a selection of 37 tequilas and 10 signature margaritas. However, the one unmissable element is wonderful **Raglan Road**, an Irish-themed pub and restaurant, with live music every

Harley-Davidson store

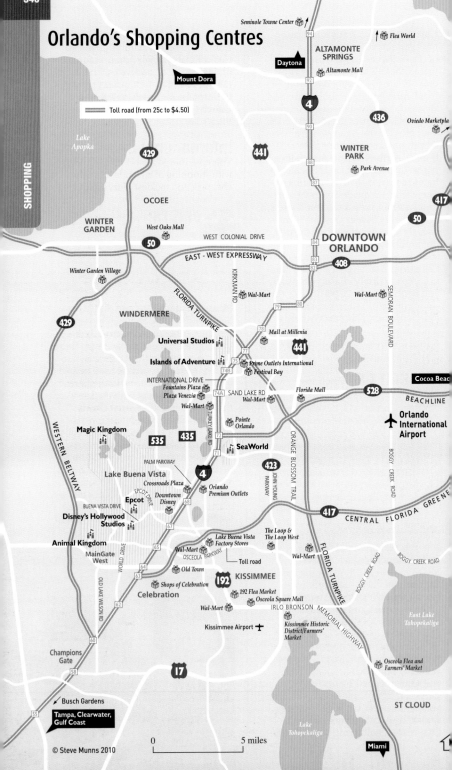

SHOPPING

Orlando's Shopping Centres

Toll road (from 25c to $4.50)

Seminole Towne Center
94
Daytona
ALTAMONTE SPRINGS
Flea World
92
Altamonte Mall
Mount Dora
4
90
441
WINTER PARK
436
Oviedo Marketpla
88
87
Park Avenue
Lake Apopka
429
417
50
OCOEE
WINTER GARDEN
West Oaks Mall
50
WEST COLONIAL DRIVE
84
DOWNTOWN ORLANDO
83
82
408
Winter Garden Village
EAST - WEST EXPRESSWAY
KIRKMAN RD
Wal-Mart
79
80
Wal-Mart
SEMORAN BOULEVARD
FLORIDA TURNPIKE
WINDERMERE
429
78
Mall at Millenia
441
Universal Studios
77
75
Islands of Adventure
74B
Prime Outlets International
Festival Bay
INTERNATIONAL DRIVE
Cocoa Beac
Fountains Plaza
74A
SAND LAKE RD
528
BEACHLINE
Plaza Venezia
Wal-Mart
Florida Mall
Wal-Mart
TURKEY LAKE RD
Pointe Orlando
Orlando International Airport
Magic Kingdom
535
435
72
SeaWorld
71
ORANGE BLOSSOM TRAIL
BOGGY CREEK ROAD
PALM PARKWAY
423
WESTERN BELTWAY
4
Lake Buena Vista
JOHN YOUNG PARKWAY
417
CENTRAL FLORIDA GREENE
Crossroads Plaza
EPCOT DRIVE
Orlando Premium Outlets
68
Epcot
Downtown Disney
BUENA VISTA DRIVE
Disney's Hollywood Studios
67
WORLD DRIVE
BOGGY CREEK ROAD
Animal Kingdom
Lake Buena Vista Factory Stores
The Loop & The Loop West
MainGate West
65
Wal-Mart
Wal-Mart
FLORIDA TURNPIKE
OLD LAKE WILSON RD
64
OSCEOLA PARKWAY
Toll road
BOGGY CREEK ROAD
63
Old Town
KISSIMMEE
Shops of Celebration
192
Celebration
62
192 Flea Market
Osceola Square Mall
East Lake Tohopekaliga
Wal-Mart
IRLO BRONSON
MEMORIAL HIGHWAY
Champions Gate
60
Kissimmee Airport
Kissimmee Historic District/Farmers' Market
58
17
Osceola Flea and Farmers' Market
ST CLOUD
Busch Gardens
55
Tampa, Clearwater, Gulf Coast
© Steve Munns 2010
0   5 miles
Lake Tohopekaliga
Miami

Up, up and away!

A recent addition to the Pleasure Island area is **Characters In Flight**, a wonderful tethered balloon ride that gently soars up to 300ft/91.5m high carrying up to 30 at a time in a 19ft/5.7m gondola on 6-minute rides. Similar to the wonderful Panoramagique balloon in the Disney Village area of *Disneyland Paris*, it provides a wonderful panorama of much of the huge extent of *Walt Disney World* and is a great photo opportunity by day or night (10.30am–11pm, to midnight Fri and Sat). It costs $18 per adult and $12 for 3–9s. Weather conditions do play a part, though, restricting the number of passengers in certain conditions, while it is grounded in high winds or heavy rain.

evening (see pages 296 and 316). No time for a sit-down meal? Try **Cookes of Dublin** for quick fish and chips. The entire area is now a more continuous part of Downtown Disney, with a large bridge to the West Side, wider walkways and a water-taxi dock.

West Side: Continuing into West Side (10.30am–11pm) gives you the superb **AMC 24** cinema complex, plus another 16 retail and dining outlets. The **Hoypoloi Gallery** is one of our favourites for an eclectic range of artwork from metal to glass, while **Magic Masters** (a wide variety of tricks and souvenirs, with demonstrations), **Mickey's Groove** (exclusively Mickey-related items), **Little Miss Matched**

(fun and funky socks, bedding and more, popular with young girls). **Pop Gallery** is also highly original. The dining choice is good, too, with **Planet Hollywood**, (Southern inspired) **House of Blues**, Latin-flavoured **Bongo's Cuban Café** and our fave, **Wolfgang Puck Café**.

International Drive

This core tourist area is simply awash with shopping of all kinds, from the cheapest and tackiest plazas, full of tourist gift shops, to 3 clever, purpose-built centres. Some of the shops just north of the Sand Lake Road junction are best avoided, while the northern end of I-Drive has undergone a major redevelopment.

This area has been renowned for discount outlet shopping – a local speciality – offering name brands at heavily reduced prices to clear.

Prime Outlets International: At the top of I-Drive, this attractive 175-shop 'lifestyle centre' has gone all out for the big, semi-open-air style that encourages people to wander the long interior promenades full of welcoming shop fronts and big-name brands. Boasting a landscaped canal running through the centre, outdoor seating, cafés, a Market Place food court and a free-standing Guest Services centre, it provides a luxury touch to its wealth of shopping opportunity. Major brands include the **Neiman Marcus Last Call Clearance Center**, which will attract

AMC 24 cinema complex

the fashion-conscious, as will the **Hugo Boss Factory Store**, **White House/Black Market**, **Esprit** and **Jones New York Outlet**. Other familiar names include **Nike Factory Store**, **Tommy Hilfiger**, **Crabtree & Evelyn** and, inevitably, **Starbucks**. Phase 2 completed the impressive picture in 2008, adding more top brands such as **Banana Republic**, **Bath & Body Works**, **Coach** and **Brooks Brothers**, while you should also look for designer stores from **Eddie Bauer** and **J Crew**. New in 2009 were an **Ed Hardy Outlet**, **L'Occitane**, **Ted Baker** and **Lacoste**. With an attractive food court, and smart new Italian restaurant **Vinito**, you have one of the area's brightest shopping centres (10am–11pm Mon–Sat, 10am–9pm Sun; 407 352 9600; **primeoutlets.com**).

Festival Bay: Also at the top end of I-Drive is this unique indoor mall. Its mix of shops and entertainment is quite unusual, and many of the stores will be unfamiliar to Brits; but don't let that put you off as there are some interesting shops to discover here and some very good value (though up to a third of the units remain empty, which can be off-putting). The emphasis here is as much on entertainment as shopping, and the village street style is aimed at the casual wanderer. The main entrance is graced by a huge fountain and multi-coloured tiling, while it also features **Ron Jon's Surf Shop** battling for prominence with **Fuddruckers** diner (superb burgers) and **Bergamo's** Italian restaurant. Pub fans will be pleased that the popular **Cricketers Arms** has relocated here from the now

Festival Bay

Festival Bay

demolished Mercado. Step inside the mall doors and you discover a huge water feature and another 45 stores and cafes, plus **Vans Skatepark** and the superb **Cinemark 20-screen Movie Complex**. The massive **Bass Pro Shops Outdoor World** is worth checking out for its range of outdoor clothing and equipment (fishing, boating, hunting and hiking) as well as the amazing themed decor, while **Shepler's Western Wear**'s range of apparel, boots and other footwear has to be seen to be believed (all at great prices, too).

> **BRIT TIP**
> Visit Bass Pro Shops at the weekend for periodic demonstrations, kids' activity days and workshops, including free in-store fishing demos (yes, really!) in its huge fish tank (407 563 5200, **basspro.com**).

The **Universal Orlando Store** is well worth seeking out for discounted merchandise, while other standouts are **Kasper** (women's attire), **Nine West** (women's shoes and accessories), **Charlotte Russe** (trendy women's clothing), **Zirbes Emporium** (an eclectic gift-and-furniture store) and **Swim Smart**, plus a unique, glow-in-the-dark mini-golf course, the **Putting Edge**, which is a great place to occupy the kids for a while. UK visitors should also note **United World Soccer** for all manner of footie-related gear and **Leader Luggage** for that extra suitcase to take home! The huge **Monkey Joe's** play centre is another ideal opportunity to let the youngsters (3–8s) run free

(with a Parent Area including TVs and relaxing seating), while there is also the **Fantasy Arcade** for video games. **Vans Skate Park** is perfect for anyone with a skateboard or roller-blade obsession (visit **vans.com**, then Skateparks, then Orlando), offering 6 2-hour sessions a day (10am–midnight) as well as a full range of safety equipment and board rentals, plus a chill-out lounge.

BRIT TIP
International visitors can go to the Guest Services booth, with photo ID, and pick up a free advantage card offering $200 in savings throughout Festival Bay.

There is no food court, but there are small dining outlets dotted around, notably **Asian Café**, **ChurroMania**, **Subway**, **A&W/Long John Silvers**, **Mike & Eddie's Ice Cream** and **Villa Pizza Cuccina**. The 3 feature restaurants up front are all great choices for a meal or just a post-shopping snack. **Fuddruckers** is a highly tempting counter-service diner offering all manner of burgers (including ostrich, turkey, salmon and vegetarian options), salads, soups and desserts; **Bergamo's** has long offered good-quality Italian dining (pasta, seafood, veal and prime Angus steaks), plus its signature singing waiters, who range from grand opera to folk songs; and **The Cricketers Arms** offers typical pub grub, plus a terrific range of local and imported beers,

as well as live entertainment and the all-important footie on TV! It even has a private function/dining room (see also page 326) (10am–9pm Mon–Sat, 11am–7pm Sun, later at the restaurants; 407 351 7718; **shopfestivalbaymall.com**).

BRIT TIP
The new-look Cricketers Arms features one of the biggest ranges of beers in Florida, with 17 on tap, including 4 hand-drawn ales.

Pointe Orlando: This is another I-Drive complex to have undergone a major change, completing a massive redevelopment in 2009. The dramatic rebuild added a new entrance plaza directly from I-Drive, as well as a wealth of new shops and especially restaurants, making this a great choice for an evening out with a bit of retail therapy. Among 20-plus smart stores, you can indulge your passion for fashion at **Victoria's Secret**, **Armani Exchange**, **Image Leather**, **Chico's** and **Hollister** or stock up on gifts and souvenirs at **Bath & Body Works**, eclectic **Artsy Abode**, T**ommy Bahamas**, **SGH sunglass hut** and the excellent **Tharoo & Co** jewellery. Don't miss **Baterbys Art Auction Gallery** for artworks by Masters such as Dali and Picasso, as well as contemporary artists, while **Brighton** (gifts, accessories and jewellery), **Millenium** (casual attire, beach accessories and shoes),

Shopping at Pointe Orlando

© OCVB

Kiehl's Since 1851 (signature beauty products) and Boardwalk Surf & Sport all offer more options. The dining choices at The Pointe are its real attraction, though, from the upscale Capital Grille (dry-aged steaks, seafood and tantalising desserts) and The Oceanaire, whose menu changes daily to highlight some of the best seafood from around the world, to Johnny Rockets American diner, Pizzeria Valdiano, Maggiano's and the stylish Cuba Libre (contemporary Cuban cuisine and authentic mojitos). Read more about The Pointe's fabulous dining choices on page 332, and you will also find plenty of entertainment by night here at BB King's Blues Club, Adobe Gila's and the Regal Cinemas Stadium 20 + IMAX Cineplex, which shows first-run movies in large screen format. Parking is at The Pointe's multi-storey car park, but several stores and restaurants will redeem your parking ticket if you shop there. It's open noon–10pm Mon–Sat, noon–8pm Sun, later at the bars and restaurants (407 248 2838, pointeorlando.com).

BRIT TIP
While you may not be able to afford some of the art on offer at Baterbys at Pointe Orlando – which includes the likes of Dali, Picasso, Miro and Peter Max – its 11,000sq ft/1,022sq m gallery offers superb viewing. Named Best Art Gallery for 2009 by *Orlando Style Magazine*, it features periodic fund-raising auctions, while its website previews many of its offerings at baterbys.com.

Kissimmee Old Town

Kissimmee

Down along the tourist territory of Highway 192, you will again find a complete mix of outlets, with a profusion of the cheap and cheerful (some of which you probably wouldn't want if they were giving it away!), but also several highly enticing possibilities.

BRIT TIP
Brit Guide readers receive FREE shopping centre coupons by turning in the ad on the back flap of this book. Take advantage of this exclusive opportunity for added savings on your holiday shopping.

Old Town: This is Kissimmee's version of the purpose-built tourist shopping centre, an antique-style offering with an eclectic mix of shops, restaurants, bars and fairground attractions, all set out along brick-built streets. The 50 shops range from standard souvenirs, novel T-shirt outlets and Disney merchandise to sportswear, motorbike fashions and other collectables (check out the Old Town General Store for a step back in time, or the Old Town Portrait Gallery for period-style photographs). The individual style of Out Of This World Embroidery offers a 'you name it, we'll stitch it' service, while Black Market Minerals, Kandlestix, Andean Manna and Magic Max are all great for novel gift ideas. There are also 16 restaurants or snack bars. Those in need of some pampering or a massage should head for the Vivian's Day Spa. For lunch or dinner try Tex Mex Mexican cuisine or Kool Katz Grill & Pub featuring American favourites in a casual atmosphere reminiscent of the Friday and Saturday Nite car cruises, while the Blue Max Tavern is another fun alternative. A&W All American Food and Old Town Chippy (British-style fish 'n' chips) are also worth trying, while there are other snack outlets, with offerings from popcorn to candy and the wonderful Old Town Ice Cream Company. Sun on the Beach is a good nightclub choice in evenings. Parking is free (10am–11pm daily; rides open noon–11pm; 407 396 4888; old-town.com).

A Kissimmee tradition

Old Town is home to some weekly events that appeal to locals and tourists alike and are well worth catching if possible. The **Saturday Nite Cruise** at 8.30pm is a drive-past of 300-plus vintage and collector cars (the biggest in America) that has become a real trademark here. A **Friday Nite Cruise** features cars built between 1973 and 1987, while every Thurs is **Motorcycle Nite** from 6pm and **Wednesday Nite** brings out the pre-1987 cars. There is live music, fairground-type stalls and prizes, and it can get fairly raucous later on, with plenty of alcoholic libations (witness the Sun on the Beach bar!).

Downtown Kissimmee offers the more local, authentic face of shopping in Florida, with the charming Main Street area featuring a range of tempting antique shops, one-off boutiques, cafes and restaurants. Much attention has been paid to the historic district in recent years, and it is now a relaxing place for a wander and a meal. The **Welcome Station** on Main Street (formerly an old fashioned petrol station) is a great place to start, and even has local crafts, keepsakes, and books focusing on Floridian history (9am–5pm Mon–Fri; 10am–2pm Sat). Then look into the likes of local landmarks **Lanier's**, **Makinson Hardware** (the oldest hardware store in Florida), and **Gallery One Artists**, while Italian restaurant **Tarantino's** is also something of a local institution. The authentic Mexican family style of **Azteca's** is worth trying, along with the casual sports-bar style of **Broadway Pizza**, while we're big fans of the smart **Chef John's Dockside Inn** (try the Grouper sandwich; just yummy!). Then, you simply must not miss the ice cream treats at **Pure Magic**. Not just a sweet way to cool down on a hot day, but truly an entertainment opportunity. Each scoop is hand-made from an ice cream base, your choice of additions are blended in, then the whole thing is flash-frozen in front of you. Brilliant! There is even a play area for youngsters to burn off a bit of energy while adults rest their weary feet. Every Thurs

(7am–1pm) you can also sample the local **Farmers' Market** on the corner of Pleasant St and Darlington Ave. Look up more at **kissimmeemainstreet.com**.

The Kissimmee area is largely short of quality shopping otherwise, but head up to the Osceola Parkway (at the junction with John Young Parkway), which runs parallel to Highway 192, and you find the extensive developments of **The Loop** and the recently added **Loop West**, which help redress the balance. This double open-air plaza offers a unique mix of shops and restaurants, plus a 16-screen **Regal Cinema**, in a pedestrian-friendly setting, with the shops grouped around 2 large car parks. Many of the shops may not mean much to UK visitors but are well worth visiting. Of note at The Loop are **Ross** (a huge discount warehouse of clothes, shoes, linens, cosmetics and more), **Kohl's** (a well-priced department store), **Bed, Bath & Beyond** (an amazing range of household wares), **Pacific Sunwear** (beach and casual wear), **Old Navy** (clothing), **Michaels** (arts and crafts), **Sports Authority** and **Famous Footwear** (discounted shoes and trainers). In addition, there is a hairdresser, nail salon, chemist (**CVS**) and a superb line-up of 10 restaurants and cafés. Look out in particular for **Johnny Rockets**, the excellent Italian style of **Macaroni Grill**, **Red Brick Pizza**, the gourmet offerings of **Chipotle Mexican Grill**, **Chili's** and the hearty fare of **Panera Bread** (great soups, salads and sandwiches). At The Loop

Kissimmee Old Town

© OCVB

Orlando Premium Outlets

West, look for the 2 big department stores of **JC Penney** (clothing and housewares) and **Belk** (home goods), plus **Ulta** (cosmetics), **Christopher & Banks** (women's clothing) and **DSW** (shoes), plus 15 additional shops and another 5 restaurants – the excellent style and value of **BJ's Restaurant and Brewhouse**, the Asian fare of **Pei Wei**, smart Mexican **Abuelo's**, **Tropical Smoothie Café** and the upmarket **Bonefish Grill**. In all, The Loop and Loop West boast 65 shopping and dining outlets and this has quickly become a major proposition, especially for the extensive dining choice (open 10am–9.30pm Mon–Sat, 11am–6pm Sun, later at the restaurants and cinemas; 407 343 9223; **attheloop.com**).

BJ's Restaurant and Brewhouse

Lake Buena Vista

The Lake Buena Vista area offers 2 of the best discount outlet centres, with a range of goods to make even the most jaded of shoppers salivate – and prices to match!

Orlando Premium Outlets: High on your list of 'must visit' shops, this is a huge hit with UK visitors – and it's still growing. With a fresh look and style, and a legion of big-name designers (from Nike, Adidas and Gap to Polo Ralph Lauren, Dior, Hugo Boss, Coach and Zegna), it can be found on Vineland Avenue between I-Drive and I-4 (just south of SeaWorld; or exit 68 off I-4).

BRIT TIP
Don't try to battle with the crowds in the main open-air car park at Orlando Premium Outlets. Instead, head towards the back of the centre where you will find the new 1,600-car multi-storey car park.

In all, it offers 150 stores of well-known brand names (like Timberland, Diesel, Burberry, Giorgio Armani, Kenneth Cole, Banana Republic, French Connection and Calvin Klein) in a semi-covered pedestrian plaza, with free parking and the added convenience of being at the south end of the I-Ride Trolley (main line). Other significant signature shops are **Samsonite**

Company Store, **Ecko Unltd** (select T-shirts, jeans and sportswear), **Fendi** (stylish women's clothing and signature handbags), **OshKosh B'Gosh** (baby/toddler clothes), **Factory Brand Shoes** (a mini-warehouse of footwear fashion) and **Perfumania**. Watch out also for big Disney bargains at the **Character Premiere**. In all, there are 75 clothing and fashion stores, 25 for shoes, 10 jewellers, 9 for children's clothing and 6 for luggage. A big 2008 expansion added another 38 upscale shops, including **J Crew**, **Diesel**, **Hurley** and **Wolford**, while new in 2009 were chic clothing outlet **Vineyard Vines** and the catwalk style of **Michael Kors**. New stores for 2010 included **Elizabeth Arden**, **Bare Escentuals**, mega sweetshop **It'Sugar** and the designer fashions of **CH Carolina Herrera**, **Talbots** and **Tory Burch**.

BRIT TIP

Brit Guide Itinerary Planner Service clients will receive Orlando Premium Outlets' special **Premier Platinum VIP Passport** voucher, for significant extra savings at many shops (see page 49).

The food court is quite tempting, too, with 10 outlets, from **JR's Steakery** and **Max Orient** to **Starbucks**, **Taco Bell** and **Subway**. There is even a beer and wine café for relaxing at your leisure. For those without a car, there is a daily free shuttle service from 15 hotels in the Lake Buena Vista area ($11/person from Highway 192 in Kissimmee). Call 407 390 0000, extension 2, for reservations, which are required at least 2 hours in advance. The Lynx bus service also stops here (407 841 2279), while Maingate Taxi as on-site taxi stands, or you could try **Star Taxi** (407 857 9999). Premium Outlets is open daily 10am–11pm (9pm Sun; 407 238 7787; **premiumoutlets.com/orlando**).

Lake Buena Vista Factory Stores: Get ready for more big-name products at discount prices here, from Fossil, Converse, Reebok, Liz Claiborne and Van Heusen to a budget-priced **Disney Character Outlet**, **OshKosh B'Gosh** superstore and (the better-priced) **Carter's For Kids**. It is another open-air plaza, with almost 50 stores spread over 6 acres/2.5ha and with plentiful, convenient parking. It's slightly off the beaten track and therefore not quite as busy as some of the others. New shops are opening all the time, and recent additions include stylish **Tommy Hilfiger**, funky **Aeropostale**, **Ecko Unltd**, **Izod**, **Avanti Sunglass Boutique**, **Eddie Bauer Outlet** and **Rawlings Factory Store** for sporting goods. There is also a decent food court and a kids' playground. Some of the stores and brand names may not be well known to us, but the likes of **Old Navy** (excellent value casual clothing), **Perfume Outlet** (heavily discounted fragrances and cosmetics), **SAS Shoes** (think Hush Puppies, only cheaper!), **Travelpro** (luggage) and **Rack Room Shoes** (big names at serious savings) are worth discovering. **Book Warehouse** offers great bargain books, **Camera Outlet** carries a large selection of European PAL systems, and **World of Coffee** is both an internet café and one of the best places you could find to sip a latte and enjoy a cake or pastry, with its outdoor terrace and bird cages. There is also a food court, a kids' play area and pleasant outdoor deck to sit with a drink. Worth noting at the neighbouring Lake Buena Vista Resort Village and Spa are the luxurious **Reflections Spa** for a bit of pampering after your day of shopping, and the new **Frankie Farrells Irish Pub & Grill**, an excellent choice for lunch or dinner in an authentic pub atmosphere (with lots of TVs showing UK sport!). Its 32 brews on tap (including Boddingtons, Guinness, Bass and Magners) complement a traditional Irish and American menu.

Frankie Farrells Irish Pub & Grill

BRIT TIP

If you are into scrapbook hobbies or other arts and crafts, you should seek out one of Orlando's 8 **Michaels** stores, which are a scrapbooking heaven!

The Factory Stores are on SR 535 (2mls/3km south off exit 68 on I-4) and are open daily 10am–9pm (to 7pm Sun). Their shuttle service picks up at hotels and condos in a 10ml/16km radius (407 238 9301, **lbvfs.com**).

BRIT TIP

Go to **lbvfs.com** for up to $400 in discount coupons.

Malls

Head out slightly beyond the main tourist territory and you will discover the further choice and style of the area's many malls, several of which are well worth adding to your holiday agenda. They contain a huge range of shops and, if you take advantage of their periodic sales, you will be firmly back on the bargain trail. The top 2 locally are the Florida Mall and the Mall at Millenia, and both offer a contrasting shopping experience.

BRIT TIP

Need a good book? Make a beeline for **Barnes & Noble,** on West Sand Lake Road in the Venezia Plaza, on the South Orange Blossom Trail opposite the Florida Mall, or at the new Winter Garden Village shops. Each has a great coffee shop, too.

Florida Mall: The largest in central Florida, this features more than 260 shops, with 6 large department stores and a 22-counter food court, plus a children's play area, the lively bar-restaurant **Ruby Tuesday**, the popular fresh offerings of **Nature's Table**, **California Pizza Kitchen** and hearty **Buca di Beppo**. Located on the South Orange Blossom Trail, on the corner of Sand Lake Road, this spacious and extremely smart mall is open 10am–9pm Mon–Sat, noon–6pm Sun. Highlights are the department stores, led by the upmarket (but expensive) **Saks Fifth Avenue** and **Macy's**, plus **JC Penney**, **Nordstrom** (which also has a sit-down café), **Sears** and **Dillard's**. Other shops worth looking out for are **Bath & Body Works**, **Williams-Sonoma** ('the place for cooks' – and how!), **PacSun** (beachwear and more) and,

Florida Mall

The Florida Mall

for kids, the **Build-a-Bear Workshop**, **Game Stop** and the wonderfully fun **M&M's World** store, plus trendy **Forever 21** and a **Zara** outlet. New in 2010 were accessory store **Charming Charlie** and the skateboard style of **CCS**. Guest services offers a discount booklet with a handy international size chart to help with American sizing, while there is also free wheelchair use, pushchair rental and foreign currency exchange. There are even spa and beauty treatments in the Lancôme Institut de Beauté in Dillard's, the JC Penney styling salon, and the Elizabeth Arden salon at Saks Fifth Avenue (407 851 6255; **simon.com**). The Mall also benefits from the integral **Florida Hotel**, with Cricket's Grille & Bar. Nearby on Sand Lake Road, you will find warehouse-like **Old Time Pottery**, a vast emporium of home goods of all kinds, from crockery to linens (**oldtimepottery.com**).

BRIT TIP
Kids – let your parents take you to the Florida Mall, then insist on visiting the huge Toys R Us store at the front and then M&M World inside the mall!

Mall at Millenia: If the Florida Mall is the biggest shopping venue in town, this is the smartest. Opened in October 2002 and located just off I-4 to the north of Universal Orlando (exit 78), it is the most upmarket, dramatic and technologically advanced shopping complex in Florida, with New York's most famous department stores – Bloomingdale's, Neiman Marcus and Macy's – among a select number of

other top-name boutiques such as Louis Vuitton and Tiffany & Co. The entrance features a 60ft/18m glass rotunda with a flowing water garden theme and a concierge desk (valet parking is also available). Then you can head in 1 of 4 directions over the marble and terrazzo floors or go upstairs to the refreshing, high-quality 12-outlet food court, **Orangerie Cafés**, where the only difficulty is deciding which tempting and health-conscious eatery to choose. Look out for **Bistro Sensations** (wonderful salads, pastas, pittas and wraps), the authentic Mandarin-style of **Chinatown**, the fresh **Greek Jalapeno** (tacos and burritos – but nothing Greek!) and the **Southwest Grill** (succulent chicken, barbecue beef and salads), plus **Tony's & Bruno's** for Italian specialities (pasta, pizza, salads and cheesecake).

BRIT TIP
Visit the concierge office at Mall at Millenia, located in the lower level, opposite the Cheesecake Factory and show this book to receive a complimentary gift and savings book!

The grand architecture is also focused on 5 separate courts along a flattened, serpentine S-shape, topped by a flowing, arched glass roof like some gigantic conservatory. On 2 airy levels (3 in Bloomingdale's and Macy's) and with 8 Juliet balconies connecting the 2 sides, the mall consists of a colossal amount of glass, plus a stunning Grand Court, featuring a dozen 20ft/6m columns capped by curved plasma

The Mall at Millenia

SHOPPING

video screens. And, while around 20% of the 150 stores are upscale and exclusive (**Cartier**, **Chanel**, **Jimmy Choo**, **Burberry** and **Gucci**), there are many unexpected options, such as **Urban Outfitters**, **Apple**, **MAC Cosmetics** and **Anthropologie**. You will also find plenty of mainstream names like **Abercrombie & Fitch**, **Hollister**, **Gap**, **Banana Republic** and **Victoria's Secret**. The 4 main restaurants are also first class: gourmet seafood **McCormick & Schmick's**, heavenly **Cheesecake Factory**, **PF Chang's China Bistro** and the stylish Italian of **Brio Tuscan Grille**. On top of that (AND the Orangerie Cafés), there is the excellent fresh sandwich style of **Panera Bread**, the **California Pizza Kitchen** and a **Johnny Rockets** diner. This is also the only mall with a US post office inside (NB: Standard postcards to the UK cost 98c, rising to $1 in Jan 2011). A currency exchange is available, as are international phone cards. Chic **Blue Martini**, a speciality martini bar, sushi-tapas restaurant and music venue, is well worth trying for a special occasion. With more than 32 unique martinis, plus premium cigars, an extensive wine list and a tapas-style menu, this is the current trendy hangout, with an outdoor terrace and indoor stage room. There's live music (8–11.30pm Mon–Thurs, 7.30–11.30pm Fri and Sat), then dance music with the house DJ (4pm–2am Mon–Fri, 1pm–2am Sat and Sun, Happy Hour 4–7pm Mon–Fri; **bluemartinilounge.com**). All in all, this takes the Florida shopping experience to a new level (10am–9pm Mon–Sat, noon–7pm Sun; 407 363 3555; **mallatmillenia.com**).

Winter Garden Village

Blue Martini

There are 4 alternatives to these popular (and busy – especially at weekends) malls: the **Altamonte Mall**, on Altamonte Avenue in the suburb of Altamonte Springs (take exit 92 off I-4 and head east for ½ml/800m on Route 436, then turn left); **Seminole Towne Center**, just off I-4 to the north of Orlando on the outskirts of Sanford (exit 101C off I-4); **Oviedo Marketplace**, to the east of Orlando (right off exit 41 of Central Florida Greeneway, 417); and **West Oaks Mall**, on West Colonial Drive (SR50), in the suburb of Ocoee, west of downtown Orlando (take the Florida Turnpike to exit 267A with SR50, and go back east on 50 for 1½mls/2.5km). The Altamonte Mall is the best of the bunch and well off the beaten tourist track, featuring 160 speciality shops, 4 major department stores – Macy's, Dillard's, JC Penney and Sears – and 19 eateries, including the fun **Bahama Breeze**, upmarket **Seasons 52** and pub-style **Orlando Ale House**. An 18-screen cinema and children's soft-play area round out the offerings. Open 10am–9pm Mon–Sat, 11am–6pm Sun, the Customer Service Centre offers a VIP savings book to visitors (**altamontemall. com**). Shop during the week and you'll feel as if you have the place to yourself!

Winter Garden Village: One last major shopping recommendation is this more offbeat offering, 5mls/8km north of *Walt Disney World* on Highway 535 at the junction with toll road 429, which is primarily a new locals' centre but still has a lot of visitor appeal. The expansive open-plan design, set around key stores like **Super Target**,

Our shopping tips

As we live locally, shopping is close to our hearts and we recommend the following as an essential slice of the Orlando retail scene:

Outlet shopping: Orlando Premium Outlets or Prime Outlets International

Mall: Mall at Millenia

Open-air centre: Winter Garden Village

Supermarket: Whole Foods Market

Chemist: Walgreens

Electronics: Best Buy

Clothing: Marshall's and Ross stores

Home goods: Old Time Pottery

Bookshop: Barnes & Noble

Specialist store: Shepler's Western Wear

Best Buy, **Ross**, **Marshall's** and **Beall's**, features a mix of the big names and smaller boutiques, as well as a tempting array of 21 cafes and restaurants sprinkled throughout. Look for the upmarket seafood choice of Bonefish Grill, the elegant Longhorn Steakhouse, family-style Chili's, Cracker Barrel, UNO Chicago Grill and Mimi's Café, or the counter-service options like Urban Flats, Quiznos, Panda Express, Coldstone Creamery and Chick-Fil-A (look up more at **wintergardenvillage.com**).

Specialist shops

Supermarkets: High on many people's lists is **Wal-Mart**, the warehouse-like American supermarket that sells just about everything. There are no fewer than 21 Wal-Marts in central Florida, 16 of which are the 24-hour Supercenter kind. The main tourist area stores are on Highway 27 (just north of 192); Highway 192 by Medieval Times (between markers 14 and 15); Osceola Parkway (at Buenaventura Lakes); John Young Parkway (at Sand Lake Road); on Kirkman Road (north of Universal Boulevard); by Highway 535 and Osceola Parkway; and on Turkey Lake Road.

There is plenty of supermarket choice, though, and you will find better-quality produce at the likes of **Publix** (throughout the main tourist areas, notably on Highway 192 and 27); **Winn-Dixie** (a major south-east US chain) and **Albertson's** (with a store at Dr Phillips Boulevard, close to I-Drive). But the real Rolls-Royce of food stores, **Whole Foods Market**, opened a new Orlando branch on Turkey Lake Road in 2008 with its signature superb fresh produce emporium and plenty of chances to sample as you go, plus a magnificent hot-food counter to grab a meal at the end (**wholefoodsmarket.com**). For clothes, DIY, home furnishings, electrical goods, household items, gifts, toys and groceries, visit **Target** (its superstores on Highway 192 just

Whole Foods Market

west of Highway 535, near Mall at Millenia and Winter Garden Village are fine examples). The big chemists ('drug stores') of **Walgreens** and **CVS** also carry a surprisingly wide range of goods and almost resemble mini-supermarkets in their own right.

BRIT TIP
If you shop at any US Wal-Mart store, you can return faulty or wrong-size goods to your local Asda for a refund, as long as you present the receipts.

Flea World: The locals also have a passion for flea markets, highlighted by America's largest covered market, with 1,700 stalls spread over 104 acres/42ha, including 3 massive (air-conditioned), themed buildings and a 7-acre/2.8ha amusement park, **Fun World**. Flea World is open 9am–6pm Fri, Sat and Sun (Fun World 9am–6pm Sat and Sun only), and can be found a 30-minute drive away on Highway 17/92 (best picked up from exit 90 on I-4) between Orlando and Sanford (to the north). The stalls include all manner of market goods (nearly all new or slight seconds), from fresh produce to antiques and jewellery, while there is a full-scale food court and a 300-seat pizza and burger eatery, the **Carousel Restaurant**, plus free entertainment on the Fun World Pavilion stage (407 330 1792; **fleaworld. com**).

BRIT TIP
Wal-Mart offers 1-hour photo processing at great savings on UK prices, as do branches of Walgreens.

Flea World

Bass Pro Shops Outdoor World

Keen shoppers will want to check out other individual outlets that might not mean much at first glance. **Ross** (10 in Orlando, see **rossstores.com**) carries a huge range of discounted brand-name clothes, shoes, linens, towels and other goods (9.30am–9.30pm Mon–Sat, 11am–8pm Sun), while **Marshalls** (5 in Orlando, **marshallsonline.com**) and **TJ Maxx** (also 5, **tjmaxx.com**) are similar. For American sports gear (shirts, caps, souvenirs, etc.) check out any **Sports Authority** shop (**sportsauthority.com**) or **Sports Dominator** (**sportsdominator. com**), while golfers should visit the **Edwin Watts Golf** stores (including the I-Drive clearance centre; **edwinwatts. com**), or any of the **Special Tee Golf & Tennis** shops. You can pick up some great deals on golf clubs in particular. By the same token, anglers can stock up on the latest gear at bargain prices at **Bass Pro Shops Outdoor World** (at the Festival Bay centre; **basspro.com**).

As a final recommendation, those staying in villas, condo-hotels or just wanting a taste of home should check out the **British Supermarket** (on Vineland Rd just east of its junction with Kirkman Ave, north of Universal Orlando). From Walkers Crisps to Daddies Sauce, Lucozade to Ribena, and proper British bacon to Irish sausages and meat pies, this is a genuine Union Jack grocery, with UK owners who stock everything for those picky eaters (not just kids!) who can't quite take American fare (10am–4pm Mon–Sat, 11am–3pm Sun; 407 370 2023, **http://britishsupermarket.com**).

But now the shopping is done, it's time to think about the journey home…

And so, dog-tired, lighter in the wallet but (hopefully) blissfully happy and with enough memories to last a lifetime, it's time to deal with that bane of all holidays – the journey home.

Now you have come through the last 2 weeks relatively unscathed, here's how to avoid any last-minute pitfalls.

The car

Returning the hire car can take time if you used an off-airport car depot, so allow ½ an hour: the process is much slicker with firms that operate directly from the airports, as nearly all of them do since the 2010 airport refurbishment. Most airlines require you to arrive 3 hours before an international flight, so don't be tempted to leave your check-in until the last minute. The off-airport check-in facilities for Virgin Holidays (at Downtown Disney by Cirque du Soleil) are a major bonus in making this aspect smoother for their passengers. Now you'll have time to kill, so here is a guide to the 2 main Orlando airports.

Orlando International Airport

Orlando International is 46mls/74km from Cocoa Beach and 54mls/87km from Daytona Beach on the east coast, 84mls/135km from Tampa and 110mls/177km from Clearwater and St Petersburg to the west,

25mls/40km from Walt Disney World and 10mls/16km from Universal Orlando; so always allow enough time for the return journey plus check-in. The Beachline Expressway (528) can get quite congested in the afternoon, for example, and the Central Florida Greeneway (417) is often better.

This modern airport is the 3rd largest in size in the USA, the 10th for number of passengers (No 1 in Florida) – and top rated for passenger satisfaction. It hit a record 36.4 million passengers in 2007 (some 100,000 a day), busier than Gatwick and San Francisco. It can get busy at peak times, but its 1,000-acre/405ha terminal complex usually handles crowds with ease, and this is one of the most comfortable airports you could ever hope to find. It boasts great facilities and its wide, airy concourses make it feel more like an elegant hotel (one end is actually the airport-owned Hyatt Hotel). Ramps, restrooms, wide lifts and large open areas ensure easy wheelchair access, and there are features like TDD and amplified telephones, wheelchair-height drinking fountains, Braille lift controls and companion-care restrooms to assist any travellers with disabilities. In keeping with the area, this airport always aims to stay a step ahead, and it is often engaged in a development project or two, including several environmentally friendly enhancements in 2009. It boasts a major food court, extra restaurant options and some superb shops. There is an emphasis on the 'green' aspect to

Orlando International, as its latest fleet of shuttle buses are hydrogen powered, with zero emissions. A convenient 'quick turnaround' area for hire cars opened in 2010, allowing 96% of hire car companies to have onsite locations, a huge boon to visitors' ease in pick-up and drop-off.

Should you have more than 3 hours to spare, it's worth taking the 15-minute taxi ride to the Florida Mall, or checking in early, keeping the car and visiting Gatorland about 20 minutes away (see pages 230–2).

BRIT TIP

You are advised to leave all luggage unlocked (no combination locks or padlocks) when you check in for your return flight, as the TSA security staff open a LOT of bags during its screening process and have the right to access any case, locked or unlocked. TSA-approved locks are suggested, if you prefer to lock your cases.

Landside

As with all international airports, there is a division between LANDSIDE (for visitors) and AIRSIDE (where you must have a ticket). There are 3 levels at Orlando's Landside.

- 1 is for ground transportation, tour operator desks, parking, buses and car rental agencies;
- 2 is for Baggage Claim, which you negotiated on your arrival) and private vehicles meeting passengers;
- 3 is where you enter on your return

Orlando International Airport

© OCVB

journey, as it holds the check-in desks, shops and restaurants.

Level 3: This divides into 5 interconnected sections:

Landside A is the check-in for **Gates 1–29** and **100–129**. Here you'll find American Airlines, Air Canada, Continental, Aer Lingus, Southwest, JetBlue and Virgin (though Virgin departs from Gates 60–99).

Landside B has check-in desks for **Gates 30–99** and the likes of Air France, BA, Delta, United, Spirit, US Airways and AirTran.

Once you've checked in, you can explore both the **East** and **West** sections of the main concourse on Level 3. These house a good mix of shops and restaurants, plus currency exchange, information desks and ATM machines, while the Hyatt Hotel is also in the East Hall. The East and West Halls are then linked by the restaurants, shops and services of the **North** and **South Walks**. In total, there are 58 places to shop and eat, including a handy food court, and it's almost like being in a smart shopping mall. There's a Suntrust bank, post office and even the relaxing **D-parture Spa and Salon** (have a massage before your flight!). Many shops feature outstanding design and even photo opportunities: see the 2 **Disney** stores, **Harley-Davidson**, **Universal**, **SeaWorld/Busch Gardens** and **Kennedy Space Center**. Other notable shops are the blissful bath products of **Lush**, the natural cosmetics of **L'Occitane**, the unique apparel of **Del Sol**, **Borders Books** (with its Seattle's Best coffee bar), **Ron Jon Surf Shop**, **Perfumania**, **Johnston & Murphy** (clothing), and **Hudson News**.

Dining: Another pleasure! The 8-counter food court features **McDonalds**, **Sbarro**, **Carvel** ice-cream, **Krispy Crème** and **Nathan's Hot Dogs**, as well as the slightly healthier option of **Chick-Fil-A**. **Macaroni Grill** is a tasty full-service Italian restaurant option, while **Fox Sports Sky Box** adds a multi-screen TV set-up plus counter and table service; and upstairs at the West Hall is **Chili's Too**, a cheerful, quick-service Tex-Mex bar-diner.

Take to the AirTran

To really make the most of your American adventure, the *Brit Guide* can thoroughly recommend exploring some other key cities direct from Orlando with **AirTran Airways**. We fly with it regularly and have found it one of the most reliable operators in the US. It offers low fares – especially if you book well in advance (sign up for its email sale alerts and special offers) – and a route network that includes Dallas, New York, Washington and Buffalo/Niagara, all non-stop from Orlando. In all, it covers more than 70 destinations in the US, Caribbean and Mexico, using a major hub at Atlanta to cities like Las Vegas, San Diego, Denver, New Orleans, Los Angeles and San Francisco, plus Aruba, San Juan, Nassau (Bahamas) and Cancun, Mexico, with a modern fleet of Boeing 717 and 737 aircraft (that all include live XM satellite radio and GoGo inflight internet, plus assigned seating). Other major US gateways include Detroit, Philadelphia, Raleigh-Durham, Boston, Minneapolis/St Paul and Chicago, which all have connecting flights to the UK for alternative transatlantic routes. For a low-cost carrier, AirTran is rare in offering a business upgrade at less than business-class prices; in fact, it puts many scheduled services to shame. Book online (**airtran.com**) for the best fares, or call 1800 247 8726 in the US, 001 678 254 7999 from the UK. If you are staying on the Florida coast, it also flies from Miami, Tampa, Sarasota/Bradenton, Fort Myers, Fort Lauderdale, West Palm Beach, Key West and Jacksonville, making it the Sunshine State's most user-friendly airline.

The **East Hall** tends to be quieter and more picturesque as it is dominated by the 8-storey Hyatt Hotel atrium. Up the escalator is the main entrance, and to see out your visit in style, **McCoy's Bar and Grill** (up and turn right) is a smart bar-restaurant with a grandstand view of the runways. To go really upmarket, take the lift to the 9th-floor **Hemispheres** (breakfast and dinner only). You'll have an even more impressive view, and its superb Continental cuisine and wine-tasting evenings offer some of the best fare in the city. It's pricey, but the service and food are 5-star.

BRIT TIP

Save some film or card space for the excellent photo opportunities at the airport: outside the Disney stores, the 2 Harley-Davidson shops and the Kennedy Space Center outlets.

Airside

Once it's time to move to your departure gate, be aware of the 4 satellite 'arms' that make up the airport's Airside. This is where you will probably need to queue as the security screening takes time, and you should allow AT LEAST 30 minutes. The arms are divided into Gates 1–29 and 30–59 at the west end, and 60–99 and 100–129 (all American domestic flights) at the east. All the departure gates are here, plus duty-free shops and more cafés.

The 4 satellites are each connected to the main building by an automated tram, so you need to be alert when it comes to finding your departure gate. There are no Tannoy announcements for flights, so you should check your departure gate and time when you check in. However, there are large monitors in the terminal with all the departure information. The usual gates are:

• Aer Lingus, American, Air Canada and Continental: 1–29;

• Spirit, United and US Airways: 30–59;

• AirTran, British Airways, Delta and Virgin: 60–99;

• JetBlue and Southwest: 100–129.

Airside at Orlando International

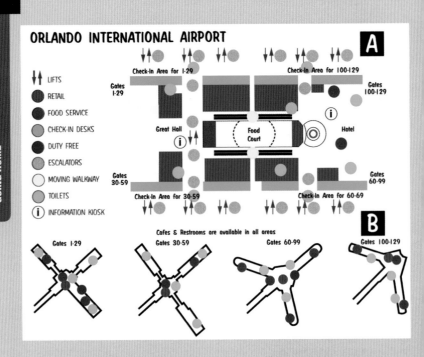

ORLANDO INTERNATIONAL AIRPORT

LIFTS
RETAIL
FOOD SERVICE
CHECK-IN DESKS
DUTY FREE
ESCALATORS
MOVING WALKWAY
TOILETS
(i) INFORMATION KIOSK

Check-In Area for 1-29
Check-In Area for 100-129
Gates 1-29
Gates 100-129
Great Hall
Food Court
Hotel
Gates 30-59
Gates 60-99
Check-In Area for 30-59
Check-In Area for 60-69

Cafes & Restrooms are available in all areas

Gates 1-29   Gates 30-59   Gates 60-99   Gates 100-129

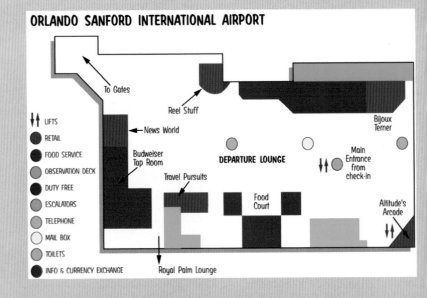

ORLANDO SANFORD INTERNATIONAL AIRPORT

To Gates
Reel Stuff
Bijoux Terner
LIFTS
RETAIL
FOOD SERVICE
OBSERVATION DECK
DUTY FREE
ESCALATORS
TELEPHONE
MAIL BOX
TOILETS
INFO & CURRENCY EXCHANGE

News World
Budweiser Tap Room
Travel Pursuits
DEPARTURE LOUNGE
Main Entrance from check-in
Food Court
Altitude's Arcade
Royal Palm Lounge

Although there isn't as much choice as at the main terminal, you should find the Airside areas just as clean and efficient, with the bonus of 2 duty-free shops (your purchases are delivered to the departure gate for you to collect as you board). Both stores have been significantly upgraded, with merchandise expanded to include designer sunglasses, jewellery, handbags, fashion watches, new perfumes and a selection of travel retail exclusives.

At **Gates 1–29**, you will find the first duty-free shop, a newsagents (the **Keys Gift Shop**), 2 **Cibo Express** gourmet markets, **Za-Za's** Cuban café and a mini food court featuring **Starbucks**, **Burger King**, **Cold Stone Creamery**, **Brioche Doree**, and **Famous Famiglia**. **Gates 30–59** have **Cibo Express**, **Pepito's Cuban Café**, **Natures Table**, **Wendy's**, **Freshens Treats**, **Za-Za's Cuban Coffee**, full service **Ruby Tuesday** and **Hudson News**. **Gates 60–99** (the main satellite for UK flights) offer another good duty-free shop, a currency exchange, **Stellar News & Gifts**, the speciality **Zoom System** shop, **The Grove** snacks and candy and a mini play area. A food court contains **Burger King**, **Nathan's Hot Dogs**, **Carvel**, **Starbucks** and **Fresh Attractions** deli, plus the excellent table service of the **Outback Steakhouse** and bar. **Gates 100–129** offer 2 **Johnny Rivers Smokehouse Express** outlets, a food court with **Freshens Treats**, **McDonald's** and **Sbarro Pizza**, plus **Starbucks** coffee shop, **Au Bon Pain** café, **Kafe Kalik** bar/lounge and 9 shops. For more details, visit **orlandoairports.net**, which includes live flight departure and arrival info.

Orlando Sanford International Airport

Returning to what is now the main Orlando gateway for British charter flights should be a relatively simple experience, providing you retrace your route on the Central Florida Greeneway (following signs for Orlando Sanford Airport, NOT Orlando International) and come off at exit 49. Turn first right at the lights, then first right again on to Lake Mary Boulevard and follow it to the airport. The efficiency of Alamo and Dollar's car return adds to the simplicity. NB: the airport turn-off sign is immediately after the toll plaza before exit 49 and is easy to miss; be aware that once you go through that toll plaza that you take the very next turn-off.

Orlando Sanford was created as a full international airport in 1996, as an initiative between the airport authorities and several British tour operators. And so Thomson, Monarch and Thomas Cook, plus the scheduled services of Icelandair, all now go for this simpler option. Of course, you are further north, so your journey time is 45 minutes longer and you have to pay an extra $3 in tolls compared with the journey to and from Orlando International, but providing you follow the simple directions, you should have no problem retracing your steps here.

And, while this charter gateway is smaller than Orlando International, it boasts a spacious check-in area and works hard to make the departure as painless as the arrival, especially with its Royal Palm Lounge facility.

Orlando Sanford Airport

Icelandair usually uses **Terminal B** for check-in: the other UK airlines check in at **Terminal A**. But all passengers use the same international departure lounge in Terminal A. It continues to grow with both domestic and international traffic, and has finished a major facility upgrade, notably in Terminal B.

There are no food or beverage outlets at the check-in level at Terminal A, but you can walk across to Terminal B where there is a **Ritazza Café** and a food court. Once checked in, you need to pass through security (again, allow a minimum of 30 minutes) to reach the International Departure Lounge. Here you have the **Budweiser Tap Room**, which serves a good selection of international beers, and the handy **Food Court**. The 4-part outlet offers American Grill (burgers and fries), Daily Specials (shepherd's pie, chicken pot pie, lasagne and more), Sweet Endings (baked goods and pastries) and the aptly named Grab-N-Go (soft drinks, bottled water and snacks). There is then an extensive **Duty Free** store (also with an increased range of merchandise), a new **Discover Orlando Sanford** shop (gifts and artwork with a 'local' flair), **Reel Stuff** character gifts from the likes of Disney, TV and film, **KidWorks**, which features educational games, books, and toys, as well as **Indulgences** for home, bath and body products. Neatly located in a corner, **Altitudes Arcade** is guaranteed to appeal to kids, while there is also an Information and **Currency Exchange** kiosk. Smoking is

Royal Palm Lounge

not permitted inside the lounge, but there is an extensive outdoor deck for smokers.

The big extra here, though, is the **Royal Palm Lounge**, a premium space available to all passengers for a modest fee. It's in a separate annexe from the main lounge and is an oasis of comfort and quiet, perfect for relaxing for the last few hours of your holiday (the only things it doesn't have are beds and shower facilities!). Split into 2 distinct halves, it boasts a pleasant café bar, where you can enjoy unlimited tea, coffee, soft drinks and snacks (plus 2 glasses of beer or wine per over-21). It also provides 2 home theatre lounges, with widescreen TV and surround-sound, for recently released films; 2 quiet reading rooms; 11 computer terminals for internet access and email; a youth entertainment centre with 14 Sony PlayStation 2 consoles; a separate toddlers' playroom with soft toys and

Orlando Sanford Airport ticket center

Your chance to give something back

After having the holiday of a lifetime, all being well, you might like to know about 2 charities helping children with serious illnesses to have a memorable time here. **Give Kids the World Village** is an amazing organisation in Kissimmee, providing a week's holiday in central Florida for children with life-threatening illnesses. GKTW works with more than 250 wish-granting foundations worldwide to provide an unforgettable Wish Vacation for children and their families. It is set up as a resort and includes meals, accommodation, transportation, whimsical venues, donated theme park tickets and many other thoughtful touches in a magical setting. It's a charity we are happy to support ourselves, and we hope you will, too. You can make a donation through its website – **gktw.org** – or send it to: Give Kids The World, 210 South Bass Road, Kissimmee, Florida 34746, USA.

Equally, **Dreamflight** is a registered UK charity taking seriously ill children aged 8–14 to Florida annually, often with the help of British Airways. It costs around £3,000 per child and, while many people generously donate their time to help, cash donations are essential. You can contribute by post: Dreamflight, 7C Hill Avenue, Amersham, Bucks HP6 5BD (01494 722733), online at **justgiving.com**, or by email to **office@dreamflight.org**. Look up more at **dreamflight.org**.

Thanks for any contributions to these worthwhile organisations.

games; a smoking lounge; and a left-luggage area. The Royal Palm Lounge is billed as an airport lounge with the comforts of home and it is well worth the extra cost ($30 per adult, $20 4–20s, under-4s free) to while away the last few hours. Most tour operators offer it in advance at a discount, or you can book on arrival or through your reps at the resort. With its extra capacity and facilities, this is a very satisfying way to conclude a holiday. See the Royal Palm Lounge, and more about the airport, at **orlandosanfordairport.com** or email **royal. palm@tbiusinc.aero**.

Whether you are using Orlando International or Orlando Sanford International, you can also expect the return flight to be about an

hour shorter than the journey out, thanks to the Atlantic jetstreams that provide tailwinds to high-level flights. Nevertheless, you'll land back at Gatwick, Manchester, Glasgow or wherever rather more jetlagged than on the trip out because the time difference is more noticeable on eastward flights, and it may take a day or so to get your body clock back on local time. It is very important not to indulge in alcohol on the flight if you will be driving when you land. By far the best way to beat Florida jetlag is to enjoy the memories from this trip – then start planning your next Orlando holiday!

Believe us, the lure of this theme park wonderland is hard to resist – you WILL be back!

See you soon!

© Disney

Your Holiday Planner

Example: 2 weeks with Disney's 5-Day Premium Ticket and Orlando FlexTicket

(Disney's 5-Day Premium Ticket gives 5 days at their 4 main theme parks, plus 4 visits to *Blizzard Beach, Typhoon Lagoon, DisneyQuest* and/or *Disney's ESPN World Of Sports*™, valid for 14 days from first use. The Orlando FlexTicket is valid for Universal Orlando's 2 parks, plus SeaWorld, Wet 'n Wild and CityWalk for 14 days from first use.)

Day	Our Example	Your Planner
ONE (Sun)	Arrive 2.40am local time, Orlando Sanford airport; transfer to resort – check out local shops and restaurants	
TWO (Mon)	Attend tour operator Welcome Meeting; rest of day at UNIVERSAL STUDIOS	
THREE (Tues)	Chill-out day at *Disney's Blizzard Beach* water park	
FOUR (Wed)	All day at MAGIC KINGDOM Park (Wishes fireworks at 9pm)	
FIVE (Thurs)	All day at DISNEY'S HOLLYWOOD STUDIOS (Fantasmic! show at 8.30pm)	
SIX (Fri)	All day at EPCOT Park (IllumiNations at 9pm)	
SEVEN (Sat)	Have a lie-in, then try some shopping at Orlando Premium Outlets and Lake Buena Vista Factory Shops	
EIGHT (Sun)	DISNEY'S ANIMAL KINGDOM Park Eve: Medieval Times Dinner Show (8pm)	
NINE (Mon)	ISLANDS OF ADVENTURE Eve: CityWalk and dinner at Hard Rock	
TEN (Tues)	Kennedy Space Center Eve: International Drive	
ELEVEN (Wed)	All day at SEAWORLD ADVENTURE PARK (Mistify at 10pm)	

Day	Our Example	Your Planner
TWELVE (Thurs)	Have a chill-out day; head for the new Aquatica water park	
THIRTEEN (Fri)	Enjoy a UNIVERSAL ORLANDO highlights day. Eve: Sleuth's Mystery dinner show	
FOURTEEN (Sat)	Have a lie-in, then head for MAGIC KINGDOM Park (Wishes fireworks at 9pm)	
FIFTEEN (Sun)	Gatorland/Back to airport; return flight at 5.30pm	

Busy Day Guide

NB: These days can change on a month-by-month basis; for the most up-to-date info, please check our website, **www.askdaisy.net/orlando**.

Day	Busiest	Average	Lightest
Mon	*Magic Kingdom; Disney's Animal Kingdom*	*Disney's Hollywood Studios*	*Epcot;* Universal Studios; Islands of Adventure; Busch Gardens; Kennedy Space Center; SeaWorld; water parks
Tues	*Epcot; Magic Kingdom*	*Disney's Animal Kingdom;* Universal Studios	*Disney's Hollywood Studios;* Busch Gardens; IoA; Kennedy Space Center; SeaWorld; Water Parks
Wed	*Disney's Hollywood Studios* (high season)	*Disney's Animal Kingdom;* Islands of Adventure; SeaWorld; water parks	*Magic Kingdom; Epcot;* Busch Gardens; Kennedy Space Center; Universal Studios
Thurs	*Magic Kingdom;* Universal Studios	*Epcot;* Busch Gardens; SeaWorld; water parks	*Disney's Hollywood Studios; Disney's Animal Kingdom;* IoA; Kennedy Space Center
Fri	*Disney's Hollywood Studios* (high season) SeaWorld; Water Parks	*Disney's Animal Kingdom;* IoA; Busch Gardens; Kennedy Space Center	*Magic Kingdom; Epcot* Universal Studios
Sat	*Disney's Animal Kingdom;* Busch Gardens; IoA; Kennedy Space Center; SeaWorld; Universal Studios; water parks	*Magic Kingdom; Epcot*	*Disney's Hollywood Studios* (high season)
Sun	*Epcot; Magic Kingdom;* IoA; Kennedy Space Center; SeaWorld; water parks	*Disney's Hollywood Studios;* Busch Gardens; Universal Studios	*Disney's Animal Kingdom*

Index

Copyright notices

The author and publisher gratefully acknowledge the provision of the following photographs.

Acknowledgements

The authors wish to acknowledge the help of the following in the production of this book: The Orlando/Orange County Convention and Visitors' Bureau, US Travel Association, Visit USA, The Kissimmee/St Cloud Convention & Visitors' Bureau, St Petersburg/Clearwater Area Convention and Visitors' Bureau, Daytona Beach Area Convention & Visitors' Bureau, Seminole County Convention & Visitors' Bureau, Mount Dora Chamber of Commerce, Walt Disney Attractions Inc., Universal Orlando, SeaWorld Parks & Entertainment, Greater Orlando Aviation Authority, Orlando Sanford International Airport and Alamo Rent A Car.

In person: Danielle Courtenay, Amy Voss (Orlando CVB), Larry White, Sylvia Oliande, Chris Long (Kissimmee CVB), Sharon Sears, Patrick Harrison (Seminole County CVB), Mary Haban (St Petersburg/Clearwater CBV), Tangela Boyd (Daytona Beach CVB), Cathy Hoechst, Paula Briskin (Mount Dora), Nina Stemson (Alamo Rent A Car), Kate Burgess (Visit USA), Todd Heiden, Sarah Hodson, Alix Vonk, Jason Lasecki, Geoff Pointon (Walt Disney), Tom Schroder, Alyson Lundell, Kristen Clarke, (Universal), Andrea Farmer (Kenney Space Center), Jackie Wallace (Legoland Florida), Carolyn Fennell, Rod Johnson (Orlando Aviation Authority), Lorraine Ellis (Get Married In Florida), Andy James, James Brown (Florida Dolphin Tours), Nick Gollattscheck, Gerard Hoeppner, Jill Revelle, Susan Flower, (SeaWorld/Discovery Cove), David Ferrara (Busch Gardens), Brooks Jordan (Silver Springs), Christine Foley (Bok Tower Gardens), Laura Richeson (Richeson Communications), Treva Marshall, Joel Kaiman (TJM Communications), Mary Kenny (Mary C Kenny & Associates), Michael Caires, Greg Dull (Orlando Sanford International Airport), Allan Oakley (Alexander Homes & Associates), Nigel Worrall (Florida Leisure), Sandy Marshall (Sky Resorts), Jason Schulke (Orlando Balloon Rides), Kay Wertz (Route 46), Bill Cowie, Chris Doran, Lee Weaver (British Homes Group), Wrenda Goodwyn (International Drive), Mark McHugh, Michelle Harris, Bret Chism (Gatorland), Donna Ernbro (Sleuths), David Walker (Titanic: The Experience), Phillip Jaffe (Pro Golf Guides of Orlando), Mary Deatrick (Deatrick PR for Rosen Hotels), Margie Long (Boggy Creek Airboats), Phil Coppen (Cricketers Arms), Kevin and Audrey Jowett (Revolution Offroad), and Jennie and Paul Skingley (Best of British Soccer World).

Reader feedback via email: Stuart Hammond, Mark, Tricia, Sophie & Rebecca Duncan, Mr and Mrs William Troman, Rupert Myers, plus many 'regulars' on the Attraction Tickets Direct forums, **wdwinfo.com** and thedibb.co.uk. You know who you are!

Other publications: Check out *Orlando Attractions Magazine* for some great info and features on this great destination – **attractionsmagazine.com**.

Got a red-hot Brit Tip to pass on? We want to hear from YOU to keep improving the guide each year. Drop us a line at: Brit's Guide (Orlando), W. Foulsham & Co. Ltd, The Oriel, Thames Valley Court, 183-187 Bath Rd, Slough, Berkshire SL1 4AA. Or e-mail **britsguide@yahoo.com**.